CAMBRIDGE
UNIVERSITY PRESS

Business Management

for the IB Diploma

COURSEBOOK

Peter Stimpson, Adamantia Malli-Charchalaki & Alexander Smith

CAMBRIDGE
UNIVERSITY PRESS & ASSESSMENT

Shaftesbury Road, Cambridge CB2 8EA, United Kingdom

One Liberty Plaza, 20th Floor, New York, NY 10006, USA

477 Williamstown Road, Port Melbourne, VIC 3207, Australia

314–321, 3rd Floor, Plot 3, Splendor Forum, Jasola District Centre, New Delhi – 110025, India

103 Penang Road, #05–06/07, Visioncrest Commercial, Singapore 238467

Cambridge University Press & Assessment is a department of the University of Cambridge.

We share the University's mission to contribute to society through the pursuit of education, learning and research at the highest international levels of excellence.

www.cambridge.org
Information on this title: www.cambridge.org/9781009053570

© Cambridge University Press & Assessment 2022

First published 2011
Second edition 2015
Third edition 2022

20 19 18 17 16 15 14 13 12 11 10 9 8 7 6 5 4

Printed in Poland by Opolgraf

A catalogue record for this publication is available from the British Library

ISBN   978-1-009-05357-0   Coursebook with digital access
ISBN   978-1-009-05446-1   Digital coursebook

Cambridge University Press & Assessment has no responsibility for the persistence or accuracy of URLs for external or third-party internet websites referred to in this publication, and does not guarantee that any content on such websites is, or will remain, accurate or appropriate. Information regarding prices, travel timetables, and other factual information given in this work is correct at the time of first printing but Cambridge University Press & Assessment does not guarantee the accuracy of such information thereafter.

This work has been developed independently from and is not endorsed by the International Baccalaureate Organization. International Baccalaureate, Baccalauréat International, Bachillerato Internacional and IB are registered trademarks owned by the International Baccalaureate Organization.

....

〉 Contents

⟩ How to use this series

This suite of resources supports students and teachers following the Business Management for the IB Diploma syllabus (M2024). The components in the series are designed to work together and help students develop the necessary knowledge and skills for Business Management. With clear language and style, they are designed for international students.

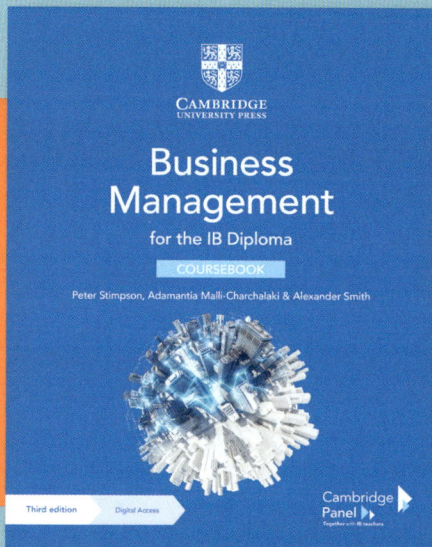

The Coursebook is designed for students to use in class with guidance from the teacher. It offers complete coverage of the Business Management for the IB Diploma syllabus (M2024). Each chapter contains clear explanations of business theory with a variety of activities, case studies and questions to engage students, help them to make real-world connections and to develop their critical thinking and evaluation skills.

The Teacher's Resource is the foundation of this series because it offers inspiring ideas about how to teach this course. Teachers will find everything they need to deliver the course in here, including teaching guidance, lesson plans, suggestions for differentiation, assessment and language support, answers and extra materials including downloadable worksheets, tests and PowerPoint slides for each chapter.

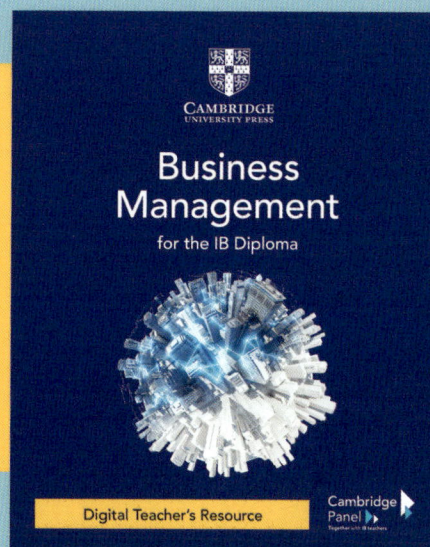

> How to use this book

Here is a brief overview of the features in this Coursebook.

LEARNING OBJECTIVES

Learning objectives help you navigate the Coursebook and indicate the important concepts in each topic.

> Higher Level Learning Objectives are marked with an arrow to allow you to easily identify Higher Level only material.

The content in this book is divided into Standard and Higher Level material. A vertical line runs down the margin of all Higher Level material, allowing you to easily identify Higher Level only material.

BUSINESS IN CONTEXT

Key ideas contained in the chapter in a real-world business context. They raise issues for discussion, with questions that allow you to look in more detail at the topic.

KEY CONCEPT LINK

These explain how the Coursebook's topics are integrated with the key concepts in the syllabus.

KEY TERMS AND FORMULAE

Key vocabulary and formulae are highlighted and explained. You will also find definitions in the Glossary.

THEORY OF KNOWLEDGE

Designed to stimulate critical thinking, allowing you to consider how you can say you know what you claim you know.

ACTIVITY

Activities include short case studies with evaluative or analytic questions, and opportunities to produce your own work individually, in pairs or in groups.

CASE STUDY

International business examples provide opportunities for you to engage with the subject, and develop your skills of application, analysis and evaluation in a real-world context.

LEARNER PROFILE

Learner profiles illustrate how the IB learner profile can be applied in different contexts.

TIPS

Tips to help with your learning cover how to avoid common errors or misconceptions, advice on essay writing, evaluation and analysis, and guidance on how answers are arrived at.

SELF-EVALUATION CHECKLIST

Statements outlining the content that you should understand by the end of the chapter. You can rate how confident you are for each of these statements when revising and re-visit topics you rated 'Needs more work' or 'Almost there'.

Higher Level only statements are marked with an arrow to allow you to easily identify Higher Level only material.

EXAM-STYLE QUESTIONS

Exam-style questions focus on knowledge and understanding, application, analysis and evaluation and may require you to use your knowledge from previous chapters.

Higher Level exam-style questions questions are marked with an arrow to allow you to easily identify Higher Level only questions.

REFLECTION

An opportunity to reflect on what you have learned and consider your own perspective on some of the issues explored.

PROJECT

Opportunities for pair or group project work to give you practice in producing different outputs, such as posters, presentations and debates, allowing you to build a range of skills.

> Introduction

Nature of the subject

The International Baccalaureate Diploma Programme course for Business Management is designed to develop an understanding of essential business theory and the ability to apply business principles, practices and skills. It encourages students to understand and analyse the diverse range of business organisations and activities, and the cultural and economic context in which businesses operate. A clear emphasis is placed on strategic decision-making both for the whole business organisation as well as within the business functions of marketing, production, human resource management and finance. Business Management is the study of both the way in which individuals and groups interact in an organisation and of the transformation of resources. It is, therefore, perfectly placed within the Group 3 subject area (Individuals and societies) of the IB Diploma Programme hexagon.

The aims of this book

As well as providing the appropriate subject content for the IB Business Management course, this book aims to:

- introduce business management as a study of ways in which individuals and groups interact in an organisation and of how resources are transformed by businesses

- explain that business management is a rigorous and rewarding subject that examines dynamic decision-making processes and assesses how decisions impact on and are affected by internal and external environments

- help students develop an understanding of business theory and the ability to apply business principles, practices and skills

- encourage students to develop international-mindedness by evaluating the activities of business in global markets and appreciating cultural diversity

- evaluate the diverse range of business organisations and activities

- develop in students an awareness of the cultural and economic context in which businesses operate

- encourage the appreciation of ethical issues and the concept of social responsibility in the global business environment

- enable the development of decision-making skills through the use of case studies that enhance students' ability to make informed business decisions

- make a clear distinction between higher-level and standard-level content, and support the higher-level material with more evaluative questions and strategic decision-based tasks

- help students improve their performance on the internal and external assessments used in the Business Management syllabus

- show how the Business Management syllabus relates to the Theory of Knowledge part of the IB Programme

- illustrate the four key concepts that underpin the Business Management syllabus (change, creativity, ethics and sustainability).

Skills

The skills acquired and developed by successful students of Business Management interlink with the IB learner profile. In particular, decision-making, risk-taking and thinking skills are needed to weigh up and make judgements on a wide range of business strategies and options. These will be transferable both to other disciplines and to higher-level undergraduate study at university.

The assessments used in the IB Business Management course will test the following skills:

- **knowledge and understanding** of business terminology, concepts, principles and theories

- **application** of skills and knowledge learnt to hypothetical and real-business situations

- **analysis and evaluation** of business decisions, strategies and practices using critical thinking

- **decision-making** by identifying the issue(s), selecting and interpreting data, applying appropriate tools and techniques, and recommending suitable solutions

- **synthesise** of knowledge in order to develop a framework for business decision-making.

Peter Stimpson, Adamantia Malli-Charchalaki, & Alexander Smith

Introduction to business management

> Chapter 1

What is a business?

BUSINESS IN CONTEXT

Enterprise in Chile

Chile is a good place for **entrepreneurs**. It was classed as the most innovative country in South America in the 2020 Global Innovation Index. According to the Global Entrepreneur Monitor (GEM), Chile is the most entrepreneurial country in the world, ahead of the US and India. Many factors explain this, such as a stable economy, several sources of start-up funding, a skilled workforce, government initiatives to support entrepreneurs and a good education system. It is possible to set up a new company in just one day. This is one reason why Chile is number one in Latin America on the 2020 World Bank's Ease of Doing Business Index.

Wheel the World is a travel company that was set up in Chile in 2017 for people with disabilities. It creates tailored travel experiences at tourist destinations around the world. The entrepreneurs who created this start-up, Alvaro Silberstein and Camilo Navarro Bustos, identified a gap in the global tourism market. The start-up raised a total of $2 million from Booking Booster, Google Launchpad Accelerator, Facebook, and Startup Chile. The company attracts disabled tourists and their families from many countries. It provides employment for an increasing number of employees who agree with Wheel the World's mission of:

- encouraging tourism for people with disabilities

- raising awareness of people with disabilities as active people who strive to live their life fully

- inspiring others with stories of overcoming, fellowship and love.

There are very few global travel companies that specialise in holidays for those with disabilities

Discuss in pairs or in a group:

- What benefits does the economy of Chile obtain from new business start-ups such as Wheel the World?

- Why is it important for entrepreneurs to identify a 'gap in the market'?

- What challenges must an entrepreneur overcome to make their business succeed?

KEY TERM

entrepreneur: someone who takes the financial risk of starting and managing a new venture

KEY CONCEPT LINK

Creativity

New enterprises need to differentiate themselves from rivals, many of whom will be well established. One way of achieving this is by innovation – providing either a different type of product or a service that is different from those of competitors, or which is delivered in a distinct way. Encouraging employees to be creative could mean they become a very useful source of ideas for new goods and services, which could help the business add value for consumers. Creativity is the ability of the mind to think freely and to generate new and original ideas. Some of the ideas of creative employees are eventually implemented on innovative products.

1.1 Introduction – what is a business?

A business is any organisation that uses resources to meet the needs of customers by providing a product or service that they demand. There are several stages in the production of finished goods. Business activity at all stages involves adding value to resources such as raw materials and semi-finished goods and making them more desirable to – and thus valued by – the customer. Without business activity we would still be entirely dependent on the goods that we could make or grow ourselves; in fact, people in some communities still are. Business activity uses the scarce resources of our planet to produce goods and services that allow us to enjoy a much higher standard of living than would be possible if we remained entirely self-sufficient.

1.2 The nature of business

Businesses identify the needs of consumers or other firms. Then they purchase resources, which are the 'inputs' of the business, or factors of production, in order to produce output. The 'outputs' of a business are the goods and services that satisfy consumers' needs, usually with the aim of making a profit. Business activity exists to produce goods or services, which can be classified in several ways: **consumer goods**, **consumer services** and **capital goods**.

Consumer goods include cars and washing machines. These two examples are referred to as durable consumer goods. Food, drink and soap are examples of non-durable consumer goods as they can only be consumed once.

1.3 What are business 'inputs'?

These are the human, physical and financial resources needed by businesses to produce goods or services. They are also known as factors of production. Businesses use different combinations of inputs,

depending on the product being produced and the size of the business. There are four main inputs:

- **Land** – this general term includes not only land itself but all of the renewable and non-renewable resources of nature such as coal, crude oil and timber.
- **Labour** – manual and skilled labour make up the workforce of the business. Some businesses are labour intensive, that is they have a high proportion of labour input compared to other factors of production. An example is house-cleaning services.
- **Capital** – this consists of the finance needed to set up a business and pay for its continuing operations. The term also includes the human-made resources used in production. These resources include capital goods such as computers, machines, factories, offices and vehicles. Some businesses are capital intensive, that is they have a high proportion of capital compared to other factors of production. An example is power stations.
- **Enterprise** – this is the driving force of business, provided by risk-taking individuals, who combine the other factors of production into a unit that is capable of producing goods and services. Enterprise provides a managing, decision-making and coordinating role. Without this essential input, even very high-quality land, labour and capital inputs will fail to provide the goods and services that customers need.

There are many other things that businesses need before they can successfully produce the goods and services demanded by customers. Figure 1.1 shows the wide range of these needs.

KEY TERMS

consumer goods: the physical and tangible goods sold to final users; these include cars, food and clothing

consumer services: non-tangible products that are sold to final users; these include hotel accommodation, insurance services and train journeys

capital goods: physical goods that are used by industry to aid in the production of other goods and services such as machines and commercial vehicles

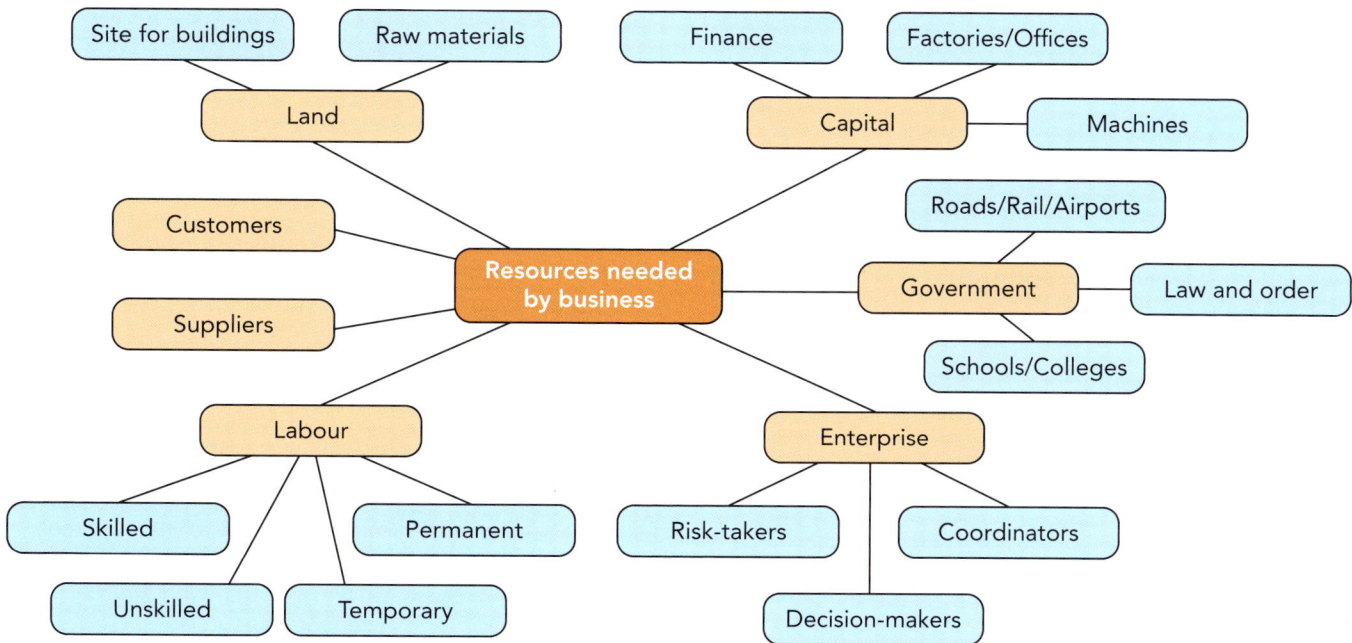

Figure 1.1: What businesses need

1.4 Business functions

Most businesses have four main functional departments. In all but very small businesses they will be staffed by people who have specific qualifications and experience in the work of the functional area.

Human resource management

Human resource (HR) management identifies the workforce needs of the business. Then it recruits, selects and trains appropriate individuals and provides motivational systems to help retain workers and encourage them to work productively. It also draws up contracts of employment and deals with the redundancy or redeployment of employees if this becomes necessary. The aim of this business function is to manage human resources to help the business achieve its overall objectives.

Finance and accounts

This function is responsible for monitoring the flow of finance into and out of the business, keeping and analysing accounts and providing financial information to both senior management and other departments. Without adequate finance, no effective decisions can be made within the other functional areas, so finance is a key division of any business.

Marketing

This function is responsible for market research and for analysing the results of such research so that consumer wants can be correctly identified. This information will then be discussed with other departments of the business so that the right product decisions are made. Once a product is available for sale, the marketing function will have to make important decisions concerning its pricing, how and where to promote it, how to sell it and how to distribute it for sale.

Operations management

Operations management is responsible for ensuring adequate resources are available for production, maintaining production and quality levels, and achieving high levels of production as efficiently as possible. This function is important in service industries as well as in traditional manufacturing. In service industries, operations management will aim to ensure that the processes for the delivery of the service are well tested, consistent and understood by all employees.

ACTIVITY 1.1

1   Identify which business function is most likely to undertake the following roles.

Role	Function
Setting prices of new products	
Recruiting a new operations manager	
Allocating resources to purchase capital equipment	
Deciding on the appropriate inventory levels of raw materials	
Finding out if consumers prefer one product design to another	
Determining the level and number of employees that the business needs for future operations	

2   The function responsible for the first role (setting prices of new products) must collaborate closely with another function before the decision is taken. Which function do you think that is?

3   How did you decide on your answer to Question 2? Did you consider the roles of all four basic business functions first to narrow your choices and to justify your answer?

1.5 Economic sectors

All production can be classified into four broad types of business activity, or economic sectors. These categories relate to the three stages involved in turning natural resources, such as oil and timber, into the finished goods and services demanded by consumers, plus the 'knowledge-based' support services that businesses require. The four sectors are **primary**, **secondary**, **tertiary** and **quaternary**.

National economic data often makes no distinction between tertiary and quaternary sectors. The balance of the primary, secondary and tertiary sectors in the economy varies substantially from country to country as it depends on the level of industrialisation in each country. The balance between the sectors is often referred to as a country's 'economic structure'. Table 1.1 shows the different economic structures of two countries.

KEY TERMS

primary sector business activity: businesses engaged in farming, fishing, oil extraction and all other industries that extract natural resources to be used and processed by other firms

secondary sector business activity: businesses that manufacture and process products from natural resources, including furniture, brewing, baking, clothing and construction

tertiary sector business activity: businesses that provide services to consumers and other businesses, such as retailing, transport, insurance, banking, hotels, tourism and telecommunications

quaternary sector business activity: this focuses on information technology (IT) businesses and information service providers such as research and development, business consulting and information gathering

Country	Primary	Secondary	Tertiary
United Kingdom	1.2	18.1	80.7
Ghana	33.8	18.6	47.6

Table 1.1: Employment data 2020 – as a percentage of total employment

CASE STUDY 1.1

Huan and Bonnie want to become entrepreneurs

Huan and Bonnie have recently graduated from university. Huan holds a degree in chemical engineering and Bonnie has graduated from a business school. They both want to become entrepreneurs, so they decided to create a start-up business producing and selling fresh ice cream. Huan will undertake the management of operations, while Bonnie will specialise in marketing.

They are worried about the management of the human resource and finance functions. They need to recruit four employees for their small production unit and two employees for the retail shop. All employees will need to be trained on the business's processes.

CONTINUED

They also need to make sure they have enough financial resources to pay for the inputs of their production.

1   Define the term 'entrepreneur'. [2]

2   In which economic sector(s) will Huan and Bonnie's start-up business operate? Justify your answer. [4]

3   Suggest two types of 'inputs' that Huan and Bonnie need in their ice-cream business. [4]

4   Using examples, explain the importance of all four business functions for the start-up ice-cream business. [4]

Changes in economic structure – sectoral change

It is very important to recognise two features of the four-sector classification of economic activity.

The first is that the importance of each sector in a country's economic structure changes over time. Industrialisation describes the growing importance of the secondary sector manufacturing industries in developing countries. The relative importance of each sector is measured in terms either of employment levels or output levels as a proportion of the whole economy. In some countries in Africa and Asia, the relative importance of secondary sector activity is increasing. This brings many benefits as well as problems.

Benefits include:

- Total national output (gross domestic product) increases and this improves average standards of living.
- The increasing output of goods can result in lower imports and higher exports of such products.
- The expansion of manufacturing businesses will result in more jobs being created.
- Expanding and profitable firms will pay more tax to the government.
- Value is added to the country's output of raw materials, such as corn processed into breakfast cereals, rather than simply exporting these as basic, unprocessed products.

Problems include:

- The chance to work in manufacturing can encourage a huge movement of people from the countryside to the towns, which leads to housing and social problems. It may also result in depopulation of rural areas, and farmers may not be able to recruit enough workers.
- The expansion of manufacturing industries may make it difficult for secondary sector businesses to recruit and retain sufficient employees.
- Imports of raw materials and components are often needed, which increases the country's import costs. Costs of imported materials vary with changes in the exchange rate.
- Pollution from factories will add to the country's environmental problems.
- Much of the growth of manufacturing industry is due to the expansion of multinational companies, which may remit all of their profits to their home countries.

In more economically developed economies, the situation is reversed. There is a general decline in the importance of secondary sector activity and an increase in the tertiary sector. This is known as deindustrialisation.

In the UK, the proportion of total output accounted for by secondary industry fell from 30% in 1970 to 17% in 2020. This decline in the relative importance of the manufacturing sector also occurred in other developed economies such as the USA, France and Germany. The reasons for and possible impact of these changes on business include the following:

- Rising incomes associated with higher living standards have led consumers to spend much of their extra income on services rather than more goods. There has been substantial growth in tourism, hotels and restaurant services, financial services and so on – yet spending on physical goods is increasing more slowly.

- As the rest of the world industrialises, manufacturing businesses in the developed countries face increased competition and these rivals tend to be more efficient and use lower-cost labour. Therefore, the growing number of imported goods are taking market away from the domestic secondary sector firms, and many have been forced to close.

- Employment patterns change – manufacturing workers may find it difficult to find employment in other sectors of industry. This is called 'structural unemployment'.

The second thing to recognise is that the relative importance of each sector varies significantly between different economies. Table 1.1 shows the differences that exist between the economies of different countries and the share of total employment accounted for by each sector of industry.

CASE STUDY 1.2

Vietnam's sectoral change

Vietnam is undergoing a swift economic transition. Historically, it has been an agricultural country, dependent on the production of rice. The country's reliance on the primary sector has been reducing over time.

The secondary sector grew fast, especially in the late 2000s. The growth of manufacturing, mostly in auxiliary industries such as textile, electronics, leather and garments has been supported by various economic policies of the Vietnamese government. Moreover, Japan offered aid of approximately $180 million to finance small and medium-sized enterprises (SMEs) in Vietnam. As a result, areas such as Que Vo district and Bac Ninh province became industrial zones. The industrialisation of Vietnam attracted big multinational firms such as the Korean company Samsung, which now assembles most of its smartphones in the country. By 2020, smartphones accounted for roughly one quarter of the country's exports.

Today, Vietnam is developing its tertiary sector fast. Some of the fastest-growing industries are finance and banking, insurance, health care, education, transportation, trade and tourism. Modern technologies in the quaternary sector are growing fast as well, with firms like Samsung investing in artificial intelligence (AI), 5G, and research and development (R&D) facilities.

Vietnam's sectoral change has improved overall welfare in the country by increasing the national output and creating new job positions in the secondary and tertiary sectors. The average

household income has increased, leading to improved living standards. Yet, Nguyen Hoang Dung, former R&D director of the Ho Chi Minh City Institute of Economy and Management in Vietnam, identified some issues along with the benefits of the sectoral change. Some of these issues are linked to the fact that most of the economic shift is led by foreign businesses. One main problem is the lack of adequate training of local manual workers by multinational companies. Also, foreign firms often do not transfer much technological know-how to Vietnamese engineers, and they are not environmentally responsible.

1 Define the term 'secondary sector'. [2]

2 With reference to the case study, identify two examples of 'sectoral change' in the Vietnamese economy. [4]

3 With reference to the case study, identify one advantage and one disadvantage of the economic transition in Vietnam. [4]

TIP

It is a good idea to read the business section of newspapers regularly. Don't forget that these are often available free online. This will help you to apply the work you have done in class to the real world, and actual business examples can be used to help answer some examination questions. For example, what was the major business story in your country this week?

ACTIVITY 1.2

Business	Primary	Secondary	Tertiary	Quaternary	Description of main activities
Coca-Cola					
HSBC					
RTZ Corporation plc					
Booking.com					
Rolls Royce Holdings plc					
Tencent					

1 Copy the table above into your notebook. Use the internet or other means of research to:

   a identify these well-known international companies

   b identify the main sector of industry that they operate in

   c give details of their main activities.

2 Have you had problems identifying the main sector of any of the companies in the table? If so, why? How did you come up with an answer?

3 Research **five** businesses that operate in your country and identify which sector of the industry they mostly operate in and what their main activities are.

1.6 Entrepreneurship – starting a business
Opportunities

The process of setting up a new business is known as entrepreneurship. Entrepreneurs have many different reasons for starting their own business but the main opportunities created by setting up a business are:

- Overcoming unemployment. Losing a job encourages many people to set up a business of their own. They could provide a product or service similar to that of their former employer, or another product, or they could provide a service based on an interest or skill they have. Talking to friends and family may reveal various products or services that an entrepreneur could offer.

- Being independent. Some people dislike the idea of being told what to do! By creating their own business they have flexibility around their work and control over their working lives. If the business is a success, the entrepreneur will no longer have to accept other managers' decisions, nor face the threat of being made redundant by an employer.

- Improving standard of living. The desire to earn more money is the main thing that drives most entrepreneurs to establish their own business. Many people setting up a business believe that they will earn a higher income working for themselves as they will be motivated to work hard and take the necessary business risks.

Knowledge question: To what extent does intuition affect entrepreneurship?

Entrepreneurs are people who are willing to take risks to turn innovative ideas into goods and services.

Start-up businesses face a high risk of failure. In order to avoid this, entrepreneurs must organise their resources and pursue their goals in the most effective way possible.

In many cases, entrepreneurs decide on appropriate business opportunities after researching the market. They examine the overall external environment to identify the potential risks. They study basic statistics such as market shares and market growth data, and in some cases they perform primary research to understand the exact wants of consumers before making any investments.

However, some famous entrepreneurs base their business plan on intuition rather than facts. Intuition – sometimes referred to as a 'gut feeling' – is not a magic ability. It is the result of accumulated knowledge, perspective, cultural background, personal ethics and experience. According to scientific evidence, the intuitive sense is the result of signals sent via neural communication channels between the gut and the brain. Richard Branson, the founder of the Virgin Group, once said: 'I rely far more on gut instinct than researching huge amounts of statistics.'

Should logic, statistics and facts overrule intuition when entrepreneurs decide on new business activities? Discuss in class.

KEY TERM

business plan: a written document that describes a business, its objectives and its strategies, the market it is in and its financial forecasts

Challenges

The potential for success when starting a new business can be considerable. However, if it was easy to set up a successful business we would all be multimillionaires! There are many challenges that new entrepreneurs have to confront and overcome when setting up a business.

Challenge 1: Do I have the appropriate personal qualities?

There are some important personal qualities that most successful entrepreneurs tend to have.

Innovation

The entrepreneur may not be a 'product inventor', but they must be able to create a new niche in the market. They need to attract consumers in innovative ways and present their business as being 'different'. This requires original ideas and an ability to do things innovatively.

Commitment and self-motivation

It is never easy to set up and run your own business. It is hard work and it may take up several hours every day. A willingness to work hard, a keen ambition to succeed, energy and focus are all essential qualities of a successful entrepreneur.

Multiple skills

An entrepreneur will have to make the product or provide the service, promote it, sell it and count the money. These different business tasks require a person with many different qualities such as being keen to learn technical skills, an ability to get on with people, and being good at handling money and keeping accounting records.

Leadership skills

An entrepreneur has to lead by example. They must have a personality that encourages people in the business to follow them and be motivated by them.

Self-belief

Many business start-ups fail, but this will not discourage a true entrepreneur. They believe in their abilities and business ideas and they will bounce back from any setbacks.

Risk-taking

Entrepreneurs must be willing to take risks in order to see results. Often the risk they take involves investing their own savings in a new business.

LEARNER PROFILE

Risk-takers

Entrepreneurs take calculated risks hoping for great rewards.

A good example is the founder of Dropbox, Drew Houston. Houston was a student at MIT and was fed up with carrying lots of USB sticks and having to email documents to himself to use of different computers. He came up with an idea for a solution and after some setbacks managed to apply to the startup hub YCominator and started Dropbox in 2007. A few years later he was contacted directly by Steve Jobs at Apply to say the market for Dropbox would be taken over by the iCloud service, but Houston refused to sell to Apple. The company he built is now worth over $1 billion.

Find examples of famous businesses which became a success a few years after their set-up. Did the entrepreneurs behind these businesses take any risks? How did the risk-taking attitude of the entrepreneurs contribute to the success of the businesses? Discuss in class.

Challenge 2: Is there a market for my product?

Many people say that they want to work for themselves. However, many fail to become entrepreneurs because they are unable to identify a market opportunity (i.e., a product or service) that is sufficiently in demand for the business to make a profit.

The original idea for most new businesses usually comes from one of the following sources:

- own skills or hobbies, e.g., dressmaking or car bodywork repairs
- previous employment experience, e.g., hairdressing
- conferences and exhibitions which offer a wide range of new business start-up ideas using franchising, e.g., fast-food restaurants

- small-budget market research. The internet allows any user to browse directories to see how many businesses of specific types there are in the local area. This low-cost research might indicate gaps in local markets that the entrepreneur could fill and make a profit.

Challenge 3: Do I have sufficient capital?

Once an entrepreneur has decided on the business idea or opportunity, the next task is to raise the necessary capital. This will come from various sources, but the business owner/entrepreneur will almost certainly have to use some of their own savings to set up the business. Friends and family might also provide financial support. Banks may provide finance by way of a loan or an overdraft facility, but they will want to check the business plan carefully. Venture capitalists may be prepared to invest if the business idea is novel, offers significant profit potential and can be legally protected by a patent so that the idea cannot be copied. Government grants might be available, perhaps as part of a policy to reduce unemployment by encouraging people to set up new businesses.

In an International Labour Organization (ILO) survey of new business start-ups, entrepreneurs said that the main difficulty they faced was getting finance. Why is obtaining finance such a major problem for entrepreneurs?

- Lack of sufficient own finance – many entrepreneurs have limited personal savings, especially if they are setting up their own business because they have been made redundant.
- Lack of awareness of the financial support and grants available.
- Lack of any trading record to present to banks as evidence of past business success – a trading record can give a bank more confidence when deciding whether to lend money for a new venture.
- A poorly produced business plan that fails to convince potential investors of the chances that the business will succeed. A lack of capital to run day-to-day business affairs is the single most common reason that businesses fail to survive in the first year. Capital is needed for day-to-day cash, in order to hold stock, and to allow the business to give trade credit to customers who then become debtors. Without sufficient working capital, the business may be unable to buy more stock or pay suppliers or offer credit to important customers.

Challenge 4: Where should I locate my business?

A suitable location is vital if the start-up business intends to sell directly to consumers. This raises the problem of costs.

Perhaps the most important consideration when choosing the location for a new business is the need to minimise fixed costs. When finance is limited, it is very important to try to keep the break-even level of output as low as possible. Break-even is the output level where enough revenue is earned to cover all costs. This will greatly increase the chances of survival.

Most entrepreneurs start their business by operating from their home. This has the advantage of keeping costs low, but there are drawbacks:

- The entrepreneur's home may not be close to the area with the biggest market potential.
- It lacks status – a business with its own prestigious premises tends to generate confidence.
- It may cause family tensions.
- It may be difficult to separate private life from working life.

If operating the business from home is not possible then the location and cost of new premises will have a big impact on the likely success of the business. New businesses that offer a consumer service need to consider location carefully. For example, a website designer could operate from home quite effectively, as communication with customers will be by electronic means. However, a hairdresser may need to consider obtaining premises in an area with the biggest number of potential customers. An alternative would be to visit customers in their own homes – this way, the entrepreneur may avoid the costs of buying or renting their own premises.

Challenge 5: How do I build a customer base?

In order to survive, a new enterprise must establish itself in the market and build up customer numbers as quickly as possible. The long-term strength of the business will depend on encouraging customers to return to purchase products again and again. Many small businesses try to encourage this by offering a better service than their larger and better-funded competitors. This might include:

- personal customer service
- knowledgeable pre- and after-sales service
- fulfilling one-off customer requests that larger firms may be reluctant to provide for.

Challenge 6: How do I compete effectively?

This is nearly always a problem for new enterprises unless the business idea is unique. Often a newly created business will experience competition from more established businesses that have more resources and market knowledge. The entrepreneur may have to offer better customer service to overcome the cost and pricing advantages of bigger businesses.

Challenge 7: Must I keep accurate business records?

Accurate records are vital in order to pay taxes and bills and chase up debtors. Many entrepreneurs fail to pay sufficient attention to this. They either believe it is less important than actually meeting customers' needs, or they think they can remember everything, which is impossible. For example, the owner of a new, busy florist's shop will not be able to remember all of the following:

- when the next delivery of fresh flowers is due to arrive
- whether the flowers for last week's big wedding have been paid for
- if the money received from an important customer has been paid into the bank
- how many hours the shop assistant worked last week.

Challenge 8: Do I have the necessary management skills?

Most entrepreneurs have had some form of work experience, but not necessarily at a management level. They may not have gained experience of:

- leadership skills
- cash handling and cash management skills
- planning and coordinating skills
- decision-making skills
- communication skills
- marketing, promotion and selling skills.

Entrepreneurs may be very keen and willing to work hard, and they may have abilities in their chosen field. For example, a new restaurant owner may be an excellent chef, but they could lack management skills. Some entrepreneurs learn these skills quickly once the business is up and running, but this is a risky strategy. Other entrepreneurs buy in the skills by employing staff with management experience, but this is an expensive option.

Just because a business is new and small it does not mean that enthusiasm, a strong personality and hard work will be sufficient to ensure success. This may prove to be the case, but often it is not. Potential entrepreneurs are encouraged to either seek management experience through employment or attend training courses to gain some of the required skills before putting their capital at risk.

Challenge 9: How do I deal with change?

Setting up a new business is risky. Not only are there the problems and challenges referred to above but there is also the risk of change, which can lead to the original business idea being less successful. New businesses may fail if any of the following changes occur, turning the venture from a successful one to a loss-making enterprise:

- new competitors appear
- legal changes, e.g., the product is banned
- economic changes that leave customers with less money to spend
- technological changes that make the methods used by the new business old-fashioned and expensive.

The list of changes could be longer, but even these four factors show that the business environment is a dynamic one, and this makes owning and running a business enterprise very risky.

Challenges and opportunities for starting a business – conclusion

This section has identified and explained the opportunities and challenges for new entrepreneurs. People who want to start a new business should always be encouraged to create a detailed business plan (see 1.7 Business management tool: Business plans). This will help to analyse how the opportunities can be exploited and the challenges overcome.

CASE STUDY 1.3

Why do start-ups fail?

Based on research performed on small businesses across various industries in the US, around 90% of start-up ventures eventually fail. In 2019, the industries in which start-up failure was especially high were grocery retailing, trucking, plumbing, air conditioning and heating, as well as security brokerage. The risk of failure was much lower in health care, social services, construction, transportation, and warehousing. The same research identified the main reasons why start-ups often fail. Some of the most significant factors are the inexperience of entrepreneurs and managers, the failure to understand the exact consumer needs and wants and the lack of adequate financial resources. On the other hand, one of the most important factors increasing the chances of success is the use of third-party experts as advisers who help the entrepreneurs to put their plans into action. Start-up businesses using professional advisers grow 3.5 times faster than start-up businesses that rely only on the know-how of their founders.

1   Define the term 'start-up business'.   [2]

2   Suggest **two** possible reasons why the probability of success varies across different industries in the USA.   [4]

3   Suggest **two** reasons why small start-ups that use third-party professional advisers grow faster than the ones which do not.   [4]

1.7 Business management tool: Business plans

Looking ahead is a key part of the effective management of any business. Making plans for the future helps to prepare finance and other resources for a new venture. Business plans are an important business management tool.

The contents of a typical business plan are:

- the executive summary – an overview of the new business and its strategies
- description of the business opportunity – details of the entrepreneur; what is going to be sold, why and to whom
- marketing and sales strategy – details of why the entrepreneur thinks customers will buy what the business intends to sell, and how the business aims to sell to them
- management team and personnel – the skills and experience of the entrepreneur and the employees they intend to recruit
- operations – premises to be used, production facilities, IT systems
- financial forecasts – the future projections of sales, profit and cash flow, for at least one year ahead.

Table 1.2 shows a typical business plan summary for a new business venture.

Name of business	Pizza Piazza Ltd
Type of organisation	Privately held company
Details of business owners	Peter Chun – chef with 15 years' experience
	Sabrina Singh – deputy manager of restaurant for three years
Business aim	To provide a high-class takeaway pizza service including home delivery
Product	High-quality home-cooked pizzas
Price	Average price of $10 with $2 delivery charge
Market aimed for	Young people and families
Market research undertaken and the results	Research in the area conducted using questionnaires
	Also, research into national trends in takeaway sales and local competitors
	Results of all research in the appendix to this plan
Human resources plan	Two workers (the business owners) to be the only staff to be employed initially
Production details and business costs	Main suppliers – R and R Wholesalers
	Fixed costs of business – $70 000 per year
	Variable costs – approximately $2 per unit sold
Location of business	Site in shopping street (Brindisi Avenue) just beyond the town centre. Leasehold site (ten years)
Main equipment required	Second-hand kitchen equipment – $6000
	Second-hand motorbike – $2000

Forecast profit	See financial appendix to this plan
	Summary: In the first year of operations the total costs are forecast to be $55 000 with revenue of $85 000. Predicted profit = $30 000
	Level of output to break even – 8750 units per year
Cash flow forecast	See financial appendix to this plan
	Due to the high set-up and promotion costs there will be negative cash flow in the first year
Finance	$10 000 invested by each of the owners
	Request to bank for a further $10 000 plus an overdraft arrangement of $5000 per month

Table 1.2: Business plan for Pizza Piazza Ltd

Importance of business plans

- Business plans are very important when setting up a new business, but they should also be referred to and updated when further important strategic choices are made. The main purpose of a business plan for a new business is to obtain finance for the start-up. Potential investors or creditors will not provide finance unless clear details about the business proposal have been written down.

- The planning process is very important too. If an entrepreneur went into a new business – even if no external finance was required – without a clear sense of purpose, direction, marketing strategies and what employees to recruit, the chances of success would be greatly reduced.

- The financial and other forecasts contained in the plan can be used as the targets that the business should aim for.

Users of business plans

Business plans may be of real benefit to the stakeholders of new businesses:

- The plan allows potential investors in the new business – and the bank – to make a judgement about the viability of the idea and the chances of the owners making a success of it. Potential shareholders will not invest without seeing a plan.

- The financial forecasts in a business plan can act as budgets and control benchmarks for the internal stakeholders such as business managers.

- Updated versions of the plan can be used to apply for additional funding, to attract more partners or to supply data for the experts if a stock market flotation becomes an option.

- Employees will find that planning helps to identify specific objectives and targets and gives focus to their work, which aids motivation.

- Suppliers may be able to tell from the parts of the business plan that are communicated externally whether it is worthwhile establishing a long-term trading relationship with the business.

Business plans as a business management tool

This business management tool can be integrated into all functional units of the IB syllabus as follows:

- A business plan for a start-up business needs to include evidence about and forecasts for human resources, finance, operations and marketing.

- A completely new venture for an established business, such as setting up operations in another country, also requires careful planning. A business plan for this type of new venture would be essential and this must draw evidence from all four main functional areas.

CASE STUDY 1.4

Does Chu Hua need a business plan?

Chu Hua is a young entrepreneur in Vietnam. Her start-up business operates in the quaternary sector, offering artificial intelligence (AI) applications such as fraud detection, security, chatbox and more to various organisations. She currently employs eight people. The Covid-19 pandemic created many opportunities in the AI industry, as businesses across all fields rushed to improve their online sales and services. Health care is just one example of an industry that needs AI applications to manage an increasing volume of data due to the pandemic.

Even though the external opportunities are excellent, Chu Hua faces many challenges when managing her start-up business. Firstly, competition in the industry is fierce. Bigger, more established competitors have already signed contracts with large customers and it is easier for them to promote their innovations through direct selling. Moreover, Chu Hua finds it difficult to attract sources of finance, as investors and traditional banks are afraid of the risk of failure, which is high for start-ups. Without enough resources, the business cannot proceed to invest in technology for innovation.

According to global research published in 2021, most start-ups eventually fail, 10% of them within the first year. In her effort to attract finance, Chu Hua is currently working closely with the finance

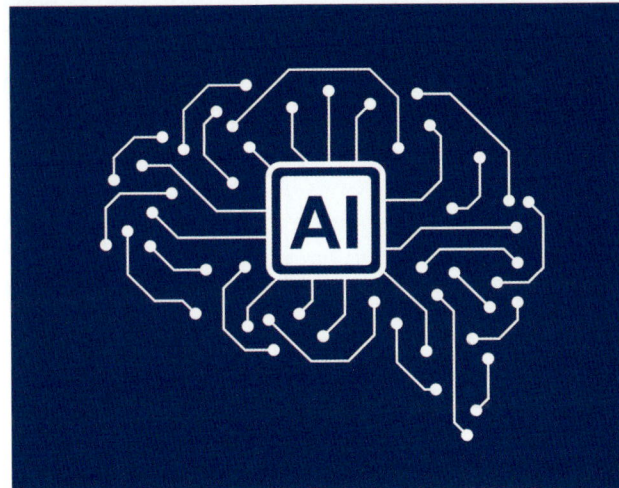

director of her business to prepare a detailed business plan. However, business planning is a difficult process, especially given that the market is very dynamic and fast changing.

1 Define the term 'quaternary sector'. [2]

2 Explain **two** reasons why the risk of failure is big for Chu Hua's start-up business. [4]

3 Identify **two** roles of Chu Hua as an entrepreneur. [4]

4 Discuss the usefulness of a business plan for Chu Hua. [10]

ACTIVITY 1.3

Quibi was a video streaming service which shut down just a few months after its launch, even though it was designed to revolutionise in the way people enjoy videos on their smartphones.

1 Find information on Quibi and do some personal research on the failed start-up business.

2 Bring your findings to class to prepare a presentation covering the reasons why the Quibi start-up failed.

3 Split into two groups. Debate the following statement: 'Quibi could have survived if it had offered its services for free like TikTok and YouTube.'

SELF-EVALUATION CHECKLIST

After studying this chapter, complete this table.

I know and understand:	Needs more work	Almost there	Ready to move on
the nature of business (AO1)			
I am able to apply and analyse:			
primary, secondary, tertiary and quaternary sectors (AO2)			
entrepreneurship – opportunities for starting a business (AO2)			
entrepreneurship – challenges of starting a business (AO2)			
I am able to select and apply the business management tool:			
business plans (AO4)			

REFLECTION

1   Assume you plan to start a new business enterprise. How would you decide which products or services to sell?

2   If you were planning to set up the business with another person, why would collaboration be important?

3   Entrepreneurs need to balance the risk involved with a new business against the potential profit. After reading this chapter, how would you attempt to do this for your new business enterprise?

PROJECT

Split into groups of four students.

1   Each group will form the management team of a start-up business. Each group member must take one of the following roles: HR director, marketing director, operations director and finance director. Each team will need to vote (or randomly select) one of its members to be the managing director.

2   Each team should decide on the type of business activity to set up and will need to prepare a brief business plan, similar to Table 1.2. In the finance section, you need to include a breakdown of your capital investment and justify why you need a loan for $50 000 from the bank.

3   Each team will prepare a class presentation on their business idea and key elements of their business plan.

4   Your teacher will act as the bank manager responsible for assessing your request for a loan to help you with your start-up plans. They will try to challenge your idea, and they can only give a loan of $50 000 to one of the teams! Prepare to receive questions on the problems you are expecting to face as a start-up business. Also, be prepared to answer any questions from the managers of the other businesses competing for the loan.

CONTINUED

Thinking about your project:

- Have you considered the risks of your business activity before you set it up as entrepreneurs? How could your business overcome such risks?

- How significant is a collaboration among the team members to create the business plan? Do you have any disagreements or problems that you have to overcome when preparing the business plan and the presentation? How can the managing director help your team deal with such issues?

EXAM-STYLE QUESTIONS

Recession sparks new business ideas

Disney, McDonald's, Burger King, Procter & Gamble, Johnson & Johnson, Microsoft – what do they all have in common? They all started during a recession or depression.

The message, delivered to around 40 would-be entrepreneurs at a workshop in Stratford, East London, is clear: do not let bad economic headlines put you off. Most of the people at this session are not aiming to create new multinational corporations. But during the coffee break, they seem pretty confident that their ideas can prosper even in the current climate. 'I'm here to find out about starting up a business providing CVs to school leavers,' says Jessica Lyons, wearing a lapel badge with My First CV, the name of the future business, written on it. 'For my particular business idea, I think this is the ideal time because there are more people than ever out there looking for work.'

The recession is causing a spike in interest in setting up small businesses. Another interesting example was from a gym instructor who wants to take his equipment to companies around London, giving people a lunchtime workout without them having to leave their offices. Most of the would-be entrepreneurs in Stratford are looking at potential opportunities in the tertiary sector which do not require large amounts of start-up finance to purchase capital equipment, and which rely more on their own skills and interests. Yet, some opportunities also arise in the secondary sector. Small producers of low-priced unbranded food products experience increasing demand for their goods, as retailers try to satisfy consumers with value-for-money offers. Overall, the demand for basic food products does not fall as much as the demand for luxury goods and services during a recession.

Even though the steps to follow to set up a business are similar under conditions of economic recession and in conditions of growth, the problems that start-ups face may be more severe when the economy is undergoing a downturn. To balance the risks of failure, some entrepreneurs employ managers who are experienced in the market and can help the business to survive and grow in the long run and can assist with the preparation of the start-up's business plan.

1	Define the term 'tertiary sector'.	[2]
2	State **two** elements of a business plan.	[2]
3	Outline the factors of production needed to set up the business providing CVs to school leavers.	[4]
4	Explain **two** reasons why new businesses might start up in the tertiary sector.	[4]
5	Suggest **two** reasons why the CV writing start-up might need a business plan.	[4]
6	Explain **two** common steps of opening a business in the tertiary sector.	[4]
7	Explain **two** common problems of start-ups that are particularly difficult to handle under conditions of economic recession.	[4]
8	Identify **two** types of resources needed for a person to open a business activity as a gym instructor.	[4]
9	Suggest **two** ways in which entrepreneurs may try to reduce the risk of failure for a start-up business.	[4]
10	Discuss the opportunities and challenges of setting up a business in a recession.	[10]

Chapter 2

Types of business entities

LEARNING OBJECTIVES

On completing this chapter you should be able to:

Apply and analyse:

- The distinction between the private and public sectors (AO2)

Evaluate:

- The main features of the following types of organisations: sole traders, partnerships, privately held companies and publicly held companies (AO3)
- The main features of the following types of for-profit social enterprises: private sector companies, public sector companies and cooperatives (AO3)
- The main features of the following types of non-profit social enterprises: non-governmental organisations (NGOs) (AO3)

BUSINESS IN CONTEXT

Pague Menos converts to public limited company

In 2020, Brazil recorded a high number of companies selling **shares** to the public for the first time. Converting a **privately held company** (private limited company) to a **publicly held company** (public limited company) is usually undertaken by arranging an **initial public offering (IPO)**. Many of these companies were originally owned and operated by families that now want to sell shares to the public to raise substantial capital sums.

One such company is Pague Menos, which operates a large chain of drug stores (pharmacies) in Brazil. The controlling **shareholders** are the Queiros family. The decision was taken in 2020 to try to raise around 1.2 billion reais (about $224 million) by selling Pague Menos shares to the public. IPOs convert privately held (owned) companies into publicly held (owned) companies. The plan was to use the capital raised to fund further growth of the business. Opportunities for increased sales of pharmaceutical products grew following public concern about health due to the Covid-19 pandemic.

Discuss in pairs or a group:

- Why do you think the owners of Pague Menos arranged an IPO?

- What are the likely advantages and disadvantages to the existing owners of a company of converting a privately held company to a publicly held company?

KEY TERMS

share: a certificate confirming part ownership of a company. Most types of share entitle shareholders to dividends paid from profits

privately held company: a business that is owned by shareholders who are often members of the same family; this company cannot sell shares to the general public

publicly held company: a limited company with the legal right to sell shares to financial institutions and the general public; its share price is quoted on the national stock exchange

initial public offering (IPO): the process of offering for sale the shares of a privately held company to financial institutions and the general public

shareholders: individuals or institutions that buy/own shares in a limited company

KEY CONCEPT LINK

Ethics

All businesses have ethical responsibilities, but the existence and long-term survival of charitable non-profit organisations relies on their ethics and transparency. If the public loses trust in charities, those charities stop receiving donations. In the US, the National Council of Nonprofits supports charities by sharing practices that demonstrate accountability, ethics and transparency to the public. This is very important from the perspective of the Council, because if one of their members behaves unethically, 'that's one too many': people could lose trust in non-profit charities overall.

2.1 Distinction between the private and public sectors

Chapter 1 looked at the classification of business into different economic sectors. This chapter further classifies business activity into:

- the **private sector** and **public sector**
- for-profit and non-profit organisations.

The relative importance of the private sector compared to the public sector is not the same in all **mixed economies**. Those that are similar to **free-market economies** have very small public sectors. Those countries with central planning **command economies** will have very few businesses in the private sector.

In most mixed economies, certain important goods and services are provided by state-run organisations – they are in the public sector. It is argued that they are too significant to be left to private sector businesses. They include health and education services, defence, and law and order (the police force). In some countries, important 'strategic' industries are also state owned and state controlled, such as energy, telecommunications and public transport. These public sector organisations therefore provide essential goods and services for individual citizens and organisations in the private sector. They often have objectives other than profit, for example:

- ensuring supplies of essential goods and services – perhaps free of charge to the user, e.g., health and education services in some countries
- preventing private sector monopolies (single firms that dominate an industry) from controlling supply
- maintaining employment
- maintaining environmental standards.

There has been a trend in many countries towards selling some public sector organisations to the private sector – called **privatisation** – and this means that profit-making becomes one of their main objectives.

Private sector organisations are owned and operated by individuals or groups of people. Most of these organisations are operated for a profit, but not all. For example, charities are non-profit making organisations in the private sector; they are not owned and controlled by the government or state.

KEY TERMS

private sector: comprises businesses owned and controlled by individuals or groups of individuals

public sector: comprises organisations accountable to and controlled by central or local government (the state)

mixed economy: economic resources are owned and controlled by both private and public sectors

free-market economy: economic resources are owned largely by the private sector, with very little state intervention

command economy: economic resources are owned, planned and controlled by the state

privatisation: the sale of public sector organisations to the private sector

---

2.2 The main features of private sector businesses

Figure 2.1 shows the main types of private sector businesses that are operated for profit.

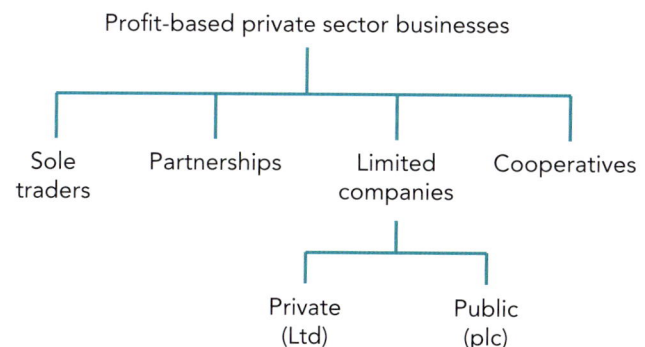

Figure 2.1: Private sector businesses that are operated for profit

Sole trader

This is the most common form of business organisation. Although there is a single owner in this business organisation, there may be employees. But the firm is likely to remain very small. While they are great in number, **sole traders** account for only a small proportion of total business turnover. All sole traders have unlimited liability. This means that the owner's personal possessions and property can be taken to pay off the debts of the business should it fail. This can discourage some potential entrepreneurs from starting their own business.

Another problem faced by sole traders involves finance for expansion. Many sole traders remain small because the owner wants to keep control of their own business. Another reason is the limitations that they have in raising additional capital. As soon as partners or shareholders are sought in order to raise finance, then the sole trader becomes another form of organisation altogether. In order to remain a sole trader, the owner is dependent on their own savings, profits made and loans for injections of capital.

This type of business organisation is most commonly established in construction, retailing, hairdressing, car servicing and catering. The advantages and disadvantages of sole traders are summarised in Table 2.1.

Partnership

A **partnership** agreement does not create a separate legal unit; a partnership is just a grouping of individuals.

Partnerships are formed in order to overcome some of the drawbacks of being a sole trader. When planning to go into partnership, it is important to choose business partners carefully – the errors and poor decisions of any one partner are considered to be the responsibility of them all. This also applies to business debts incurred by one partner. In most countries there is unlimited liability for all partners should the business venture fail. It is usual, although not a legal requirement, to draw up a formal Deed of Partnership between all of the partners. This provides agreement on issues such as voting rights, the distribution of profits, the management role of each partner and who has authority to sign contracts.

Partnerships are the most common form of business organisation in some professions, such as law and accountancy. Small building firms are often partnerships too. The advantages and disadvantages of partnerships are summarised in Table 2.2.

> **KEY TERMS**
>
> **sole trader:** a business that is exclusively owned by one person who has full control of it and is entitled to all of the profit (after tax)
>
> **partnership:** a business formed by two or more people to carry on a business together, with shared capital investment and, usually, shared responsibilities

Advantages	Disadvantages
Easy to set up – no legal formalities	Unlimited liability – all of owner's assets are potentially at risk
Owner has complete control – not answerable to anyone else	Often faces intense competition from bigger firms, e.g. food retailing
Owner keeps all profits	Owner of a small business may have responsibility for all aspects of management and may therefore be unable to specialise
Able to choose times and patterns of working	
Able to establish close personal relationships with staff (if any are employed) and customers	Difficult to raise additional capital
	Long hours are often necessary to make the business pay
Rather than working as an employee for a larger firm, the sole trader can use their skills in their own business	Lack of continuity – as the business does not have separate legal status, when the owner dies the business ends too

Table 2.1 Sole traders – advantages and disadvantages

Advantages	Disadvantages
Partners may specialise in different areas of business management	Unlimited liability for all partners (with some exceptions)
Shared decision-making	Profits are shared
Additional capital can be injected by each partner	As with sole traders, there is no continuity and the partnership will have to be reformed in the event of the death of one of the partners
Business losses are shared between partners	All partners are bound by the decisions of any one of them
Greater privacy and fewer legal formalities than corporate organisations (companies)	Not possible to raise capital by selling shares
	Partners need to discuss and agree major decisions which might take a long time

Table 2.2: Partnerships – advantages and disadvantages

CASE STUDY 2.1

Martha's digital marketing agency

After being crowned entrepreneur of the year at the 2020 'Women in Business' Awards, Martha's digital marketing agency has gone on to beat her revenue target and win new clients. She has been nominated for the awards again this year, in the small business of the year and inspirational woman categories. Martha set up 'Catchy Internet' as a sole trader in 2009 to help businesses be more successful on the internet. She decided to grow the business in 2015, and by 2020 the business has expanded from 3 employees to 18.

She said: 'I am very pleased to be nominated again this year. The awards ceremony itself is a great chance to network with other successful businesspeople. Winning the award raised the visibility of Catchy Internet, which is growing fast. We are working with a lot of exciting clients. Our goal was a revenue of $1 million in 2021 but we are already ahead of that target. The next goal is to grow outside our local geographical area. We have already signed contracts with two multinational customers.'

Martha is now considering the possibility of changing the type of organisation from a sole trader business to a partnership with her friend Alan, who specialises in financial management and business planning. But Martha has been advised by one of her most loyal employees to avoid the disadvantages of a partnership by turning the business into a privately held company.

1   Define the term 'privately held company'.   [2]

2   Outline **two** advantages for Martha of running her business as a sole trader.   [4]

3   Outline **two** problems that Martha may face due to being a sole trader.   [4]

4   Discuss the possible advantages and disadvantages for Martha if she decides to change her business organisation from a sole trader business to a partnership.   [10]

Limited companies

There are three important differences between companies (privately held companies and publicly held companies) and sole traders and partnerships:

- company shareholders have **limited liability**, but sole traders and partners do not (apart from the case of limited liability partnerships)
- companies have legal personality but sole traders and partnerships do not
- companies can continue after the death of one of the owners, unlike sole traders and partnerships.

KEY TERM

limited liability: the only liability – or potential loss – a shareholder (or partner in a limited liability partnership) has if the company fails is the amount invested in the company, not the total wealth of the shareholder

---

- **Limited liability:** The ownership of companies is divided into small units called shares. People can buy these and become 'shareholders' – they are part-owners of the business. It is possible to buy just one share, but some shareholders will own many shares. It is possible for one person or organisation to have complete control if they own more than 50% of the shares in a company. Individuals with a large number of shares often become directors of the business. All shareholders benefit from the advantage of limited liability. Nobody can make any further claim against shareholders should the company fail. This has two important effects:

  - People are prepared to provide finance to enable companies to expand as the risk of losing capital is limited to the investment in shares.

  - The greater risk of the company failing to pay its debts is now transferred from investors to creditors (those suppliers/lenders who have not been paid). So creditors may be keen to check if the word 'limited' appears in the company name and to scrutinise the company's accounts for signs of potential future weakness.

- **Legal personality:** A company is legally recognised as having an identity separate from that of its owners. This means, for example, that if the products sold by a company are found to be dangerous or faulty, the company itself can be prosecuted but not the owners, as would be the case with either a sole trader or a partnership. A company can be sued and it can sue others through the courts.

- **Continuity:** In a company, the death of an owner or director does not lead to its break-up or dissolution. All that happens is that ownership continues through the inheritance of the shares, and there is no break in ownership.

Privately held companies

The protection that comes from forming a company is therefore substantial. Small firms can gain this protection when the owner(s) create(s) a privately held company. In many countries these are referred to as private limited companies.

Usually the shares will be owned by the original sole trader (who may hold the majority of the shares to keep control of the company), relatives, friends and employees. New issues of shares cannot be sold on the open market to the public. Existing shareholders may only sell their shares with the agreement of the other shareholders.

Legal formalities must be followed when setting up a privately held company and these can be expensive and time-consuming in some countries. The advantages and disadvantages of privately held companies are summarised in Table 2.3.

Publicly held companies

Publicly held companies (known as 'plcs') are the most common form of legal organisation for large businesses because they have access to substantial funds for expansion. Converting a privately held company to publicly held company status is referred to as a stock market flotation.

A publicly held company has all the advantages of privately held company status plus the right to advertise its shares for sale and have them quoted on the stock exchange. Publicly held companies have the potential to raise large sums of money from public issues of shares. Existing shareholders can sell their shares quickly if they want to. This flexibility of share buying and selling encourages the public to purchase the shares in the first instance and thus invest in the business.

Advantages	Disadvantages
Shareholders have limited liability	There are legal formalities involved in establishing the business
Separate legal personality	
Continuity in the event of the death of a shareholder	Capital cannot be raised by the sale of shares to the general public
The original owner is often still able to retain control	It is quite difficult for shareholders to sell shares
Ability to raise capital from the sale of shares to family, friends and employees	In the UK, end-of-year accounts must be sent to Companies House – they are available for public inspection there (there is less secrecy over financial affairs than for sole traders or partnerships)
Greater status than a non-company or unincorporated business	

Table 2.3: Privately held companies – advantages and disadvantages

Advantages	Disadvantages
Limited liability	There are legal formalities in formation
Separate legal identity	Cost of business consultants and financial advisers when creating a plc
Continuity	Share prices are subject to fluctuation, sometimes for reasons beyond the business's control, e.g. the state of the economy
Ease of buying and selling of shares for shareholders – this encourages investment in plcs	
Access to substantial capital sources due to the ability to issue a prospectus to the public, giving full details of a potential investment in the company, and to offer shares for sale	Legal requirements concerning disclosure of information to shareholders and the public, e.g. annual publication of detailed report and accounts
	Risk of takeover due to the availability of the shares on the stock exchange
	Directors are influenced by short-term objectives of major investors

Table 2.4: Publicly held companies – advantages and disadvantages

The other main difference between these two types of company organisations concerns the 'divorce between ownership and control'. The original owners of a business are usually still able to retain a majority of shares and continue to exercise management control when the business converts to privately held company status. This is most unlikely with publicly held companies due to the volume of shares issued and the number of people and institutions investing. These shareholders own the company, but at the annual general meeting they appoint a board of directors who control the management and decision-making of the business.

This clear distinction between ownership and control can lead to conflicts over the objectives to be set and direction to be taken by some publicly held companies. The shareholders might prefer short-term maximum-profit strategies, but the directors may aim for long-term growth of the business, perhaps in order to increase their own power and status. Many privately held companies convert to publicly held status to gain the benefits referred to in Table 2.4. It is also possible for the directors or the original owners of a business to convert it back from public ownership to privately held company status. Richard Branson and the Virgin group is one of the best-known examples of this. The reasons for doing this are largely to overcome the divorce between ownership and control – in a privately held company it is normal for the senior executives to be the majority shareholders. In addition, the owner of a privately held company can take a long-term planning view of the business. It is often said that the major investors in a publicly held company are only interested in short-term gains. 'Short-termism' can be damaging to the long-term investment plans of any business.

A summary of the advantages and disadvantages of publicly held companies is given in Table 2.4.

CASE STUDY 2.2

Airbnb 'Goes Public'

Airbnb went public in December 2020, amid conditions of reduced demand for travelling due to the public health crisis. The initial public offering (IPO) was very successful and Airbnb shares traded at $146, more than doubling the price of $68 per share set for the IPO one day earlier. The decision of Airbnb to become a public limited company offered a great financial return to its investors. The financial resources raised from the stock market will help Airbnb's management to invest in more innovation around its cloud-based application, offering advanced services for vacation rentals and tourism activities to its users in a market which is becoming increasingly competitive.

1 Define the term 'publicly held company'. [2]

2 Analyse **two** potential advantages to Airbnb of becoming a publicly held company. [4]

3 Analyse **two** potential disadvantages to Airbnb of becoming a publicly held company. [4]

THEORY OF KNOWLEDGE

Knowledge question: How can we decide whether a type of business activity is ethical or not? For example, can the price of the product be a criterion?

The personal loan market in many economies has seen the emergence of a huge number of so-called 'payday' lenders. These organisations provide very short-term loans (up to 30–40 days) to borrowers who urgently need cash to cover their living costs or a particular expense until, in theory, they get paid.

Research conducted in the US suggests that 12 million Americans take out payday loans each year, with interest rates ranging from 300% to 500%, which are commonly disguised as 'fees'. Compare this with 15–30% interest rates on credit cards and it is easy to see how customers are financially drained by payday lenders.

The main targeted consumers are low- to medium-income workers who do not qualify for credit cards or personal loans due to financial problems.

A typical reason that consumers use payday loans is to pay utility bills and rent.

'Payday' loans are legal in 32 states in the US. Payday lenders claim that the very high rates are justified by the very high risk of borrowers eventually not being able to repay the loans. Moreover, lenders say that payday loans are a valuable service for US society. Numerous low-income consumers have avoided eviction and homelessness because they have received payday loans while they were being denied access to the traditional banking system.

Discuss in class:

1 Is it unethical to charge high interest to consumers if they are willing to accept it?

2 Is it ethical for 'payday' businesses to trap consumers in loans that are very expensive and hard to repay, to save them from huge problems such as homelessness?

ACTIVITY 2.1

The graph shows the return to shareholders on a monthly basis between 29 June 2010 (the day Tesla Motors floated in the NASDAQ stock exchange) and 29 June 2020.

1   If an investor had spent $100 on Tesla shares on the day of the IPO, how much would their return be if they sold their shares on 29 June 2020?

   a   More than $400

   b   More than $1000

   c   More than $4000

2   Which other two car manufacturers appear on the share price performance graph? How do they perform in terms of returns to the shareholders compared to Tesla?

3   Which factors do you think explain the difference between the returns on Tesla shares and the returns of the other two car manufacturers?

4   What does Tesla's soaring share price mean for the business as a plc and its ability to raise money through the stock exchange?

5   Would you have bought Tesla shares on 29 June 2020 if you were an investor? Justify your answer.

Tesla's soaring share price

Share price performance since Tesla's IPO date of 29 June 2010

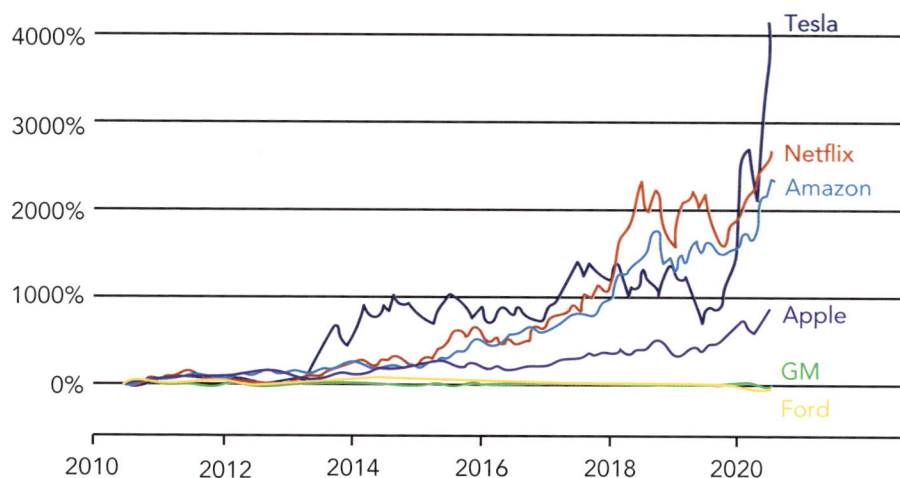

2.3 Types of for-profit social enterprises

Private sector companies as Social enterprises

Social enterprises are not charities, but they have objectives that are often different from those of an entrepreneur who is only motivated by profit. Making a profit may be one of the objectives of a social enterprise, but it is usually less important than the organisation's social objectives. However, **social entrepreneurs** cannot abandon the financial disciplines of business in their desire to improve society as they need to earn profits to allow them to survive and grow.

A social enterprise is therefore a business that makes its money in socially responsible ways and uses most of any surplus made to benefit society. Social entrepreneurs are not running a charity – they can and often do keep some of the profit made for themselves.

Social enterprises compete with other businesses in the same market or industry. They use business principles to achieve social objectives. Most social enterprises have these common features:

- They directly produce goods or provide services.
- They have social aims and use ethical ways of achieving them.
- They need to make a surplus or profit in order to survive as they cannot rely on donations as charities do.

Objectives of social enterprises

Social enterprises often have three main aims:

- Economic – to make a profit or surplus to reinvest back into the business and provide some return to the owners.
- Social – to provide jobs or support for local, often disadvantaged, communities.
- Environmental – to protect the environment and to manage the business in an environmentally sustainable way.

These aims are often referred to as the triple bottom line. This means that profit is not the sole objective of these enterprises.

Here are two examples of social enterprises.

- SELCO in India provides sustainable energy solutions to low-income households and small businesses. In one scheme, solar-powered lighting was provided by SELCO to a silkworm farmer who depended on dangerous and polluting kerosene lamps. The farmer could not afford the initial capital cost of solar power, so SELCO helped with the finance too.
- The KASHF Foundation in Pakistan provides very small loans and social support services to women entrepreneurs who traditionally find it difficult to obtain help. This enables the women to set up their own businesses in food production, cloth-making and other industries. The loans have to be repaid with interest, but the interest rates are much lower than an international bank would charge.

The advantages and disadvantages of the social enterprise form of business organisation are summarised in Table 2.5.

As with all business owners in the private sector, social entrepreneurs must establish their businesses with a legally recognised structure. Most social enterprises operate in the private sector. They can be organised as sole traders, partnerships, limited companies or mutual organisations such as cooperatives.

> **KEY TERMS**
>
> **charity:** an organisation set up to raise money to help people in need or to support causes that require funding
>
> **triple bottom line:** the three objectives of social enterprises: economic, social and environmental

Advantages	Disadvantages
Most governments want to encourage this form of business structure so they provide a range of financial incentives to social entrepreneurs	Social enterprises have to compete with other businesses and organisations whose costs may be lower due to their reduced social/environmental objectives
The objectives of social enterprises attract like-minded and committed people who want to be employed by them, and this helps to create a cohesive workforce	Social enterprises often offer unusual products that are targeted towards particular communities. Since communities and consumer tastes are always changing, social enterprises have to constantly research and monitor their target market
There are increasing trends towards 'responsible consumerism' so marketing social enterprises and their products may become easier because there is a growing potential market	Investors, employees and customers need to trust that the social mission is being pursued effectively, so complete transparency of the operations of the enterprise is essential

Table 2.5: Social enterprises – advantages and disadvantages

Economy

47% of social enterprises are under five years old

74% made a profit or broke even last year

44% of social enterprises grew their turnover over the last year

66% of social enterprises introduced a new product or service in the last year

Society

47% of social enterprises are led by women

31% of social enterprises have directors from ethnically diverse backgrounds

72% of social enterprises said that they were a Living Wage employer

22% of social enterprises operate in the most deprived areas of the UK

Environment

84% of social enterprises believe that buying products that are socially responsible and environmentally friendly is as important – or more important – than cost

20% of social enterprises are addressing the climate emergency as part of their core social/environmental mission

67% of social enterprises have or plan to embed tackling climate change/climate emergency into their constitution/articles of association

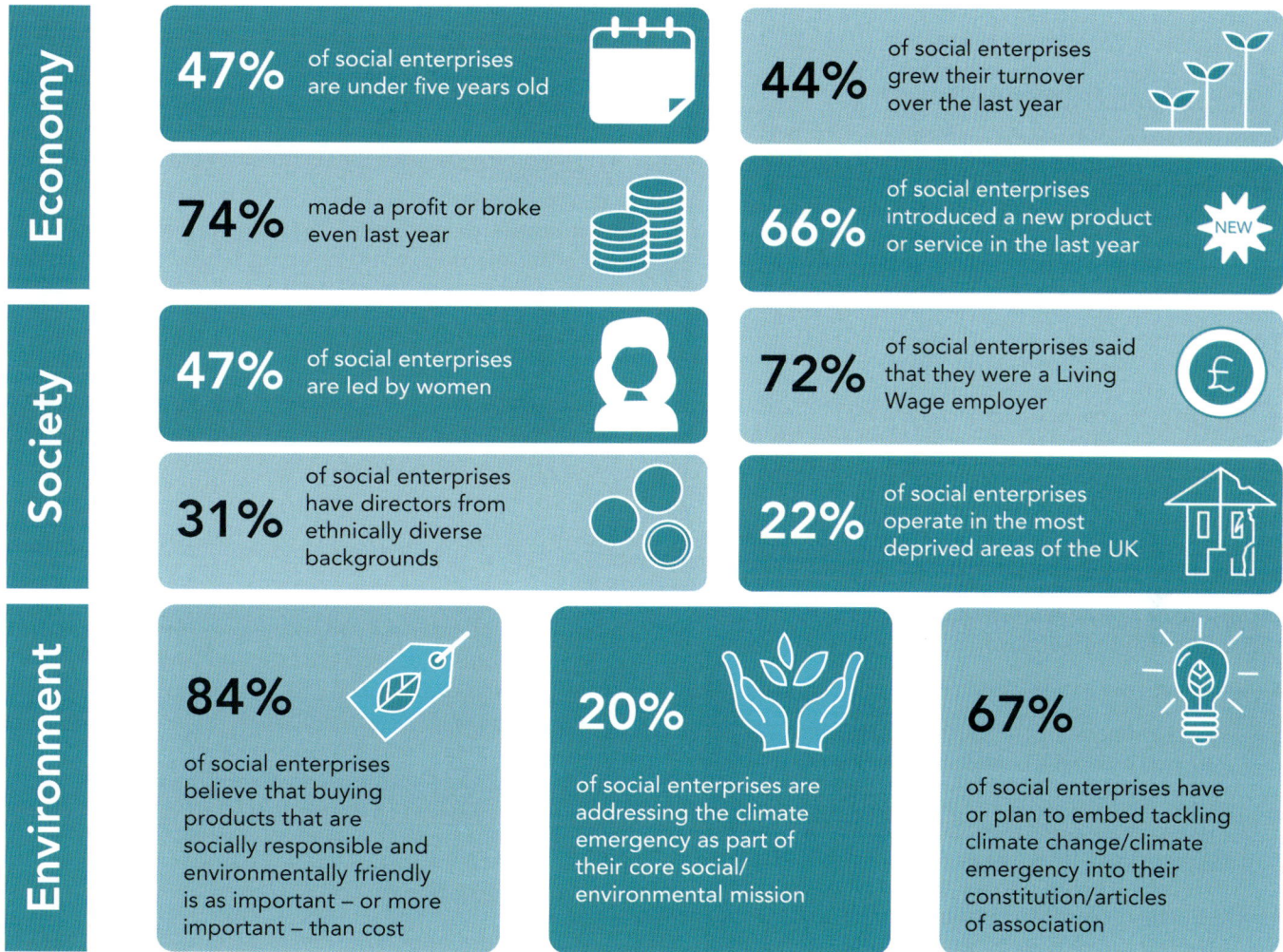

Figure 2.2: Results of a 2021 report on private sector social enterprises

Public sector companies as social enterprises

Every country will have some enterprises that are owned by the state – usually central or local government. These organisations are therefore in the public sector and they are referred to as **public corporations**.

Public sector organisations can be operated as social enterprises. Often they do not have profit as a major objective. For example, in many countries the main focus of the publicly owned TV channels is the quality of public service programmes and state-owned airlines have safety as a priority. When public corporations are sold to the private sector, known as privatisation, the objectives often change from socially orientated ones

to profit-driven goals. A summary of the potential advantages and disadvantages of public corporations as social enterprises is given in Table 2.6.

KEY TERM

public corporation: a business enterprise owned and controlled by the state – also known as nationalised industry or public sector enterprise

TIP

Avoid a common error by remembering that publicly held companies are in the private sector of industry – but public corporations are not.

Advantages	Disadvantages
They are managed with social objectives rather than solely with profit objectives	There is a tendency towards inefficiency due to lack of competition and lack of strict profit targets
Loss-making services might continue to operate if the social benefit is great enough	Subsidies from government can encourage inefficiencies
Finance is raised mainly from the government, so they are not subject to limitations from banks or shareholders	Government may interfere in business decisions for political reasons, e.g., by opening a new branch in a certain area to gain popularity

Table 2.6: Public sector social enterprises – advantages and disadvantages

Cooperatives as social enterprises

Cooperatives are not about making big profits for shareholders. They aim to create value for customers and secure employment for workers. This is what gives cooperatives a social enterprise character, and influences their values and principles.

Cooperatives tend to fall into one of these three groups:

- Retail cooperatives – also called consumers' cooperatives. This is a cooperative business owned by customers for their mutual benefit. It is a private sector enterprise that is oriented towards service rather than financial profit. It often takes the form of retail outlets operated and owned by the consumers. The consumers or customers are the people who have provided the capital required to launch or purchase the enterprise. Profits are shared either by way of discounts on products or by a payout to customer-owners each year.

- Agricultural cooperatives – these exist when farmers pool resources for mutual benefit, for example in the buying of fertiliser or the marketing of key food products.

- Worker cooperatives – often these are manufacturing businesses. Workers collectively own the business and make the important decisions.

KEY TERM

cooperative: a group of people acting together to meet the common needs and aspirations of the members, sharing ownership and making decisions democratically

ACTIVITY 2.2

The privatisation of British Rail started back in the 1990s and it has been the subject of much debate. Supporters of the decision identified benefits for the public such as improved customer services and increased capital investment in infrastructure. But some stakeholders disagree and say the 'private sector efficiency vision' did not work well for this example of privatisation.

1   Find more information about the privatisation of British Rail.

2   Search for evidence of the impact of this privatisation on stakeholders.

3   Discuss your findings in class.

Reflection

- When looking for information, did you make sure that you used a variety of sources and not just one article?

- Is the evidence you collected trustworthy? Does it include any statistical data or research evidence, for example on the evolution of ticket prices after privatisation?

- Have you tried to identify both positive and negative aspects of the privatisation example being discussed?

CASE STUDY 2.3

The Aegina Agricultural Cooperative of Pistachio Growers

Pistachio trees arrived in Greece in around 1850. Aegina is a small Greek island where local farmers have a special variety of tree and produce superb pistachio nuts. Today, the Aegina Agricultural Cooperative of Pistachio Growers handles harvesting, packaging and distribution of Aegina pistachios all over Greece and the rest of the world.

The cooperative was first set up in 1947 and initially there were many problems, such as the lack of marketing skills. Through the effective collaboration of its members, the cooperative grew, and by 2020 there were 347 members producing roughly 30% of the island's pistachio production.

Many of the members of the cooperative are not full-time professional farmers; they are just small-scale producers who want to sell their products to increase their household income. The members pool resources for mutual benefit for the production, distribution and promotion of their products. However, the democratic management of the cooperative is not without problems. There are often disagreements among the members on issues such as the growth and marketing strategy of the

cooperative. Producers outside the cooperative prefer to remain free to decide on how to package, promote and price their products.

1 Define the term 'agricultural cooperative'. [2]

2 Suggest the advantages for pistachio producers of joining the Aegina Agricultural Cooperative of Pistachio Growers. [6]

3 With reference to the case study, identify two problems associated with agricultural cooperatives. [4]

2.4 Non-profit social enterprises

Not all organisations in the world aim to make profits. There are thousands of **non-profit organisations** that have objectives other than profit – for example, charities and pressure groups. Many of these are also called **non-governmental organisations (NGOs)**.

Non-governmental organisations (NGOs)

A non-governmental organisation (NGO) is a not-for-profit group, independent from government, which is organised on a local, national or international level to tackle issues that support the public good. They are task focused and made up of people sharing a common interest. NGOs perform a variety of services and

humanitarian functions. They bring public concerns to the attention of governments and encourage community participation by stakeholders. The objectives of NGOs are not profit based; they are specifically focused on social, environmental or humanitarian objectives.

KEY TERMS

non-profit organisation: any organisation that has aims other than making and distributing profit and which is usually governed by a voluntary board

non-governmental organisation (NGO): a legally constituted body that functions independently of any government and that has a specific humanitarian or social aim/purpose, e.g., supporting disadvantaged groups in developing countries or advocating the protection of human rights

Examples of NGOs include the following:

- Amnesty International is a worldwide campaigning movement that works to promote internationally recognised human rights for all. It undertakes research and action focused on preventing and ending serious abuses of human rights to physical and mental integrity, ensuring freedom of conscience and expression, and freedom from discrimination.

- Article 19 is a human rights organisation with a specific mandate and focus on the defence and promotion of freedom of expression and freedom of information worldwide.

- Avocats Sans Frontières (ASF – 'Lawyers Without Borders') is mostly made up of lawyers, solicitors and magistrates who aim to contribute, completely independently, to the establishment of a fair, equitable and united society.

- Médecins Sans Frontières (MSF – 'Doctors Without Borders') is an international humanitarian aid organisation that provides emergency medical assistance to populations in danger in more than 70 countries.

Médecins Sans Frontières (MSF) is an international humanitarian aid organisation

- The Ford Foundation is a resource for innovative people and institutions worldwide that aim to strengthen democratic values, reduce poverty and injustice, promote international cooperation and advance human achievement.

- The MacArthur Foundation supports creative people and effective institutions committed to building a more just, verdant and peaceful world. Among other things, it seeks to further the development of an international system of justice and advance human rights around the globe.

- The International Committee of the Red Cross (ICRC) is an 'impartial, neutral and independent organisation whose exclusively humanitarian mission is to protect the lives and dignity of victims of armed conflict and other situations of violence and to provide them with assistance.'

LEARNER PROFILE

Principled

Médecins Sans Frontières (MSF) is a not-for-profit NGO that provides medical aid and support to developing countries in conflict situations and humanitarian crises. Between March and August 2021, it provided medical care to 6000 malnourished children across Madagascar, a country that was hit by the worst food and nutrition crisis in its recent history. To deal with the humanitarian crisis, MSF set up mobile clinics in 20 locations. It had to overcome many problems, including the country's geography, which makes it difficult to access remote villages.

MSF's actions are based on the principles of medical ethics, independence and impartiality. Its primary aim is to go to the most difficult places and situations around the world and provide support to sick and injured people.

Why can the people of Médecins Sans Frontières be described as 'principled'? Discuss in class.

Find another example of an organisation that you would describe as principled and explain to your class why you think it is.

Charities

Most countries have laws about what constitutes charitable work as charities are usually allowed tax benefits. The following list is typical of activities accepted as being for 'charitable purposes':

- prevention or relief of poverty
- advancement of education
- advancement of religion
- advancement of health or the saving of lives
- advancement of citizenship or community development
- advancement of the arts, culture, heritage or science
- advancement of human rights conflict resolution or reconciliation, or the promotion of religious or racial harmony or equality and diversity

- advancement of environmental protection or improvement
- relief of those in need, by reason of youth, age, ill health, disability, financial hardship or other disadvantage
- advancement of animal welfare.

Charities often perform useful social and environmental functions that would not be undertaken by private businesses or government-funded organisations. They are dependent on private contributions and these can vary in amount, making it difficult for charity managers to plan. Some charitable work is duplicated – for example, in social care or medical research – and it is argued that such situations can lead to wasteful duplication.

ACTIVITY 2.3

1   Identify the type of business activity that is most likely to match the description provided.

	For-profit private sector	For-profit social enterprise	Non-profit	Public sector business
Women's Legal and Human Rights Bureau				
Production of straws made from sugarcane				
Ophthalmic hospital				
National Statistical Institute				
Financial consulting				

2   One of the business activities above can be either a for-profit private sector or a public sector business. Which one do you think it is, and why?

SELF-EVALUATION CHECKLIST

After studying this chapter, complete this table.

I am able to apply and analyse:	Needs more work	Almost there	Ready to move on
the distinction between the private sector and public sector (AO2)			
I am able to evaluate:			
the main features of the following types of organisations: sole traders, partnerships, and privately held companies and publicly held companies (AO3)			
the main features of the following types of for-profit social enterprises: private sector companies, public sector companies, cooperatives (AO3)			
the main features of the following type of non-profit social enterprises: non-governmental organisations (AO3)			

REFLECTION

1   If you were planning to set up a business, would you create a social enterprise? Justify your decision to another learner.

2   What factors did you consider when making this decision? Which was the most important factor, and why?

PROJECT

1   As a class, find an NGO specialising in any social cause that you think is important in your country.

2   Find as much information as you can about this NGO and its goals from the internet.

3   Split into two groups. One group should organise a meeting with the NGO for an interview with a manager. The interview should include structured open and closed questions, aiming to understand:

   a   the scope of the business activity

   b   how it is organised

   c   how it differs from for-profit businesses

   d   how it finds resources to cover its needs

   e   what kind of problems it has when trying to reach its goals

The interview findings should be presented to the other group, which will need to organise a practical way to support the NGO. Some ideas are to offer voluntary work or to organise lotteries, etc.

4   The two groups meet to create a visual presentation of the project, e.g. a video, to be shared with their peers at school to increase awareness of the social goals of the non-profit organisation.

EXAM-STYLE QUESTIONS

Alejandro and Santiago become partners

Alejandro and Santiago are graduates from the same university. They have decided to set up a partnership to start a business organising experiential events. They came up with the idea when they saw a video on YouTube, in which IKEA offered a sleepover event to 100 people in one of its stores. They were also inspired by the fact that some famous partnerships were so successful that they ended up becoming huge public limited companies, such as the partnership between Larry Page and Sergey Brin, who founded Google. However, they also read statistics which suggest that partnerships have many disadvantages and that only 30% survive in the long term.

In 2018, they started the partnership, under the name XEvent. As a start-up, XEvent faced many problems. Competition in the market was more intense than the partners expected. The business had cash flow problems, and banks were not prepared to offer a loan. The business plan initially set up by the partners proved inaccurate. In 2020, Alejandro convinced a friend, Maria, to invest in the business. However, Maria demanded that the business be incorporated by becoming a private limited company. Initially the partners were sceptical about this because the incorporation process is quite costly. But they knew that the decision would solve many of their problems. Eventually the partners became shareholders with limited liability in XEvent.

The business started to grow and soon became very profitable. Maria was interested in transforming XEvent from a traditional for-profit business to a for-profit social enterprise by investing some of their profit in organising events for children with special needs as part of their social integration programme. Santiago and Alejandro also suggested that XEvent could help non-profit businesses by supporting them with their goals. Alejandro contacted an NGO working on animal rights and volunteered to organise an event to help them spread awareness.

1	Define the term 'partnership'.	[2]
2	Identify the economic sector in which XEvent operates.	[2]
3	Suggest **two** reasons why Santiago and Alejandro decided to set up their business as a partnership.	[4]
4	Suggest **two** problems the two owners faced from setting up XEvent as a partnership.	[4]
5	Describe **two** common steps of setting up a new business that the partners must have followed when starting XEvent.	[4]
6	Suggest **two** reasons why Maria did not want to invest in a partnership but wanted XEvent to become a private limited company.	[4]
7	Explain **two** possible disadvantages for Alexander and Santiago from changing their partnership into a private limited company.	[4]
8	Explain **one** difference and **one** similarity between a typical for-profit business and a for-profit social enterprise.	[4]
9	With reference to the case study, explain **one** difference and **one** similarity between an NGO and a for-profit business.	[4]
10	Should XEvent become a social enterprise? Justify your answer.	[10]

> Chapter 3

Business objectives

BUSINESS IN CONTEXT

Daimler AG – objectives and strategy

Daimler AG is one of the world's most successful automotive companies. With its Mercedes-Benz Cars & Vans, Daimler Trucks & Buses and Daimler Mobility divisions, the Group is one of the leading global suppliers of premium cars and one of the world's largest manufacturer of commercial vehicles.

The Group's strategic approach can be summarised in three core statements:

Move: *Reinvent the invention*

As the inventor of the automobile, it is in our nature to repeatedly reinvent mobility. Our aspiration is to offer environmentally sustainable solutions for mobility and the transport of goods in the future. . . . We are working systematically to achieve our "Ambition 2039" goal of CO_2-neutral mobility. To do so, we are also utilising the potential offered by automated driving and digital services.

Perform: *We create sustainable value*

We aim to create value that is sustainable. Our business is grounded in what we do best – delighting our customers with fascinating vehicles. Here, the attainment of our profitability targets and the maintenance of a solid cash flow remain top priorities for the short and medium term. ...

Transform: *Reinvent ourselves*

Our transformation is a long-term process of adapting the implementation of our structures and processes in cooperation with our employees. We have a workforce that is agile and willing to learn . . .

Our corporate culture creates the foundation for the outstanding innovative capability displayed by our employees. We put diversity into practice, . . . and the principle of integrity guides our actions and our relationships with our business partners.

Daimler-Benz's chairman has stated that the overall business has an objective of reaching an average 8–9% profit return on sales. This objective is broken down into specific profit targets for each division of the business such as cars, trucks and buses.

Discuss in pairs or a group:

- What are the likely benefits to a business of having a 'strategic vision'?

- Why is it important for a business to have environmental objectives as well as financial ones?

- What is the purpose of setting profit objectives for each division of a business?

KEY CONCEPT LINK

Change

Strategic objectives are long term in nature, but nothing is forever. As external and internal conditions change, business objectives need to change as well.

But not all businesses are able to cope with change. Many factors affect a business's adaptability.

Some of these factors are the size of the business, the culture and attitudes of employees, the way the business is organised and the availability of financial resources to invest in change.

3.1 Vision statement and mission statement

Mission statements outline the overall purpose of the organisation. A **vision statement**, on the other hand, describes a picture of the 'preferred future' and outlines how the future will look if the organisation achieves its mission. It is a statement of the future position that describes what owners and directors ideally want their business organisation to become.

KEY TERMS

mission statement: a statement of the business's core aims, phrased in a way to motivate employees and to stimulate interest from outside groups

vision statement: a statement of what the organisation would like to achieve or accomplish in the long term

---

A mission statement is an attempt to condense the central purpose of a business's existence into one short paragraph. It is not concerned with specific, quantifiable goals, but it tries to sum up the aims of the business in a motivating and appealing way. It can be summed up as a statement about 'who we are and what we do'.

Here are some examples of mission statements.

- **An A Level/IB college:** 'To provide an academic curriculum in a caring and supportive environment.'

- **Samsung:** 'to devote its talent and technology to creating superior products and services that contribute to a better global society.'

- **Huawei:** 'To invest resources in the making of a digitally connected world.'

- **Microsoft:** 'To empower every person and every organization on the planet to achieve more.'

- **Google:** 'To organize the world's information and make it universally accessible and useful.'

- **Merck:** 'To discover, develop and provide innovative products and services that save and improve lives around the world.'

An effective mission statement should answer three key questions:

- What do we do?

- For whom do we do it?

- What is the benefit?

Table 3.1 compares the vision and mission statements of three organisations.

So what is the link between vision statements, mission statements and strategies? It is simple. Without the direction and focus brought to an organisation by vision and mission statements, planning new strategies will be like trying to steer a ship with no idea of either where it is or the direction in which it is meant to be heading. Vision and mission statements give the organisation a sense of purpose and can prevent it from drifting between the tides and currents of powerful events.

Organisation	Vision statement	Mission statement
Alibaba	We envision that our customers will meet, work and live at Alibaba, and that we will be a company that lasts at least 100 years.	To make it easy to do business anywhere.
Minnesota Department of Health (USA)	Health equity in Minnesota where all communities thrive and everyone has what they need to be healthy.	Protecting, maintaining and improving the health of all Minnesotans.
McDonald's restaurants	To move with velocity to drive profitable growth and become an even better McDonald's serving more customers delicious food each day around the world.	Our mission is to make delicious feel-good moments easy for everyone.

Table 3.1: Comparing vision and mission statements

Knowledge question: How can we evaluate the usefulness of evidence in strategic decision-making?

Firms are constantly trying to find evidence before taking major strategic decisions. Coca-Cola has developed sugar-free soft drinks based on evidence that consumers are pursuing a healthier lifestyle. It decided to diversify into coffee, by acquiring Costa Coffee, given strong evidence about a growing global coffee market. Volkswagen invested in a huge 'electrification plan' based on facts showing how the global market for electric vehicles is expected to expand due to changing consumer wants and government policies favouring electric mobility.

Evidence is crucial for businesses, especially when they decide on their long-term strategy and need to invest billions of dollars on their growth plans. But evidence is sometimes conflicting. It is not uncommon for professional market reports to provide contradictory evidence which can be misleading for businesses. Many firms are producing premium-priced environmentally friendly products, based on research suggesting that consumers are happy to pay higher prices for 'green' goods. Yet, they soon find out that consumers are not actually willing or able to pay a premium for sustainability – at least not for their products.

Discuss in class:

1   Before making strategic decisions, can businesses be sure that the evidence they have is reliable?

2   How much 'evidence' is enough before a big strategic decision is taken?

3   Should a business take decisions when there is conflicting evidence?

Effectiveness of these statements

Virtually every organisation of a reasonable size has developed a vision statement and a mission statement. Do they perform a useful function or are they just another management fad? Here are some arguments in favour of these statements.

- They quickly inform groups outside the business what the central aims and vision are.
- They help to motivate employees. This is particularly true where an organisation is looked upon as a caring and environmentally friendly body as a result of its mission statement. Employees will then be associated with these positive qualities.
- Where they include ethical statements, they can help to guide and direct individual employee behaviour at work.
- They help other groups to establish what the business is about.

On the other hand, these statements are often criticised for being:

- too vague and general; they lack specific information about the business or its future plans
- based on a public relations exercise to make stakeholder groups feel good about the organisation
- virtually impossible to analyse or disagree with
- too similar – it is common for two completely different businesses to have very similar mission statements, which may lead to stakeholders being confused about the real purpose of each business.

Communicating mission and vision statements is almost as important as establishing them. There is little point in identifying the central vision for a business if nobody else knows about it. Businesses communicate their mission statements in a number of ways, for example in published accounts, communications to shareholders and the corporate plans of the business. Internal company newsletters and magazines may draw their title from part of the mission statement. Advertising slogans or posters are frequently based around the themes of the mission statements. For example, The Body Shop is very effective at incorporating its mission into its eco-friendly campaigns.

On their own, mission statements are insufficient for operational guidelines. They do not tell managers what decisions to take or how to manage the business.

Their role is to provide direction for the future and an overall sense of purpose, and in public relations terms, at least, they can prove very worthwhile. It is important that both vision and mission statements are applicable to the business, understood by employees and convertible into genuine strategic actions.

CASE STUDY 3.1

Starbucks's mission

Starbucks is the largest coffee chain in the world, with more than 30 000 stores in 83 markets. Its mission is 'to inspire and nurture the human spirit – one person, one cup and one neighborhood at a time'. This non-conventional mission statement reflects the unique strategy of the business, which aims to provide products of excellent quality but also a 'third place' experience to consumers away from home and work. The megabrand combines the magnitude of a truly global name with localised services to satisfy individualised consumer wants.

Starbucks coffee wants to 'inspire and nurture the human spirit' not only of its customers but primarily of its employees. The business calls its employees 'partners', and they are at the heart of the 'Starbucks Experience'.

The mission statement is not typical as it does not inform targeted consumers and other stakeholders about the overall business activity and types of products offered. Nonetheless, the business is already leading the industry, so it does not feel the need to introduce itself to the market. The mission statement is designed to reflect the business culture and philosophy rather than describe the operations of the business. Moreover, it is abstract enough to cover the needs of the business in case of changes in future objectives.

The company's strategy, as confirmed by CEO Kevin Johnson and Starbucks leaders in December 2020,

can be summarised as 'continued growth at scale'. Its vision is reflected through the following statement:

Starbucks 'aims to drive consistent and predictable sales growth and margin expansion while continuing to create significant value for all stakeholders.'

1 Define the term 'mission statement'. [2]

2 Suggest **two** groups of people (stakeholder groups) that Starbucks wants to attract with its mission statement. [4]

3 With reference to the case study, explain the difference between a mission statement and a vision statement. [4]

4 Evaluate the effectiveness of Starbucks's mission statement. [10]

ACTIVITY 3.1

Netflix is a subscription-based online streaming service business.

Netflix's mission: At Netflix, we want to entertain the world. Whatever your taste, and no matter where you live, we give you access to best-in-class TV shows, movies and documentaries. Our members control what they want to watch, when they want it, with no ads, in one simple subscription. We're streaming in more than 30 languages and 190 countries, because great stories can come from anywhere and be loved everywhere. We are the world's biggest fans of entertainment, and we're always looking to help you find your next favorite story.

CONTINUED

TED is a non-profit business, organising powerful talks on new ideas in any area of science and other disciplines, to spread knowledge around the world.

TED's mission: Spread ideas

1   What is similar and what is different between these two mission statements?

2   Netflix is a for-profit business, while TED is a non-profit. Can this difference partially explain the variations in the mission statements of the two businesses? Explain your answer.

3.2 Common business objectives

The hierarchy of objectives

Before analysing the most common objectives that are set for business organisations, it is useful to consider the nature of business aims and objectives and the benefits of establishing them. All objectives are targets. Most businesses will set targets not only for the whole business, based on the overall business aim, but also for each division or department. This leads to a hierarchy of objectives, as shown in Figure 3.1.

Corporate aims

The core of a business's activity is expressed in its corporate aims. A typical corporate aim is: 'To increase shareholder returns each year through business expansion'. This statement tells us that the company aims to give shareholders maximum returns on their investment by expanding the business. Other corporate aims can concentrate on customer-based goals, such as 'meeting customers' needs', or market-based goals, such as 'becoming the world leader'. Corporate aims are all-embracing, and are designed to provide guidance to the whole organisation, not just a part of it.

Establishing a corporate aim allows the senior managers to focus on setting more specific and measurable business objectives. These objectives have several benefits. They:

- can help develop a sense of purpose and direction for the whole organisation if they are communicated clearly and unambiguously to the workforce

- allow an assessment to be made, in the future, of how successful the business has been in reaching its targets

- provide the framework within which the strategies of the business can be drawn up.

A business without a long-term aim and specific business objectives is likely to drift from event to event without a clear sense of purpose. This will become obvious to the workforce and customers, who may respond in adverse ways.

Figure 3.1: The hierarchy of objectives

(Pyramid, top to bottom: Aim / Mission / Corporate objectives / Divisional objectives / Departmental objectives / Individual targets)

KEY TERMS

corporate aims: the long-term goals which a business hopes to achieve

business objectives: short- or medium-term goals or targets – usually specific in nature – which must be achieved in order for an organisation to attain its overall corporate aim

Business objectives should be 'SMART'

Business objectives help to direct, control and review the success of business activity.

The most effective business objectives usually meet the following SMART criteria:

- **S – Specific** Objectives should focus on what the business does and should apply directly to that business. For example, a hotel may set an objective of 75% bed occupancy over the winter period – the objective is specific to this business.

- **M – Measurable** Objectives that have a quantitative value are likely to be more effective targets for directors and staff to work towards – for example, to increase sales in the south-east region by 15% this year.

- **A – Achievable** Objectives must be achievable. Setting objectives that are almost impossible to achieve in a given time will be pointless. They will demotivate staff who have the task of trying to reach these targets.

- **R – Realistic and relevant** Objectives should be realistic when compared with the resources of the company, and should be expressed in terms relevant to the people who have to carry them out. For example, informing a factory cleaner about 'increasing market share' is less relevant than a target of reducing usage of cleaning materials by 20%.

- **T – Time-specific** A time limit should be set when an objective is established. For example, by when does the business expect to increase profits by 5%? Without a time limit it will be impossible to assess whether the objective has actually been met.

> **TIP**
>
> Remember the acronym: SMART, and the meaning of each individual letter.

> **ACTIVITY 3.2**
>
> The following are departmental objectives of ICY, a business producing and selling fresh ice cream. The market is growing fast, and the owners want to capture the opportunities available for growth.

> **CONTINUED**
>
> ICY has the internal resources needed to support growth.
>
> - To expand in five new geographical locations by 2025.
> - To increase the sales of sugar-free ice cream products by 5% in the current year compared to the previous year.
> - To add ten more ice-cream flavours to the product portfolio by the end of the month.
>
> 1 Are all the above objectives SMART? Justify your answer.
>
> 2 How could you improve the phrasing of the objectives that are not SMART enough? Give appropriate examples.

Profit objective

Profits are essential for rewarding investors in a business and for financing further growth. They are also necessary to persuade business owners and entrepreneurs to take risks. Some businesses aim to achieve profit maximisation. This means producing at the level of output where the greatest positive difference between total revenue and total costs is achieved – see Figure 3.2.

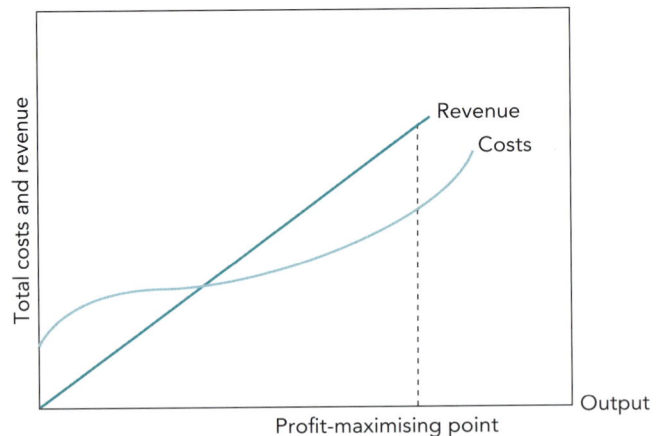

Figure 3.2: Profit maximisation – the greatest possible difference between total revenue and total cost

It seems rational to seek the maximum profit available from a given business operation. Not to maximise profit is seen as a missed opportunity, but there are limitations with this business objective:

- Achieving high short-term profits may lead competitors to enter the market.

- Many businesses seek to maximise sales in order to secure the greatest market share possible, rather than maximise profits. The business would expect to make a target rate of profit from these sales.

- Owners of smaller businesses may be more concerned with issues of independence and keeping control – these may be of more importance than making higher profits.

- Most business analysts assess business performance through return on capital employed – the rate of profit returned on each dollar invested in the business – rather than through total profit.

- In practice, it is very difficult to assess whether the point of profit maximisation has been reached, and constant changes to prices or output to attempt to achieve it may well lead to negative consumer reactions.

An alternative profit objective is profit satisficing. This means aiming to achieve enough profit to keep the owners happy but not aiming to work flat out to make as much profit as possible. This is often the objective of owners of small businesses who wish to live comfortably but do not want to work very long hours in order to earn more profit.

Growth objective

The growth of a business – in terms of sales units or value of sales – has many potential benefits for the managers and owners. Larger firms will be less likely to be taken over and should be able to benefit from economies of scale. Managers may gain higher salaries and fringe benefits. Businesses that do not attempt to grow may cease to be competitive and, eventually, will become less appealing to new investors. Business objectives based on growth have limitations:

- Over-rapid expansion can lead to cash flow problems.

- Sales growth might be achieved at the expense of lower profit margins.

- Larger businesses can experience diseconomies of scale.

- Using profits to finance growth – retained profits – can lead to lower short-term returns to shareholders.

- Growth into new business areas and activities can result in a loss of focus and direction for the whole organisation.

An alternative way to assess business growth is to measure **market share**.

Market share is closely linked to the overall growth of a business. However, it is possible for an expanding business to suffer a loss of market share if the market is growing at a faster rate than the business itself. Increasing market share indicates that the marketing mix of the business is proving to be more successful than that of its competitors. Benefits resulting from being the business with the highest market share include:

- Retailers will be keen to stock and promote the best-selling brand.

- Profit margins offered to retailers may be lower than for competing brands as the shops are so keen to stock it – this leaves more profit for the producer.

- Effective promotional campaigns are often based on 'buy our product with confidence – it is the brand leader'.

Protecting shareholder value

Investors buy shares in companies to benefit from an increase in **shareholder value**.

Shareholders can gain financially from owning shares by receiving regular dividend payments from the profit of the business and from increases in the market price of the company's shares. Management, especially in public limited companies, take decisions that aim to increase the company share price and dividends paid to shareholders. These targets might be achieved by pursuing the objectives of growth and profit maximisation.

> ### KEY TERMS
>
> **market share:** sales of the business as a proportion of total market size, in a given period
>
> **shareholder value:** the financial gains received by the owners of a company's shares

Pursuing the objective of protecting or increasing shareholder value may create conflicts between the interests of shareholders and those of other groups involved in the business. Some business analysts claim that the shareholder value objective puts the interests of shareholders above those of other stakeholders. For instance, shareholder value might be increased by:

- increasing business efficiency which results in some employees losing their jobs
- increasing consumer prices for products with few competitors, raising company profit, but impacting negatively on consumers
- constructing a new operating facility to achieve growth which may damage the environment.

As a consequence of this apparent conflict between shareholder interests and those of other groups in society, greater emphasis is being placed on ethical business objectives.

Ethical objectives

Ethics are moral guidelines, and ethical objectives are targets based on a moral code for the business – for example, 'doing the right thing'. The growing acceptance of corporate social responsibility has led to businesses adopting an **ethical code** to influence the way in which decisions are taken.

> ## KEY TERMS
>
> **ethics:** moral guidelines that determine decision-making
>
> **ethical code (code of conduct):** a document detailing a company's rules and guidelines on staff behaviour that must be followed by all employees

Most decisions have an ethical or moral dimension. For example:

- Should a toy company advertise products to young children so that they pester their parents into buying them?
- Is it acceptable to take bribes when deciding whether to place a contract with a company?
- Should a bank invest in a company that manufactures weapons or tests new chemicals on animals?

- Is it acceptable to feed genetically modified food to cattle?
- Do we accept lower profits in the short term by purchasing less-polluting production equipment?
- Should directors receive substantial pay rises and bonuses when other workers in the business are facing redundancy?
- Is it acceptable to close a factory to save costs and increase profits, even though many jobs will be lost and workers may find it hard to get other jobs?
- If legal controls and inspections are weak in a country, is it acceptable to pay very low wages for long hours of work as this policy will reduce the firm's costs?
- Should a business employ child labour to reduce costs rather than employing adults?
- Should a business continue to produce potentially dangerous goods as long as no one finds out?

These are all examples of ethical dilemmas. The way in which employees behave and take decisions in these cases should be covered and explained by a company's ethical code of conduct. To what extent should businesses take ethics into consideration when making decisions? There is now considerable evidence that more and more companies are considering the ethical dimension of their actions – not just the impact they might have on profits.

Different people will have different answers to these dilemmas. Some managers will argue that any business decision that reduces costs and increases profits is acceptable as long as it is legal – and some might argue that even illegal actions could be justified. Other managers will operate their business according to strict ethical rules and will argue that, even if certain actions are not illegal, they are not right. Morally, they cannot be justified even if they might cut costs and increase sales.

Assessing ethical objectives

Adopting and keeping to a strict ethical code in decision-making can be expensive in the short term. For example:

- Using ethical and Fairtrade suppliers can add to a business's costs.
- Not taking bribes to secure business contracts can mean losing out on significant sales.

- Limiting the advertising of toys and other child-related products to an adult audience to reduce 'pester power' may result in lost sales.

- Accepting that it is wrong to fix prices with competitors might lead to lower prices and profits.

- Paying fair wages – even in very low-wage economies – increases costs and may reduce a firm's competitiveness against businesses that exploit workers.

However, in the long term there could be substantial benefits from acting ethically. For example:

- Avoiding potentially expensive court cases can reduce the costs of fines.

- While bad publicity as a result of being caught acting unethically can lead to lost consumer loyalty and long-term reductions in sales, ethical policies will lead to good publicity and increased sales.

- Ethical businesses attract ethical customers and, as global pressure grows for corporate social responsibility, this group of consumers is increasing.

- Ethical businesses are more likely to be awarded government contracts.

- Well-qualified employees may be attracted to work for companies that have ethical and socially responsible policies.

CASE STUDY 3.2

The principles of business ethics for real-estate agencies in Dubai

Apart from being lawful, the Dubai Land Department (DLD) has urged real-estate companies operating in Dubai to follow certain ethical principles to ensure high standards of business ethics in the market. Some of the basic ethical rules set by the DLD are:

- Trust: All real-estate businesses should enhance the public trust in Dubai's real-estate market, and employ the highest global standards.

- Confidentiality and privacy: Businesses should not disclose customers' private information without permission.

- Honesty and fairness towards customers: To ensure foreign direct investment (FDI) is attracted in Dubai, to further strengthen the national economy.

- Professionalism: High-quality services must be offered by all real-estate firms to ensure customer satisfaction.

- Social responsibility: Real-estate businesses should operate as active members of society and support making Dubai 'the happiest city in the world', as per the vision of Dubai's leadership and the National Program for Happiness and Positivity, which aims to improve the happiness and welfare of residents, citizens and visitors in the emirate.

DLD plays a crucial role in Dubai, regulating the property industry while keeping pace with the ever-changing market conditions and customer needs.

1 Define the term 'business ethics'. [2]

2 Suggest **two** reasons why DLD has urged real-estate businesses to follow a set of ethical rules in Dubai. [4]

3 Suggest **one** possible advantage and **one** disadvantage for real-estate businesses trying to follow DLD's ethical code in Dubai. [4]

4 With reference to the case study, explain the difference between being a 'lawful' business activity and being an 'ethical' business activity. [4]

3.3 Strategic objectives and tactical objectives – the key differences

As Figure 3.1 outlines, trying to meet the overall company aim will require the setting of many subsidiary objectives at business, departmental and even small team levels. Some of these objectives will be focused on the long term and will require substantial resources if they are to be achieved. Other targets will be smaller scale and for shorter time periods. Table 3.2 outlines the key differences between **strategic objectives** and **tactical objectives**.

Strategic objectives	Tactical objectives
Long-term targets, e.g. increase market share by 10% over next three years	Short to medium term, e.g. increase sales by 5% to south-eastern region in three months
Difficult to reverse once the objective is set – departments will have committed considerable long-term resources to achieving the objective	More likely to be reversible or changeable as the time period is shorter and fewer resources are likely to be allocated to achieving them
These objectives are set by directors and/or senior managers	These objectives are likely to be set by less senior managers and subordinates with delegated authority
Often involve coordination with other business functions/ departments	The impact of tactical objectives may often be on just one department

Table 3.2: Key differences between strategic objectives and tactical objectives

KEY TERMS

strategic objective: a long-term target for the whole organisation, designed to achieve the corporate aim

tactical objective: a short-term target aimed at resolving a particular problem or meeting a specific part of a longer-term strategic objective

ACTIVITY 3.3

Juan owns a Mexican restaurant.

1. Characterise Juan's following business decisions as strategic, tactical or purely operational (day to day).

   a. Offering a free drink to all customers on Tuesday afternoons, when the restaurant is usually empty.

   b. Deciding on the weekly schedules of workers in the kitchen.

   c. Deciding to redecorate the restaurant to attract business executives.

   d. Changing the type of business from 'Mexican' to 'South American' cuisine.

2. Explain your thought process behind each of your choices.

CASE STUDY 3.3

Business objectives of Domestic Detergents Inc.

Domestic Detergents Inc. (DD) produces household cleaning products in a very competitive market. The firm enjoys strong demand from a loyal clientele and shareholders are expecting strong returns. DD's directors have agreed on the following corporate objectives:

- to increase annual sales from $1 billion to $2 billion by the end of 2023

CONTINUED

- to enter a new market every 18–24 months

- to launch new products in the detergents market

- to be the lowest-cost, highest-quality producer in the household products industry

- to achieve a 15% growth rate per year in profit and earnings per share.

The marketing director is very optimistic about the future sales of DD Bright, a biological washing liquid which was launched three months ago.

But to encourage consumers to try the product, the DD Bright's brand manager believes that the firm should temporarily sell DD Bright at a low promotional price.

1   Define the term 'SMART' objectives.   [2]

2   With reference to the case study, explain the difference between strategies and tactics.   [4]

3   Suggest **one** advantage and **one** disadvantage for DD of trying to set SMART corporate objectives.   [4]

4   Discuss the extent to which the corporate objectives of DD are SMART.   [10]

3.4 Corporate social responsibility (CSR)

Objectives that focus on meeting social responsibilities are becoming increasingly important for most business organisations.

To whom is business answerable? Should business activity be concerned solely with making profits to meet the objectives of shareholders and investors, or should business decisions also be influenced by the needs of other stakeholders? When a business fully accepts its legal and moral obligations to stakeholders other than investors, it is said to be accepting corporate social responsibility (CSR).

KEY TERMS

stakeholders: people or groups of people who can be affected by, and therefore have an interest in, any action taken by an organisation

corporate social responsibility: this concept applies to those businesses that consider the interests of society by taking responsibility for the impact of their decisions and activities on customers, employees, communities and the environment

One important measure of a business's attitude to its social responsibility is the way in which it deals with environmental issues. Our environment can be greatly affected by business activity. Air and noise pollution from manufacturing processes, road congestion caused by heavy trucks, business expansion into country areas, emissions of gases that can lead to global warming, and the use of scarce non-renewable natural resources are all environmental issues that are of increasing concern to people and governments all over the world. How should business managers react to these concerns? Should they respond by adopting environmentally safe or green policies, even if these are expensive? Or should they always take the cheapest option, no matter what the consequences for the environment might be?

Other issues connected with the concept of CSR cross over into ethical decisions. In fact, the two concepts are closely linked. Examples of CSR developments include:

- the growth in the number of firms that promote organic and vegetarian foods

- increasing numbers of retailers emphasising the proportion of their products made from recycled materials

- businesses that refuse to stock goods that have been tested on animals or foods based on genetically modified ingredients.

In these cases, is the action being taken in order to retain trade and reputation? Or is it being taken because such action is increasingly profitable? Might businesses be criticised for simply trying to create positive publicity for their CSR strategy rather than being praised for their genuine concern for society and the environment? It is conceivable that businesses are being ethical or environmentally conscious because they *want* to behave in that way. They have an objective that Peter Drucker (a famous writer on management) calls 'public

Advantages	Disadvantages
The image of the business and its products can be improved with a green or socially responsible approach. This could become a major competitive advantage, attracting new customers and loyalty from existing customers. Attracting the best-motivated and most efficient employees may become easier as many workers will prefer to work for and be associated with socially aware businesses. Bad publicity and pressure group activity resulting from socially irresponsible behaviour should not arise. The goodwill of other stakeholder groups, resulting from socially responsible behaviour, could lead to better relations with workers, suppliers, customers and the local community. Higher long-term profitability should result from all of the factors here.	Short-run costs could increase, e.g., fitting anti-pollution equipment, paying workers above poverty wage levels, paying suppliers promptly, not exploiting vulnerable groups when advertising. Shareholders may be reluctant to accept lower short-run profits (even though long-run profitability might increase). Loss of cost and price competitiveness if rival businesses do not accept social responsibilities and have lower costs as a result. Consumers may be prepared to pay higher prices for products made in a socially responsible manner, but during an economic recession they might prefer low prices and worry less about how products were made. There could be a considerable social backlash against a business that *claims* to be socially responsible but is discovered to operate in socially irresponsible ways, e.g., a furniture maker claims to use sustainable timber but buys from rainforest suppliers – this is sometimes referred to as 'greenwash'.

Table 3.3: Advantages and disadvantages of corporate social responsibility

responsibility'. However, many consumer groups and pressure groups are still dubious as to whether these objectives are based on genuinely held beliefs.

Table 3.3 looks at the advantages and disadvantages for businesses of adopting CSR policies.

Changes in corporate responsibility

Attitudes towards corporate responsibility have changed over time. The standards that companies are expected to reach are determined by societal norms, and in most countries these now focus on stakeholders rather than shareholders.

The main reasons for changing corporate approaches to social responsibility include:

- increasing publicity from international pressure groups that use the internet to communicate, blog, raise funds and organise boycotts
- the United Nations Millennium Development Goals include 'environmentally sustainable growth' – this has forced many developing

nations to insist that new company investment in their economy takes environmental concerns into consideration

- global concern over climate change and the impact this could have on social and economic development – this is forcing companies to confront the climatic consequences of their actions and investments, e.g., the rapid increase in wind-power farms in Germany
- legal changes at local, national and international level – these have forced businesses to refrain from certain practices. In most countries, businesses can no longer pay staff very low wages or avoid legal responsibility for their products.

CSR and corporate strategy changes

The changing corporate strategies of the world's mining companies are an excellent example of how firms may adopt different strategies towards their social responsibilities in response to pressure. In the 1970s and 1980s, many mining companies signed mineral extraction deals with undemocratic political regimes. Environmental concerns were given very low priority and the interests of the local or indigenous peoples (displaced by the mine workings) were ignored. The Grasberg (West Papua) and Bougainville (Papua New Guinea) gold and copper mines are useful case studies.

- In Bougainville, joint owners of the mine, RTZ and Freeport, allowed the government to use force to put down civil unrest caused by the displacement of people by the mine and its environmental damage. The company took a very tough line and military action took place next to the mine. Eventually, the company was forced to close it.

- The Grasberg mine opened later than Bougainville. As a result of the poor publicity relating to the Bougainville mine policy in Papua New Guinea, RTZ took a very different approach to its social responsibilities, and it has benefited from this. A trust fund has been set up to spend 1% of total mine revenue to fund village development. In addition, one quarter of the total workforce is drawn from local communities.

- RTZ went even further with the Jabiluka uranium mine in a protected National Park in northern Australia. Publicity by the local Mirrar tribe and their supporters, campaigning about the environmental impact of the mine, led to an unprecedented extraordinary general meeting of shareholders. This caused the mine to be closed; it has never reopened.

Measuring CSR – social audits

Social audits report on a firm's 'social' performance and they are becoming an important way for businesses to report on their corporate social responsibility record. They assess the impact a business has on society and how effectively its ethical behaviour matches up to its ethical objectives. Social audits can include an environmental audit, but they give details of other impacts on society too. These include:

- health and safety record, e.g. number of accidents and fatalities
- contributions to local community events and charities
- proportion of supplies that come from ethical sources, e.g. Fairtrade Foundation suppliers
- employee benefit schemes
- feedback from customers and suppliers on how they perceive the ethical nature of the business's activities.

> **KEY TERM**
>
> **social audit:** an independent report on the impact a business has on society. This can cover pollution levels, health and safety record, sources of supplies, customer satisfaction and contribution to the community

The social audit will also contain annual targets to be reached to improve a firm's level of social responsibility and details of the policies to be followed to achieve these aims. By researching and publishing these reports, businesses are often able to identify potentially antisocial behaviour and take steps to find and remove this from the company's practices. Publishing detailed and independently verified social audits can improve a business's public image, increase consumer loyalty and give the business a clear direction for future improvements in its social responsibility achievements. The advantages and disadvantages of social audits are considered in Table 3.4.

Advantages	Disadvantages
Identify what social responsibilities the business is meeting and what still needs to be achieved	If the social audit is not independently checked – as published accounts must be – will it be taken seriously by stakeholders?
Set targets for improvement in social performance by comparing audits with the best-performing firms in the industry	Time and money must be devoted to producing a detailed social audit – is this really necessary if it is not legally required?
Give direction to the action plans a business still needs to put into effect to achieve its social/ethical objectives	Many consumers may just be interested in cheap goods, not whether the businesses they buy from are socially responsible
Improve a company's public image and this can be used as a marketing tool to increase sales	A social audit does not prove that a business is being socially responsible

Table 3.4: Advantages and disadvantages of social audits

Evaluation of social audits

- Until social audits are made compulsory and there is general agreement about what they should include and how the contents will be verified, some observers will not take them seriously.

- Companies have been accused of using them as a publicity stunt or a way to disguise or hide their true intentions and potentially damaging practices.

- They can be very time-consuming and expensive to produce and publish, and this may make them of limited value to small businesses or those with limited finance.

LEARNER PROFILE

Open-minded

OpenMinds is an NGO with a mission to assist people with special needs in Lebanon, not only by providing financial support to families and to neurodevelopmental disorder research, but also by promoting the integration of people with disabilities in society. OpenMinds envisions a community in which people with special needs will be accepted and included like everyone else, and it designs appropriate activities to make this happen.

OpenMinds is not the only NGO in the world dealing with the social problems facing people with special conditions, especially in schools, education and the workplace. Many non-profit organisations have the vision to support communities to become more aware and open-minded on issues of disability, understanding how the uniqueness of people with special needs does not mean they cannot become functioning members of society.

Find examples of other non-profit businesses whose mission is to help society to become more open-minded on any matter of social interest. Discuss in class the significance of such organisations.

3.5 Business management tools

The following business management tools can be used to help business managers identify an appropriate **strategy** or strategies to adopt once the business objectives have been set. They are all forms of **strategic analysis**.

SWOT analysis

A **SWOT analysis** provides information that can be helpful in matching the resources and strengths of the business to the competitive environment in which it operates. So it is useful in strategy formulation and selection. It comprises:

- **S – strengths** These are the internal factors of a business that can be looked upon as real advantages. These could be used as a basis for developing a competitive advantage. They might include experienced management, product patents, loyal workforce and good product range. These factors are identified by undertaking an internal audit of the firm. This is often undertaken by specialist management consultants who analyse the effectiveness of the business and the effectiveness of each of its departments and major product ranges.

- **W – weaknesses** These are the internal factors of a business that can be seen as negative factors. In some cases they can be the flip side of a strength. For example, whereas a large amount of spare manufacturing capacity might be a strength in times of a rapid economic upturn, if it continues to be unused it could add substantially to a firm's

---

KEY TERMS

strategy: a plan of action designed to help achieve an objective

strategic analysis: conducting research into the business environment and into the business itself to help identify future strategies

SWOT analysis: a form of strategic analysis that identifies and analyses the main internal strengths and weaknesses and external opportunities and threats that will influence the future direction and success of a business

average costs of production. Weaknesses might include: poorly trained workforce, limited production capacity and ageing equipment. This information would also have been obtained from an internal audit.

- **O – opportunities** These are the potential areas for expansion of the business and future profits. These factors are identified by an external audit of the market the firm operates in and its major competitors. Examples include: new technologies, export markets expanding faster than domestic markets, and lower rates of interest increasing consumer demand.

- **T – threats** These are also external factors, gained from an external audit. This audit analyses the business and economic environment, market conditions and the strength of competitors. Examples of threats are: new competitors entering the market, globalisation driving down prices, changes in the law regarding the sale of the firm's products, and changes in government economic policy.

This information is usually presented in the form of a four-box grid, as shown in Table 3.5.

SWOT and business objectives

The SWOT diagram focuses on the key issues under each heading. A brief outline of each of these could then accompany the grid to make it more useful to the managers responsible for strategic planning. This approach helps managers assess the most likely successful future strategies and the constraints on them. A business should not necessarily pursue the most profitable opportunities. It may stand a better chance of developing a competitive advantage by identifying a good 'fit' between the business's strengths and potential opportunities. In many cases, a business may need to overcome a perceived weakness in order to take advantage of a potential opportunity. SWOT is a common starting point for developing new corporate strategies, but it is rarely sufficient. Further analysis and planning are usually needed before strategic choices can be made.

	Strengths	Weaknesses
Internal	Specialist marketing expertise	Lack of marketing expertise
	A new, innovative product or service	Undifferentiated products or services (i.e. in relation to competitors)
	Location of the business	Location of the business
	Quality products and processes	Poor-quality goods or services
	Any other aspect of the business that adds value to the product or service	Damaged reputation
	Opportunities	**Threats**
External	A developing market such as the internet	A new competitor in the home market
	Mergers, joint ventures or strategic alliances	Price wars with competitors
	Moving into new market segments that offer improved profits	A competitor has a new, innovative product or service
	A new international market	Competitors have superior access to channels of distribution
	A market vacated by an ineffective competitor	Taxation of the product or service

Table 3.5: SWOT analysis – some common issues

SWOT evaluation

Subjectivity is often a limitation of a SWOT analysis as no two managers will necessarily arrive at the same assessment of the company they work for. It is not a quantitative form of assessment, so the 'cost' of correcting a weakness cannot be compared with the potential 'profit' from pursuing an opportunity. SWOT should be used as a management guide for future strategies, not a prescription. Part of the value of the process of SWOT analysis is the clarification and mutual understanding that senior managers gain by the focus that the analysis provides.

SWOT as a business management tool

This business management tool can be integrated into all functional units of the IB syllabus. This is because:

- evidence from all departments is required in developing a SWOT analysis
- SWOT should be used before developing any major strategy for the business such as an HR strategy, operations strategy, finance strategy or marketing strategy.

TIP

Some examination questions may ask you to undertake a SWOT analysis while others will ask you to evaluate the technique for a particular business. Read the question carefully to grasp its key requirements.

STEEPLE analysis

STEEPLE analysis is another form of strategic analysis. It focuses on analysing the external macro-environment in which a business operates. The macro environment means the wide-ranging and major factors that could influence the future strategies of a business.

KEY TERM

STEEPLE analysis: the strategic analysis of the macro-environment in which a business operates, including social, technological, economic, environmental, political, legal and ethical factors

- **S – social** Changes in society, including cultural trends, influence customers' buying behaviour, attitudes and interests. It is important for a business to analyse these social and cultural changes to assess their likely impact on a new strategy. These social factors contain: structure of population, birth rates, level of education and cultural diversity.

- **T – technological** Advances in technology have an impact on all aspects of business activity. Any new business strategy that fails to consider these is likely to fail. New technologies such as artificial intelligence (AI) will increasingly impact on the marketing, human resources and operations strategies of most businesses.

- **E – economic** The state of the economy that a business operates in (or plans to operate in) is of crucial importance to the future strategies it might implement. Economic factors include: rate of inflation, interest rates; exchange rates, tax rates, economic growth and the purchasing power of consumers. All of these economic factors will impact on the potential demand for the products of a business.

- **E – environmental** Increasing environmental pressure group activity against businesses that damage the environment is causing substantial changes in business strategy. Other environmental factors include climate change, international agreements to limit carbon emissions, consumers switching to 'green' businesses, and stakeholder pressure on business to become more sustainable.

- **P – political** Political issues and government decisions can create many opportunities or potential threats for organisations. These factors include: political stability, state interference in business decisions, nationalisation, market regulations and international trade agreements.

- **L – legal** These factors involve all regulatory and legal constraints that can negatively or positively affect business activity and management decisions. They include: consumer protection laws, environmental protection laws, location of industry controls, minimum wages and controls over working conditions. These factors may be very different for each of the countries that a multinational company operates in.

- **E – ethical** Ethical factors include standards of morality, integrity and behaviour, and they are of growing importance in many countries. Managers must determine what is good and bad for their company, stakeholders and society as a whole.

S Social	T Technological	E Economical	E Environmental	P Political	L Legal	E Ethical
Demographics	Technological growth	Economic growth	Weather	Government policy	The court system	Bribery
Population growth	New innovation	Exchange rates	Climate change	Taxation	Employment law	Intellectual property
Age distribution	Skilled resources	Interest rates	Environmental policy	Political stability	Discrimination law	Reputation
Education	Automation	Inflation	Atmospheric emissions	Foreign trade	Antitrust law	Business ethics
Cultural differences	Research	Purchasing power		Trade restrictions	Trade unions	Confidentiality
Lifestyle trends	Technology awareness	Unemployment rates			Consumer protection	
Health & welfare		Income			Health & safety	
Career attitudes		Investment opps			Copyright law	

Figure 3.3: Assessing the STEEPLE factors is a key part of strategic analysis

All of the factors referred to in the STEEPLE analysis of external environment factors can have both positive influence (opportunities) or negative influence (threats) on future business strategies.

STEEPLE analysis plays an important role in assessing the likely chances of a new business strategy being successful.

The seven key areas covered by it are clearly external to the business and beyond its control. STEEPLE is complementary to SWOT; it is not an alternative.

Figure 3.3 illustrates the main factors that a business would consider when planning a new strategy. In this case, the business is considering operating in a different country for the first time.

Evaluation of STEEPLE analysis

Any significant new business strategy should be preceded by a detailed analysis of the wider environment in which the strategy has to operate and be successful.

The use of STEEPLE analysis formalises this process. The results of the analysis should be an important part of developing strategies for the future.

Once completed, STEEPLE analysis does not just stop. It may need to be constantly updated and reviewed, especially in a rapidly changing wider environment. For multinational businesses, or for a business considering foreign expansion for the first time, it will be important to undertake STEEPLE analysis for each country in which it operates.

STEEPLE as a business management tool

This business management tool can be integrated into the following functional areas of business (Units 1, 2 and 4 of the IB syllabus):

- Unit 1 – setting up a business and business objectives
- Unit 2 – developing new human resources strategies, e.g. before expanding into a different country
- Unit 4 – developing new marketing strategies e.g. before diversifying into a completely different market.

Ansoff matrix

This management tool for strategic analysis is one of the most widely referred-to means of portraying alternative corporate growth strategies.

Igor Ansoff popularised the idea that long-term business success was dependent upon establishing business strategies and planning for their introduction. His best-known contribution to strategic planning was the development of the **Ansoff matrix**, which represented the different options open to a marketing manager when considering new opportunities for sales growth.

KEY TERM

Ansoff matrix: a model used to show the degree of risk associated with the four growth strategies of: market penetration, market development, product development and diversification

He considered that the two main variables in a strategic marketing decision are:

- the market in which the firm is going to operate
- the product(s) intended for sale.

In terms of the market, managers have two options:

- to remain in the existing market
- to enter new ones.

In terms of the product, the two options are:

- selling existing products
- developing new ones.

When put on a matrix, these options can be presented as shown in Figure 3.4.

As there are two options each for markets and for products, this gives a total of four distinct strategies that businesses can adopt when planning to increase sales. These are shown on the matrix and can be summarised as follows.

Market penetration

In 2021, Samsung reduced the European prices of its range of 4K TVs by up to €1200. This was in response to price cuts by other manufacturers – but Samsung's reductions were larger in an attempt to increase market share. **Market penetration** is the least risky of all the four possible strategies in that there are fewer 'unknowns' – the market and product parameters remain the same. However, it is not risk-free as, if low prices are the method used to penetrate the market, they could lead to a potentially damaging price war that reduces the profit margins of all businesses in the industry.

Product development

The mobile phone market is changing rapidly and Apple updates its product ranges frequently. When this book was written (in 2021), the iPhone 13 had just been developed and launched. What is the latest Apple iPhone as you read this? **Product development** often involves innovation – as with electric vehicles – and these brand new products can offer a distinctive identity to a business.

KEY TERMS

market penetration: achieving higher market shares in existing markets with existing products

product development: the development and sale of new products or new developments of existing products in existing markets

---

PRODUCTS

Existing ← → New

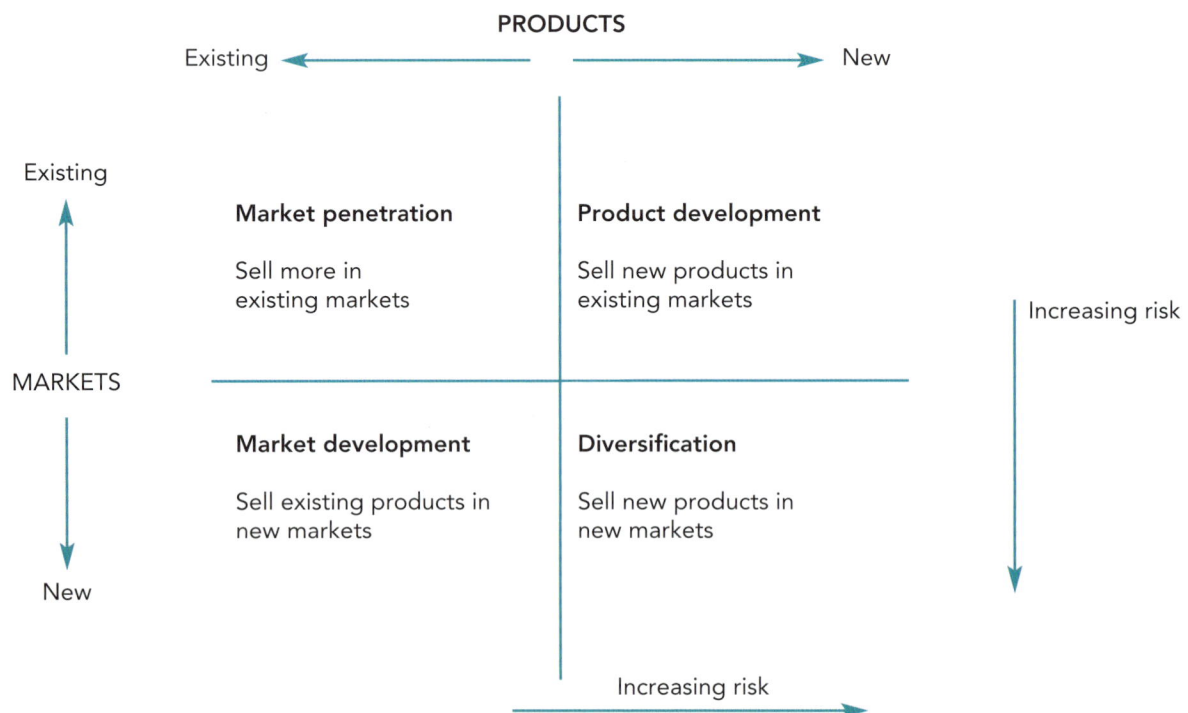

Figure 3.4: Ansoff's matrix

Market development

Market development could include exporting existing designs of products to overseas markets or selling to a new market segment. The rapid growth of McDonald's has been driven by the opening of its fast-food restaurants in 100 countries. It could expand further by opening branches in Cambodia, one of the countries it does not currently operate in.

Diversification

The **diversification** strategy involves accepting new challenges in both markets and products. It is the most risky of the four strategies. It is often a growth strategy that results in a business moving away from its original core competences. However, diversification may be a possible option if the high risk is balanced out by the chance of a high profit. Other advantages of diversification include the potential to gain a foothold in an expanding industry and the reduction of overall business portfolio risk.

Tata is one of the largest companies based in India. It has pursued a growth strategy based on diversification. Its operations now include business divisions in car manufacturing, chemicals, hotels, communications and steel making.

Related diversification, e.g., vertical integration with suppliers of retailers in the existing industry, can be less risky than unrelated diversification, which takes the business into a completely different industry.

> ### KEY TERMS
>
> **market development:** the strategy of selling existing products in new markets
>
> **diversification:** the process of selling different, unrelated goods or services in new markets

Evaluation of Ansoff matrix

Clearly, the risks involved in these four strategies differ substantially. By opening up these options, Ansoff's matrix does not direct a business towards one particular future strategy. However, by identifying the different strategic areas in which a business could expand, the matrix allows managers to analyse the degree of risk associated with each one. Managers can then apply decision-making techniques to assess the costs, potential gains and risks associated with all options. In practice, it is common for large businesses in today's fiercely competitive world to adopt multiple strategies for growth at the same time.

While Ansoff's analysis helps to map the strategic business options, it has limitations too. It only considers two main factors in the strategic analysis of a business's options – it is important to consider SWOT and STEEPLE analysis too in order to give a more complete picture. Recommendations based purely on Ansoff would tend to lack depth and hard environmental evidence.

Management judgement, especially based on experience of the risks and returns from the four options, may be just as important as any one analytical tool when making the final choice.

The matrix does not suggest actual detailed marketing options – and to be fair to Ansoff, it was never intended to. For instance, market development may seem to be the best option, but which market/country and with which of the existing products produced by the business? Further research and analysis will be needed to supply answers to these questions.

Ansoff matrix as a business management tool

This business management tool can be integrated into Unit 1 and Unit 2 of the IB syllabus as follows:

- challenges and opportunities of starting up a business
- developing marketing strategies, e.g., international marketing.

CASE STUDY 3.4

Beauty plc wants to grow

Beauty plc is a firm producing natural organic cosmetics for the competitive UK consumer market. Its mission statement is as follows:

'We offer every type of natural cosmetic that consumers want, preserving the Earth and its resources and investing in what is most valued in our business: our employees.'

Beauty plc has adopted corporate social responsibility (CSR), which attracts loyal consumers and employees and a lot of positive publicity. A big NGO aiming to improve animal welfare awarded a prize to Beauty plc for stopping animal testing.

Beauty plc donates part of its profit each year to the NGO. This is a valuable source of revenue for the not-for-profit organisation, which has 200 employees and maintains facilities to accommodate abused animals.

Even though Beauty plc has spent a huge amount on 'green' production technologies, it remains profitable and returns considerable value to its shareholders. But the market is becoming increasingly saturated, so the business is now seeking growth. Many competitors are trying to penetrate the profitable cosmetics market, especially with natural and organic products.

One growth option considered by Beauty plc's managers is to invest in research and development so that the business produces a new line of organic cosmetics. Market research will be required to identify the exact needs and wants of British consumers. Another option for the business is to enter the growing market of organic food supplements. Beauty plc knows that the second strategy is riskier yet more promising because of increasing consumer demand and less competition in the supplements market.

1 Define the term 'corporate social responsibility'. [2]

2 Describe **one** strength and **one** opportunity that a manager of Beauty plc would consider in a SWOT analysis. [4]

3 With reference to the case study, explain **one** difference and **one** similarity between an NGO and a 'for-profit' business organisation. [4]

4 Using an Ansoff matrix framework, discuss the **two** growth options considered by Beauty plc. [10]

SELF-EVALUATION CHECKLIST

After studying this chapter, complete this table.

I am able to apply and analyse:	Needs more work	Almost there	Ready to move on
vision statement and mission statement (AO2)			
common business objectives including: growth, profit, protecting shareholder value and ethical objectives (AO2)			

CONTINUED

I am able to synthesise and evaluate:			
strategic objectives and tactical objectives (AO3)			
corporate social responsibility CSR (AO3)			
I am able to select and apply the following business management tools:			
SWOT analysis			
STEEPLE analysis			
Ansoff matrix			

REFLECTION

1   List three of your personal objectives for the next five years. How might having these objectives help you decide what important decisions to take in your life?

2   Do you think businesses should become more concerned about ethical issues in their decision-making? How would you justify your views to another learner?

PROJECT

You are starting up a social enterprise which produces clothes and accessories purely from recycled materials, such as old tyres and ocean waste, and will sell its products domestically and abroad. Some of the profits of the social enterprise will be invested to upgrade the recycling facilities in your home country.

1   Split into teams.

- **Team 1:** Decide the name and write a mission statement appropriate for your business.

- **Team 2:** Identify at least four corporate objectives for your start-up, to link to the mission.

- **Team 3:** Decide on appropriate geographic regions to structure your startup and decide on divisional objectives to support the strategic objectives.

- **Team 4:** Decide on appropriate departmental objectives to link to the regional objectives.

- **Team 5:** Give examples of SMART individual objectives to support the departmental objectives.

2   Create a conceptual map with your objectives in a hierarchy, using sticky notes.

Thinking about your project:

- When phrasing the mission statement, did you try to express the business's aim through it?

- Does it have the characteristics of successful mission statements, for example is it brief enough for stakeholders to remember it?

- When phrasing corporate, divisional, departmental and individual objectives, did you phrase them to be SMART enough?

EXAM-STYLE QUESTIONS

Is STS plc successful?

STS plc collects waste from houses, offices and factories. Most of the waste is burned to produce heat and electricity for the company's own use. This saves costs and reduces the impact on the environment by not using areas of land to bury the rubbish. A recent increase in customers has meant that not all of the waste can be burned and the company has dumped it in old quarries where it causes smells and gas emissions.

Investment in new equipment has allowed the business to save on production costs. The company's new mission statement is 'to be the country's number one waste business and to protect the environment for our children's benefit'. This has been explained to all shareholders in a recent letter to them, but the workers of the company were not involved in helping to create the mission statement and they have not been informed of it.

The latest company accounts stated: 'Our vision is to maximise the shareholder's value through a strategy of aggressive growth. Our objectives are to expand year on year.'

The increasing profits of STS will be used for further market penetration and market development, as the business plans to expand into new cities and smaller towns where there is not a lot of competition in the waste collection market. STS's CEO also announced the plans of the business to diversify in new markets by setting up a factory producing environmentally friendly garbage bags.

These accounts contained the following data.

	2019	2020	2021	2022
Sales revenue ($m)	22	27	38	42
Profit before tax and interest ($m)	5	9	11	22
Total value of country's waste market ($m)	129	147	168	192

A stock market analyst commented that the growth strategy of STS hides significant risks and that STC needs to prioritise CSR rather than growth. The company's lack of consistency in terms of social responsibility has recently led to poor publicity and social backlash. The analyst suggested that the firm should arrange for a social audit to identify the areas of improvement so that its ethical behaviour matches the ethical objectives expressed in its mission statement.

1	Define the term 'diversification'.	[2]
2	Define the term 'social audit'.	[2]
3	Explain the term 'shareholder's value'.	[2]
4	Suggest **two** reasons why STS needs a mission statement.	[4]
5	With reference to the case study, explain the difference between a mission and a vision statement.	[4]
6	Explain **one** advantage and **one** limitation for STS from setting CSR objectives.	[4]
7	Discuss **one** advantage and **one** disadvantage for STS for conducting a social audit.	[4]
8	Using a SWOT framework, explain **one** strength and **one** weakness of STS.	[4]
9	Using a SWOT framework, explain **one** opportunity and **one** threat faced by STS.	[4]
10	Using Ansoff's matrix, evaluate the 'aggressive growth strategy' of STS.	[10]

Chapter 4
Stakeholders

LEARNING OBJECTIVES

On completing this chapter you should be able to:

Apply and analyse:

- Internal and external stakeholders (AO2)
- Conflict between stakeholders (AO2)

BUSINESS IN CONTEXT

Stakeholder conflicts over airport near World Heritage site

Machu Picchu is one of the world's best-known heritage and cultural sites. The decision to build a new airport a few kilometres from this site was never going to be popular with all groups. The tourist industry and hotel companies have been campaigning for an airport to bring thousands more foreign travellers into the region. The government wants the economy to grow to create more jobs and increase tax revenues.

Archaeologists, historians, conservationists and local community groups opposed to pollution were all against the construction of the airport.

'This is a built landscape; there are terraces and routes which were designed by the Incas,' said a Peruvian art historian at Cambridge University who organised a petition against the new airport. 'Putting an airport here would destroy it.'

The new airport is expected to receive more than six million visitors a year. It is claimed that it will not only threaten the environment around Machu Picchu but put at risk the traditional cultures and way of lives of the inhabitants of the village of Chinchero.

New roads and hotels will also have to be constructed. These developments will cause further conflict with environmentalists and conservationists.

Discuss in pairs or in a group:

- Why do you think the government of Peru agreed to the construction of the Chinchero airport?

- Is conflict between stakeholder groups inevitable with all large infrastructure projects such as this?

KEY CONCEPT LINK

Sustainability

According to the 'triple bottom line' approach, sustainability for businesses has three dimensions: ecological sustainability, social sustainability and economic sustainability.

All three areas of sustainability have the potential to become typical areas of stakeholder conflicts. Managers of businesses that pollute the environment are often in conflict with pressure groups interested in preserving the environment's resources for ecological sustainability. Owners of factories often conflict with local communities on issues of overall community well-being, labour standards, and health and safety issues, which are linked to social sustainability. Finally, shareholders' interests often conflict with the interests of workers on the level of wages and benefits, which affect the economic sustainability of the business activity.

4.1 Internal and external stakeholders

The traditional view of business is often referred to as the shareholder concept. As the shareholders are the owners of the company, the firm has a legally binding duty to take decisions that will increase shareholders' value. Since directors and managers ultimately owe their position to shareholders, it is important to keep them satisfied. For most business managers, this limited view of business responsibility has been extended to include the interests not just of the investors/owners but also of suppliers, employees and customers.

This approach to business responsibilities does not end with these four groups, however. The **stakeholder concept** or theory is that there are many other parties involved and interested in business activity and that the interests of these groups – local communities, the public, government and pressure groups such as environmental lobbyists – should be considered by business decision-makers.

> **KEY TERM**
>
> **stakeholder concept:** the view that businesses and their managers have responsibilities to a wide range of groups, not just shareholders

Internal stakeholders

There are three main groups of internal stakeholders, each with their own set of interests in the business's activities. They include:

- employees
- managers
- shareholders.

> **TIP**
>
> Do not confuse the terms 'stakeholder' and 'shareholder'. Stakeholder is a much broader term that covers many groups, including shareholders.

External stakeholders

The external stakeholders include:

- customers
- suppliers
- government
- banks and other creditors
- special interest groups such as:
  - pressure groups that want to change a business's policy towards pollution or testing of chemicals on animals
  - community action groups concerned about the local impact of business activity
- competitors – fairness of competitive practices, strategic plans of the business.

4.2 Conflict between stakeholders

Business decisions and activities can have both positive and negative effects on stakeholders, but it is rare for all stakeholders to be either positively or negatively affected by any one business activity. It is also possible for any one stakeholder group to experience both negative and positive effects from the same business decision. This is why conflicts of interest between stakeholder groups, with different objectives and interests, can arise.

Table 4.1 outlines specific interests that each stakeholder group has. It also outlines the responsibilities that businesses are often considered to have towards stakeholders.

Table 4.2 outlines some business decisions and the conflict of stakeholder interests that can result.

> **TIP**
>
> Many examination questions involve conflict of stakeholders' objectives. It is difficult for a business to meet all of its responsibilities to all of the stakeholders at any one time. Compromise might be necessary – meeting as many stakeholders' objectives as possible or meeting the needs of the most important group in each situation.

THEORY OF KNOWLEDGE

Knowledge question: How do managers know which group's interests to prioritise in the case of stakeholder conflict? Is it a matter of reason or a matter of ethics?

In the case of stakeholder conflict, senior managers must establish priorities. They need to decide which stakeholder group is more important in each case, in the sense of how much damage the stakeholder group could cause to the business if their interests are not satisfied. But what roles do ethics and reason play for managers when they take such a decision?

Let's take the example of the common conflict between shareholders and employees. Shareholders seek the maximum possible profit, so they want to pay the minimum possible wages. Employees want the maximum possible personal income, so they ask for the maximum possible wages. Which group's interests should managers prioritise?

For many decades, the prevailing business principle was the notion of 'shareholder primacy', supported by the Nobel laureate economist Milton Friedman. According to his perspective, it is the profit incentive that creates business activities in the first place, so shareholders are always 'right' when they try to make the maximum possible profit. In fact, he wrote that 'the social responsibility of a business is to make profits'.

Milton Friedman's 'shareholder approach' has been gradually replaced by a 'stakeholder approach', especially in the social democracies of Northern and Western Europe. In such a system, shareholders are not always justified in seeking maximum profits. The needs of all stakeholders are treated as equally important to maximise long-term value in a business. In such an approach, the ethical obligations of businesses to their stakeholders are usually more important than shareholder's short-term profit.

Split into two groups. Debate the notion of the 'shareholder approach' against the 'stakeholder approach' for multinational companies that address thousands of shareholders through the stock market.

	Stakeholders' interests	Business responsibilities to stakeholders
Employees	Employment security Wage levels and benefits that compare well with similar jobs in other businesses Good conditions of employment, e.g., health and safety Some participation in decision-making	Observe employment laws, e.g., minimum wages Offer job security and training
Managers	Employment security Salary and benefits that compare well to similar posts of responsibility Responsibilities offered and status of the post Profit sharing or share purchase scheme	Job security Competitive salaries and other benefits Opportunities for responsibility and career advancement

	Stakeholders' interests	Business responsibilities to stakeholders
Shareholders	Pay annual dividends Share price increasing over time Security of investment Ability to sell shares when necessary	Observe company laws Annual accounts presented to shareholders Strategies used to increase shareholder value over time
Customers	Value for money Product quality and safety Guarantees Service levels Long-term rewards for loyalty	Observe consumer protection laws Avoid exploitation of consumers Assurances about quality, customer services and delivery dates
Suppliers	Speed of payment Level and regularity of orders Fair treatment, e.g., not being exploited by a customer whose business is large	Avoid excessive pressure on smaller or weaker suppliers to cut prices Pay fair prices and pay invoices promptly
Government	Creation of jobs and incomes that boost the economy Taxes paid, e.g., tax on profit Value of output produced (adds to GDP) Impact on wider society, e.g., is production environmentally sustainable?	Pay tax on profit Keep accurate accounting records so true profit can be shown Provide information to the government as requested Observe all applicable laws
Banks and other creditors	Security of their loans and the ability of the business to repay them Prompt payment of interest and capital owed by the business	Pay interest Pay back capital owed
Special interest groups	Pressure groups – campaigning to achieve a change in business decisions/activities Local community – encouraging businesses to act in the community's interests and to avoid harmful production methods	Respond to pressure group concerns when appropriate Local community – avoid pollution and other damaging operations; support for local groups
Competitors	Fairness of competitive practices Strategic plans of the business	To compete fairly and within the law It is not a responsibility of business to provide details of its strategic plans to competitors

Table 4.1: Stakeholders' interests and businesses' responsibilities to stakeholders

---

CASE STUDY 4.1

Major palm oil companies accused of breaking ethical promises

Palm oil is one of the world's most versatile raw materials. It is estimated that it is an ingredient in 50% of all products sold by a typical supermarket. It is used in a wide range of products from margarine, cereals, crisps, sweets and baked goods to soaps, washing powders and cosmetics, but it is often listed as just 'vegetable oil'. So its production benefits the customers of these products. In addition, an estimated 1.5 million small farmers grow the crop in Indonesia, and about 500 000 people are directly employed in the sector in Malaysia plus those connected with related industries. The governments of these countries have encouraged production as it is a major export for these economies.

However, the industry has a poor image. Palm oil production has led to deforestation, with a resulting negative impact on climate change. There has been substantial loss of wildlife habitat, even endangering the orangutan. Palm oil companies have been accused by community groups of driving native people off their land, which is then used for palm oil production. Socially responsible businesses, such as KL Kepong in Malaysia, have agreed a code of ethics which aims to make palm oil production 'sustainable', with fair treatment for all local populations affected by it. However, many companies have been accused of breaking the code as there is no strong world body to stop them behaving irresponsibly. In any

case, final consumers and food manufacturers aiming for profit maximisation want the cheapest raw materials possible.

Due to the many areas of possible expansion for the palm oil industry, investments are constantly growing in Malaysia. In 2021, Malaysia's crude palm oil (CPO) exports are expected to grow by more than 20% compared to 2020.

1 Define the following terms used in the article:

    a 'code of ethics' [2]

    b 'profit maximisation'. [2]

2 Explain the interests of any **two** of KL Kepong's stakeholder groups. [4]

3 Discuss the impact of the growing Malaysian crude palm oil market on its major stakeholders. [10]

ACTIVITY 4.1

Business decision/activity	Impact on:	
	Employees	Local community
Expansion of the business by investing in bigger production units, to increase the range of products and the quantity produced	✓ More job and career opportunities ✗ More complex lines of communication after expansion	✓ More jobs for local residents and increased spending in other local businesses ✗ External costs caused by increased traffic and loss of green fields for amenity use

CONTINUED

Business decision/activity	Impact on:	
	Employees	Local community
Merging with another business (the two businesses will become one new, fully integrated bigger organisation)	✓ The larger business may be more secure and offer career promotion opportunities ✗ Rationalisation may occur to avoid waste and cut costs – jobs might be lost	✓ If the business expands on the existing site, local job vacancies and incomes might increase ✗ Rationalisation of duplicated offices or factories might lead to closures and job losses
New IT introduced into production methods	✓ Training and promotion opportunities might be offered ✗ Fewer untrained staff will be required and those unable to learn new skills may be made redundant	✓ Local businesses providing IT services could benefit from increased orders ✗ Specialist workers may not be available locally, so more staff may need to commute

Table 4.2: Potential conflicts of interest between stakeholder groups

1   In the three examples above, analyse the likely positive or negative effects on one other stakeholder group.

2   Which of the above three decisions is likely to better satisfy the overall interests of employees? Discuss in class.

CASE STUDY 4.2

VestMe fires 150 factory workers

VestMe is a big cloth manufacturing business, producing men's and women's products for the global fast-fashion market. The Covid-19 pandemic hit VestMe hard. In 2020, sales dropped by 12% and in 2021 by another 15%, due to reducing consumer demand.

To protect the profits of the shareholders, VestMe had to cut costs. It started by negotiating the prices of raw materials with its suppliers. Abdul Aziz , CEO of Threadit, which supplies VestMe with processed cotton cloth, complained that the business 'demands cost cuts which are cutthroat for the suppliers. How could we maintain the excellent quality that VestMe wants at such low prices?'

CONTINUED

VestMe middle managers experienced reductions in their fringe benefits and received no bonus payments for 2020 and 2021. In January 2022, VestMe directors announced the compulsory redundancy of 150 factory workers. 'This is not a decision we wanted to take. However, it's a matter of survival,' said Gurmeet Sondh, VestMe's CEO. The redundancy decision brought a strong reaction from the factory workers' trade union, which threatened to go on strike. The factory workers complained that the business remains profitable even after the sales reduction, and that the management shows no ethics regarding its

employees, some of whom have been working for VestMe for more than 20 years.

1   With reference to the case study, explain the difference between internal and external stakeholders.   [4]

2   Explain why there is a conflict of interests between VestMe's shareholders and the business's suppliers.   [4]

3   Identify **two** possible threats for VestMe from the conflict between the management and the factory workers.   [4]

Resolving stakeholder conflict

One way of reducing conflict is to compromise. For example, a business aiming to reduce costs may close one of its factories in stages rather than immediately, in order to allow workers time to find other jobs. However, as a result, business costs will fall more slowly. Plans to build a new chemical plant may have to be adapted to move the main site away from a housing estate to protect the local community, but the new site might be more expensive. The introduction of 24-hour flights at an airport – which will benefit the airlines and passengers – may only be accepted if local residents are offered sound insulation in their homes, thereby increasing costs for the airport and airlines.

Clearly, senior management must establish its priorities in these situations. They need to decide who the most important stakeholders are in each case, what the extra cost of meeting the needs of each stakeholder group will be, and whether bad publicity resulting from failure to meet the interests of one group will lead to lost revenue – perhaps this will be greater than the cost savings of not satisfying this group.

Table 4.3 considers methods available to businesses to reduce stakeholder conflict, and the potential advantages and disadvantages of each.

Method of conflict resolution	Advantages	Disadvantages
Arbitration – to resolve industrial disputes between workers and managers.	An independent arbitrator will hear the arguments from both sides and decide on what they consider to be a fair solution. Both sides can agree beforehand whether this settlement is binding, i.e., they have to accept it.	Neither stakeholder group is likely to receive exactly what they want The costs of the business might increase if the arbitrator proposes higher wages or better work conditions than the employer was originally offering.
Worker participation – to improve communication and decision-making and reduce potential conflicts between workers and managers, e.g., works councils, employee directors.	Workers have a real contribution to make to many business decisions. Participation can motivate employees to work more effectively.	Some managers believe that participation wastes time and resources and that it is the managers' role to manage, not the workers' Some information cannot be disclosed to employees other than senior managers, e.g., sensitive details about future product launches.
Profit-sharing schemes – to reduce conflict between workers and shareholders over the allocation of profits and to share the benefits of company success.	The workforce is allocated a share of annual profits before these are paid out in dividends to shareholders. Sharing business profits can encourage workers to work in ways that will increase long-term profitability.	Paying workers a share of the profits can reduce retained profits (used for expansion of the business) and/or profits paid out to shareholders, unless the scheme results in higher profits due to increased employee motivation.
Share-ownership schemes – to reduce conflict between workers, managers and shareholders.	These schemes, including share options (the right to buy shares at a specified price in the future), aim to allow employees (at all levels, including directors) as well as shareholders to benefit from the success of the business. Share ownership should help to align the interests of employees with those of shareholders.	Administration costs, negative impact on employee motivation if the share price falls, dilution of ownership – the issue of additional shares means that each owns a smaller share of the company Employees may have to stay with the company for a certain number of years before they qualify, so the motivation effect on new staff may be limited.

Table 4.3: Methods to reduce stakeholder conflict – advantages and disadvantages

ACTIVITY 4.2

On 28 August 2021, about 70 000 people gathered to form a human chain along the coastline of Spain's Mar Menor, a coastal saltwater lagoon in the Iberian Peninsula located south-east of the Autonomous Community of Murcia. The human chain was there to protest against an environmental disaster in the area.

Work in pairs:

1 Do your research to find out what the environmental problem was that the region faced.

2 Identify and explain a conflict of interest between a specific industry operating in the area and the 'Ecologists in Action' NGO.

3 What was the role of the government to solve such a conflict? Discuss in class.

CASE STUDY 4.3

BP goes 'green'

On 4 August 2020, BP started a new chapter in the world's energy market. It announced its plan to produce much less oil and promised a real breakthrough in the fight against climate change. More specifically, BP announced that by 2030 it will:

- produce 40% less gas and oil
- produce 20 times more renewable energy
- invest 10 times more in low-carbon technology.

Stakeholders are sceptical about BP's announcements. It is not the first time in the energy giant's corporate history that it has promised the world a 'green future'. In March 2002, BP's former chief executive, Lord John Browne, declared BP needed to 'go beyond petroleum'. However, BP soon abandoned its aspiring plans to become a steward to the environment. In 2010, BP's lack of adequate safety measures led to the DB Deepwater Horizon disaster, the worst oil spill in US history, in the Gulf of Mexico. In this dreadful incident, 11 workers died and millions of barrels of crude oil poured into the sea, causing unprecedented ecological damage.

Nonetheless, with its new announcements, BP has become the first oil company to commit to reducing its fossil fuel business by setting specific objectives.

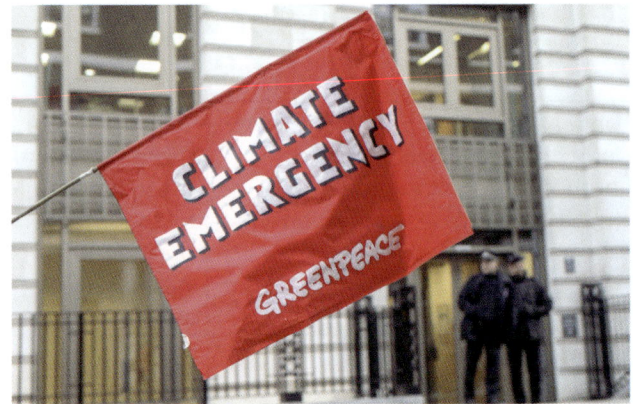

This progress did not just happen. It is the result of the relentless pressure from individuals and groups such as Greenpeace, demanding socially responsible business practices from the oil industry.

1 Define the term 'stakeholders'. [2]

2 Explain the impact of BP's plans to reduce oil production on any **two** stakeholder groups. [4]

3 Suggest **two** possible reasons why BP failed to deliver its 'Go Beyond Petroleum' strategy announced in 2002. [4]

4 Discuss the significance of social responsibility for a business such as BP. [10]

ACTIVITY 4.3

When the customer comes first, the customer will last.

Robert Half

I am convinced that companies should put staff first, customers second and shareholders third – ultimately that's in the best interest of customers and shareholders.

Richard Branson

1   Split into two groups, based on which of the two quotes you most agree with. If any of you disagree with both quotes and you believe that shareholders must come first, form a third group.

2   Each group should prepare a list of arguments to support their view. Debate in class.

3   Do you think there is a right or wrong answer to which shareholder group should be placed as a priority in a business? What are the factors affecting this choice? Discuss in class.

SELF-EVALUATION CHECKLIST

After studying this chapter, complete this table.

I am able to apply and analyse:	Needs more work	Almost there	Ready to move on
internal and external stakeholders (AO2)			
conflict between stakeholders (AO2)			

REFLECTION

How could you assess whether your school or college's responsibilities to its main stakeholder groups are being fulfilled?

PROJECT

Split into three groups.

Group 1: You are the social entrepreneurs and managers of PenFG, a social enterprise that produces stationery and school accessories from environmentally friendly materials and uses its profit to support underprivileged children in your country. You operate a production unit and own three shops. Some of your goods are sold through big retailers. PenFG employs 100 people in total.

Your business was growing fast until the Covid-19 pandemic hit the stationery market. As students moved from physical to online classes, the demand for PenFG's products fell dramatically. Your revenues dropped by 45% in 2020 and by another 26% in 2021. PenFG is facing a survival issue. You have announced the following to your employees:

- The temporary contracts of workers in the factory will not be renewed.

- The salaries of full-time employees will be cut by 15%, as PenFG cannot offer anything more than the legal minimum wage.

- The business will stop offering some benefits such as free lunch to all employees.

Even though you promised your employees that all their benefits will be re-established when the crisis is over, the trade union reacted negatively to your decisions.

Group 2: You are the members of the trade union, and you need to protect the interests of all employees in PenFG. You are preparing your arguments against the management's decisions along with proposals on how to solve the conflict. You are considering the option of a strike if your interests are not satisfied.

Group 3: You are independent arbitrators, and your role is to facilitate the two groups out of their conflict. You try to help them to negotiate and find a solution, otherwise the business may shut down.

Organise a formal meeting, so that Group 1 and Group 2 negotiate to find a solution to the conflict. Group 3 will facilitate the process and help to avoid a further escalation of the conflict. If no solution is reached through negotiations, Group 3 will need to decide on a solution that Group 1 and 2 must accept.

Thinking about your project:

- Before starting negotiations, have you thought about how the conflict affects the interests of the opposing group? During negotiations, are you prepared to hear (and keep detailed notes about) what the other group has to say, before expressing your point of view?

EXAM-STYLE QUESTIONS

Tencent's online games

Tencent is a public limited company and a world-leading internet and technology company. It publishes some of the world's most popular video games and other high-quality digital content, as well as a range of services in the quaternary sector such as cloud computing, fintech (technology enabling banking and financial services), and other B2B services. The business maintains offices around the world and employs a large number of people.

One of Tencent's most popular products is the *Honor of Kings* blockbuster video game. Worldwide, the game has more than 100 million users a day. *Honor of Kings*, which is particularly appealing to minors, is one of the world's highest-earning mobile games, offering a great return to Tencent's shareholders.

Yet not all stakeholders are happy with Tencent's products. The business has serious stakeholder conflicts to handle. In 2021, NGO Beijing Children's Law Aid and Research Centre (BCLARC) filed a lawsuit against Tencent for violating the rights of children by 'encouraging addictive behaviour and showing inappropriate content'. Some media characterised the role-playing *Honour of Kings* as a type of 'drug'. The business is expected to pay millions in fines for creative content that is potentially addictive for young people.

Tencent's response was immediate, starting with the implementation of verification systems to check the real name ID of users and to limit the playing time for minors. In addition, the business announced its collaboration with scientists and researchers to create games that do more than entertain. Such games will have a significant educational role and will add social value, as they will focus on various areas of science, art and technology. With such decisions, Tencent tries to communicate its intention to focus on Tencent group's mission and vision – 'Value for Users, Tech for Good' through its commitment to social responsibility.

The new plans can offer benefits to shareholders as well, as the 'serious games' market is growing fast worldwide.

1   Define the term 'stakeholder conflict'. [2]

2   Identify **one** internal and **one** external stakeholder group in Tencent and explain their interests. [4]

3   Explain **one** conflict of interest that arises from the article. [2]

4   Suggest **two** reasons why Tencent's managers should resolve the conflict of interest as soon as possible. [4]

5   By applying Ansoff's matrix, suggest **one** advantage and **one** disadvantage of the growth strategy that Tencent will use by creating educational games. [4]

6   Suggest **one** advantage and **one** disadvantage for Tencent from setting social responsibility as a corporate objective. [4]

7   With reference to the case study, explain how 'pressure groups' are stakeholders of business activities. [4]

8   Suggest **one** advantage and **one** disadvantage for Tencent from using only one statement to express both its mission and its vision. [4]

9   With reference to the case study, explain the difference between the tertiary and the quaternary sectors. [4]

10 Evaluate the extent to which the two decisions Tencent took as an immediate response to the lawsuit are enough for the business to solve the stakeholder conflict. [10]

Chapter 5

Growth and evolution

BUSINESS IN CONTEXT

Mergers and acquisitions drive business growth

Wellversed, one of India's most successful nutritional food and supplements businesses, has acquired Sportfit with the agreement of Sportfit's owners and managers. Sportfit provides clients with 'customised fitness solutions' to achieve transformations in their fitness and health. Sportfit offers different fitness programmes for each client, which include dietary recommendations. The **acquisition** means that Sportsfit gym instructors and diet specialists will now be recommending Wellversed's large range of products, helping to boost sales and profits.

'The acquisition strengthens our position as the fastest-growing health transformation player in the country,' Aanan Khurma, co-founder and chief executive officer at Wellversed, said. 'Along with Sportfit, we are now equipped to cater to all kinds of fitness outcomes that the consumers need. We welcome the Sportfit team to Wellversed and look forward to creating the desired **synergies** with them.' Business analysts agreed that this was a mutually agreed acquisition and not a hostile **takeover**.

Gojek, a ride-hailing and payment provider in Indonesia, and PT Tokopedia, a leader in e-commerce in the region, are in discussion about a **merger**. If this merger is agreed, the directors of the business could plan to convert it into a public limited company with an initial public offering of shares. The merger would allow a faster rate of expansion for Gojek than could be achieved from **internal growth**. Synergies that might result include cost savings from reducing duplication of services and revenue gains from cross-selling in each other's markets.

The combined value of the merged business would be in excess of $18 billion. The activities of the combined business would range from ride-hailing and payments to online shopping and delivery – a localised version of Uber Technologies, PayPal Holdings, Amazon.com and DoorDash. Business analysts believe that the combined business will be more able to compete effectively with these and other global tech giants.

Discuss in pairs or a group:

- What are the possible advantages and limitations for a business of expanding by merging with or acquiring other businesses rather than growing internally?

- Why will some stakeholder groups benefit from mergers and acquisitions but other groups' interests are damaged?

KEY TERMS

acquisition: when a company buys at least 50% of the shares of another company and becomes the controlling owner – with the agreement of the existing owner(s)/managers

synergy: the concept that, following a merger or acquisition, the combined value and performance of two businesses will be greater than the sum of the separate individual businesses

takeover: when a business wishes to acquire another company but this is opposed by that company's managers – often referred to as a 'hostile takeover'

merger: an agreement by shareholders and managers of two businesses to bring both businesses together under a common board of directors with shareholders in both businesses owning shares in the newly merged business

internal growth: expansion of a business by means of opening new branches, shops or factories (also known as organic growth)

Sustainability

Multinationals are typically accused of depleting natural resources and polluting the environment when they undertake direct investment in foreign countries, especially in countries that are less developed. However, nowadays many multinational corporations try to consider the environment and reduce the impact of their activities, contributing to ecological sustainability. For example, both Nike and Adidas invest heavily in technology to produce sustainable products using tonnes of recycled materials. They have also committed themselves to engage more resources on environmentally safe production methods.

5.1 Internal and external economies and diseconomies of scale

There is a huge difference between the **scale of operations** of a small business – perhaps operated by just one person – and the largest companies in the world. Some of the largest companies have total annual sales exceeding the GDP of many countries! In 2020 Walmart recorded sales of over $523 billion, yet the GDP of Vietnam, for example, was $345 billion.

There are risks and costs involved in increasing the scale of production (e.g., purchasing land, buildings and equipment, and employing more staff) and the capital used for this will always have alternative uses. Businesses expand capacity by increasing the scale of production so that they can avoid turning business away and increase market share. But they also benefit from the advantages of large-scale production – these are called economies of scale. They can be classified as **internal economies of scale** and **external economies of scale**.

Internal economies of scale

These cost benefits can be so substantial in some industries that smaller businesses are unlikely to survive due to lack of competitiveness, such as in oil refining or soft-drink production. The cost benefits arise for five main reasons.

1 Purchasing economies

These economies are often known as bulk-buying economies. Suppliers often offer substantial discounts for large orders. This is because it is cheaper for them to process and deliver one large order than several smaller ones.

2 Technical economies

There are two main sources of technical economies. Large businesses are more likely to be able to justify the cost of mass production lines. If these are worked at a high capacity level, then they offer lower unit costs than other production methods. The latest and most advanced technical equipment – such as computer systems – is often expensive and can usually only be afforded by big businesses. Such expense can only be justified by larger businesses with high output levels – so that average fixed costs can be reduced.

scale of operation: the maximum output that can be achieved using the available inputs (resources) – this scale can only be increased in the long term by employing more of all inputs

internal economies of scale: reductions in unit (average) costs of production that result from an increase in the scale of operations of a business

external economies of scale: reductions in unit (average) costs of production of a business that result from growth of the industry, often in one particular region

3 Financial economies

Large organisations have two cost advantages when it comes to raising finance. First, banks often prefer lending to a big business with a proven track record and a diversified range of products. Interest rates charged to these businesses are often lower than the rate charged to small businesses, especially newly formed ones. Secondly, raising finance by 'going public' or by further public issues of shares for existing public limited companies is very expensive. As this cost does not increase much when a large number of shares is sold, this benefits a big business raising a considerable capital sum.

> **TIP**
>
> Do not confuse 'producing more' with increasing the scale of operation. More can be produced from existing resources by increasing capacity utilisation. Changing the scale of operation means using more (or less) of all resources – for example, opening a new factory with additional machines and workers.

4 Marketing economies

Marketing costs obviously increase with the size of a business, but not at the same rate that the business grows. Even a small enterprise will need a sales force to cover the whole of the sales area. It may employ an advertising agency to design adverts and arrange a promotional campaign. These costs can be spread over more sales for a big business, and this offers a substantial economy of scale.

5 Managerial economies

Small businesses often employ general managers who have a range of management functions to perform. As a business expands, it should be able to afford to attract specialist functional managers who should operate more efficiently than general managers, helping to reduce average costs.

> **TIP**
>
> When answering questions about economies of scale, make sure your answer is applied to the business in the question.

Internal diseconomies of scale

If there were no disadvantages to large-scale operations, nearly all industries would be dominated by huge corporations. Some are, of course, as with oil exploration, refining and retailing – the benefits of large-scale production are so substantial that smaller businesses find it increasingly difficult to operate profitably. In other industries, the impact of **internal diseconomies of scale** prevents one or just a few businesses from being able to completely dominate.

> **KEY TERM**
>
> **internal diseconomies of scale:** factors that cause unit (average) costs of production to rise when the scale of operation of a business is increased

Diseconomies of scale are those factors that increase unit costs as a business's scale of operation increases beyond a certain size. These diseconomies are related to the management problems of trying to control and direct an organisation with many thousands of workers, in many separate divisions, often operating in several different countries. There are three main causes of management problems.

1 Communication problems

Large-scale operations will often lead to poor feedback to workers, excessive use of non-personal communication media, communication overload with the volume of messages being sent, and distortion of messages caused by the long chain of command. Poor feedback reduces worker incentives.

These problems may lead to poor decisions being made, due to inadequate or delayed information, and management inefficiency.

2 Alienation of the workforce

The bigger the organisation, the more difficult it is to directly involve every worker and to give them a sense of purpose and achievement. They may feel insignificant in the overall business plan and become demotivated, failing to do their best. Larger manufacturing businesses are the ones most likely to adopt flow-line production, and workforce alienation is a real problem due to repetitive and boring tasks.

3 Poor coordination and slow decision-making

Business expansion often leads to many departments, divisions and products. The number of countries a business operates in often increases too. The problems for senior management relate to coordinating these operations and taking rapid decisions in such a complex organisation. Smaller businesses with greater control over operations and much quicker and more flexible decision-making may benefit from lower average production costs as a result.

Large-scale production – impact on unit costs

The combined effect of economies of scale and diseconomies of scale on unit (average) costs of production is shown in Figure 5.1. There is not a particular point of operation at which economies of scale cease and diseconomies begin. The process is more difficult to measure than this, as certain economies of scale may continue to be received as scale increases, but the growing significance of diseconomies gradually begins to take over and average costs may rise. It is often impossible to state at what level of output this process occurs, which is why many managers may continue to expand their business, unaware that the forces causing diseconomies are building up.

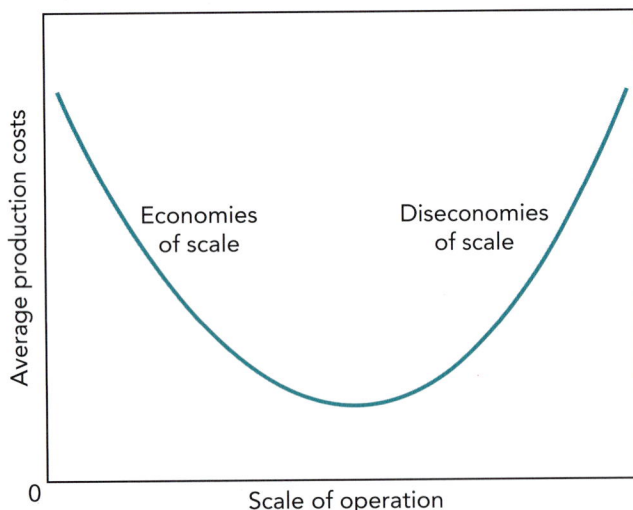

Figure 5.1: The impact of economies and diseconomies of scale on average costs

External economies of scale

The growth of a business is not the only source of potential average cost savings. When a business operates in an expanding industry, especially when it is concentrated in one particular region, further cost benefits might be gained. It is quite common for businesses in the same industry to be clustered in the same region. Silicon Valley in the USA and Bengaluru in India have a very high concentration of IT-focused businesses. The Laphu region in Vietnam has 136 knitwear businesses within a relatively small geographical area, and many of them are expanding rapidly.

What benefits do IT businesses gain in Silicon Valley and Bengaluru, and what benefits do textile manufacturers gain from being based in the Laphu region of Vietnam?

Businesses in these industries will be able to attract a large pool of qualified and experienced workers to the area, drawn by the prospect of employment. Local college and university courses will often focus on the specific skill requirements of industries clustered in the region. These courses will increase the supply of well-qualified employees able to offer creative ideas and productive working practices. A network of supplying businesses will exist, able to meet the companies' needs for specialist machines, components, maintenance and support services. It will also be relatively easy to arrange cooperation and joint ventures on projects when businesses are located close to each other. All of these factors that result from the regional growth of an industry can lead to cost savings for all businesses in the industry. The reductions in average costs are referred to as external economies of scale.

External diseconomies of scale

If an industry continues to grow in one region it can lead to cost increases for the businesses operating in the industry. There will be increased demand for land or property, suitable labour and other resources needed for production. These demand pressures will cause unit costs to rise and might make the area a less competitive region for businesses to locate in. These cost disadvantages are called **external diseconomies of scale**.

> **KEY TERM**
>
> **external diseconomies of scale:** factors causing unit costs for a business to rise as an industry expands, especially in a given region

5.2 The difference between internal and external growth

Business growth can be achieved in a number of ways, and these forms of growth can lead to differing effects on stakeholder groups, such as customers, workers and competitors. The different forms of growth can be grouped into internal and external growth, as shown in Figure 5.2.

KEY TERM

external growth: business expansion achieved by means of merging with or taking over another business, from either the same or a different industry

---

An example of internal growth would be a retailing business opening more shops in towns and cities where it previously had none. Compared to external growth, internal (or organic) growth can have the following benefits:

- Expansion of the business is slower and more manageable.
- The need for very large sums of finance is likely to be less as there is no takeover or acquisition involved.
- There is no risk of a culture clash with managers from a business that is being integrated.

See 5.4 Reasons for business to stay small for an evaluation of why businesses might remain small rather than expand externally.

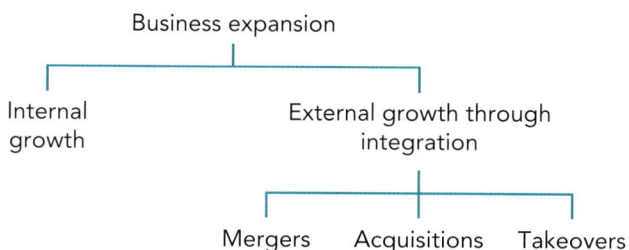

Figure 5.2: Different forms of growth

5.3 Reasons for businesses to grow

There are several reasons why the managers of a business might want their business to grow. These include:

- To benefit from unit cost advantages. If internal economies of scale drive down unit costs, a large business will gain considerable competitive advantages over smaller firms in the same industry. These cost advantages can make the business more profitable and help managers expand the business by being able to offer lower prices to customers.

- To increase market share and market power. When a business grows faster than the market it operates in, it will increase market share and market power and influence. For example, this means having greater control over setting prices. A large business may be able to afford to set very low prices for a period of time in order to weaken or even eliminate competitors. It might then be able to increase prices in future to make a higher profit.

- To reduce risk. Expanding a business into new markets, different stages of the production process or even into completely different industries are all forms of diversification. Any reduction in sales of the original products of the business might be counterbalanced by sales growth in the new markets that the business is developing.

- Managerial motives. The potential for conflict resulting from the 'divorce between ownership and control' (see Chapter 2) might mean that the management team are largely interested in their own status and recognition. Managing a growing business can result in higher salaries and a wider recognition in the business world for the senior decision-makers within that business.

- To increase profits. This is likely to be the long-term reason why businesses plan to expand. By reducing unit costs, gaining market power and diversifying into new markets, the potential for increased profit levels should be achieved.

- To reduce the risk of takeover. By increasing the size of the business, and in the longer term its profitability, a management team will make the business less likely to become a takeover target. This is for two reasons. Firstly, the business will cost much more to take over, which means that many potential 'predators' will not be able to afford this. Secondly, increasing profit raises shareholder value so the owners of expanding companies are much less likely to accept a takeover bid if they consider that their long-term interests are best served with the existing management team.

5.4 Reasons for businesses to stay small

Despite the potential benefits from business expansion, many businesses remain small. The main reasons for this are:

- The market that the business operates in is small. The size of the market for repairing antique clocks is small. There are likely to be several specialist clock repairers in the market so each business will have to remain small – as measured by sales value or employment – unless the owner considers diversification. This is such a specialist and technical service that most owners of clock repairing businesses might be unwilling to learn other skills in order to diversify effectively. Hence, businesses in these market scenarios will remain small.

- The lifestyle choice of the owner. The owners of many small businesses want to maintain sole control over the firm and to have a happy work–life balance. If the business expands, other managers might be required and the owner might find that they are spending too much time on business affairs. Keeping the business small is often a choice made by the owner.

- Desire to keep overhead costs low and reduce financial risks. Some small business owners do not want the anxiety that can result from moving to larger premises with high fixed costs. They may not want to borrow finance for expansion and will therefore keep risks low by not expanding the business.

- Maintaining a personal service to customers. Owners of small businesses often value the personal contact they enjoy with customers. This is not only sociable but also helps the owner maintain quality control over the goods or service being provided. These advantages could be lost if the growing sales of an expanding business require employees to be recruited to serve customers.

- Keeping the business flexible and adaptable to market conditions. Small businesses often have just one key decision-maker – the owner. This means that quick and effective decisions can be made in response to changing market conditions such as different customer requirements or increased competition. This benefit of small business operation is often lost if it expands beyond a certain point at which decision-making becomes the responsibility of several people. This can lead to disagreements and time spent on discussions before important decisions to change the products or operations of the business can be made.

Comparing the benefits of small and large businesses

The reasons why some businesses expand and others remain small can be summarised by considering the advantages and disadvantages of small and large businesses (see Tables 5.1 and 5.2).

Small businesses	Large businesses
Can be managed and controlled by the owner(s)	Can afford to employ specialist professional managers
Are often able to adapt quickly to meet changing customer needs/market conditions	Benefit from cost reductions associated with large-scale production
Offer personal service to customers	May be able to set prices that other businesses have to follow
Find it easier to know each worker, and many staff prefer to work for a smaller, more 'human' business	Have access to several different sources of finance
Average costs may be low due to no diseconomies of scale and low overheads	May be diversified in several markets and products, so risks are spread
Easier communication with workers and customers	Are more likely to be able to afford research and development into new products and processes

Table 5.1: Potential advantages of small and large businesses

Small businesses	Large businesses
May have limited access to sources of finance	May be difficult to manage, especially if geographically spread
May find the owner has to carry a large burden of responsibility if unable to afford to employ specialist managers	May have potential cost increases associated with large-scale production
May not be diversified, so there are greater risks of negative impact of external change	May suffer from slow decision-making and poor communication due to the structure of the large organisation
Unlikely to benefit from economies of scale	May often suffer from a divorce between ownership and control that can lead to conflicting objectives

Table 5.2: Potential disadvantages of small and large businesses

CASE STUDY 5.1

Should Hasan grow his shoe factory?

Hasan owns a small footwear manufacturing unit in Jakarta, Indonesia. In his production unit, he makes leather shoes of high quality for men and women. The factory employs 60 workers. Even though wages in Indonesia are relatively low, Hasan's production cost per unit is higher compared to competitive local businesses.

To reduce the production cost, the finance director advised Hasan to grow his factory by investing in advanced technology, which would allow the production process to become more capital intensive. In such a factory, a greater quantity would be produced to be exported abroad for more revenue and profit, while economies of scale would occur. The finance director believes that suppliers would be happy to offer Hasan better prices per unit for the larger quantities offered. The transportation cost per unit would also fall.

Hasan is not convinced that he should turn his medium-sized business into a large-scale organisation. He is afraid of the managerial complexity that could appear in a big factory. He is currently managing most of the business activities alone and he is in charge of all strategic decisions. If the business grows, Hasan will lose direct control. Moreover, he currently has a personal relationship with all his workers. This would not be possible in a large business unit where employees are often alienated.

1   Define the term 'economies of scale'. [2]

2   Suggest **two** types of economies of scale that could appear in the business, if Hasan grows the production unit. [4]

3   Suggest **two** advantages of growth for Hasan's business, **other than** economies of scale. [4]

4   Discuss the advantages and disadvantages for Hasan's business if he invests in a large-scale production unit. [10]

ACTIVITY 5.1

Top 10 of the Fortune Global 500*						
Rank	Company	Country	Revenues ($ Mil.)	Revenues (% Change)	Profits ($ Mil.)	Profits (% Change)
1	Walmart	USA	559 151	6.7	13 510	–9.2
2	State Grid	China	386 618	0.7	5 580	–30
3	Amazon	USA	386 064	37.6	21 331	84.1
4	China National Petroleum	China	283 958	–25.1	4 575	3
5	Sinopec Group	China	283 728	–30.3	6 205	–8.7
6	Apple	USA	274 515	5.5	57 411	3.9
7	CVC Health	USA	268 706	4.6	7 179	8.2
8	United Health Group	USA	257 141	6.2	15 403	11.3
9	Toyota Motor	Japan	256 722	–6.5	21 180	13.1
10	Volkswagen	Germany	253 965	–10.2	10 103	–35

*Fiscal year ended on or before March 31, 2021.

1   Find out what the Fortune Global 500 is and describe what the table shows.

2   Which was the biggest business in the world by 31 March in terms of revenues?

3   Which was the biggest business in the world by 31 March in terms of profits?

4   Why do you think the world's biggest business in terms of revenues is not the biggest in terms of profit?

5   Amazon's revenue grew by the astonishing 37.6% during the Covid-19 pandemic. Can you suggest any external factor that helped it to grow so much?

THEORY OF KNOWLEDGE

Knowledge question: To what extent is the belief that market leaders are better than followers a matter of perception and perspective?

Consumers often follow the market leaders because they believe they are better than competitors. The biggest players in the market have a position of strength. That is why it is typical for firms to intensively promote their leadership.

There are many reasons why market leaders might indeed be better than followers. Leaders are commonly huge business organisations that have financial resources available to spend on improving

CONTINUED

the quality of the factors of production. They are often able to spend heavily on innovation and possess superior management know-how. But there are many cases where the market leaders are simply big producers with huge economies of scale who manage to dominate the industry just because of their low prices.

Suggest brands that lead their markets and are commonly believed to be superior to competitors. Discuss in class whether this belief is a matter of facts or the result of perceptions.

5.5 External growth methods

Mergers and acquisitions

Rapid growth can be achieved by using external growth such as merging with or acquiring another business. Both of these forms of external growth assume a certain level of agreement between the managers and owners of the businesses involved.

A merger occurs when individual businesses decide to join their resources together to create a new business entity. The new entity might be given a name made up of the two business names or it may be given a completely new identity.

On the other hand, an acquisition is a situation in which a larger, financially stronger organisation takes over a smaller one. The smaller organisation ceases to exist as a business entity, and all of its operations and resources are acquired and managed by the larger business. Both mergers and acquisitions aim to achieve higher synergy levels within the expanded organisation with the aim of increasing efficiency and competitiveness.

Takeover

A takeover is an acquisition which is contested. The managers and owners of the 'victim' business originally had no intention of losing control of the firm. However, publicity issued by the predator business about the

reasons for the takeover bid combined with a high share price offer is often effective in encouraging sufficient shareholders to sell their shares (51% of shares are required).

See Table 5.3 for a summary of the key differences between merger, acquisition and takeover.

Mergers, acquisitions and takeovers are often referred to as forms of business integration.

Figure 5.3 illustrates the different types of integration resulting from external growth. Table 5.4 provides a guide to the different types of integration, their common advantages and disadvantages, and the impact they often have on stakeholder groups.

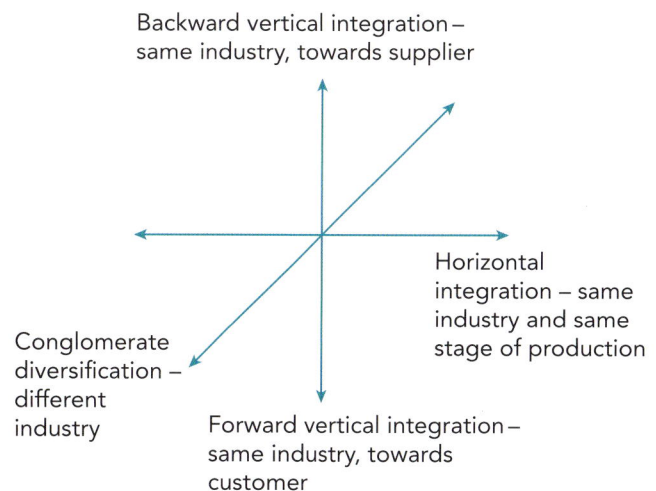

Backward vertical integration – same industry, towards supplier

Horizontal integration – same industry and same stage of production

Conglomerate diversification – different industry

Forward vertical integration – same industry, towards customer

Figure 5.3: Forms of external growth

	Merger	Acquisition	Takeover
Procedure	Two businesses (it could be more) form a new, larger business entity	One company takes over the operations of another business that is usually smaller in size	One company takes over the operations of another business that is usually smaller in size
Decision	A mutually agreed decision	Usually mutually agreed – e.g., if a family wishes to sell its family business	Hostile takeover bid which is initially opposed by the managers/owners of the business that is eventually taken over
Name of company	Operates under a new name	Acquired company may use the name of the other business – but it may operate under its own name if it has a strong brand image	Existing name of the acquiring business is usually used
Relative power/ status of the businesses involved	Likely to have equal status, with managers from both businesses being offered posts	The acquiring company is usually larger – it may not retain all managers and employees of the other business	Managers of the acquired business may not be retained – and some of the assets of this business might be sold
Shares	The merged company will issue new shares in the new company name to both groups of shareholders	New shares might be issued to swap for the shares of the business being acquired – reducing the cash outlay of the acquiring business	New shares might be issued to swap for the shares of the business being taken over – reducing the cash outlay of the acquiring business

Table 5.3: The main differences between merger, acquisition and takeover

---

TIP

If an examination question refers to a merger **or** acquisition, you should start by identifying what type of integration it is. Do not forget that mergers and acquisitions (takeovers) often cause businesses as many problems as they solve.

Type of integration	Advantages	Disadvantages	Impact on stakeholders
Horizontal integration	Eliminates one competitor Possible economies of scale Scope for rationalising production, e.g., concentrating output on one site instead of two Increased power over suppliers	Rationalisation may bring bad publicity May lead to monopoly investigation if the combined business exceeds certain size limits	Consumers have less choice Workers may lose job security as a result of rationalisation

Type of integration	Advantages	Disadvantages	Impact on stakeholders
Forward vertical integration	Business is able to control the promotion and pricing of its own products Secures an outlet for the business's products – may now exclude competitors' products	Consumers may suspect uncompetitive activity and react negatively Lack of experience in this sector of the industry – a successful manufacturer does not necessarily make a good retailer	Workers may have greater job security because the business has secure outlets There may be more varied career opportunities Consumers may resent lack of competition in the retail outlet because of the withdrawal of competitor products
Backward vertical integration	Gives control over quality, price and delivery times of supplies Encourages joint research and development into improved quality of supplies of components Business may control supplies of materials to competitors	May lack experience of managing a supplying company – e.g., a successful steel producer will not necessarily make a good manager of a coal mine Supplying business may become complacent having a guaranteed customer	Possibility of greater career opportunities for workers Consumers may obtain improved quality and more innovative products Control over supplies to competitors may limit competition and choice for consumers
Conglomerate integration	Diversifies the business away from its original industry and markets This should spread risk and may take the business into a faster-growing market	Lack of management experience in the acquired business sector There could be a lack of clear focus and direction now that the business is spread across more than one industry	Greater career opportunities for workers More job security because risks are spread across more than one industry

Table 5.4: Types of business integration

KEY TERMS

horizontal integration: integration with a business that is in the same industry and at the same stage of production

forward vertical integration: integration with a business that is in the same industry but a customer of the existing business

backward vertical integration: integration with a business that is in the same industry but a supplier of the existing business

conglomerate integration: merger with or takeover of a business that is in a different industry

Why mergers, acquisitions and takeovers can fail

If external growth was always successful in achieving its aims of increased efficiency, competitiveness and profitability, there would undoubtedly be many more mergers, acquisitions and takeovers than there are. The fact is that on many occasions, external growth fails to reach some or all of its objectives. There are several possible reasons for this:

- The newly integrated business is too large to control and manage effectively. This is a diseconomy of scale, but it might also be caused by the management team not being experienced or capable enough to take the appropriate decisions that the newly expanded business needs for success.

- There could be a serious culture clash between the two management teams involved – especially with a merger where most members of both management teams are likely to retain their positions. For example, the approach each company took (before integration) towards environmental or ethical issues may be very different. In the newly integrated business these differences could cause such tensions that management teams and groups of workers from both companies find it very difficult to set common objectives and to work together.

- There may be only a few potential cost savings to be gained from merging key departments of the two businesses. This might apply to the marketing department if, before the integration, both companies operated in very different markets/countries.

- Government regulatory controls might limit the opportunities for higher profit. Governments of most countries will investigate the potential impact on the market and consumer interests of large mergers, acquisitions and takeovers. If a government considers that competition will be too seriously affected, it might place conditions on the integration, such as selling some retail stores or production capacity. This will eventually make the combined bigger business less profitable than it would otherwise have been.

LEARNER PROFILE

Risk taker

Samsung, the giant electronics manufacturer, has announced it will invest $206 billion by 2023 to achieve growth in the post-pandemic era. The investments will focus on artificial intelligence, biopharmaceuticals, semiconductors and robotics.

Samsung is the biggest conglomerate in South Korea and the world's largest memory chip maker. Even though the firm did not provide any breakdown of the investment figures, it announced that its goal is to strengthen its global position in existing markets such as the production of chips and to diversify into new areas such as robotics for long-term growth. The investments will be mostly in the form of mergers and acquisitions.

Even though the investment in new technologies hides very significant risks, it is considered necessary by Samsung's management. 'The chip industry is the safety plate of the Korean economy... Our aggressive investment is a survival strategy in the sense that once we lose our competitiveness, it is almost impossible to make a comeback,' Samsung Electronics said in a statement.

What kind of risks do you think Samsung is taking in its post-pandemic growth plan? Do you agree with Samsung's statement about the need to proceed to aggressive investment for survival purposes, regardless of the risks? Discuss in class.

CASE STUDY 5.2

Coca-Cola's efforts to diversify are paying off as beverage maker tops forecast

In 2018, Coca-Cola public limited company (plc) grew significantly through product development and diversification.

The management had to inform its shareholders in a press release that net revenues declined by 15% to $9.1 billion in the first nine months of 2017 compared to the same period of the previous year. Given that more consumers moved away from Coke's signature beverages as part of a broader effort to cut back on sugar, the beverage giant focused its attention on improving its existing portfolio and adding more 'better-for-you' products to the mix. Coca-Cola has also reduced the amount of added sugar in its products. Its Coca-Cola Zero Sugar, which launched in the US in August 2017, posted double-digit growth during the quarter compared to the year before. By the first quarter of 2018, the company planned to introduce the product internationally. At that time, analysts suggested that the global Gross Domestic Product (GDP) was projected to rise by 3.7% in 2018 compared to 2017.

The manufacturer continued to expand its reach beyond soda, by entering new industries with innovative products. Apart from attempting to diversify organically, Coca-Cola invested in external growth as well. In early October 2017, the company announced that it had acquired the Topo Chico premium sparkling mineral water brand for $220 million.

Efforts to diversify beyond the sodas that are synonymous with Coca-Cola appear to be paying off. The Atlanta company gained or maintained its market share in sparkling soft drinks, juices, sports drinks and ready-to-drink tea. In August 2018, Coca-Cola announced the acquisition of the British coffee-shop chain Costa Coffee for $5.1 billion. But the market of coffee is significantly different from the soft-drinks market, and competition in this industry from giants such as Starbucks is a big threat.

1   With reference to the case study, outline **one** disadvantage of public limited companies.   [2]

2   With reference to the case study, explain the difference between internal and external growth.   [4]

3   Explain **two** STEEPLE factors that affect Coca-Cola's growth strategy.   [4]

4   Evaluate Coca-Cola's decision to diversify beyond the soft-drinks market.   [10]

ACTIVITY 5.2

In May 2020, Facebook announced the acquisition of Giphy and its plan to fully integrate it with Instagram. The deal is estimated to be worth $400 million. However, the UK antitrust authorities reacted against the decision.

1   Research project

    Use internet-based sources to research this example of acquisition. Create a report to describe the deal, the possible effects on stakeholders and the reasons behind the reaction of the UK regulators.

2   Reflection

    In your report, did you discuss both the positive and the negative effects on a variety of different stakeholders?

Joint ventures

A **joint venture** is not the same as a merger, but it may lead to a merger of the businesses if their joint interests coincide and if the joint venture is successful. The reasons for joint ventures are:

- Costs and risks of a new business venture are shared – this is a major consideration when the cost of developing new products is rising rapidly.

- Different companies might have different strengths and experiences, so they fit together well.

- They might have their major markets in different countries and they could exploit these with the new product more effectively than if they both decided to 'go it alone'.

Such ventures can lead to the following problems:

- Styles of management and culture might be so different that the two teams do not blend together well.

- Errors and mistakes might lead to one blaming the other.

- The business failure of one of the partners would put the whole project at risk.

Strategic alliances

Strategic alliances can be made with a wide variety of stakeholders, for example:

- With a university – finance provided by the business to allow new specialist training courses that will increase the supply of suitable employees for the business.

- With a supplier – to join forces in order to design and produce components and materials that will be used in a new range of products. This may help to reduce the total development time for getting the new products to market, gaining a competitive advantage.

- With a competitor – to reduce the risks of entering a market that neither business currently operates in. Care must be taken that, in these cases, the actions are not seen as being 'anti-competitive' and, as a result, against the laws of the country whose market is being entered.

KEY TERMS

joint venture: two or more businesses agree to work closely together on a particular project and create a separate business division to do so

strategic alliance: an arrangement between businesses in which each agrees to commit resources to achieve an agreed set of objectives

---

ACTIVITY 5.3

The following are some growth options that Coca-Cola has followed in its history.

1   Tick the box(es) that describe the growth strategies used.

	Internal growth (organic)	External growth (inorganic)	Horizontal integration	Conglomerate integration	Vertical integration
The development of Coca-Cola Diet and Zero					
The acquisition of Costa Coffee					
The acquisition of Monster Beverage					
The acquisition of the North American Coca-Cola bottling company					
The Coca-Cola and Nestlé partnership on the Nestea ready-to-drink products					

CONTINUED

2 Why do you think Coca-Cola combines many growth methods? Discuss in class.

CASE STUDY 5.3

Nestlé's growth strategy

Nestlé S.A. is a Swiss multinational conglomerate business. It is headquartered in Switzerland, and has 376 factories in over 80 countries worldwide. Nestlé is a global market leader and its product catalogue consists of highly recognisable brands such as Nescafe, KitKat, bottled water brands, etc. Nestlé's vision is 'to be a leading, competitive, Nutrition, Health and Wellness Company delivering improved shareholder value by being a preferred corporate citizen, preferred employer, preferred supplier selling preferred products.'

On 28 August 2018, Nestlé and Starbucks closed a deal which legally allowed the Swiss multinational to globally market Starbucks – labelled, packaged, consumer goods as well as foodservice products outside of the popular American coffee house chain's physical coffee shops – as part of a $7.15 billion global strategic alliance. In 2020, Nestlé announced the acquisition of Aimmune Therapeutics Inc., a biopharmaceutical company developing and commercialising treatments for potentially life-threatening food allergies.

The combination of internal and external growth strategies has allowed the business to experience increasing sales and significant economies of scale. Nestlé's factories are among the most technologically advanced and fully automated food manufacturing units in the world. Nestlé is among the world's largest milk companies, sourcing more than 12 million tonnes of fresh milk

equivalents every year from farmers in more than 30 countries.

Growth has helped Nestlé to reach its aim to deliver high shareholder value over time. The Nestlé Group's net profit rose from about 7 billion Swiss Francs in 2017 to roughly 13 billion in 2019. However, the huge size of the business has led to diseconomies of scale. The significant managerial complexity within the expanding conglomerate has forced the business to sell some of its business units.

1 Define the term 'conglomerate' business. [2]

2 Describe **two** methods of external growth used by Nestlé. [4]

3 Explain **two** types of economies of scale relevant to Nestlé. [4]

4 Evaluate Nestlé's growth strategy. [10]

Franchising

A **franchise** contract allows the franchisee to use the name, logo and marketing methods of the franchiser. The franchisee can decide which form of legal structure to adopt. Franchises are a rapidly expanding form of business operation. They have allowed certain multinational businesses, such as McDonald's and Ben and Jerry's, to expand much more rapidly than they could otherwise have done. Why would a business entrepreneur want to use the name, style and products of another business?

Table 5.5 outlines the main advantages and disadvantages of franchising to the business using this expansion method (the franchiser).

Table 5.6 summarises the advantages and disadvantages of a franchised business for the franchisee.

> ### KEY TERM
>
> **franchise:** a business that uses the name, logo and trading systems of an existing successful business

Advantages	Disadvantages
Business expansion is largely financed by the franchisee	Franchisees have to be selected carefully to ensure the quality image of the business is maintained
Some business risk is taken by the franchisee	Unethical practices by one franchisee will cause bad publicity for the whole business
Franchisees have a high level of motivation for their franchise to be successful	Only a share of the profit is paid – the franchisee retains the rest
If used in other countries, the franchisee will have local knowledge, e.g., about culture and consumer tastes	Extensive training and support might need to be provided to franchisees to help ensure common standards of customer service are maintained
A share of the sales or profit of the franchise will be received every year	There will be legal costs for preparing detailed franchise contracts
Central control over products, suppliers, decor, prices and other key issues ensure that a clear brand image is maintained	It is not a solution for a failing business – other key elements of the business model have to be effective in order for franchising to be successful

Table 5.5: Advantages and disadvantages of franchising to the franchiser

Advantages	Disadvantages
Less chance of the new business failing as an established brand and product are being used	Share of profits or sales revenue has to be paid to franchiser each year
Advice and training offered by the franchiser	Initial franchise licence fee can be expensive
National advertising paid for by franchiser	Local promotions may still have to be paid for by franchisee
Supplies obtained from established and quality-checked suppliers	No choice of supplies or suppliers to be used
Franchiser agrees not to open another branch in the local area	Strict rules over pricing and layout of the outlet reduce owners' control over own business

Table 5.6: Advantages and disadvantages of franchising to the franchisee

CASE STUDY 5.4

Harry goes it alone

Harry was really bored with his job as second chef in a top-of-the-market hotel. He did not like being ordered around by the head chef. He hoped to use his talents preparing food for customers in his own restaurant. The main problem was his lack of business experience. Harry had just been to a business conference and had been interested in the franchising exhibition there. One of the businesses offering to sell franchises was Pizza Delight. This business sold a new type of pizza recipe to franchisees and provided all the ingredients, marketing support and help with staff training. It had already opened 100 restaurants in other countries and offered to sell new franchises for a one-off payment of $100 000. If Harry signed one of these franchising contracts, then he would have to agree to:

- buy materials only from Pizza Delight

- fit out the restaurant in exactly the way the franchiser wanted

- pay a percentage of annual turnover to Pizza Delight every year.

Harry would have to find and pay for suitable premises and recruit and motivate staff. Pizza Delight claimed that its brand and products were so well known that 'success was guaranteed'. As the product had been tested already, there would be none of the initial problems that small businesses often experience, and Pizza Delight would pay for national advertising campaigns. Harry was told that no other Pizza Delight restaurant could open within five kilometres of one that was already operating.

1   Define the term 'franchise'. [2]

2   Explain **two** potential benefits Harry would enjoy if he were to open a franchised Pizza Delight restaurant. [4]

3   Analyse **two** potential drawbacks to Harry if he agreed to the terms of the franchise contract. [4]

4   Using all of the evidence, advise Harry on whether he should take out a franchise with Pizza Delight. Justify your answer. [10]

SELF-EVALUATION CHECKLIST

After studying this chapter, complete this table.

I am able to analyse and apply:	Needs more work	Almost there	Ready to move on
internal and external economies and diseconomies of scale (AO2)			
the difference between internal and external growth (AO2)			
I am able to synthesise and evaluate:			
reasons for businesses to grow (AO3)			
reasons for businesses to stay small (AO3)			
external growth methods: mergers and acquisitions (M&As), takeovers, joint ventures, strategic alliances and franchising (AO3)			

REFLECTION

Assume your school or college has plans to expand. It has sufficient funds to buy another organisation. It could buy a private school with good facilities; it could buy a supplier of educational resources; or it could buy a privately owned higher education college.

Which of these three growth options would you recommend for you school or college and why? Compare your ideas with those of another learner.

PROJECT

Not many for-profit social enterprises are very big. Most remain small- to medium-sized. But there are exceptions to the rule. Why do most social enterprises remain small and how could they benefit from growth? How do some social enterprises manage to grow bigger and what are the advantages and disadvantages from such a decision?

Split into two groups.

Group 1: Find a social enterprise that has managed to grow big over time.

Explain the reasons why growth became one of its objectives and describe the methods the business used for growth. Identify advantages and disadvantages for its stakeholders as a result of the

decision of the social enterprise to grow. Prepare a presentation with your findings.

Group 2: Find a social enterprise that operates in your home country and remains small.

Explain the reasons why growth is not one of its objectives. Identify advantages and disadvantages for its stakeholders as a result of its decision to remain small. If you cannot find a lot of published data about the business, you may want to try to contact the social entrepreneur who is behind your chosen enterprise. Prepare a presentation with your findings.

Groups 1 and 2 together: Prepare a poster for your class with the two social enterprises, their goals, their main similarities and their differences.

CONTINUED

Thinking about your project:

- When evaluating growth as an option for your chosen social enterprise, did you first clearly identify the other important strategic objectives of the business and how growth affects them?

EXAM PRACTICE QUESTION

PepsiCo to sell Tropicana and other juice brands for about $3.3 billion

PepsiCo has agreed to sell Tropicana and other juice brands to PAI Partners, a French private equity firm. The transaction is expected to be concluded by the end of 2021 or early 2022. 'This joint venture with PAI enables us to realise significant upfront value, whilst providing the focus and resources necessary to drive additional long-term growth for these beloved brands,' said Ramon Laguarta, PepsiCo's CEO. The deal is described as a 'joint venture' because PepsiCo will maintain a 39% stake and the exclusive distribution rights for the products in the US.

But why would a business sell profitable, world-famous brands to another business? PepsiCo's decision can be explained as an effort to rationalise its product portfolio based on changing consumer trends. The demand for juices was strong in 2020, with consumers seeking more vitamin C for immune support due to the Covid-19 pandemic, but the long-term trend of juices is one of decline because juices are rich in sugar. The business will use the proceeds of the sale to invest in healthier products, mainly by acquiring smaller firms producing low-sugar beverages and low-fat snacks.

The business is constantly searching for innovative and sustainable products for consumers. In early 2021, PepsiCo joined forces with Beyond Meat Inc. to launch The PLANeT Partnership, a joint venture to develop, produce and market innovative snack and beverage products made from plant-based protein.

Another reason why PepsiCo is selling the juice products is to improve managerial efficiency by reducing operational complexity, and to help the business to focus on its vision, which is to 'be the global leader in convenient foods and beverages by winning with purpose.' Over the years, PepsiCo has grown both internally (for example, by expanding its Pepsi and Lays ranges) and externally, mainly through horizontal integration. Today, PepsiCo has a wide range of foods and beverages, including 23 brands such as Pepsi, Lays, Doritos, Gatorade, 7Up and many more, sold in more than 200 countries. It all started many decades ago when Pepsi merged with Frito-Lay, a growth option which the CEOs of the two businesses called 'a marriage made in heaven'. Since then, PepsiCo has made many acquisitions, some of the most notable being the acquisition of Quaker Oats and Tropicana. When businesses such as PepsiCo grow to become so big, they often face diseconomies of scale, some of which are reduced through the selling of products that show no long-term growth potential.

1 Define the term 'diseconomies of scale'. [2]
2 Define the term 'horizontal integration'. [2]
3 Explain **two** external growth strategies used by PepsiCo. [4]
4 Suggest **two** reasons why PepsiCo depends heavily on acquisitions as a growth strategy. [4]
5 Explain **two** types of diseconomies of scale that PepsiCo could face. [4]
6 Suggest **two** advantages for PepsiCo as a result of growing to become one of the biggest competitors in its industry. [4]
7 Suggest **two** possible reasons why the merger between PepsiCo and Lays proved to be a successful growth decision. [4]
8 Identify **one** internal weakness and **one** external opportunity for PepsiCo selling the juice brands. [4]
9 With reference to the case study, explain the difference between a merger and an acquisition. [4]
10 Evaluate PepsiCo's decision to sell Tropicana and other juice brands. [10]

> Chapter 6

Multinational companies (MNCs)

BUSINESS IN CONTEXT

Nestlé's impact on emerging market economies

Nestlé, the Swiss-based manufacturer of food and drink, is one of the world's largest **multinational companies**. In 2020 it had a total turnover of three billion Swiss francs ($3.25 billion). It sells products in 187 countries and has manufacturing operations in 83 of those countries. Nestlé employs 320 000 workers, most of them based in countries other than Switzerland. For example, it employs 2300 workers in Nigeria in three manufacturing sites, seven branch offices and one head office. Its operations in this West African country result in substantial tax revenues for the government. Many of the products made in Nestlé's Nigerian operations are exported to neighbouring countries. The company claims to have one of the best employee training schemes in Africa. It is aiming to make all of its operations in Nigeria sustainable with the target of zero carbon emissions.

As with all other MNCs, Nestlé's operations have come in for criticism. The company has been accused of using aggressive marketing tactics in selling tinned baby milk products to mothers in **emerging market economies**. This was despite the scientific evidence that natural mothers' milk is safer for babies. Also, it is claimed that the company's demand for water has led to droughts and water shortages in some of the countries it operates in. According to some reports, the supply of cocoa used by Nestlé and other MNC food manufacturers is still dependent on child labour. In addition, it is alleged that the efficiency of Nestlé's operations makes it increasingly difficult for locally based food producers and processors to survive. As with the majority of other subsidiary operations of MNCs in host countries, most profits are sent back to the company's home country.

Discuss in pairs or a group:

- Why do many businesses, such as Nestlé, operate in more than one country rather than export products from their home country?

- On balance, should the Nigerian government encourage further investment by MNCs in its economy?

KEY TERMS

multinational company or business: business organisation that has its headquarters in one country, but with operating branches, factories and assembly plants in other countries

emerging market economy: a country with an economic system which results in low to middle income per head of population

KEY CONCEPT LINK

Ethics

One of the main reasons why multinational companies (MNCs) are attracted to developing countries is the low production cost. There are still countries around the world that have a very low minimum wage, or even no minimum wage to support workers. Under such circumstances, labour has no protection from being offered very low pay that cannot cover their basic needs. It is an ethical obligation for MNCs to protect the right of workers, even in countries where labour laws are weak. Similar considerations apply in countries where environmental laws are weak. Multinationals should still operate in sustainable ways to demonstrate high ethical standards.

6.1 Multinational companies (MNCs)

Multinational companies have benefited greatly from the freedoms offered by **globalisation**. They are more than just importers and exporters; they actually produce goods and services in more than one country. The biggest multinationals have annual sales turnovers exceeding the size of many countries' entire economies. This sheer size – and the power and influence it can bring – can lead to numerous problems for nations that deal with such companies. Many multinationals have their head offices in Western European countries or in the USA, but they have several of their operating bases in less-developed countries with much smaller economies. If the companies need to save costs by reducing the size of their workforces, often the last countries to lose jobs will be the ones where the head offices are based.

LEARNER PROFILE

Principled

The Organisation for Economic Co-operation and Development (OECD) has issued guidelines for multinational enterprises, in the form of recommended principles to enhance responsible business conduct in the host countries. These recommendations reflect the shared values of most governments involved in foreign direct investment transactions. The goal of the guidelines is to make the contribution of MNCs as positive as possible for the economic and social global welfare. There are 15 general recommended policies, including the responsibility of multinational companies for sustainable development, recognition of human rights, creation of employment and training opportunities and development of good corporate governance principles.

Why do you think the OECD decided to create specific guiding principles for multinational enterprises? To what extent do you believe such recommended principles help host countries to avoid the potential negative effects of foreign direct investment? Discuss in class.

KEY TERM

globalisation: the growing interaction and integration between markets, businesses, people and governments worldwide

Why become a multinational?

There are several reasons why businesses start to operate in countries other than their main base.

- They are closer to main markets – this will have a number of advantages:
  - lower transport costs for the finished goods
  - better market information about consumer tastes as a result of operating closer to them
  - may be viewed as a local company and gain customer loyalty as a result.
- Lower costs of production – apart from lower transport costs for the completed items, there are likely to be other cost savings:
  - lower labour rates, e.g., much lower demand for local labour in developing countries compared to developed economies which keeps wage rates low
  - cheaper rent and site costs, again resulting from lower demand for commercial property – these cost savings can make the 'local' production very efficient in terms of the market in the rest of the world and can lead to substantial exports
  - government grants and tax incentives designed to encourage the industrialisation of such countries.
- Avoidance of import restrictions – items produced in the local country are not subject to import duties or import restrictions.
- Access to local natural resources – these might not be available in the company's main operating country.

TIP

When defining a multinational business, it is not enough to state that such businesses 'sell products in more than one country'.

Potential problems for multinationals

Setting up operating plants in foreign countries is not without risks. Communication links with headquarters may be poor. Language, legal and cultural differences with local workers and government officials could lead to misunderstandings. Coordination with other plants in the multinational group will need to be monitored carefully to ensure that products that might compete with each other on world markets are not produced and that conflicting policies are not adopted. Finally, it is likely that the skill levels of the local employees will be low and this could require substantial investment in training programmes.

The impact on 'host' countries of multinational companies

The potential benefits to a host country of inward investment by multinationals are:

- The investment will bring in foreign currency and, if output from the plant is exported, further foreign exchange can be earned.
- Employment opportunities will be created and training programmes will improve the quality and efficiency of the local workforce.
- Local businesses are likely to benefit from supplying services and components to the new factory and this will generate additional jobs and incomes.
- Local businesses will be forced to bring their quality and productivity up to international standards either to compete with the multinational or to supply to it.
- Tax revenues to the government will be boosted from any profits made by the multinational and by taxing the incomes of local workers employed by the MNC
- Management expertise in the community will slowly improve when and if the 'foreign' supervisors and managers are replaced by local staff (once they are suitably qualified).
- The total output of the economy will be increased and this will raise gross domestic product.

However, there are potential disadvantages to a country of allowing multinational expansion. The expansion of multinational companies into a country could lead to the following drawbacks:

- Exploitation of the local workforce might take place. Due to the absence of strict labour and health and safety rules in some countries (particularly some emerging market economies), multinationals or their suppliers can employ cheap labour for long hours with few of the benefits that the employees in their 'home' country would demand. There is also a risk that child workers will be employed by unethical MNCs. For example, recent research has established that children work in all stages of the supply chain in the international fashion industry, from production of cotton in Benin, harvesting in Uzbekistan, yarn spinning in India and garment making in Bangladesh. How many large multinational clothing chains care about these practices, especially as the child workers and producers are so far removed from Western media investigation?
- Pollution from plants might be at higher levels than allowed in other countries. This could be ecause of slack rules or because the 'host' government is afraid of driving the multinational away if it insists on environmentally acceptable practices. This is a sign of the huge influence multinationals can have.
- Local competing businesses may be squeezed out of business if they are unable to compete effectively. This might be due to lower levels of efficiency as a result of inferior equipment and much smaller resources than large multinationals.
- Some large Western-based businesses, such as McDonald's and Coca-Cola, have been accused of imposing 'Western' culture on other societies by the power of advertising and promotion. This could lead to a reduction in cultural identity.
- Profits may be sent back to the country where the head office of the company is based, rather than kept for reinvestment in the host nation.
- Extensive depletion of the limited natural resources of some countries has been blamed on some large multinational corporations. The argument is that they have little incentive to conserve these resources, as they are able to relocate quickly to other countries once resources have run out.

THEORY OF KNOWLEDGE

Knowledge question: How can we decide whether the activities of multinational companies are ethical or not?

Samsung, the Korean electronics manufacturer, started investing in Vietnam in 2009. Ten years later, Shim Won Hwan, The President of Samsung Electronics Vietnam Complex stated that 'we have fulfilled all our promises to Vietnam'. Indeed, Samsung's sales in 2019 accounted for 28% of Vietnam's GDP. The MNC created thousands of jobs in the country and helped Vietnam to achieve a sectoral change towards high technology.

However, the Vietnamese government has also supported Samsung with tax breaks and other financial benefits, such as a rent exemption for the site of their factory. The four major subsidiaries of Samsung in the country earned a revenue of $63.25 billion in 2020 and a profit of $3.8 billion. But 2020 revenues fell for the second year in a row.

Samsung also faced supply issues due to the Covid-19 pandemic restrictions along with an increasing labour cost in Vietnam. As result, it reduced its reliance on the country for smartphone manufacture by moving some of the production to other countries such as Indonesia. Analysts have commented about the ethics of this decision, as it will lead to job losses in Vietnam.

Is it ethical for a business such as Samsung, that has contributed so much to the growth of Vietnam, to eventually change its growth strategy? Does the decision to shift part of the investment to other countries contradict Samsung's President's statement that it has fulfilled its promises to Vietnam? Discuss in class.

CASE STUDY 6.1

Foreign investment in Mozambique

Mozambique is a key destination country for Foreign Direct Investment (FDI) in South-East Africa. Multinational companies are primarily interested in Mozambique's mining, hydrocarbon and energy sectors. The country has abundant natural resources and offers access to the sea, which gives it an advantage in transportation compared to neighbouring countries.

The Mozambican government has tried to attract FDI by facilitating visas for investment purposes. It also offers fiscal incentives to businesses interested in investing in geographical areas with rich resources but poor infrastructure. The young and growing population offers is a pool of labour for businesses interested in employing them.

Investors from many countries have decided to take the risk despite the fragile political situation in the country. They have had to overcome problems such as the lack of land property rights in Mozambique. However, the level of FDI has been falling since 2013 due to a drop in global commodity prices. Local officials hope that the relative economic stability of the country through the Covid-19 crisis

and the abundance of liquified natural gas (LNG) will bring a new increase in foreign investments in the near future.

1   Define the term 'multinational company'.   [2]

2   Suggest **two** reasons why foreign firms are interested in investing in Mozambique.   [4]

3   Suggest **two** problems that foreign firms face when investing in Mozambique.   [4]

4   Evaluate the impact of FDI in the mining sector on the host country (Mozambique).   [10]

TIP

In case study questions on multinational business activity, you may have the opportunity to use examples from your own country as well as from the case study to support your answers.

ACTIVITY 6.1

LATIN AMERICA AND THE CARIBBEAN

FDI flows, top 5 host economies, 2019 (Value and change)

2019 Inflows
$ 164.2 bn

2019 Increase
+10.3%

Share in world
10.7%

Mexico
$32.9 bn
−5.3%

Colombia
$14.5 bn
+25.6%

Peru
$8.9 bn
+37.1%

Brazil
$72.0 bn
+20.4%

Chile
$11.4 bn
+62.9%

Flows, by range

- Above $10 bn
- $5.0 to $9.9 bn
- $1 to $4.9 bn
- $0.1 to $0.9 bn
- Below $0.1 bn

Top 5 host economies

Economy
$ Value of inflows
2019 % change

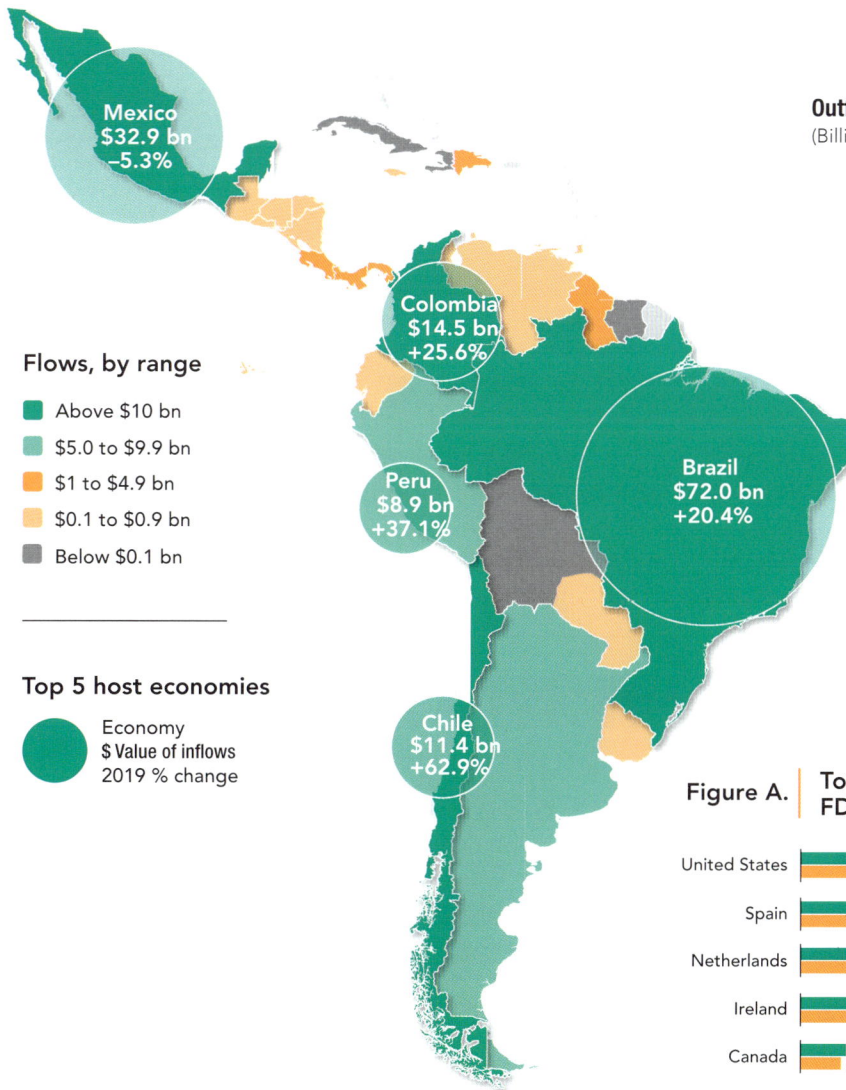

Outflows: top 5 home economies
(Billions of dollars and 2019 growth)

Brazil	$15.5	..
Mexico	$10.2	+32.6%
Chile	$7.9	+2 753.6%
Colombia	$3.2	−37.3%
Argentina	$1.6	−12.7%

Figure A.   **Top 10 investor economies by FDI stock, 2014 and 2018** (Billions of dollars)

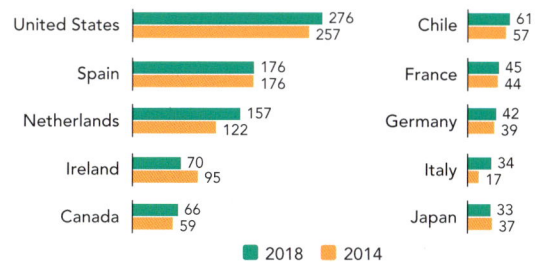

Economy	2018	2014
United States	276	257
Spain	176	176
Netherlands	157	122
Ireland	70	95
Canada	66	59
Chile	61	57
France	45	44
Germany	42	39
Italy	34	17
Japan	33	37

■ 2018   ■ 2014

Source: UNCTAD.

Note: The boundaries and names shown and the designations used on this map do not imply official endorsement or acceptance by the United Nations.

CONTINUED

The picture of Latin American and the Caribbean comes from the World Investment Report 2020, published by the United Nations Conference on Trade and Development (UNCTAD). It illustrates the flows of Foreign Direct Investment (FDI) in Latin America and the Caribbean in 2019.

1   Split into two groups:

- **Group 1**: Research the major reasons behind the increase in FDI in Brazil, Chile, Peru and Colombia. Which factors seem to have attracted multinational corporations to invest in these countries?

- **Group 2**: Research the major reasons behind the decrease in FDI in Mexico. Why did multinational companies decide to invest less in this country?

2   What are the main possible positive and negative effects of the increasing levels of FDI on the overall geographical area? Discuss in class.

SELF-EVALUATION CHECKLIST

After studying this chapter, complete this table:

I am able to synthesise and evaluate:	Needs more work	Almost there	Ready to move on
the impact of multinational companies (MNCs) on the host countries (AO3)			

REFLECTION

Assume you are a government minister responsible for industry. What would be the most important factor you would consider in deciding whether to allow a large food processing multinational to set up in the country? Explain your answer to another learner.

PROJECT

Engine No. 1 is an 'activist investor' group. This small hedge fund believes that businesses should invest for social good and that this would eventually translate to higher profits for the shareholders. In June 2021, Engine No. 1 managed to get three directors onto the elected board of directors of Exxon Mobil, the multinational oil giant. Analysts suggest that the activist investors may help Exxon to change the way it works. This is important, given the increasing pressure on the business to become more ecologically sustainable.

Split into two groups.

- **Group 1**: Research the concept of activist investors. Prepare a presentation showing the main aims of shareholder activist groups. Include one or two examples of activist investors that have social, cultural and environmental goals for the firms in which they invest.

CONTINUED

- **Group 2**: Research NGOs that conflict with MNCs on issues of social, cultural or environmental impact in the host countries. Identify one to two examples of such NGOs and present their goals and methods to achieve them.

Discuss in class:

- Why do activist investors such as Engine No. 1 emphasise social good? Isn't this detrimental to the profits of multinational corporations?

- How much power do NGOs have to affect the long-term strategy of MNCs and to reduce the negative impact of multinationals on the host countries?

EXAM-STYLE QUESTIONS

Should Indonesia attract more FDI?

Indonesia is one of the most attractive destinations in the world for FDI. Many multinationals are attracted to the country, which is the largest economy in Southeast Asia. The climate of political stability and the availability of young workers in the country with the fourth biggest population in the world are also important reasons why foreign producers choose Indonesia to open factories. Finally, investments seem highly rewarding in Indonesia because it is rich in natural resources, including natural gas, petroleum and minerals. It is also the world's biggest producer and exporter of palm oil, a basic commodity used in food manufacturing, personal care and cosmetics, biofuel and energy, and many more industries.

But investments in Indonesia entail certain risks. Corruption is still a problem for MNCs that want to invest in the country, even though it is gradually improving. Infrastructure is insufficient, and the country is located on the Pacific Ring of Fire so it often suffers from natural disasters such as earthquakes and tsunamis. Moreover, the business environment is complex and there are many entry requirements for foreign businesses that want to invest.

The Covid-19 pandemic restrictions reduced FDI in the country from 2019 and onwards. This is a problem for Indonesia, which depends heavily on FDI for growth. According to OECD Policy Reviews 2020, FDI in Indonesia played a key role in increasing employment, productivity and exports. However, rapid growth (from investments in manufacturing) has created sustainability problems in Indonesia. The country is one of the biggest global emitters of greenhouse gases, 60% of which are caused by forest degradation, deforestation and peatland conversion. According to the International Energy Agency, Indonesia's share of renewable energy sources is still low.

In 2019, the country announced a deductible tax of up to 200% for businesses investing in research and development (R&D) to attract FDI and to improve the productivity of capital in the country. Many policymakers in Indonesia stress the need for the country to deregulate its complex business environment to attract more investors and to increase FDI to pre-pandemic levels. However, not all agree. Opponents of FDI claim that the negative effects of multinationals in the country outweigh the advantages. They believe that the government should focus on policies to support domestic production and consumption for further economic growth.

1 Define the term 'foreign direct investment'. [2]

2 By applying a STEEPLE framework, identify **two** reasons why MNCs are attracted in Indonesia. [4]

3 By applying a STEEPLE framework, analyse **two** risks for businesses interested in investing in Indonesia. [4]

4 Explain **two** reasons why the government of Indonesia depends on FDI for growth. [4]

5 Evaluate whether or not Indonesia should continue relying on MNCs for economic growth. [10]

> Unit 2

Human resource management

Introduction to human resource management

BUSINESS IN CONTEXT

The management of human resources

Sharon Yam, managing director of TMF Malaysia, has this to say about TMF employees:

Our biggest competitive advantage, our best product and our Unique Selling Proposition are definitely our employees. We invest in them, we engage them and we nurture them. These are our utmost priorities.

The Huawei company website says:

We have launched many diversity initiatives focusing on nationality, gender, age, race, and religion. For example, we emphasize gender equality in employment and prohibit gender bias, in strict compliance with all applicable international conventions as well as local laws and regulations.

And from Shell.com we have:

Employee Health and Welfare: Keeping our employees safe and well is our top priority, no matter where they are working. Thousands of our employees work on construction sites away from home – good working and living conditions help to bring about a safer and more productive working environment.

Discuss in pairs or a group:

- Why is the 'management of human resources' important to these three businesses?

- Should all businesses aim to 'nurture employees', emphasise 'gender equality' and 'keep their employees safe' – or should they aim to keep labour costs as low as possible?

KEY CONCEPT LINK

Ethics

Human resource management is very sensitive to ethical issues, as the organisation tries to achieve its objectives by increasing the productivity of employees. If we take the example of human resource planning as part of human resource management, we can identify many ethical dimensions in the efforts of businesses to ensure the availability of employees in the short and long term. One such issue is the decision to declare people redundant when new technology replaces expensive labour with cost-efficient capital. In the USA alone, it is estimated that 100 000 positions could be lost from the banking sector between 2022 and 2027, as banks invest more and more in e-banking technology. If the employees who lose these jobs are not provided with redundancy payments and support to find other work, could the banks be considered to be acting unethically?

Ethical businesses must take measures to support employees through redundancy, for example by helping them to find new jobs within or outside the business organisation through training or upskilling opportunities.

7.1 The role of human resource management

Human resource management (HRM) aims to recruit capable, flexible and committed people, managing and rewarding their performance and developing their key skills to the benefit of the organisation.

This suggests that HRM is of crucial importance to the long-term performance and success of businesses and is not just about 'hiring, paying and firing' workers. This list of HRM functions give an indication of the range and significance of the role of HRM:

- Human resource planning (see 7.2).

- Talent management – recruiting and retaining high-quality employees, developing their skills, and continuously motivating them to improve their performance. The primary objective of talent management is to create a workforce who are highly motivated to perform well and stay with the business in the long term.

- Training and development of employees – this involves identifying the skills needs of the business and resourcing training courses for employees that will give them these skills. This is also an important aspect of motivating workers as when they are offered opportunities for developing their own skills it will be seen as a recognition of their important role in the business.

- Reward and performance management – paying employees an appropriate level of remuneration using a payment system which stimulates and motivates them to perform well is a key HRM role. Benefits in addition to pay are frequently expected by many employees. Monitoring employee performance, perhaps through a regular appraisal system, provides clear objectives for employees to work towards.

- Employee relations (see Chapter 13).

- Employee welfare – this means providing facilities which allow employees to perform their work in a healthy environment. It includes providing sanitation, drinking water, access to a canteen and first aid in the event of a work accident. These facilities are for the benefit of workers but they can result in improved employee morale and motivation which will have positive outcomes for employers too. One aspect of employee welfare that is receiving much attention at present is work–life balance, and many employers are offering more flexi-time contracts and the opportunities to work from home to attempt to improve the welfare of employees who may be over-stressed in their current roles.

- Human resource compliance – this involves HRM in developing policies and practices to ensure that the employment and work practices of the organisation meet all legal controls and regulations such as minimum wage law and health and safety at work laws.

The starting point for effective HRM is to stablish what the employees need from the business now and what they are likely to need in the future. This requires detailed human resource planning.

7.2 Factors that influence human resource planning

What is human resource planning?

Effective HRM requires careful planning of the number and skills of people needed by the organisation. **Human resource planning** aims to get the right number of people with the right skills, experience and competencies in the right jobs at the right time at the right cost.

KEY TERM

human resource management (HRM): the strategic approach to the effective management of an organisation's workers so that they help the business achieve its objectives and gain a competitive advantage

human resource planning: also known as workforce planning – analysing and forecasting the numbers of workers and the skills of those workers that will be required by the organisation to achieve its objectives

---

HR departments need to assess the future labour resource needs of the business to try to avoid having too few or too many employees or employees with the wrong skills. HR departments must respond to the corporate plan of the business and the objectives this contains. If the overall business plan is to expand production and develop products for foreign markets, then this must be reflected in the **workforce plan**. The starting point for HR planning is always a **workforce audit**.

Human resource planning involves two main stages.

1. Forecasting the number of employees required. This will depend on several internal factors:

   a. Forecasting demand for the product – this will be influenced by market conditions, seasonal factors, competitors' actions and trends in consumer tastes. It could be a mistake to replace a worker who decides to leave the firm if consumer demand is falling or if there is likely to be a seasonal downturn in demand. Demand forecasts may be necessary to help establish workforce planning needs.

   b. The productivity levels of employees – if productivity (output per worker) is forecast to increase, perhaps as a result of more efficient machinery, then fewer workers will be needed to produce the same level of output.

   c. The objectives of the business – these could influence future workforce numbers in two main ways. First, if the business plans to expand over the coming years, then employee numbers will have to increase to accommodate this growth. Secondly, if the business intends to increase customer service levels, possibly at the expense of short-term profits, then more workers might need to be recruited. A workforce plan cannot be devised without consideration of business objectives.

   d. Changes in the law regarding workers' rights – if the government of a country decides to pass laws which establish a shorter maximum working week or introduce a minimum wage level, then there will be a considerable impact on the workforce plan. A shorter working week might lead to a greater demand for employees to ensure that all the available work is completed on time. A minimum wage might encourage businesses to employ fewer workers and to substitute them with machines.

   e. **Labour turnover** and absenteeism rate – the higher the rate at which employees leave a business, the greater will be the need for the business to recruit replacement workers. If the level of employee absenteeism is high then a greater number of employees will be needed to ensure that adequate numbers of workers are available at any one time.

2. Forecasting the skills required. The need for better-qualified employees or for employees with different skills is a constant factor in the minds of HR managers. The importance of these issues will depend upon on the following:

   a. The pace of technological change in the business, e.g., production methods and the complexity of the machinery used. The application of IT in offices has meant that traditional typists or clerks are now rarely required – skilled computer operators and web designers are in greater demand than ever.

   b. The need for flexible or multi-skilled employees in the operations of the business. Workers can become over-specialised, finding it difficult to adapt when demand conditions change. Most businesses need to recruit employees or train them with more than one skill that can be applied in a variety of different ways. This gives the firm greater adaptability when market conditions change – and it makes the workers' jobs more rewarding.

External factors

Demographic change

The potential supply of labour to any organisation is affected by demographic changes. Table 7.1 summarises three of these changes and their potential opportunities and constraints supply

---

KEY TERMS

workforce plan: numbers of workers and skills of those workers required over a future time period

workforce audit: a check on the skills and qualifications of all existing employees

labour turnover: measures the rate at which employees are leaving an organisation

Example of demographic change	Opportunities	Constraints
Natural population growth (or decline) – birth rate exceeds death rate (or vice versa)	May be easier to recruit effective employees as the working population increases	Increased birth rates may take years before they impact on the working population
Net migration (immigration compared with emigration)	May be easier to recruit effective employees from other countries at lower rates of pay Highly qualified employees might be recruited from other countries	Some qualified and experienced employees may move to other countries, which will reduce the competitiveness of the business Immigrants may need more training, e.g., in language and cultural issues
Ageing population (the average age of the population increases as a result of rising life expectancy)	It is often claimed that older employees are more loyal and reliable than younger workers Older employees may have experience and 'people' skills that younger employees may have not yet developed	Older employees may be less flexible and adaptable, e.g., to the introduction of new workplace technologies

Table 7.1: The effect of demographic change on labour supply

Changes in labour mobility

High **occupational mobility of labour** helps a country to achieve economic efficiency. A mobile workforce means that if jobs are lost in one industry or region, workers are willing and able to move to other jobs and/or other occupations. This helps to keep structural unemployment low.

In developed economies, labour tends to be relatively immobile because:

- high levels of home ownership mean that workers are reluctant to pay the cost in time and money of arranging a house sale and purchase in another region
- high skill levels in one occupation may mean that workers are not equipped to deal with machines, processes and technologies in other industries and occupations.

In emerging market countries, despite strong family or ethnic ties to one area, mobility tends to be higher because:

- home ownership is low
- low skill levels mean that workers can undertake low-skilled jobs in many different industries.

However, a high degree of **geographical mobility of labour**, especially between rural and urban areas, can lead to overcrowding and poor living conditions in towns and cities.

Many governments pursue policies to attempt to increase labour mobility. These include:

- relocation grants for key public sector workers
- job centres and other government offices to advertise job vacancies nationally
- training and retraining programmes for the unemployed.

KEY TERMS

occupational mobility of labour: extent to which workers are willing and able to move to different jobs requiring different skills

geographical mobility of labour: extent to which workers are willing and able to move geographical region to take up new jobs

---

CASE STUDY 7.1

Global labour mobility

One of the consequences of globalisation has been a shift in the global demand for labour. Since the beginning of the 21st century, many richer economies have suffered declining birth rates and shifts in types of industry creating new work opportunities. At the same time, development and increasingly open borders in emerging economies have created a labour force more eager to migrate to take advantage of these opportunities. The result has been a significant expansion of global labour mobility. Governments in both origin and destination countries have encouraged this trend. Temporary work visas in both the USA and Germany have opened the door to increasing numbers of skilled non-permanent residents. Several origin countries in Asia, including India and the Philippines, actively seek labour markets for their workers overseas.

The benefits of these policies to businesses and to the world economy are becoming clearer. Research conducted in 2021 estimated that an increase of 3% in the workforce in high-income countries through migration by 2027 could increase global real income by $386 billion.

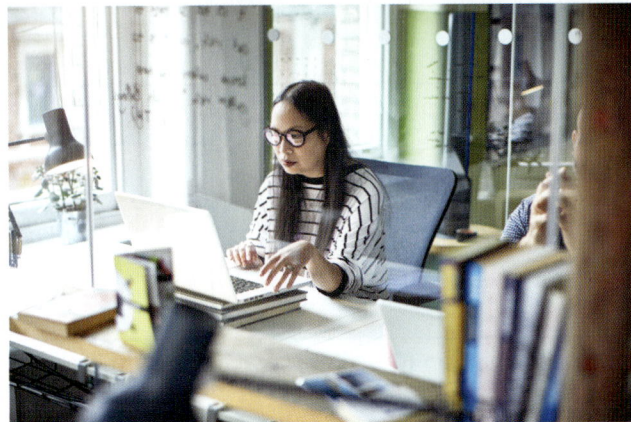

1 Define the term 'labour mobility'. [2]

2 Outline **two** benefits to businesses in a developed country like Germany of migrant labour entering the German labour market. [4]

3 Explain **two** ways a developed country like Germany might attract migrant workers with appropriate skills. [4]

4 Examine the advantages and disadvantages to a country like the Philippines of migrant workers leaving the Philippines to find employment abroad. [10]

Internal factors

Flexi-time

Flexi-time is a way of working which allows employees to fit their working hours around their individual needs, and accommodate other commitments outside of work.

This flexibility is achieved by asking the employer to create an adaptable work schedule that is different to the set timings of the standard working day (e.g., 9 to 5). Flexi-time may involve working from home, or adjusting starting and finishing times around the core hours (e.g., 10 to 4).

It would then be up to the employee to choose when they work, with their employer's permission, provided the total hours worked add up to the amount required by their contract.

The use of flexi-time by employers impacts on the workforce plan because:

- there must always be sufficient employees available at key times of the day
- flexi-time is more successful if employees are multi-skilled and able to provide cover for those workers who are undertaking commitments outside of work.

KEY TERM

flexi-time: a flexible way of working that allows employees to fit their working hours around their individual needs to allow for other commitments outside of work

ACTIVITY 7.1

Google is one of the many big multinational firms that have embraced flexi-time by allowing employees to decide on their own working hours.

1   Split into two groups.

- **Group 1:** Prepare a brief presentation on how Google applies flexi-time, along with the advantages and disadvantages for the business from this decision.

- **Group 2:** Prepare a brief presentation with the main advantages and disadvantages of flexi-time for the employees of Google.

2   Overall, does Google benefit from applying flexi-time? Why is it typical for businesses in the quaternary sector to allow flexi-time to their employees? Discuss in class.

Gig economy

A **gig economy** exists when employers not only have workers who are on permanent or temporary employment contracts, but also use the services of individuals as independent contractors or freelance workers. These freelance workers – sometimes referred to as 'contract labour' – are only required to fulfil a particular task, will not be guaranteed employment after the task is completed and have no formal contract of employment.

The impact of the gig economy on human resource planning includes:

- The use of freelance contractors can reduce overall labour costs as they are only contracted when specifically required.

- Accurate scheduling of work is essential if freelance workers are to be available exactly when required and for their contract to end as soon as the task finished, e.g., wall plasterers in the construction of a new house.

KEY TERM

gig economy: a labour market characterised by the widespread use of short-term contracts or freelance work rather than jobs with permanent contracts

- Motivation levels may be low as the workers do not have secure, permanent jobs; but on the other hand, they will be incentivised by the need to gain further freelance contracts in the future.

- The lack of permanent contracts means that a business might find it difficult to recruit gig workers as and when needed if demand for their services is high.

ACTIVITY 7.2

1   Split into three groups. Prepare a brief presentation for the following gig economy applications:

- Uber (transportation services)

- Amazon Flex (pick-up and delivery services)

- 99 Designs (graphic design services)

Each presentation should include a description of the business activity and the reasons why these three businesses choose the gig economy model.

2   Why is the gig economy often chosen by businesses that rely on big data and internet applications? What are the limitations for these businesses from using the gig economy? Discuss in class.

7.3 Resistance to change in the workforce

The dynamic nature of business activity means that nearly all businesses will have to change over time in order to be competitive and to survive and thrive. Change within business organisations can be necessary for many reasons including:

- relocation
- change of ownership, e.g., takeover
- change of senior management
- new working practices and employment contracts
- changes in technology and the workplace skills required.

Most changes can create as many opportunities as threats, but there will nearly always be some resistance to changes which affect employees directly. This resistance can be one of the biggest problems any organisation will face when it attempts to respond to the dynamic business environment. The managers and other employees of a business may resent and resist change for any of the following reasons:

- **Fear of the unknown** Change means uncertainty and this is uncomfortable for some people. Not knowing what may happen to their job or what the future of the business might be leads to increased anxiety – this results in resistance.

- **Fear of failure** The changes may require new skills and abilities that, despite training, may be beyond a worker's capabilities. People know how the current system works – but will they be able to cope with the new one?

- **Self-interest – losing something of value** Workers could lose status or job security as a result of change and they want to know precisely how the change will affect them.

- **Misinformation – false beliefs about the need for change** To put themselves at ease and to avoid the risks of change, some people fool themselves into believing that the existing system will 'work out someday' without the need for radical change.

- **Low tolerance – lack of trust** Perhaps because of past experiences there may be a lack of trust between workers and managers who are introducing the change. Workers may not believe the reasons

given to them for change or the reassurances from managers about its impact.

- **Inertia** Many people suffer from inertia or reluctance to change and try to maintain the status quo. Change often requires considerable effort, so the fear of having to work harder to introduce it may cause resistance.

> **TIP**
>
> When discussing the possible resistance to changes proposed by management, try to think of the leadership style being used to implement the change. This could be a major contributory factor in determining the degree of resistance.

The importance of these 'resistance factors' will vary from business to business. In those organisations where previous change has gone well, where workers are kept informed and even consulted about change, and where managers offer support and training to the workforce involved, resistance to change is likely to be low. In contrast to this is the likely resistance to change in businesses where there is a lack of trust and little communication.

7.4 Human resource strategies for reducing the impact of change

An important role of HRM is to reduce employees' resistance to change and encourage them to embrace it positively. The following strategies might be used by HRM to convince the workforce that change will potentially be beneficial for the business and the employees.

Understand what change means

Change is the continuous adoption of business strategies and structures in response to changing internal pressures or external forces. Change happens whether we encourage and welcome it or not. To take control of it and to ensure that it is a positive process and not a negative one, businesses must have a vision, a strategy, and a proven and adaptable process for managing change.

Change in business is no longer the exception but the rule – it has become an accelerating and ongoing process. Table 7.2 gives some common causes of change. 'Business as usual' will become increasingly rare as global, economic and technological upheavals necessitate a business response. **Change management** requires firms to be able to cope with dramatic one-off changes as well as more gradual evolutionary change.

- Evolutionary or incremental change occurs quite slowly over time – for example, the swing towards more fuel-efficient cars has been happening for several years. These changes can be anticipated or unexpected – the decision to increase the London congestion charge was announced months in advance, but a sudden oil-price increase may not have been expected. Obviously, incremental changes that are easy to anticipate tend to be the easiest to manage.

- Dramatic or revolutionary change, especially if unanticipated, causes many more problems. The Covid-19 pandemic forced many holiday companies to re-establish themselves in new markets or countries which were less affected by this health crisis. In extreme cases, these dramatic changes might lead to totally rethinking the operation of an organisation. This is called business process re-engineering.

KEY TERM

change management: planning, implementing, controlling and reviewing the movement of an organisation from its current state to a new one

TIP

When discussing how change will affect a business and its strategies, try to analyse whether the change is incremental or dramatic, anticipated or unanticipated.

LEARNER PROFILE

Open-minded

Leaders who manage change need to help people to become less resistant to changes. To achieve that, they need to be open-minded and ready to accept change themselves.

A leader who has been famous for his open-mindedness and ability to drive change is Howard Schultz, the heart and soul of the modern Starbucks organisation and its CEO until 2017. Inspired by the Italian coffee culture, Schultz led the organisation through the globalisation era, transforming it from a local Seattle coffee shop to a world-leading multinational coffee chain. Moreover, he guided the organisation through technological changes, such as the shift from physical to mobile order and pay systems.

Do you think Howard Schultz faced resistance to change from Starbucks employees when trying to implement changes such as innovative mobile order and pay systems in the stores? If yes, why? In what way does the open-mindedness of the leader help an organisation to implement such changes successfully?

Recognise major causes of change

Nature of change	Examples of change	Managing change
Technological innovation – leading to new products and new processes	Products – new computer games, the latest iPhone, hydrogen-powered cars Processes – AI and robots in production; CAD in design offices and computer systems for inventory control	Need for employee retraining Purchase of new equipment – any necessary redundancies must be explained and managed sensitively Need for quicker product development, which may need new organisational structures and teams – social needs of workers should be recognised

Nature of change	Examples of change	Managing change
Macroeconomic changes – fiscal policy, interest rates, fluctuations in the business cycle	Changes in consumers' disposable incomes – and demand patterns that result from this Boom or recession conditions – need for extra capacity or rationalisation	Need for flexible production systems – including employee flexibility – to cope with demand changes. Training should be offered to allow multi-skills to be learned Explain the need for extra capacity or the need to rationalise Deal with workforce cutbacks in a way that encourages employees who remain to accept change
Takeover by another business	New leadership style Different management culture Might be employee rationalisation, e.g., competing for jobs which are now duplicated May need to relocate	Inform employees of reasons for takeover Reassure employees, as far as possible on issues such as job security and remuneration levels Meetings with new management team to discuss its future plans Training and guidance on new corporate culture Financial assistance for relocation, if necessary

Table 7.2: Examples of change impact on employees.

Understand the stages of the change process

Here is a checklist of essential points that managers should consider before attempting to introduce significant changes in an organisation:

- **Where are we now and why is change necessary?** It is important to recognise why a business needs to introduce change from its current situation.

- **New vision and objectives** For substantial changes, a new vision for the business may be needed – and this must be communicated to those affected by the change.

- **Ensure resources are in place to enable change to happen** Starting a change and then finding that there is too little finance to complete it could be disastrous.

- **Plan the timing of the change** Workers in particular should not be taken by surprise by change – this will increase their resistance to it.

- **Involve workers in the plan for change and its implementation** This will encourage them to accept change and develop a sense of 'ownership' of it. This may also lead to proposals from them to improve the change process.

- **Communicate** The vital importance of communication with the workforce runs through all of these other stages – unless employees are kept up to date with the pace and scope of change then resistance will build against it.

- **Introduce initial changes that bring quick results** This will help all involved in the change to see the point of it.

- **Focus on training** This will allow staff to feel that they are able to make a real contribution to the changed organisation.

- **Sell the benefits** Staff and other stakeholders may benefit directly from changes – these need to be explained to them.

- **Always remember the effects on individuals** A 'soft' human resource approach will often bring future rewards in terms of staff loyalty when they have been supported and communicated with during the change process.

- **Check how individuals are coping and remember to support them** Some people will need more support than others – a 'sink or swim' philosophy will damage the business if it leads to low-quality output or poor customer service because staff were poorly supported during the change period.

Lead change, do not just manage it

All business change – especially significant strategic changes – must be 'managed'. This means that:

- New objectives need to be established that recognise the need for change.

- Resources – finance and employees – need to be made available for the change to be implemented.

- Appropriate action needs to be taken – and checked on – to ensure that the planned changes are introduced.

CASE STUDY 7.2

LB handbags and accessories must change

Chiara and Giovanni are siblings and have inherited LB, their family business that produces leather handbags and accessories in Italy.
LB used to be a recognisable brand name, but the business is now facing declining sales and profits. The vegan leather industry is growing fast, as consumers increasingly favour sustainable products. Moreover, LB has not invested in modern technology in the production process and is still very dependent on expensive manual labour.

Giovanni believes that radical changes need to be implemented at LB to allow the business to survive the competition. He is trying to get a big bank loan to buy automated machines which would produce many items through the help of 3D printing technology. He thinks that some of the existing employees could be trained on the new production methods, but many would have to be declared redundant. He wants the change to be implemented within the following three months.

Chiara agrees with Giovanni that changes should be made to make the business more competitive, but she is worried about the employees' resistance to change. Many workers have been with LB for more than 20 years and are not expected to react positively to the new technology. Those people believe that only hand-made work can offer high quality to the business. Moreover, the redundancies could seriously demotivate the personnel and have a big impact on the local community. Chiara wants

to avoid stakeholder conflicts. The business has always been socially responsible, and she does not want to risk their image. Giovanni's plans could push the trade union into industrial action. She believes that change management is needed to support the organisation through such a big change. This would not be possible within just three months.

1   Explain what 'change management' means. **[2]**

2   Explain **two** reasons why employees at LB are resistant to technological change. **[4]**

3   Identify **two** possible areas for stakeholder conflict that could result from Giovanni's plan. **[4]**

4   Evaluate the significance of change management in LB to support the organisation in the process of introducing new production methods. **[10]**

THEORY OF KNOWLEDGE

Knowledge question: To what extent is reason more important than emotion when managing dramatic changes?

The Covid-19 pandemic led to dramatic changes in education. It is estimated that in 2020 more than 1.2 billion children in the world were out of the classroom due to lockdowns.

The management of schools and colleges around the world had to adjust fast to e-learning through digital platforms. Even before the pandemic, many organisations were slowly preparing for the technological evolution in education. But due to the crisis, many educational bodies had no time to manage the change on an incremental basis. To avoid students losing a whole academic year, organisations had to adapt to the new reality without adequate training and with little time for preparation. Effective change management required

that teachers and students were supported on an emotional basis, given the social and psychological impact of the crisis. Some of the strategies used to support students and teachers throughout the change process were the creation of online professional learning communities for teachers and the provision of online social and emotional support for students by professional counsellors and psychologists.

In your class consider the following questions:

1 Why may the workforce of a school be resistant to the change brought about by e-learning technology?

2 The stages of change management are planning, implementing, controlling and reviewing. In which of these stages could emotion be more important than reason and why?

Managing change effectively is important to successful implementation. However, managing change is not the same as leading change. Leading strategic change is much more than just managing resources. Change leadership involves having a much greater vision than just making sure the right resources are available to deal with change. Leading change means:

- dynamic leaders who will shake an organisation out of its complacency and away from resistance to change ('corporate inertia')
- motivation of staff at all levels of the organisation so that change is looked upon as a positive force that could improve people's lives – this motivation will lead to significant changes in the behaviour of workers
- ensuring that acceptance of change is part of the culture of the organisation
- visible support of all senior managers who will help the change process to be accepted at all levels and within all departments of the business.

Use project champions

A **project champion** is often appointed by senior management to help drive a programme of change through a business.

A project champion will come from within the organisation and be appointed from middle to senior management – they need to have enough influence within the organisation to make sure that 'things get done'. They are like 'cheerleaders' for the project, but they will not necessarily be involved in the day-to-day planning and implementation of the new scheme. They will smooth the path of the project team investigating and planning the change, and they will remove as many obstacles as possible. For example, at board or other meetings of senior managers they will speak up for the changes being suggested, they will try to ensure that sufficient resources are put in place and they will try to make sure that everyone understands the project's goals and objectives.

KEY TERM

project champion: a person assigned to support and drive a project forward and who explains the benefits of change and assists and supports the team putting change into practice

---

CASE STUDY 7.3

Project champions

Zhan is the operations director within the restaurant business Dining Group. She has acted as a project champion for the implementation of an electronic ordering process that will allow the business to place orders for raw materials with suppliers online. 'Being a project champion allows you to get involved in high-value-added activities. Project champions organise efficient teams, and that will help the whole organisation to embrace change and to become more productive,' she said. 'But it's a demanding role, requiring certain skills and most importantly the ability to motivate project team members while getting all stakeholders on board', she added.

Not all the restaurant managers of the Dining Group chain saw the value of the project, which was supposed to make the ordering process faster and to allow the business to reduce excessive stock levels. Moreover, the group's finance director was not sure if the business had to prioritise this project over other initiatives that also required the investment of scarce financial resources.

1   Define the term 'project champion'.   **[2]**

2   With reference to the case study, outline **two** roles of a project champion.   **[4]**

3   Analyse **two** factors that would make Zhan a successful project champion.   **[4]**

Use project groups or teams

'Problem-solving through team-building' is a structured way of making a breakthrough on a difficult change situation by using the power of a team.

When a difficult problem arises regarding a major change in a business's strategy or structure, one of the most common ways to analyse it and suggest solutions is to organise a **project group**. Project groups should work with the manager responsible for introducing the change. A team meeting of experts should provide a rigorous exchange of views that may well lead to an appropriate action plan being developed and agreed. The responsibility for carrying out the plan still lies with the original manager. Now, though, the manager will be better equipped to solve the problem that was preventing change from being implemented effectively.

KEY TERM

project groups: these are created by an organisation to address a problem that requires input from different specialists

---

Planning and promoting change

Planning and promoting change are important strategies for HRM. The timing of change is important in order to gain acceptance for it. Introducing big changes too quickly in response to a crisis within the business – such as a collapse in sales and profit – will lead to greater resistance than change which is planned for and explained in good time to all those affected by it.

Gaining acceptance of change – by both the workforce and other stakeholders – will be much more likely to lead to a positive outcome than imposing change on unwilling groups. According to John Kotter, a leading writer on organisational change, the best way to promote it in any organisation is to adopt the following eight-stage process:

1   establish a sense of urgency

2   create an effective project team to lead the change

3   develop a vision and a strategy for change

4   communicate this change vision

5   empower people to take action

6 generate short-term gains from change that benefit as many people as possible

7 consolidate these gains and produce even more changes

8 build change into the culture of the organisation so that it becomes a natural process.

If change is not 'sold' or promoted to the people most affected by it so that they develop a sense of ownership of it, then there will almost certainly be damaging resistance that could increase the chances of failure.

> **TIP**
>
> Effective management of change should, where possible, focus on the positive benefits of change to the stakeholders most affected by it.

7.5 Business management tools – force field analysis

Lewin's force field analysis

Force field analysis, first developed by Kurt Lewin, provides a framework for looking at the factors (forces) that influence change. These forces can either be 'driving forces for change' that help the organisation towards a goal or 'restraining forces against change' that might prevent an organisation reaching its goal.

> **KEY TERM**
>
> **force field analysis:** an analytical process used to map the opposing forces within a business where change is taking place

Steps in force field analysis

1 Outline the proposal for change – insert in the middle of a force field diagram, as shown in Figure 7.1.

2 List forces for change in one column and forces against change in the other.

3 Assign an estimated score for each force, with 1 being weak and 5 being strong.

Figure 7.1 shows a proposal for installing IT-controlled manufacturing equipment in a factory. The numerical scores indicate whether the forces are weak (e.g., 1) or strong (e.g., 5).

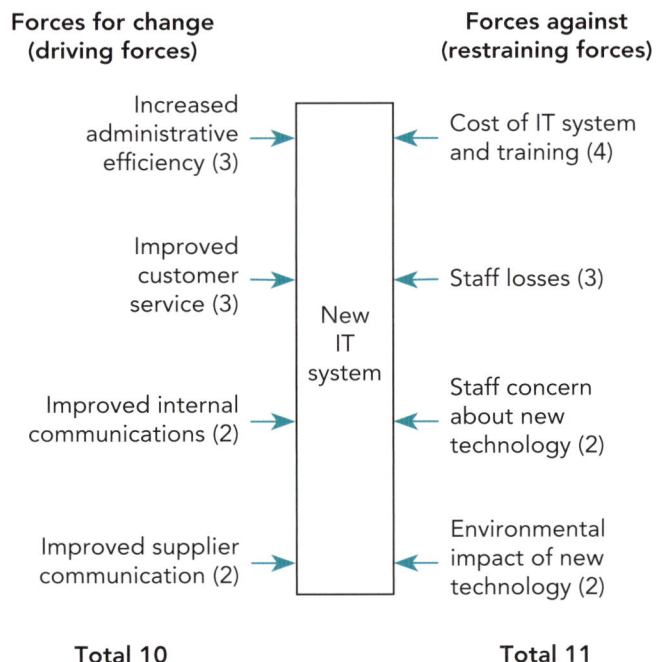

Figure 7.1: Force field analysis of an IT-controlled machinery proposal

Once the analysis has been carried out, the process can help management improve the probability of success of this major change. For example, by training staff (which might increase cost by +1) their concern about new technology could be reduced (reducing staff concern by −2).

Usefulness of Lewin's model

- The force field diagram helps managers weigh up the importance of these two types of forces.

- It helps identify the people most likely to be affected by the change.

- It encourages an examination of how to strengthen the forces supporting the decision and reduce the forces opposed to it.

- The use of a leadership style that reduces opposition and resistance to change is highlighted as being more effective than forcing through unpopular changes in an autocratic manner.

Force field analysis – possible limitations

Force field analysis requires the full participation of everyone involved to provide the accurate information required for an effective analysis. This can be a disadvantage when full participation is not possible, resulting in an analysis that does not provide a realistic picture of the supporting and opposing forces. Another disadvantage is the possibility that the analysis will not result in a consensus among the group. In fact, a force field analysis may actually cause a division in the group between those who support the decision and those who oppose it.

One of the key things to keep in mind when using force field analysis is that the analysis developed is entirely dependent upon the skill level and knowledge of the group working on the analysis. In most cases, force field analysis is based on assumptions, not facts. Even if the assumptions are based on experience, the interpretation of the evidence should not necessarily be seen as being objective within the overall process of evaluating the driving and restraining forces.

Force field analysis as a business management tool

The technique of force field analysis can be integrated into any functional area of business which is planning a significant change. For example, in operations management, the driving and restraining forces of a plan to relocate the business could be analysed. If one of the main restraining forces is employee resistance to relocation, then this factor could be made less influential by offering work-from-home contracts to some workers or financial assistance with the removal costs.

ACTIVITY 7.3

Evaluate the usefulness of force field analysis for planning and managing a major change within your school or college. For example, the introduction of IT-based lessons with students working from home on one day per week, downloading lecturers' video lessons.

SELF-EVALUATION CHECKLIST

After studying this chapter, complete this table.

I am able to analyse and apply:	Needs more work	Almost there	Ready to move on
the role of human resource management (AO2)			
internal and external factors that influence human resource planning (AO2)			
reasons for resistance to change in the workplace (AO2)			
I am able to synthesise and evaluate:			
human resource strategies for reducing the impact of change and resistance to change (AO3)			
I am able to select and apply:			
Force Field Analysis (AO4)			

REFLECTION

- How do you think HR management might be affected by increasing use of flexi-time and gig contracts?

- Are these effects likely to be positive or negative for employees?

- How would you justify your answers to these questions to another learner?

PROJECT

You are managing a for-profit employment agency which is also a social enterprise interested in reducing unemployment amongst young people. Your customers are big business organisations across many different sectors of the economy, which use your services to recruit employees. You have set a goal to find jobs for at least 30 young homeless people, who have just graduated from school and have no work experience.

Split into three groups:

- **Group 1:** Your task is to help young people to improve their CVs by offering to pay for training programmes. You need to decide on the exact types of training that could help the candidates become attractive to employers who are offering sales positions in retail.

- **Group 2:** Create a letter to be sent to the customers of your business to promote your initiative. Your goal is to positively affect the potential employers so that they give the candidates the opportunity of an interview after they conclude their training programme.

- **Group 3:** Do some internet research to identify two potential employers that could hire the graduates as gig workers. Prepare a presentation for the graduates on the possible advantages and limitations of the gig economy.

Thinking about your project:

- **Group 1:** When you design the training programme, have you thought about how to help the candidates improve a wide range of skills?

- **Group 2:** When writing a letter, have you thought about the needs of employers in retail in terms of employee skills and qualifications?

- **Group 3:** When creating the presentation for the graduates, have you taken into consideration both their short-term and their long-term career needs?

EXAM-STYLE QUESTIONS

Extract 1: Things top employers do to attract and retain their employees

A study performed by a research centre on a global scale and across many industries in the secondary and tertiary economic sectors, suggests that only about 13% of employees feel engaged at work. The other 87% seems to suffer from a lower level of motivation and productivity. This phenomenon typically leads to high labour turnover and, as a result, businesses need to be constantly searching for new employees.

Are businesses that cannot engage employees 'bad' employers? Not necessarily. Sometimes, the problem is created because of inefficient human resource planning. The same research identified the things that 'top employers' do in terms of human resource planning to increase labour retention and improve employee engagement at work:

- They offer valuable training to employees, addressing both personal and professional needs, and spend time and resources to appraise their employees professionally. They use appraisal not only to spot any areas of improvement for employees but also to reward them for excellent performance.

CONTINUED

- They adopt flexible employment patterns not only to benefit the business with cost savings, but also to improve the ability of employees to achieve work–life balance.

Extract 2: Changes in the restaurant industry

Research on the impact of the Covid-19 pandemic in business activity identified the various changes it brought to the restaurant industry:

- Dining in restaurants declined, especially in indoor settings. Businesses relying solely on indoor dining as a source of revenue need to proceed to business process re-engineering by completely changing the way they work.

- There are opportunities in takeaway and drive-through methods of distribution.

- Contactless online food ordering and delivery services are increasing and taking advantage of the gig economy. However, the gig economy is restricted in many countries around the world where the occupational mobility of labour is limited by laws that do not allow flexible employment patterns. Such laws force businesses to hire delivery workers instead of contracting them as freelancers. In countries where laws allow the gig economy, delivery workers are often resisting the change of their employment contracts from permanent to temporary or freelance arrangements.

Even though big restaurant chains such as McDonald's employee many people, they are sometimes more effective in terms of change management compared to small restaurants. This happens mainly because of their ability to recognise the need for change faster, to plan for it and to engage resources for it to happen successfully. They are also able to hire project champions to support the organisation through the required changes. But most of all, these organisations are led by managers who embrace change, so the workforce is more flexible and less resistant to changes compared to smaller organisations that are not accustomed to change.

When asked how the multinational fast-food chain managed to adjust to the pandemic reality, Nitin Chaturvedi, chief digital and technology officer at KFC Global, stated the following:

'In terms of business model shifts, we went from having no delivery, click-and-collect or curb-side pick-up in many parts of the world, to standing up all these channels overnight, or at most, in a few months. In terms of [the] business and operating model, it was a very, very big shift'.

On the other hand, small restaurants rarely apply professional change management principles and tools such as the force field analysis to plan for a change. The extent to which they adapt to the pandemic challenges relies heavily on the change leadership skills of their owner.

1 Define the term 'gig economy'. [2]
2 Define the term 'human resource planning'. [2]
3 With reference to extract 1, explain **two** reasons why human resource planning is an important part of human resource management [4]
4 Explain **one** advantage and **one** limitation for the restaurant industry from the evolution of the gig economy. [4]
5 Suggest **two** reasons why bigger restaurant chains may be more effective in change management than small restaurants. [4]
6 Analyse **two** reasons why employees in the food delivery service may resist the evolution of the gig economy. [4]
7 Suggest **two** ways in which a project champion may help a big restaurant chain to upgrade its online order and delivery system. [4]
8 Discuss the usefulness of the force field analysis as a tool for small restaurants when managing changes brought about by the Covid-19 pandemic. [10]

> # Chapter 8

Organisational structure

BUSINESS IN CONTEXT

Tata's organisational structure

Tata Motors has adopted a new, flat **organisational structure**. The change is being made to:

- improve communications between different levels of the organisation

- develop faster and more flexible decision-making

- improve customer focus of decisions.

The structural changes eliminate several layers of middle management so that employees in each business unit are empowered and have clear accountability. The company is already organised on a product division basis with separate structures for passenger vehicles and commercial vehicles. Tata Motors is one of India's largest automobile manufacturers by revenue, but its market shares have fallen: passenger vehicles are down 5% from as high as 16%, and commercial vehicles are down to 46%, the lowest in decades. The company has set itself a target of breaking into the top three car makers in the country and top three commercial vehicles makers globally in three years. The new organisational structure is designed to help the business achieve these new objectives.

Discuss in pairs or a group:

- Why does Tata need an organisational structure at all?

- How can a change to the structure of a business help it achieve its objectives?

Tata trucks and Tata cars are two separate divisions of Tata Motors

KEY TERM

organisational structure: the internal, formal framework of a business that shows the way in which management is organised and linked together and how authority is passed through the organisation

KEY CONCEPT LINK

Change

These days, multinational businesses trying to become as adaptable to change as possible create the 'network' organisational structure. Such a structure relates to businesses that do not have all their operations under one roof but operate as a complicated network of retailers, subcontractors, freelancers, etc. In practice, in a network structure a core company creates networks with other peripheral companies through outsourcing or partnerships. H&M is an example of a network organisational structure, as it distributes its functions to different companies in different countries, such as a product development company in Australia, a call centre in New Zealand, a manufacturing company in Malaysia.

8.1 Organisational structures

A sole trader with no employees needs no organisational structure. Even if this sole owner were to take on just one worker or one partner, a sense of formal structure would become necessary. Who is to do what job? Who is responsible to whom and for which decisions? If the business expanded further with more workers – including supervisory staff, different departments or divisions – then the need for a structure would be even greater. This would allow the division of tasks and responsibilities to be made clear to everyone. So what is meant by 'organisational structure'? What would happen if it was confused or misunderstood? How does the structure impact on workers and managers? What are the key principles of designing and analysing an organisation's structure?

Delegation

This is a very important concept which can have far-reaching effects on both the organisational structure and the motivation levels of subordinate employees. As Herzberg and other researchers have pointed out, the process of delegation, requiring workers to be accountable for their work, can be very beneficial to motivation. Generally, the flatter and wider the organisation structure, the greater is the degree of delegation. Figure 8.1, which shows a wide span of control of eight, is likely to encourage delegation, whereas Figure 8.2, which shows a narrow span of control of three, is likely to lead to close control of subordinates.

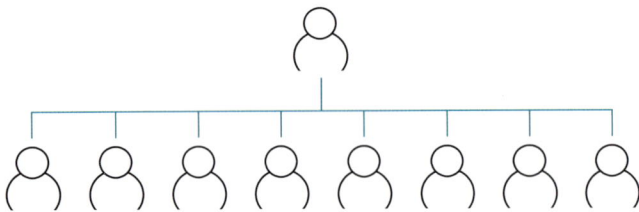

Figure 8.1: Wide span of control of eight – high level of delegation likely

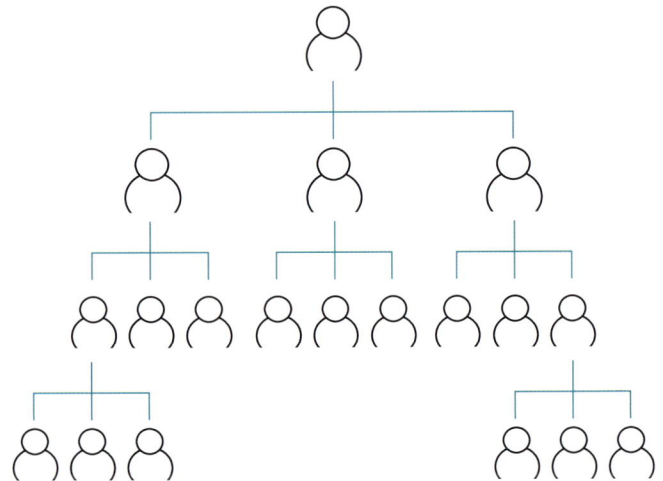

Figure 8.2: Narrow span of control of three – likely to be limited delegation

Imagine a manager with a span of control of 15 subordinates. It might be impossible to closely supervise the work of each of these every day – the manager would have no time for more important 'strategic' matters. Thus, the manager will delegate authority to their subordinate employees, and will trust them to perform well. Clearly, the subordinate employees are accountable to the manager for good performance; but the manager retains ultimate responsibility for the work done in the department whether it was delegated to others or not. Table 8.1 summarises the advantages and limitations of delegation.

KEY TERMS

delegation: passing authority down the organisational hierarchy

accountability: the obligation of an individual to account for his or her activities and to disclose results in a transparent way

---

Advantages of delegation	Limitations of delegation
Gives senior managers more time to focus on important, strategic roles	If the task is not well defined or if inadequate training is given, then delegation will be unlikely to succeed
Shows trust in subordinates, and this can motivate and challenge them	Delegation will be unsuccessful if insufficient authority (power) is given to the subordinate who is performing the tasks
Develops and trains employees for more senior positions	Managers may only delegate the boring jobs that they do not want to do – this will not be motivating
Helps empoyees to achieve fulfilment through their work (self-actualisation)	Delegation requires managers to exercise less control over the work of subordinates and some find this difficult to accept
Encourages employees to be accountable for their work-based activities	

Table 8.1: The advantages and limitations of delegation

Span of control

Spans of control can be wide (with a manager being directly responsible for many subordinates) or narrow (a manager has direct responsibility for a few subordinates). The wider the average span of control, the fewer the **levels of hierarchy**, other things being equal. This concept is clearly linked to the degree of delegation within the organisation. A small or narrow span of control suggests that managers want to keep close control over their subordinates by not taking the opportunity to delegate many tasks.

KEY TERMS

span of control: the number of subordinates reporting directly to a manager

level of hierarchy: a stage of the organisational structure at which the personnel on it have equal status and authority

Levels of hierarchy

Each level in the hierarchy represents a grade or rank of staff. Lower ranks are subordinate to superiors of a higher rank. The more levels, the greater the number of different grades or ranks in the organisation is. A **tall organisational structure** has a large number of levels of hierarchy and this creates three main problems:

- Communication through the organisation can become slow with messages becoming distorted or 'filtered' in some way.
- Spans of control are likely to be narrow.
- There is likely to be a greater sense of remoteness, among those on lower levels, from the decision-making power at the top.

In contrast, a **flat organisational structure** will have few levels of hierarchy but will tend to have wider spans of control. This will encourage managers/supervisors to delegate more extensively as they cannot effectively control the work of a large number of employees. It will also have a short chain of command and, potentially, better communication between the top of the hierarchy and the lower levels.

Chain of command

Typically, instructions are passed down the hierarchy; information, for example about sales or output levels, is sent upwards. The taller the organisational structure, the longer the **chain of command** will be and this can potentially slow down communications.

KEY TERMS

tall (vertical) organisational structure: one with many levels of hierarchy and, usually, narrow spans of control

flat (horizontal) organisational structure: one with few levels of hierarchy and wide spans of control

chain of command: this is the route through which authority is passed down an organisation – from the chief executive and the board of directors

Bureaucracy

Bureaucracy is a system that is most commonly found in government organisations. It discourages initiative and enterprise as decisions are taken centrally and then put into effect by staff following set procedures and protocols. Max Weber, the sociologist, identified the main attributes of bureaucracy as rationality and efficiency. However, he also recognised its impersonality and ineffectiveness when a decision needed to be adapted to suit an individual case.

Centralisation and decentralisation

Centralised businesses want to maintain exactly the same image and product range in all areas – perhaps because of cost savings or to retain a carefully created business identity in all markets. Examples of **decentralised** businesses are those multinationals that allow regional and cultural differences to be reflected in the products and services they provide. Clothing retailers with operations in several countries often allow local managers to decide on the exact range of clothing to be sold in each country – it could be disastrous for a business to sell European winter clothes in Singapore for example. See Table 8.2 for the advantages of centralisation and decentralisation.

Advantages of centralisation	Advantages of decentralisation
A fixed set of rules and procedures in all areas of the firm should lead to rapid decision-making – there is little scope for discussion	More local decisions can be made which reflect different conditions – the managers who take the decisions will have local knowledge and are likely to have closer contact with consumers
The business has consistent policies throughout the organisation. This prevents any conflicts between the divisions and avoids confusion in the minds of consumers	More junior managers can develop skills and this prepares them for more challenging roles.
Senior managers take decisions in the interest of the whole business – not just one division of it	Delegation and empowerment are made easier and these will have positive effects on motivation
Central buying should allow for greater economies of scale	Decision-making in response to changes, e.g., in local market conditions, should be quicker and more flexible as head office will not have to be involved every time
Senior managers at head office will be experienced decision-makers	

Table 8.2: The advantages of centralisation and decentralisation

---

> KEY TERMS

bureaucracy: an organisational system with standardised procedures and rules

centralisation: keeping all of the important decision-making powers within head office or the centre of the organisation

decentralisation: decision-making powers are passed down the organisation to empower subordinates and regional/product managers

---

CASE STUDY 8.1

Should all big businesses decentralise the decision-making process?

Centralisation is a common phenomenon in small business organisations that are typically managed by one or a few individuals. However, there are also big business organisations that are quite centralised. In Apple, much of the decision-making rests in the hands of CEO Tim Cook. In fact, many businesses in the fast-changing information technology industry centralise decisions to streamline policies across the organisation and to enhance clarity and simplicity in the decision-making process.

CONTINUED

However, often centralisation does not work for multinational organisations operating in consumer markets where localisation is essential to better satisfy consumers' wants at a country level. Starbucks maintains a fairly decentralised management approach, where CEO Kevin Johnson sets the tone and the vision of the organisation, but many decisions (especially the operational ones) are taken even at a local store level. The decentralisation approach within Starbucks has helped to create motivated employees who contribute to the success of the giant coffee chain.

1   Define the term 'centralisation'.   [2]

2   Suggest **two** reasons why centralisation is more common in small rather than in big businesses.   [4]

3   Explain **one** advantage and **one** disadvantage from decentralisation for multinational organisations.   [4]

Delayering

Many businesses aim for a flatter organisational structure to reduce the costs of management salaries. This process is known as **delayering** (see Table 8.3). It leads to wider spans of control and increased delegation to subordinates. This development in organisational structures has been assisted by improvements in IT and communication technology, which better enable senior managers to communicate with and monitor

the performance of junior staff and widely dispersed departments. This has had the effect of diminishing the importance of the role of middle managers.

Advantages of delayering	Disadvantages of delayering
Reduces business costs	Could be one-off costs of making managers redundant, e.g., redundancy payments
Shortens the chain of command and should improve communication through the organisation	Increased workloads for managers who remain – this could lead to overwork and stress
Increases spans of control and opportunities for delegation	
May increase workforce motivation due to less remoteness from top management and greater chance of having more responsible work to perform	Fear that redundancies might be used to cut costs could reduce the sense of security of the whole workforce – one of Maslow's needs (see Chapter 10)

Table 8.3: The advantages and disadvantages of delayering

The matrix structure

The **matrix structure** approach to organising businesses aims to eliminate many of the problems associated with the hierarchical structure. This type of structure cuts across the departmental lines of a hierarchical chart and creates project teams made up of people from all departments or divisions. The basic idea is shown in Figure 8.3.

This method of organising a business is task or project focused. Instead of highlighting the role or status of individuals it gathers together a team of specialists with the objective of completing a task or a project successfully. Emphasis is placed on an individual's

KEY TERMS

delayering: removal of one or more of the levels of hierarchy from an organisational structure

matrix structure: an organisational structure that creates project teams from across traditional functional departments

	Finance Dept	Production Dept	Marketing Dept	Human Resources	Research & Development
Project Team 1					
Project Team 2					
Project Team 3					

Figure 8.3: A matrix organisational structure

ability to contribute to the team rather than their position in the hierarchy. The use of matrix project teams has been championed by Tom Peters, one of the best-known writers on organisational structure. In his book *In Search of Excellence* (1982) he suggested that:

- organisations need flexible structures that remove as much bureaucracy as possible by getting rid of as many rigid rules and regulations as possible
- the use of project teams should lead to more innovative and creative ideas as employees will be more motivated to contribute.

Advantages:

- It allows total communication between all members of the team, cutting across traditional boundaries between departments in a hierarchy where only senior managers are designed to link with and talk to each other.
- There is less chance of people focusing on just what is good for their department. This is replaced with a feeling of what is good for the project and the business as a whole.
- The crossover of ideas between people with specialist knowledge in different areas tends to create more successful solutions.
- As new project teams can be created quickly, this system is well designed to respond to changing markets or technological conditions.

Disadvantages:

- There is less direct control from the 'top' as the teams may be empowered to undertake and complete a project. This passing down of authority to more junior employees could be difficult for some managers to come to terms with.

- The benefit of faster reaction to new situations is, therefore, at the expense of reduced bureaucratic control, and this trend may be resisted by some senior managers.
- In effect, team members may have two leaders if the business retains levels of hierarchy for departments but allows cross-departmental teams to be created. This could cause a conflict of interests.

8.2 Organisation charts

The hierarchical structure

Many businesses are still organised in a traditional **hierarchical structure**, as decision-making power starts at the top but may be passed down to lower levels. The rungs on the career ladder for an ambitious employee are illustrated by the different levels of hierarchy. The role of each individual will be clear and well defined, and there is a clearly identifiable chain of command. This traditional hierarchy is most frequently used by organisations based on a 'role culture', where the importance of the role determines the position in the hierarchy.

> **KEY TERM**
>
> **hierarchical structure:** a structure in which power and responsibility are clearly specified and allocated to individuals according to their standing or position in the hierarchy

This structure has different layers of the organisation with fewer and fewer people on each higher level. Figure 8.4 shows an example of this, organised by function or department.

In general terms, it is often presented as a pyramid, as shown in Figure 8.5.

The organisational structure chart displays a number of important points about the formal organisation of any business. It indicates:

- who has overall responsibility for decision-making
- the number of levels of hierarchy on which people have similar degrees of decision-making power

- the formal relationships between people and departments – workers can identify their position in the business and who is their immediate 'line' manager
- how accountability and authority are passed down the organisation – the chain of command
- the number of subordinates reporting to each more senior manager – the span of control
- formal channels of communication, both vertical and horizontal
- the identity of the supervisor or manager to whom each worker is answerable and should report.

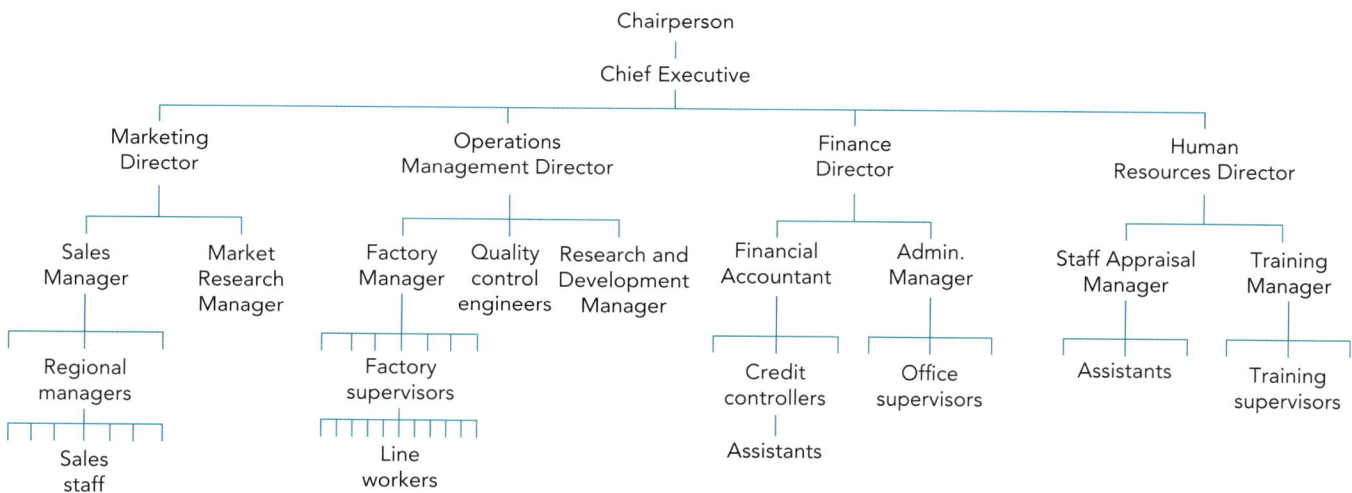

Figure 8.4: An example of an organisational structure organised by function

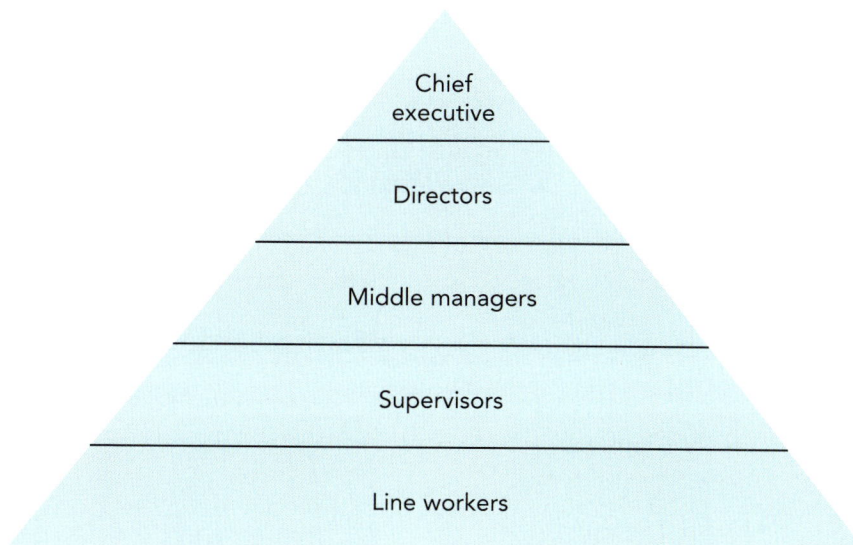

Figure 8.5: A typical hierarchical pyramid

Flat and tall structures

As already discussed, the traditional organisation structure can be either flat (horizontal) or tall (vertical). The key features of these two versions of the pyramid structure are outlined in Table 8.4.

Structure by product, function or region

The traditional pyramid-based organisational structure can be based on product, function or region.

Product-based structure

An organisational structure based on products usually consists of several parallel teams focusing on a single product or service line. Examples of a product line are the different car brands under General Motors or Microsoft's software platforms. One example of a service line is Bank of America's retail, commercial,

Flat or horizontal structure	Tall or vertical structure
Few levels of hierarchy	Many levels of hierarchy
Short chain of command	Long chain of command
Wide spans of control	Narrow spans of control
Delegation likely to be widely used	Delegation likely to be limited

Table 8.4: Key features of tall and flat structures

investing and asset management arms. An example of a product-based structure is shown in Figure 8.6.

An organisational structure based on product divisions gives a larger business the ability to segregate large sections of the company into semi-autonomous groups. These groups are often mostly self-managed and focus on a narrow aspect of the company's products or services. As with any organisational structure, divisions have both strengths and weaknesses.

Unlike functional departments, product divisions tend to be more autonomous, each with its own top executive. They typically manage their own recruitment, budgeting and advertising. Though small businesses rarely use a product divisional structure, it can work for such firms as advertising agencies which have dedicated staff and budgets that focus on major clients or industries.

Advantages:

- Product divisions can work well because they allow a team to focus on a single product or service, with an appropriate leadership structure.

- Having a senior executive – often a member of the board of directors – makes it more likely the division will receive the resources it needs from the company.

- A product division's focus allows it to build a common culture and team spirit that contributes both to higher morale and a better knowledge of the division's range of products. This is preferable to having its product or service managed by multiple departments through the organisation.

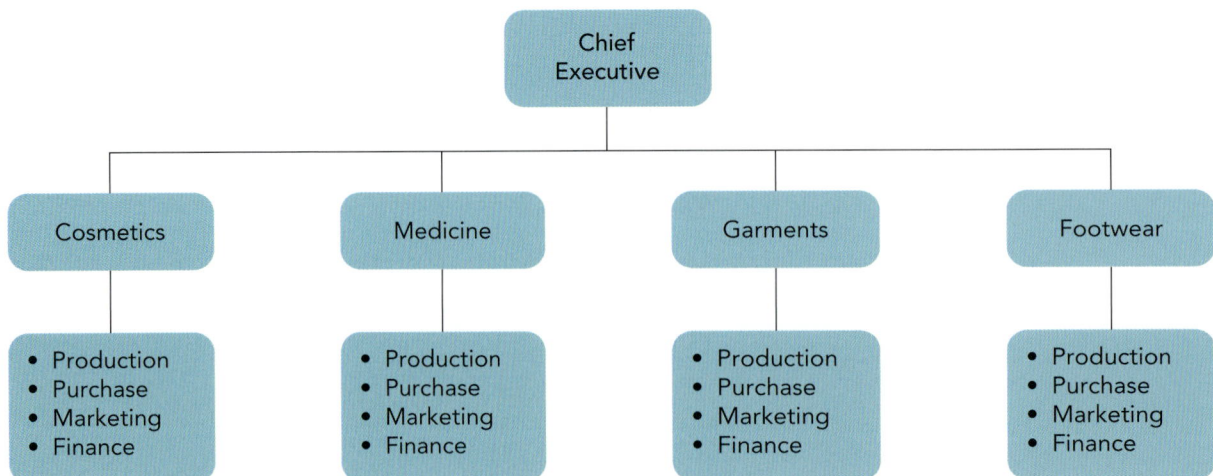

Figure 8.6: Organisational structure by product division

Disadvantages:

- Product divisions may compete with each other for available financial resources and this might reduce cooperation between them.

- Divisions can result in compartmentalisation that results in lack of coordination or even duplication of developments. For example, Microsoft's business-software division developed the Social Connector in Microsoft Office Outlook. It was unable to integrate Microsoft SharePoint and Windows Live until several months after Social Connector could interface with MySpace and LinkedIn. Some experts suggested that Microsoft's divisional structure contributed to a situation where its own products were incompatible across internal business units.

Functional-based structure

This form of organisational structure is illustrated in Figure 8.4.

Advantages:

- Grouping employees by functional skills, e.g., marketing, can improve efficiency. Specialists are clustered together, which promotes collaboration and the opportunity for the further development of professional expertise.

- Employees can capitalise on their specialised skills as a means to progress in a given department.

- As each department specialises in a specific function, managers train and develop employees within their unit to be proficient in their given role.

Disadvantages:

- Such a structure tends to suggest that one-way (top downwards) communication is the norm – this is rarely the most efficient form.

- There are few horizontal links between the departments, and this can lead to lack of coordination between them.

- Managers are often accused of tunnel vision because they are not encouraged to look at problems in any way other than through the eyes of their own department. They can become too focused on departmental objectives and not overall corporate aims.

- This type of structure is very inflexible and often leads to change resistance. This is because all managers tend to be defending both their own position in the hierarchy and the importance of their own department.

Regional-based structure

Multinational businesses are often structured using regional divisions. Large businesses that only operate in one country might also divide the structure into different regions of that country.

Advantages:

- Communication between representatives can be very direct and personal in a geographical organisational structure – rather than having to establish working relationships with people on the other side of the world via email and telephone.

- Grouping employees into regional sections can encourage the formation of strong, collaborative teams that work effectively together and engage in planning and decision-making together.

- The ability to recruit local management offers companies the advantage of having leaders who are completely familiar with the local business environment, culture and legal climate.

- Better decisions can result from relying on the knowledge and experience of regional managers who are aware of specific cultural factors. Recruiting a mix of local and head-office managers to lead a geographical unit has the advantage of linking local culture with company culture. Customers can feel more at ease when speaking with local representatives who fully understand their language and forms of expression.

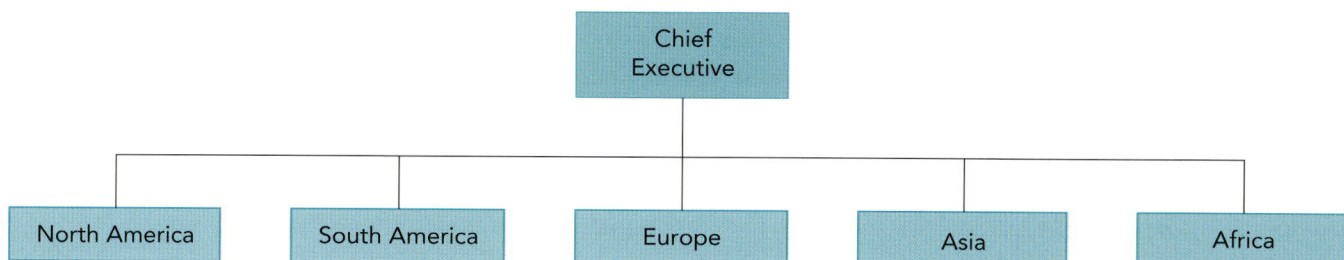

Figure 8.7: Organisational structure by region

- Tracking the performance of individual regional markets is simplified under this structure, as measures such as revenues, profit margins, costs and performance improvements can be tracked to specific regions.

Disadvantages:

- Some disadvantages of the regional/geographical structure may include the duplication of personnel between head office and regional offices.

- There may be conflict and unhealthy competition between different regional divisions of the business.

- It could make it more difficult to be consistent in core company beliefs, e.g., applying the same ethical code of practice from one region to the next.

- Inconsistent company strategies might be adopted in different regions as a result of poor coordination between regional offices.

ACTIVITY 8.1

Starbucks' organisation maintains a hybrid organisational structure, which combines traditional hierarchy 'by function', 'by geographical division' and ' by product', as well as the matrix structure.

Do some research on the organisational structure of Starbucks. Why do you think the business needs to combine all these types in a unique hybrid organisational structure? What are the advantages and disadvantages of such a hierarchy?

CASE STUDY 8.2

How will the Covid-19 related teleworking policies affect middle management?

Middle managers have been under 'attack' since tall organisations started valuing the role of delayering to make organisations more agile and efficient in decision-making, to enhance delegation and to reduce the cost of labour. Middle managers have even been blamed for obstructing both top-down and bottom-up communication.

But the Covid-19 crisis and the subsequent shift to new employment patterns such as teleworking affected the role of managers as well. In many organisations, middle managers became more critical than ever in supervising and coaching employees when working away from the office. The smooth transition of the labour force to the teleworking era has relied heavily on their support and guidance. Thus, many businesses had to postpone or even reverse their delayering plans.

However, as communication becomes more and more 'electronic', the notion of 'chain of command' becomes less and less important. Middle managers become just names among the many recipients of top-management emails addressed to all personnel.

Information technology allows senior managers to communicate directly with the 'shop-floor' employees, who become increasingly trained and accustomed to teleworking methods. The exact

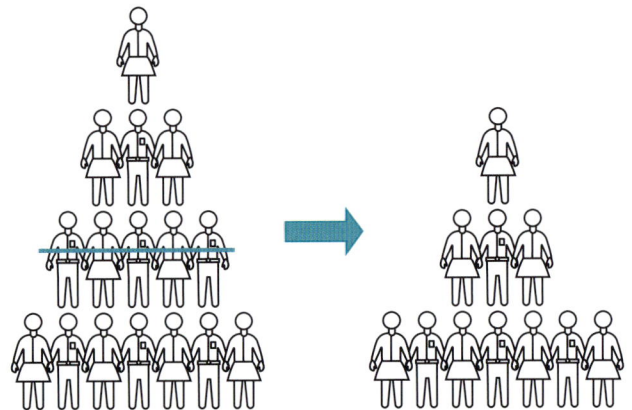

effect of the changing work patterns on middle management, in the long run, is yet to be seen.

1 Define the term 'delayering'. [2]

2 With reference to the case study, suggest **two** reasons why firms often remove middle-management levels from the organisation. [4]

3 Explain why the notion of the 'chain of command' becomes less and less important in the era of teleworking, where communication becomes 'electronic'. [4]

4 'The delayering of tall organisations is vital to improving their efficiency'. Discuss this statement. [10]

8.3 External factors influencing organisational structure

Changes in the external environment in which a business operates can lead to the present organisational structure being less appropriate than it once was. Most business leaders recognise that to never change the structure of their organisation would be a mistake. Changes in the economy, competitors' actions, legal controls and globalisation could all contribute to a decision to adapt the internal structure of a business to a more appropriate one. Here are some examples:

Economic changes

A long-term downturn or recession in the economy of the country or countries in which a business operates could make the following changes to structure appropriate:

- Delayering of the organisation – perhaps as part of a larger retrenchment programme – would take out one or more levels of hierarchy and would reduce overhead salary and other labour-related costs. This revised and 'leaner' structure would give the business a better chance of remaining profitable during a period of difficult trading conditions.

- Adopting a regional structure to allow for expansion in other countries that might be less affected by an economic recession. This revised structure might allow the business to revise its marketing mix quickly to successfully exploit foreign markets which might still be expanding.

Technological changes

When rapid and significant technological change occurs – such as in electric vehicle production or mobile phone capabilities – senior management could consider the following changes to organisation structure:

- Greater use of research and development requiring, perhaps, the creation of a separate department for the scientific research and technical development of new products which would help to restore business competitiveness.

- Employment of more specialist employees experienced in IT and other developments to advise senior management on how the business could respond to technological changes. These specialists might report directly to senior management, in which case they become 'staff managers' and will not be assigned to the existing functional departments.

- A matrix or project-based structure to focus teams of specialists from different functional areas tasked with developing new products which embrace the latest technology. The aim of this change to structure would be to make the business more flexible and fluid in response to technological change and to speed up the organisation's response to it.

Legal changes

Most governments are making legal changes that impact on how businesses operate. Many of these legal changes affect the environmental responsibilities of businesses and their responsibility to their employees on matters of equality and inclusion. Appropriate changes to the organisation could include:

- The creation of a compliance unit to monitor and oversee whether all departments and employees of the business are aware of their legal responsibilities. The work of a typical compliance unit is to identify risks that an organisation faces resulting from leal regulations and advise on how to avoid or address these risks. Compliance officers provide an in-house service that effectively supports other business departments in their duty to comply with relevant laws and regulations and internal procedures.

Competitors' actions

Some markets are relatively stable with few external changes occurring, e.g., the domestic furniture market or washing detergent market. The structure of businesses that operate in markets such as these does not have to be very flexible or adaptable to rapid change. In contrast, some markets are unstable. For example, new competitors frequently enter the market with new ideas, such as digital technology and online retailing. An appropriate organisation structure could be a decentralised one because:

- Businesses operating in these markets need to be able to introduce rapid and significant changes in strategy. Rapid strategic changes such as decisions to diversify product lines or markets require decentralised structures as decision-making is done at a level of the organisation closer to the market and the customers. Some businesses are also adopting the project-based approach to provide solutions to particular aspects of market change.

In contrast, businesses that do not often need to diversify their operations could justify the use of a centralised organisational structure.

LEARNER PROFILE

Principled

Hierarchical structures serve the principles of authority, responsibility and accountability.

Through organising people in a traditional hierarchy, businesses aim to maintain managerial integrity. When a person becomes a manager, they must follow the principles of professional management as underlined by their position in the structure, to be competent in their roles and to avoid high employee turnover.

On the other hand, a clear hierarchy enables managers to keep employees accountable for errors or omissions in a fair manner, in the sense that roles and responsibilities are clearly and explicitly defined. Therefore, businesses usually maintain the traditional hierarchy, even when the focus is shifted towards a matrix structure. Yet, it must be said that even in the most rigidly structured organisations, fairness and accountability is not guaranteed if it is not reflected by the personal principles of managers and employees.

In small organisations with an informal hierarchy in place, accountability depends solely on personal integrity, as roles and responsibilities are not so clear.

Take the example of a small business offering computer technical services, owned by five partners, and maintaining an informal organisational structure. What kind of problems do you think may arise in this case if one owner is not a principled person? Discuss in class.

Globalisation

The growing trend towards international marketing brought about by globalisation is having the following impact on organisational structure:

- To become a successful global business operating in several national or regional markets, the organisational structure needs to be flexible enough to allow for decisions to be taken locally that reflect market conditions and local cultures. Many multinational companies have adopted a regional structure with decentralised decision-making. This should allow local differences in market conditions, culture and consumer preferences to be accurately reflected in the marketing mix adopted by the business.

8.4 Changes in organisational structures

There are alternative organisational structures, other than the hierarchical type.

Handy's Shamrock organisation

Charles Handy is a well-known writer on organisational structure who has focused on the changes being introduced into many business organisations as a result of greater cost pressures and the need for greater flexibility.

He first used the term the 'Shamrock organisation' (see Figure 8.8) with the three leaves made up of the following:

- Core managerial and technical staff, who must be offered full-time, permanent contracts with competitive salaries and benefits. These workers are central to the survival and growth of the organisation. In return for high rewards they are expected to be loyal and work long hours when needed. As core workers are expensive, their numbers are being reduced in most organisations.
- Outsourced functions by independent providers, who may once have been employed by the company. Also known as the 'contractual fringe', these workers provide specific services that do not have to be kept within the core. These may include payroll services, transport, catering and IT.

- Flexible workers on temporary and part-time contracts, who are called on when the situation demands their labour. As the organisation demonstrates little concern or loyalty towards these workers, they often respond in kind. These workers are most likely to lose their jobs in an economic downturn.

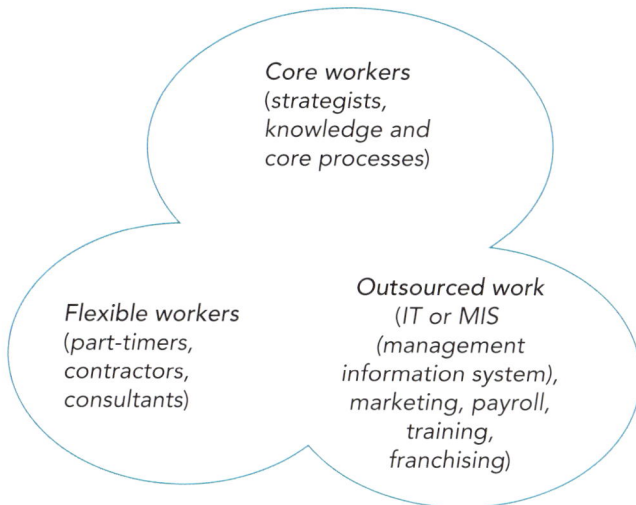

Core workers
(strategists, knowledge and core processes)

Flexible workers
(part-timers, contractors, consultants)

Outsourced work
(IT or MIS
(management information system), marketing, payroll, training, franchising)

Figure 8.8: Charles Handy's Shamrock organisation

ACTIVITY 8.2

How did the Covid-19 pandemic affect the organisational structure of businesses?

The Covid-19 pandemic forced many businesses to quickly change the way they operated.

Organisations suddenly realised they needed to speed up decision-making to adapt to the fast-changing reality resulting from Covid-19. Urgent changes that had to be made ranged from adopting new technologies fast to producing new goods and services, often within just a few days.

What kind of changes do you think the pandemic brought to organisational structures of big, hierarchical organisations? Discuss in class.

Project-based organisation

Some businesses have always adopted a project-based structure. For example, advertising agencies will use a team of creative employees for each major promotion campaign contract, and events-organising firms will use a group of people to organise and manage a major event such as an international conference. The project-based organisation (PBO) has become a more widely adopted form of structure as an alternative to traditional organisational structures. It is claimed that it better allows businesses to deal with demands that are often quite short term and one-off, within a dynamic market. As a consequence of the trend towards increased globalisation, application of new technologies, rapid changes in the economic environment and unstable markets, organisations must be flexible enough to adapt to continual transformational process.

KEY TERM

project based organisation (PBO): undertake most of their activities through temporary project teams, often with a small central administrative department overseeing them.

Project-based structures often use a matrix organisation with several distinct project teams, but essential company functions are maintained by a central core of managers. As was noted when discussing matrix structures, an employee can have one manager for project-related work but another for issues such as pay and working conditions. Senior managers could have several project groups reporting to them on specific tasks, such as a strategy to enter a new market or a plan to reduce operating costs by 10%. At the same time, the business would maintain core functions (such as human resources) outside the project groups.

One of the key benefits of a project-based organisation is its flexibility. Employees best suited to a particular project are assigned to it and there will be a mix of people from different functional areas. Within each project team there is likely to be a hierarchical structure but, typically, with very few levels of hierarchy.

Another benefit is that the focus of the organisation changes compared to traditional structures. Instead of being concerned with department responsibilities, projects are focused on solving problems and devising new strategies. It is argued that solution and strategies are arrived at more quickly using a project manager and a team of people most suited to each job.

Critics of the project-based organisation suggest that each project team might feel isolated from others.

They become task focused and do not concentrate of coordinating with other teams or the rest of the organisation. Continuity and loyalty to the company could become a problem too. Employees might change project teams quite frequently as their role ends, reporting to different managers all the time. In addition, specialist employees might be more loyal to their team than the overall business organisation, and when their project ends they could look for challenges in other organisations.

THEORY OF KNOWLEDGE

Knowledge question: How do we know what makes teams work?

When managers organise people in a matrix structure, they hope that such a decision will work miracles in enabling horizontal communication and making the organisation much faster to solve problems and respond to fast-changing market conditions. However, this is not always true.

Based on research performed in the USA in 2018, more than 40% of the managers surveyed on the effectiveness of matrix organisations stated that they believed the matrix 'made the organisational hierarchy more complex' and the decision-making 'more difficult'. According to the same research, the degree of success in a matrix does not depend only on project management effectiveness. Two common problems when people work in teams are the quality of communication and the clarity of accountability of the members, which depend on leadership and culture and not on planning. Moreover, in businesses where people have received training on working in teams, the matrix seemed to work better. Employees felt less stressed about collaborating with other people on shared targets.

What is the role of employees' attitudes when a business tries to embed the matrix? What can leaders do to improve the effectiveness of teamwork, other than training their employees? Discuss in class.

CASE STUDY 8.3

New organisational structure for the pharmaceutical company

Riaz has been appointed as the HR director of a pharmaceutical company employing about 2000 people. The business has a very traditional organisational structure by function. The grouping of employees by functional skills has enabled specialisation and has created the advantage of clarity and simplicity in the chain of command.

However, Riaz wants to change the way the organisation is organised. The business is growing by opening a second factory abroad. Riaz is considering the option of creating a regional organisational structure to facilitate communication and decision-making under the new environment. Riaz is also worried about the bureaucracy that has been created in the home country. Horizontal communication is practically non-existent in the company, as employees focus mostly on the goals of their department and do not have many opportunities to collaborate with other functions. The business needs innovation in order to remain competitive in a dynamic market

where rivals come up with creative ideas, especially in the 'non-prescription' category with products such as medication for the common cold.

Riaz is thinking of embedding the matrix structure in the business. However, his predecessor failed when he tried to apply the matrix in the organisation. Some senior managers resisted the change, which required training of employees and the shift of focus away from the departmental objectives.

CONTINUED

1 Define the term 'matrix structure'. [2]

2 Suggest **one** advantage and **one** disadvantage from the traditional hierarchy by function currently maintained in the business. [4]

3 Explain **two** possible reasons why Riaz wants to create a regional structure in the business. [4]

4 Evaluate Riaz's plan to embed a matrix structure in the pharmaceutical company. [10]

ACTIVITY 8.3

1 Match the business problems shown in the left column with the possible solutions in the right column.

Problem	Possible solution
The managing director cannot communicate effectively with the shop-floor employees in a traditional hierarchy that has five layers	Delegation of responsibilities
Managers concentrate decisions and employees feel left out of the decision-making process	Delayering
Horizontal communication is weak and the organisation is slow in responding to changing consumer wants with new products	Centralisation of the strategic decision-making process
The regional offices of a big multinational business are not aligned with each another in terms of corporate strategy. The business loses the opportunity to get the maximum possible economies of scale from ordering supplies centrally for all subsidiary businesses	Forming a matrix structure

2 How likely is it that the above problems would be seen in small businesses with few employees? Discuss in class.

SELF-EVALUATION CHECKLIST

After studying this chapter, complete this table.

I am able to apply and analyse:	Needs more work	Almost there	Ready to move on
terminology in relation to different types of organisational structures (AO2)			
the following types of organisational charts: • flat/horizontal • tall/vertical • by product, by function or by region (AO2)			
I am able to synthesise and evaluate:			
appropriateness of different organisational structures given a change in external factors (AO3)			
changes in organisational structures (for example, Charles Handy's Shamrock Organisation and Project-based organisation) (AO3)			
I am able to use and apply:			
the following types of organisation charts: • flat/horizontal • tall/vertical • by product, by function or by region (AO4)			

REFLECTION

To what extent should a multinational business have different organisational structures for its operations in different countries which have important cultural distinctions?

How would you justify your answer to another learner?

PROJECT

Electra and Penelope started LittlePaws in 2015 as a social enterprise producing and selling pet food, toys and accessories for the very competitive domestic market. The entrepreneurs keep 40% of the profit, while 60% is used on activities related to stray animals. Figure 8.9 demonstrates the organisational structure of LittlePaws.

The Covid-19 pandemic brought significant changes in consumer demand due to reducing household income, which forced pet owners to cut their spending. On the other hand, the number of stray dogs increased dramatically. Electra and Penelope found themselves with marginal profit, unable to serve their social goals.

Ben, a friend of the owners who specialises in organisational structure, has suggested that the business should undertake a radical restructuring from a traditional hierarchy to a flexible form such as the Shamrock organisation. In his opinion, only two core employees (decision-makers) should remain in the business, i.e., Electra and Penelope. The owners should subcontract the production to third parties.

Electra and Penelope are not very open to the radical change proposed by Ben. They believe that in order to improve organisational structure the business should delayer, to cut costs.

Split into three groups:

- **Group 1:** Debate in favour of restructuring the business into a Shamrock organisation.

- **Group 2:** Debate against the restructuring of the business into a Shamrock organisation.

- **Group 3:** Decide which of the two groups wins the debate. Select some specific criteria for your decision (e.g., quality of arguments regarding short-term and long-term consequences, recognition of impact on stakeholders, identification of the implications on the competitiveness of the business, recognition of the ethical dimensions of the decision).

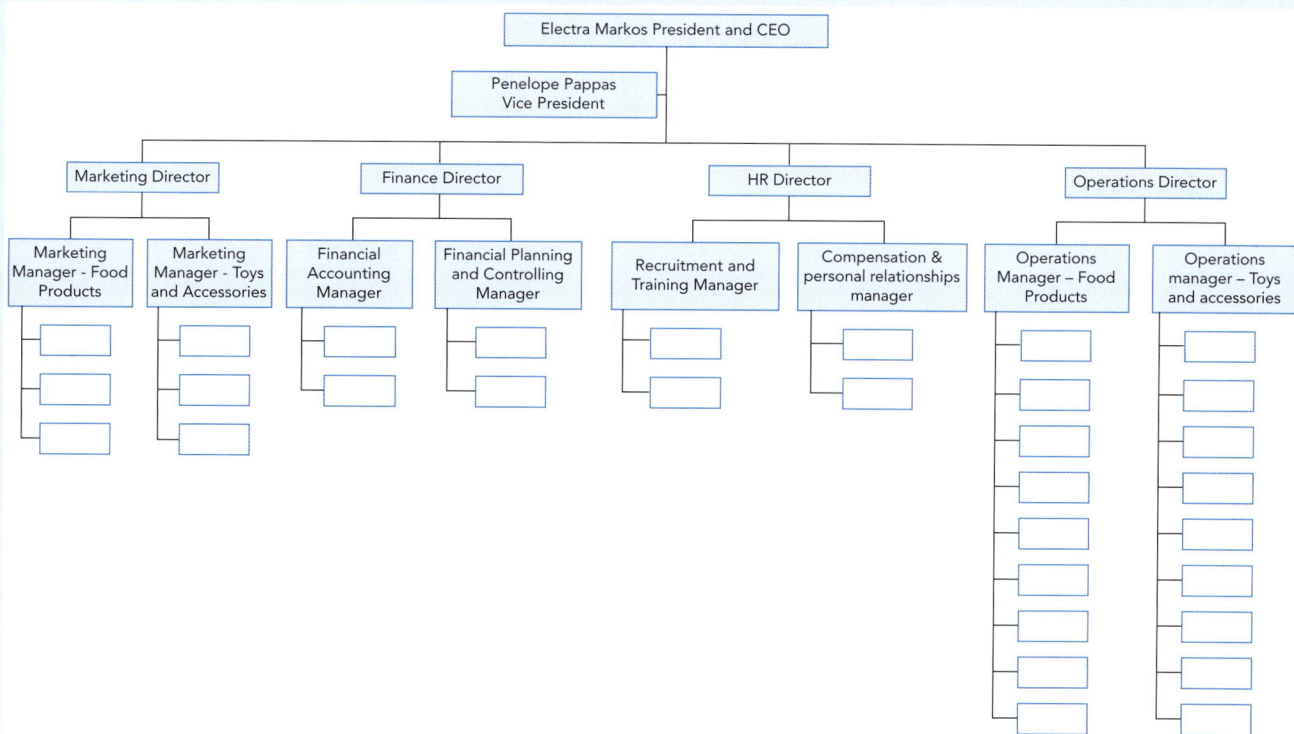

Figure 8.9: LittlePaws organisational chart

EXAM-STYLE QUESTIONS

Nassim was recruited as an HR consultant for Chocolate Flavors (CF) Plc, a multinational business producing chocolates. Nassim has ten years' experience in the soft-drinks industry, and his responsibility is to guide CF to improve its organisational structure.

CF grew significantly because of globalisation between 1990 and 2010. It has gradually developed across 60 countries, and along its growth process it became taller and taller by adding more middle management levels in its traditional hierarchy. The narrow span of control allows managers to specialise in their area of focus. There are processes for everything, and new recruits quickly become familiar with the clear chain of command. The lines of promotion are also clear, which motivates the employees interested in climbing the hierarchy ladder.

The chocolate market is becoming very competitive. Rivals are quick to produce new flavours and innovative products such as sugarless chocolates. CF is slow to respond. The bureaucracy created through the hierarchical structure blocks the creativity of employees. Horizontal communication is almost non-existent, and employees have never worked in teams. Most decisions are centralised in the hands of the senior managers, while middle managers hesitate to take the initiative. Such an environment does not promote change in the organisation.

CF faces financial problems as well. The finance director complains that the many layers in the hierarchy are the main reason the net profit margin is lower than the industry average. Most of CF's main competitors maintain flatter hierarchies and respond to market changes faster, while they have lower indirect costs. A few competitive rivals operate as Shamrock organisations. According to the finance director, such businesses tend to be cost-effective mainly because they outsource their production processes.

CF's board of directors asked Nessim to examine the two following options for the business:

- Delayer the organisation by removing one level from the traditional hierarchy. This layer consists of experienced middle managers with years of service in CF who are not very productive and are close to retirement. The finance director suggests offering those managers 50% higher compensation than the minimum legal requirement if they decide to leave the business voluntarily.

- Embed the matrix structure in the organisation without delayering. There are many projects that CF needs to launch, including the development of two new products.

1	Define the term 'traditional hierarchy'.	[2]
2	Define the term 'span of control'.	[2]
3	Explain **one** advantage and **one** disadvantage for CF from maintaining a tall traditional hierarchy.	[4]
4	Explain **one** advantage and **one** disadvantage from the narrow span of control prevailing at CF.	[4]
5	Explain how the many levels of hierarchy in CF affect:	
	a the profit of the business, and	
	b the profitability of the business.	[4]
6	Suggest **one** possible reason why Shamrock organisations are characterised by the finance director as 'cost-effective'.	[2]
7	Suggest **two** possible disadvantages for CF from the centralisation of decisions by senior managers	[4]
8	Suggest how the delayering of CF is likely to affect:	
	a the span of control, and	
	b the extent to which managers delegate responsibilities to subordinates.	[4]
9	Suggest one reason why bureaucracy may not be desirable in CF.	[2]
10	Advise Nassim which of the two restructuring options is the most appropriate for CF.	[10]

Chapter 9

Leadership and management

LEARNING OBJECTIVES

On completing this chapter you should be able to:

Apply and analyse:

> Scientific and intuitive thinking/management (AO2)

- Management and leadership (AO2)

Synthesise and evaluate:
- The following leadership styles:
  - Autocratic
  - Paternalistic
  - Democratic
  - Laissez-faire
  - Situational (AO3)

BUSINESS IN CONTEXT

What makes a good leader?

The question is eternal: what makes a good leader? There is no definitive answer, but here are four quotes about leaders or **leadership**:

- Seth Godin: 'The secret of leadership is simple: Do what you believe in. Paint a picture of the future. Go there. People will follow.'

- Ted Devine, CEO Insureon: 'Having a completely open plan office says this about leadership: No walls, no barriers, no hierarchy. Everybody can talk to everybody. Everybody can participate in a decision. We work together, and that's very important in leadership.'

- Zappos senior **manager** about CEO, Tony Hsieh: 'Our culture was inspired by how he does business and the people he hires. He takes a hands-off approach to leadership that requires effective delegation. He is more of an architect; he designs the big vision and then gets out of the way so that everyone can make the things happen.'

- Tom Peters: 'Management is about arranging and telling. Leadership is about nurturing and enhancing.'

What do chief executive officers (CEOs) do?

CEO's are the top managers of public companies. A Harvard Business Review study of 27 CEOs found that their work is varied: 25% of their time is spent on people and relationships – guiding and liaising with senior managers; 25% on controlling departmental and business activities through reviews; 16% on organisation and culture; and 21% on strategic decision-making. Only 3% of their time is spent on professional development, 1% on crisis management, 4% on mergers and acquisitions, while another 5% is spent planning.

Meetings make up much of a CEO's day – 72% of their time is spent in meetings. The study found that

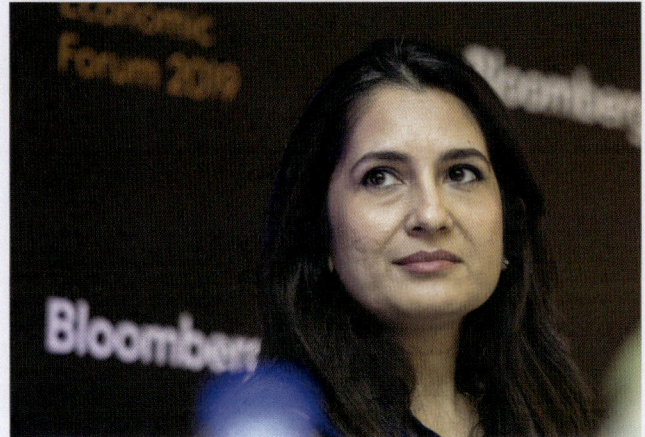

Mahreen Rahman, CEO of Alfalah Investment

CEOs believe having direct contact with employees is very important. Some 61% of their communication with employees was face to face, 24% was electronic, and 15% was by phone and letter.

Discuss in pairs or a group:

- Select one of the four quotes which you think best explains leadership. Justify your choice to a friend or the class. After your discussion, write down your own definition of leadership.

- What do you think are the most important functions of managers? Make a list.

- What do you think are the differences between 'leadership' and 'management'? Justify your answer.

KEY TERMS

leadership: the act of motivating a group of people towards achieving a common objective

manager: responsible for setting objectives, organising resources and motivating employees so that the organisation's aims are met

9.1 Scientific and intuitive thinking/ management

There are two extreme approaches to **management**. One is based on **scientific management** and the other is based on **intuitive management**.

F.W. Taylor was the first management analyst to use the term 'scientific management' when he proposed giving workers clear tasks, matching workers to each task, insisting on a set way of undertaking jobs and then measuring workers' performance against pre-set targets

KEY TERMS

management: directing and controlling a group of people or an organisation to reach a goal by using the resources available to the organisation

scientific management: management of a business which follows the principles of efficiency derived from scientific experiments to improve productivity, especially those based on time-and-motion studies

intuitive management: decision-making based on the hunches and subconscious expertise of managers

(see Chapter 10). This scientific approach to using data, measurement and problem-solving techniques to deal with business problems (which Taylor usually narrowed down to low productivity) has been widened to include all business decision-making based on data analysis.

Decision-making is a key element of effective management. Business decision-making requires a manager to consider alternatives and use their skills and judgement to choose an appropriate, cost-effective course of action. Making effective decisions as a manager is a significant challenge. The business environment is changing fast and managers have to make decisions under conditions of uncertainty or limited information, which have a big impact at every stage of the decision-making process. Managers have to apply their skills and experience to select the most appropriate course of action for the problem they are trying to overcome and for the context the business is operating in. Usually this will involve finding a balance between the two extremes of scientific decision-making and intuitive decision-making.

Scientific management and decision-making

This approach to taking business decisions uses a logical process that is heavily dependent on data. Figure 9.1 shows a typical decision-making cycle or process. Information is needed at each stage of this cycle to allow logical and data driven decisions to be made.

The stages of the scientific decision-making process

Business objectives

Scientific management is based on setting and attempting to achieve clear business objectives. These are the starting point for scientific decision-making as the courses of action which are selected should be those which have the best chance of helping the business to achieve its objectives.

Define the problem

What is the issue that senior managers want to find a solution to? Is business growth slowing down? Are profits below forecasts? Has a new competitor entered the market with a technically advanced rival product? The exact nature of the problem that needs to be resolved must be identified and defined by management considering relevant data.

Process of scientific decision-making

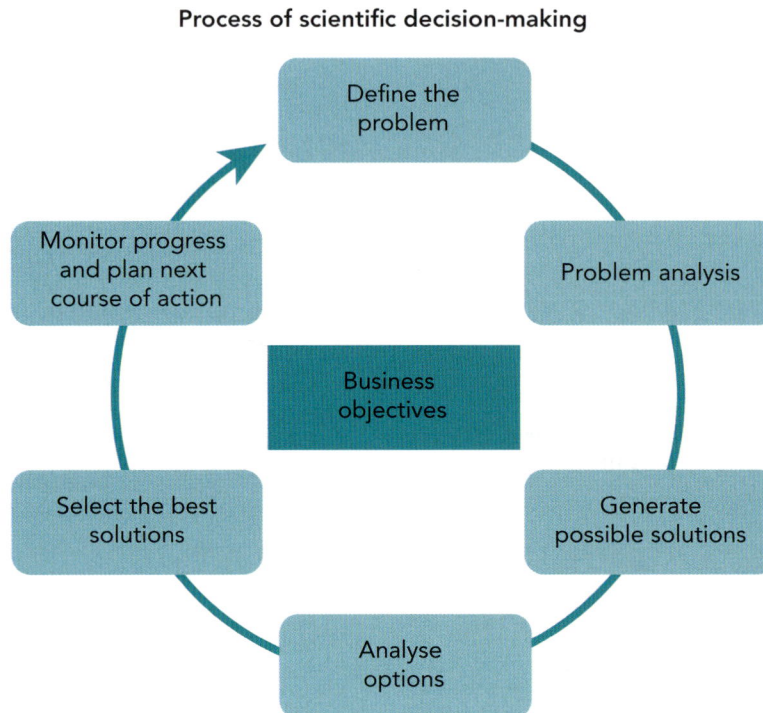

Figure 9.1: The process of scientific decision-making

Problem analysis

Data will be needed by managers in order to assess the scale, importance and duration of the problem or issue that requires a corrective decision to be made. Have sales been falling over the short or long term? Are sales falling for all products or just some product ranges? Are sales falling in all of the countries and regions that the business operates in? These are just some of the detailed questions that managers need answers to before they are able to analyse, in detail, what problem has to be solved by the decision that they are about to make.

Generate possible solutions

There is nearly always more than one approach that can be used to solve a business problem. Managers need to consider as many realistic options for action as possible. Information about possible solutions might be obtained from previous decisions or from decisions taken by comparable businesses when confronted with similar issues. Information about these previous situations and decisions will need to be considered.

Analyse options

Once the range of options for solving the problem have been identified then the likely impact of pursuing each course of action needs to be analysed. This stage with

be heavily data dependent and might involve techniques such as different costing approaches, decision trees, investment appraisal and force field analysis.

Select the best solution

The final decision will be based on the results of the data analysis. If one of the options clearly performs better when its likely outcome has been analysed quantitatively, then this should be chosen. The decision will need to be implemented effectively and this might require careful management of change within the business.

Monitor progress and plan the next course of action

This stage is vital as the decision-making process does not end once the decision has been made. Data needs to be gathered constantly and analysed to measure the effectiveness of the decision. Are the objectives for the decision being met? Is the original problem being solved? Are some parts of the new course of action proving to be more successful than others? By monitoring performance through the analysis of data, managers can start to plan the next course of action – because the process of decision-making is usually a continuous one.

Potential advantages of scientific management

- By setting objectives there is a clear sense of direction and a way to assess performance.
- Decisions are based on business logic and analysis of data.
- It is probable that more than one manager will be involved in the process, which will reduce the possibility of bias.
- It requires decisions, and their outcomes to be monitored continually and reviewed.
- When decisions are based on rational thinking, overall business success should be more likely.

Scientific management is most likely to be used when:

- Strategic decisions are required which have long-term consequences and involve substantial resources.
- The consequences of failure could be significant.
- The business has the management and other resources to gather and analyse quantities of data.
- The business is controlled by professional managers and not the owner. Investors will expect to see evidence that major decisions are supported by data analysis.

Intuitive management and decision-making

In some business situations, most decisions are not taken on the basis of data analysis and the application of decision-making techniques. Instead, decisions are taken using managers' 'sixth sense' or 'gut instincts'. Intuitive management and decision-making refers to the use of a manager's feelings or hunches to make decisions rather than rely on a scientific approach using data. The scientific approach relies on quantitative evidence, supported by logical, rational decision-making models.

Potential advantages of intuitive management:

- Decisions can be taken very quickly and this might be important when managers have to react fast, perhaps following a decision by a competitor to reduce prices by 10%.

- Decisions are often based on the personal experience of managers. This might be more effective than using just the results of data analysis if the hunch of an experienced manager appears to contradict data results.

Intuitive management is most likely to be used when:

- the business owner still controls major decisions and has great experience of the business environment
- the business is a family owned and controlled organisation and qualitative factors such as customer relations or employee welfare and job security might be more significant factors in some decisions than analysis of numerical data
- the data is out of date, unreliable or not available
- the business environment is changing rapidly and a situation has arisen – perhaps a pandemic – for which there is no data.

In many business situations, intuition and hunches are combined with scientific approaches to reach the most effective decision. A good example of this is when deciding between two investment projects for expansion of the business. The scientific approach will use investment appraisal, involving identifying and quantifying the costs and revenues from each investment. Intuition will be used to weigh up the importance of qualitative factors, such as the impact on the local environment and the community's welfare. Also management intuition will be used to help determine the appropriate discount factors (see Chapter 21) and judgement will be needed to interpret the quantitative results.

9.2 Management and leadership

A good manager does not always make an effective leader. According to John Kotter, former Konosuke Matsushita professor of leadership at Harvard University, there is often a problem understanding the difference between management and leadership. He fears that too often the terms are used synonymously.

Management is a set of processes that keep an organisation functioning. They make it work today – they make it hit this quarter's numbers. The processes are about planning, budgeting, staffing, clarifying jobs, measuring performance and problem-solving when results did not go to plan.

CASE STUDY 9.1

Big coffee chain is hiring a store manager

Indah has worked in retailing for three years and she is now looking for a job. She just saw a job advertisement from a multinational coffee chain operating in Indonesia which is hiring a store manager.

According to the job description, the position requires the store manager to take responsibility for hiring and directing six employees, under the guiding principles of the parent company. The ideal candidate will have good organisational and communication skills so that their staff receive clear and concise guidance on their priorities. The store manager will be responsible for the financial performance of the store and will have to establish measurable sales targets for the group.

According to the person specification, the manager should have a university degree, at least three years of experience in a similar position, and adequate leadership skills to inspire and motivate their staff.

Indah feels confident that she fits the role. She holds a business degree, and she is a hard worker and a sociable young person. Her previous employer praised her for her communication skills and her professionalism. However, she has not managed other people before and she is not sure if she could

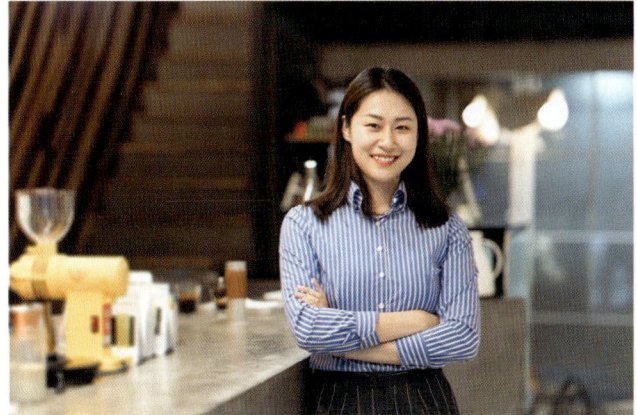

handle the store's financial management. The job description states that the store manager should plan the store's financial forecast and present it to the chain's regional head.

1   Define the term 'manager'.   [2]

2   Explain **two** managerial roles for Indah
    if she gets the job at the coffee chain.   [4]

3   Explain why financial budgeting is typically
    one of the roles of a store manager.   [2]

4   Is Indah the ideal candidate for the
    position of store manager? Discuss.   [10]

LEARNER PROFILE

Risk-takers

'Our history is about taking risks,' said Jeff Bezos in his final shareholder meeting before stepping down from the position of Amazon's CEO to give his position to Andy Jassy. As one of the most powerful and influential leaders in the world, Bezos always believed in the power of taking risks despite the possibility of failing. The e-commerce global leader is moving into areas such as telehealth, after facing challenges in many diverse markets with products such as Alexa, Kindle, Fire TV, Amazon Fresh, Amazon Prime, etc.

'Let me assure you, I can guarantee you that none of these ideas are guaranteed to work,' Bezos said.

In the past Amazon has had many successes, but not all of its goods and services managed to survive in the market. For example, in 2014 Amazon's Fire Phone (which was an attempt by the business to enter the smartphone market) failed, forcing Amazon to report a $170 million write off in its financial accounts.

How important for the success of Amazon was Jeff Bezos's willingness to take risks? Do you think the business would have been as successful as it is today without its leader taking risks? How do you think leaders such as Bezos overcome failure in order to remain focused on their vision? Discuss in class.

Leadership is very different, Kotter believes. He considers it to be about aligning people to the vision of the business which means communication, motivation and inspiration.

Table 9.1 summarises some of the key differences between leaders and managers.

Leaders	Managers
Motivate and inspire others	Direct and monitor others
They are innovators who encourage others to accept change	They are problem-solvers
Leadership stems from personal qualities or traits	They have an official position of responsibility in the organisation
They have natural abilities and instincts	They are skilled and qualified to perform a role
They believe in doing the right thing	They believes in doing things right
They are respected and trusted by followers – they want to follow because of leader's personality	They are listened to by others because of their status – not necessarily because of their personality
They create and develop a culture of change	They accept and conform to the 'norms' of the organisation

Table 9.1: Differences between leaders and managers

The key functions of management are common to all managers in any size of organisation. Henri Fayol, a management theorist, analysed the following management functions:

- **Setting objectives and planning** – all good managers think ahead. Senior management will establish overall strategic objectives and these will be translated into tactical objectives for the less senior managerial employees. The planning needed to put these objectives into effect is also important. A new production or marketing objective will require the planning and preparation of sufficient resources.
- **Organising resources to meet the objectives** – this is not just about giving instructions. People throughout the business need to be carefully recruited and encouraged to take some authority

and to accept some accountability via delegation. Senior managers will ensure that the structure of the business allows for a clear division of tasks and that each department is organised to allow them to work towards the common objectives.

- **Directing and motivating employees** – this involves guiding, leading and overseeing employees to ensure that organisational goals are met. The significance of developing employees so that they are motivated to employ all of their abilities at work is now widely recognised. This will make it more likely that organisational aims are achieved.
- **Coordinating activities** – as the average size of business units increases, especially in multinationals, so the need to ensure consistency and coordination between different parts of the organisation increases. The goals of each branch, division, region and even all of the employees must be welded together to achieve a common sense of purpose. At a practical level this means, for example, preventing two divisions of the same company spending money on research into similar new products, resulting in wasteful duplication of effort.
- **Controlling and measuring performance against targets** – it is management's responsibility to appraise performance against targets and to take action if underperformance occurs. As the motivational theorist Herzberg pointed out, it is just as important to provide positive feedback when things are going right.

All of these functions are performed by managers at all levels of an organisation. Senior managers will also be involved in strategic decision-making. Once important decisions have been taken, these managers and their more junior colleagues, will need to undertake the functions listed above to try to ensure that the strategy achieves the objectives set for it.

Leadership, in contrast, involves setting a clear direction and vision for an organisation that others will be prepared to follow. Employees will want to follow a good leader and will respond positively to them. A poor leader will fail to win over employees and will have problems communicating with and organising workers effectively. Many good managers are also good leaders – but some managers are not. Managers who focus on control of people and allocation of resources can fail to provide a sense of purpose or focus that others will understand and be prepared to follow.

1 Quiz: Leaders or managers?

Which option, a or b, best describes what a successful leader does?

a **i** Sets a vision

  ii Sets goals

b **i** Asks 'why'

  ii Asks 'how'

c **i** Maintains and administers

  ii Develops and innovates

d **i** Has employees

  ii Has followers

e **i** Shapes the organisation's culture

  ii Shapes the organisation's procedures

f **i** Aligns people

  ii Arranges people

2 'A good leader must have managerial abilities, and a good manager must have leadership skills.' Do you agree with this statement? Explain your answer.

Without clear and charismatic leadership workers may be very well 'managed', but will they be inspired to help the leader and the business take a fresh direction and achieve new goals?

What makes a good leader?

Many studies have been conducted on this point – some argue that leaders are 'born' with natural assets that create an aura or charisma that others will find appealing. This is the essential idea behind trait theory, which suggests that effective leaders are in some ways naturally different from other people. A number of personal characteristics have been identified as being common among effective leaders, including:

- A desire to succeed and natural self-confidence that they will succeed.

- The ability to think beyond the obvious – to be creative – and to encourage others to do the same.

- Being multitalented, enabling them to understand discussions about a wide range of issues affecting their business.

- An incisive mind that enables the heart of an issue to be identified rather than unnecessary details.

Not all leaders or managers will have all of these important characteristics. Other research is more inclined to support the view that leaders can be trained to adopt the key attributes of good leadership. Indeed, critics of trait theory argue that it ignores the impact of life's experiences on the quality of leadership.

9.3 Leadership styles

There are five distinct leadership (or management) styles.

Autocratic leaders

Autocratic leaders will take decisions on their own with no discussion. They set business objectives themselves, issue instructions to workers and check to ensure that they are carried out. Workers can become so accustomed to this style that they are dependent on their leaders for all guidance and will not show any initiative. Motivation levels are likely to be low, so supervision of employees will be essential. Managers using this style are likely to use only one-way communication – that is, they will issue instructions but will not encourage any feedback from the workforce.

This style of management does have some applications. Armed forces and the police are likely to adopt this approach, as orders may need to be issued quickly with immediate response. Also, in crises, such as an oil tanker disaster or a railway accident, leaders may have to take full charge and issue orders to reduce the unfortunate consequences of the incident. It would be inappropriate to discuss these instructions with the employees concerned before they are put into effect.

> **KEY TERM**
>
> **autocratic leadership:** a style of leadership that keeps all decision-making at the centre of the organisation

Paternalistic leaders

A **paternalistic leadership** style is a form of management whereby managers pay more attention to the social aspects of their employees; they are concerned with keeping them happy and motivated, and act as a sort of parental figure to the employees. With this leadership style, decisions are made with the best interests of the workers at heart – as perceived by the management. Feedback is invited, improving morale, but the final decisions are still taken by senior management. Employee loyalty and motivation might be higher than in cases where autocratic leadership is adopted. However, there is no true participation in management decisions and this could lead to a sense of frustration in employees especially if their feedback seems to have been ignored when important decisions are made.

Democratic leaders

Democratic leaders will engage in discussion with workers before taking decisions. Communication links will be established on the two-way principle, with every opportunity for employees to respond to and initiate discussion. Managers using this approach need good communication skills themselves to be able to explain issues clearly and to understand responses from the workforce. Full participation in the decision-making process is encouraged. This may lead to better final decisions, as the employees have much to contribute and can offer valuable work experience to new situations. In light of research by Herzberg, this style of management should improve employee motivation, as they are being given some responsibility for the objectives and strategy of the business. Workers should feel more committed to ensuring that decisions that they have influenced are put into effect successfully. However, employing the democratic approach can be a slow process, and this could make it unsuitable in certain situations.

Democratic – or participative – leadership is increasingly common for a number of reasons. Working people are better educated than ever before and have higher expectations of their experience from work – they expect complex human needs to be partly satisfied at work. Many managers have realised that the rapid pace of change at work, as a result of technological and other factors, has increased the need to consult and involve workers in the process of change. People find change less threatening and more acceptable if they have been involved in some meaningful way in managing it. Despite these factors many managers will still avoid consultation and employee participation, perhaps because they find it very difficult to adapt to these ways. Others may so doubt their own ability to discuss and persuade that they would rather issue instructions that do not allow for any feedback from employees.

Laissez-faire leadership

Laissez-faire literally means 'let them do it' – or allow workers to carry out tasks and take decisions themselves within very broad limits. This is an extreme version of democratic management. There will be very little input from management into the work to be undertaken by subordinates. This style could be particularly effective in the case of research or design teams where creativity is an important element in success. Experts in these fields often work best when they are not tightly supervised and when they are given the freedom to work on an original project. Many scientific discoveries would have been prevented if the researchers concerned had been restricted in their work by senior management. In other cases, a laissez-faire management style could be a disaster. Leaving workers to their own devices with little direction or supervision might lead to a lack of confidence, poor decisions and poor motivation as they are never sure if what they are doing is right.

Situational leaders

Situational leaders will adapt their style of leadership to the task or job that needs to be undertaken and the

---

KEY TERMS

paternalistic leadership: a type of fatherly/ motherly style typically used by dominant leaders where their power is used to control and protect subordinate employees who are expected to be loyal and obedient

democratic leadership: a leadership style that promotes the active participation of workers in taking decisions

laissez-faire leadership: a leadership style that leaves much of the business decision-making to the workforce – a 'hands-off' approach and the reverse of the autocratic style

situational leadership: effective leadership varies with the task in hand and situational leaders adapt their leadership style to each situation

CASE STUDY 9.2

Leadership styles at Fast Nuggets

Fast Nuggets, a large fast-food chain in Asia, has a reputation for cheap meals of consistent quality with rapid customer service. Surveys suggest that the public appreciate that, no matter which restaurant they are in, they can always depend on finding exactly the same range of dishes, at similar prices with the same quality standards. This reputation is built on a detailed training programme for staff – failure to pass the end-of-course test or failure to observe the methods and practices taught leads to demotion or dismissal. Every activity of the workers is laid down in company regulations. For example:

- all customers to be greeted with the same welcome

- chicken nuggets to be cooked for exactly two minutes in oil at 100°C

- a portion of French fries to contain 150 grams, to be salted with 4 grams of salt and to be kept for no more than 5 minutes before sale – after 5 minutes they would have to be disposed of

- staff to be trained to specialise in undertaking two tasks within the restaurant.

The managers at Fast Nuggets believe they have 'thought of everything' and that workers do not have to show initiative – there is a set procedure to deal with any problem.

Workers are well looked after. The pay rate per hour is competitive, there are free uniforms and staff meals, and bonus systems are paid to staff who, in the manager's view, have given the best customer service each month.

Regular meetings with staff discuss information about branch performance. They are encouraged to air their views but are told that they cannot, under any circumstances, change the method of working laid down by Fast Nuggets' head office.

Despite what the managers consider to be good working conditions, staff turnover is high, and absenteeism is a problem. Fast Nuggets' HR director has started thinking of ways to change the leadership style used in the business, especially given the opening of stores in Europe where employees in a big competitive fast-food chain are involved in the decision-making process.

1 Explain the leadership style that most closely fits Fast Nuggets. [2]

2 Analyse **one** advantage and **one** problem for Fast Nuggets of using this leadership style. [4]

3 Suggest **two** consequences for Fast Nuggets of changing its leadership style. [4]

4 To what extent might Fast Nuggets have to adapt its leadership style if it opens branches in Europe? [10]

skills and experience of the group being led. If the group contains workers who lack specific skills and are unable or unwilling to accept responsibility for the task, then a high level of directive leadership will be needed. If, however, the workers are experienced and willing and able to perform a task and take responsibility for it, then a more participative or democratic style of leadership will be appropriate.

Table 9.2 provides a summary of these five leadership styles.

Leadership style	Main features	Drawbacks	Possible applications
Autocratic	Leader takes all decisions Gives little information to employees Supervises workers closely Only one-way communication Workers are only given limited information about the business	Demotivates employees who want to contribute and accept responsibility Decisions do not benefit from employee input	Defence forces and police where quick decisions are needed and the scope for 'discussion' must be limited In times of crisis when decisive action might be needed to limit damage to the business or danger to others
Paternalistic	Strong 'parent-like' figure takes key decisions but in interests of employees Some feedback and consultation encouraged – but not participative decision-making	Low employee motivation if loyal connection to leader is not established Increasing dependency of employees on the leader, leading to more supervision being required Employee dissatisfaction if bad decisions are made	Family-owned businesses where leaders still want to take decisions themselves but value employee loyalty and low labour turnover In a business with a formal and hierarchical structure where creative thinking is not required of employees
Democratic	Participation encouraged Two-way communication used, which allows feedback from employees Workers given information about the business to allow full employee involvement	Consultation with employees can be time-consuming On occasions, quick decision-making will be required Level of involvement – some issues might be too sensitive, e.g., job losses, or too secret, e.g., development of new products	Most likely to be useful in businesses that expect workers to contribute fully to the production and decision-making processes, thereby satisfying their complex human needs An experienced and flexible workforce will be likely to benefit most from this style In situations that demand a new way of thinking or a new solution, then workforce input can be very valuable
Laissez-faire	Managers delegate virtually all authority and decision-making powers Very broad criteria or limits might be established for the employees to work within	Workers may not appreciate the lack of structure and direction in their work – this could lead to a loss of security Lack of feedback – as managers will not be closely monitoring progress – may be demotivating	When managers are too busy (or too lazy) to intervene May be appropriate in research institutions where experts are more likely to arrive at solutions when not constrained by narrow rules or management controls

Leadership style	Main features	Drawbacks	Possible applications
Situational	Style of leadership used will depend on the nature of the task and the work group's skills and willingness to accept responsibility	Varying the style of leadership may be difficult for some workers to accept and they may become uncertain of how they will be led in different situations	By allowing flexibility of leadership style, different leadership approaches can be used in different situations and with different groups of people

Table 9.2: Summary of leadership styles

Effectiveness of leadership styles

There is no single leadership style which is best in all circumstances and for all businesses. The most appropriate style used will depend on many factors, including:

- the training and experience of the workforce and the degree of responsibility that they are prepared to take on

- the amount of time available for consultation and participation

- the management culture and business background of the managers, e.g., whether they have always worked in an autocratically run organisation

- personality of managers – do they have the confidence and strength of character to lead by persuading and motivating people to follow them or must they hide behind the authority of their role to dictate what needs to be done?

- the importance of the issue – different styles may be used in the same business in different situations; if there is great risk to the business when a poor or slow decision is taken, then it is more likely that management will make the choice in an autocratic way.

ACTIVITY 9.2

1 Identify all the roles of your business teacher as a manager in your IB Business class. Prepare a poster with these roles.

2 How important are leadership skills for teachers? Discuss in class.

ACTIVITY 9.3

Mary Barra is Chair and Chief Executive Officer of General Motors. She was elected Chair of the GM Board of Directors on Jan. 4, 2016, and has served as CEO of GM since Jan. 15, 2014. She is focused on improving the customer experience and strengthening GM's core vehicle and services business, while also working to lead the transformation of personal mobility through advanced technologies like connectivity, electrification and autonomous driving.

Mary Barra is described as an 'inclusive' leader. Do your own research about 'inclusive leadership' and how Mary Barra applies this leadership style in GM. Do you think this leadership style is effective in a huge car manufacturing company like GM? Discuss in class.

CASE STUDY 9.3

Waves nonprofit needs a new CEO

Waves is a philanthropic non-profit organisation dedicated to building a fair world for everyone.

The mission of Waves is to 'accelerate social change, by solving society's biggest problems'.

Waves is currently dealing with the recruitment of a new CEO to bring strategic and inspiring leadership. As a champion of social justice, philanthropy, inclusion and innovation this individual will ensure that the staff and partners are guided with respect and support and are encouraged to participate in the decision-making process. The CEO reports to the board of directors and has overall responsibility for managing strategic, financial and management operations. As a senior manager, the new CEO must ensure that Waves will have enough income from donations to cover both its costs and its philanthropic goals. They will also be responsible for organising meetings across all departments to ensure enough resources are available to guarantee operations and will coordinate activities to embed a 'common sense of purpose'.

The new CEO is expected to manage a change within the organisation to improve efficiency in communication. Waves has become quite tall and

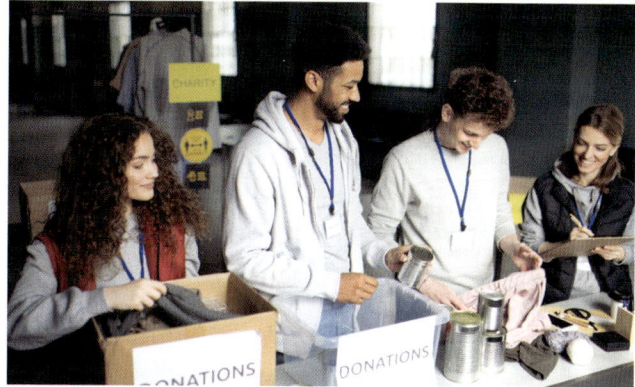

bureaucratic, and the organisational structure is characterised by various stakeholders as being 'too hierarchical'.

1   Define the term 'recruitment'. [2]

2   Identify the leadership style that the new CEO is expected to adopt. [2]

3   Suggest **two** methods that the new CEO could implement to improve efficiency in communication at Waves. [2]

4   Compare and contrast the role of the new CEO as a leader and their role as a manager at Waves. [10]

THEORY OF KNOWLEDGE

Knowledge question: Is leadership without ethics really leadership?

Leaders set a vision in their organisations and inspire people towards a given direction. But do leaders need to apply ethics in their effort to motivate employees to reach goals? Is 'morality' a necessary element of leadership?

For example, a leader in a top car manufacturing business is excellent at promoting strategic thinking and innovation at the workplace. They have set a clear vision for global market leadership for their organisation and take action to make this a reality by investing in electric mobility and

self-driving technology. Their team is inspired by their commitment to success. But the leader is not prioritising ethics in their agenda. They do not recognise the emotions of their subordinates and they are not open and honest in their communication. Employees who struggle with personal problems and underperform are typically degraded, or even dismissed. Productivity has been prioritised in the business over the welfare of employees.

Is the person described above a real leader or just a person in a position of power, manipulating and exploiting employees to accomplish a set of goals? Discuss in class.

SELF-EVALUATION CHECKLIST

After studying this chapter, complete this table.

I am able to analyse and apply the:	Needs more work	Almost there	Ready to move on
scientific and intuitive thinking/management (AO2)			
management and leadership (AO2)			
I am able to synthesise and evaluate:			
the following leadership styles: • autocratic • paternalistic • democratic • laissez-faire • situational (AO3)			

REFLECTION

Suggest five qualities that you think effective managers should have. To what extent do you think you have these qualities? How do you know that you have them? Ask another learner whether they agree with your assessment of your management qualities.

PROJECT

1 Split into four groups. Each group should research one of the following social entrepreneurs:
- Muhammad Yunus
- Jazzmine Raine
- Blake Mycoskie
- Trinity Heavenz.

2 Prepare a presentation for each of the social entrepreneurs above, including the following:
- a brief presentation of their goals and how they try to achieve them
- the leadership traits, skills and approaches that help them to pursue their goals
- an evaluation of their social impact.

3 After watching all four presentations in class, discuss the following:
- Are there any similarities in the leadership characteristics of the four social entrepreneurs? What motivates them to pursue social goals? Do you think that social leaders are different from the leaders of for-profit businesses and, if yes, in what way?

Thinking about your project:
- When evaluating the social impact of the social entrepreneurs, did you search for any criticism about their activities or leadership approaches?

EXAM-STYLE QUESTIONS

Catering at Le Menu

Le Menu is a catering company that was founded by brothers Oscar and Pierre Decaux. The business specialises in providing high-quality catering for corporate hospitality and private clients. This is a high-pressure operation. A client company will, for example, hire Le Menu to cater for 200 guests at a race meeting. This will involve setting up a mobile kitchen at the racecourse the day before the event and then producing 200 five-course meals, along with canapés and drinks on the day.

Apart from Oscar and Pierre, the business has four other permanent staff including a head chef, an assistant chef, an administrative assistant and a driver. When Le Menu is catering a large function, such as the racecourse event, it hires temporary staff from an agency. Some of the temporary staff will have worked for Le Menu regularly, but often there will be new staff as well.

Oscar is a tough, direct manager, who believes in scientific thinking and collects data on the productivity of workers before making decisions related to human resource planning. He tells workers exactly what he wants and then expects them always to meet his high standards. If they do not, he is quick to let them know; he has a reputation for dismissing temporary workers part-way through an event.

Pierre is much calmer, prefers to consult with his staff and tends to make decisions based on intuition. While Oscar takes the lead during events, Pierre is more involved with strategy. Pierre will, for example, work with Le Menu's chefs on the type of food to prepare for an event. He often allows chefs to make decisions without consulting him. He knows that in some cases chefs know better than him what to do, as they have a great deal of experience in the market.

Le Menu currently faces two major problems:

- It struggles to recruit agency staff because temporary workers do not like Oscar's management.
- Some customers have commented that employees seem too distant, too stressed and too overworked.

Le Menu has never received complaints about the quality of the food. On the contrary, in a consumer survey organised by Oscar, the menu was rated as 'superior and creative'.

Pierre suggested that Oscar should adopt a more democratic approach in leadership to solve the problems of Le Menu. Oscar disagrees. He believes democratic leadership is not suitable when employing temporary workers.

1   Define the term 'scientific thinking'. [2]
2   Define the term 'human resource planning'. [2]
3   Suggest **one** advantage and **one** disadvantage for Le Menu of the fact that Oscar takes decisions in HR planning based on scientific thinking. [4]
4   Identify the leadership style that describes Oscar's leadership approach. [2]
5   Identify the leadership style that describes Pierre's leadership approach. [2]
6   Suggest **one** advantage and **one** disadvantage of the leadership approach applied by Pierre with his chefs. [4]
7   Using appropriate motivation theory, suggest **one** positive and **one** negative effect on the motivation of workers at Le Menu, resulting from the leadership approach of the two owners. [4]
8   Explain **two** reasons why Oscar thinks that democratic leadership might not be appropriate when employing temporary workers. [4]
9   Suggest **one** advantage and **one** disadvantage from intuitive decision-making applied by Pierre. [4]
10 Discuss Pierre's suggestion to Oscar as a solution for the problems of Le Menu. [10]

Chapter 10

Motivation and demotivation

LEARNING OBJECTIVES

On completing this chapter you should be able to:

Apply and analyse:

> Labour turnover (AO2)

> The following types of appraisal: formative; summative; 360-degree feedback; self-appraisal (AO2)

> Methods of recruitment (AO2)

- The following types of financial rewards: salary, wages (time and piece rates), commission, performance-related pay (PRP), profit-related pay, employee share ownership schemes (AO2)
- The following types of non-financial rewards: job enrichment, job rotation, job enlargement, empowerment, purpose/the opportunity to make a difference, teamwork (AO2)
- The following types of training: induction, on the job, off the job (AO2)

Synthesise and evaluate:

- The following motivation theories: Taylor; Maslow; Herzberg (motivation-hygiene theory) (AO3)

> The following motivation theories: McClelland's acquired needs theory; Deci and Ryan's self-determination theory; equity and expectancy theory (AO3)

> Internal and external recruitment (AO3)

CONTINUED

Use and apply:

> Labour turnover (AO4)

BUSINESS IN CONTEXT

Motivating employees in different countries

What encourages people to work hard and be happy to stay with their existing employer? Is giving higher pay the best way to motivate?

Many studies have been undertaken to try to explain what motivates workers. Most agree that 'just paying workers more' is not necessarily the best way of motivating them. Researchers have established that workers from different countries have different needs and respond to different motivational factors. Understanding these different needs is vital for businesses such as multinational corporations that employ ethnically and culturally diverse workers.

Employees from different countries have different views on what is needed to achieve 'job satisfaction'. It has been claimed that workers in Thailand will not respond to bonus systems based on a worker's own achievements as this reduces the strength of the team. Some researchers have suggested that Chinese, Israeli and Korean employees believe that 'a sense of achievement at work' is the most important factor as it can bring great 'self-fulfilment'. However, for employees from a German, Dutch or American cultural background, 'the fun of work' is the most important motivating factor.

Japanese enterprises tend to show their recognition of employees through medals, attention and applause. Some Japanese employees may even be angry when they receive financial bonuses. This kind of reward means that they have to work harder to get material rewards in future. Japanese companies focus on overall goals of the team or the enterprise, while US-owned businesses usually focus on individual goals, achievements and material rewards.

Even with these cultural differences, researchers agree that all business managers can improve worker motivation by showing more recognition for the work and achievements of their employees – and not just through higher pay.

Discuss in pairs or in a group:

- What needs do people try to satisfy from work?
- Why is it important for businesses with employees from many different countries to be aware of their different needs?
- Why do you think 'recognition' is important to employees? Is it important to you?

KEY CONCEPT LINK

Creativity

Creativity is affected greatly by motivation. Research across different industries shows the level of interest and satisfaction that people get from work determines their ability to innovate. Challenging work may lead to higher levels of creativity than a well-paying but repetitive and boring job. However, is it ethical for a business to reduce the financial rewards offered to an employee in exchange for a more challenging work?

10.1 Motivation theories

Well-motivated workers will help an organisation to achieve its objectives as cost-effectively as possible. Motivated workers will also try to reach their own personal goals by satisfying their own needs. Employers need to be aware of **extrinsic motivation** and needs, such as pay, which can provide **motivation** even if the job itself does not. **Intrinsic motivation** stems from the nature of the job itself, but this does not mean that employers can pay workers doing interesting work nothing at all! Some rewards will be needed even for workers driven by the fulfilment of intrinsic needs.

Unmotivated or demotivated employees will not perform effectively, offering only the minimum of what is expected. Motivation levels have a direct impact on productivity levels and the competitiveness of the business – highly motivated workers have high productivity and this reduces unit costs. Motivated employees will be keen to stay with the firm, reducing the costs of **labour turnover**. They will be more likely to offer useful suggestions and to contribute in ways other than their contractual obligations. They will often actively seek promotion and responsibility. In contrast, some indicators of poor employee motivation are shown in Table 10.1.

Many social psychologists and behavourial scientists have developed theories, as a result of research, into the factors most likely to lead to motivated employees or – in contrast – most likely to demotivate them if they are not present.

Indicator	Explanation
Absenteeism	Deliberate absence for which there is not a satisfactory explanation; often follows a pattern
Lateness	Often becomes habitual
Poor performance	Poor-quality work; low levels of work or greater waste of materials
Accidents	Poorly motivated workers are often more careless, concentrate less on their work or distract others, and this increases the likelihood of accidents
Labour turnover	People leave for reasons that are not positive; even if they do not get other jobs, they spend time trying to do so
Grievances	There are more complaints raised within the workforce and there might be more union disputes
Poor response rate	Workers do not respond well to orders or leadership and any response is often slow

Table 10.1: Some indicators of poor employee motivation

F. W. Taylor and scientific management

Taylor made the first serious attempt to analyse worker motivation. He aimed to advise management on the best ways to increase worker performance and productivity. The techniques he used – of establishing an idea or hypothesis, studying and recording performance at work, altering working methods and re-recording performance – are still used in modern industry. This approach has become known as 'scientific management' due to the detailed recording and analysis of results that it involves.

Taylor's main aim was to reduce the level of inefficiency that existed in the US manufacturing industry. Any productivity gains could then, he argued, be shared between business owners and workers. The scope for efficiency gains in early 20th-century manufacturing plants was huge. Most workers were untrained and non-specialised. They were poorly led by supervisors and managers with little or no formal **training** in dealing with people. There was usually no formal selection or appraisal system of employees and many were recruited on a daily or weekly basis with no security of employment.

> ### KEY TERMS
>
> **extrinsic motivation:** comes from external rewards associated with working on a task, for example pay and other benefits
>
> **motivation:** the factors that stimulate people to take actions that lead to the achievement of a goal
>
> **intrinsic motivation:** comes from the satisfaction derived from working on and completing a task
>
> **labour turnover:** measures the rate at which employees are leaving an organisation
>
> **training:** work-related education to increase workforce skills and efficiency

How to improve worker productivity

Taylor's scientific approach identified seven steps to improving worker productivity:

1 Select workers to perform a task.
2 Observe them performing the task and note the key elements of it.
3 Record the time taken to do each part of the task.
4 Identify the quickest method recorded.
5 Train all workers in the quickest method and do not allow them to make any changes to it.
6 Supervise workers to ensure that this 'best way' is being carried out and time them to check that the set time is not being exceeded.
7 Pay workers on the basis of results – based on the theory of 'economic man'.

Taylor believed in the theory of 'economic man', which stated that humans were driven or motivated by money alone and the only factor that could stimulate further effort was the chance of earning extra money. This formed the basis of Taylor's main motivational suggestion – wage levels based on output. He always maintained that workers should be paid a 'fair day's pay for a fair day's work' and that the amount should be directly linked to output through a system known as '**piece rate**'. This means paying workers a certain amount for each unit produced. To encourage high output a low rate per unit can be set for the first units produced and then higher rates become payable if output targets are exceeded. Table 10.2 summarises the relevance of Taylor's approach to modern industry and identifies its limitations.

> ### KEY TERM
>
> **piece rate:** a payment to a worker for each unit produced

Taylor's approach	Relevance to modern industry	Limitations
Economic man	Some managers still believe that money is the only way to motivate employees.	Workers have a wide range of needs, not just extrinsic needs of money, which can be met, in part at least, from work.
Select the right people for each job	Before Taylor, there had been few attempts to identify the principles of employee selection. The importance he gave to this is still reflected in the significance given to careful employee selection in nearly all businesses.	This requires an appropriate selection procedure.
Observe and record the performance of employees	This was widely adopted and became known as 'time and motion study'. It is still employed but often with the cooperation and involvement of employees.	Taylor's autocratic use of this technique was regarded with suspicion among workers who saw it as a way of making them work harder.
Establish the best method of doing a job – method study	This is still accepted as being important as efficiency depends on the best ways of working being adopted.	The Taylor approach, which involved giving instructions to workers with no discussion or feedback, is considered undesirable. Worker participation in devising best work practices is now encouraged.
Piece-rate payment systems – to maximise output through motivating workers to produce more	This is often of limited relevance as it has become difficult to identify the output of each worker.	This is not now widely used. Quality may be sacrificed in the pursuit of quantity – workers will vary output according to their financial needs and it discourages them from accepting changes at work in case they lose pay. In most modern industries, especially service industries, it has become very difficult to identify the output of individual workers.

Table 10.2: Evaluation of how relevant Taylor's views and methods are today

Maslow's hierarchy of human needs

Abraham Maslow's research was not based solely on people in the work environment and his findings have significance for students of psychology and sociology too. He was concerned with trying to identify and classify the main needs that humans have. Our needs determine our actions – we will always try to satisfy them and we will be motivated to do so. If work can be organised so that we can satisfy some or all of our needs at work, then we will become more productive and satisfied. Maslow summarised these human needs in the form of a hierarchy – see Figure 10.1 and Table 10.3.

This hierarchy was interpreted by Maslow as follows:

- Individuals' needs start on the lowest level.
- Once one level of need has been satisfied, humans will strive to achieve the next level.
- **Self-actualisation** is not reached by many people, but everyone is capable of reaching their potential.
- Once a need has been satisfied, it will no longer motivate individuals to action – thus, when material needs have been satisfied, the offer of more money will not increase productivity.

- Reversion is possible – it is possible for satisfaction at one level to be withdrawn, e.g., a loss of job security, and for individuals to move down a level.

Limitations of Maslow's approach

Criticism of Maslow's hierarchy includes:

- Not everyone has the same needs as are assumed by the hierarchy.
- In practice it can be very difficult to identify the degree to which each need has been met and which level a worker is at.
- Money is necessary to satisfy physical needs, yet it might also play a role in satisfying the other levels of needs, such as status and esteem.
- Self-actualisation is never permanently achieved – as some observers of the hierarchy have suggested. Jobs must continually offer challenges and opportunities for fulfilment, otherwise regression will occur.

> **KEY TERM**
>
> **self-actualisation:** a sense of self-fulfilment reached by feeling enriched and developed by what a person has learnt and achieved

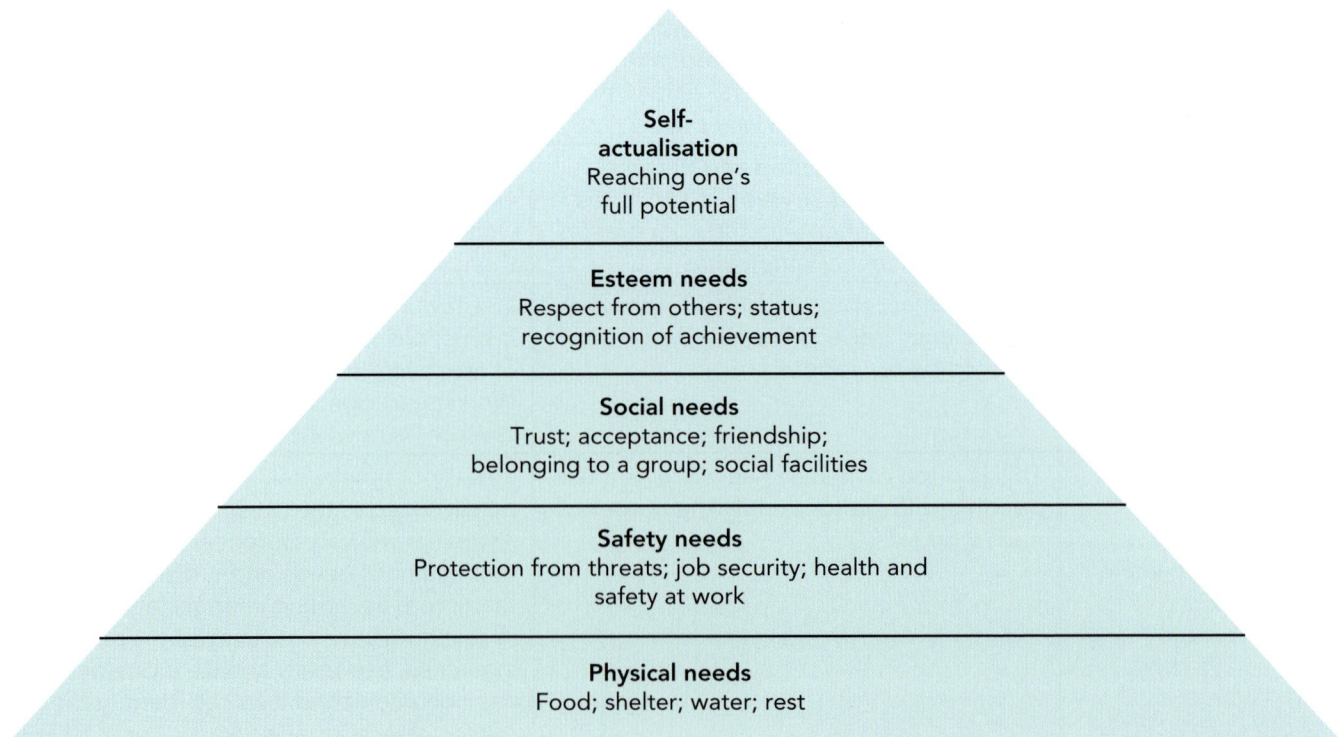

Figure 10.1: Maslow's hierarchy of needs

Level of need	Business conditions which could allow for the needs to be met
Self-actualisation – fulfilment of potential	Challenging work that stretches the individual – this will give a sense of achievement. Opportunities to develop and apply new skills will increase potential.
Esteem needs	Recognition for work done well – status, advancement and responsibility will gain the respect of others.
Social needs	Working in teams or groups and ensuring good communication to make workers feel involved.
Safety needs	A contract of employment with some job security – a structured organisation that gives clear lines of authority to reduce uncertainty. Ensuring health and safety conditions are met.
Physical needs	Income from employment high enough to meet essential needs.

Table 10.3: Significance of the hierarchy of needs to business

---

CASE STUDY 10.1

Piece rates at FreshF

Eva and Mary have set up FreshF Ltd, producing and selling organic food products and beverages in Brazil. With the industry sales being at least 55% higher than other countries in Latin America and growing fast, the market outlook for FreshF is excellent.

FreshF employs many manual workers who produce handmade food products, and offers them piece rate pay. This payment system allows the business to observe and reward the employees based on their performance. According to Eva's perspective, which is in line with Taylor's approach to motivation, workers are expected to work hard in their effort to maximise their daily pay. This is very important for FreshF, which faces increasing demand.

But Mary has observed some quality problems. Some workers, in their effort to increase the quantity produced sacrifice the quality of the meals prepared. Moreover, she is worried by the fact that two of FreshF's best employees recently resigned. They complained that Eva had an autocratic approach in the way she supervised them and showed them no respect.

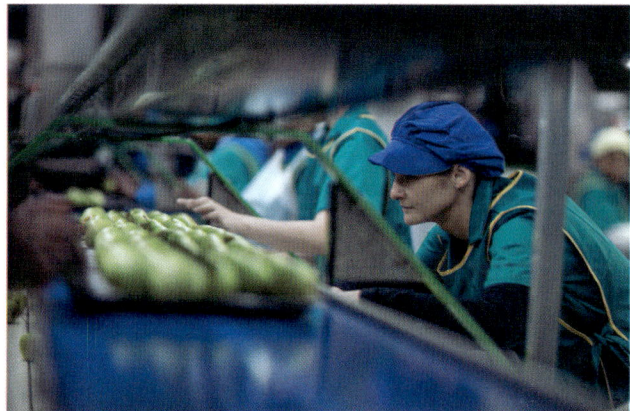

1   Define the term 'piece rate'. [2]

2   Identify **one** advantage and **one** disadvantage for FreshF adopting Taylor's approach to motivation. [4]

3   Use Maslows' motivation theory to suggest **one** reason why FreshF's employees resigned. [4]

4   Discuss the appropriateness of Taylor's approach to motivation for a contemporary business such as FreshF. [10]

Herzberg and the 'two-factor theory'

Despite basing his research on just 200 professionally qualified workers, Herzberg's conclusions and famous two-factor theory have had the greatest impact on motivational practices since Taylor's work almost 60 years earlier. Herzberg used worker questionnaires to discover:

- those factors that led to them having very good feelings about their jobs
- those factors that led to them having very negative feelings about their jobs.

These were his conclusions:

- Job satisfaction resulted from five main factors – achievement, recognition for achievement, the work itself, responsibility and advancement. He called these factors the '**motivators**'. He considered the last three to be the most significant.
- Job dissatisfaction also resulted from five main factors – company policy and administration, supervision, salary, relationships with others and working conditions. He termed these '**hygiene factors**'. These factors surround the job itself (extrinsic factors) rather than the work (intrinsic factors). Herzberg considered that the hygiene factors had to be addressed by management to

prevent dissatisfaction, but even if they were in place, they would not, by themselves, create a well-motivated workforce. (see Figure 10.2).

Consequences of Herzberg's theory

- Pay and working conditions can be improved and these will help to remove dissatisfaction about work; but they will not, on their own, provide conditions for motivation to exist. Herzberg argued that it was possible to encourage someone to do a job by paying them – he called this 'movement'. However, movement does not mean that someone wants to do the job – that would require motivation. Motivation to do the job, and to do it well, would only exist if the motivators were

> ### KEY TERMS
>
> **motivating factors (motivators):** aspects of a worker's job that can lead to positive job satisfaction, such as achievement, recognition, meaningful and interesting work and advancement at work
>
> **hygiene factors:** aspects of a worker's job that have the potential to cause dissatisfaction, such as pay, working conditions, status and over-supervision by managers

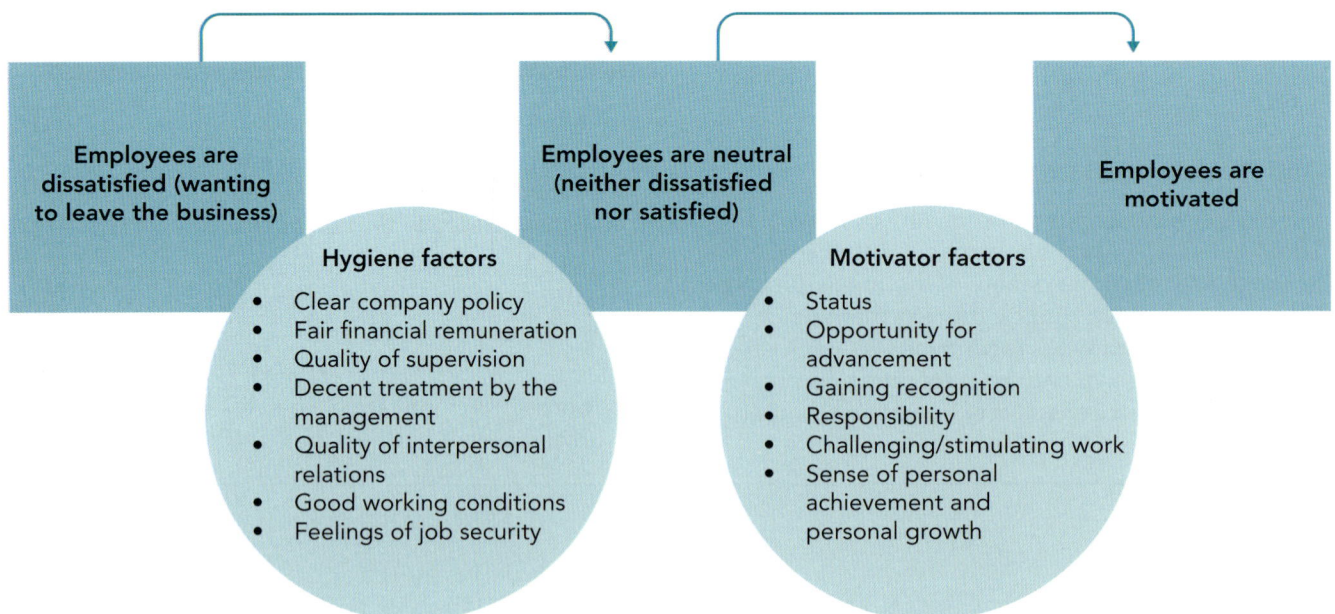

Employees are dissatisfied (wanting to leave the business)

Employees are neutral (neither dissatisfied nor satisfied)

Employees are motivated

Hygiene factors
- Clear company policy
- Fair financial remuneration
- Quality of supervision
- Decent treatment by the management
- Quality of interpersonal relations
- Good working conditions
- Feelings of job security

Motivator factors
- Status
- Opportunity for advancement
- Gaining recognition
- Responsibility
- Challenging/stimulating work
- Sense of personal achievement and personal growth

Figure 10.2: Herzberg's hygiene and motivator factors

in place. Herzberg did not claim that pay did not matter, but that it moves people to do a job and does not motivate them to do it well.

- The motivators need to be in place for workers to be prepared to work willingly and always to give their best. Herzberg suggested that motivators could be provided by adopting the principles of 'job enrichment'. There are three main features of job enrichment:

  - Assign workers complete units of work – typical mass-production methods leave workers to assemble one small part of the finished product. This is not rewarding, can be boring and repetitive and prevents the worker from appreciating the importance of what they are doing as part of the overall production system. Herzberg argued that complete and identifiable units of work should be assigned to workers, and that this might involve teams of workers rather than individuals on their own.

These complete units of work could be whole sub-assemblies of manufactured goods, such as a complete engine assembly in a car plant. In service industries it could mean that a small team of multi-skilled people, such as waiters, chefs and technicians for IT/video equipment, provide all of the conference facilities in a hotel for a business conference rather than many people doing just one small and relatively unimportant task before moving on to another part of the hotel. 'If you want people motivated to do a good job, give them a good job to do,' said Herzberg.

> ### KEY TERM
>
> **job enrichment:** aims to use the full capabilities of workers by giving them the opportunity to do more challenging and fulfilling work

CASE STUDY 10.2

High labour turnover in trucking and warehousing

We live in an e-commerce world. People order a huge variety of goods online, and these must be transported and delivered on time. While engineers are looking for automation solutions to increase efficiency in the trucking and warehousing industry, employees suffer from job insecurity. Companies in this industry are facing increasing competition and try hard to cut costs. Workers around the globe are complaining about bad working conditions, as the industry adopts an 'expendable workforce' mindset. Workers are typically offered only part-time or temporary employment contracts and low wages. This has led to high labour turnover in the industry in most countries around the world.

CleverLog is a startup business in Singapore, offering trucking and warehousing services to big customers. Cheng, the founder and CEO of CleverLog, wants to keep the labour turnover low in his business. He tries to boost motivation in the business by offering wages that are higher than the industry average. He also tries to make the manual jobs more interesting, mainly through job rotation. However, he is worried about the effect of his decision on the profitability and competitiveness of his business.

1   Define the term 'motivation'.   [2]

2   Using Herzberg's theory of motivation, explain **two** hygiene factors that lead to job dissatisfaction and high labour turnover in the trucking and warehousing industries.   [4]

3   Suggest one advantage and one disadvantage of using job rotation as a method to increase motivation at CleverLog.   [4]

4   Discuss the importance of employee motivation for a business such as CleverLog.   [10]

ACTIVITY 10.1

Having studied computer science at university, Carla could not wait to find her first full-time job. She was recruited by a software developing business. Initially, she was very excited. Her first salary allowed her to share an apartment with a friend and to pay most of her bills. She met many other computer professionals and enjoyed the social life around her new job. However, her manager was rather autocratic and unappreciative. She instructed Carla to do her work exactly as told and was not open to new ideas. Carla found the job to be repetitive and boring. The lack of challenge and the bad treatment by the management made Carla want to leave her job just two years after she got it.

1   Split in two groups.

- **Group 1:** Apply Maslow's Theory to explain Carla's demotivation two years after she was recruited.

- **Group 2:** Apply Herzberg's Theory to explain Carla's job dissatisfaction two years after she was recruited.

2   What are the similarities and what are the differences between the two approaches to motivation observed by the two groups? Discuss.

Reflection

- **Group 1:** While answering question 1, have you clearly identified the level of Maslow's hierarchy on which Carla seems to be standing?

- **Group 2:** While answering question 1, have you clearly distinguished the 'hygiene' factors from the 'motivator' factors affecting Carla's job satisfaction?

CASE STUDY 10.3

Teamwork at Puerto Rico's Fantasy

Alondra is a young entrepreneur and chef who has opened Puerto Rico's Fantasy, a new luxury restaurant in a business area in Puerto Rico. Her start-up was a big success. Consumers enjoy the quality of food and the excellent service. Alondra believes that her success is the result of strong teamworking among her employees. Her ten employees have become close friends and enjoy working together. This improves their productivity and creativity, leading to excellent customer ratings.

As Puerto Rico's Fantasy enjoys increasing demand, Alondra is ready to buy the premises next to her current business to increase her capacity. But she is worried about how new employees would fit the established team, as they might feel left out. Also, she knows that teamworking might not be enough to motivate her employees after the

business grows. She is now thinking of possibilities for job enrichment for at least four of her most talented workers.

1   Define the term 'job enrichment'. [2]

2   Suggest **one** advantage and **one** disadvantage of teamworking as a method used to motivate employees at Puerto Rico's Fantasy. [4]

3   Suggest **two** methods of intrinsic motivation, other than job enrichment and team working, that could be used to motivate employees at Puerto Rico's Fantasy. [4]

4   Evaluate 'job enrichment' as a method to motivate employees at a restaurant such as Puerto Rico's Fantasy. [10]

- Provide feedback on performance – this type of communication could give recognition for work well done and could provide incentives to achieve even more.

- Give workers a range of tasks – to challenge and stretch the individual, a range of tasks should be given, some of which may be, at least initially, beyond the workers' current experience. This, in quite a large measure, ties in with the 'self-actualisation' level in Maslow's hierarchy.

- A business could offer higher pay, improved working conditions and less heavy-handed supervision of work. These would all help to remove dissatisfaction, but they would all be quickly taken for granted. If work is not interesting, rewarding or challenging, then workers will not be satisfied or will not be motivated to offer their full potential whatever the pay level offered to them.

Evaluation of Herzberg's work

- Team working is now much more widespread as a consequence of Herzberg's findings, with whole units of work being delegated to these groups.

- Workers tend to be made much more responsible for the quality of their own work rather than being closely supervised by a quality-controlling inspectorate.

- Most firms are continually looking for ways to improve effective communication, and group meetings allowing two-way communication are often favoured.

	Taylor	Maslow	Herzberg
Basic assumptions	Work is unpleasant Workers are rational Managers need to only supervise workers who should not be trusted	Human needs are classified in a pyramid containing: physiological needs; safety needs; social needs; esteem needs; self-actualisation.	Factors affecting the morale of the employees are classified in two factors: a) hygiene factors b) motivator factors
Motivational factors	Financial rewards	Fulfilling each level of needs according to the pyramid	Provide adequate hygiene factors so that employees are not dissatisfied. Offer motivator factors to motivate them
Main limitations of the theories	Differences among individuals are not recognised Money is not the only motivator The role of the managers as cold-hearted supervisors	It is complicated to apply Employees needs differ (may be on different 'levels') so trying to satisfy all workers is difficult Each individual responds differently to different needs	Assumes that increasing job satisfaction of employees will always lead to increased productivity
Examples of practical tools for managers to apply	All types of financial rewards, primarily piece rates but also time rates, commission, profit-related pay, performance-related pay, share ownership schemes and fringe benefits	Managers should focus on identifying the needs of each employee and make appropriate opportunities for them to satisfy these needs at work; adequate pay and job security essential starting points	Non-financial rewards such as job enlargement, job enrichment, job rotation, promotion, recognition, empowerment, team working training

Table 10.4: Summary of the key motivation theories (SL and HL)

10.2 Further motivation theories

McClelland and acquired needs theory

David McClelland pioneered workplace motivational thinking, developed an achievement-based motivational theory and promoted improvements in employee assessment methods. He is best known for describing three types of acquired motivational need, which he identified in his book *The Achieving Society* (1961).

- **Achievement motivation:** A person with the strong motivational need for achievement will seek to reach realistic and challenging goals and job advancement. There is a constant need for feedback regarding progress and achievement. This helps to provide a sense of accomplishment. Research suggests that this result-driven attitude is almost always a common characteristic of successful business people and entrepreneurs.

- **Authority/power motivation:** A person with this dominant need is motivated by having authority. The desire to control others is a powerful motivating force. This includes the need to be influential, to be effective and to make an impact. Such a person has a strong leadership instinct, and when they have authority over others they value the personal status and prestige gained.

- **Affiliation motivation:** A person whose strongest motivator is the need for affiliation has a need for friendly relationships and is motivated by interaction with other people. These people tend to be good team members as they need to be liked, popular and held in high regard.

McClelland stated that these three motivational needs are found to varying degrees in all workers and managers. The mix of needs characterises a worker's or manager's behaviour, both in terms of what motivates them and how they believe other people should be motivated.

The acquired-needs theory does not claim that people can be precisely classified into one of three types. Instead, an individual's balance of these needs forms a psychological profile that can be useful in creating a tailored motivational strategy for them. McClelland stressed that it is important to note that needs do not necessarily correlate with an individual's competencies. It is possible, for example, for an employee to be strongly affiliation motivated but still be successful in a situation in which affiliation needs are not met.

McClelland suggested that those in top management positions generally have a high need for power and a low need for affiliation. He also believed that although individuals with a need for achievement can make good managers, they are not generally suited to being in top management positions. He believed that achievement-motivated people are generally the ones who make things happen and get results. However, they can demand too much of their subordinate employees in the achievement of targets and prioritise this above the many and varied needs of their workers.

Deci and Ryan's self-determination theory

Self-determination is a theory of human motivation developed by psychologists Edward Deci and Richard Ryan. The theory looks at the inherent, positive human tendency to move towards self-development and growth. It outlines three core needs which facilitate that growth. Those needs are competence, autonomy and relatedness.

- **Competence:** The need to experience that our behaviour and performance at work are of a high standard.

- **Autonomy:** The need to experience behaviour as voluntary and to feel that we have control over what tasks we perform.

- **Relatedness:** The need to interact and be connected to others. This could involve having meaningful relationships and interactions with other people.

Self-determination outlines the two types of motivation (intrinsic and extrinsic) that were considered in section 10.1. The three needs promote intrinsic motivation. This type of motivation encourages us to behave in a certain way for its own sake because it is inherently satisfying or inwardly rewarding. The natural human tendency to move towards growth or self-fulfilment is, essentially, intrinsic motivation.

There are two key assumptions of the self-determination theory:

- The need for personal growth drives behaviour. People are naturally actively directed towards growth. Gaining mastery over new challenges and accepting new experiences are essential for developing a sense of self-fulfilment.

- Autonomous motivation is important. While people are often motivated to act by external rewards such as money, bonuses and fringe benefits, self-determination theory focuses primarily on internal sources of motivation such as a need to gain knowledge or independence, i.e., intrinsic motivation.

Deci and Ryan stress that it is important to realise that the psychological growth described by self-determination theory does not happen automatically. While people might be oriented toward such growth, it requires continual support in a business context by appropriate reward systems. For example:

- **Extrinsic motivators can lead to reduced self-determination.** According to Deci and Ryan, if managers continually focus on giving employees extrinsic rewards for intrinsically motivated behaviour, then autonomy can be undermined. As the behaviour becomes increasingly controlled by external rewards, employees may consider that they are less in control of their own behaviour and intrinsic motivation is reduced.

- **Positive feedback can boost self-determination.** Deci and Ryan also suggest that offering unexpected positive encouragement and feedback on an employee's performance can increase intrinsic motivation. This type of feedback helps workers to feel more competent, which is one of the key needs for personal growth.

Vroom and expectancy theory

Victor Vroom suggested that individuals choose to behave in ways which they believe will lead to results that they value. His expectancy theory states that individuals have different sets of goals. They can be motivated if they believe that:

- there is a positive link between effort and performance
- favourable performance will result in a desirable reward
- the reward will satisfy an important need
- the desire to satisfy the need is strong enough to make the work effort worthwhile.

His expectancy theory is based on the following three beliefs:

- Valence: the depth of the desire of an employee for an extrinsic reward, such as money, or an intrinsic reward, such as satisfaction.

- Expectancy: the degree to which people believe that putting effort into work will lead to a given level of performance.

- Instrumentality: the confidence of employees that they will actually get what they desire, even if it has been promised by the manager.

Vroom argued that if even one of these conditions or beliefs is missing, workers will not have the motivation to do the job well. Therefore, according to Vroom, managers should try to ensure that employees believe that increased work effort will improve performance and that this performance will lead to valued rewards.

> **TIP**
>
> if you are answering a question about motivational theorists, try to do more than just list their main findings. It is much better to apply their ideas to the business situation given.

John Adams and equity theory

John Adams' equity theory is built on the belief that employees become demotivated towards their jobs and employer if they feel that their inputs are greater than their outputs. Inputs include effort, loyalty, commitment and skill. Outputs include financial rewards, recognition, security and sense of achievement.

While many of these factors cannot be quantified, Adams argued that employers should attempt to achieve a fair balance between what the employee gives an organisation and what they receive in return. If workers consider that their inputs are greater than the outputs received, they will move to try to redress this imbalance. When a balance is reached, then employees will consider their treatment to be fair and will respond with positive attitudes and high levels of motivation (see Figure 10.3).

The key difference between expectancy theory and equity theory

According to expectancy theory, employees may perform effectively at work in exchange for rewards based on their clear expectations. So, the argument goes, an employee will exert more effort when they believe that their increased effort will result in a positive reward. For instance, if an employee believes they will receive a pay raise or a promotion if they have a very good performance appraisal, they will be motivated to improve

Figure 10.3: Adam's equity theory of motivation

their overall job performance. However, if the employee receives no reward following a positive appraisal, they will be demotivated to continue working at a higher level.

Equity theory suggests that employees are more likely to derive job satisfaction by comparing their effort and reward ratio with that of others and analysing whether equity exists. It recognises that individuals are concerned with both the absolute amount of rewards and the relationship of that amount to what others receive. Employees compare their own job inputs and outcomes with those of others, and any inequities impact on the effort that employees put into their work. If the income : output ratios between themselves and other workers are unequal, inequity exists and employees will perceive themselves as either under-rewarded or over-rewarded.

10.3 Labour turnover

If a business employed, on average, 200 employees last year and 30 left during the year, then the labour turnover rate would be 15%. If this result is high and increasing over time, then it is a good indicator of employee discontent, low morale and, possibly, a **recruitment** policy that leads to the wrong people being employed. High labour turnover is more likely in areas of low unemployment too, as there may be many better-paid

and more attractive jobs available in the local area. It is also true that some industries typically have higher labour turnover rates than others. The fact that so many students, looking for part-time and temporary employment, find jobs in fast-food restaurants leads to labour turnover rates that can exceed 100% in one year. In other organisations, labour turnover rates can be very low; this is typical in law practices and in scientific research.

Table 10.5 summarises the potential problems from both high and low labour turnover.

> **KEY TERM**
>
> **recruitment:** the process of identifying the need for a new employee, defining the job to be filled and the type of person needed to fill it, attracting suitable candidates for the job and selecting the best one

Labour turnover is measured by:

> **KEY FORMULA**
>
> $$\frac{\text{number of employees leaving in 1 year}}{\text{average number of people employed}} \times 100$$

CASE STUDY 10.4

What people want from work

'I was asked by the principal of my university to form a committee of ten lecturers to discuss holiday dates, student enrolment and ways to check on the quality of lectures. He told us it was a very important committee; we would receive recognition and our views would influence future decisions. We had many meetings, agreed a written report, and sent it to the principal. We heard nothing back – no feedback, no thanks and no decisions made on our recommendations. I would not do it again if I was asked.'

Many motivation theorists believe that giving people what they want from work is quite easy, although it depends on the type of work situation and on the individual person. A research performed across several industries at a global scale identified the following factors as important motivators for most individuals:

- Some control of their work, including control over job enrichment; the responsibility for a well-defined task, the need for achievement and recognition from others.

- Good communication from management and some participation opportunities.

- The opportunity for growth and development to help employees to gain 'mastery', including education, career paths and team working. Employees need to believe that if they try harder, they will have what it takes to perform better.

- Leadership providing clear targets and appropriate rewards if these targets are met.

Of course, money is important, because if employees do not receive remuneration that is perceived by them as 'fair' based on what other people get in similar positions, they become demotivated. But once workers are satisfied with fair financial rewards, they look for other things from work. Most employees want involvement in decisions that affect their work. Those who contribute ideas should be recognised and rewarded. Effective employee participation assumes that workers are very competent and experienced to be able to make decisions about their work.

For some employees, especially in managerial levels, the desire to control and lead their teams could be a strong motivator as it gives the sense of personal status. For others, the sense of belonging in a team and the creation of friendly relationships is a more important motivator.

Lastly, many employees are motivated through autonomy and the desire to control their own working environment as much as possible.

1   With reference to the case study and by applying McClelland's motivation theory, explain **two** factors affecting motivation at work. [4]

2   With reference to the case study and by applying Deci and Ryan's motivation theory, explain **two** factors affecting motivation at work. [4]

3   With reference to the case study and by applying Vroom's motivation theory, explain **two** factors affecting motivation at work. [4]

4   With reference to the case study and by applying Adam's motivation theory, explain **one** factor affecting motivation at work. [2]

CASE STUDY 10.5

High labour turnover at Electro plc

Advika is the HR director of Electro plc which produces home appliances. The business has been dealing with the problem of high labour turnover in its factory. Employees complain about bad working conditions and low wages.

Devansh, the operations director, is worried about the consequences of high labour turnover on the production unit. Retailers have recently informed him about delays in the delivery of orders. However, Advika sees an opportunity in the fact that workers leave the factory. She is considering the recruitment of younger employees as she thinks they are more motivated and happier to accept part-time employment contracts.

Devansh disagrees. He is worried that the recruits would need a lot of on-the-job training, which would then make them attractive to competitive businesses offering better wages. In the last meeting held by the board of directors, Devansh came with suggestions about how to reduce labour turnover in the factory, including better pay and benefits for manual workers.

Jaya, the CEO of Electro plc., said that before taking any decisions regarding the solution of the problem, the board of directors should discuss the implications of high labour turnover on the financial performance and the overall image of the business.

1 Define the term 'labour turnover'. [2]

2 Suggest **two** disadvantages of high labour turnover for Electro plc. [4]

3 Suggest **two** benefits of high labour turnover for Electro plc. [4]

4 Evaluate Devansh's suggestion to reduce labour turnover in Electro plc by offering better pay and benefits to manual workers. [10]

Drawbacks of high labour turnover	Potential benefits of high labour turnover
Costs of recruiting, selecting and training new staff	Low-skilled and less-productive staff might be leaving – they could be replaced with more carefully selected workers
Poor output levels and customer service due to staff vacancies before new recruits are appointed	New ideas and practices are brought into an organisation by new workers
Difficult to establish loyalty and regular, familiar contact with customers	A business that plans to reduce staff numbers anyway – due to rationalisation – will find that high labour turnover will do this, as leaving staff will not be replaced
Difficult to establish team spirit and stable work groups	

Table 10.5: Drawbacks and potential benefits of high labour turnover

10.4 Appraisal of employees

Employee appraisal is often undertaken annually. It is an essential component of an employee development programme. The analysis of performance against preset and agreed targets combined with the setting of new targets allows the future performance of the worker to be linked to the objectives of the business. Both appraisal and employee development are important features of Herzberg's motivators – those intrinsic factors that can provide the conditions for effective motivation at work. An appraisal form is often used which will comment on the worker's ability to meet certain criteria

KEY TERM

employee appraisal: the process of assessing the effectiveness of an employee judged against preset objectives and may suggest areas for action and improvement or recommendations for training or promotion. Figure 10.4 shows some examples of questions from appraisal forms.

Formative appraisal

Formative appraisal is based on a range of formal and informal assessment methods employed by supervisors not only to monitor an employee's progress but also to support and provide guidance for improvement. It typically involves qualitative feedback (rather than scores or grades for achievement) that focuses on the details of performance and ways of improving it. Formative appraisal – if done well – should be a supportive learning process for the employee and there should be no sense of overall failure or success.

In essence, the goal of formative assessment is to gather feedback that can be used by the instructor/supervisors and the employees to guide improvements in the ongoing work being undertaken by the workers.

Summative appraisal

In contrast, the goal of summative assessment is to measure the level of an employee's success or proficiency in meeting predetermined benchmarks. To be effective, these benchmarks should have been discussed and agreed with each employee before the time period over which assessment is to be made. The outcome of a summative assessment could be used to influence an employee's pay grade, annual bonus or chances of internal promotion.

360-degree feedback

Performance-appraisal summative assessments are collected from 'all around' an employee. The key feature of this form of appraisal is not to use a supervisor as the sole means of providing appraisal feedback, but to use many people who come into contact with the employee as sources of appraisal feedback information. These people often include:

- the employee's 'line' work colleagues and peers
- subordinates
- supervisors
- internal and external customers.

The main objective of 360-degree appraisal is usually to assess training and development needs and to provide competence-related information for succession planning, not promotion or pay increases.

It is also known as multi-source assessment or multi-source feedback.

A1 Score your own capability or knowledge in the following areas in terms of your current role requirements (1–3 = poor, 4–6 = satisfactory, 7–9 = good, 10 = excellent). If appropriate, bring evidence with you to the appraisal to support your assessment. The second section can be used if working towards new role requirements.

1 commercial judgement	10	creativity
2 product/technical knowledge	11	problem-solving and decision-making
3 time management	12	team-working and developing others
4 planning, budgeting and forecasting	13	energy, determination and work rate
5 reporting and administration	14	steadiness under pressure
6 communication skills	15	leadership and integrity
7 delegation skills	16	adaptability, flexibility and mobility
8 IT/equipment/machinery skills	17	personal appearance and image.
9 meeting deadlines/commitments		

A2 In light of your current capabilities, your performance against past objectives, and your future personal growth and/or job aspirations, what activities and tasks would you like to focus on during the next year? Again, also think of development and experiences outside job skills – related to personal aims, fulfilment, passions.

Figure 10.4: Examples of questions from appraisal forms

Self-appraisal

Employee self-appraisal, within a performance management or annual performance review system, involves asking the employee to self-evaluate his or her job performance. Typically, prior to meeting with an employee, the supervisor will ask the employee to complete an evaluation form. This will be used as a basis for discussion during the annual performance review meeting. Then at the meeting, the manager and employee discuss the self-appraisal results, and negotiate final evaluations based on both the manager's perceptions and those of the employee. Self-appraisal or self-evaluation results should be used after discussion and negotiation. Actual self-evaluation as part of performance management can take the form of evaluating progress towards predefined annual objectives and performance standards. The employee may be asked to rate themself using the same rating form the manager uses, or even undertake self-ranking against a preset scale of attainment levels.

10.5 Recruitment

Organisations need to obtain the best workforce available if they are to meet their objectives and be competitive. Workers need to be chosen so that they meet the needs of the organisation exactly, in order to reduce the risk of conflict between their personal objectives and those of the business. The recruitment and selection process involves the following steps:

1   Establish the exact nature of the job vacancy and draw up a **job description**. The job description provides a complete picture of the job and includes:

   a   job title
   b   details of the tasks to be performed
   c   responsibilities involved
   d   place in the hierarchical structure
   e   working conditions
   f   how the job will be assessed and performance measured.

The advantage of the job description is that it should attract the right type of people to apply for the job, as potential recruits will have an idea of whether they are suited to the position or not.

2   Draw up a person specification. This analyses the qualities and skills being looked for in suitable applicants. It is clearly based on the job description because these skills can only be assessed once the nature and complexity of the job have been identified. The **person specification** is like a 'person profile' and helps in the selection process by eliminating applicants who do not match up to the necessary requirements.

> **KEY TERMS**
>
> **job description:** a detailed list of the key points about the job to be filled, stating all the key tasks and responsibilities of it
>
> **person specification:** a detailed list of the qualities, skills and qualifications that a successful applicant will need to have

3   Prepare a job advertisement reflecting the requirements of the job and the personal qualities desired. The job advertisement can be displayed within the business premises – particularly if an internal appointment is being sought – on the firm's website or in government job centres, recruitment agencies and/or newspapers. Care must be taken to ensure that there is no element of discrimination implied by the advertisement as nearly all countries outlaw unfair selection on the basis of race, gender or religion.

> **TIP**
>
> Do not confuse the job description and the person specification.

4   Draw up a shortlist of applicants. A few applicants are chosen based on their application forms and personal details, often contained in a CV (curriculum vitae). References may have been obtained in order to check on the character and previous work performance of the applicants.

> **TIP**
>
> The disadvantages of each method of recruitment are the reverse of the advantages of the other method. For example, a drawback of external recruitment is that it does not give internal staff a career structure or a chance to progress.

5   Conduct interviews. Interviews are designed to question the applicant on their skills, experience and character to see if they are likely to perform well and fit into the organisation. Some interviewers use a seven-point plan to carry out a methodical interview. Candidates are assessed according to achievements, intelligence, skills, interests, personal manner, physical appearance and personal circumstances.

10.6 Internal and external recruitment

An important decision that HR managers often have to make is whether to go down the route of **internal recruitment** (i.e. recruiting a person to a post who is already working in the organisation) or **external recruitment** (recruiting an external candidate). Some businesses will nearly always try to recruit internally as this can provide a career ladder for employees and a real chance of advancement. Other businesses, perhaps more focused on rapidly developing technology or involved in advanced research, will nearly always appoint external candidates to fill vacant posts.

It might be unwise for a business to adopt a very inflexible rule as to which type of recruitment to use. A business that normally uses internal recruitment might be unwise to not appoint a truly outstanding candidate from another organisation. Similarly, a business that usually focuses on external recruitment might be advised to appoint a very deserving, capable and ambitious internal candidate if they were well suited to the vacant post. Table 10.6 outlines some of the advantages of these two approaches to recruitment.

> ## KEY TERMS
>
> **internal recruitment:** filling vacant posts by appointing existing employees
>
> **external recruitment:** filling vacant posts by appointing candidates from outside the organisation

Internal recruitment	External recruitment
Applicants may already be well known to the selection team and there might be less risk than appointing someone with unknown qualities and skills	External applicants will bring new ideas and practices to the business – this helps to keep existing employees focused on the future rather than 'the ways things have always been done'
Applicant will already know the organisation and its internal methods. There should be little need for induction training	New ideas and practices can be particularly important for businesses operating in fast-changing markets or in technologically advanced industries
The culture of the organisation will be well understood by the applicant and this avoids the risk of a culture clash with the views and beliefs of an external candidate	There should be a wide choice of potential applicants – not limited to internal employees – so the overall quality of applicants might be high
Often it is quicker than external recruitment as outside agencies and advertising might not be necessary	It avoids resentment sometimes felt by existing employees if one of their former colleagues is promoted above them
Likely to be lower cost than using external advertising and recruitment agencies	If a business or a department within it has not been performing well, selecting an external candidate for a senior management post is likely to lead to new ways of working which might reverse this disappointing performance. Internal candidates might be too closely associated with existing under-performance
Gives internal employees a career structure and a chance to progress, and this encourages high levels of motivation amongst those keen to advance in the organisation	
Employees may be less likely to have to get used to a new style of management approach if the vacancy is a senior post	

Table 10.6: The advantages of internal and external recruitment

ACTIVITY 10.2

1 Draw up a job description for the head teacher or principal's post at your school or college.

2 Draw up a detailed person specification for this post.

3 Produce an eye-catching and effective newspaper advertisement for this post (use IT if you can) including key features from the job description and person specification.

Reflection

When designing the person specification, did you ensure that it would appeal to a diverse pool of candidates from different age, gender and/or ethnic groups? Why would diversity be important among the faculty of a school or college? Discuss in class.

LEARNER PROFILE

Knowledgeable

Spanx founder and CEO Sara Blakely takes a step back and lets candidates ask the questions

As the founder of Spanx and one of the world's most influential businesswomen, Sara Blakely . . . knows a thing or two about what it takes to make a great hire, especially when it comes to hiring executives for her own company. One of her favourite interviewing strategies is to step back and see how the candidate fills moments of silence – including what questions they ask.

'You can learn the most about a person by the questions he or she asks or doesn't ask,'

Sara explains. . . . Sara also has another piece of advice that has inspired the likes of Richard Branson: Great leaders should hire 'for their weaknesses.' In other words, to create a well-rounded company, business leaders need to recognize and communicate their own strengths and shortcomings so their recruiters can find talent to fill those gaps.

'I surround myself with people who have knowledge and talents in areas where I might not be so well versed,' Richard adds.

Do you think that becoming knowledgeable will be important for you and your classmates in your future careers? Discuss in class.

THEORY OF KNOWLEDGE

Knowledge question: How important are reason, emotion and intuition when evaluating someone in an interview?

You are preparing to interview a new graduate for a management trainee job with your multinational media organisation.

The first candidate enters the interview room. They have a superb academic background that includes a first-class degree from a top university; they have completed plenty of relevant work experience, speak three languages fluently and have a wide range of other interests including high-level sports. On paper, they are the best candidate for the job. The trouble is you do not really like them and would not want to work with them. Even though they have a polite smile on their face, you sense

they might be arrogant and not a good fit for the company's culture.

The second candidate is less qualified and experienced for the job. Yet, they seem friendly and open-minded, and you love their sense of humour. You feel that they must be offered the position. For some reason, you trust that they would fit the organisation fast and that they will prove to be an asset for the business.

In your class consider the following questions:

1 Which candidate would you offer the job to and why?

2 Should professional recruiters trust their intuition and emotion, or should they just hire employees based on reason?

10.7 Payment or financial reward systems

The most common payment systems are:

- salary
- wage: time-based wage rate and piece rate
- commission
- performance-related pay
- profit-related pay
- employee share-ownership schemes
- fringe payments (perks).

Salary

A **salary** is the most common form of payment for professional, supervisory and management employees The salary level is fixed each year and it is not dependent on the number of hours worked or the number of units produced. The fixing of the salary level for each job is a very important process because it helps to determine the status of that post in the whole organisation.

Job evaluation techniques may be used to assist in deciding the salary bands and the differences between them. In most organisations, all jobs will be put into one of a number of salary bands and the precise income earned within each band will depend upon experience and progress. It is always possible to gain promotion to another job in a higher salary band. Firms that are interested in creating a 'single status' within their organisation are now increasingly putting all staff – manual and managerial – on to annual salaries to give the benefits of security and status to all employees. The advantages and disadvantages of a salary system are outlined in Table 10.8.

Job grade	Salary band (per year)
E, e.g., regional heads	$50 000–$75 900
D, e.g., departmental heads	$30 000–$49 900
C, e.g., office managers	$20 000–$29 900
B, e.g., secretaries	$10 000–$19 900
A, e.g., junior clerical staff	$5 000–$9 900

Table 10.7: Salary bands – typical example

Advantages	Disadvantages
Salary gives security of income	Income is not related to effort levels or productivity
It gives status compared to time-rate or piece-rate payment systems	It may lead to complacency of the salary earner
It aids in costing – the salaries will not vary for one year	Regular appraisal may be needed to assess whether an individual should move up a salary band, although this could be an advantage if this becomes a positive form of worker appraisal
It is suitable for jobs where output is not measurable	
It is suitable for management positions where staff are expected to put in extra time to complete a task or assignment	

Table 10.8: Advantages and disadvantages of salary system

Wage

Time-based wage rate

An **hourly wage rate** or 'time rate' is set for the job – perhaps by comparing with other firms or similar jobs. The wage level is determined by multiplying this by the number of hours worked and is usually paid weekly. Although there is more income security than with piece rate, speed of work is not rewarded with this payment system – indeed, the opportunity to earn overtime might encourage workers to stretch work out unproductively.

> **KEY TERMS**
>
> **salary:** annual income that is usually paid on a monthly basis
>
> **hourly wage rate:** payment to a worker made for each hour worked

Piece rate

A rate is fixed for the production of each unit, and the workers' wages therefore depend on the quantity of output produced. The **piece rate** can be adjusted to reflect the difficulty of the job and the 'standard' time needed to complete it. The level of the rate can be very important. If set too low, it could demotivate the workers, but if it is too high, it could reduce the incentives because workers will be able to meet their target wage level by producing relatively few units (see Table 10.9).

Advantages	Disadvantages
It encourages greater effort and faster working The labour cost for each unit is determined in advance and this helps to set a price for the product	It requires output to be measurable and standardised – if each product is different, then piece work is inappropriate It may lead to falling quality and safety levels as workers rush to complete units Workers may settle for a certain pay level and will therefore not be motivated to produce more than a certain level It provides little security over pay level, e.g., in the event of a production breakdown

Table 10.9: Advantages and disadvantages of the piece rate

Commission

Commission can make up 100% of the total income of direct sales employees – it reduces security as there is no 'basic' or flat-rate payment if nothing is sold during a particular period – or it can be paid in addition to a basic salary. It has the same advantages and disadvantages as the piece rate used in production industries, except that the potential drawback of low quality of production may be replaced by the risk of high-pressure selling, where sales staff try so hard to convince a customer to buy a product or service that they simply create a bad impression of the company. Commission-based pay also does not encourage teamwork – each individual sales person will be keen to hold on to each new customer for themselves to earn more commission!

Performance-related pay (PRP)

Performance-related pay is usually in the form of a bonus payable in addition to the basic salary. It is widely used for those workers whose 'output' is not measurable in quantitative terms, such as management, supervisory and clerical posts. It requires the following procedure:

- regular target setting, establishing specific objectives for the individual
- annual appraisals of the worker's performance against the preset targets
- paying each worker a bonus according to the degree to which the targets have been exceeded.

The main aim is to provide further financial incentives and to encourage staff to meet agreed targets. Bonuses are usually paid on an individual basis, but they can also be calculated and awarded on the basis of teams or even whole departments.

There are problems with PRP schemes (see Table 10.10). The main issue is one that Herzberg would recognise – does the chance of additional pay 'motivate' or just temporarily 'move' a worker to perform better? As there is no change in the nature of the work being undertaken most of the 'motivators' recognised by Herzberg would not be satisfied by PRP. In addition, the concentration on individual performance can create divisions within teams and groups. There is also a widely held view that PRP bonuses are often inadequate, even to achieve short-term productivity gains or improvements in effort. The last problem concerns the style of management that PRP can lead to. By giving senior managers the power to decide which subordinates have achieved performances above target, it can lead to claims of favouritism and the ability to control staff by means of the 'carrot' of extra rewards.

KEY TERMS

piece rate: a payment to a worker for each unit produced

commission: a payment to a sales person for each sale made

performance-related pay: a bonus scheme to reward staff for above-average work performance

---

Advantages	Disadvantages
Employees are motivated to improve performance if they are seeking increases in financial rewards	It can fail to motivate if employees are not driven by the need to earn additional financial rewards
Target setting can help to give purpose and direction to the work of an individual	Team spirit can be damaged by the rivalry generated by the competitive nature of PRP
Annual appraisal offers the opportunity for feedback on the performance of an individual, but as it tends to occur only once a year this is not usually sufficient to achieve a key feature of job enrichment	Claims of manager favouritism can harm manager–subordinate relationships
	It may lead to increased control over workers by managers because of the danger that bonuses may not be awarded if workers do not 'conform'

Table 10.10: Advantages and disadvantages of performance-related pay

Profit-related pay

The essential idea behind profit-sharing arrangements (and **profit-related pay**) is that staff will feel more committed to the success of the business and will strive to achieve higher performances and cost savings (see Table 10.11). Some shareholder groups, however, claim that profits should only be considered as being the return to the owners of the business and are a reward to them for taking risks with their own capital.

> **KEY TERM**
>
> **profit-related pay:** a bonus for employees based on the profits of the business – usually paid as a proportion of basic salary

Employee share-ownership schemes

Some profit-sharing schemes do not offer cash but instead offer shares in the business to each worker when the firm declares a profit. This is designed to establish the workers as part-owners of the business and reduce the conflict that might exist between 'them' (the owners and managers) and 'us' (the workers). In practice, many of the shares in such schemes are quickly sold by the workers, thus reducing the hoped-for long-term impact on motivation (see Table 10.11).

Advantages	Disadvantages
Potential conflict between owners and workers is reduced as everyone now has an interest in higher profits	The reward offered is not closely related to individual effort – why should one worker put in greater effort when everyone will be benefiting?
They are designed to lead to increased effort by workers and a greater willingness to accept cost-reduction measures and changes that benefit the business	The schemes can be costly to set up and operate, especially in large firms with many employees
The business is likely to attract better recruits drawn by the chance of sharing profits or owning shares in the firm	Small profit shares paid at the end of the financial year are unlikely to promote motivation throughout the year
As the bonuses are paid out of profits, the scheme does not add to business costs, unlike a normal increase in pay levels	Profit-sharing schemes will reduce profits available to be paid to owners (reducing dividends) and to be reinvested in the business (retained profits)
If successful in improving motivation, then the schemes could lead to an increase in overall business profitability	Worker share-ownership schemes can increase the total number of shares issued and dilute the value of existing shares

Table 10.11: Advantages and disadvantages of profit sharing and employee share ownership

Fringe payments (benefits)

These are non-cash forms of reward – and there are many alternatives that can be used. They include company cars, free insurance and pension schemes, private health insurance, discounts on company products and low-interest rate loans. These are sometimes referred to as 'perks'. They are used by businesses in addition to normal payment systems in order to give status to higher-level employees and to recruit and retain the best staff. Some of these fringe benefits are taxed, but others are not. That gives the employees an added benefit, because to purchase these perks from after-tax income would be very expensive. It is difficult to assess the impact of these benefits on productivity.

ACTIVITY 10.3

Different jobs, different pay systems

Look at the job adverts and then answer the questions that follow.

Human resources director – Singapore

Diverse Portfolio of International Businesses

Our client is an undisputed leader in the private equity market. It has financed the acquisition of a wide variety of businesses with a presence in more than 50 countries, an annual turnover in excess of $3.5 billion and 50 000 employees. Key to the group's success has been its close financial management and the assistance it has given portfolio companies in areas such as human resources and IT. Due to continuing growth, an HR director is now sought to add value across the group.

The position

- Optimise the deployment of HR to add value within the portfolio businesses and support the group's overall objectives.

- Provide business and HR support to operating company management teams. Emphasis on management development, leadership teams and compensation.

- Active involvement in evaluation of potential acquisition targets. Provide critical analysis of management strengths and weaknesses.

Qualifications

- Outstanding HR professional with a minimum of 15 years' experience, a demonstrable record at group and divisional levels in an international business.

- Practical understanding of business drivers and HR issues within large and small organisations. Highly influential with outstanding business management toolkit.

- Specific experience in Asia is required, with fluency in an Asian language a distinct advantage.

Please send full CV and current salary details to S. Amm at the address below.

Alternatively email: samm@partnership.com

THE PACIFIC RECRUITMENT AGENCY

Driver wanted

- Must have clean driving licence

- Light removal work

- Overalls provided

- Ring: 0837 5108 if interested

1 Suggest which of the two job positions above is likely to be paid with an hourly wage and which with a yearly salary. Justify your answer.

2 One of the job positions above offers fringe benefits, such as a company car and private health insurance. Suggest which one and why.

3 Explain the possible reasons why the second job position pays for overtime work, but the first does not.

10.8 Non-financial rewards

It is now widely recognised that businesses cannot use money alone to create the necessary motivation for employees to complete jobs efficiently. Non-financial motivators include:

- job enlargement
- job enrichment
- job rotation
- team work
- empowerment
- purpose (the opportunity to make a difference).

Job enlargement

Job enlargement can include both job rotation and job enrichment, but it also refers to increasing the 'loading' of tasks on existing workers, perhaps as a result of a shortage of staff or redundancies. It is unlikely to lead to long-term job satisfaction unless the principles of job enrichment are adopted.

Job enrichment

This involves the principle of organising work so that employees are encouraged and allowed to use their full abilities – not just physical effort. The process often involves a slackening of direct supervision as workers take more responsibility for their own work and are allowed some degree of decision-making authority. Herzberg's findings formed the basis of the job enrichment principle. Its three key features are not always easy to apply in practice, but employers are increasingly recognising the benefits to be gained by attempting to implement them:

- complete units of work so that the contribution of the worker can be identified and more challenging work offered, e.g., cell production
- direct feedback on performance to allow each worker to have an awareness of their own progress, e.g., two-way communication
- challenging tasks offered as part of a range of activities, some of which are beyond the worker's recent experience – these tasks will require training and the learning of new skills. Gaining further

skills and qualifications is a form of gaining status and recognition – see Maslow's hierarchy of human needs.

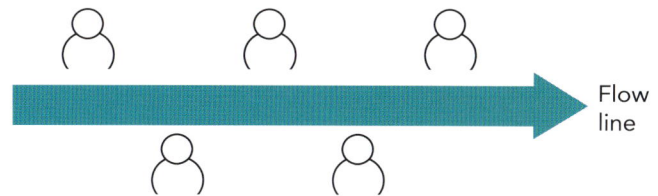

Figure 10.5: Traditional mass production – each worker performs a single task

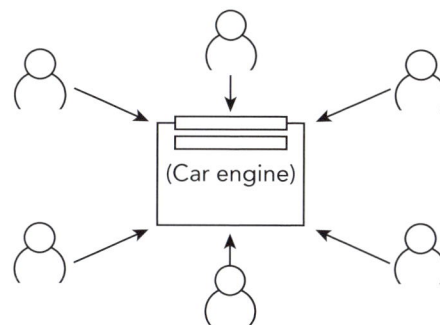

Figure 10.6: Team production allowing for job enrichment – all workers contribute to producing the completed unit

Job rotation

The practice of job rotation is widespread in businesses that have production processes where several different jobs – of similar degrees of difficulty and challenge –

KEY TERMS

job enlargement: attempting to increase the scope of a job by broadening or deepening the tasks undertaken

job enrichment: attempting to motivate employees by giving them opportunities to use the full range of their abilities

cell production: flow production split into self-contained work groups that are responsible for a complete unit of work

job rotation: the practice of moving employees between different tasks to promote experience and variety

exist. It is argued that workers are less likely to become bored if they are given a range of different tasks to undertake.

Although this approach can increase variety and, possibly, the number of skills workers are required to use, it does not offer true challenge or enrichment from the work experience.

> **TIP**
>
> Do not confuse job enlargement with job rotation. Job rotation offers variety but does not necessarily provide more stimulating or challenging work.

Team working

The **team working** approach to work places each member of staff into a small team of employees. Some traditionalists argue that moving away from 'pure division of labour', where one worker performs just one simple task all the time, will result in lower productivity and time-wasting team meetings. Supporters of job enrichment would respond by claiming that more challenging and interesting work, as allowed by team working or 'cell' production, will lead to:

- lower labour turnover
- more and better ideas from the workforce on improving the product and the manufacturing process
- consistently higher quality, especially when total quality management (TQM) is incorporated.

Table 10.12 summarises the advantages and disadvantages of team working.

There are a number of benefits to the organisation from team working:

- Team spirit should improve motivation of staff
- Teams are more flexible than hierarchical systems
- New teams can be formed and redundant teams disbanded as the needs of the organisation change
- Management costs may be reduced as fewer middle managers and supervisory staff are required.

> **KEY TERM**
>
> **team working:** production is organised so that groups of workers undertake complete units of work

Advantages	Disadvantages
Workers are likely to be better motivated as social and esteem needs (see Maslow) are more likely to be met. By empowering workers within teams, job enrichment can be achieved (see Herzberg).	Not everyone is a team player – some individuals are more effective working alone. When teams are formed, this point must be considered and training may need to be offered to team members who are not used to working collaboratively in groups. Some workers may feel 'left out' of the team meetings unless efforts are made to involve and encourage all team members.
Better-motivated employees should increase productivity and reduce labour turnover – both will help to reduce business costs.	
Team working makes fuller use of all of the talents of the workforce. Better solutions to problems will be found as those most closely connected with the work participate in suggesting answers.	Teams can develop a set of values and attitudes which may contrast or conflict with those of the organisation itself, particularly if there is a dominant personality in the group. Teams will need clear goals and assessment procedures to ensure that they are working towards the objectives of the organisation at all times.
Team working can reduce management costs as it is often associated with delayering of the organisation – fewer middle managers will be required.	
Complete units of work can be given to teams – a key feature of job enrichment.	The introduction of team working will incur training costs and there may be some disruption to production as the teams establish themselves.

Table 10.12: Advantages and disadvantages of working in teams

Making a difference

If employees are allocated roles and given the appropriate authority to perform them, they can make a significant difference to certain aspects of the operation of a business. The areas of business activity where the 'making a difference' idea has been most effective include:

- customer service – dealing with issues without always having to consult with supervisor or manager
- quality improvements – as with quality circles (see Chapter 30)
- productivity improvements – by having direct experience of the operations process, employees can often make effective suggestions for improvements.

Giving employees these opportunities relates effectively to Herzberg's motivator factors and the Deci and Ryan concept of intrinsic motivation.

Empowerment

Empowerment is closely linked to delegation (see Chapter 9) as it allows employees s some degree of control over how a particular task should be undertaken and the resources needed to complete it.

KEY TERM

empowerment: delegating to an employee or group of employees the authority to perform a task and to take appropriate decisions to be able to complete it

In a customer-focused business, customers often prefer having their questions and needs met immediately by the first employee they contact. The customer should not be turned away if a manager is not available. From a motivational point of view, the reasoning is that front-line employees become more committed and motivated when their role includes showing initiative, creative thinking and decision-making.

Evaluation of financial and non-financial motivational methods

If it is accepted that pay is not the only motivating factor for people to work effectively and to be satisfied in their jobs, then managers need to take a critical look at all of the payment and non-financial methods of motivating staff. What works for some groups of workers will not be effective with others. Managers need to be flexible and adapt the methods and approaches that are available to motivate employees to the particular circumstances of their business and their workforce. The main factors that influence the different degrees of emphasis on pay and non-pay motivational methods include the leadership style of management and the culture of the organisation.

If managers have the attitude that workers are naturally lazy and cannot be trusted, then a 'piece rate or payment by results' system with close supervision will be adopted. If the culture views workers as partners or associates in the business, then production will be organised to encourage intrinsic motivation and give workers a chance to accept responsibility and to participate. A monthly salary payment system is likely under these circumstances. As with so many important decisions made within a business, a great deal depends on the attitudes and beliefs of senior managers – and the business culture they adopt.

10.9 Training

Having recruited and selected the right staff, the HR department must ensure that they are well equipped to perform the duties and undertake the responsibilities expected of them. This will nearly always involve training in order to develop the full abilities of the worker.

There are three main types of training:

- **Induction training:** this should be given to all new recruits although those appointed to a new post internally may require less of it than external recruits.

  Induction training aims to introduce new recruits to the people they will be working with most closely, to explain the organisational structure, outline the layout of the premises and make clear the essential health and safety issues, such as procedures during a fire emergency.

  When it is done well, induction training makes a new recruit feel part of the organisation quickly and it allows them to make an effective contribution earlier than if they had to find out these important details for themselves in the first few weeks of employment.

- **On-the-job training:** this involves instruction at the place of work. This is often conducted by either the HR managers or departmental training officers. Watching or working closely with existing experienced members of staff is a frequent component of this form of training. It is cheaper than sending recruits on external training courses and the content is controlled by the business itself.

- **Off-the-job training:** this entails any course of instruction away from the place of work. This could be a specialist training centre belonging to the firm itself or a course organised by an outside body, such as a university or computer manufacturer, to introduce new ideas that no-one in the firm currently has knowledge of. These courses can be expensive, yet they may be indispensable if the firm lacks anyone with this degree of technical knowledge.

KEY TERMS

induction training: introductory training programme to familiarise new recruits with the systems used in the business and the layout of the business site; this form of training is usually on the job

on-the-job training: instruction at the place of work on how a job should be carried out

off-the-job training: all training undertaken away from the business, e.g., work-related college courses

---

Training evaluation

Training can be expensive. It can also lead to well-qualified staff leaving for a better-paid job once they have gained qualifications from a business with a good training structure. This is sometimes referred to as 'poaching' of well-trained staff and it can discourage some businesses from setting up expensive training programmes.

The costs of not training are also substantial. Untrained staff will be less productive, less able to do a variety of tasks (inflexible) and will give less satisfactory customer service. Without being pushed to achieve a higher standard or other skills, workers may become bored and demotivated. Training and a sense of achievement can lead to what were identified by both Maslow and Herzberg as important motivators. Finally, accidents are likely to result from staff who are not trained on safety matters.

TIP

When discussing the costs and benefits of training remember that the risk of 'poaching' is a reason often given by firms for not training their employees well. Perhaps they ought to do more to keep their well-trained employees.

CASE STUDY 10.6

Fresh Food (FF) social enterprise needs a chef

Fresh Food is a chain of 'avant-garde' restaurants, serving only locally sourced food and training a new generation of chefs who cannot pay for their own professional training. Some 80% of FF's profits are donated to charities, and customers can even decide where the money goes.

CONTINUED

FF urgently needs to recruit a chef for its biggest restaurant in the heart of the city. This specific venue generates 25% of the profits of the whole restaurant chain. Many business executives have become loyal customers of the restaurant and word has spread regarding the excellent food and the social purpose of FF.

Inessa, the restaurant's manager, does not know what the best way is to recruit a new chef for the position. One choice is to offer the position to one of the three sous chefs working for the restaurant. All three employees would love to be promoted to head chef, but none is ready for the position. They all need off-the-job training to get the skills required to meet FF's high-quality standards. Even though the training of employees is one of the main aims of FF as a social enterprise, Inessa believes that at this point the business should recruit a professional chef externally.

1   Define the term 'off-the-job training'.   [2]

2   With reference to the case study, identify the difference between internal and external recruitment.   [4]

3   Suggest **two** steps in the recruitment process to be followed by Inessa for the chef's position.   [4]

4   Suggest whether Inessa should promote one of the sous chefs or whether she should hire a chef externally. Justify your answer.   [10]

10.10 Business management tools
Hofstede's cultural dimensions

Hofstede's cultural dimensions theory was developed by Geert Hofstede. It is a model that can be used to understand the differences in culture between countries and to compare and contrast the ways that business is conducted in different cultures. Hofstede's framework can therefore be used to distinguish between different national cultures and assess the impact these differences

might have on business activities such as employee motivation and forms of marketing promotion.

Hofstede identified and analysed six dimensions in which cultures vary.

These are:

- power distance index
- collectivism vs individualism
- uncertainty avoidance index
- femininity vs masculinity
- short-term orientation vs long-term orientation
- restraint vs indulgence.

  - **Power distance index:** The power distance index assesses the extent to which inequality and power are tolerated in national society. A high power distance index indicates that a nation's culture accepts inequalities and power differences, encourages bureaucracy, and shows high respect for rank and authority. A low power distance index indicates that a culture encourages organisational structures that are flat and feature decentralised decision-making responsibility, participative style of management, and stress the importance of the distribution of power. Saudi Arabia is a country with a high power distance index.

  - **Collectivism vs individualism:** The individualism vs collectivism dimension assesses the extent to which societies are integrated into groups and the obligations to and dependence on groups. A society which features a high degree of individualism indicates that greater importance is placed on attaining personal goals. Collectivism indicates that greater importance is placed on the goals and well-being of the group. The USA is considered one of the most individualistic countries in the world.

  - **Uncertainty avoidance index:** The uncertainty avoidance index assesses whether uncertainty and ambiguity are tolerated. This dimension considers how unknown situations and unexpected events are dealt with by a nation's population. A high uncertainty avoidance index indicates a low tolerance for uncertainty, ambiguity and risk-taking. In this culture there are likely to be rules and regulations to reduce uncertainty. A low uncertainty avoidance index indicates a high tolerance for uncertainty, ambiguity and risk-taking. The unknown is more widely and willingly accepted, so there may be much less emphasis on rules and regulations. South American countries such as Chile, Peru and Argentina are countries that score high on the uncertainty avoidance index

- **Femininity vs masculinity:** The masculinity vs femininity dimension is also referred to as 'tough vs tender'. It attempts to assess the preference of society for achievement, and attitudes towards sexuality equality, According to Hofstede, masculinity is associated with distinct gender roles and assertiveness, and it is focused on material achievements and wealth building. Femininity is associated with the following characteristics: fluid gender roles, modesty, nurturing and concern for the quality of life. Japan is considered to be a very masculine country, whereas Scandinavian countries such as Norway and Sweden are considered highly feminine.

- **Short-term orientation vs long-term orientation:** The long-term orientation vs short-term orientation dimension analyses whether society focuses on short-term or long-term issues. Long-term orientation suggests a focus on the future. This is associated with delaying short-

term success or gratification in order to achieve long-term success. Long-term orientation emphasises persistence, perseverance and long-term growth. Short-term orientation emphasises the near future, and society prefers short-term success and gratification. Short-term orientation emphasises quick results and respect for tradition. Asian countries such as Japan are known for their long-term orientation. Morocco is a short-term oriented country.

- **Restraint vs indulgence:** The indulgence vs restraint dimension assesses the inclination of a society to fulfil its desires. This dimension analyses how societies can control their impulses and desires. Indulgence indicates that a society allows relatively free gratification related to enjoying life and having fun. Restraint indicates that a society suppresses gratification of needs and wants and tends to regulate it through norms of social behaviour. According to Hofstede, most East Asian countries have low scores on the 'indulgence' cultural dimension. For example, with a low score of 29, the South Korean society is shown to be one of the most 'restrained countries'.

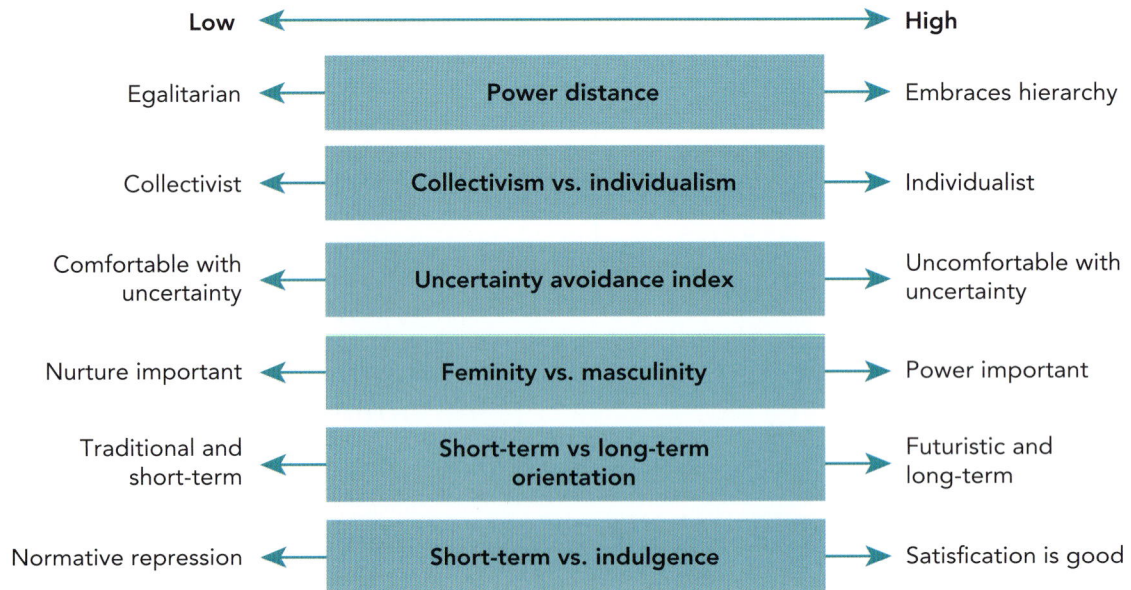

Figure 10.7: A visual representation of Hofstede's six cultural dimensions

Country comparisons

Figure 10.8 compares the cultural dimension scores of two countries: Argentina and New Zealand.

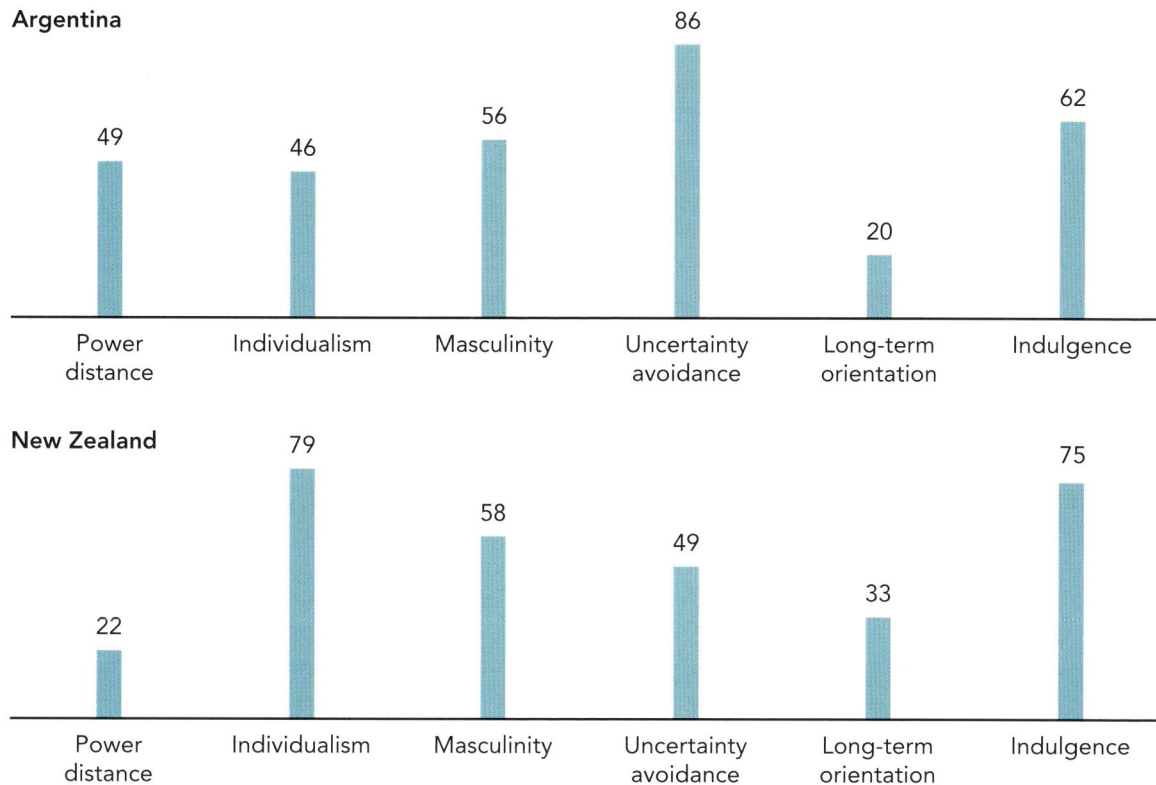

Argentina

New Zealand

Figure 10.8: Hofstede's cultural dimensions for Argentina and New Zealand

Cultural differences and HRM

An awareness of these cultural dimensions is very important for effective HRM, especially in a multinational corporation. Even a business based only in one country is likely to employ people from many different cultural backgrounds, and understanding national differences in culture is important for effective leadership of employees and for deciding on appropriate reward systems.

Is it appropriate to use the same reward systems in divisions of a business that operate in different countries around the world? Do employees everywhere respond in the same way to changes in financial and non-financial reward systems? Do people from every culture respond in the same way to a particular style of leadership?

Hofstede's work helps managers to answer these questions in the negative. Managers of any business that has a multicultural workforce need to be prepared to adapt their systems to those which are most likely to be effective within the different cultures represented by

their workers. Here are some examples of how HRM may need to adapt to different cultures:

- **'Masculine' performance orientation:** the extent to which performance improvement, innovation and striving for excellence is encouraged. This cultural feature is strongest in Germanic Europe and the UK but weakest in Latin America. In the countries where 'masculine performance orientation' is strongest, there is likely to be much greater emphasis on performance-related pay, bonus payments and share purchase schemes. In Sweden, where there is a feminine focus to the culture, the use of supportive appraisal techniques to help mentor subordinates is likely to be more effective than a harsh 'hire and fire' approach.

- **Future orientation:** the degree to which individuals are focused on delaying immediate reward and engaging in future-oriented behaviour such as planning and investing for the future. In countries with a long-term orientation, the use of individual incentive schemes based on future business performance such as share ownership schemes of management might be effective methods of reward. In countries with short-term orientation, recruitment is often based on merit, but in long-term orientation societies it might be based more on loyalty of long-serving employees.

- **Collectivism:** this cultural feature was found to be strongest in Nordic Europe and Germanic Europe and weakest in Asia. In the countries where this is a powerful cultural force, the use of team-based incentives and employee profit-sharing schemes has been found to be particularly significant. In individualistic societies, teamworking may be less effective than ways of working which focus on individual performance.

- **Uncertainty avoidance:** in societies that have a high tendency to avoid uncertainty and risk, such as Peru, the use of temporary employment contracts would be demotivating and a financial reward system relying heavily on irregular bonus payments might be unpopular.

- **Power distance:** a Danish manager may willingly accept working in a cross-functional team and take advice and suggestions from employees as this country has a low power distance culture. In Saudi Arabia managers may have real problems coping with informal relationships with employees because of high power distance.

Links between business management tools and other units of the IB syllabus

Hofstede's cultural dimensions analysis can also be linked to other units of the IB syllabus. For example:

- Unit 4 Marketing – different cultures will respond in different ways to product names and promotion campaigns. Failure to recognise these cultural differences could mean that a product does not sell well in certain countries unless the marketing is localised towards different countries' cultures.

- Unit 5 Operations management – international location decisions might be influenced by a country's prevailing culture. If it seems likely that a national culture may clash with the way the business operates, organises production and manages employees, then locating in that country might be unsuccessful.

SELF-EVALUATION CHECKLIST

After studying this chapter, complete this table.

I am able to apply and analyse:	Needs more work	Almost there	Ready to move on
the nature of business (AO1)			
labour turnover (AO2)			
appraisal (AO2)			
methods of recruitment (AO2)			
The following types of financial rewards: salary, wages (time and piece rates), commission, performance-related pay (PRP), profit-related pay, employee share ownership schemes (AO2)			
The following types of non-financial rewards: job enrichment, job rotation, job enlargement, empowerment, purpose/the opportunity to make a difference, teamwork			
The following types of training: induction, on the job, off the job (AO2)			

CONTINUED

I am able to synthesies and evaluate:			
the following motivation theories: • Taylor • Maslow • Herzberg (motivation-hygiene theory) (AO3)			
the following motivation theories: McClelland's acquired needs theory; Deci and Ryan's self-determination theory; Equity and expectancy theory (AO3)			
internal and external recruitment (AO3)			
I am able to use and apply:			
labour turnover (AO4)			

REFLECTION

Assume you are in full-time employment, earning what you consider to be an appropriate income from your work. What are the key factors that will determine your level of motivation? Compare your ideas with those of another learner.

PROJECT

What motivates social entrepreneurs?

When Jeff Bezos of Amazon speaks with entrepreneurs interested in working with his business, he tells them that he is looking for 'missionaries' rather than 'mercenaries'. According to his point of view, successful start-ups are the ones which try to make excellent products and to 'change the world for the better'. Then, profit will 'take care of itself'.

If intrinsic motivation is important for entrepreneurs of for-profit business organisations, then one would assume that it is absolutely vital for social entrepreneurs. This assumption can be made because of the very definition of social entrepreneurship, which is about contributing to the society before making any profit. However, is this supposition true?

Research has examined what motivates social entrepreneurs by involving more than 400 participants. The research indicated that a big proportion of start-up social enterprises are attracted by extrinsic motivators, such as grants. Social entrepreneurs that are attracted by extrinsic motivators to start a business activity, often start with excellent business ideas. But most of them were found to be less successful one year later compared to social entrepreneurs who are less money oriented.

1   Split into two groups. The first group should present a social enterprise of their own choice to the second group. The second group should create a poster with the extrinsic and intrinsic factors that seem to have motivated the social entrepreneur to set up the business activity.

2   Which factors were the most important to motivate the social entrepreneur in your example social enterprise? Discuss as a class.

EXAM-STYLE QUESTIONS

Extract 1: Why women are happier in their work than men

The world of work is a better experience for women than it is for men, according to a survey. Asked to rate their job satisfaction on a scale of one to seven, they scored an average of 5.56, while males scored 5.22. Experts appear divided over the reasons why women appear to get more out of their work than men do. Many women work part time and have job-sharing schemes, which, the survey found, increased job satisfaction as they could pursue other interests too. In addition, older workers get the greatest satisfaction from their jobs, while university graduates are the most dissatisfied of all, according to the survey of 30 000 employees. Employees generally enjoy their first years at work, but then job satisfaction falls between the ages of 30 and 40. However, employees over 60 gain the greatest satisfaction from their work.

Professor Andrew Oswald of Warwick University, who conducted the survey, said, 'The young are just happy to have a job. As they grow older they realise that ambitions and needs may not be so easily fulfilled.' It seems that we all begin thinking we will reach the top in our careers, but most of us are forced to adjust. 'The older we get, the more settled and content with our role at work we get,' he added. Graduates are often frustrated by the lack of challenging work on offer. They are often forced to take low-skilled jobs for which they are over-qualified in order to pay off debts.

Employees of small businesses were more motivated and happier at work than those working for big companies. David Hands, of the Federation of Small Businesses, said, 'There is a greater camaraderie (friendship) in small firms than in big companies.' Workers feel less involved and less secure in bigger firms. He added, 'It is more relaxed in small firms and people enjoy it more. Many also get more responsibility which adds to their satisfaction.' Moreover, employees of charities and other non-for-profit organisations are usually more motivated than employees of big for-profit businesses. This can be explained by the strong purpose behind these business activities, which makes people feel that they work for something higher than the profit of shareholders or their personal financial gain. For many people, this is a matter of self-actualisation.

1 Define what you understand by the terms:

    a   motivation

    b   responsibility   **[4]**

2 Identify **two** factors that seem to influence job satisfaction and explain them in terms of Maslow's hierarchy of needs.   **[4]**

3 Explain in terms of the features of job enrichment why it might be easier for small firms to motivate staff than big businesses.   **[4]**

4 By applying Adams' equity theory, explain why graduates are often demotivated at the workplace.   **[4]**

5 Discuss the extent to which it might be possible for large firms to use Herzberg's motivators to improve the level of worker motivation.   **[10]**

Extract 2: Things top employers do to attract and retain their employees

A study performed by a research centre at a global scale and across many industries in the secondary and tertiary economic sectors, suggests that only about 13% of employees feel engaged at work. The other 87% seems to suffer from a lower level of motivation and productivity. This phenomenon typically leads to high labour turnover, and as a result businesses need to be constantly searching for new employees.

CONTINUED

The same research identified the things that 'top employers' do in terms of human resource planning to increase labour retention and improve employee engagement at work:

- Top employers have advanced recruitment methods. They use internal recruitment, when possible, to show appreciation to existing employees and to motivate them with new responsibilities. When the business needs new ideas and know-how, they use external recruitment. They produce detailed and clear job descriptions, and they inform the candidate if the business expects them to accept flexible employment patterns. In the selection process, top employers value the candidates' personality equally if not more than the hard skills written on the CV. This way, they avoid the problem of recruits leaving the business because of not fitting the business culture. They also make sure that ethics are followed across the recruitment process, for example by ensuring adequate diversity among the shortlisted candidates.

- Top employers offer valuable training to employees, on the job and off the job, addressing both personal and professional needs. This way they attract the most talented employees, while they help their existing staff to stay competent and productive. They also understand the value of organised induction training to engage recruits as soon as possible and to help them to integrate with the rest of the organisation quickly.

- Top employers spend time and resources to appraise their employees professionally. They combine informal methods with formal appraisal methods, and they make sure that employees are always appraised fairly. They use appraisal not only to spot any areas of improvement for employees but also to reward them for excellent performance.

Excellent human resource planning does not come without disadvantages. Recruitment involves many steps, while businesses might be in a hurry to fill vacant positions. The cost of recruitment and training can be high and there is always a risk that well-trained employees will become attractive to competitive firms. Small business organisations cannot spend as many resources as big firms to recruit, train and formally appraise their employees.

1   Define the term 'induction training'. [2]

2   Explain **two** problems associated with high labour turnover, other than the business having to find and recruit new employees. [4]

3   With reference to the case study, explain why firms cannot always rely on internal recruitment. [4]

4   Suggest **two** reasons why appraisal is considered a very important process by top employers. [4]

5   Evaluate the advantages and disadvantages for businesses of spending resources on the recruitment, training and appraisal of employees. [10]

> Chapter 11

Organisational (corporate) culture

Higher-level

LEARNING OBJECTIVES

On completing this chapter you should be able to:

Know and understand:

> Organisational culture (AO1)

Apply and analyse:

> Types of organisational culture, e.g., Charles Handy's 'Gods of management' (AO2)

Synthesise and evaluate:

> Cultural clashes when organisations change, including but not limited to, when organisations grow and merge and when leadership styles change (AO3)

BUSINESS IN CONTEXT

Changing organisational (corporate) culture at Microsoft helps achieve rapid growth

Several studies have identified a direct correlation between a company's culture and its business performance. High-performing corporations – those that have higher revenue growth, market share and customer satisfaction than competitors – are more likely to exhibit cultural traits which bring out the best in employees, nurture innovation, encourage collaboration and support diversity and inclusion. Many companies adapt their **organisational (corporate) culture** to reflect the changing norms and standards of the societies in which they operate.

However, it is not easy to change the culture of a corporation the size of Microsoft. When Satya Nadella was appointed as CEO in 2014 he told employees that renewing the company's culture was his highest priority. Nadella has been credited with a virtual reinvention of Microsoft. Its market value now exceeds $1.7 trillion. When Nadella first took over, its market value was around $300 billion.

Before Nadella's appointment, Microsoft's culture featured fierce internal competition between different teams and departments and an aggressive employee performance review system. The rivalry between teams was intended to promote the best creative ideas, and the review system aimed to identify the strongest and weakest employees.

Nadella analysed the consequences of internal rivalry at Microsoft in his 2017 memoir manifesto, 'Hit Refresh: Innovation was being replaced by bureaucracy. Teamwork was being replaced by internal politics. We were falling behind.'

He introduced a much more supportive and collaborative approach, provided more positive feedback to product development teams, and introduced a 'learn-it-all' rather than 'know-it-all' philosophy within the company.

Discuss in pairs or a group:

- Explain why a new CEO might need to change the culture of an organisation.

- Is collaboration between teams and departments always likely to achieve better results than internal rivalry? Justify your answer.

- How can the culture of an organisation influence its performance?

KEY TERM

organisational (corporate) culture: the shared values, attitudes and beliefs of the people working in an organisation that influence how they interact with each other and with external stakeholder groups

KEY CONCEPT LINK

Creativity

Creativity in an organisation is a matter of culture. In tall bureaucratic businesses, creativity is not rewarded. In such organisations 'success' is measured in terms of compliance to procedures. Businesses that enhance creativity embrace diversity and teamwork among people who feel free to express different points of view. They value disagreement as a source of power for continuous improvement. They encourage risk-taking behaviour and are not afraid of failure; if things go wrong after an innovative decision is implemented, they value the learning opportunity this provides.

11.1 Organisational culture

A commonly used definition of organisational culture is 'the way we do things around here'. This means, how people within the organisation view the world and respond to it in trying to achieve certain goals.

It is widely understood that different organisations have distinctive cultures. This is true of businesses as well as other organisations such as schools and colleges. The culture of a steel company will be very different from that of a nursing home, for example. Similarly, some schools' culture is driven by the need for better examination results while others maintain that educating the 'complete person' is more important. The culture of an organisation gives it a sense of identity and is based on the values, attitudes and beliefs of the people who work in it, especially senior management.

Values, attitudes and beliefs have a very powerful influence on the way staff in a business will act, take decisions and relate to others in the organisation. They define what is 'normal' in an organisation, so it is possible for the same person to act in different ways in different organisations. What we do and how we behave – in society in general and in business in particular – are largely determined by our culture.

> **TIP**
>
> Culture is such a powerful force in any organisation that you should take every opportunity in your answers to refer to it as a factor that helps explain managers' decisions and behaviour.

Elements of organisational culture

An understanding of the culture of an organisation can be gained through:

- mission and vision statements – these inform employees and other stakeholders about what the business is trying to achieve
- the record of senior managers , e.g., in handling ethical issues – the directors and other senior managers will be one of the main influencing factors in an organisation's culture

- the organisation's ethical code of conduct – this lists the dos and don'ts that must be observed by employees when dealing with external stakeholders
- strategies on social and environmental issues – these will provide a clear guide to the organisation's social and environmental values and beliefs
- the example set by senior managers, e.g., how they treat subordinates, how they take decisions and how these are announced and introduced.

The industry that the business operates in will also influence the values and beliefs of the organisation. For instance, the culture of a weapons manufacturer or a tobacco company is likely to be very different from that of a workers' cooperative or a business operating homes for the elderly.

The legal constraints, social norms and cultural values of countries vary markedly, and these are likely to be reflected in the culture of organisations that are based there.

11.2 Types of organisational culture

Many management writers have used different ways to identify and classify different types of organisational culture, especially Charles Handy. Here are the most widely identified classifications of corporate culture.

Power culture

Power culture is associated with autocratic leadership. Power is concentrated at the centre of the organisation. Decisions can be made swiftly as so few people are involved in making them. Managers are judged by results rather than the means they used to obtain them. Autocratic leadership and hierarchical structures are features of organisations with a power culture.

Charles Handy uses the analogy of a spider's web – the spider at the centre of the web has all the power, and the web has little purpose without the spider. Motivational methods are likely to focus on financial incentives

> **KEY TERM**
>
> **power culture:** concentrating power among a few people

and bonuses to reward exceptional performance – and this can encourage risky and, in the longer term, inappropriate decisions.

Role culture

Role culture is usually associated with bureaucratic organisations. Employees operate within the rules and show little creativity. The structure of the organisation is well defined and each individual has clear delegated authority. Power and influence come from a person's position within the organisation. Decision-making is often slow and risk-taking is frowned upon.

Tall hierarchical structures are used in organisations with a powerful role culture. Handy uses the image of a substantial building to represent this form of culture – solid and dependable but not going anywhere fast.

Task culture

Organisations adopting this culture are likely to use groups to solve particular problems, and lines of communication are similar to a matrix structure (see Chapter 8). Such teams often develop a distinctive culture because they have been empowered to take decisions. Team members are encouraged to be creative and there may be a strong team spirit, which can lead to a very motivating environment – based on meeting workers' intrinsic needs.

Handy uses the image of a net to represent **task culture** – the net's strength is derived from the many strands.

Person culture

There may be some conflict between individual goals and those of the whole organisation, but **person culture** is the most creative type of culture. There is no emphasis on teamwork as each individual is focused on their own tasks and projects. This type of culture might be found in a scientific research environment or in a professional partnership such as lawyers and architects. Individuals who thrive in this type of environment will often find it difficult to work effectively in a more structured organisation.

Handy depicts this type of culture as a constellation of stars – each person is different from everyone else and operates alone.

ACTIVITY 11.1

Look at the two images showing people in business meetings. Just by looking at these pictures, can you identify possible differences in the organisational culture between the organisations? Discuss in class.

CASE STUDY 11.1

Marks & Spencer reinvents itself

Marks & Spencer (M&S) group plc is a major British retailer with a long heritage dating back to 1884. It sells clothing, home and food products globally. By 2021, M&S operated more than 1500 stores and employed more than 78 000 people around the world.

In 2018, after a year of declining profits, M&S announced a 'radical plan' to reshape the company's organisational culture, to become more agile and faster to respond to the changing consumer patterns. This plan would also help the business to compete online.

M&S's chief executive Steve Rowe admitted that the business had become too bureaucratic and slow, with a very tall organisational structure which made it too 'corporate' and hierarchical. Before the cultural change, many managers within M&S maintained roles with no true accountability. The new culture would be shaped across a simpler organisational structure, in which people would work in effective teams to accelerate change.

The culture change attempted by M&S is a difficult task and a long-term process. Part of it involves the closing of stores and redundancies in managerial positions. In May 2020, the business announced it was cutting 7000 jobs as the Covid-19 crisis forced

M&S to accelerate its turnaround. CEO Steve Rowe labelled the effort of M&S to reinvent itself as the 'never the same again' programme.

1   Define the term 'organisational culture'.   [2]

2   Using Handy's theory on types of culture, suggest the type of culture that best described M&S until 2018.   [4]

3   Suggest **two** reasons why CEO Steve Rowe wants to change the organisational culture at M&S.   [4]

4   Explain **two** problems that CEO Steve Rowe might encounter in his effort to change M&S's culture.   [4]

Entrepreneurial culture

In this culture, success is rewarded, but failure is not necessarily criticised since it is considered a consequence of enterprise and risk-taking. Although Handy did not specifically identify **entrepreneurial culture**, other theorists consider it to be important for certain types of organisations. This type of culture is usually found in flexible organisational structures. Motivation levels are likely to be high among people who enjoy the challenge of innovative risk-taking.

KEY TERM

entrepreneurial culture: encourages management and workers to take risks, to come up with new ideas and test out new business ventures

TIP

- As with leadership styles, there is no one right or wrong culture for a business. The appropriate culture will depend on the objectives of the organisation, the type of market it operates in, and the values and expectations of managers and employees.

- Do not expect all departments in a business to have the same culture. They may be very different. A team working with IT all day will be unlikely to have the same jargon, patterns of behaviour, values and beliefs as HR staff or marketing teams.

Balanced

CB Insights creates a culture that helps people to grow both on a personal and a professional level. The business competes in data analytics, and it offers services to companies that want to understand industry trends before taking important marketing decisions. CB Insights has created a learning culture, prioritising not only the technical training of employees but also any aspect of individual development and personal success. The employees within the business are encouraged to be hungry for knowledge and to work hard for success, but always with humility and by helping one another.

Managers in CB Insights have regular discussions with employees about their future career paths, personal passion and areas for development. They encourage employees to work on projects that interest them, hosting a quarterly 'Hack Day' in which employees focus on any type of work they want. Moreover, CB Insights has launched a 'culture for service' programme, through which its employees are given the opportunity to serve the local community with meaningful initiatives, such as technology education for children.

Why do you think CB Insights creates a culture that emphasises both the professional and the personal growth of its employees? How can a business in technology benefit from employing mentally and emotionally balanced people? Discuss in class.

'Gods of management'

Management thinker Charles Handy wrote a very influential book called *Gods of Management* (1978). In it, he argued that organisations and the culture of their managers can be classified by referring to Greek gods as metaphors: Zeus, Apollo, Athena and Dionysus.

According to Handy, Zeus represents leadership by trust. 'Zeus' managers can be dynamic entrepreneurs who make snap, intuitive decisions. This culture often arises under a dominant and successful business founder. Apollo manages through bureaucracy and a role culture. Managers who can be classified as 'Apollo like' demand consistency, order and employees who keep to their job descriptions. Individuality and personality

will not be strong qualities of these managers. Athena is the goddess of problem-solving, so managers who conform to this style will recognise expertise amongst subordinates and will create a task culture. Dionysus is the god of individualism, and using this approach will lead managers to create an organisation that serves the individual, not the other way round. There may be no clearly identified 'leader'. Employees will be unlikely to owe much allegiance to any one manager. This culture can lead to managers encouraging creative freedom, but it can also lead to internal conflicts and unproductive competition.

Handy continued his analysis by arguing that each organisation and each manager is guided by one of these gods. For example, a charity that favours processes and systems is influenced by Apollo. A Dionysian organisation, perhaps an advertising agency, might focus on creativity as each person is left to do their own thing. Employees might only join together to share resources.

Handy believes that many organisations are influenced by more than one of these classifications. In fact, he suggests it is important to realise that the most effective organisations are the ones that create a balance of power between each of the classifications. The manager they place in the prime leadership role should have the characteristics required for the task that needs to be done. For example, there would be little point in putting a charismatic Zeus leader in charge of the accounts department as the scope for original thinking is so limited. In contrast, it would be unwise to put a bureaucracy-loving Apollo in charge of developing original new product ideas.

Handy advocates a 'best fit' approach to organisational culture. According to him, most effective organisations have an appropriate fit between employees, the type of work, the business environment and the culture. This implies that changes in the work or the business environment may lead to a requirement for culture change as well.

11.3 Reasons for and consequences of cultural clashes

In most organisations it is likely that not all employees will share exactly the same values, attitudes and beliefs. These differences only become a problem if they lead to clashes between employees that result in demotivation, disaffection, and serious and unresolvable disagreements. Culture conflicts – or clashes – are most likely to arise when:

- A business changes rapidly and there is conflict between the established employees and the new managers and other employees who are recruited. This can be a particular problem for family businesses when they start to recruit external professional managers, and for loss-making businesses when a new CEO is appointed with the aim of cutting costs rapidly.

- A business merges with or acquires another business and the prevailing cultures of the two organisations cause such serious conflicts that synergy is unlikely to be achieved (see the examples that follow).

- A new leader is appointed or the existing leaders adopt a new style of leadership – the values and beliefs of a new leader may differ from those of the former 'boss'.

Here are some examples:

- A traditional family firm, which has favoured members of the family for promotion into senior posts, converts to a public limited company. New investors demand more transparency and recognition of natural talent from recruited employees. A different leadership style may lead to a clash with the existing culture of the business – hence the need to change existing values and beliefs.

- A product-led business needs to respond to changing market conditions by encouraging more employee involvement. A team or task culture may need to be adopted which some employees might find it difficult to adapt to.

- A recently privatised business, formerly managed on bureaucratic principles, needs to become more profit orientated and customer focused. An entrepreneurial culture may need to be introduced for the first time and existing managers and other employees may find this difficult to cope with.

- A merger or takeover may result in one of the businesses having to adapt its culture to ensure consistency within the newly created larger business unit. The danger of culture clashes as a result of mergers and takeovers is very real and Activity 11.2 gives an example of this between Amazon and

Whole Foods. The problem of culture clashes resulting from a merger or takeover involving businesses based in different countries can be even more acute. The culture clash between the management team at Mercedes (Germany) and Chrysler (USA) is often used as an example of how cross-border integration sometimes fails.

- Declining profits and market share may be the consequences of poorly motivated employees and a lack of interest in quality and customer service. A person culture may help to transform the prospects of this business, but existing employees may resist this unless they are trained in taking responsibility and in participating in decision-making.

> ### KEY TERM
>
> **culture clash:** a conflict arising from the interaction of people with different values, attitude and beliefs

Consequences of culture clashes

The consequences of not responding to these and other examples of culture clashes can be very serious. Disagreements over business objectives, the most appropriate strategies, ways of taking decisions and the very nature of those decisions will result from culture clashes between senior managers or between managers and other employees. The consequences of culture conflicts can be reduced or eliminated by encouraging all members of an organisation to adapt to and accept the same cultural values.

It could take several years before all employees and processes have fully adapted to the new culture and the values that senior management want to introduce. It means changing the way people think and react to problem situations. It can mean directly challenging the way things have been done for years. It can also involve substantial changes of personnel, job descriptions, communication methods and working practices.

The key common elements in effective cultural change to minimise clashes are:

- Concentrate on the positive aspects of the business and how it currently operates, and grow and adapt these. This will be much easier and more popular with employees than focusing on, and trying to change, negative aspects.

- Obtain the full commitment of people at the top of the business and all key personnel. These can become the 'influencers' during the change process. However, if they cannot or will not change, it might be easier to replace them altogether. Unless the key personnel model the behaviour they expect to see in others, change will be very difficult to achieve.

- Establish new objectives and a mission statement that accurately reflect the new values and attitudes that are to be adopted – then communicate these to all staff.

- Encourage 'bottom-up' participation of workers when culture clashes occur or when developing a new set of values or beliefs. The biggest mistake could be to try to impose a new culture on workers without explaining the need for change or without giving them the opportunity to propose alternative ways of working.

- Train employees in new procedures and new ways of working to reflect the changed value system of the business. If people believe in the change and understand the benefits of it, then it will become more acceptable to them.

- Change the employee reward system to avoid rewarding success in the 'old ways' and ensure that appropriate behaviour that should be encouraged receives recognition. People need to be reassured that if they adjust to the new approach they will gain from it.

CASE STUDY 11.2

Amazon's acquisition of Whole Foods 'killed' by cultural clash

Amazon's Whole Foods deal in 2017 was an example of integration which was supposed to allow Amazon to go beyond e-commerce by selling groceries in physical stores. Amazon was always interested in becoming a bigger player in food and beverages, given the sheer size of the market. The acquisition, which was worth $13.4 billion, also gave Amazon an advantage over Walmart, the largest grocery retailer in the USA, which is struggling to enter the e-commerce distribution channel.

However, market analysts have identified a cultural clash between the two businesses. Amazon is about low cost, efficiency and technology, it does not maintain a personalised culture, and it enforces strict employee discipline. Whole Foods was driven by idealistic values and approaches. It maintained high standards for quality and it decentralised decisions so that employees were empowered to build relationships and to offer creative health-food offerings at a local store level.

The cultural clash meant that decisions taken by Amazon's management were not compatible with the way things were done at Whole Foods. In Amazon, success means standardisation of processes for low cost, and data analysis for optimum performance measurement. So a new inventory system was implemented on Whole Foods.

This system centralised product selection decisions and forced prices down on many items. Employees started complaining about loads of paperwork and the fact that they no longer had time to provide good customer service. Whole Foods dropped from 'Fortune's best companies to work for' list for the first time in 20 years.

1 Explain what a 'cultural clash' is. [2]

2 Explain **two** advantages for Amazon of growing by acquiring Whole Foods. [4]

3 Suggest **two** opposing elements of organisational culture which created a cultural clash between Amazon and Whole Foods. [4]

4 Discuss the significance of the cultural clash in the Amazon–Whole Foods integration as a determinant of its long-term success. [10]

ACTIVITY 11.2

This is the first sign language Starbucks shop in China. There are more similar stores around the world. This store is an example of the practical application of the 'inclusion and diversity culture' that prevails at Starbucks.

1   Do your own research to find out what 'inclusion and diversity' mean from the perspective of the Starbucks organisation.

2   Find more examples of Starbucks' strategic decisions which reflect its 'inclusion and diversity' culture.

3   Find out what the mission of Starbucks is. Does 'inclusion and diversity' fit the mission of the business? Discuss in class.

ACTIVITY 11.3

The statements in the table reflect elements of organisational culture that may affect employee motivation. Use appropriate motivation theory to explain the possible positive or negative effects. The first one has been completed for you.

Element of organisational culture	Effect on employee motivation
In a fast-food restaurant, employees do not smile at customers because of a strong power culture in place. Their supervisor, who controls everything his subordinates do, talks down to them and does not allow them to connect with consumers.	Dissatisfaction according to Herzberg's theory, because decent treatment by management is a hygiene factor.
In a digital marketing agency, all employees are free to decide their own work schedule. There is no dress code, and people occasionally take the initiative to rearrange their seating arrangements.	
In a factory, when new employees are recruited the supervisor organises a lunch to introduce them to the rest of the workers. Teamwork is embedded in the production unit and many employees become best friends for life.	
In a big business selling clothes, all employees are treated as junior assistants. Supervisors are always polite, but no employee feels that their job is secure. They know that the slightest mistake will mean that their temporary contracts will not be renewed.	

THEORY OF KNOWLEDGE

Knowledge question: How important are reason, emotion and ethics in the creation of a successful business culture?

Which tech business has the best organisational culture in the world? Comparably has been awarding Google for many years as a 'Best Company' in terms of performing culture, based on real feedback from its employees. In 2021, Google won 14 Comparably awards, including the award for 'Best Company – Perks & Benefits', 'Best Company – Happiness' and 'Best Company – Leadership'.

Google embraces maximum flexibility at work, with people able to work in any way they wish, e.g., from home, or outside of usual working hours. Google's offices feature video games, ping-pong and nap pods, and such culture enhances creativity. Many micro-kitchens are found around the Google campus to bring people together, and employees are free to behave how they feel – they can even bring their dogs to work. Google aims to create a culture of inclusion with a clear set of values, emphasising ethics. The goal is to create an environment of constant innovation, which is key to the success and market leadership of the tech giant.

How do ethics and emotion shape the distinct organisational culture within Google? What role does reason play in the way culture is developed at Google? Are all three elements (reason, emotion and ethics) equally important to determine the culture which has been rated by employees as the best organisational culture in high technology? Discuss in class.

CASE STUDY 11.3

Can Bandile change the corporate culture of PEarth50?

PEarth50 is an NGO, the mission of which is 'a sustainable future for all creatures on earth'. The organisation was first established in South Africa but grew to become a multinational corporation, with offices around the world. To raise funds, PEarth50 sells toys, stationery and accessories produced by subcontractors. However, since 2018 the NGO has been failing to reach its strategic goals, and this led the CEO to resign.

Bandile Shosi took over as the new CEO of PEarth50. On the day he joined the organisation he observed a power culture, shaped around a few managers who had positions of authority in the business. The autocratic approach was even implemented in the marketing department, where the marketing director made all decisions and expected obedience from his subordinates. PEarth50 was not attracting enough volunteers, and this meant that the NGO had to employ several people at a high cost.

Bandile understood the need to change the organisational culture into one that would be task-oriented. He realised that an NGO dealing with hard-to-solve environmental problems needed the creativity that results from motivated and effective self-managed teams. As a first step, he communicated the following set of values, common for all employees and volunteers working for PEarth50:

- collaboration: finding solutions to environmental problems through teamworking

- ethics: acting with integrity, transparency and accountability

- inclusion: everyone is given an opportunity to contribute to PEarth50's effort and high purpose to serve the planet.

CONTINUED

1   State **two** characteristics of the 'power culture'. [2]

2   Explain **one** possible advantage and one disadvantage of the power culture prevailing at PEarth50. [4]

3   Suggest **two** reasons why Bandile believed that PEarth50 needed a common set of values. [4]

4   To what extent can the new chief executive influence the culture of PEarth50? [10]

SELF-EVALUATION CHECKLIST

After studying this chapter, complete this table.

I know and understand:	Needs more work	Almost there	Ready to move on
organisational culture (AO1)			
I am able to apply and analyse:			
types of organisational culture, e.g., Charles Handy's 'Gods of management' (AO2)			
I am able to synthesise and evaluate:			
the reasons for and consequences of cultural clashes (AO3)			

REFLECTION

How would you explain the culture of your school or college to someone who does not attend it?

Compare your view of its culture with another student's view.

PROJECT

Split into two groups.

1   Each group needs to choose a for-profit social enterprise.

2   Find evidence of the prevailing culture in your chosen organisation.

3   Prepare a presentation to describe the culture of your chosen organisation, using Handy's types of organisational culture.

4   Compare and contrast the two cultures. Are there any similarities? If yes, does this have to do with the fact that both businesses are social enterprises? Discuss in class.

Thinking about your project:

*   When researching the corporate culture, did you research the mission and/or vision statements and stated values to see how these reflect the organisational culture?

EXAM-STYLE QUESTIONS

Prestige Supermarkets – a case study in cultural change

As one of the country's largest family-owned chain of supermarket stores, Prestige Supermarkets had established a culture amongst its staff that had contributed to its success and growth. Loyalty to the family managers was high. Staff often commented on the whole business being like a 'big family'. Promotion was based on long service and loyalty. Relationships with suppliers had been built up over many years and long-term supply contracts were in place. Customer service was a priority and as Prestige never intended to be the cheapest shop in the towns it operated in. Its mission statement was: 'Always caring about our customers by offering excellent services and products' and it reflected the company's culture. Employees received both on-the-job and off-the-job training. However, profits were low, and the younger members of the owning family lacked the skills to take over.

It was clear to some industry experts that some of these values and attitudes had to change once it was sold and converted into a public limited company. The new chief executive, Josefina Dominquez, had experience as an operations manager for the biggest supermarket competitor in the market. On the first day of her appointment, she announced to the press: 'There is a lot of potential to unlock within Prestige. I intend to improve the shareholders' value and to increase dividends starting from this year, by finding ways to cut costs and to boost the efficiency of the business. There are also many opportunities for us to capture in the growing online grocery sales channel.'

Within five weeks, half of the directors and key managers had been replaced. Suppliers' terms were changed, on Josefina's insistence, to '5% below the cheapest'. Suppliers not complying with this requirement were dropped. Staff salary and pension schemes were replaced for new recruits with flexible pay and temporary employment contracts. All employees had to follow the rules determined by Josefina. Labour turnover increased sharply.

Josefina had not predicted the adverse media coverage of these changes. She said, 'I am only trying to change our corporate culture to one which is more efficient and flexible. Competition is intense and consumers demand good quality at low prices.'

1	Define the term 'corporate culture'.	[2]
2	Explain **one** possible reason why Josefina thought it necessary to change the organisational culture of Prestige Supermarkets.	[2]
3	Outline the type of culture that Josefina seems to be introducing at Prestige Supermarkets.	[2]
4	Explain **one** possible advantage and **one** disadvantage for Prestige Supermarkets of offering training to their employees.	[4]
5	By using appropriate motivation theory, explain why labour turnover increased in prestige supermarkets after Josefina was appointed as the new CEO.	[4]
6	Suggest **one** possible advantage and **one** disadvantage for Prestige Supermarkets of the increase in labour turnover.	[4]
7	Identify and outline **two** areas of stakeholder conflict in Prestige Supermarkets, resulting from Josefina's effort to change the organisational culture.	[4]
8	Explain **one** advantage and **one** disadvantage for Prestige Supermarkets of Josefina's decision to focus on protecting the shareholders' value.	[4]
9	Explain **two** reasons why the mission statement of a business such as Prestige Supermarket should reflect its organisational culture.	[4]
10	To what extent can Josefina, as a new chief executive, influence the culture of the organisation?	[10]

> Chapter 12

Communication

LEARNING OBJECTIVES

On completing this chapter you should be able to:

Apply and analyse:

- Barriers to communication (AO2)

Synthesise and evaluate:

- Formal and informal methods of communication for an organisation in a given situation (AO3)

BUSINESS IN CONTEXT

Technology and business communication

The latest technological advances have had an immense impact on how a business communicates with its stakeholders. Smartphones, iPads, tablets, networks, cloud computing, VR (virtual reality), Zoom and Microsoft Teams are some of the developments that allow businesses to communicate in ways that, even in the early 2000s, would have been unimaginable.

Networking promotes collaboration on reports, programming and other document production. Cloud computing allows businesses to operate globally without sacrificing security or limiting user access. Some businesses – such as LinkedIn and Kaplan – give employees iPads to allow easier internal communication and constant web access.

Intranets are helping to drastically reduce many administrative jobs. Once online, employees can take training courses, communicate with colleagues, find out how much holiday they have or check internal job vacancies. M2M (machine to machine) technology provides the ability to collect important business data on a continual basis. VR is used in many business applications. For example, construction businesses use VR produce a virtual 3D tour of a property that has not yet been built in order to show potential clients what it will look like. The 'work from home' trend, boosted by the global pandemic, has led to most meetings in some businesses being conducted online.

With all of this technology, perhaps a stage will be reached when we never have to meet with people at work in order to communicate with them. But this could have serious human and social consequences. Zoom's chief financial officer, Kelly Steckelberg, has said: 'We certainly understand that being on video all day long can be challenging'. She said that Zoom encourages its employees to take some calls while out walking and to shorten scheduled online meetings to prevent burnout.

Discuss in pairs or a group:

- Do you think technologically advanced methods of communication are always the best ones to use?

- What would be the disadvantages of never having to meet with people at work in order to communicate with them?

KEY CONCEPT LINK

Creativity

Effective communication enables the transparent transmission of instructions and facts within an organisation, but it also enhances creativity. This is especially important in businesses that increasingly rely on technology. Effective communication is what distinguishes people from machines and it is the only way to build relationships. Communication can create strong teams, able to generate ideas through collaboration. Good communicators often link together to share expertise, which can generate new products and solutions to problems.

12.1 Business communication

All businesses need to communicate with stakeholders. Some communication is internal (between managers and other employees for example) and some is external, such as between the business and customers or suppliers. Business efficiency depends greatly on **effective communication** with all of these groups. Communication is only effective if the message has been received and understood by the receiver, and the sender knows that it has been understood. Figure 12.1 shows the key stages of effective communication:

- sender (or transmitter) of the message
- clear message
- appropriate medium (way in which the message is sent)
- receiver
- **feedback** to confirm receipt and understanding.

If the message has been sent, but there has been no feedback, then the effectiveness of the communication cannot be judged.

KEY TERMS

effective communication: the exchange of information between people or groups, with feedback

feedback: information given by the receiver in response to a message

---

Importance of effective business communication

The effectiveness of internal communication can have an impact on many areas of business.

- Employee motivation and labour productivity – if employees are encouraged to participate through group discussion, for example, then effective communication will aid motivation.

- The number and quality of ideas generated by the workforce – if employees are asked for their ideas this can assist with problem-solving and management decision-making.

- Speed of decision-making – the more people who have to be communicated with, the slower the decision-making system, so directing messages just to those who 'need to know' will speed up this process.

- Speed of response to market changes – if changes in consumer tastes take a long time to be communicated to the main decision-makers, then the business will be slow to respond with appropriate products.

- Reducing errors – incorrect understanding of a poorly expressed message will lead to potentially serious errors. This could lead to many internal problems, such as the wrong products being made or incorrect prices being set.

- Effective coordination between departments – this will be helped by good communication links between them.

Poor communication will lead to demotivated workers, uncoordinated departments, poor customer service and a lack of overall direction for the organisation.

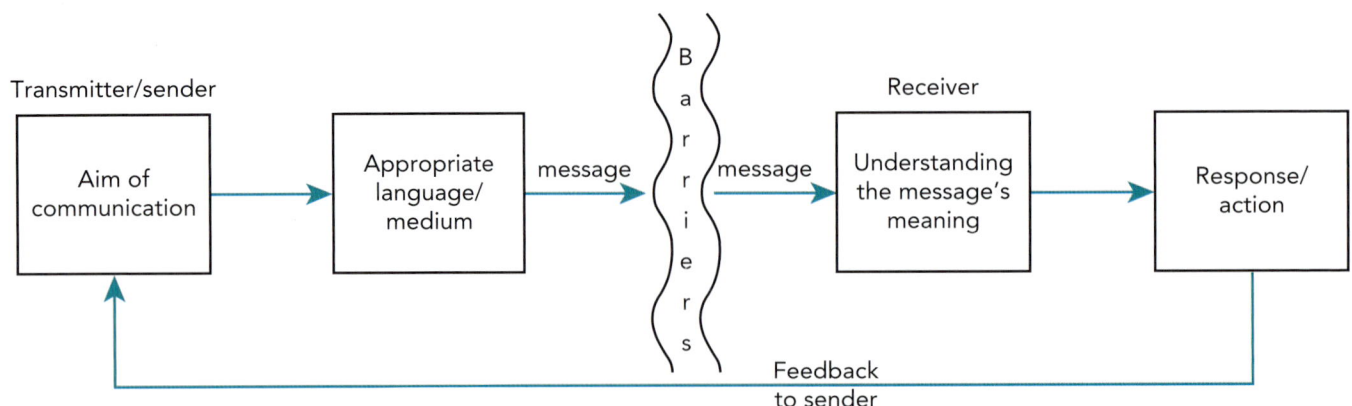

Figure 12.1: Effective communication – barriers must be reduced or eliminated

LEARNER PROFILE

Communicators

The best leaders are great communicators

David Nelms is the former CEO of Discover Financial with 17 000 employees. Communication is a hallmark of David's leadership style and played a huge role in growing his company and creating an engaged and productive workforce. He realises that the importance of communication will only grow as how we communicate changes.

David said: 'A leader who doesn't adapt to the new ways of communication will never be heard.

We aren't getting and sharing information the same way we used to. Understanding the various tools we have to communicate as well as how to communicate across different channels is essential, and as the number of ways to communicate increases, this skill will only become more valuable.'

'A leader who doesn't adapt to the new ways of communication will never be heard.' Discuss this quote in class. Do you agree that leaders should always find new ways to communicate? If yes, why? Are there any disadvantages for leaders when they change their methods of communication?

CASE STUDY 12.1

Why is communication in GIdea ineffective?

Vicente is the CEO of GIdea Inc., a medium-sized business organisation producing home decoration and accessories sold through premium concept stores and GIdea's online store. The business employs 120 people, organised in a traditional, by-function hierarchy. Vicente always believed in the power of **formal communication** and asked his subordinates to put everything in writing. 'Sending emails helps us reduce errors and misunderstandings,' he said in a meeting. 'What is discussed in the corridor is easily forgotten. If you have an idea for a new product to add to our portfolio, please do not just come to me to discuss it in person. First, send me an email with all the details: product description, photos, cost of production, suggested price and any other information related to it.'

Even though communication in GIdea is primarily electronic, Vicente is still not happy with its effectiveness. He cannot understand why he is gradually receiving fewer and fewer ideas for new products, even though he wants to motivate people and encourage employees' participation in the decision-making process. He is also afraid that the business is becoming slower in responding to market changes, which is a big problem because GIdea competes with many small and big competitors.

1   Define the term 'formal communication'.   [2]

2   With reference to the case study, explain the difference between formal and informal communication.   [4]

3   Suggest **two** reasons why the effectiveness of communication is essential for GIdea.   [4]

4   Evaluate the effectiveness of formal communication through emails in GIdea.   [10]

KEY TERM

formal communication: information that flows through well-defined official channels

Methods of formal communication

Formal communication is used when people in an organisation need to communicate with others through official channels. Much formal communication is initiated by managers or supervisors with the aim of giving information to other employees, perhaps in a subordinate position. Some formal communication can be in the other direction, still vertical within the organisational structure, but from employees to managers, such as a daily report on production levels or customer numbers. Communication can also be horizontal, e.g., between managers in different functional departments.

The choice of the method used to communicate a message can have a significant impact on effectiveness. The range of formal **communication methods** available can be classified as follows.

Spoken communication

This can be undertaken by one-to-one conversations, interviews, appraisal sessions, group meetings or team briefings.

Strengths:

- It allows for two-way communication and feedback and this should encourage good motivation. Herzberg considered that frequent feedback was a powerful motivational factor. **Spoken communication** is instantaneous – there is no delay between sending and receiving the message.
- Evidence of who attended the meeting, and therefore who received the message, can be kept for future reference.
- If any points are not made clearly, then the receiver(s) should be able to ask for immediate clarification.
- It allows the sender or the transmitter to reinforce the message with an appropriate tone of voice or, if visible to the receiver, with body language.

Weaknesses:

- Some spoken communication can be ambiguous, and in a large group some receivers may be reluctant to ask for further detail.
- There may be no written record of what was said.
- It might not be appropriate for complicated and technical matters, which would be better sent in a written format.

- Spoken communication, especially on a one-to-one basis, can be time consuming.

> ### KEY TERMS
>
> **communication methods:** the media used to convey a message
>
> **spoken communication:** oral way of sending information between two or more people

Written communication

Many managers still like everything to be in writing. So they will tend to use letters, memos, notices on boards, reports, minutes of meetings, and diagrams for technical matters such as house plans. Many written messages are sent electronically.

Strengths:

- Written messages can be referred to more than once to aid the understanding of the receiver.
- Written communication allows detailed information, figures and diagrams to be sent.
- It provides a permanent record which might be useful legally e.g., with employment contracts.

Weaknesses:

- Non-verbal communication, such as body language, cannot be used to support the message.
- It does not allow for immediate feedback, and clarification of the message cannot be obtained quickly.
- There is evidence that the message has been sent but not that it has been received and/or understood.

IT – electronic communication

Electronic communication includes email, instant messaging, websites, blogs, text messaging, voicemail, videoconferencing and video messaging. Electronic communication has changed the way businesses communicate with each other and the way they communicate internally.

Strengths:

- Message are transmitted rapidly as it requires only a few seconds to communicate via electronic media.

- Global coverage is possible as the internet allows communication with, potentially, millions of 'receivers' all over the world.

- Once the hardware and training costs have been covered, electronic communication is low cost. It can save time and money compared to more traditional methods. For example, text SMS is cheaper than a traditional letter, and a videoconference can save thousands of dollars in transport costs transporting delegates to one geographical location.

- Electronic communication allows for instant exchange of feedback.

- It increases information so that managers can control a large, perhaps global, business. Business managers can now control operations more easily around the world.

- Most countries' legal systems now allow emails to be used as evidence and legal proof of contracts and transactions.

- Online videoconferences allow employees to work from home, potentially reducing the need for costly office space. Employees can spend less time and money on travelling to work too.

Weaknesses:

- The various methods may require employees to be trained, and the young are usually much more proficient in their use than older employees.

- They reduce social contact and can create a sense of isolation. An important social need may go unsatisfied.

- Employees may send personal messages during company time.

- Direct interpersonal contact is lost and most of these media do not facilitate the use of body language to help convey messages.

- There are security and technical issues with computer technology, and hard copies of important messages are often kept too in case of a computer virus.

- There is increasing evidence that IT can lead to **information overload** as a result of the speed and low usage cost of these methods. Too many messages can prevent the really important communication from being noticed and acted upon. For example, the sheer volume of email messages can take some workers several hours to reply to each day. Too much information can also cause stress and a feeling of overwork.

- Online videoconferences can lead to excess time spent in front of computer screens. The social interactions between employees are fewer than when they meet in person, and this can reduce the creativity and interaction between work groups.

> ### KEY TERM
>
> **information overload**: so much information and so many messages are received that the most important ones cannot be easily identified and quickly acted on – most likely to occur with electronic media

Visual communication

This form of communication makes an impact on the receiver by presenting information in a non-verbal form. This method includes: maps, charts, posters graphic design, animation, short films, diagrams, pictures, charts and other computer images.

Strengths:

- It is effective for receivers who do not speak the same language as the communicator – at least, in the language being used for communication. Visual communication may be more effective to exchange information when communicating with people from several different countries.

- It supports oral communication which becomes more meaningful if graphs, pictures and diagrams are used with it. They can create a real impact to support the sender's message.

- It is a simple way of presenting complex information – such as an organisational chart.

- The receiver can understand messages presented in this form more quickly than if they were transmitted in pages of text.

Weaknesses:

- Visual methods of communication can be more costly and time consuming to produce, for example a video to be used in training.

- They cannot be the only method used when detailed technical data or accounting information needs to be transmitted.

- They do not allow for non-verbal communication such as body language.

- The visual images used might be so dramatic that they take the receiver's attention away for the information they are meant to transmit.

Interpersonal communication

Interpersonal communication can take place without a single word being spoken. When two or more people are in the same room, non-verbal communication can send messages between them. The way people stand or sit, their facial expressions and appearance can send messages to others and allow them to form an impression about that person's role, personality, intentions or even emotional state. Although there might not be an intention to communicate, people receive messages through these non-verbal indicators.

Once verbal communication begins, it is not just what is said that impacts on communication. How it is said, the emphasis put on certain words, the gestures that are used and other forms of body language will all impact on how effective the communication is.

Factors influencing choice of communication method

Managers will consider these factors before deciding on the best communication method:

- The importance of a written record that the message has been sent and received, for example an important new legal contract.
- The advantages to be gained from employee input or two-way communication. For example, a new employee shift system proposal could be discussed with workers before implementation.
- Cost. Electronic media often require expensive capital resources, but once these are obtained, electronic communication is cost-effective. The cost of management time in meetings should not be overlooked. For example, it would be quicker and cheaper, but may be less effective, to email all of those concerned instead. If videoconferences were adopted in preference to meetings in person, it could lead to reduced overhead costs as less office space will be needed.
- Speed. Electronic means of communication can be quick, but is this more important than allowing time for opinions to be discussed at a meeting?

- Quantity of data to be communicated. The longer and more detailed the message, the less likely it is that oral communication will be effective.
- Whether more than one method should be used for clarity and to be sure that the message has been received. A quick telephone call followed up by an official letter or order form will achieve both speed and accuracy.
- Size and geographical spread of the business. Regular and frequent meetings of senior regional managers may be impossible in a multinational business.
- Health issues. The global pandemic meant that many workers felt safer working from home using online methods of communication.

Methods of informal communication

Have you ever heard about important events in, or decisions about, your school or college through the 'grapevine' before any official announcements? If so, you have been part of an **informal communication** channel. There is unofficial communication in every organisation – it takes place in the rest room or at the lunch table, in the queue next to the photocopier or in meetings before the official agenda begins. Some of it may be no more than gossip, but a lot of it can be well-informed information about the organisation. In fact, much informal communication is not necessarily about work at all – it might just be social interactive chat.

Whatever managers might think about informal communication, they will find it very hard to stop people chatting in groups or with friends at work. After all, communication is a natural human activity.

KEY TERMS

interpersonal communication: exchange of information between two or more people

informal communication: the sending of unofficial messages between informal groups within an organisation

---

Table 12.1 summarises alternative views of informal communication.

Some managers restrict informal communication because:	Some managers encourage informal communication because:
It wastes valuable working time	Informal communication can help create important feelings of belonging, teamwork and social cohesion
It spreads gossip and rumours, and these can be unsettling and lead to feelings of insecurity	Management can use the grapevine to 'test out' new ideas and see what the unofficial reaction might be – if it is too negative, they might never make an official announcement
It may result in informal groups banding together to resist management decisions – even though they may not have been officially communicated yet	It can help to reduce barriers between departments and encourage development of new ideas
The unofficial information might be inaccurate and this could lead to misunderstandings and unnecessary conflicts with management	Studies have shown it can be faster than formal communication

Table 12.1: Alternative views of informal communication

Informal communication networks do not exist within the structure of the organisational hierarchy. Informal meetings between two or more employees can take place anywhere at the place of work, such as the canteen or even the elevator! Often informal communication networks have been referred to as 'grapevine communication' or 'water-cooler communication' or 'photocopier communication.' Some business analysts suggest that up to 70% of all internal communication could be classified as informal.

Davis, K. (1969) has argued that there are four types of informal communication methods or networks. In a single channel (or strand) network, the process of communication is linear and information travels from one person to the next person. This approach means that the message will take some time to reach a number of people and it could become distorted along the way.

THEORY OF KNOWLEDGE

Knowledge question: Does emotion play an equally important role to language in business communication?

Language facilitates the effectiveness of communication to a great extent, especially in multicultural environments. In multinational organisations, employees with exceptional language skills are often offered opportunities for cross-functional job rotations and careers abroad in subsidiary businesses as ex-patriots. On the other hand, the lack of language skills often prevents workers from building relationships with colleagues and customers, especially when differences in culture act as a barrier to communication in the first place.

Emotion affects communication as well. Anxiety, anger, pride, frustration, depression and trauma are examples of emotions that can raise barriers to communication. Emotions also affect non-verbal communication, the so-called 'body language', which is expressed through body posture, gestures, eye contact and tone of voice. Non-verbal communication is critical in determining attitudes and, thus, the ability of people to communicate with others.

Research suggests that communication gaps between employees and their managers result from problematic non-verbal communication and the inability of people to control their emotions. Therefore, leaders should receive training in effective non-verbal communication.

'Language barriers to communication are more difficult to overcome compared to emotional barriers.' To what extent is this true? Discuss in class.

The second type of informal communication network that Davis identified is the gossip communication network. Using this approach, there is one individual who acts as the source of the message and who transmits the message to a number of people directly.

The third type of informal communication described by Davis is referred to as the probability communication network. In this system, there is one individual who acts as the primary source of the information. They randomly select people within their work or social group to communicate the message. These people then also randomly pick other people to transmit the message. As with an email 'spam' message, there is no way for the source of the message to be tracked or the content to be verified, as the message is communicated randomly.

The final form of informal communication network identified by Davis is the cluster network. With this, the transmitter of the message chooses a number of pre-selected people to communicate a message to. The secondary people then pass on the message to a group of people who have also been pre-selected to receive the message. This can lead to rapid communication to a large number of people.

ACTIVITY 12.1

Microsoft's mission statement:

'Empower every person and every organisation on the planet to achieve more.'

Discuss in class:

1 This mission statement appears on a wall in one of Microsoft's offices. What is the business trying to achieve?

2 Why do mission and vision statements typically appear first on the official web pages of businesses?

12.2 Barriers to effective communication

Any factor that prevents a message being received or correctly understood is called a 'barrier to communication'. These **communication barriers** are often much more of a problem for large businesses with operations in more than one location and with several levels of hierarchy.

KEY TERM

communication barrier: something that gets in the way of a message being received

---

There are four broad reasons why barriers to communication occur.

1 Failure in one of the stages of the communication process:

- The method chosen might be inappropriate. If the message contained detailed technical language and flow diagrams, trying to explain these over a smartphone could lead to incorrect understanding.

- If a receiver forgot part of a long message given to them orally, then a written version would have been more appropriate.

- A misleading or an incomplete message would result in poor understanding – 'send the goods soon' may be interpreted as being tomorrow when in fact the sender meant 'now' or 'as soon as possible'.

- The excessive use of technical language or jargon (terms that are understood by a specific group but not by others) may prevent the receiver from being able to comprehend what is required. Messages sent to branches or employees in another country may not be understood unless they are translated into the local language.

- If there is too much information – perhaps more than is actually necessary for the receiver to respond in the right way – the threat of information overload leads to what is known as 'noise'. This is unnecessary information that actually prevents the receiver from grasping the important elements of the message.

- If the channel of communication is too long from the sender to the receiver, messages will be slow to reach their intended receiver and they may become distorted or the meaning may change along the way. This problem is particularly significant in large organisations with long chains of command.

2 Poor attitudes of either the sender or the receiver:

- If the sender is not trusted – perhaps because of previous misleading messages or unpopular decisions – then the receiver may be unwilling to listen to or read the message carefully.

- Unmotivated or alienated workers make poor receivers. If workers have never been consulted on important issues before, then they may become very suspicious if the management style seems to be changing towards a more participative one. Workers with little interest in their work will not want to take the trouble to ensure that communication is effective.

- Intermediaries – people on the communication channel – may decide not to pass on a message, or to change it, if they are poorly motivated. This could occur, for example, if there has been a supplier query about an order or a customer complaint.
- The sender may have such a poor opinion or perception of the receiver that no effort is made to ensure clarity of message or to check on understanding.

3 Physical reasons:

- Noisy factories are not the best environment for communication. This is an example that shows that the poor quality of the external environment can limit effective communication.
- Geographical distance can inhibit effective communication – certainly interpersonal communication will be very difficult. Modern electronic methods, such as videoconferencing, are designed to overcome some of these problems, but these depend on reliable internet links.

4 Failure to consider different cultures:

- Ignoring culture in business communication can lead to problems and communication disruptions. Internal business communication can be disrupted or misinterpreted if workers do not share the same understanding of goals, expectations and processes as managers. Understanding a culture can help businesses anticipate potential challenges or barriers in the adoption of new policies or processes before efforts break down. For example, some business cultures such as in Western Europe may thrive in an exchange- and dialogue-based communication system while other cultures (e.g., Japanese and Arab cultures) rely more heavily on subtext. If new information or ideas are suddenly imposed on employees who are accustomed to a participative business culture, there may be a deep-seated resistance and the project could fail.
- The impact of cultural differences on communication methods can be huge,

and failure to recognise this can lead to a significant barrier. The choice of communication method can have cultural overtones. The determining factor may not be the degree of industrialisation, but rather whether the country falls into a 'high-context' or 'low-context culture'.

- High-context cultures (Mediterranean, Slav, Central European, Latin American, African, Arab, Asian, American–Indian) leave much of the message unspecified, to be understood through context, non-verbal cues, and between-the-lines interpretation of what is actually said. By contrast, low-context cultures (most Germanic and English-speaking countries) expect messages to be explicit and specific. Therefore, culture directly affects verbal and non-verbal business communication. Some cultures, including Australia, the UK and Germany, place high significance on the words actually spoken. Other cultures, including Japanese and Arab cultures, still place significance on the spoken word, but also place great significance on the context of the conversation. Silence carries significance in all cultures, and this might be interpreted in different ways during cross-cultural business meetings.
- In **sequential cultures** (like North America, the UK, Germany, Sweden and the Netherlands), business people give full attention to one agenda item after another.
- In **synchronic cultures** (including South America, southern Europe and Asia) the flow of time is viewed as a sort of circle, with the past, present and future all interrelated. This viewpoint influences how organisations in those cultures approach deadlines, strategic thinking, investments and the concept of 'long-term' planning.

Reducing communication barriers

One of the important roles of management in facilitating communication is to minimise communication barriers. If managers are successful in reducing or eliminating barriers, then communication will be improved in all situations.

There are six steps managers should take to minimise the impact of communication barriers:

- Ensure the message is clear and precise but adequately detailed.

- Keep the communication channel short, for example by having as few intermediaries as possible between the original transmitter and the eventual receiver of the message.

- Make sure that the method of communication used is appropriate for the information to be transmitted and the culture of the receiver.

- Ensure feedback is part of the communication process so that problems with receipt or understanding of the message can be checked quickly.

- Establish trust between senders and receivers – this could be most easily achieved in a business where the culture is to accept all employees as being important and as having useful contributions to make.

- Ensure that physical conditions are appropriate so that messages can be heard or received effectively.

CASE STUDY 12.2

The 'Zoom fatigue' phenomenon: when videoconferencing replaces physical interaction and communication

Angelique works for a computer software company. She manages a team of five computer engineers who develop software for big multinational companies. When the Covid-19 pandemic forced everyone out of the office due to lockdown, Angelique saw an opportunity to replace physical meetings with Zoom calls. 'We are computer scientists,' she said. 'We do not need to have face-to-face meetings in the office. Videoconferences are much more effective. We can interact as we do in person. And at the same time we can record our meetings for future reference, as well as instantly sharing documents and other resources online'.

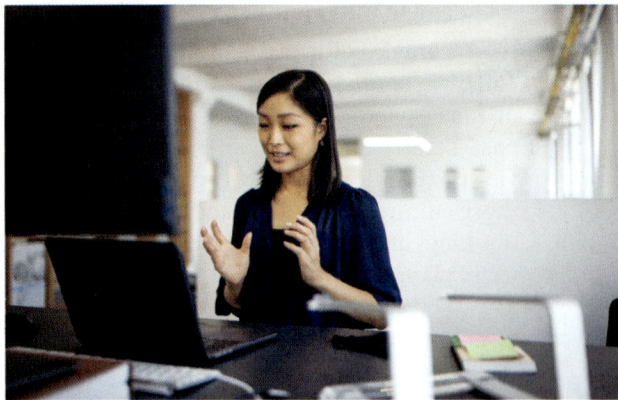

However, two months later her team showed signs of what researchers describe as 'Zoom fatigue': people started feeling exhausted from overusing virtual work meetings as a means of communication. One reason behind this phenomenon is the information overload in Zoom meetings. Another is that non-verbal communication is very different behind the camera, while the process is less natural and does not help people bond as teams. Team building is better achieved through informal communication channels and face-to-face meetings.

When people communicate through Zoom, they can get distracted by their environment, especially when working from home. One of the engineers has developed a negative attitude towards video meetings. He has become alienated and often fails to connect on time, claiming technical problems. Angelique called a meeting with her team to see if they should continue relying on videoconferencing and how they can improve communication efficiency in the department.

1   Define the term 'non-verbal communication'. [2]

2   Explain **one** advantage and **one** disadvantage of videoconferencing as a method of communication for Angelique and her team. [4]

3   Identify **two** barriers to communication in Angelique's job environment. [4]

4   Suggest **two** methods to improve communication effectiveness in Angelique's department. [4]

ACTIVITY 12.2

Amazon's Alexa changes the way things are done in a business

Alexa for Business lets employees reserve meeting rooms and start conference calls using intuitive voice commands. Employees do not need to use remote controls and manually dial in to meetings or look up room availability on the calendar. Employees can just say: 'Alexa, join the meeting' to start their online meeting, or: 'Alexa, is this room booked?' to check if the meeting room is free, or: 'Alexa, who booked the room?' to find who made the booking, and: 'Alexa, book the room' to book a meeting room. Alexa for Business also provides end-of-meeting reminders a few minutes prior to the start of the next meeting. This encourages employees to end their meetings promptly and allows the next meeting to start on time.

How does it work?

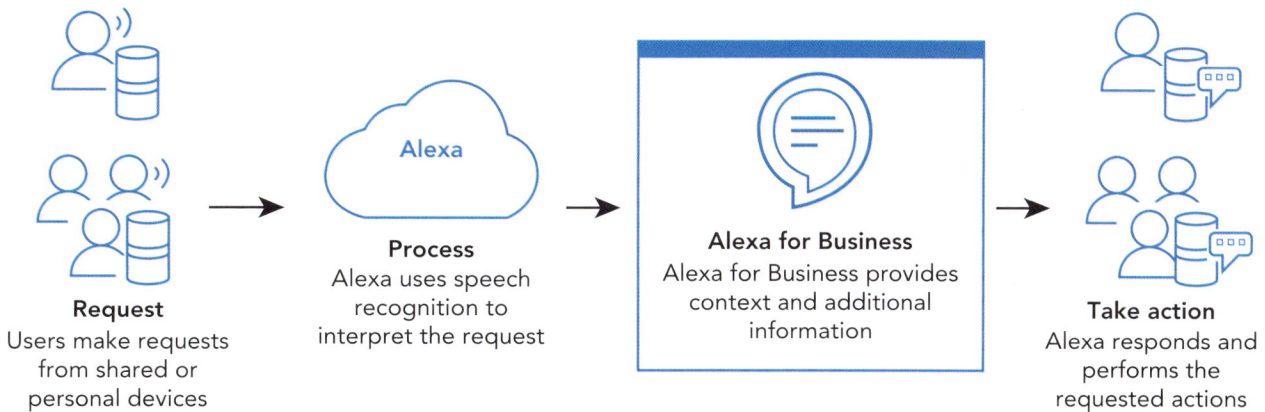

Request
Users make requests from shared or personal devices

Process
Alexa uses speech recognition to interpret the request

Alexa for Business
Alexa for Business provides context and additional information

Take action
Alexa responds and performs the requested actions

1   Find more information about Alexa For Business and identify how it can help businesses improve communication efficiency and productivity at work.

2   Does technology such as Alexa For Business create any new type of communication problems at work? Discuss in class.

SELF-EVALUATION CHECKLIST

After studying this chapter, complete this table.

I am able to apply and analyse:	Needs more work	Almost there	Ready to move on
barriers to communication (AO2)			
I am able to synthesise and evaluate:			
formal and informal methods of communication for an organisation in a given situation (AO3)			

REFLECTION

Your school or college is planning to allow some teachers to work some days each week from home. Your only contact with teachers during these days will by online messaging and video lessons. Write a report to the head teacher/principal, explaining what you consider to be the advantages and disadvantages of these methods of communication between teachers and students. Compare your ideas with those of another learner.

PROJECT

You are working for CFG, a big for-profit business organisation producing cosmetics. The board of directors has decided to turn the organisation from one focused on shareholders and their profits to a social enterprise, caring for the environment and spending part of its profit to empower young women with initiatives such as sourcing ingredients from women's cooperatives in developing countries.

The change in the strategy is dramatic and is reflected in the change of a mission statement from: 'We make women beautiful by creating innovative luxury cosmetics' to: 'We exist to make the world beautiful and fair'.

Split into two groups.

- **Group 1:** Prepare a press conference to present your business and its new corporate objectives. Use a variety of communication media during the conference (e.g., PowerPoint presentation, poster, etc.) to communicate the new mission effectively to the representatives of the press.

- **Group 2:** You are the audience at the press conference. Be ready to ask questions about the reasons for the change in the strategy and the problems that the business is expected to face during this change.

Thinking about your project:

- **Group 1:** When preparing for the press conference, have you clearly presented the current corporate objectives and how these change as the business becomes a social enterprise? Are your new objectives SMART?

- **Group 2:** Are you equipped to keep notes during the presentation to help you ask effective questions and provide feedback to CFG managers?

EXAM-STYLE QUESTIONS

Communication inefficiency within Trench plc

Trench plc is a multinational company producing heavy equipment for the construction industry. Its four main markets are the USA, Australia, India and Nigeria. It employs 9000 employees, and it has more than 100 000 industrial customers worldwide. The HR department in the head office, in the USA, surveyed regional offices to identify the extent to which communication is effective in the organisation.

The main findings were as follows.

- Horizontal communication across functions is relatively poor. People communicate more efficiently within their departments.

- Senior managers are not aware of any complaints or suggestions coming from the customers. The sales people receive feedback from the market but do not effectively escalate the information upwards through the tall organisational structure.

- In counties such as Nigeria, where the business culture is rather hierarchical, younger employees find it hard to 'open up' and work in teams with older colleagues, especially with managers who are from other countries.

CONTINUED

Trench fails to consider differences in culture and their effect on business communication. Both creativity and productivity in such countries tend to be lower than average.

- Most office communication is done through emails. Employees complain of receiving hundreds of emails per week making it difficult to separate the important and urgent messages from the less-significant ones.

- Workers in the factories feel 'left out of what is happening in the business'. More than 40% of people working in the factory were unaware of the business's mission statement.

To improve communication, the management decided to delayer by cutting one layer off the traditional hierarchy. They also decided to train workers in the factory to use emails and videoconferences. So the CEO would share with them important messages. However, according to the survey results, employees believed that the business needed more informal communication, rather than formal – especially in the factory. They also complained about other problems such as noise in the production unit, which is detrimental to the working conditions and constitutes a barrier to communication. However, the management does not favour informal communication on the premises.

1 Explain what is meant by 'effective communication'.   [2]
2 Identify **two** communication issues in Trench that are linked to problems in the organisational structure.   [4]
3 Suggest **one** advantage and **one** disadvantage for Trench of relying on emails for office communication.   [4]
4 Suggest **two** ways for Trench to correct the problem of factory workers feeling 'left out of what happens in the business'.   [4]
5 Identify **two** problems for Trench as a result of ignoring the effect of cultural differences in communication.   [4]
6 Suggest **two** reasons why Trench needs to make communication more effective across the organisation.   [4]
7 Discuss the decision of Trench's managers not to encourage informal communication in the business.   [10]
   Exam-style Questions

> Chapter 13

Industrial/ employee relations

Higher-level

LEARNING OBJECTIVES

On completing this chapter you should be able to:

Apply and analyse:

> Sources of conflict in the workplace (AO2)

Synthesise and evaluate:

> Approaches to conflict in the workplace by:

- employees – collective bargaining, work-to-rule and strike action

- employers – collective bargaining, threats of redundancies, changes of contract, closure and lockouts (AO3)

CONTINUED

> The following approaches to conflict resolution.

- conciliation and arbitration

- employee participation and industrial democracy

- no-strike agreement

- single-union agreement (AO3)

BUSINESS IN CONTEXT

Conflict within Petrobas

In 2020, Petrobas, the state-owned Brazilian energy business, closed some of its production facilities and sold assets to raise finance. The redundancies resulting from these actions were opposed by the main **trade union** of energy workers, the Oil Workers Federation or FUP. The FUP called a **strike** to protest against the closure of a fertiliser plant and organised groups of union members to try to encourage all Petrobas workers to join the industrial action. These groups are called 'picket lines'.

Senior managers within Petrobas reported that the strike action and picket lines had very little impact: 'Our units are operating within normal safety parameters, with contingency teams activated when necessary,' was the news from one Petrobas press release in 2020.

This strike came during a long-term conflict between Petrobras and oil workers unions which had lost much of their negotiating power. This was because Petrobras had made many of its own contracted workers redundant under cost-cutting measures and outsourced much of the production to third-party service companies such as SBM Offshore and Modec.

The **industrial action** followed similar action that union officials referred to as 'warning strikes'. The warning strikes typically included a refusal to report for shift changes at refineries, terminals and platforms as well as work-to-rule actions at other sites that maintained operational security.

The unions, however, faced increased legal challenges to industrial action from Petrobras. A similar five-day

An FUP picket line outside a Petrobas production facility

strike was stopped early after Petrobras won a legal ruling that blocked the walkout. According to Petrobras, the 2020 industrial action was illegal because oil workers agreed to a new collective bargaining agreement the previous year.

KEY TERMS

trade union (labour union): an organisation of working people with the objective of improving the pay and working conditions of its members and providing them with support and legal services

strike: a form of industrial action in which workers, often trade union members, withdraw their labour services

industrial action: measures taken by the workforce or trade union to put pressure on management to settle an industrial dispute in favour of employees

---

CONTINUED

Discuss in pairs or a group:

- Should governments intervene in management-labour relations with laws to protect employees or prevent strikes?

- Discuss how employee/management relations could be improved within Petrobas or any other business you have knowledge of.

KEY CONCEPT LINK

Change

Industrial relations have been changing rapidly in the 21st century. One reason is the evolution of new, flexible work patterns which make the formation of trade unions very difficult. For example, in industries such as catering that depend on part-time or temporary workers, labour unions are often weak or non-existent. Moreover, many businesses increasingly adopt socially responsible practices in favour of their workforce, applying methods such as worker participation and profit sharing, which help to avoid stakeholder conflicts and reduce the need for workers to form unions. On the other hand, there are industries in which trade unions are being born for the first time, such as high technology. Such unions can protect the employees of the quaternary sector from practices that deprive them of basic worker rights. The idea that labour unionism is relevant only to unskilled workers or public-sector employees is gradually being reversed.

13.1 Sources of conflict in the workplace

It is often assumed that conflict at work is only between employers and employees (or 'management' and 'labour'). Employers aim to achieve satisfactory profit levels by keeping costs as low as possible, including labour costs which can form a high proportion of total costs,. However, workers will seek to obtain high pay, shorter working hours and improvements in their working conditions, often through unions acting on their behalf.

There are obvious potential conflicts of interest between these two groups – employers and employees – and some of the most common are explained in Table 13.1.

Conflict can also occur between employees or between groups of employees. Here are four reasons why potentially damaging conflict might exist in the workplace between employees.

Poor communication

Poor communication can result in serious misunderstandings. For example, a manager reallocated an employee's task to another worker but failed to communicate this to the employee. This may cause the employee to feel rejected, which can lead to bad feelings between the two employees and between them and the manager.

Difference in personalities

Employees come from different backgrounds and experiences, which play a role in shaping their personalities. When employees fail to understand or accept the differences in each other's personalities, problems arise in the workplace. For example, an employee may possess a confident personality that leads to him speaking his mind directly and leading discussions, even if the timing is poor. This employee could offend other workers who prefer a more cooperative and thoughtful approach to problem-solving and communication. The co-workers may feel that the employee is rude or they may feel they lack the authority to deal with this personality.

Different values

One cause of different values amongst employees is when a generational gap is present. Young workers may possess different workplace values from those of older workers. The difference in values is not necessarily the cause of employee conflict in the workplace, but the failure to accept the differences is. When employees fail to accept the differences, co-workers may insult

Cause of conflict	Common management view	Common employee view
Business change, e.g., relocation or new technology.	Change is necessary to remain competitive and profitable.	Change can lead to job losses, may result in retraining in new skills that causes uncertainty over ability to cope. Demands for increased 'flexibility' from employees may reduce job security.
Rationalisation and organisational change.	Business needs to cut costs and be flexible and adaptable to compete effectively with 'globalised' low-cost rival businesses.	Cost cuts and rationalisation always seem to fall on employees – not the senior managers or owners of the business. Reduced pay or job security will damage employee motivation.
Pay levels and working conditions.	The market determines what the appropriate pay level should be. An unjustified increase in pay or costly improvements in working conditions might make the business uncompetitive. This is more likely when there is no increase in productivity.	If profits and managers' bonuses are rising, then employees deserve pay increases. At least, wages should rise in line with inflation to maintain the real value of incomes.

Table 13.1: Common causes of labour–management conflict

each other's characters and experiences. This tends to intensify the conflict until the right solution is offered and accepted.

Internal rivalry

Excessive workplace competition is a cause of employee conflict. Some businesses deliberately foster competitive environments to encourage workers or teams to out-perform each other. When salary is linked to employee production, a workplace may experience strong competition between employees. Competition that is not properly managed for the good of the whole business can result in employees sabotaging efforts by other groups or not cooperating with them. This can create a hostile work environment, discouraging teamwork and promoting individualism.

These and other internal business conflicts can lead to low productivity, high labour turnover and demotivated employees. The following sections evaluate how managers and employees might respond to conflict and how these clashes can be resolved or their impact reduced.

13.2 Approaches to workplace conflict

Approaches by employees

What happens when a conflict between employees and employers occurs? This depends greatly on whether the employees belong to trade unions. If they do not, then an individual worker will probably have little influence over the employer. This assumes the employer is meeting minimum legal standards for issues such as pay and work health and safety. If this is not the case, then the worker may be able to seek support through legal channels such as taking their grievance to an industrial tribunal, if these have been established by the government in the country.

So, if minimum legal standards are being met by the employer, a serious conflict is likely to lead to an individual worker leaving the business – perhaps to seek employment in another organisation offering higher pay, better working conditions or both. When many employees are involved in the conflict, if they are not organised into trade unions, they are likely to have to either accept the terms and conditions laid down by the employer or, over time, seek other employment. Obviously in some economic situations this could be difficult, and this would strengthen the position of the employer.

In most countries, workers are legally free to join trade unions and if several employees in a business do this, the approach to conflict is likely to change.

Union membership and collective bargaining

Trade unions exist to allow workers to collectively negotiate with their employer on issues such as pay, working conditions and job security.

Why workers join trade unions

- 'Power through solidarity' has been the basis of union influence and this is best illustrated by their ability to engage in 'collective bargaining'. This is when trade unions negotiate on behalf of all of their members in a business, putting workers in a stronger position than if they negotiated individually to gain higher pay deals and better working conditions.

- Individual industrial action – one worker going on strike, for example, is not likely to be very effective. Collective industrial action could result in much more influence over employers during industrial disputes.

- Unions provide legal support to employees who claim unfair dismissal or poor conditions of work.

Unions pressurise employers to ensure that all legal requirements are met, such as health and safety rules regarding the use of machinery.

CASE STUDY 13.1

Tech workers are interested in employee unions

In 2021 more than 400 engineers and other employees at Google announced they were forming a trade union in the USA. They called it the Alphabet Workers Union.

Unions are rare in the tech industry, which is normally averse to them. The Alphabet Workers Union came about because workers wanted to make management more accountable and ethical in its dealings both inside and outside the organisation.

Over one hundred thousand full-time staff were employed by Google at the time, and only a small proportion of them joined the union. But the development was watched with interest by labour economists in India. Unions for blue-collar and public sector workers have a long history in India, but recently there has been more interest among white-collar and service sector employees.

The developments at Google were followed by members of the All India IT and ITES Employee's Union (AIITEU), which is based in Kolkata and has around 1500 members across the country. The AIITEU is particularly focused on discrimination and issues with remote working.

1 Define the term 'trade union'. [2]

2 Explain **two** reasons why tech workers in Google decided to form a trade union. [4]

3 Suggest **two** possible reasons why organisations in the tech industry are 'averse' to employee unions. [4]

4 Suggest **two** reasons why the blue-collar workforce in India has been more active in unionism compared to white-collar employees. [4]

ACTIVITY 13.1

Investigate a recent industrial dispute in your country. Analyse the causes of the dispute, what actions were taken by employees and employers to settle the dispute and how it ended.

Collective bargaining

Collective bargaining is widely used by trade unions to attempt to prevent conflicts from occurring with an employer and, if a clash does exist, to try to resolve it. It is the opposite of individual bargaining, where each worker discusses separately with their employer issues such as pay and conditions. This process becomes impossibly time consuming in large organisations and each worker has relatively little bargaining power. Instead, many employees belong to trade unions and these organisations bargain or negotiate on their behalf. In some countries, employers also belong to employers' associations that negotiate with unions and any agreements made will cover all firms that belong to the association.

> ### KEY TERM
>
> **collective bargaining:** the negotiations between employees' representatives (trade unions) and employers on issues of common interest such as pay and conditions of work

The growing power and membership of trade unions in the 20th century in the USA and Europe led to the widespread development of national collective bargaining. These collective negotiations can make trade union leaders very powerful as they may be able to threaten and actually call for industrial action from all of their members, which could bring the entire industry to a standstill.

This form of collective bargaining has never been used in some countries where unions are weak or illegal. Even in Europe and the USA, national collective bargaining is now much less common as national agreements are not always suitable or affordable for smaller or less-profitable businesses. Agreements are now often made by individual businesses or business units negotiating with union representatives regionally or locally.

The benefits claimed for collective bargaining are:

- it leads to higher wages and better working conditions than individual bargaining
- all workers in the business will benefit from the results of collective bargaining
- it can lead to long-term agreements between union representatives and employers which will provide some security and stability for both employees and employers

- employers may be able to recruit better-qualified workers if the collective bargaining deals lead to better pay and conditions
- employers do not have to use managerial time in negotiating separately with each employee.

Work to rule

If collective bargaining fails to achieve the specific aims of the union representatives, then the union can decide to encourage its members to take some form of industrial action.

Work to rule is a form of industrial action in which employees refuse to do any work outside the precise terms of the employment contract. Overtime will not be worked and all non-contractual cooperation will be withdrawn. During busy times of year in particular, this could lead to lost output and lost sales for the employer. The lack of cooperation between workers and employers, other than following the strict terms of the employment contracts, can greatly reduce the level of productivity and operational flexibility with a business. The trade union's aim is to create a situation where the financial losses of this withdrawal of cooperation encourage the employer to meet its demands.

Strike action

This is the most extreme form of industrial action that employees can undertake. By totally withdrawing their labour for a period of time, production is likely to stop altogether, causing substantial disruption and financial losses for the employer. Strike action can lead to the business shutting down during the industrial action and, if the business has limited financial resources, it may never reopen. As strike action can have such serious consequences, many governments have limited the ability of trade unions to ask their members to refuse to work. It is now a legal requirement in many countries for unions to hold a secret ballot (vote) of all members working for an employer. Only if a majority agree to strike action will the union be able to instruct members to withdraw their labour in that business.

Approaches by employers

Settling disputes with unions can increase the long-term profitability of businesses. Industrial action by trade unions can damage the long-term viability of a business. Employers can adopt the following approaches in an effort to resolve harmful industrial disputes.

Collective bargaining

The potential benefits of reaching an agreement through collective bargaining have already been outlined. Individual businesses usually agree to negotiate with union officials as they recognise the right of the trade union to represent its members during negotiations. Employers may belong to an industrywide organisation, such as Gesamtmetall in Germany. This is the Federation of German Employers' Associations in the Metal and Electrical Engineering Industries and it bargains collectively, with union representatives, on behalf of several thousand employers. The benefits to employers of such an approach is that they do not have to spend time negotiating with unions separately, and the agreements reached will apply to all businesses in the same industry.

If agreements cannot be reached between unions and employers during negotiations, then employers can adopt the following approaches.

Threat of redundancies

If agreement cannot be reached an employer might threaten to make some, perhaps a large number, of workers redundant. The employer might claim that without common agreement on key issues, the business will become less competitive and so will need a smaller workforce. These threats would put pressure on unions to agree to a settlement of the dispute. However, the threats might inflame opinions on the employees' side; it could be seen as 'bullying' and lead to poor publicity for the employer.

Changes of employment contract

If employees are taking advantage of their employment contracts to work to rule or ban overtime, when the current contracts are due for renewal the new contracts could insist on higher work rates or overtime working. If unions are calling for strike action, then employers might try to force workers to accept temporary and more flexible contracts which would weaken their job security. These new contracts would discourage workers from taking strike action as their employment security might be put at risk.

Closure

Closure of the business or the factory/office where the industrial dispute takes place would certainly end the dispute at that location, but it could create poor industrial relations at other locations operated by the business. Closure would lead to redundancy for all of the workers and no output or profit for the business owners. This is an extreme measure and would only be threatened or used if the demands of the union were so costly for the employer that they would lead to a large loss being made by the business or factory.

Lockouts

A lockout is short-term closure of the business or factory to prevent employees from working and being paid. Some workers who are not keen on losing pay for long periods may put pressure on their union leaders to agree to a reasonable settlement of the dispute.

ACTIVITY 13.2

1   Split into two groups.

- **Group 1:** Find examples of one major trade union in your country. Prepare a presentation showing its history and main goals.

- **Group 2:** Find an example of an employers' association in your country. Prepare a presentation showing its history and main goals.

2   After both groups have presented in class, discuss the power of trade unions versus employers' associations in your country.

LEARNER PROFILE

Caring

Research on industrial relationships indicated that employers in manufacturing who manage to avoid the creation of conflicts with their employees and have a lower possibility of industrial action, practice two important things: empathy and employee autonomy.

Empathy at the workplace means that managers can sense the views and attitudes of the workers, they are proactive in finding solutions to problems and help employees to solve disputes before these escalate. If trade unions feel that the management simply does not care, they are more likely to adopt a similar stance. Moreover, employees want to be

CONTINUED

respected for their contribution to the business's success, according to Wayne Ranick, director of communications for United Steel Workers (USW) International. Arrogant attitudes, whereby workers are treated as a 'bottom-line cost', create feelings of resentment and may lead to damaged industrial relations.

The autonomy of workers is vital in creating a healthy working environment. In the era of advanced technology, it becomes gradually easier for managers to trust employees with autonomy without relying on 'micromanagement' which is considered disrespectful, especially by experienced workers. By creating conditions that allow workers to manage their own working environment and to take initiatives at work, employers show that they care about the need of employees for 'self-esteem' or even 'self-actualisation' through work, as per Maslow's hierarchy of needs. To avoid conflicts with employees, an employer needs to remember that people do not work only for money.

- Find big real-world businesses that prioritise 'empathy' or 'autonomy' of employees, as reflected in their mission statements or core values.

- Try to find information about the status of industrial relationships in these businesses. Have they faced conflict with their employees at any point? What else do these businesses do to maintain good relationships with their workers? Discuss in class.

Which factors influence the relative strength of employers and unions?

The power and influence of employers and unions during an industrial dispute will depend on a number of factors, as outlined in Table 13.2.

Union/employee power will be strong when:	Employer power will be strong when:
Most workers in a business belong to one union	Unemployment is high – there are few alternative jobs for workers to take
All workers agree to take the industrial action decided on	The employer takes rapid action, e.g., lock-out has a very quick impact on workers' wages
The business is experiencing high demand for its products, operating close to full capacity, does not want to disappoint customers and profits are high	There is public support for the employer, e.g., when unions are asking for rises much higher than other workers receive
Industrial action rapidly leads to substantial reductions in output/revenue/profits. There is public support for the union case, e.g., for very low-paid workers	Profits are low and threats of redundancies and closure are taken seriously
Inflation is high, so a high wage increase would seem 'reasonable' to maintain living standards	Threats of relocation to low-cost countries are taken seriously, e.g., the business has already closed other plants and relocated them
Labour costs are a low proportion of total costs.	Legal restrictions exist which limit the scope and extent of industrial action

Table 13.2: The relative strength of unions and employers

THEORY OF KNOWLEDGE

Knowledge question: To what extent should trade union recognition by employers rely merely on business ethics?

The Malaysian constitution guarantees the rights to all workers to form or join a trade union. But in 2017, the Trade Union Affairs Department in the country reported that only 6% of the roughly 14.5million workers in the country were union members and that the union membership rates in the private sector fell considerably between

CONTINUED

2009 and 2017. With Malaysian trade union and labour laws being rather weak compared to the minimum international standards, workers in Malaysia face problems when they ask for trade union recognition, and even if there are reported violations of worker rights, they rarely proceed to industrial action.

Under such circumstances, trade union recognition and the conduct of collective bargaining in Malaysia depends heavily on the ethical code of individual businesses operating in the country. But this does not seem enough. International organisations of human and labour rights have called for a radical labour law reform in the country. The low rate of unionisation has left most workers unprotected, especially during the Covid-19 pandemic, when the government opened the way for employers to negotiate wages with workers.

How important is the legal framework to protect the rights of employees and to guarantee the smooth operation of trade unions? Why are there problems in trade union recognition and participation in countries such as Malaysia, even though the constitution protects the right of workers to unionise? Could businesses with strong business ethics help to improve worker rights in such cases and if yes, how? Discuss in class.

13.3 Approaches to conflict resolution

It is likely that many of the approaches referred to in 13.2 will lead to poor relations between employees and employers, especially if a strike or lockout has lasted for a long time. The following approaches are designed to stop this problem from arising by preventing or resolving conflicts before serious industrial action takes place.

Conciliation and arbitration

In most countries the government encourages the resolution of industrial disputes through **conciliation** and **arbitration**. Governments may create a state-funded department to offer these services to unions and employers that are unable to resolve their own disputes. Such a department would give advice to employers and employees and their representatives on issues likely to cause disputes between them. A conciliator in industrial disputes will listen to both sides of the argument – perhaps relating to pay or working conditions – and attempt to find common ground. This might be used as a basis for an eventual compromise agreement.

Arbitration is different. An arbitrator will listen to both sides of a dispute, but they will make a decision for resolving the disagreement. This might be a compromise between the opposing views of employers and union officials. If both parties agree to accept this, then this becomes a binding arbitration. The risk if the arbitrator sets the compromise more in favour of one side than the other is that both groups may establish extreme negotiating positions. For example, in wage negotiations a union might ask for a pay rise of 10% rather than a more realistic figure of, say, 5%. This is in the hope that the final decision of the arbitrator may be influenced by the high pay claim, and they will set a 'compromise' figure of 7.5% – which is what the union was hoping to achieve anyway.

An alternative form of arbitration, designed to prevent this union strategy (and also to discourage employers from offering a very low increase) is called 'pendulum arbitration'. In this case, both sides must accept the decision of the arbitrator and the arbitrator is forced to accept either the union's pay claim or the employer's pay offer because no compromise is allowed. Thus, if a union submitted a very high claim or if employers offered a very low pay rise, then the arbitrator would be tempted to 'swing' the decision towards the other side.

It has become increasingly common for businesses to insert 'mandatory arbitration' as a clause into contracts with employees and customers. Such clauses prevent customers and employees from going to court if there is a dispute. If a conflict arises, the issue is transferred to privatised organisations who undertake arbitration.

1   Do your own research on 'mandatory arbitration'. Discuss in class the possible advantages and disadvantages of such clauses for employees.

2   The state of California in the USA banned most mandatory arbitration agreements for employees in 2019. Why do you think that happened? Do you think trade unions in the USA embraced this decision? Justify your answer.

Employee participation and industrial democracy

These are attempts to reduce industrial conflict by building a closer working relationship between employees and employers. This might lead to commonly agreed objectives and it should mean that workers and employers will be keen to avoid conflict which would prevent these objectives from being reached. Participation at work by employees can take different forms:

- Industrial democracy, in its purest form, implies workers' control over industry, perhaps linked to workers' ownership of the business, e.g., producer cooperatives.

- Employee or trade union directors on the company's board of directors represent the workers' approach to major company issues at the highest decision-making level. These 'workers' directors' would have the same right to discuss and vote on company policies as all other directors. They could use this voting power to influence company policy towards redundancies, employment contracts, pay levels and working conditions.

- Works councils, e.g., European Works Councils, discuss issues such as the employment situation, major investment projects planned by the business, major organisational changes and health and safety. The councils are made up of representatives from employers and employees, and often union representatives too. The agreements of these councils are rarely binding on either employers and employees but the meetings are useful opportunities to engage in discussion and frank exchanges of views on important issues of common interest.

- Autonomous work groups and quality circles lead to employee participation in decision-making and help to avoid the 'us and them' environment. By involving workers in everyday decisions that impact on their working lives, such as work schedules, improvements in work practices and how to plan team working, the threat of industrial disputes is reduced.

Single-union agreement

Single-union agreements are a strategy to reduce conflict at work. One cause of conflict can be between different trade unions representing different groups of workers within a business. In some countries it is possible for the workforce of one business to have members in several different unions. This makes collective bargaining much more difficult and time-consuming. In addition, it can lead to inter-union disputes over which skills or grades of workers should get the highest pay rise. It can also reduce the flexibility of a workforce if members of one union are prevented from doing the work of other workers belonging to another union. This is called a demarcation dispute and it reduces total productivity.

Many employers now insist on signing recognition deals with just one union. Two potential consequences of such deals are that the newly united workforce and its union representatives may be able to exert greater influence during collective bargaining, and that just one union may not effectively represent the range of skilled staff, and their needs at work, that exist in most businesses. The growth of single-union agreements has led to further mergers between unions to prevent smaller unions being gradually excluded from all such industrial deals.

KEY TERM

single-union agreement: an employer recognises just one union for purposes of collective bargaining

No-strike agreements

At first glance, it might seem strange for a union to sign a **no-strike agreement** with an employer. Why should it give up the most effective form of industrial action? There are two main reasons:

- It improves the image of the union as being a responsible representative body, and this could encourage employees to become members.

- These deals are often agreed to in exchange for greater union involvement in both decision-making and in representing employees in important negotiations. This has led to union–employer agreements to change working methods and increase labour flexibility that leads to higher productivity, higher profits *and* higher pay and worker participation. This is sometimes referred to as a win–win settlement as both employer and employee will gain from this new partnership approach to industrial relations.

> ### KEY TERM
>
> **no-strike agreement:** unions sign an agreement with employers not to strike in exchange for greater involvement in decisions that affect the workforce

CASE STUDY 13.2

ScotRail Passengers face service disruption as engineering workers vote for strike action

Hundreds of Scotland's railway engineering workers, conductors, ticket examiners and cleaners voted to take industrial action after the collective bargaining process on pay terms collapsed. Abellio, the Dutch state-owned transport firm which manages ScotRail, said industrial action is 'completely wrong', especially as services are being increasingly used by the public with the easing of the lockdown due to the pandemic. Pat McIlvogue, Unite industrial officer, said: 'The reality is the working relationship between Unite, and for that matter all trade unions, with Abellio is virtually non-existent . . . Unite's members have had their terms and conditions cut, while Abellio also refuses to offer a decent pay rise . . ..
The ballot result is the inevitable outcome when workers are treated with no respect.'

Abellio reported falling revenues in 2020 because of the pandemic. However, rail operators receive heavy government subsidies, and an EMA (emergency measures agreement) has been put in place to support the industry in September 2021. Abellio will have access to part of these emergence payouts.

1 Define the term 'industrial action'. [2]

2 Explain **two** possible reasons why the collective bargaining between ScotRail's trade union and Abellio's management collapsed. [4]

3 Suggest **two** reasons why ScotRail's employees decided to go on strike. [4]

4 Describe **two** possible methods to be used by Abellio's management to stop the employees from going on strike. [4]

SELF-EVALUATION CHECKLIST

After studying this chapter, complete this table.

I am able to apply and analyse:	Needs more work	Almost there	Ready to move on
sources of conflict in the workplace (AO2)			
I am able to synthesise and evaluate:			
approaches to conflict resolution in the workplace by: • employees – collective bargaining, work to rule, strike action • employers – collective bargaining, threats of redundancies, changes of contract, closure and lockouts (AO3)			
the following approaches to conflict resolution: conciliation and arbitration, employee participation and industrial democracy, no-strike agreement, single-union agreement (AO3)			

REFLECTION

To what extent do you think governments should be involved in industrial relations, for example by limiting the power of trade unions or insisting that employers take industrial disputes to arbitration?

PROJECT

1   As a class, organise a workshop on the role of the International Labour Organization (ILO) (the United Nations Agency responsible for setting the international labour standards) and its effectiveness in promoting women's empowerment at work. Invite to your workshop other IB students studying business management at standard level and/or economics or any other social science.

2   As workshop leaders, split into teams to prepare the following:

  • A presentation on the ILO, its history, its functions, and its significance in terms of advancing social and economic justice around the world. The presentation should also include its role in promoting and safeguarding trade unions at a global level, as well as its limitations as a non-profit organisation.

  • Handouts for your audience showing the key functions of the ILO.

3   After your presentation, distribute to the participants a summary of a paper published by the ILO in 2020 called 'Empowering Women at work – Trade Union Policies and Practices for Gender Equality'. After the audience reads the summary, split into two groups to debate the following statement: 'The empowerment of women at work is better achieved through trade union activities rather than through government regulations'.

Thinking about your project:

  • When preparing your presentation, did you highlight the tripartite structure of the ILO, by which all of its policies and standards require the collaboration and the approval of governments, employers and workers?

EXAM-STYLE QUESTIONS

The workers of C-Real Company, one of the biggest makers of breakfast cereals in the country, go on strike

The trade union of workers in the National Food Manufacturing Industry said in a press release on Monday that the worker's council of C-Real, with 1000 members, is going on a strike. The workers complain that they have been working long hours throughout the Covid-19 pandemic to produce the popular products of C-Real, to keep up with the increased demand during the lockdown. However, instead of rewarding them for their hard work and commitment, the management cancelled their health care and retirement benefits.

In a statement, Garry Barton, C-Real's spokesperson characterised the demands of the employees as 'outrageous'. 'We are very disappointed by the union's decision to proceed to industrial action. Our workers are getting a total remuneration which is way higher than the industry average, including paid vacations. We have paid a bonus in 2020 for the increased productivity of the workers during the difficult Covid-19 conditions, so we cannot understand their decision to go on a strike. We believe that the trade union is simply taking advantage of the shortage of available workers in the country this year, to push the business beyond its limits. A strike will disrupt the production process and will create shortages in the supply chain. Under such conditions, we will be forced to start thinking about relocating the production facility to another country.'

The conflict escalated after a full year of negotiations, but the collective bargaining failed to lead to a collective agreement, while the proposal of the management of C-Real for a single-union agreement was rejected by the workers. However, 12 months later and given the threat of redundancies, the trade union might now be willing to cooperate. For this to happen the management must demonstrate interest in resolving the disagreement. However, it is very unlikely that the management will continue the negotiations without a no-strike agreement in place.

1 Define the term 'collective bargaining'. [2]

2 Define the term 'single-union agreement'. [2]

3 Explain **two** negative consequences for C-Real, if the workers go on strike. [4]

4 Explain **one** more method of industrial action, other than the strike, available to the workers of C-Real. [2]

5 Explain **one** potential advantage and **one** disadvantage for the employees of C-Real from their decision to go on strike. [4]

6 Explain **one** more method available to the management of C-real other than the threat of redundancies to put pressure on the trade union not to strike. [2]

7 Explain **one** possible advantage and **one** disadvantage for the workers from accepting a no-strike agreement. [4]

8 By using appropriate motivation theory, explain why workers feel dissatisfied and want to go on strike. [4]

9 Suggest **two** more methods to resolve the conflict, other than no-strike agreement and single-union agreement. [4]

10 Discuss whether employees of C-Real should sign a no-strike agreement to continue the collective bargaining with the management. [10]

Finance and accounts

Chapter 14

Introduction to finance and sources of finance

LEARNING OBJECTIVES

On completing this chapter you should be able to:

Apply and analyse:

- Role of finance for businesses: capital expenditure; revenue expenditure (AO2)
- The following internal sources of finance: personal funds (for sole traders), retained profit, sale of assets (AO2)
- The following external sources of finance: share capital, loan capital, overdrafts, trade credit, crowdfunding, leasing, microfinance providers, business angels (AO2)

Synthesise and evaluate:

- The appropriateness of short- or long-term sources of finance for a given situation (AO3)

BUSINESS IN CONTEXT

Finance needed – but the amount is not the same!

Interloop, a public limited company in Pakistan, has raised $51m from the sale of additional shares to the public. The company makes socks for some of the biggest brands in sportwear, including Adidas and Nike. Interloop needs the finance as it has ambitious plans for organic growth. It aims to increase sock manufacturing capacity by 20% and enter the denim market for the first time.

Advanced Technologies Europe is a UK-based private limited company that designs and manufactures high technology lithium-ion battery packs and fast rate chargers for medical respirators, portable life saving devices and other applications.

The directors obtained a bank loan of $6m to finance a management buy-out of the company from the former owners. An additional loan was used to finance expansion of the company's manufacturing facilities from 2000 to 8000 square metres.

Aala Aziz lives in Sahiwal, Pakistan. She decided to start her own business when her husband became unable to earn enough to support her and her daughters. Aala is a skilled seamstress, so she makes and repairs clothes. She borrowed $150 from the local microfinance bank to buy material and a sewing machine. She was surprised how quickly she gained a large number of customers. She was

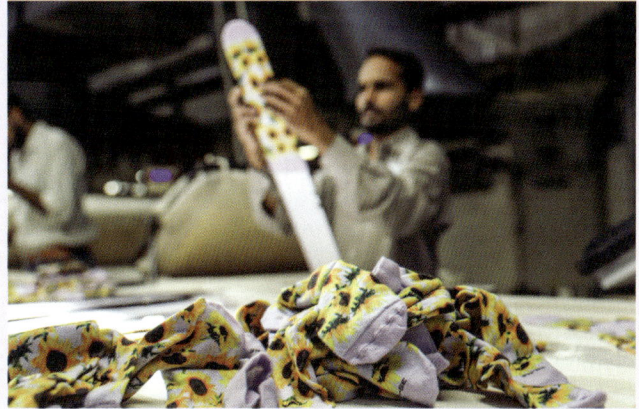

able to easily pay back the loan. She can now earn essential income to help support her family. Nearly 85% of microfinance loans are made to women like Aala.

Discuss in pairs or a group:

- Why do all businesses, at different stages of their development and growth, need finance?

- Is it advisable to take out a bank loan or sell shares in the business to raise long-term finance? Explain your answer.

- Why might a traditional commercial bank have been unwilling to lend the finance required to Aala?

KEY CONCEPT LINK

Change

Crowdfunding roots go back to the 1700s when Jonah Swift established the Irish Loan Fund as a method to collect funds from the wealthier 'crowd' in favour of the less-advantaged citizens. Modern-day 'crowdfunding' started to emerge after the big recession in 2008, when the collapse of the real-estate market brought dramatic changes to the finance industry and firms were forced to seek funding through non-traditional ways. Banks became

less able or willing to take the risks associated with lending money to small business ventures, and the evolution of internet technology allowed entrepreneurs with good business ideas to seek finance from the crowd.

The growth of crowdfunding platforms has been massive. In 2009, crowdfunding raised $530 million. By 2015, global crowdfunding funds had reached $24.4 billion.

14.1 Why businesses need finance

Finance is required for many business activities, for example:

- Setting up a business will require **start-up capital** involving cash injections from the owner(s) to purchase essential capital equipment and possibly premises.

- Businesses need to finance their **working capital** – the day-to-day finance needed to pay bills and expenses and to build up stocks.

- Business expansion needs finance to increase the capital assets held by the firm, and often expansion will involve higher working capital needs.

- Expansion can be achieved by taking over other businesses. Finance is needed to buy out the owners of the other business.

- When the management of a business decides to purchase it from the existing owners in a **management buy-out**, finance will be required.

- Special situations will often lead to a need for greater finance. A decline in sales, possibly as a result of economic recession, could lead to a need for cash to keep the business stable. Or a large customer could fail to pay for goods, and finance may be needed quickly to pay essential expenses.

- Apart from purchasing fixed assets, finance is often used to pay for research and development into new products or to invest in new marketing strategies, such as expanding into overseas markets.

> ### KEY TERMS
>
> **start-up capital:** capital needed by an entrepreneur to set up a business
>
> **working capital:** the capital needed to pay for raw materials, day-to-day running costs and credit offered to customers. In accounting terms: working capital = current assets − current liabilities
>
> **management buy-out:** the existing managers of a business purchase it from the owners to take full control

Some of these situations will need investment in the business for many years. Others will need only short-term funding – for around one year or less. Some finance requirements of the business are for between one and five years – medium-term finance. The important point to note about the list is that all of these situations will need different types of finance. In practice, this means that no one source or type of finance is likely to be suitable in all cases.

Capital expenditure and revenue expenditure

Capital expenditure is the purchase of assets that are expected to last for more than one year, such as buildings and machinery. Revenue expenditure is spending on all costs and assets other than fixed assets, and it includes wages and salaries, and materials bought for stock. These two types of spending will be financed in different ways as the length of time that the money is required for will be very different.

14.2 Sources of finance

Businesses are able to raise finance from a wide range of sources. It is useful to classify these sources into **internal finance** and **external finance**.

Another classification is also often made – that of short-, medium- and long-term finance. The time period refers to the length of time that the finance is needed/used for. Short term is up to one year, medium term is one to five years and long term is more than five years. This distinction is made clearer in Figure 14.1.

> ### KEY TERMS
>
> **internal finance:** raised from the business's own assets or from profits left in the business (ploughed-back or retained profits)
>
> **external finance:** raised from sources outside the business

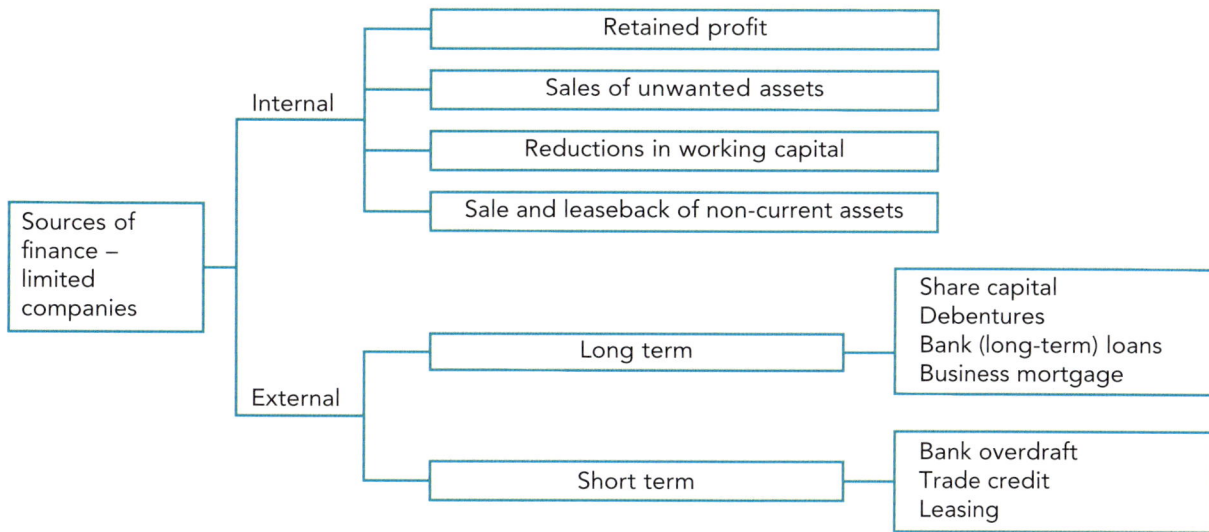

Figure 14.1: Sources of finance for limited companies

14.3 Internal sources of finance

Personal funds (for sole traders)

The owner's savings are a commonly used as a source of finance for sole-trader businesses – especially for starting up new businesses. If the sole trader finances the business from their own resources it adds to the business risk for the entrepreneur. It also means that the finances of the business, at least initially, are limited to the amount the owner has in the form of savings. Advantages of using this source include:

- the fact that no interest payments have to be made to a lender (although interest might be given up as an opportunity cost if the owner's savings were held in a bank account) and
- the control the owner has over the business, being the sole or main source of finance, compared with taking on new partners for example.

Profits retained in the business

If a company is trading profitably, some of these profits will be used to pay tax to the government (corporation tax) and some is nearly always paid out to the owners or shareholders (dividends). If any profit remains, it is kept in the business and this **retained profit** becomes a source of finance for future activities. Clearly, a newly formed company or one trading at a loss will not have access to this source of finance. For other companies, retained profits are a significant source of funds for expansion, i.e. they are invested back into the business. These retained profits will not be paid out to shareholders, so they represent a permanent source of finance.

TIP

Do not assume that a profitable business is cash rich and that it can use all of its profits as a source of finance for future projects. In practice, profits are often tied up in money owed to the business by debtors or have been used to finance increased stocks or replace equipment.

KEY TERM

retained profit: the profit left after all deductions, including dividends, have been made; this is invested back into the company as a source of finance

---

Sale of assets

Established companies often find that they have assets that are no longer fully used. These could be sold to raise cash. In addition, some businesses will sell assets that they still intend to use but which they do not need to own. In these cases, the assets might be sold to a leasing specialist and leased back by the company. This will raise capital – but there will be an additional fixed cost in the leasing and rental payment.

In 2021, Indian low-cost airline IndiGo signed a sale-and-leaseback agreement with BOC Aviation for eight new A320neos (a type of aircraft). Since many airlines order hundreds of aircraft at a time, they usually receive significant discounts on the list price. With a sale-and-leaseback deal, an airline can make a profit from selling the plane to lessors, who will then lease it back to the airline. Airlines are able to operate many aircraft with lower initial capital costs, and they can continue to grow. These deals also help to keep the age of aircraft fleets down as airlines can return their planes to the lessor after a fixed period.

Managing working capital more efficiently

When businesses increase inventory levels or sell goods on credit to customers (debtors), they need to use a source of finance. When companies reduce these assets – by reducing their working capital – capital is released, which acts as a source of finance for other uses. There are risks in cutting down on working capital, however. Managing working capital by cutting back on current assets by selling stocks or reducing debts owed to the business may reduce the firm's **liquidity** debts – its ability to pay short-term debts – to risky levels.

Internal sources of finance – an evaluation

This type of capital has no direct cost to the business, although there may be an opportunity cost, and if assets are leased back after being sold, there will be leasing charges. Internal finance does not increase the liabilities or debts of the business. There is no risk of loss of control by the original owners as no shares are sold. However, it is not available for all companies, for example newly formed ones or unprofitable ones with few spare assets. Depending solely on internal sources of finance for expansion can slow down business growth as the pace of development will be limited by the annual profits or the value of assets to be sold. Thus, rapidly expanding companies are often dependent on external sources for much of their finance.

TIP

Do not make the mistake of suggesting that selling shares is a form of internal finance for companies. Although the shareholders own the business, the company is a separate legal unit and, therefore, the shareholders are 'outside' it.

CASE STUDY 14.1

Ernesto wants to grow Tasty Ltd

Ernesto is thinking about growing Tasty Ltd, the online food ordering and delivery business in which he owns 98% of the shares. The external market conditions are excellent, and online sales for all products including restaurant food are growing fast, especially after the first wave of lockdowns due to the Covid-19 pandemic. Ernesto's business is offering a different daily menu to consumers. The food is prepared by small local restaurants that will form a joint venture with Tasty Ltd. Ernesto earns a commission for every meal delivered. He now wants to expand the services into one more geographical location.

Ernesto needs finance for the capital expenditure related to this growth option. He needs to set up an office in the new town where he wants to operate, and he will need to buy ten scooters for the delivery drivers. He would need to hire ten employees to drive the scooters (they will be paid an hourly rate) and two office-based assistants (who will be paid a yearly salary).

KEY TERM

liquidity: the ability of a firm to pay its short-term debts

CONTINUED

To finance the investment, Ernesto prefers to use internal sources of finance. He is thinking about using $50 000 from Tasty's retained profit.

1   Define the term 'retained profit'.   [2]

2   Identify **two** possible reasons why Ernesto prefers to use internal sources of finance to grow his business.   [4]

3   With reference to Tasty Ltd, distinguish between capital and revenue expenditure.   [4]

4   Suggest **one** advantage and **one** disadvantage for Ernesto of using retained profit to finance Tasty's growth.   [4]

14.4 Sources of finance – external

Short-term finance

There are three main sources of short-term external finance:

- Bank **overdrafts**
- Trade credit
- Leasing.

Bank overdrafts

A bank overdraft is the most 'flexible' of all sources of finance. The amount of finance can vary from day to day, depending on the needs of the business. The bank allows the business to overdraw on its account at the bank by writing cheques to a greater value than the balance in the account. This overdrawn amount should always be agreed in advance and it always has a limit beyond which the firm should not go. Businesses may need to increase the overdraft for short periods of time, e.g., if customers do not pay as quickly as expected or if a large delivery of stock has to be paid for. This form of finance often carries high interest charges. In addition, if a bank becomes concerned about the stability of one of its customers, it can 'call in' the overdraft and force the business to pay it back. In extreme cases, this may lead to the failure of the business.

Trade credit

By delaying the payment of bills for goods or services received, a business is, in effect, obtaining finance. Its suppliers, or creditors, are providing goods and services without receiving immediate payment. Many businesses aim to pay their suppliers within one to two months. Further lengthening of this trade credit period effectively becomes a source of finance for the debtor business. The downside to these periods of credit is that they are not free – discounts for quick payment and supplier confidence are often lost if the business takes too long to pay its suppliers.

Leasing is used to acquire assets with a medium life span – usually up to five years. It involves a contract with a leasing or finance company to acquire, but not necessarily to purchase, assets over the medium term. A periodic payment is made over the life of the agreement, but the business does not have to purchase the asset at the end. This agreement allows the firm to avoid purchasing the asset using cash. The risk of

KEY TERMS

overdraft: an arrangement with a bank that their customer can withdraw up to an agreed limit from their account as and when required; this is a form of borrowing

leasing: obtaining the use of equipment or vehicles and paying a rental or leasing charge over a fixed period. This avoids the need for the business to raise long-term capital to buy the asset; ownership remains with the leasing company

having unreliable or outdated equipment is reduced as the leasing company will repair and update the asset as part of the agreement.

Leasing is not a low cost option but it does improve the short-term cash-flow position of a business compared to outright purchase of an asset for cash.

Long-term finance

The two main choices here are debt or **equity finance**. Debt finance increases the liabilities of a company. Debt finance can be raised in two main ways:

- **long-term loans** from banks
- **debentures** (also known as loan stock or corporate bonds).

Long-term loans from banks

These may be offered at either a variable or a fixed interest rate. Fixed rates provide more certainty, but they can turn out to be expensive if the loan is agreed at a time of high interest rates. Companies borrowing from banks will often have to provide security or collateral for the loan. This means that if the company cannot repay the debt the bank has the right to sell the asset that was provided as security. Businesses that have few assets to act as security may find it difficult to obtain loans – or they may be asked to pay higher rates of interest.

Debentures

A company wishing to raise funds will issue or sell debentures to interested investors. The company agrees to pay a fixed rate of interest each year for the life of the debenture, which can be up to 25 years. The buyers may resell them to other investors if they do not wish to wait until maturity before getting their original investment back. Debentures are usually not 'secured' on a particular asset. When they are secured, the debentures are known as mortgage debentures.

Debentures can be an important source of long-term finance. In 2021, Chilean lender Banco de Credito e Inversiones issued $54 million of debentures in the European market, which offer a rate of 2.365% for a term of nine years.

LEARNER PROFILE

Risk-taker

Business angels take risks. They often provide unsecured finance to start-ups or established businesses that have a promising business idea but no access to the traditional banking system. Even though the beneficiaries of finance by business angels are expected to have growth potential, the projections can prove wrong for several reasons, varying from internal factors such as lack of management inexperience to external factors such as unpredictable consumer wants.

So, is the risk worth it from the perspective of the business angels? Many firms receiving support from them eventually fail. However, if the companies succeed the return is massive. Some of the most successful businesses of all time, including tech giants such as Meta (formerly Facebook) and Google have returned extraordinary profits to the business angels who have made it possible for them to survive and grow.

If you were a business angel, your goal would be to increase the possibility of a high return, while reducing the risk of failure in your investments. Which criteria would you consider when finding a new start-up business to invest in? Discuss in class.

CASE STUDY 14.2

Healing Ltd opens a new physical therapy centre

Faizal and Fatima are best friends. They graduated from university with degrees in physical therapy and set up Healing Ltd, offering a variety of services such as orthopaedic and sports physical therapy and orthotics. The business was a success and gained the trust of loyal customers. Fatima, who is the finance director, is now looking for growth opportunities and she is currently seeking the appropriate sources of finance to cover the following expenses:

- Opening one more fully equipped centre for physical therapy, an investment of $60 000.

- Replacing two biofeedback machines in the current premises, at a cost of $4,000 each.

- Paying a creditor who has provided Healing with equipment such as yoga straps and mattresses. The supplier is due to be paid $3000 in four days, but Healing does not have available cash right now.

Fatima tries to convince Faizal to get a long-term loan to finance the opening of the new physical therapy centre. The bank through which Healing does all of its transactions and pays its employees and suppliers is already providing an overdraft and is expected to be willing to offer loan capital for the growth of the business.

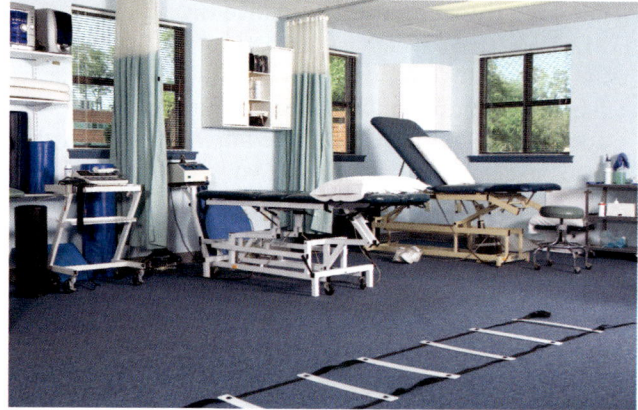

Faizal disagrees. He is worried about future interest rates and possible problems repaying the loan in the long run. He believes that they should try to attract one more investor in the business to share the capital expenditure with them.

1 Define the term 'overdraft'. [2]
2 Suggest **two** appropriate external sources of finance to replace the two biofeedback machines. [4]
3 Suggest **two** appropriate external sources of finance to pay the creditor. [4]
4 Discuss Fatima's suggestion to finance the opening of a new centre for physical therapy through a long-term loan. [10]

If the borrower wishes, convertible debentures can be switched into shares in the issuing company after a certain period of time and this means that the company issuing them will never have to pay the debenture back.

Equity finance

Sale of shares

All limited companies issue shares when they are first formed. The capital raised will be used to purchase essential assets. Both private and public limited companies are able to sell further shares – up to the limit of their authorised share capital – in order to raise additional permanent finance. This capital never has to be repaid unless the company is completely wound up as a result of ceasing to trade. Private limited companies can sell further shares to existing shareholders. This has the advantage of not changing the control or ownership of the company – as long as all shareholders buy shares in the same proportion to those already owned. Owners of a private limited company can also decide to 'go public' and obtain the necessary authority to sell shares to the wider public. This would have the potential to raise much more capital than from just the existing shareholders, but with the risk of some loss of control to the new shareholders.

In the UK (and many other countries), this can be done in two ways:

1   Obtain a listing on the Alternative Investment Market (AIM), which is that part of the London Stock Exchange concerned with smaller companies that want to raise only limited amounts of additional capital. The strict requirements for a full stock exchange listing are relaxed.

2   Apply for a full listing on the London Stock Exchange by satisfying the criteria of:

    a   selling at least £50 000 worth of shares and

    b   having a satisfactory trading record to give investors some confidence in the security of their investment.

This sale of shares can be undertaken in two main ways:

*   Public issue by prospectus – this advertises the company and its share sale to the public and invites them to apply for the new shares. This is expensive, as the prospectus has to be prepared and issued. The share issue is often underwritten or guaranteed by a merchant bank, which charges for its services.

*   Arranging a placing of shares with institutional investors without the expense of a full public issue – once a company has gained plc status, it is still possible for it to raise further capital by selling additional shares. This is often done by means of a **rights issue** of shares.

By not introducing new shareholders, the ownership of the business does not change and the company raises capital relatively cheaply as no public promotion or advertising of the share offer is necessary. However, as the rights issue increases the supply of shares to the stock exchange, the short-term effect is often to reduce the existing share price. Existing shareholders could lose confidence in the business if the share price falls too sharply.

KEY TERM

rights issue: existing shareholders are given the right to buy additional shares at a discounted price

business angel: an individual, usually with business experience, who directly invests part of their wealth in new and growing businesses

---

Debt or equity finance – an evaluation

Which method of long-term finance should a company choose? There is no easy answer to this question, and, as seen above, some businesses will use both debt and equity finance for very large projects.

Debt finance has the following advantages:

*   As no shares are sold, the ownership of the company does not change and is not 'diluted' by the issue of additional shares.

*   Loans will be repaid eventually (apart from convertible debentures), so there is no permanent increase in the liabilities of the business.

*   Lenders have no voting rights at annual general meetings.

*   Interest charges are an expense of the business and are paid out before corporation tax is deducted, while dividends on shares have to be paid from profits after tax.

*   The gearing of the company increases and this gives shareholders the chance of higher returns in the future. This point is dealt with more fully in Chapter 18.

Equity finance has the following advantages:

*   It never has to be repaid – it is permanent capital.

*   Dividends do not have to be paid every year. In contrast, interest on loans must be paid in accordance with the lender's terms.

Other sources of long-term finance

Business angels

Most of these are successful business people who would like to help other entrepreneurs start their own business. Generally they offer continuing support from the initial stage of the business and carry on to the point at which the business requires a greater level of funding than the **business angel** investors can offer.

Advantages of business angel investors include:

*   The business angel investor can easily make an investment decision rapidly as they will be experienced in assessing the likely chances of success for a new venture. However, it will still be necessary for the entrepreneur to draw up a professional and tailored business plan.

- The personal experience of these investors helps the business when taking critical decisions. Their prior knowledge of working in a small business or running their own business establishments can be used effectively.
- Angels usually concentrate their investments within a small geographical area, hence they have better local knowledge.

Disadvantages of business angel investors include:

- Angel investors will want to share ownership and will require a certain part of the profit of the business. While to most entrepreneurs, this is more than compensated for by the finance and experience of the angels, some entrepreneurs will strongly resist any loss of ownership.
- Business owners still need to gain the angel investors' trust. They might have to pitch to get the funding they need, i.e., present, in person, the plans for the business and what benefits the angel is likely to receive from the investment.

Crowdfunding

Entrepreneurs rarely have sufficient finance to set up their business, banks may be unwilling to lend and other external sources of finance may be expensive. **Crowdfunding** websites, such as Kickstarter and Crowdcube, are an increasingly significant source of finance for new business start-ups. They allow an individual to explain their business, its objectives and why finance is needed. Investors can commit small sums (such as $10) until the target is reached. The publicity generated can also promote the new business or product.

> **KEY TERMS**
>
> **crowdfunding:** the use of small sums of capital from a large number of individuals to finance a new business venture

---

THEORY OF KNOWLEDGE

Knowledge question: Are objective facts or appeals to emotion more effective when applying for an external source of finance?

In 2021, Cargill was the largest private company in the USA.

The company was originally a grain storage facility, founded by William Wallace Cargill at the end of the American Civil War. His descendants have held common equity in the firm for more than 140 years. Cargill is now a producer and international distributor of products including chocolate, turkey, sugar and refined oil, as well as providing transportation services, risk management and commodities trading.

With a revenue of around $134.4 billion, it is interesting to examine why Cargill remains a private limited company. A world-famous business of this size could have tried to raise huge amounts of money through the stock market. Cargill's CEO

David MacLennan announced to the press that the family owners are committed to keeping the business private.

One reason why Cargill has averted pressures for an IPO in the past is the massive size of its assets, which make its valuation very difficult. Another reason is that the business has focused on paying down debt as per schedule, maintaining an excellent debt rating, which allows it to have access to low-interest bank loans. However, some analysts suggest that the decision of Cargill to stay private is mostly the result of the emotion of the family members who own about 90% of the business, rather than a decision based on objective facts.

How likely do you think is it for owners of a successful family business to deny access to huge sources of finance through the stock market? If they do deny an IPO, is it purely a matter of emotion or are there objective risks and disadvantages that they are not willing to accept? Discuss in class.

Some businesses, such as not-for-profit social enterprises, do not aim to make profits so investors are, in effect, just making a donation. In other cases, investors will expect a return on their investment. However, the failure rate of new business start-ups is high. If the business does succeed, the investors will receive one of the following:

- their initial capital back, plus interest (called loan-based crowdfunding)
- an equity stake in the business and a share of the eventual profit (called equity-based crowdfunding)
- a reward instead of a financial return, for example a free product (called reward-based crowdfunding).

CASE STUDY 14.3

PopSocket successful Kickstarter crowdfunding campaign

The first version of Popsocket was created in 2010 by David Barnett who was a professor of philosophy in Colorado. David was looking for a way to stop his earbud cord from getting tangled. He achieved this by glueing two buttons to the back of his phone and wrapping the earbud cord around them.

Ideas such as the PopSocket have little chance of attracting traditional sources of finance such as bank loans. David decided to go for crowdfunding. The campaign for PopSocket was launched on Kickstarter in 2012, and raised $18 592 from 520 people, making it one of the most successful crowdfunded businesses. PopSocket is still one of the best-selling mobile phone accessories on Amazon.

CONTINUED

1 Define the term 'crowdfunding'. [2]

2 Suggest **two** possible reasons why innovative products such as the PopSocket have limited access to traditional sources of finance. [4]

3 Explain **one** advantage and **one** disadvantage for David using crowdfunding as a source of finance for PopSocket. [4]

ACTIVITY 14.1

Suggest one appropriate source of finance for the following scenarios, based on the description provided. Justify your suggestion.

1 The finance director of a family-owned limited company producing shoes wants to increase the productive capacity of the factory without creating a liability to third parties.

2 A sole trader is starting up a business as a private tutor teaching English to primary school students. She needs a laptop, a printer and some books.

3 A plc producing food products needs 20 cars for its sales force in Dubai. The CEO does not see any reason why the firm should own the assets and is against hiring an extra employee for the administration of the car fleet.

The entrepreneur should make clear which form of crowdfunding is being used. Crowdfunding allows small businesses to benefit from capital that might otherwise be impossible to obtain, but they must keep accurate records to pay back capital and interest or a share of the profit to multiple investors. With equity-based crowdfunding, the entrepreneur may end up with only a small stake in their business. Also, exposing a new product idea online means it may be copied before the entrepreneur is able to start the business.

TIP

When answering case study examination questions, you should analyse what type of legal structure the business has and what sources of finance are available to it. Unincorporated businesses – sole traders and partnerships – cannot issue shares, for example.

Microfinance

Microfinance is an approach to providing small capital sums to entrepreneurs that has grown in importance. In 1974, an economics lecturer at the University of Chittagong, Bangladesh, lent $27 to a group of very poor villagers. They repaid this loan in full after their business ideas became successful. The lecturer, Muhammad Yunus, went on to win the Nobel Peace Prize. He founded the Grameen Bank in 1983 to make very small loans – perhaps $20 a time – to poor people with no bank accounts and no chance of obtaining finance through traditional means. Since its foundation, the Grameen Bank has lent more than $21 billion to over eight million Asian people, many of whom have set up their own small enterprises with the capital.

Many business entrepreneurs in Bangladesh and other Asian countries have received microfinance to help start their business.

ACTIVITY 14.2

Some celebrities act as business angels, with significant activity across various industries. One example is the tennis player Serena Williams.

1   Find examples of the activity of Serena Williams as a business angel.

2   Find examples of other celebrities acting as business angels.

3   Why do you think celebrities such as Serena Williams become business angels? Are they attracted to supporting businesses that are not traditional 'for profit', such as social enterprises, and if yes, why? What are the risks that celebrities face when they decide to finance business activities as business angels? Discuss in class.

TIP

You should be able to recommend appropriate sources of finance for businesses needing capital in different situations.

KEY TERM

microfinance: the provision of very small loans by specialist finance businesses, usually not traditional commercial banks

14.5 Choosing appropriate finance sources

The size and profitability of the business are clearly key considerations when managers make a financing choice. Small businesses are unlikely to be able to justify the costs of converting to plc status. They might also have limited internal funds available if the existing profit levels are low. These and other factors that are considered before making the appropriate financing choice are analysed in Tables 14.1 and 14.2.

Source of finance	Short, medium or long term	Advantages	Disadvantages	Most appropriate for	Least appropriate for
Sale of shares	Long	Permanent capital No interest charges	Some loss of control by original owners Dividends will be expected by shareholders	Long-term expansion of the business Taking over another business	Buying inventories (stocks) Temporary increase in working capital needs
Sale of debentures	Long	Fixed interest paid	Must be repaid at end of term Interest rate payable has to be competitive	Long-term uses such as expansion or purchase of equipment expected to last several years	Short-term financing needs, e.g., paying for unforeseen maintenance
Leasing	Medium	Gives business full use of an asset without the need to finance the purchase	Asset is never owned/purchased Expensive	Vehicles Equipment Computers	Major expansion or takeover project
Bank overdraft	Short	Flexible amount can vary with daily needs	High interest Bank can call in the overdraft if it is concerned about the liquidity of the business	When the amount of finance needed varies on a regular basis, e.g., daily expenses might exceed daily cash revenue	Major expansion or takeover project Purchase of equipment (because it is too expensive)
Business angel	Long	Provide finance when other sources might not be available due to risk	Some loss of ownership Share of profits is payable to business angel	To finance a relatively risky business start-up or expansion of a recently formed business	A profitable family business in which the family owners want to retain full control
Bank loan	Medium or long	Fixed interest (usually)	Interest payments must be made on time or assets provided as security might be repossessed and sold by the bank	Finance expansion that is expected to lead to higher revenue to allow for the loan to be repaid in the time limit agreed with the bank, e.g., a new factory	Purchasing inventories to meet higher expected demand over a festival period

Source of finance	Short, medium or long term	Advantages	Disadvantages	Most appropriate for	Least appropriate for
Trade credit	Short	Finances the purchase of inventories with no interest costs	Possible loss of discounts for rapid payment of invoices	To finance an increase in inventory held or sales – especially when the sales are on credit and cash will not be received quickly	Purchasing land on which to build an extension to the factory or offices of the business

Table 14.1: An analysis of different sources of finance

Factor influencing finance choice	Significance
Short-term or long-term finance need	It is very risky and expensive to borrow long-term finance to pay for short-term needs. Businesses should match the sources of finance to the requirement. Permanent capital may be needed for long-term business expansion. Short-term finance could finance a short-term need to increase stocks or pay creditors.
Cost	Obtaining finance is never 'free' – even internal finance may have an opportunity cost. Loans may become very expensive during a period of rising interest rates. A stock market flotation can cost millions of dollars in fees and promotion of the share sale.
Amount required	Share issues and sales of debentures, because of the administration and other costs, would generally only be used for large capital sums. Small bank loans or reducing debtors' payment period could raise small sums.
Legal structure and desire to retain control	Share issues can only be used by limited companies – and only public limited companies can sell shares directly to the public. Doing this runs the risk of the current owners losing some control – except if a rights issue is used. If the owners want to retain control of the business, a sale of shares may be unwise.
Size of existing borrowing	This is a key issue – the higher the existing debts of a business (compared to its size), the greater the risk to the lender of lending more. Banks and other lenders will become anxious about lending more finance. This concept is referred to as gearing and is fully covered in Chapter 18.
Flexibility	When a firm has a variable need for finance – for example, it has a seasonal pattern of sales and cash receipts – a flexible form of finance is better than a long-term and inflexible source.

Table 14.2: Factors to be considered in making the 'source of finance' decision

ACTIVITY 14.3

CrowdCube is an example of an equity crowdfunding platform.

1 Research the concept of 'equity crowdfunding'.

2 Prepare a presentation about equity crowdfunding to show in class.

3 What are the advantages and disadvantages of businesses using equity crowdfunding to finance their business activities? Discuss in class.

Reflection

When discussing the advantages and disadvantages of businesses using equity crowdfunding, have you first identified the profile of businesses that are likely to turn to equity crowdfunding and their alternative options to raise sources of finance?

SELF-EVALUATION CHECKLIST

After studying this chapter, complete this table.

I am able to apply and analyse:	Needs more work	Almost there	Ready to move on
role of finance for businesses: capital expenditure; revenue expenditure (AO2)			
the following external sources of finance: share capital, loan capital, overdrafts, trade credit, crowdfunding, leasing, microfinance providers, business angels (AO2)			
I am able to synthesise and evaluate:			
the appropriateness of short- or long-term sources of finance for a given situation (AO3)			

REFLECTION

Personal finance decisions are often influenced by the same principles followed by businesses. For example, do you think it would ever be a good idea to take out a long term loan to pay for a holiday?

PROJECT

Crowdfunding has been a popular source of finance for social entrepreneurs. Some of the crowdfunding online platforms used most by non-profit organisations and for-profit social enterprises are Indiego, Chuffed, Mightycause and UpEffect.

1   Split into three groups:

- **Group 1:** Prepare a presentation for your classmates on a for-profit social enterprise successfully financed through crowdfunding.

- **Group 2:** Prepare a presentation for your classmates on a non-profit organisation successfully financed through crowdfunding.

- **Group 3:** Prepare two posters based on the presentations of groups 1 and 2, with:

    a   the possible advantages and disadvantages of crowdfunding as a source of finance for the two organisations presented

    b   other sources of finance that these businesses could have used instead of crowdfunding.

2   As a class, discuss the role and significance of crowdfunding for social enterprises.

Thinking about your project:

- **Groups 1 and 2:** Have you included a brief description of the business activity, its mission and/or vision and the main arguments in its crowdfunding campaign to attract contributors?

- **Group 3:** Are your posters well balanced with the advantages and disadvantages of both crowdfunding and alternative sources? Have you made sure that the alternative sources proposed apply to the presented case studies?

Financing the Fitness Club

Murad and George work together as gym instructors. The friends decide to open their own fitness club by sharing responsibilities and profits on an equal basis. Murad is certain that their business will soon become a success, as both owners are professionals with an excellent reputation in the market. He thinks they should start the business as a partnership financed through their personal savings and then change to a private limited company after profits appear.

George disagrees. He is afraid of unlimited liability and difficulties in decision-making in partnerships, so he wants the business to be incorporated from the very beginning. However, the two friends have limited personal savings to invest. The capital expenditure associated with the investment is big, as they are dreaming of having technologically advanced equipment, large and modern shower areas, and attractive changing rooms in their facilities. He is thinking of two possible sources of finance: rewards-based crowdfunding or business angels.

Murad does not agree with rewards-based crowdfunding as a method to finance the new fitness club. He believes that this source is more suitable for innovative business ideas. He also does not want business angels in the business, as they tend to ask for a very high return for helping start-ups.

The friends decided to consult Andrea, a finance manager, to advise them on appropriate sources of finance. Andrea agrees with George that the business should be incorporated because private limited companies have better access to external sources of finance compared to partnerships. She also suggests that the best way to finance the start-up fitness club is to find shareholders to invest in their private company. However, George and Murad are not sure if they want to share the ownership of their new business with other people. Andrea advises them to prepare a detailed business plan and to see if the bank would offer them a long-term loan but, she stresses that this financing option is risky, especially for start-up businesses.

1 Define the term 'long-term loan'. [2]

2 Outline the concept of 'rewards-based crowdfunding'. [2]

3 State **one** feature of business angels as a source of finance. [2]

4 Suggest **two** possible reasons why Murad thinks a partnership is an appropriate business type for the new fitness club. [4]

5 Explain **one** advantage and **one** disadvantage of financing the start-up business through the personal savings of the owners. [4]

6 Explain **one** possible advantage and **one** disadvantage for the business by using rewards-based crowdfunding as a source of finance. [4]

7 Explain **one** possible advantage and **one** disadvantage for the business by using business angels as a source of finance. [4]

8 Analyse **two** reasons why incorporated businesses may attract sources of finance more easily than partnerships. [4]

9 Explain **two** reasons why start-ups such as the business of Murad and George may have problems attracting external sources of finance. [4]

10 Discuss loan capital and share capital as long-term sources of finance and recommend the best option for the start-up fitness club. [10]

Chapter 15

Costs and revenues

BUSINESS IN CONTEXT

Costs and revenues for Singapore-based businesses

A report from the Singapore Ministry of Manpower (MOM) stated that over 6000 businesses have indicated that they are taking cost-cutting measures. This is in response to an economic downturn which has reduced revenue for businesses, particularly those in the following sectors: hotel and catering; construction and retail.

The cost-cutting measures include employee leave without pay and shorter working weeks. Nearly 225 000 workers are thought to be affected.

In 2020, financial data from Dyson Holdings included a 17% increase in profit. Despite the high costs of discontinuing its electric car project, profit increased due to a 23% increase in annual revenue to $7.0billion. The home appliance maker has its headquarters in Singapore. The founder and owner of the company, James Dyson, was hoping that electric vehicles would create an additional **revenue stream** for the business but the **fixed costs** of research and factory construction were considered to be too high for the project to proceed.

Discuss in pairs or in a group:

- Why is it important for a business to be able to identify and calculate its costs?

James Dyson has expanded his business to achieve annual revenue in excess of $8 billion

- Why do you think it is important for businesses to cut costs during periods of low sales?

- What are the benefits Dyson might have received from developing an additional revenue stream from electric vehicles?

KEY TERMS

revenue stream: a source of income received over time from the sale of a product

fixed costs: costs that do not vary with output or sales in the short term

KEY CONCEPT LINK

Sustainability

One of the dimensions of sustainability relates to the ability of the business to operate in a way that is profitable for its owners/shareholders. Economic sustainability involves managing revenues and costs in a way that their difference (which is the profit of the business) is as high as possible. However, when trying to maximise profit, firms must also make sure their decisions would also be environmentally and socially sustainable. This can explain why firms often decide to bear a cost that is not the minimum possible. For example by choosing expensive but environmentally safe production methods or paying their employees more than the minimum wage.

Caring

'Certified B' Corporations are a new kind of business, balancing purpose with profit. Such businesses are a special type of social enterprise as they have the legal obligation to consider their impact on various social groups, such as their employees and the community, as well as the environment. Businesses that are Certified B show a practical commitment to the creation of a more equitable economy through the support of appropriate legislative and regulatory changes.

Cotopaxi is a 'Certified B' Corporation producing outdoor clothing and accessories. It puts 1% of its revenue 'toward addressing poverty and supporting community involvement'. It also chooses socially responsible production practices, ranging from the use of recycled raw materials to treating and paying employees fairly. Thus, the business operates in a way that prioritises caring for society over maximising revenues and minimising costs.

Find examples of world-famous businesses that are Certified B. How does their effort to do good in the world affect their revenues and costs? Why do you think an increasing number of businesses want to become Certified B corporations? Discuss this in class.

15.1 Different types of costs

Management often require cost data for business decision-making. These business decisions include location of the operations, which method of production to use, which products to continue to make and whether to buy in components or make them within the business. Such decisions would not be possible without cost data. Here are some of the major uses of cost data:

- Business costs are a key factor in the 'profit equation'. Profits or losses cannot be calculated without accurate cost data. If businesses do not keep a record of their costs, then they will be unable to take profitable decisions, such as where to locate.

- Cost data are important to departments such as marketing. Marketing managers will use cost data to help inform their pricing decisions.

- Keeping cost records also allows comparisons to be made with past periods of time so that the efficiency of a department or a product's profitability can be measured and assessed over time.

- Past cost data can help to set budgets for the future. These will act as targets to work towards for the departments concerned.

- Cost variances can be calculated by comparing cost budgets with actual data.

- Comparing cost data can help a manager make decisions about resource use. For example, if wage rates are very low, then labour-intensive methods of production may be preferred over capital-intensive ones.

- Calculating the costs of different options can assist managers in their decision-making and help improve business performance.

The financial costs incurred in making a product or providing a service can be classified in several ways. Cost classification is not always straightforward and allocating costs to each product is not usually easy in a business with more than one product.

The main types of costs are:

- fixed costs
- **variable costs**
- **direct costs**
- **indirect costs**.

KEY TERMS

variable costs: costs which vary with output

direct costs: costs that can be clearly identified with each unit of production and can be traced back or allocated to a cost centre

indirect costs: costs which cannot be identified with a unit of production or allocated accurately to a cost centre – also known as overhead costs

---

Some costs are difficult to classify as they may have both a fixed and a variable element to them. These are referred to as semi-variable costs. Examples include the electricity standing charge per month plus cost per unit used; the sales person's fixed basic wage plus a commission that varies with sales.

Fixed costs

These remain fixed, in the short term, no matter what the level of sales or output, such as the rent of premises. If a retail shop sold no items at all in one trading day, the costs of the shop (such as rent and property tax) would still have to be paid for that day. If the shop sold 1000 items, these costs would not change.

In the long term, decisions can be made about changing the size of the business, either growing it or cutting some of its operations. This period of time will vary from business to business. For example, it will take much longer to expand the capacity of a steelworks than to open a new clothing store. Over this long period of time, costs that were once fixed can be increased or reduced, for example by renting an additional premises or closing down a branch of the business. This is why, when the classification of fixed costs is referred to, it is important to remember that they are fixed and cannot change in the short term.

Variable costs

These vary as output changes, such as the direct cost of materials used in making a washing machine or the electricity used to cook a fast-food meal. If nothing is produced or sold then variable costs will be zero. Some costs increase as output increases – so they are variable – but they do not increase directly (i.e., at exactly the same rate as output). Costs such as machine maintenance or the cost of employing production supervisors will rise if output is increased, but they will not change at exactly the same rate as output changes.

CASE STUDY 15.1

Harry's coffee shop seeks to cost cuts

Coffee roasters and retailers around the world face a significant problem as the price of coffee beans is rising. One of the reasons why coffee beans are becoming more expensive is that extreme weather conditions destroyed crops in Brazil, the world's largest coffee exporter. Moreover, political protests delayed Colombia's coffee exports. The net result was an increase in the price of beans by more than 40%.

Harry, the owner of a small coffee shop in Chelsea, London, is very worried about the increase in the variable costs of his business. 'We cannot afford to pass the higher cost on to the consumers,' he said. 'We have to compete with huge chains such as Starbucks and Costa Coffee that have economies of scale. In addition, such chains often buy their coffee supplies far in advance. It's easier for our big competitors to absorb the higher price of beans. Small shops like mine have high overheads. Certain indirect costs can be squeezed, but others cannot. For example, our rent is fixed based on a contract and we cannot change that for the next two years.'

1 Define the term 'variable cost'. [2]

2 Suggest **two** types of the direct cost for a coffee shop like Harry's. [4]

3 Explain **two** types of economies of scale that huge coffee shops may enjoy. [4]

4 With reference to the case study, explain the difference between variable and fixed costs. [4]

Direct costs

These costs can be directly identified with each unit of output and can be traced back to a cost centre. They may be variable or they may be fixed, in the short term. The two most common direct costs in a manufacturing business are labour and materials. The most important direct cost in a service business, such as retailing, is the cost of the goods being sold. Here are some examples:

- One of the direct costs of a hamburger in a fast-food restaurant is the cost of the meat.
- One of the direct costs for a garage when servicing a car is the labour cost of the mechanic.
- One of the direct costs of the business studies department is the salary of the business studies teacher.

Indirect costs

Indirect costs are often referred to as overheads. Examples of indirect costs include:

- the purchase of a tractor for a farm
- promotional expenditure in a supermarket
- the rent paid for a garage
- the cost of cleaning a school.

So any cost which cannot be identified with each product or traced back to a cost centre is referred to as an indirect cost. Another example in a school or college would the salaries of administration and office employees.

Overheads are usually classified into four main groups:

- Production overheads – these include factory rent and rates, depreciation of equipment and power.
- Selling and distribution overheads – these include warehouse, packing and distribution costs, and salaries of sales staff.
- Administration overheads – these include office rent and rates, clerical and executive salaries.
- Finance overheads – these include the interest paid on loans.

15.2 Total revenue and revenue streams

Revenue is *not* the same as cash in a cash flow forecast *unless* all goods have been sold for cash. Revenue is recorded on a firm's accounts whether the cash has been received from the customer/debtor or not. Revenue is *not* the same as profit either. All costs of operating the business during a time period have to be subtracted from **total revenue** to obtain the profit figure. The selling price of a product is the revenue earnt from that product. Total revenue can be calculated by multiplying the quantity of products sold by the selling price.

A business may develop a range of trading activities which can all result in revenue streams. For example, internet-based businesses could develop the following activities which could all lead to income:

- services requiring a subscription
- advertisement
- transaction fees
- syndication and franchise
- sponsorship and co-marketing.

The benefits of having more than one source of income include:

- it should lead to higher total revenue for the business
- it is a form of diversification, so other incomes could be a useful source of finance when one of the business's operations is struggling to gain customers.

The potential drawbacks to developing a range of income-generating activities include:

- Each activity needs to be managed and controlled and this makes more work – and this could be a significant drawback for an entrepreneur or sole trader.

KEY TERMS

revenue (or sales turnover): the value of sales made during the trading period = selling price × quantity sold

total revenue: total income from the sale of all units of a product during a given time period

- A large number of activities can result in a business losing focus and being less likely to make a success of its central and original business activity.

- Accounts need to be kept separate so that each activity's performance can be measured and monitored – this means separate profit centres will need to be established. An IT-based accounting system is likely to be essential.

Businesses may receive income from revenue streams other than their normal operating or trading activities, for example from:

- rent from factory or office space that is rented to another business

- dividends on shares held in another business

- interest on deposits held in a bank.

ACTIVITY 15.1

Conglomerate businesses have the advantage of generating many different revenue streams.

One of the most famous conglomerate businesses is the Virgin Group.

1   Find information about the Virgin Group and identify its main revenue streams.

2   What are the advantages of the group from having so many revenue streams? What disadvantages do you think the group is facing?

3   Since the turn of the century, many conglomerates have decided to sell some of their activities, focusing only on one or a few main revenue streams. Why do you think this is? Discuss in class.

CASE STUDY 15.2

Twitter's new revenue streams look promising

When Twitter announced its proposals to sell shares to the public (to 'go public') in 2013, analysts were surprised not only by the forecast of the rising total revenue of $200 million that it reported – but also by the forecast loss it was expected to make. What Twitter did not draw attention to was the surprise that it had for new investors: new sources of income that would grow hugely over the next few years.

By 2021, Twitter had revenues from the following streams:

- Advertising services for promoted accounts, trends and Tweets. This was Twitter's original revenue stream.

- Data licensing, as Twitter sells subscriptions to public data to companies seeking to use and analyse historic and real-time data.

- Fees from subscriptions to the MoPub, an application helping mobile publishers to manage their advertising inventory. The acquisition of MoPub cost Twitter $350 million

To support its expanding revenue-earning activities, Twitter massively increased its staff levels.

In 2011 the business employed just 350 employees. By the end of 2020, it employed 5500 people.

1   Define the term 'total revenue'. **[2]**

2   Explain how Twitter can report an overall loss when total revenue is rising. **[4]**

3   Analyse **one** advantage and **one** limitation for Twitter of developing new revenue streams. **[4]**

4   Evaluate Twitter's decision to increase its scale of operations so quickly. **[10]**

THEORY OF KNOWLEDGE

Knowledge question: What roles do ethics and reason play when businesses try to control their costs?

Famous businesses such as Nike, Burberry, H&M, Amazon and many more have come under fire for destroying their own products. The practice has been widely used during the Covid-19 pandemic when firms found themselves with lots of unsold inventory. Amazon reportedly destroyed 130 000 items in a single week, including both returned and unsold goods. But why do firms do this?

The answer is clear: the cost to destroy these goods is smaller than the cost of warehousing them in the hope of selling them in the future. Some businesses such as Burberry recycle their clothes into energy. But the energy spent to produce these items far exceeds the energy produced through their recycling.

Many ethical questions arise from the fact that famous businesses destroy their own goods. Why can't these businesses donate their products to charities or other non-profit organisations for free? It seems that such a practice could destroy the perceived value of the products, especially luxury ones. Producers could have problems in the future, pricing their goods in a way that would generate enough revenue. In the long term, advanced stock controlling methods could help businesses to produce a smaller quantity of unwanted stock. For the time being, the practice of destroying goods creates a serious social backlash. Environmental pressure groups also react against this practice, which is not ecologically sustainable.

How significant are the ethical dimensions related to the practice of destroying excessive stock of products? What would you do if you were the CEO of a business producing luxury goods if these goods remained unsold? Would you consider the possibility of donating them? Discuss in class.

ACTIVITY 15.2

Classifying costs

The management of a furniture-manufacturing business is trying to classify the costs of the business to help with future decision-making. It makes a range of wooden tables and chairs. You have been asked to assist.

1   Classify these costs by ticking the appropriate boxes in the table.

2   Explain why you have classified these costs in the way you have.

Cost	Direct	Indirect	Fixed	Variable	Semi-variable
Rent of factory					
Management salaries					
Electricity					
Piece-rate labour wages of production employees					
Lease of company vehicles					
Wood and other materials used in production					
Maintenance cost of special machine used to make one type of wooden chair					

CASE STUDY 15.3

New revenue streams for Bliss Inn

Dajuan is the owner of Bliss Inn, a small hotel in Negril, Jamaica, that offers bed and breakfast services. Bliss Inn faces a lot of competition. The price charged per room is $50 and the capacity of the hotel is 20 rooms. However, Bliss Inn is rarely fully booked, except for a few days per year during the high season.

Dajuan is looking for new revenue streams. One option is to organise guided walking tours. This service seems to be popular among visitors, but competitors are already offering similar tours to their customers. To make a real difference and to stand out from the competition, he is thinking of opening a small concept shop in Bliss Inn, selling vintage Jamaican accessories and clothes. The second option is possibly riskier, but it could help Dajuan to significantly increase the total revenues of his business.

1 Define the term 'revenue streams'. [2]

2 Calculate the maximum revenue that Bliss Inn can earn per day. [2]

3 Suggest **two** reasons why adding more revenue streams might be important for Bliss Inn. [4]

4 Explain **two** possible disadvantages of adding new revenue streams to Bliss Inn. [4]

ACTIVITY 15.3

1 Suggest new revenue streams that could be considered by business activities, as per the example provided.

Activity	New revenue streams
A hotel offering accommodation only	Include spa services, restaurant services, etc.
A popular burger restaurant chain	
A beauty salon for ladies	
An online store selling organic food products	
A gym	

2 What would be the possible advantages and disadvantages of the new revenue streams that you propose in each case? Discuss in class.

SELF-EVALUATION CHECKLIST

After studying this chapter, complete this table.

I am able to apply and analyse:	Needs more work	Almost there	Ready to move on
the following types of costs, using examples: • fixed • variable • direct • indirect/overhead (AO2)			
total revenue and revenue streams, using examples (AO2)			

REFLECTION

Dyson took the decision to stop the electric car project in 2020. In light of developments since then, do you think this was the right decision?

Explain your answer by referring to: revenue streams; the costs of research; the high cost of vehicle batteries.

PROJECT

You are setting up a for-profit social enterprise café in your local town. Your goal is to reinvest most of your profits to deliver community benefit.

Organise a workshop for your class to:

• Discuss examples of similar social enterprises around the world.

• Name your business and decide on your exact social goals.

• Decide on different revenue streams for your café. Choose at least two, but no more than three.

• Identify the types of capital and revenue expenditures for your café.

• Categorise the costs of your business between direct and indirect.

• Create a workshop report and use it as a basis to design a crowdfunding campaign to finance your social enterprise.

Thinking about your project:

• When deciding about the revenue streams, did you first discuss both their advantages and their limitations?

EXAM-STYLE QUESTIONS

How will MyToys remain competitive in the market?

MyToys Ltd is a business producing toys. Parents trust MyToys for its excellent products that are safe for children, innovative and environmentally friendly. The products of MyToys are premium priced.

The business is facing the problem of falling sales revenue. One reason is the fierce competition from low-cost multinational companies, which experience big economies of scale. Another reason is changing consumer tastes. Children over the age of six are increasingly more attracted by electronic games rather than physical toys.

CONTINUED

MyToys is also facing the problem of high production costs. One reason for this is that the business uses expensive, environmentally friendly materials to build attractive and environmentally sustainable toys, and it promotes them through social media. Being a socially responsible business, MyToys spends money on many activities that benefit the local community around its factory. In 2021, it supported the construction of a school for children with special needs and donated specially designed educational toys for the students. This activity cost $150 000, 15% of the firm's total indirect costs for the year. Moreover, MyToys does not employ part-time workers. All employees are offered full-time employment contracts and receive a profit-related bonus each year.

MyToys hired Yichen as the new finance director to help them manage their financial performance. The shareholders are worried about the falling revenues, which are now only just covering the increasing costs. Yichen had worked for years for a big multinational toy company that has been returning high value to its shareholders.

In the meeting of the board of directors, Yichen proposed the following:

- Replace wood, the raw material used to produce most products, with recyclable plastic.
- Cut some indirect costs, such as the spending on CSR.
- Reduce the fixed costs of the business by reducing the number of full-time employees working in the offices of MyToys.
- All new recruits in the factory should be offered temporary employment contracts and be paid by the hour (time wages).

Yichen said that the efforts of the business to cut costs should be a priority, to help it to compete with the huge toy producers and to free up resources to develop new revenue streams. More specifically, Yichen believes that MyToys should:

- open two fun parks for children, one close to the factory and one in a centre of the city
- create multiplayer video games and e-sports for children over six years of age and young adults.

The board of directors was not enthusiastic about the cost cuts proposed by Yichen. The marketing director said that such cuts could cause the business to lose its identity. However, they agreed that the business needs new revenue streams, and asked Yichen to propose appropriate external sources of finance to support his two proposed investments.

1 Define the term 'indirect cost'. [2]
2 With reference to the case study, identify **two** types of indirect costs for MyToys. [4]
3 With reference to the case study, explain the difference between variable and fixed costs. [2]
4 Suggest **two** possible reasons why multinational competitors of MyToys are experiencing lower production costs. [4]
5 Explain **two** reasons why firms such as MyToys need to cut costs in periods of low sales. [4]
6 Analyse **two** problems MyToys might encounter when trying to reduce its direct production cost. [4]
7 Explain the impact that a reduction in corporate social responsibility (CSR) spending is likely to have on a) the costs of MyToys, and b) the revenues of MyToys. [4]
8 Explain **one** advantage and **one** disadvantage for MyToys of adding new revenue streams in the business. [4]
9 Suggest **two** appropriate external sources of finance for the new revenue streams of MyToys. [4]
10 Evaluate Yichen's proposal to cut costs and add new revenue streams as a method to improve the financial performance of MyToys. [10]

› Chapter 16
Final accounts

LEARNING OBJECTIVES

On completing this chapter you should be able to:

Apply and analyse:

- The purpose of accounts to different stakeholders (AO2)
- Final accounts:
  - profit and loss account
  - statement of financial position (AO2)
- Different types of intangible assets (AO2)

› Depreciation using the following methods:

- straight line

- units of production (AO2)

Synthesise and evaluate:

› Appropriateness of each depreciation method (AO3)

Use and apply:

- Final accounts: profit and loss account and statement of financial position (AO4)

› Depreciation methods: straight line and units of production (AO4)

BUSINESS IN CONTEXT

Final accounts – what do they tell us about a business?

Nimir Industrial Chemicals is an important limited company that operates in Pakistan's chemical industry. As with all limited companies, Nimir has to produce detailed published or **final accounts** each year. Table 16.1 and Figure 16.1 show important information from recent published accounts for Nimir Industrial Chemicals.

Earnings in Rupees (millions)	2015	2016	2017	2018	2019	2020
Revenue	3663	5011	7369	12154	14850	17173
Gross profit	561	972	1065	1612	2030	2546
Profit before tax	294	603	701	887	1159	1349
Long-term loans and leases	166	348	354	480	592	1004
Equity	1681	1788	2144	2615	3035	3623
Earnings per share (rupees)	2.0	4.0	4.3	6.3	7.3	8.4

Table 16.1: Summary of Nimir Industrial Chemicals accounting data

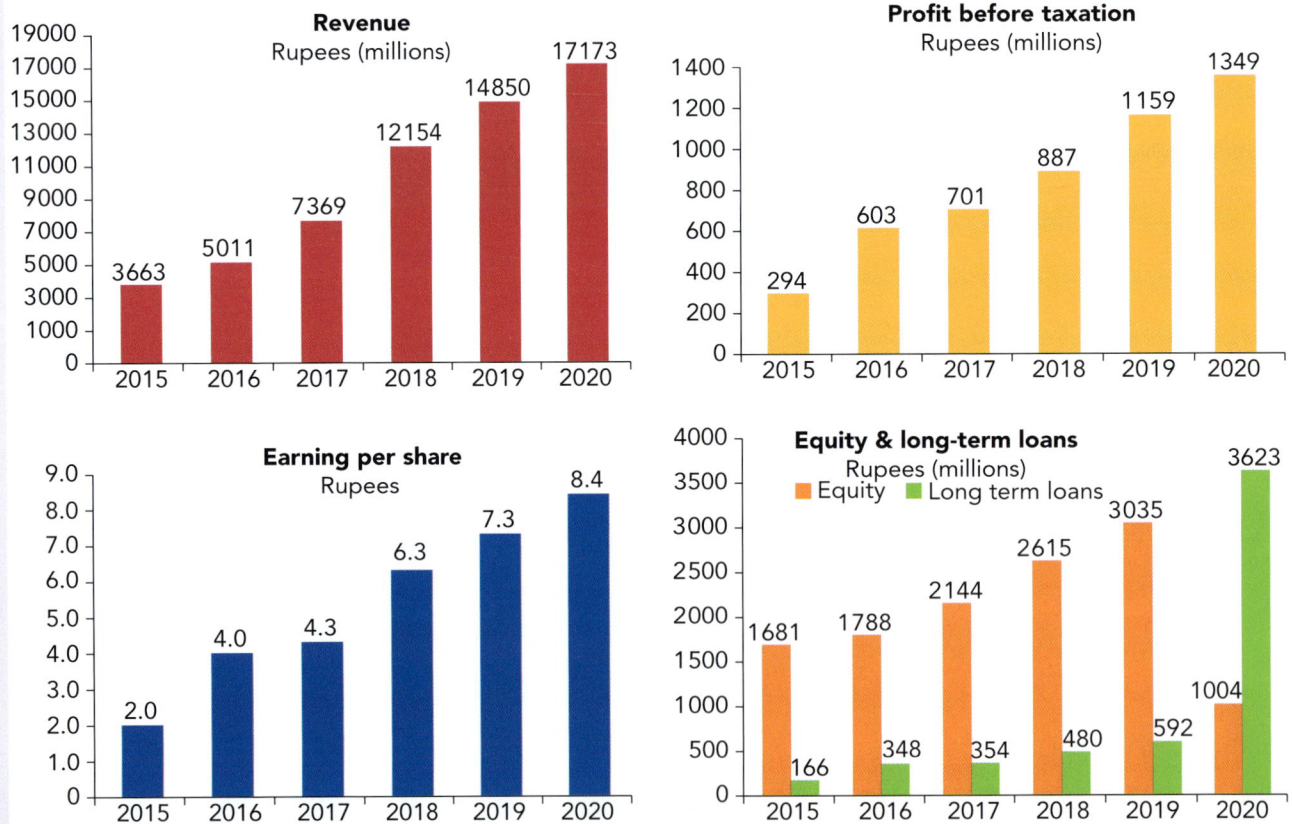

Figure 16.1: Extract from Nimir Industrial Chemicals accounts

Discuss in pairs or in a group:

- Why do you think public limited companies have to produce and publish annual final accounts?

- Do you think the management of Nimir Industrial Chemicals should be satisfied with the financial performance of the business?

- Explain why any two groups of stakeholders would find this information useful.

KEY TERM

final accounts: the end of year financial accounts produced by a business

KEY CONCEPT LINK

Sustainability

The economic sustainability of a business depends on its ability to generate profits in the long term. Profit is a survival condition for 'for-profit' business activities. It is also a valuable internal source of finance that can be retained and accumulated to cover the business's long-term financial needs. Non-profit entities are not aiming for profit, but they need revenues to be economically sustainable, as they also have costs and expenses to cover in order to reach their social goals.

16.1 The purposes of accounts to different stakeholders

All businesses have to keep detailed records of purchases, sales and other financial transactions. Table 16.2 lists some problems that would immediately arise if accounts were not kept. We can therefore say that accounts are financial records of business transactions, which are needed to provide essential information to stakeholder groups both within and outside the organisation.

Problem arising without accounting data	Stakeholder groups affected
How much did we buy from our suppliers and have they been paid yet?	Managers and suppliers (creditors)
How much profit did the business make last year?	Managers, shareholders and the tax authorities
Is the business able to repay the loan to the bank?	Managers and the bank
Did we pay wages to the workers last week?	Managers and workers
What is the value of the fixed assets and by how much did they depreciate last year?	Managers and shareholders

Table 16.2: Accounting data and the interests of stakeholders

It is therefore important that both internal and external stakeholder groups have access to accurate and up-to- date accounts – or at least a summary of them. The managers, as internal users, will have access to much more detailed and current data than other groups. External users include banks, government, employees, shareholders and other stakeholders of the business. These groups will have access to the published accounts of the company. The following list identifies the main stakeholders and the purposes of accounts to these groups.

The main stakeholders and the purposes of accounts to these groups

Business managers

- Measure the performance of the business to compare against targets, previous time periods and competitors.
- Provide information for taking decisions such as new investments, closing branches and launching new products.
- Control and monitor the operation of each department and division of the business.
- Set targets or budgets for the future and review these against actual performance.

Workforce

- Assess whether the business is secure enough to pay wages and salaries.
- Determine whether the business is likely to expand or be reduced in size.
- Determine whether jobs are secure.
- Find out whether, if profits are rising, a wage increase can be afforded.
- Find out how the average wage in the business compares with the salaries of directors.

Banks

- Decide whether to lend money to the business.
- Assess whether to allow an increase in overdraft facilities.
- Decide whether to continue an overdraft facility or a loan.

Creditors such as suppliers

- Assess whether the business is secure and has sufficient cash to pay off its debts.
- Assess whether the business is a good credit risk.
- Decide whether to press for early repayment of outstanding debts.

Customers

- Assess whether the business is secure.
- Determine whether they will be assured of future supplies of the goods they are purchasing.

- Establish whether there will be security of spare parts and service facilities.

Government and tax authorities

- Calculate how much tax is due from the business.
- Determine whether the business is likely to expand and create more jobs.
- Assess whether the business is in danger of closing down, creating economic problems.
- Confirm that the business is staying within the law in terms of accounting regulations.

Investors and potential investors in a business

- Assess the value of the business and their investment in it.
- Establish whether the business is becoming more or less profitable.
- Determine what share of the profits investors are receiving.
- Decide whether the business has potential for growth.
- As potential investors, compare these details with those from other businesses before making a decision to buy shares in a company.
- As actual investors, decide whether to consider selling all or part of their holding.

Local community

- See if the business is profitable and likely to expand, which could be good for the local economy.
- Determine whether the business is making losses and whether this could lead to closure.

Limitations of accounting information to stakeholders

It is common for stakeholders to believe that, because accounts are based on numbers and not descriptive words, they must be accurate and fair. Unfortunately, this is often not the case. Although, in theory, there can be no secrets in these accounts, they show the headline figures rather than the specific detail. This limits the usefulness of accounting information provided to stakeholders.

The following factors need to be remembered by stakeholders when they use the accounts provided by a business to make judgements and assessments.

One set of accounts is of limited use

A series of accounts is needed to be able to compare the performance of a business over time and with other similar businesses. One year's accounts are of limited value as they provide no trend picture over time of whether the business is becoming more or less profitable and more or less liquid. External stakeholders such as investors should have access to the full set of accounts of a business for a number of years.

Accounts do not measure items which cannot be expressed in monetary terms

For instance, accounts do not indicate the state of technology within the business or the ability and skills of the management team. The reputation of the business cannot be valued but this is often the most important consideration for customers and potential **creditors** to the business. The absence of any 'valuation of employees' can be crucial when analysing a business where the creativity of staff is important. With an advertising agency, for example, its strength depends on its key creative staff. If they leave, the prospects for the firm are poor, even though the accounts, which are always historic, covering previous time periods, may not show this until it is too late for potential investors.

The accounts of one business do not allow for comparisons

Effective assessment of a business performance can only be made in comparison with other firms engaged in similar activities. One set of one business's accounts will not allow for these comparisons to be made.

Business accounts will only publish the minimum information required by law

Managers would not be impressed with their accountants if they published accounts data that was very detailed and specific, beyond legal requirements, as this could help their competitors. So published accounts are a summary and they do not tell the whole story about a business.

Accounts are historic

Accounts can be up to six months out of date at the time of publication and they never contain the future financial plans or budgets of a business – these are not legally required. Accounts report what *has happened*, not what is going to happen. Only management accounts, which are intended for internal stakeholder use, look ahead. These accounts are used as planning and budgeting documents for the management and are not available to the external stakeholders.

Window dressing

In public companies, **window dressing** is a type of 'creative accounting' and it can amount to fraud – which is, of course, illegal. However, there is often very little difference between illegal accounts reporting and 'trying to give a favourable gloss' to the accounts. The latter may be unethical but it may not be against the law.

16.2 The final accounts

At the end of each accounting period, usually one year, accountants will draw up the financial statements of the business. For companies, these will be included in the annual report and accounts, which are not only sent to every shareholder but also in the public domain and can be accessed by any external stakeholder. Table 16.3 gives details of the financial statements of limited companies, as these are the accounts you are most likely to come across in IB Business Management.

Layout changes

There have been many changes to the layout of published accounts to comply with the International Financial Reporting Standards (IFRS Standards). These changes include different titles to important items on published accounts. This book employs the traditional layouts and titles, as used by the IB examinations, but you should be aware that accounts may be presented in slightly different ways and using slightly different terminology.

> **KEY TERMS**
>
> **creditors:** suppliers to a business who have not yet been paid
>
> **window dressing:** presenting the accounts of a business in the best possible, or most flattering, way which could potentially mislead users of accounts

LEARNER PROFILE

Principled

The goal of the International Standard-Setting Boards is to set internationally acceptable standards of financial reporting. 'Transparent, high-quality international standards are essential pillars of the global financial architecture. Their adoption and implementation improves the availability of high-quality financial information for stakeholders, investors and the public, which result in greater economic growth, development and accountability.

The independent, international standard-setting boards are responsible for issuing high-quality international standards in the public interest as well as non-authoritative pronouncements, such as guidance material for implementation.'

The International Ethics Board of Accountants (IESBA) has created a Code of Ethics to set a conceptual framework for all professional accountants to ensure compliance with the five fundamental principles of ethics.

Why do you think professional accountants need a code of ethics? To what extent do you think accountants can use 'window dressing' of the final accounts without being considered unethical by the IESBA? Discuss in class.

The account	What it shows	Other names for this account
Profit and loss account	The gross and operating profit of the company	Income statement
	Details of how the operating profit and profit before interest and tax is split up (or appropriated) between dividends to shareholders and retained profits	Statement of profit or loss Statement of comprehensive income
Statement of financial position	The net worth of the company. This is the difference between the value of what a company owns (assets) and what it owes (**liabilities**)	Statement of financial position

Table 16.3: Final accounts of limited companies – what they contain

The profit and loss account

When referring to published accounts from companies in many countries, the terms 'income statement' or 'statement of comprehensive income' will be used instead of 'profit and loss account'.

- A detailed profit and loss account is produced for internal use because managers will need as much information as possible. It may be produced as frequently as managers need the information – perhaps once a month.
- A less detailed summary will appear in the published accounts of companies for external users. It will be produced at least once a year. The content of this is laid down by the laws of each country or by international accounting standards, and it provides a minimum of information to prevent competitors having insight into their rivals' strengths and weaknesses.

Table 16.4 shows the simplified layout of a profit and loss account for a profit-seeking business. The title of it may be either 'Profit and loss account' or 'Statement of profit or loss'. The version used in this chapter is the one laid down by the 2023 IB syllabus. Additional information has been added where this aids understanding.

KEY TERMS

profit and loss account: records the revenue, costs and profit (or loss) of a business over a given period of time

liabilities: financial obligations of a business that it is required to pay in the future

XYZ plc Statement of profit or loss for the year ending 31/12/22	$m
Revenue	3060
Cost of sales	(1840)
Gross profit	1220
Expenses	(580)
Profit before tax and interest	640
Interest	(80)
Profit before tax	560
Tax	(112)
Profit for period	448
Dividends	(200)
Retained profit	248

Table 16.4: The simplified layout of a profit and loss account for a profit-seeking business

Note: all negative figures in accounting are denoted with ( ).

Explaining the profit and loss account

The trading section

This shows how **gross profit** (or loss) has been made from the trading activities of the business.

It is important to understand that, as not all sales are for cash in most businesses, the revenue figure is not the same as cash received by the business. The formula for calculating sales revenue is: selling price × quantity sold. Therefore, if 120 items are sold at $2 each, the sales revenue (also known as the sales turnover) is $240.

Profit and loss section

This section of the profit and loss account calculates both the **profit before interest and taxation** and the **profit after tax** of the business.

Overheads are costs or expenses of the business that are not directly related to the number of items made or sold. These can include rent and business rates, management salaries, lighting costs and depreciation. Profit before interest and taxation is the profit made before tax and interest have been subtracted, but after all costs of sales and overheads have been deducted from sales revenue. For many businesses this is exactly the same as operating profit as all revenue has been made from normal operating activities. If a business also has non-operating

CASE STUDY 16.1

Calculating Gross Profit

Cosy Corner Retailers Ltd has just completed its first year of trading. The managing director is keen to learn whether a profit has been made.

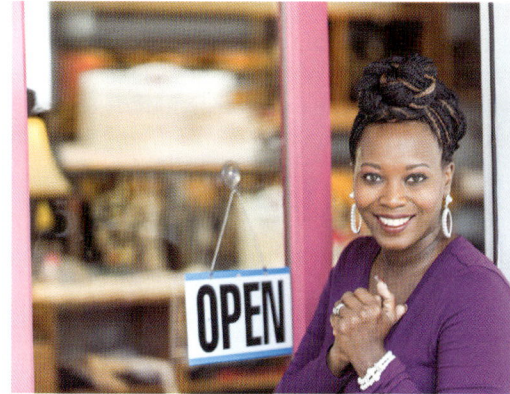

1   1500 items were sold for $5 each; cost of goods sold = $2 per unit. Calculate gross profit for Cosy Corner Retailers Ltd for the financial year ending 31 March 2023. Show all workings. [2]

2   State **two** reasons why you think it is important for any for-profit business to make a profit. [2]

3   Calculate Cosy Corner Retailers' gross profit for the following financial year, if the sales quantity rises by 20%. Show all your workings. [2]

KEY TERMS

gross profit: equal to sales revenue minus cost of sales

profit before interest and taxation: gross profit minus overhead expenses

profit after tax: profit made after corporation tax has been deducted

income – such as the rent on an unused warehouse – then this will be included in profit before interest and tax but not operating income. Interest is deducted to give the profit before tax figure. Corporation tax is deduced from this to arrive at profit for the year. Limited companies pay this corporation tax on their profit before paying **dividends** to shareholders.

Appropriation section

This final section of the profit and loss account shows how the profit for the year of the business is distributed between the owners – in the form of dividends to company shareholders – and as **retained profits**.

Profit and loss accounts – non-profit seeking organisations

Organisations which do not seek to make a profit, such as charities, are also likely to prepare annual accounts. The profit and loss accounts of these entities will be different from the example given in Table 16.4 in the following ways:

- the term 'surplus' will be used instead of 'profit'
- no dividends will be payable, so the 'surplus for the period' will be the same figure as 'retained surplus'.

TIP

When answering questions that ask for amendments to existing profit and loss accounts and statement of financial position, keep exactly the same layout and structure as contained in the case study.

KEY TERMS

dividends: the share of the profits paid to shareholders as a return for investing in the company

retained profit: the profit left after all deductions, including dividends, have been made; this is 'ploughed back' into the company as a source of finance

cost of sales (or cost of goods sold): this is the direct cost of purchasing the goods that were sold during the financial year

---

CASE STUDY 16.2

Sun Ltd

Sun Ltd produces sunglasses. In 2021 its revenues amounted to $228 000. The **cost of sales** (also called the cost of goods sold) was 40% of the selling price. The firm paid $50 000 in overheads and $20 000 in other one-off expenses. It also paid $10 000 on interest for a long-term loan that it took back in 2013. The corporate tax rate in the country is 25%. The shareholders decided to retain half of the profit to finance the business in the future.

1 Define the term 'overheads'. **[2]**

2 Prepare the P&L statement for Sun Ltd for the financial year ended 31/12/2021. **[6]**

3 Suggest **one** stakeholder group that is interested in the P&L statement of Sun Ltd. **[2]**

ACTIVITY 16.1

1 Do your own research to find the final accounts published by Amazon.com Inc. for the financial years ended 31/12/2018, 31/12/2019 and 31/12/2020.

2 What do you observe about the revenues of the business? Did they increase during the period?

3 Do you think Covid-19 affected Amazon's revenue, and if so, how?

4 Calculate a) the percentage change in sales revenue between 2019 and 2020, and b) the percentage change in net profit before interest and tax between 2019 and 2020. What do you observe? Discuss in class.

The statement of financial position

The statement of financial position (**balance sheet**) records the net wealth or shareholders' equity of a business at one moment in time. In a company, this net wealth 'belongs' to the shareholders. The aim of most businesses is to increase the **shareholders' equity** by raising the value of the business's assets more than any increase in the value of liabilities. Shareholders' equity comes from two main sources:

- The first and original source was the capital originally invested in the company through the purchase of shares. This is called '**share capital**'.
- The second source is the retained earnings of the company accumulated over time through its operations. These are sometimes referred to as reserves – which is rather misleading as they are not reserves of cash.

Further points to note:

- Companies have to publish the profit and loss account and the statement of financial position for the previous financial year as well in order to allow easy comparison.
- The titles of both accounts are very important as they identify both the account and the company.
- Whereas the profit and loss account covers the whole financial year, the statement of financial position is a statement of the estimated value of the company at one moment in time – the end of the financial year.

Non-current assets

The most common examples of non-current assets are land, buildings, vehicles and machinery. These are all tangible assets as they have a physical existence and are expected to be retained and used by the business for more than 12 months. Businesses can also own intangible assets – these cannot be seen but still have value in the business.

Current assets

Current assets are very important to a business, as will be seen when liquidity is assessed later in this chapter. The most common examples are inventories (stocks), accounts payable (**debtors** who have bought goods on credit) and cash/bank balance.

Current liabilities

Typical **current liabilities** include creditors, bank overdraft, unpaid dividends and unpaid tax.

Shareholders' equity

Shareholders' equity is sometimes referred to as shareholders' funds. It represents the capital originally paid into the business when the shareholders bought shares (share capital) or the retained earnings/profits of the business that the shareholders have accepted should be kept in the business. These are also known as reserves. Other reserves can also appear on the statement of financial position if a company believes that its fixed assets have increased in value (revaluation reserve) or if it sells additional shares for more than their 'nominal' value (share premium reserve). Shareholders' equity is the permanent capital of the business – it will not be repaid to shareholders (unless the company ceases trading altogether), unlike loans that are repaid to creditors.

The most common misunderstanding regarding reserves is that they are 'cash reserves' that can be called upon as a source of finance. They are not. Retained earnings arise due to profits being made which are not paid out in tax or dividends, but they have nearly always been invested back into the business through the purchase of additional assets. They are, therefore, no longer available as a source of liquid funds. The only cash funds available in the business are those indicated under 'cash' in the current assets section.

KEY TERMS

statement of financial position (balance sheet): an accounting statement that records the values of a business's assets, liabilities and shareholders' equity at one point in time

shareholders' equity: total value of assets less total value of liabilities

share capital: the total value of capital raised from shareholders by the issue of shares

current assets: the value of all assets that could reasonably be expected to be converted into cash within one year

debtors: customers who have bought products on credit and will pay cash at an agreed date in the future

current liabilities: debts of the business that will usually have to be paid within one year

shareholders' equity: total value of capital invested in the business by shareholders either in the form of share capital or retained profits

Table 16.5 shows an example of the layout of a statement of financial position (balance sheet). The explanatory notes in italics are included to help understanding, but these would not be part of the final accounts of a business.

XYZ plc Statement of financial position as at 31/12/21	$m	$m	Explanatory notes
Non-current assets:			assets to be kept and used by the business for more than one year
Property, plant, equipment	542		
Accumulated depreciation	(100)		
Non-current assets		**442**	
Current assets:			assets that are likely to be turned into cash before the next statement of financial position date
Stocks	34		stocks held by the business in the form of materials, work in progress and finished goods
Debtors (trade receivables)	28		the value of payments to be received from customers who have bought goods on credit
Cash	4		
Current assets		**66**	
Total assets		**508**	
Current liabilities			debts of the business that will usually have to be paid within one year
Creditors (trade payables)	42		value of debts for goods bought on credit payable to suppliers
Bank overdraft	28		
Other short-term loans	3		
Current liabilities		**73**	
Non-current (long-term) liabilities:		**125**	value of debts of the business that will be payable after more than one year
Total liabilities		**198**	
Net assets		**310**	total assets less total liabilities
Shareholders' equity			
Share capital	200		
Retained earnings	110		
Total shareholders' equity		**310**	

Table 16.5: Example of a statement of financial position with explanatory notes

Non-current liabilities

These are the long-term loans owed by the business. They are due to be paid over a period of time greater than one year and include loans, commercial mortgages and debentures. The value of non-current liabilities compared to the total capital employed by the business is a very important measure of the degree of risk being taken by the company's management, and this is explained in Chapter 18.

CASE STUDY 16.3

'Care' for animal welfare

This is an extract from the final accounts of Care, a non-profit business organisation that focuses on animal welfare and sells T-shirts and mugs to raise funds.

Financial Year Ended 31/12/2021	
Figures in $000	
Overheads:	35
Sales revenue:	420
Overdraft:	15
Machinery:	320
Equipment:	190
Buildings:	300
Retained earnings:	200
Debtors:	30
Direct cost:	170
Stock:	70
Cash	30
Creditors:	55
Tax:	0%
Accumulated depreciation:	70
Interest:	40
Non-current liabilities:	?
Short-term loans:	10

1   Prepare the profit and loss statement for Care for the financial year ended 31/12/2021. **[6]**

2   Construct the statement of financial position for Care as at 31/12/2021. Non-current liabilities must be calculated. **[8]**

16.3 Different types of intangible assets

Intangible assets are assets that have no physical substance and are not financial instruments (such as bank accounts and accounts receivables). They include asset types such as copyrights and goodwill.

Marketing-related intangible assets

Marketing-related intangible assets are used to market or promote products or services. Trademarks, logos or trade names are words, phrases or symbols that distinguish or identify a company or its products. They can be renewed indefinitely for periods of ten years at a time. Internet domain names and companies' names also qualify as marketing-related intangible assets that no other businesses have the right to use.

Customer-related intangible assets

Customer-related intangible assets result from business relationships with outside parties. They include lists of regular and reliable customers and contracts gained through long term customer relationships.

Artistic-related intangible assets

Artistic-related intangible assets give ownership rights to plays, literary works, musical works, pictures, photographs, and video and audiovisual material. A copyright protecting these ownership rights can be granted for the life of the creator plus 70 years.

Contract-related intangible assets

Contract-related intangible assets come from the value of rights arising from contractual arrangements, such as franchises, licensing agreements, construction permits, broadcasting rights, and service or supply contracts.

KEY TERM

Intangible asset: an identifiable non-monetary asset without physical substance

Technology-related intangible assets

Technology-related intangible assets arise from patents taken out on innovations or technological advances. A patent gives its holder the exclusive right to use, manufacture and sell a product or process for a period of 20 years without any interference or infringement by others. Accountants reduce the value of technology-related intangible assets on statement of financial position over their legal life or useful life, whichever is shorter.

Goodwill

This is another intangible asset that can arise when buying out another company. **Goodwill** is the value paid for the company in excess of the fair market value of the net assets acquired. For example, suppose you are paying $2 million for a company with net assets worth $1.6 million. Goodwill in the acquisition is equal to $400 000 = $2 000 000 − $1 600 000). Goodwill may only be recorded as part of an acquisition of another company. Accountants never recognise internally generated goodwill.

Intangible assets – conclusion

Intangible assets are difficult to put a value on as they are rarely bought and sold on the open market. In addition, unlike buildings or equipment which can be valued by specialist surveyors who can be fairly confident in their assessment, the value of intangible assets can fluctuate wildly. The damage to Tesla's brand image (and hence brand valuation) by the 2022 recall for safety reasons of millions of cars worldwide is a good example. Disputes can arise between accountants about the valuation of intangible assets and there is a current debate regarding the asset value of well-known brand names. There is scope for varying the value of these and other intangibles on the statement of financial position in order to give a better picture of the company's position. This is one aspect of 'window dressing' of accounts that can reduce the objectivity of published accounts.

Statements of financial position prepared under normally accepted accounting rules do not usually record these assets – often known as **intellectual property** – unless acquired through takeover or merger.

KEY TERMS

goodwill: arises when a business is valued at or sold for more than the statement of financial position value of its assets

intellectual property: an intangible asset that has been developed from human ideas and knowledge

ACTIVITY 16.2

Briefly explain the expected effects and impacts that the changes described are likely to have on the final accounts of a school that operates as a non-profit business. The school's revenues come from tuition, as students are charged a small yearly fee.

Change	Account(s) affected	Description of the expected impact
Enrolling more students in the school	Profit and loss statement	Higher sales revenue
Taking a short-term loan to pay its creditors		
Increasing the yearly salaries of teaching personnel		
Making better deals with suppliers to buy raw materials at lower prices		
Buying a new printer for the school head's office		

ACTIVITY 16.3

Understanding statements of financial position

Copy out this table and indicate in which category the following items would appear in on a for-profit company's statement of financial position.

	Fixed tangible assets	Fixed intangible assets	Current assets	Current liabilities	Non-current liabilities	Shareholders' equity
Company's car						
Work in progress						
Four-year bank loan						
Money owed to suppliers						
Issued share capital						
Dividends owed to shareholders						
Value of patents						
Payments due from customers						
Retained earnings						
Cash in bank						

For many companies, intangible assets are their main source of future earnings, especially in a world increasingly dominated by the 'knowledge-based economy', e.g., scientific research companies, publishing and music companies, companies with famous brand names and so on. The **market value** of companies with many intangible assets will be much greater than the statement of financial position or book value.

KEY TERM

market value: the estimated total value of a company if it were taken over

16.4 Depreciation of assets

Nearly all fixed/non-current assets will depreciate or decline in value over time. It seems reasonable, therefore, to record only the value of each year's depreciation as a cost on each year's profit and loss account. The key principles of depreciation are:

- Annual depreciation attempts to record capital expenditure over the useful life of an asset and avoids recording this expenditure as a one-off cost when the asset is purchased.

- The assets will retain some value on the statement of financial position each year until fully depreciated or sold off.

- The profits will be reduced by the amount of that year's depreciation and will not be under- or over-recorded.

Assets decline in value for two main reasons:

- normal wear and tear through usage
- technological change over time, making either the asset, or the product it is used to make, obsolete.

Technological change makes office equipment obsolete, even if it was purchased quite recently.

Knowledge question: How do our expectations and assumptions have an impact on how we read company accounts?

On 23 October 2019, Tesla reported 'surprise profits' to shareholders, after years of fluctuating operating results and many quarters of reported losses. This date was marked as a milestone for the financial performance of the company and created expectations for shareholders. By January 2020, Tesla's share price more than doubled.

But Tesla lagged behind the steady profits of major competitors such as Porche Automotive, BMW and Mercedez Benz. The supporters of Tesla's strategy welcomed the high profits reported as the beginning of an era for improvement in the financial performance of the business. However, many investors are still worried about Tesla missing targets in recent years. Between 30 December 2020 and 28 January 2021, stock market analysts were seriously divided in terms of their recommendations to investors. Some recommended buying Tesla shares, but others recommended selling – or provided neutral ratings.

How do the expectations and the assumptions of different investors and stock market analysts affect the way they read company accounts? How can it be that the same set of financial results is read differently by different people? How does the interpretation of the financial results affect the share price of plcs? Discuss in class.

Calculating depreciation – straight line and units of production methods

There are a number of different methods that accountants can use to calculate depreciation – but only two will be tested by the IB examination papers: **straight line depreciation** and the **units of production method**.

straight-line depreciation: a constant amount of depreciation is subtracted from the value of the asset each year

units of production method: depreciating an asset on the basis of its usage

Straight-line method of depreciation

The title of this method indicates the way in which depreciation is calculated.

To calculate the annual amount of depreciation the following information will be needed:

- the original or historical cost of the asset
- the expected useful life of the asset
- an estimation of the value of the asset at the end of its useful life – this is known as the residual value of the asset.

The following formula is then used to calculate the annual depreciation charge:

$$\text{annual depreciation charge} = \frac{\text{historic cost of asset} - \text{residual value}}{\text{useful life of asset (years)}}$$

Calculating depreciation using the straight-line method

A firm of lawyers purchases three new computers costing $3000 each. Experience with previous computers suggests that they will need to be updated after four years. At the end of this period, the second-hand value of each machine is estimated to be just $200. Using straight-line depreciation, the annual depreciation charge will be:

$$\frac{\$9000 - \$600}{4} = \frac{\$8400}{4} = \$2100$$

CONTINUED

So an annual depreciation charge of $2100 will be made. This will be included in the firm's overhead expenses on the profit and loss account. On the statement of financial position, the annual depreciation charge will be subtracted from the value of the computers. At the end of four years, each computer will be valued at $200 on the statement of financial position. Table 16.6 shows how the **net book value** of the computers reduces over the four-year period.

Year	Annual depreciation charge	Net book value of the three computers
Present	0	$9000
1	$2100	$6900
2	$2100	$4800
3	$2100	$2700
4	$2100	$600

Table 16.6: Net book value declines with each annual depreciation

KEY TERM

net book value: the current statement of financial position value of a non-current asset = original cost − accumulated depreciation

Suppose that at the end of the fourth year, the computers are sold for more than their expected residual value. If they are sold for a total of $900, then the business has made a surplus of $300. If, however, the computers were scrapped, because they had become so out of date compared with more recent models, the business would have to record a loss, in the fourth year, on the disposal of these assets.

Units of production method

This method is based on the assumption that the more an asset is used the faster it will depreciate. By focusing on asset usage, it ignores the number of years an asset is owned for – unlike straight-line depreciation. Since this method uses actual production levels produced by an asset to calculate its annual depreciation, the depreciation expense is likely to vary each year as in some years the asset will be used more than in others.

Again, this is unlike the straight-line method which depreciates an asset by the same amount each year.

The units of production method is calculated in a two stage process. Firstly, the depreciation per unit of output is calculated by using the following formula:

KEY FORMULA

$$\text{depreciation per unit} = \frac{\text{cost of asset} - \text{residual value}}{\text{total units of production}}$$

The second stage is to calculate the annual depreciation using the following formula:

annual depreciation = depreciation per unit × annual units produced

WORKED EXAMPLE 16.2

Calculating depreciation using the units of production method

Assume a machine is bought for $400 000 by an engineering business. The company's accountants believe that it has a residual or salvage value of $40 000. Based on previous experience, the company considers that the machine is capable of producing 20 000 units during its lifetime.

$$\text{Depreciation per unit} = \frac{\$400\,000 - \$40\,000}{20\,000} = \$18$$

In the current year, the engineering business produced 5000 units with this machine. The annual depreciation charge will be:

annual depreciation with production level of 5000 units = $18 × 5000 = $90 000

Table 16.7 shows the annual depreciation and the net book value of this machine during its working life.

Year and output level	Depreciation	Net book value
1 – 5000	5000 × $18 = $90 000	$310 000
2 – 5000	5000 × $18 = $90 000	$220 000
3 – 8000	8000 × $18 = $144 000	$76 000
4 – 2000	2000 × $18 = $36 000	$40 000

Table 16.7: Net book value declines with each annual depreciation

Note that:

- the amount of annual depreciation varies depending on output level
- the residual value at the end of year 4 is equal to the original estimate of the engineering company's accountants.

16.5 Appropriateness of each depreciation method

Each of these two methods have advantages and disadvantages:

Advantages of straight-line depreciation:

- It is easy to calculate and understand. It is widely used by limited companies and is accepted by tax authorities for the calculation of depreciation expenses. You can check this for yourself. Look in the annual accounts of any plc and you will find a statement about the depreciation methods it has used – more often than not, it will have used this method.

Limitations of straight-line depreciation:

- It requires estimates to be made regarding both life expectancy and residual value. Mistakes at this stage will lead to inaccurate depreciation charges being calculated.
- In addition, production equipment, trucks and computers are examples of assets that tend to depreciate much more quickly in the first and second years and with the rate at which the assets are used. This is not reflected in the straight-line method of calculation – all annual depreciation charges are the same. The units of production method of depreciation depreciates assets by a greater amount in those years in which production is greatest.
- There is no recognition of the rapid pace at which advances in modern technology tend to make existing assets redundant.
- The repairs and the maintenance costs of an asset usually increase with usage and this will reduce the profitability of the asset in the period when it is most used. This is not adjusted for by the fixed depreciation charge of the straight-line method.

Advantages of the units of production method:

- For manufacturing businesses it can be more accurate than the straight-line method, especially where assets lose greater value the more they are used.
- Another rationale for using this method is that the profit made from an asset largely depends on how much it is used. Most assets are more profitable when used intensively so it is logical to 'match' a higher amount of the cost of the asset against the higher profit made when it is used most.

Limitations of the units of production method:

- It is slightly more difficult to calculate than the straight-line method and needs to be recalculated each year.
- It cannot be used by businesses that do not manufacture or produce easily identifiable 'units of output', and other depreciation methods must be used.
- If a machine proves to be much less reliable and productive than expected, the unit rate of depreciation used may be insufficient to fully depreciate the asset before it has to be prematurely disposed of.
- Output data for each machine has to be recorded and used to recalculate depreciation during each time period.
- This method of accounting for depreciation is not accepted by tax authorities in calculating profit before tax, so it can only be used for internal accounting records.

In general terms the use of these two methods would be appropriate in different circumstances.

- The straight-line method would be advised for assets that fall in value fairly constantly over their useful lives or which give approximately the same level of benefit to the business each year, such as furniture and fittings in a shop premises. It would also be preferred by owners of small businesses which might have a relatively low value of equipment and other non-current assets and for which speed and ease of calculation is important.
- The units of production method is most appropriate when an asset's value is more closely related to the number of units it produces rather than the number of years it is in use. This method often results in greater deductions being made for depreciation in years when the asset is heavily

used, which can then offset those periods when the equipment experiences less use.

This method is particularly appropriate for assets that experience a high degree of wear and tear based on actual use per unit. This would apply to most items of production equipment. The method more accurately reflects the declining physical value of an asset than the straight-line method. The units of production method also allows companies to show higher depreciation expenses in more productive years when revenue and gross profit are likely to be highest.

CASE STUDY 16.4

Which depreciation method is best for HTprints Ltd?

HTprints Ltd offers printing services. In 2020 John, who owns the business together with his sister Margaret, bought a specialist printer for $32 000. The residual value of this asset is estimated at $8000 after four years of use. The business's accountant uses the straight-line method of depreciation for the machines and equipment of the business. Margaret, who has studied finance, believes that HTprints should also calculate depreciation of all its assets, including the new printer, by applying the units of production method.

Margaret has come up with a forecast of the total professional printouts to be produced by the newly acquired printer throughout its useful life:

Year	Forecasted units of professional printouts
1	12 000
2	10 000
3	6 000
4	2 000

John believes that the business should only use one method, the one that is the most straightforward. He does not agree with maintaining two depreciation methods, one for internal book-keeping purposes and one for the official final accounts and tax declaration. He believes it is a waste of time.

1   Define the term 'depreciation'. [2]

2   Calculate the annual depreciation charge, if the business uses the straight-line method of depreciation for the new printer. [2]

3   Calculate the annual depreciation charge for years 1 and 2 if the business uses the units of production method for the new printer. [4]

4   Discuss Margaret's idea to introduce the units of production method for the calculation of depreciation in HTprints. [10]

SELF-EVALUATION CHECKLIST

After studying this chapter, complete this table.

I am able to apply and analyse:	Needs more work	Almost there	Ready to move on
the purpose of accounts to different stakeholder groups (AO2)			
final accounts: • profit and loss account • statement of financial position (AO2)			

CONTINUED

different types of intangible assets (AO2)			
depreciation using the following methods: • straight line • units of production (AO2)			
I am able to synthesise and evaluate:			
the appropriateness of each depreciation method (AO3)			
I am able to use and apply:			
final accounts: profit and loss account and statement of financial position (AO4)			
depreciation methods: straight line and units of production (AO4)			

REFLECTION

Assume that you are advising an entrepreneur establishing a business for the first time.
Explain to them:

- the reasons for keeping financial records (accounts)

- the importance of preparing accounts showing profit or loss and the net worth of the business.

PROJECT

1 Split into two groups.

- **Group 1:** Prepare a presentation with the income statements of the Médecins Sans Frontières NGO for the two latest available financial years. Ask your teacher to help you put the income statement into the format provided by the International Baccalaureate Organization (IBO).

- **Group 2:** Prepare a presentation with the statement of financial position of the Médecins Sans Frontières NGO for the two latest available financial years. Ask your teacher to help you put the statement of financial position into the format provided by the IBO.

2 Discuss in class:

1 The changes in the NGO's revenues, costs, expenses and surplus before interest between the two financial years. What are the reasons behind these changes?

2 The changes in the non-current assets and liabilities between the two financial years. Have there been any significant changes, and if yes, what kind of changes are they?

3 The overall financial position of the NGO: to what extent is the financial performance indicating a business that reaches its goals?

Thinking about your project:

- Before doing your presentations, have you first done some research on the nature of the business activity of the 'Doctors Without Borders' and their long-term aim?

EXAM-STYLE QUESTIONS

Natcloth Ltd needs to expand

Natcloth Ltd is a family-owned business that produces clothes from organic fabric. The business was set up five years ago and its profits are growing. The market was initially a niche, but now it is growing fast and becoming very competitive, even though the economy is showing signs of economic slowdown.

The family has set growth as the main aim for Natcloth. They want to open a second production unit to double the production capacity and to explore substantial economies of scale, especially in the form of bulk-buying economies and technical economies.

Mary, one of the shareholders of the business, believes that the firm should seek a long-term loan to finance the investment, given the low cost of borrowing money (interest rates are at low levels). John, her father, does not want to increase the long-term liabilities of the firm and is considering attracting new shareholders to the company.

Mary and John are also discussing the depreciation method used to depreciate the machinery and equipment in the factory. So far, the accountant has been using the straight-line method of depreciation for all assets. However, the capital to be acquired for the new production unit is going to be technologically advanced and the straight-line method would not be efficient to realistically reflect the lost value of the assets over time. The depreciation of the new assets one year after their purchase would be $16 000 by using the straight-line method.

The extract below is from the final accounts of Natcloth Ltd.

Financial Year Ended 31/12/2021	
Figures in $000	
Indirect cost	40
Sales revenue	410
Share capital	?
Dividends: 40% on profit after interest and tax	
Machinery	300
Equipment	200
Buildings	300
Accumulated Retained profit	190
Debtors	35
Direct cost	170
Inventory	60
Cash	40
Creditors	50
Tax: 20% on profit before tax	
Accumulated Depreciation	80
Interest	50
Long-term loans	115
Short-term loans	8

CONTINUED

1   Define the term 'final accounts'. [2]

2   Define the term 'debtors'. [2]

3   By applying a STEEPLE framework, explain two factors affecting the growth strategy of Natcloth Ltd. [4]

4   Prepare the profit and loss statement of Natcloth Ltd for the financial year ended 31/12/2021. [6]

5   Construct the statement of financial position of Natcloth Ltd as at 31/12/2021. Share capital must be calculated. [8]

6   Explain how the depreciation of the new assets will appear on a) the profit and loss statement and b) the statement of financial position of Natcloth Ltd. [4]

7   Analyse **one** advantage and **one** limitation for Natcloth Ltd from using the straight-line method for the depreciation of the new assets. [4]

8   Suggest **two** external stakeholder groups that are interested in the final accounts of Natcloth Ltd. [4]

9   Explain the likely effect of economies of scale on the cost of goods sold of Natcloth Ltd. [4]

10 Discuss the appropriateness of a long-term loan as a source of finance, for Natcloth Ltd to reach its aim. [10]

Profitability and liquidity ratio analysis

CONTINUED

Use and apply:

- The following profitability ratios:
    - gross profit margin
    - profit margin
    - return on capital employed (ROCE) (AO4)
- The following liquidity ratios:
    - current ratio
    - acid test (quick) ratio (AO4)

BUSINESS IN CONTEXT

Comparing the accounts of the cola giants

How can stakeholders in PepsiCo and Coca-Cola, the world's two best-known soft-drink businesses, compare their performances?

One way is to analyse their accounting results. Ratio analysis is widely used by shareholders, banks and creditors – as well as the management of the business – to assess and compare performances of different businesses.

Here are extracts from both companies' published accounts as at the end of December 2021 (in $ million).

The **liquidity** of both companies can be assessed by comparing current assets with current liabilities. This analysis would indicate how able the companies were to pay off short-term debts. The gross and profit before tax and interest data can be compared with revenue to calculate **profit margin** ratios. These results would be a good starting point in comparing the performances of these two businesses. But these ratios do not give us the whole picture. Which company is making more profitable use of the capital invested in it? Which one seems to handle inventories more effectively? Does Coca-Cola or PepsiCo manage its trade receivables more efficiently? These and other questions can be answered by detailed ratio analysis of published accounts.

Discuss in pairs or in a group:

- Would it be useful to compare these two companies' accounts with those of a construction company? Explain your answer.
- How important is the ability to pay short-term debts to the survival of a business?
- Why would it be useful for stakeholders to make a comparison between profit and capital invested into a business?

KEY TERMS

liquidity: the ability of a business to pay its short-term debts

profit margin: this ratio compares operating profit with revenue

CONTINUED

	Revenue	Cost of goods sold	Operating profit	Current assets	Current liabilities	Stocks (inventories)	Trade accounts receivable	Capital employed
PepsiCo	79 474	37 075	31 237	21 783	26 220	4 347	8 680	66 049
Coca-Cola	38 655	15 357	10 308	22 545	19 950	3 414	3 512	74 404

KEY CONCEPT LINK

Change

The constant changes in the wider environment affect the **profitability** and liquidity of businesses. Some external changes bring improvement to the financial ratios. For example, technological evolution allows many firms to improve their net profit margin by replacing human labour, which is the most expensive factor of production per unit produced. The gradual shift of consumers from physical shops to online purchases, along with the evolution of internet technology, has allowed many industries to close their bricks-and-mortar stores and thus to cut overheads and enjoy improved profitability. But other external changes cause profit margins to deteriorate. For example, in an economic recession, many businesses are forced to reduce their selling price but they are unable to cut their costs by the same proportion, and as a result their profit margins deteriorate.

KEY TERM

profitability: a relative measure of a business's ability to make a profit from sales or a capital investment

17.1 Profitability ratios

There are three main groups of ratios to be studied on the IB syllabus:

- profitability ratios
- liquidity ratios
- debt/equity ratios (see chapter 18).

This section calculates and evaluates profitability ratios.

How much can we tell about a company's performance by studying the published accounts? It is easy to compare one year's profit figure with the previous year. Changes in revenue can also be identified, as can differences from one year to the next in current assets, current liabilities and shareholders' equity. Similar comparisons can be made between different companies too. However, when making these comparisons one essential problem arises. Look at the company results from two printing firms:

	Gross profit 2023 ($m)
Nairobi Press	125
Port Louis Press	800

How much can we tell about the performance of these two companies from these results? Is Port Louis Press more successful than Nairobi Press? Are the managers of Nairobi Press less effective? Are the companies becoming more profitable? Would they make good investments for future shareholders? Are the strategies adopted by Port Louis Press much more successful than those of Nairobi Press?

The answer to all of these questions is the same – we cannot tell from the information given. The only correct statement that can be made is that one company (Port Louis Press) made an gross profit 6.4 times greater than that of the Nairobi Press (NP).

Now look at other information about these two businesses:

	Revenue, 2023 ($000)
Nairobi Press (NP)	250
Port Louis Press (PLP)	3200

This additional data starts to give us a more detailed picture of the performance of these two businesses. The comparison would be even clearer if we analysed the data together with the profit results already given. Which management team has been more effective at converting revenue into profit? Accountants make this assessment by relating two accounting results to each other in the form of a ratio.

LEARNER PROFILE

Thinkers

Finance managers need to synthesise and evaluate the information revealed through the final accounts and to develop courses of action to help the business to improve its financial performance. This is done with the help of ratio analysis.

In 2014, Amazon's net profit margin was very low – close to zero. Since then, the profitability has improved spectacularly and on 30 June 2021 the business reported a record-high operating profit margin of 6.68%.

This improvement was not a coincidence; it was the result of deliberate business decisions to boost the profitability of Amazon. The business has been investing heavily in high-profit margin business sectors and has focused on improving customer satisfaction rates. This has allowed Amazon to charge premium prices for services such as third-party e-commerce transactions and digital advertising. Moreover, Amazon Web services in a cloud infrastructure has continued to grow and this division generates high margins for the business.

At the same time, Amazon is always looking for ways to cut costs and increase the productivity of workers. As an example, in 2020 Amazon reportedly started testing a concept by which independent contractors would pick products at Whole Foods Market stores and then deliver them in their own vehicles, to help the business cut costs in the growing grocery delivery service segment.

How important is the role of finance managers as thinkers who can analyse the financial performance of a business in order to make improvements? Are there ethical considerations in the process of decision-making to improve the profitability of organisations such as Amazon? Discuss in class.

A high level of profit does not necessarily mean a high level of profitability, as the following example shows. There are three profitability ratios included in the syllabus.

Gross profit margin ratio

This is used to assess how successful the management of a business has been at converting revenue into gross profit. It is widely used to measure the performance of a company and its management team.

KEY TERM

gross profit margin: this ratio compares gross profit (profit before deduction of overhead expenses) with revenue

The gross profit margin is calculated by the following formula:

KEY FORMULA

$$\text{gross profit margin}\% = \frac{\text{gross profit}}{\text{sales revenue}} \times 100$$

Using the two businesses already referred to – Nairobi Press and Port Louis Press – the gross profit margin can be calculated as follows (all figures are for 2023):

	Gross profit ($m)	Revenue ($m)	Gross profit margin
NP	125	250	$\frac{125}{250} \times 100 = 50\%$
PLP	800	3200	$\frac{800}{3200} \times 100 = 25\%$

Points to note:

- Higher profit does not necessarily mean higher profitability. Although Port Louis Press recorded a much higher gross profit figure it has a lower gross profit margin. This is because its revenue was 12.8 times greater than that of Nairobi Press but its gross profit was only 6.4 times greater.
- The lower gross profit margin could result from a PLP adopting a lower because Port Louis Press is adopting a low-price strategy to increase sales or because it has higher cost of sales per unit.
- Higher cost of sales per unit could be the result of higher material costs or higher direct labour costs compared with Nairobi Press. Perhaps the

management of this company is less effective in controlling costs than managers at Nairobi Press.

- The gross profit margin is a good indicator of how effectively managers have added value to the cost of sales.
- Methods that could be used to improve profitability are analysed in section 17.2.
- It is misleading to compare the ratios of firms in different industries because the level of risk and gross profit margin will differ greatly.

ACTIVITY 17.1

The table shows the average gross profit margin by industry in the USA for 2020.

Industry title	Gross profit margin 2020 (%)
Agricultural production crops	10.3
Metal mining	8.7
Building, construction, general contractors and operative builders	24.4
Apparel and other finished products made from fabrics and similar materials	48.3
Chemicals and allied products	54.8
Health services	33.7
Communications	54.1

Why do you think the average gross profit margin varies so much among different industries? Discuss the possible reasons affecting the gross profit margin at an industry level.

Profit margin

This ratio uses profit before tax and interest data. This is calculated by subtracting expenses from gross profit, adding non-operating income and subtracting

KEY FORMULA

$$\text{profit margin}\% = \frac{\text{profit before interest and tax}}{\text{sales revenue}} \times 100$$

non-operating expenses. The profit margin (also known as net profit margin) measures how successful a business is at converting revenue into operating profit before interest and tax are deducted.

Using the same two businesses (all figures for 2023):

	Profit before interest and tax ($m)	Revenue ($m)	Profit margin
NP	50	250	$\frac{50}{250} \times 100 = 20\%$
PLP	500	3200	$\frac{500}{3200} \times 100 = 15.6\%$

Points to note:

- The profitability gap between these two businesses has narrowed. The difference in gross profit margins is substantial but the difference in profit margins is much less. This suggests that Nairobi Press has relatively high overhead expenses, causing much lower profit before interest and tax compared with revenue, than Port Louis. The difference might also have been caused by higher non-operating income for Port Louis.
- Port Louis could narrow the gap further by reducing overhead expenses while maintaining revenue, or by increasing revenue without increasing overhead expenses.
- A comparison of results with those of previous years would indicate whether the performance and profitability of either company was improving or worsening. This would give a more complete analysis of the level of management performance.
- The profit margin – and the trend in this ratio over time – indicates management effectiveness at converting revenue into profit (operating and non-operating) after all costs and expenses have been subtracted.

TIP

Many students state that to 'increase profit margins the business should increase sales'. This is an incomplete answer because revenue needs to increase at a greater rate than the costs of the business in order for profit margins to rise.

CASE STUDY 17.1

Energy company needs to improve their profitability

Energia Ltd is an energy company currently engaged in the marketing and distribution of oil-based products including petrol, diesel, heating oil and jet fuel.

Two business analysts have obtained the following information from Energia's accounts (shown in $000). One of the two experts believes that the business could increase profitability by increasing prices. The other one thinks profitability could be best increased by reducing non-essential indirect costs such as marketing expenses.

	2020	2019	2018
Revenue	4 215 879	3 915 779	4 127 654
Gross profit	125 847	119 822	132 997
Profit before interest and tax	31 870	30 826	41 972

1 Calculate the gross and net profit margin ratios of Energia for all **three** years. [6]

2 Comment on Energia's profitability over the period shown. [4]

3 Evaluate the **two** proposals of the business analysts for increasing Energia's profitability. [10]

Return on capital employed (ROCE)

Return on capital employed is the most commonly used measure of the profitability of a business. It is often referred to as the primary efficiency ratio. It compares profit with the capital that has been invested in the business (the **capital employed**).

KEY TERMS AND FORMULA

return on capital employed: this compares operating profit and the capital employed in the business

Return on capital employed (%)

$$= \frac{\text{profit before interest and tax}}{\text{capital employed}} \times 100$$

capital employed: the total value of all long-term finance invested in the business = non-current liabilities + equity

	Profit before interest and tax ($m)	Capital employed ($m)	Return on capital employed ROCE
NP	50	400	$\frac{50}{400} \times 100 = 12.5\%$
PLP	500	5000	$\frac{500}{5000} \times 100 = 10\%$

From these results it is clear that the management of Nairobi Press is more effective at making the capital invested in the business earn profit.

Points to note:

- The higher the value of this ratio, the greater the return on the capital invested in the business.

- The return can be compared both with other companies and with the ROCE of the previous year. Making comparisons over time allows the trend of profitability in the company to be identified.

- The result can also be compared with the return from interest-bearing accounts – could the capital be invested in a bank at a higher rate of interest with no risk?

- ROCE results should be compared with the interest cost of borrowing finance. If it is less than this interest rate, an increase in borrowing will reduce returns to shareholders.
- The ROCE of a business can be raised by increasing the profitable, efficient use of the assets owned by the business, which were purchased by the capital employed.

17.2 Possible strategies to improve these ratios

Tables 17.1 and 17.2 provide an evaluation of methods to increase profitability and improve these ratios.

Methods to increase profit margins	Examples	Evaluation of method
Reduce direct costs	Use lower-cost materials	Quality image may be damaged; the product's reputation could be damaged
	Cut labour costs, e.g., relocate production to low-labour-cost countries	Quality may be at risk; communication and supply problems with distant factories
	Cut labour costs by increasing productivity through automation	Purchasing machinery will increase overhead costs; workers will need retraining – short-term profits may be reduced
	Cut wage costs by reducing workers' pay	Motivation levels might fall, which could reduce productivity and quality
Increase prices	Will increase profit on each item sold	Total revenue and profit could fall if too many consumers switch to competitors – this links to price elasticity
Increase profit margin by reducing overhead costs	Relocate to low-cost site	Lower rental costs could mean moving to a less attractive area, which could damage image
	Reduce promotion costs	Cutting promotion costs could lead to sales falling by more than fixed costs
	Delayer the organisation	Fewer managers could reduce the efficient operation of the business
	Increase non-operating income	Existing assets might be fully employed in the operations of the business

Table 17.1: Evaluating methods to increase profit margins

Methods to increase ROCE	Evaluation of method
Increase profit before interest and tax without increasing capital employed, for example:	
• raise prices	Demand could be price elastic
• reduce direct costs per unit	Cheaper materials could reduce quality
• reduce overheads, such as delayering or reducing promotion costs	May not be effective in increasing profit in the short term and may have drawbacks, e.g., less promotion could reduce sales
Reduce capital employed, for example:	Assets may be needed in the future, e.g., for expansion of the business
• sell assets that contribute nothing or little to sales/profit – use the capital raised to reduce debts	

Table 17.2: Evaluating methods for increasing ROCE

TIP

Many examination questions will ask for methods of increasing profitability of a business. If the question needs an evaluative answer, it is very important that you consider at least one reason why your suggestion might not be effective.

CASE STUDY 17.2

Should DairyFun Ltd grow in order to improve its profitability?

DairyFun Ltd is a small business producing dairy products that it sells in a very competitive market. Karim, the finance director, is worried about the profitability of the business. He managed to get some information about the industry average profitability ratios to compare DairyFun's performance.

Year: 2020	DairyFun Ltd	Industry average
Gross profit margin	24.3%	25.1%
Net profit margin	4.2%	5.7%
ROCE	4.8%	4.1%

Karim believes that the only way to improve the profitability of the business is to grow in a way that DairyFun would enjoy economies of scale.

Zoya, the operations management director disagrees. She believes that the business should stay small and focus on the production of high-quality premium-priced products in small quantities. According to her perspective, management has been very efficient in the way they have used the available financial resources to generate profits. This efficiency could be lost through growth, which could lead to diseconomies of scale. Zoya suggests that the business should look for other ways to improve profitability ratios.

1   Comment on the profitability of DairyFun compared to the industry average profitability ratios.   [6]

2   Suggest **two** types of economies of scale that could improve DairyFun's profitability ratios.   [4]

3   Suggest **two** ways in which DairyFun could improve its profitability, other than economies of scale.   [4]

4   Discuss Karim's suggestion to pursue growth as a way to improve DairyFun's profitability.   [10]

17.3 Liquidity ratios

These ratios measure how easily a business could meet its short-term debts and liabilities – or its **liquidity**. The liquidity ratios are, therefore, concerned with the current assets and liabilities of a business. If the level of current assets is relatively low, then the business could have problems paying its short-term debts – a situation known as 'being illiquid'. Suppliers would refuse to deliver more materials and banks would refuse more loans. If it has too much money tied up in current assets, then this could be used more effectively and profitably by investing in other assets.

> **KEY TERM**
>
> **liquidity:** ability of a business to pay its short-term debts

Current ratio

The **current ratio** is calculated by the following formula:

> **KEY FORMULA**
>
> $$\text{current ratio} = \frac{\text{current assets}}{\text{current liabilities}}$$

> **KEY TERM**
>
> **current ratio:** this compares the current assets with the current liabilities of the business

The result can be expressed either as a ratio (e.g., 2 : 1) or just as a number (e.g., 2). These two results show that this business could pay for its short-term debts twice over. It is in a very liquid position. There is no particular result that can be considered a universal and reliable guide to a firm's liquidity. Many accountants recommend a result of around 1.5–2, but much depends on the industry the firm operates in and the recent trend in the current ratio. For instance, a result of around 1.5 could be a cause of concern if, last year, the current ratio had been much higher.

The current ratios for the printing companies can be calculated as follows (all figures as at 31 December 2023, $m):

	Current assets	Current liabilities	Current ratio
NP	100	50	$\frac{100}{50} = 2:1$
PLP	1000	1000	$\frac{1000}{1000} = 1:1$

Points to note:

- Nairobi Press is in a more liquid position than Port Louis Press. Nairobi Press has twice as many current assets as current liabilities. For every $1 of short-term debts it has $2 of current assets to pay for them. This is a relatively 'safe' position – indeed, many accountants advise firms to aim for current ratios between 1.5 and 2.0.

- The current ratio of Port Louis Press is more worrying. It only has $1 of current assets to pay for each $1 of short-term debt. In the unlikely event that all of its short-term creditors demanded repayment at the same time, it would struggle to pay them all. This would be even more of a problem if some of its current assets could not be converted into cash quickly.

- Very low current ratios might not be unusual for businesses, such as food retailers, that have regular inflows of cash which they can rely on to pay short-term debts.

- Current ratio results over 2 might suggest that too many funds are tied up in unprofitable inventories, trade receivables and cash. It might be better to place some of these current assets in a more profitable form, such as equipment to increase efficiency.

- A low ratio might lead to corrective management action to increase current assets held by the business.

Acid test ratio

The **acid test ratio** is a stricter test of liquidity and is sometimes referred to as the 'quick ratio'. It ignores the least liquid of the firm's current assets – stocks. Stocks, by definition, have not yet been sold and there can be no certainty that they will be sold in the short term. By eliminating the value of stocks from the acid test ratio, the users of accounts are given a clearer picture of the firm's ability to pay short-term debts.

acid test ratio: this compares the liquid assets of a business with its current liabilities.

The acid test ratio is calculated using the following formula:

$$\text{acid test ratio} = \frac{\text{current assets} - \text{stock}}{\text{current liabilities}}$$

The acid test ratios for the printing companies may be calculated as follows (all figures as at 31 December 2023, $m):

	Liquid assets	Current liabilities	Acid test ratio
NP	70	50	$\frac{70}{50} = 1.4$
PLP	400	1000	$\frac{400}{1000} = 0.4$

Points to note:

- Results below 1 are often viewed with caution by accountants. They mean that the business has less than $1 of liquid assets to pay each $1 of short-term debt. Therefore, Port Louis Press may well have a liquidity problem.

- The full picture needs to be gained by looking at previous years' results. For example, if Port Louis Press had an acid test of 0.3 in 2022, this means that over the past 12 months its liquidity has actually improved. This is more favourable than if its result in 2022 had been 1, showing a decline in liquidity in the current year.

- Businesses with high stock levels will record very different current and acid test ratios. This is not a problem if stock levels are always high for this type of business, such as a furniture retailer. It would be a cause for concern for other types of businesses, such as computer manufacturers, where stocks lose value rapidly due to technological changes.

- Selling inventories for cash *will not* improve the current ratio – both items are included in current assets. However, it *will* improve the acid test ratio as cash is a liquid asset but stocks are not.

17.4 Possible strategies to improve these ratios

Table 17.3 provides an evaluation of methods to improve business liquidity and improve these ratio results.

Method to increase liquidity	Examples	Evaluation of method
Sell off fixed assets for cash – these could be leased these back if still needed by the business	Land and property could be sold to a leasing company	If assets are sold quickly, they might not be sold for their true value If assets are still needed, then leasing charges will add to overheads and reduce operating profit margin
Sell off stocks for cash (note: this will improve the acid test ratio, but not the current ratio) or use JIT (just-in-time) stock management (see Chapter 30)	Stocks of finished goods could be sold off at a discount to raise cash JIT stock management will reduce the stock held	This will reduce the gross profit margin if inventories are sold at a discount Brand image could be damaged if inventories are sold off at low prices Inventories might be needed to meet changing customer demand levels – JIT might be difficult to adopt in some industries
Increase loans to inject cash into the business and increase working capital	Long-term loans could be taken out if the bank is confident of the company's prospects	These will increase the gearing ratio Increased interest costs will reduce profit for the year

Table 17.3: Evaluating strategies to increase liquidity and improve ratio results

ACTIVITY 17.2

1   Split into two groups.

- **Group 1:** Find the final accounts of the Coca-Cola Company.

   Calculate the following ratios for the three latest financial years:

   a   profit margin

   b   current ratio

   c   ROCE

- **Group 2:** Find the same information as Group 1 for PepsiCo.

2   Compare and contrast the two businesses in terms of profitability and liquidity.

3   If you were an investor, how would these ratios help you with your decision about which of the two businesses to invest in? Are these ratios enough for you to make a decision? Suggest other information, financial or non-financial, that you would like to have before deciding.

TIP

When commenting on ratio results, it is often advisable to question the accuracy of the data used and the limitations of using just a limited number of ratio results in your analysis.

CASE STUDY 17.3

How is my business doing?

Mohammed Ahmed is the chief executive of Ahmed Builders plc. The company specialises in quality fitting out of shops for internationally famous retailers. These customers demand that work is finished to very tight time limits, so it is important for Ahmed Builders to keep stocks of important materials. Ahmed is keen to compare the performance and liquidity of his company with those of another building company that does similar work. He obtained a set of published

CONTINUED

accounts for Flash Builders plc and used ratios to help him in the comparison. These were the figures he used from both companies:

	Ahmed ($000)	Flash ($000)
Gross profit (2022)	100	150
Profit before tax and interest (2022)	20	60
Revenue (2022)	350	600
Current assets (as at 31 December 2022)	100	150
Inventories (as at 31 December 2022)	50	60
Current liabilities (as at 31 December 2022)	45	120

1   Using the data for Ahmed Builders plc and Flash Builders plc, calculate their profit margin.   [4]

2   Suggest **two** ways in which Ahmed might attempt to increase the net profit margin ratio for his business.   [4]

3   Using the data for Ahmed Builders plc and Flash Builders plc, calculate each company's:

   a   current ratio

   b   acid test ratio   [4]

4   Suggest **two** ways in which Flash Builders plc might be able to improve its liquidity position.   [4]

THEORY OF KNOWLEDGE

Knowledge question: To what extent is ratio analysis open to interpretation?

Profitability and liquidity ratios are calculated based on facts and figures, as these appear on the final accounts of business organisations. When it comes to plcs, the validity of these figures has also been audited by independent auditors. Thus, it could be said that the information revealed through ratio analysis is always clear and objective and cannot be subject to interpretation. But this is not always true.

Take for example the ROCE ratio. Many stock market analysts and investors regard ROCE as one of the most important ratios, as it can be used as an indicator of the company's overall performance. The ROCE does not only indicate the extent to which a company enjoys good profitability. It is also a very good indicator of the management's efficiency to generate profits as a proportion of capital investments. However, not all agree. Some shareholders do not place much trust in ROCE because they know that the ratio is subject to interpretation. For example, a business with a falling ROCE is not necessarily losing its ability to generate profit as a percentage of total capital employed because of ineffective management decisions. It could be a business that has recently invested for long-term growth, the profits of which have not yet appeared but are expected in the long term.

Think of other examples of how profitability and liquidity ratios are open to interpretation. Does the fact that ratios can be interpreted differently by different people reduce the value of ratio analysis? Split into two groups to debate the significance of ratio analysis.

ACTIVITY 17.3

The Steel Authority of India operates in a market affected by cyclical demand for its steel products. Material costs also vary from one year to the next – particularly energy costs and iron ore costs. The business invests regularly to improve the productivity of the mines and to increase their capacity. Its ROCE between 2017 and 2021 has been:

	2021	2020	2019	2018	2017
ROCE (%)	10.37	7.92	7.89	2.44	−2.87

Discuss in pairs or in a group: Why is the ROCE significant for a firm such as the Steel Authority in India? How can a business try to achieve a high and consistent return on capital employed in highly cyclical markets?

TIP

When commenting on ratio results, it is often advisable to question the accuracy of the data used and the limitations of using a limited number of ratio results in your analysis.

SELF-EVALUATION CHECKLIST

After studying this chapter, complete this table.

I am able to apply and analyse:	Needs more work	Almost there	Ready to move on
the following profitability ratios: • gross profit margin • profit margin • return on capital employed (ROCE) (AO2)			
the following liquidity ratios: • current ratio • acid test ratio (AO2)			
I am able to synthesise and evaluate:			
strategies to improve these ratios (AO3)			
I am able to use and apply:			
the following profitability ratios: • gross profit margin • profit margin • return on capital employed (ROCE) (AO4)			
the following liquidity ratios: • current ratio • acid test ratio (AO4)			

REFLECTION

Select one public limited company that operates in your country. Research its financial accounts for the last five years. Using profitability and liquidity ratio analysis, explain to another learner whether the performance of this business is improving or worsening over time.

PROJECT

Traditional financial ratio analysis is not efficient to evaluate the financial performance of non-profit social enterprises. Some values are not reflected in financial statements, such as the social benefits derived from the activities of a social enterprise. One ratio to measure the effectiveness of such businesses from this perspective is the social return on investment (SROI).

1   Split into two groups:

  • **Group 1:** Do some research on the SROI. Prepare a poster of what it measures and some points for discussion about its usefulness.

  • **Group 2:** Find other financial ratios that are commonly used by social enterprises. Prepare a poster to present them and compare and contrast them with the ratios used by for-profit businesses.

CONTINUED

2 Discuss in class: Which ratios are most useful in understanding the financial performance of social enterprises? Why are they different from the ratios used by for-profit businesses?

EXAM-STYLE QUESTIONS

Has Royal Paint's performance improved in 2021?

Royal Paint (RP) Plc is one of the biggest producers of paint and other chemicals in a competitive market. Annelise, RP's CEO, has been very worried about the financial performance of the business in the aftermath of the Covid-19 pandemic. In an effort to control profitability, the business tried to reduce spending on certain overheads. However, the cost of raw materials rose because of supply shortages. Given all of these problems, Annelise was thrilled when the financial results for 2021 showed an increase in both revenues and net profit. However, analysts in the stock market have identified some problems with the profitability and liquidity of RP.

Annelise is planning to issue more share capital to finance the future growth plans of RP.

	Year ending 31 December 2021 ($m)	Year ending 31 December 2020 ($m)
Revenue	400	370
Cost of sales	120	100
Profit before tax and interest	35	34
Inventories (stock)	58	36
Accounts receivable (debtors)	80	70
Current assets	140	120
Current liabilities	140	120
Long-term (non-current) liabilities	150	120
Capital employed	300	260

1 Define the term 'current assets'. [2]
2 Define the term 'capital employed'. [2]
3 Comment on the business's liquidity by using the current ratio. [4]
4 Comment on the business's liquidity by using the acid test. [4]
5 Calculate the following ratios for 2020 and 2021:
   a return on capital employed
   b gross profit margin
   c profit margin [6]
6 Based on the change in ROCE between 2020 and 2021, comment on management efficiency at RP Plc. [2]
7 Outline how the overheads cut has affected the three profitability ratios of RP. [3]
8 Suggest how the increase in inventories affects the statement of financial position of RP. [2]
9 Explain how the ROCE of RP could change, if the business decides to raise more share capital. [4]
10 Use the financial data provided and the ratios you have calculated and evaluate the change in performance of RP over the two years. [10]

Chapter 18

Debt/equity ratio analysis

Higher-level

LEARNING OBJECTIVES

On completing this chapter you should be able to:

Apply and analyse:

> The following efficiency ratios:
>   • stock turnover
>   • debtor days
>   • creditor days
>   • gearing ratio (AO2)

> Insolvency versus bankruptcy (AO2)

Synthesise and evaluate:

> Possible strategies to improve these ratios (AO3)

CONTINUED

Use and apply:

> The following efficiency ratios:
> - stock turnover
> - debtor days
> - creditor days
> - gearing ratio (AO4)

BUSINESS IN CONTEXT

Comparing the financial efficiency of the cola giants

Stakeholders in PepsiCo and Coca-Cola will often need more information about the performance of these two companies than the liquidity and profitability ratios can provide. Here are other questions that stakeholders would like to see answered by analysing final accounts:

- How efficient is the management at managing **working capital** and paying creditors?

- Are debtors allowed too long to pay the companies?

- Do the companies depend greatly on external loans to finance their assets?

These questions can be answered by further ratio analysis. Here are extracts from the published accounts for both companies as at the end of December 2021 (in $ million):

KEY TERM

working capital: the capital needed to pay for raw materials, day-to-day running costs and credit offered to customers. In accounting terms: working capital = current assets − current liabilities

Discuss in pairs or in a group:

- Which stakeholders would be interested in the level of borrowing compared to capital employed in these businesses and why?

- Should management of either business be worried about the level of inventories being held? Explain your answer.

- Why should business managers try to manage both trade receivables and trade payables efficiently?

	Revenue	Cost of goods sold	Average stock (inventory) held during year	Creditors	Debtors	Long-term liabilities	Capital employed
PepsiCo	79 474	37 075	4 259	21 159	8 680	50 006	66 049
Coca-Cola	38 655	15 357	3 340	14 619	3 512	49 644	74 404

18.1 Financial efficiency ratios

There are several ratios that can be used to assess how efficiently the assets or resources of a business are being used by management. High levels of financial efficiency mean that managers are using the assets of the business effectively and minimising the amount that needs to be borrowed.

Stock turnover ratio

This is also known as the inventory turnover ratio.

In principle, the lower the amount of capital used to finance the holding of stocks, the better. Modern stock-control theory focuses on minimising the finance tied up in stocks. This ratio records the number of times the stock of a business is bought in and resold in a period of time. If this ratio increases over time then the business is increasing the efficiency of its stock management and is reducing the finance used to hold inventories. This is being financially efficient. If a business bought stock just once each year, sufficient for the whole year, its inventory turnover would be 1 and investment in stocks would be high.

Stock turnover is measured by the ratio:

$$\text{stock turnover (number of times)} = \frac{\text{cost of sales}}{\text{average value of stock}}$$

The average value of stocks held during the year is calculated by the formula:

$$\frac{\text{opening stock (at start of year)} + \text{closing stock (at end of year)}}{2}$$

The calculations in this book use the formula given above, but an alternative formula for stock turnover calculates the average number of days stocks are held by the business.

The stock turnover ratio (days) formula is:

$$\frac{\text{average stock}}{\text{cost of sales}} \times 365$$

The following examples use this ratio to compare the stock turnover between two companies.

	Cost of sales $m (2023)	Average stock value $m	Stock turnover ratio
Nairobi Press Ltd	125	25	$\frac{125}{25} = 5$
Port Louis Press Ltd	2400	600	$\frac{2400}{600} = 4$

According to the 2023 stock turnover ratio, NP has more efficient stock management as it turns over its stock five times in one year compared to four times for PLP. It has a lower level of stocks compared to cost of sales than Port Louis Press. If Port Louis Press introduced a system of just-in-time (JIT) stock management, then suppliers' deliveries would be more frequent but smaller in size. This would increase its stock turnover ratio.

Points to note:

- The result is not a percentage but the number of times stock turns over (i.e., is sold and replaced) in the time period – usually one year.
- The higher the number, the more efficient the managers are at selling stock rapidly. Very efficient management, by using JIT – will give a high stock turnover ratio.
- The 'normal' result for a business depends very much on the industry it operates in. For example, a fresh-fish retailer would (hopefully) have a much higher stock turnover ratio than a car dealer! Comparisons with businesses in other industries is therefore difficult.
- For service-sector firms, such as insurance companies, this ratio has little relevance as they are not selling 'products' held in stock.

ACTIVITY 18.2

Dell, Toyota, Harley Davison and McDonald's are companies that use just-in-time stock management to improve their stock turnover.

In pairs or as a group, research another business that uses just-in-time stock management and discuss the impact its use will have on stock turnover in that business.

Improving stock turnover

Table 18.1 outlines some strategies that a business could adopt to attempt to improve its stock turnover ratio.

Debtor days

The **debtor days ratio** measures how long, on average, it takes the business to recover payment from customers who have bought goods on credit – the debtors of the business. The shorter this time period is, the better management is at controlling its working capital. This ratio is also known as trade receivables turnover.

KEY TERM

debtor days: how long, on average, it takes the business to recover payment from customers who have bought goods on credit

KEY FORMULA

$$\text{debtor days} = \frac{\text{debtors}}{\text{total revenue}} \times 365$$

TIP

As cash sales do not create debtors, the total revenue figure will be used in IB examinations as an approximation for the total value of sales on credit.

Strategies to improve this ratio result	Evaluation
Reduce stocks of finished goods, e.g., in retail outlets	Offering consumers less choice might reduce sales If revenue falls, then even with lower stocks, the ratio will not improve
Reduce stocks of raw materials/components	Unless this reduction is well managed it could lead to production hold-ups and delays – customers may not wait for products to be produced
Introduce an effective just-in-time stock management system that should allow lower stock levels throughout the chain of production	This requires investment in IT, very reliable suppliers, flexible production machinery, adaptable workforce and excellent infrastructure – to allow for frequent, small stock deliveries

Table 18.1: Strategies to improve stock turnover

It can also be calculated by using total sales on credit, thus excluding sales for cash from the calculation. This could be more accurate, as cash sales will never lead to trade receivables.

	Debtors (31/12/23) $m	Revenue for year ending 31/12/23 $m	Debtor days
NP	65	250	$\frac{65}{250} \times 365 =$ 94.9 days
PLP	400	3200	$\frac{400}{3200} \times 365 =$ 45.6 days

These results show that both companies give their customers a long time to pay debts. Perhaps the publishing market is very competitive in these cities, and in order to gain business long credit periods have to be offered. However, debtor days as high as these increase companies' working capital requirements.

THEORY OF KNOWLEDGE

Nike's struggles to manage its inventory

As one of the most recognised sports brands in the world, Nike has a lot of goods to manage. In the early 2000s, Nike estimated the business was losing around $100 million a year because it failed to manage its inventory effectively. In response to this, Nike has invested heavily in a state-of-the-art inventory management software system that can track and manage its stock more efficiently. The software promised to help Nike predict items that would sell best and prepare the company to meet consumer demand, order stock effectively and manage the movement of inventory through the business. Despite the cost of new software system, bugs and data errors have resulted in incorrect forecasts and led to millions more being lost.

In pairs or as a group discuss the following question: To what extent are businesses over-reliant on technology to solve business problems?

Points to note:

- There is no right or wrong result – it will vary from business to business and industry to industry. A business selling almost exclusively for cash will have a very low ratio result.

- If the number of debtor days is high, this may be a deliberate management strategy. Customers will be attracted to businesses that give extended credit. Despite this, the results shown for NP and PLP here are higher than average for most businesses. They could result from poor management of debtors and repayment periods.

- The value of this ratio could be reduced by giving shorter credit terms. Customers could be asked to pay in 30 days instead of more than 45 days. Improved credit control could involve refusing to offer credit terms to frequent late payers. The impact on sales of such policies must always be analysed. Perhaps the marketing department wants to increase credit terms for customers to sell more, but the finance department wants all customers to pay for products as soon as possible.

Creditor days

Creditor days measures the average length of time the business takes to pay its suppliers. The longer this period is, the lower the working capital needs of the business will be.

KEY TERM

creditor days: the average length of time taken to pay suppliers

KEY FORMULA

$$\text{creditor days} = \frac{\text{creditors}}{\text{cost of sales}} \times 365$$

Creditor days can also be measured using the value of all credit purchases, as any purchases made for cash will not create creditors.

TIP

In the IB examinations, cost of sales is used as an approximation for credit purchases during the year.

	Creditors (31/12/23) $m	Cost of sales	Creditor days
NP	18	125	$\frac{18}{125} \times 365 =$ 52.5 days
PLP	240	2400	$\frac{240}{2400} \times 365 =$ 36.5 days

Points to note:

- Port Louis Press pays its suppliers more quickly than Nairobi Press. This would not usually be a problem except that PLP allows its customers much longer to pay. This creates a cash flow problem. Paying suppliers more quickly than customers pay the business leads to a greater need for working capital finance. This is not good financial efficiency!

- Although Nairobi Press takes much longer to pay its suppliers it still has the same problem. It must find additional finance to cover the very long period before it receives payment from its customers.

- Both businesses would benefit from methods to improve financial efficiency. See Table 18.2.

Strategies to improve debtor days and creditor days ratios

Financial efficiency as measured by these two ratios can be improved in several ways. These would all reduce the need for high levels of working capital. See Table 18.2.

Gearing ratio

The **gearing ratio** measures the degree to which the capital of the business is financed from long-term loans. The greater the reliance of a business on loan capital, the more highly geared it is said to be. A highly geared business runs the risk of not being able to pay interest expenses or repay the loans if profits fall significantly.

Nairobi Press is less dependent on long-term loans to finance its assets than Port Louis Press is. This is a less risky business strategy. However, the directors of Nairobi Press could be missing some potentially profitable investment opportunities due to their reluctance to increase debts.

KEY TERM

gearing ratio: measures the proportion of long-term capital invested in the business that is borrowed

KEY FORMULA

$$\text{gearing ratio (\%)} = \frac{\text{non-current liabilities}}{\text{capital employed}} \times 100$$

Strategy	Evaluation
Reduce credit period offered to customers – this will reduce the number of days allowed for them to pay back	Customers may switch to another business that offers a longer credit period
Stop offering trade credit to customers and insist on cash payments	Customers may switch to a business that offers trade credit
Sell claims on creditors (invoices) to a debt factoring business	Although cash is received quickly, only a proportion of the debt outstanding will be received by the business
Delay payment to suppliers – this will increase the creditor days period	Discounts from suppliers for quick payment might be reduced. Suppliers may refuse to supply unless quick payment is made
Only purchase supplies from businesses that offer long credit periods	This may reduce the choice of suppliers and it will not help to develop long-term relationships with essential suppliers
Ask all suppliers for extended credit terms	Some may be unwilling to do this and refuse to supply important materials/components

Table 18.2: Strategies to improve the debtor days and creditor days ratios

	Non-current liabilities 2023 ($m)	Capital employed (shareholders' equity + non-current liabilities) 2023 ($m)	Gearing ratio
NP	40	400	$\frac{40}{400} \times 100 = 10\%$
PLP	2000	5000	$\frac{2000}{5000} \times 100 = 40\%$

On the other hand, if interest rates and company profits fell during a recession, the directors of Port Louis Press might regret their decision to raise finance from debts to this extent.

Points to note:

- The ratio shows the extent to which the company's assets are financed from external long-term borrowing. A result of over 50% would indicate a highly geared business.

CASE STUDY 18.1

Measuring Fencing Solutions' efficiency

Fencing Solutions is small business that specialises in garden fencing. Table 18.3 shows financial data for year ended 31 January 2020 and 31 January 2021.

	30/1/20 $000	31/1/21 $000
Revenue	625	765
Costs of sales	354	369
Stocks	34	42
Trade payables	23	26
Trade receivables	27	26

Table 18.3: Fencing Solutions: financial data, 2020–21

1   Define the term stock turnover ratio.   **[2]**

2   State the following equations:
   a   trade receivables turnover (debtor days)   **[1]**
   b   trade payables turnover (creditor days)   **[1]**

3   Using the data for Fencing Solutions in Table 18.3, calculate the following for 2020 and 2021:
   a   stock turnover ratio   **[2]**
   b   trade receivables turnover (debtor days)   **[2]**
   c   trade payables turnover (creditor days)   **[2]**

4   Using the data from the ratios you have calculated, evaluate the performance of Fencing Solutions over the two-year period.   **[10]**

- The higher this ratio, the greater the risk taken by shareholders when investing in the business. This risk arises for two main reasons:
  - The higher the borrowings of the business, the more interest must be paid. This will affect the ability of the company to pay dividends and gain retained earnings. This is a particular problem when interest rates are high and company profits are low.
  - Interest will still have to be paid even if profit is falling.
- Debts have to be repaid eventually, and the strain of paying back high debts could leave a business with low liquidity.
- A low gearing ratio is an indication of a safe business strategy. It also suggests that management are not borrowing to invest in, or to expand, the business. This could also be a problem for shareholders if they want rapid and increasing returns on their investment. The returns to shareholders will not increase by as much as they would for a highly

geared business pursuing a strategy of rapid growth. Shareholders in a company following a successful growth strategy financed by high debt will find their returns increasing much faster than in a slower-growth company with low gearing.

Strategies to improve gearing

A highly geared business may want to reduce its dependence on loans when economic conditions are difficult or interest rates are high. Table 18.4 evaluates methods to improve gearing.

Limitations of ratio analysis

- One ratio result is not very helpful – to allow meaningful analysis to be made, a comparison needs to be made between this one result and either:
  - other businesses, called inter-firm comparisons, or
  - other time periods, called trend analysis.

Strategy	Evaluation
Sell more shares and use capital raised to pay back loans	Dilutes control of existing shareholders
	Dividend payments will have to increase to maintain dividend yield
	Poor economic conditions might mean that additional shares are sold at a low price
Retain more profit and use this finance to repay loans	Profit may be very low and some is used to pay dividends – retaining more profit will cut dividends, which could impact on the share price
	If dividends are reduced then returns to shareholders will fall
Sell assets to raise finance which is then used to repay loans	If assets have to be sold quickly then a high price might not be achieved
	This reduces the value of the business and limits its ability to expand unless the assets sold are no longer required, such as an empty office building

Table 18.4: Strategies to improve (reduce) gearing

TIP

If you are asked to compare the results of these ratios with those of another business, you could suggest that comparisons only have real significance when the businesses are operating in the same industry.

- Inter-firm comparisons need to be used with caution and are most effective when companies in the same industry are being compared. Financial years end at different times for businesses and a rapid change in the economic environment could have an adverse impact on a company publishing its accounts in June compared to a January publication for another company.

- Trend analysis needs to take into account changing circumstances over time which could have affected the ratio results. These factors may be outside the companies' control, such as an economic recession.

- As already noted, some ratios can be calculated using slightly different formulas, and care must be taken only to make comparisons with results calculated using the same ratio formula.

- Companies can value their assets in different ways, and different depreciation methods can lead to different capital employed totals, which will affect certain ratio results. Deliberate window dressing of accounts would obviously make a company's key ratios look more favourable, at least in the short term.

- Ratios are only concerned with accounting items to which a numerical value can be given. Increasingly, observers of company performance and strategy are becoming more concerned with non-numerical aspects of business performance, such as environmental audits and human rights abuses in developing countries that the firms may operate in. Indicators other than ratios must be used for these assessments.

- Ratios are useful analytical tools, but they do not solve business problems. Ratio analysis can highlight issues that need to be tackled – such as falling profitability or liquidity – and these problems can be tracked back over time and compared with other businesses. On their own, ratios do not necessarily indicate the true cause of business problems and it is up to good managers to locate these and form effective strategies to overcome them.

CASE STUDY 18.2

Financial efficiency in the confectionery business

The Orange and Green Confectionery (OGC) business is concerned about is efficiency. It has brought in an accountancy firm to analyse its efficiency. The data in Table 18.5 sets out the position of OGC in financial terms relative to the industry average.

	OGC 2021	Industry average 2021
Stock turnover ratio	4.5	6.3
Debtor days	36 days	32 days
Creditor days	31 days	34 days
Gearing ratio	27%	23%

Table 18.5: OGC financial efficiency compared to industry average, 2021

1   Define the term 'debtors'.   [2]

2   The value of OGC's stock is $1.3 million and its capital employed is $5.4 million. Using the data in Table 18.5 calculate the value of the following:
   a   cost of sales   [2]
   b   non-current assets.   [2]

3   Outline what the value OGC's trade payables ratio shows.   [4]

4   Explain two ways OGC might reduce its trade receivables turnover.   [4]

ACTIVITY 18.3

'There is no ratio that measures effort, imagination or creativity in a business – if I'm honest, they are pretty useless at measuring business performance.'

In pairs or as a group, produce a short presentation on the strengths and weaknesses of ratio analysis.

LEARNER PROFILE

Inquirers

If you speak to many small business owners, they will tell you that it is easy to sell a product, but getting a customer to pay for it is more difficult. There are many stories of young growing businesses who will do business with anyone who comes to them. Many of these businesses sell on credit, build up large debtors and end up being owed a lot of money. The business looks profitable but it is in a risky position. If one major customer or a group of customers does not pay, then the business risks not being able to pay its suppliers and there is then a threat of bankruptcy.

The key is research and patience. Businesses need to research suppliers and make informed judgements about who they sell to.

In pairs or in groups, discuss the importance of business people being inquirers when they are managing stock, debtors and creditors.

CASE STUDY 18.3

A&L is a furniture retailer that specialises in household furniture and is based in Vietnam. The management is concerned about the cash flow of the business. The business's CFO Bian Nguyen has put forward a strategy to improve A&L's cash flow position which focuses on increasing the firm's stock turnover.

1   Define the term 'stock turnover'. [2]

2   State the equation used to measure stock turnover. [2]

3   State the equation used to measure the stock turnover ratio (in days). [2]

4   Explain two ways that A&L might improve its stock turnover to improve its cash flow. [4]

18.2 Insolvency versus bankruptcy

If a business experiences serious financial problems so that it cannot pay its debts, it is said to be insolvent. If the business is a sole trader or partnership then these individuals can ask to be declared bankrupt. In the UK and many other countries, the term 'bankruptcy' is only applicable to individuals, including sole traders and members of partnerships. For a limited company, a process known as liquidation would be the equivalent of bankruptcy.

An individual or company becomes cash-flow insolvent when their assets are greater than their liabilities, but their liquid assets are insufficient to pay short-term debts. So, the individual or business owns assets worth more than the total outstanding debt, but there is insufficient cash available to service that debt. This is usually a problem that can be resolved through negotiation, whereby a creditor may choose to wait for assets to be sold instead of taking further action.

KEY TERMS

bankruptcy: a legal proceeding carried out to allow individuals or businesses freedom from their debts, while simultaneously providing creditors an opportunity for repayment

liquidation: the process of bringing a business to an end and distributing its assets to claimants such as creditors – usually done by selling the assets of the business and distributing the cash raised

insolvency: a state of financial distress in which a person or business is unable to pay their debts. This can lead to liquidation

---

Statement of financial position insolvency is when the debts outstanding are greater than the total value of assets owned. A statement of financial position insolvency does not necessarily mean the end of the business, as there may still be sufficient cash flow to keep paying day-to-day expenses.

Common causes of insolvency are:

- a cash flow crisis, e.g., an unplanned overspend or customers who are late paying

- loss of business contract: an important customer could suddenly change suppliers

- loss of customers: customers may switch to a different product, or the service provided by the business could become unpopular as a result of changing needs and markets.

As already explained, bankruptcy is a type of insolvency usually applied to an individual, including owners of unlimited liability businesses. Bankruptcy generally means there is no chance of creditors receiving any of the outstanding sums owed by the individual. Usually, it is a situation decided by law courts because either assets are worth less than liabilities or the individual/business is unable to meet their debts.

Courts usually determine the period of bankruptcy as being one year, after which it is discharged. This means the bankruptcy conditions end. During this time any money the bankrupt individual earns may be taken to pay back outstanding debts or to pay the interest on them. They may also lose valuable assets.

However, if someone is declared bankrupt, some pressure is taken off. The bankrupt will not have to deal with creditors and they can keep some personal property as well as general living expenses. At the end of the bankruptcy period, any outstanding debts are cancelled or discharged.

SELF-EVALUATION CHECKLIST

After studying this chapter, complete this table.

I am able to apply and analyse:	Needs more work	Almost there	Ready to move on
the following efficiency ratios: • stock turnover • debtor days • creditor days • gearing ratio (AO2)			
insolvency versus bankruptcy (AO2)			
I am able to synthesise and evaluate:			
possible strategies to improve these ratios (AO3)			
I am able to use and apply			
the following efficiency ratios: • stock turnover • debtor days • creditor days • gearing ratio (AO4)			

REFLECTION

Use the same public limited company that you selected in Chapter 17. Analyse the four financial efficiency ratios for that company over the last five years. Explain to another learner whether this business has become more or less financially efficient over this period.

PROJECT

A new trend in business which many suppliers are not happy about is late payment from customers. This applies particularly to large industrial buyers who squeeze smaller suppliers. According to a study from The Hackett Group, the 1000 largest US public companies delayed payment to their suppliers.

On the buyers' side, the logic of such late practices is easy to follow. By delaying payments, companies can increase the cash they have for use in other areas of the business, which enables them to expand. Theoretically, this expansion creates opportunities that extends to the suppliers as well.

One well-known power tool manufacturer, for example, has increased its payment delays to component suppliers and this has increased its cash flow at the expense of its component suppliers. The company's delayed payments, which are among the highest in the United States, have freed up $500 million in capital. According to the company's chief financial officer (CFO), this increase in capital has created valuable investment opportunities.

According to Atradius, a global credit insurer, 90% of suppliers are reporting late payments. With average payment duration increasing from 61 to 63 days. The bad debts resulting from late payment continues

CONTINUED

to plague business-to-business (B2B) markets, with 51% of companies having a customer that suffers bankruptcy.

In pairs or as a group, produce a video presentation on the importance of effective management of creditors (accounts payable), debtors (accounts receivable) and stock. Areas to cover in your presentation should include: cashflow; profits; business security; stakeholder interests.

Thinking about your project:

- Once you have completed your video presentation, do you feel your understanding of the management of creditors, debtors and stock has improved?

- How good was your video presentation compared to those of the other groups in the class?

- How could you improve your video presentation?

EXAM-STYLE QUESTIONS

The Cape Town Furniture Company (CTFC)

CTFC is a furniture manufacturer based in South Africa. It specialises in making furniture from materials sourced from sustainable producers. It is the leading company in the sector, and it has received many awards for its furniture designs using sustainable materials. The market is becoming more competitive, with other furniture manufacturers switching to sustainable production methods. The are some concerns about interest rates in South Africa which have started to rise due to inflation.

	Year ending 31 December 2020 ($m)	Year ending 31 December 2021 ($m)
Revenue	30.2	35.3
Cost of sales	15.4	17.2
Credit purchases	14.8	15.1
Creditors	1.4	1.6
Inventories (stock)	1.5	1.1
Debtors	3.2	2.9
Long-term (non-current) liabilities	15.5	15.1
Capital employed	34.4	34.5

Table 18.6: CTFC financial data

1   Define the term 'capital employed'.   [2]
2   a   Calculate CTFC's gearing ratio in 2020 and 2021.   [2]
    b   Describe the change in CTFC's gearing ratio.   [2]
    c   Explain two benefits of the change in CTFC's gearing ratio.   [4]
3   Using the data in Table 18.6 calculate the following ratios for CTFC for 2020 and 2021:
    a   stock turnover   [2]
    b   debtor days   [2]
    c   creditor days   [2]
4   Explain one reason why CTFC's trade payables turnover has changed.   [4]
5   Evaluate the view that CTFC has become more efficient over the period 2020–21.   [10]

> Chapter 19
Cash flow

LEARNING OBJECTIVES

On completing this chapter you should be able to:

Apply and analyse:

- The difference between profit and cash flow (AO2)
- Cash flow forecasts (AO2)
- The relationship between investment, profit and cash flow (AO2)
- Working capital (AO2)
- Liquidity (AO2)

Synthesise and evaluate:

- Strategies for dealing with cash flow problems (AO3)

Use and apply:

- Cash flow forecasts (AO4)
- Working capital (AO4)

BUSINESS IN CONTEXT

Cash flow is vital

Managing **cash flow** can be one of the biggest challenges business owners face. A 2020 study from Intuit, a financial software business, found that 61% of small businesses around the world struggle with cash flow. Nearly one-third of businesses in the survey were unable to pay suppliers, repay loans or pay their employees due to cash flow problems. The first step in dealing with these problems is to determine cash flow needs.

Jay Singer, vice president for small business at Mastercard, said this is done by analysing the current state of a business.

It's important to understand how much cash you've been using and plan to use, as well as the length of time it will take to acquire more cash. While every business's needs are different, it would be wise to have enough cash on hand to cover up to six months of your average. **cash outflow**.

Banks advise their business customers to:

- Borrow money *before* it is absolutely necessary.

- Reduce costs and other outflows and consider outsourcing some operations.

- Restructure payments to suppliers or change suppliers to those giving longer credit.

- Avoid rapid expansion financed only from loans. Interest payments will become a large cash outflow before the benefits from the expansion are received.

- Take advantage of technological advances and AI-enabled solutions, like new apps and software updates. These can streamline business processes, increase efficiency and reduce costs.

Cash flow is not the same as profit. However, all banks and business analysts agree that managing cash flow is critically important to sustain a profitable business in the long term.

Discuss in pairs or a group:

- Why do small businesses in particular have cash flow problems?

- Examine two ways in which a new business start-up could minimise the risk of experiencing cash flow problems.

KEY TERMS

cash flow: the sum of cash payments to a business less the sum of cash payments from the business

cash outflow: payments in cash made by a business, such as those to suppliers and workers

KEY CONCEPT LINK

Change

The ultimate challenge that a business can face is the threat of running out of cash and bankruptcy. Sudden market changes can make this happen. The abrupt rise in petrol and diesel prices in 2022 put all road transport businesses in a perilous position and many may go bankrupt. The rise in petrol and diesel prices highlights why all businesses must be able to react to change.

19.1 The difference between profit and cash flow

It is very common for profitable businesses to run short of cash. However, it is also possible for loss-making businesses to have high cash inflows in the short term. The essential difference between cash and profit can be explained with a simple example.

Example

Shula owns Fine Foods, a specialist delicatessen. Last month she bought $500 of fresh goods from a supplier who offers her one month's credit. The goods sold very slowly during the month and she was forced to cut her prices several times. Eventually, she sold them all for only $300, paid in cash by her customers.

- What was Shula's profit or loss (ignoring all other costs)? Answer: a loss of $200 – because even though she has not yet paid for the goods they are still recorded as a cost.
- What was the difference between her cash outflow and **cash inflow**? Answer: a positive inflow of $300 – because she has not paid the supplier yet. So Shula has a positive cash flow from these goods this month even though she made a loss on them.
- Cash was not the same as profit for this business.

Profitable businesses can have cash flow problems. Profit does not pay the bills and expenses of running a business – but cash does. Of course, profit is important, especially in the long term when investors expect rewards and the business needs additional finance for investment. Cash is always important in both the short and long term.

Cash flow relates to the timing of payments to workers and suppliers and receipts from customers. If a business does not plan the timing of these payments and receipts carefully, it may run out of cash even though it is operating profitably. If suppliers and creditors are not paid in time, they can force the business to liquidate its assets if it appears to be insolvent. Monitoring the weekly or monthly **net cash flow** is a key responsibility for finance managers.

> **ACTIVITY 19.1**
>
> In pairs or as a group, discuss how the cash flow position of a household is determined. Consider the different sources of household income that lead to an inflow of cash and the different types of household spending that lead to an outflow of cash. Think about the reasons households run into cash flow problems and the way a household might overcome cash flow difficulties.

> **KEY TERMS**
>
> **cash inflows:** payments in cash received by a business, such as those from customers (debtors) or from the bank, e.g., receiving a loan
>
> **net cash flow:** the sum of cash payments to a business (inflows) minus the sum of cash payments made by it (outflows)

So, cash flow is certainly important, especially to small business start-ups. Cash flow planning is vital for entrepreneurs for several reasons:

- Business start-ups are often offered much less time to pay suppliers than larger, well-established firms – they are given shorter credit periods.
- Banks and other lenders may not believe the promises of new business owners as they have no trading record. They will expect payment at the agreed time.
- Finance is often very tight at start-up, so not planning accurately is of even more significance for new businesses.

19.2 Cash flow forecasts

Forecasting cash flow is about estimating future cash inflows and cash outflows, usually on a month-by-month basis. Let's take the case of Keon, an entrepreneur planning to open a car-valeting service offering car cleaning to individual customers and owners of car fleets, such as taxi firms.

Forecasting cash inflows

The business owner will probably start by attempting to forecast cash inflows. Some will be easier to forecast than others. Here are some examples of cash inflows and how they might be forecast:

- Owner's own capital injection – easy to forecast as this is under Keon's direct control.

- Bank loan payments – easy to forecast if they have been agreed with the bank in advance, both in terms of amount and timing.

- Customers' cash purchases – difficult to forecast as they depend on sales, so a sales forecast will be necessary – but how accurate might this be?

CASE STUDY 19.1

Poor cash flow in Brazil

Reports have suggested that many Brazilian businesses have been under cash flow pressure and several are operating in negative cash flow positions. This is a concern for the Brazilian government because a large proportion of business failure is due to poor cash flow rather than poor sales. Many firms with large profits fail to manage their cash payments because they do not collect their cash quickly enough. Because of credit sales, profitable businesses can still be a risk of failure of they manage their cash flow poorly. It only takes a few major customers to pay late or default on payments and a business can be in financial difficulty. It is estimated that it takes the average Brazilian business 52 days to pay an outstanding debt, and this is a figure the government would like to be much lower.

1   Define the term 'cash flow'.   [2]

2   Outline how late payment of debt can cause Brazilian businesses cash flow problems.   [4]

3   Explain how rising sales in Brazil can lead to cash flow problems for a business.   [4]

- Debtors' payments – difficult to forecast as these depend on two unknowns. First, what is the likely level of sales on credit and, second, when will debtors actually pay? One month's credit may have been agreed with them, but payment after this period can never be guaranteed.

> **TIP**
>
> Never fall into the trap of referring to forecasts as actual accounts – they are financial estimates that are dealing with the future.

Forecasting cash outflows

Again, some cash outflows will be much easier to forecast than others. Here are some examples:

- Lease payment for premises – easy to forecast as this will be in the estate agent's details of the property.
- Annual rent payment – easy to forecast as this will be fixed and agreed for a certain time period. However, the landlord may increase the rent after this period.
- Electricity, gas, water and telephone bills – difficult to forecast as these will vary with several different factors such as the number of customers, seasonal weather conditions and energy prices.
- Labour cost payments – these forecasts will be based largely on demand forecasts and the hourly wage rate that is to be paid. These payments could vary from week to week if demand fluctuates and if staff are on flexible contracts.
- Variable cost payments such as cleaning materials – the cost of these should vary consistently with demand, so revenue forecasts could be used to assess variable costs too. How much credit will be offered by suppliers? The longer the period of credit offered, the lower the start-up cash needs of the business will be.

Structure of cash flow forecasts

Due to the crucial importance of cash (it is the lifeblood of any successful business), all firms should engage in **cash flow forecasting** to help identify cash flow problems before it is too late.

A simplified cash flow forecast is shown in Table 19.1. It is based on an online business selling protective covers for mobile phones.. Although there are different styles of presenting this information, all cash flow forecasts have three basic sections:

- **Section 1 Opening cash balance.** This is the amount of cash forecast to be held by the business at the start of each period. It will be the same as the closing cash balance of the previous period. With a new business start-up it is assumed that the opening cash balance is zero before owners inject their start-up capital.
- **Section 2 Cash inflows.** This section records the cash payments to the business, including cash sales, payments for credit sales and capital inflows.
- **Section 3 Cash outflows.** This section records the cash payments made by the business, including wages, materials, rent and other costs.
- **Section 4 Net cash flow and closing balance.** This shows the net cash flow for the period (often monthly) and the cash balance at the end of the period – the closing cash balance. If the closing balance is negative (shown by a figure in brackets), then a bank overdraft will almost certainly be necessary to finance this. The closing cash balance for one month becomes the opening cash balance for the next month.

> **KEY TERMS**
>
> **cash flow forecast:** estimate of a firm's future cash inflows and outflows
>
> **opening cash balance:** cash held by the business at the start of the month
>
> **closing balance:** cash held at the end of the month becomes next month's opening balance

	January	February	March	April
Opening balance	0	(3)	(2)	(2.5)
Cash inflows				
Owners' capital injection	6	0	0	0
Cash sales	3	7	8	14
Payments by debtors	0	2	3	3
Total cash inflows	9	9	11	17
Cash outflows				
Lease of equipment	4	0	0	0
Rent	1	1	1	1
Cost of sales/materials	1.5	1	3	5
Salaries and wages	2	2	3	3
Packaging and transport	0.5	1	1	3
Heating and lighting	1	1	1.5	1
Other costs	2	2	2	1
Total cash outflows	12	8	11.5	14
Net monthly cash flow	(3)	1	(0.5)	3
Closing balance	(3)	(2)	(2.5)	0.5

Table 19.1: Cash flow forecast for the first four months of operating the online business ($000; figures in brackets are negative)

KEY TERM

net monthly cash flow: estimated difference between monthly cash inflows and outflows

What does the forecast in Table 19.1 tell the business owner about the prospects for his business? In cash terms, the business appears to be in a good position at the end of four months. This is because:

- in April the closing cash balance is positive, so the bank overdraft is fully repaid
- there are two months – January and March – in which the monthly net cash flow is negative
- the monthly net cash flow improves substantially in April.

Remember, these are only forecasts – the accuracy of the cash flow forecast will depend greatly on how accurate the business owner's demand, revenue and material cost forecasts are.

CASE STUDY 19.2

Cash flow at Pro-printing

Pro-printing is a business that specialises in small printing jobs for commercial and domestic consumers. The business is meticulous at managing cash flow because it sees the firm's cash flow security as crucial for the small business. The cash flow data in Table 19.2 has been forecast by Pro-printing for the first four months of the year.

The business has been approached by a large company with a $10 000 order, which is nearly two-months' business for Pro-printing. The management are excited about the additional revenue the order would bring to Pro-printing, but they are concerned about the credit history of the buyer.

Table 19.2 sets out the forecasted cash flow data for Pro-printing for the first four months of the year.

1   Define the term 'debtor'. [2]

2   Outline why Pro-printing might forecast its monthly cash inflows. [4]

3   Using the cash flow data in Table 19.2 calculate the following:

   a   monthly total cash inflow [2]

   b   monthly cash outflow [2]

   c   net monthly cash flow [2]

   d   opening balance each month [2]

   e   closing balance each month [2]

4   Explain why accepting the order from the large company might be a risk for Pro-printing's cash flow position. [4]

	January ($000)	February ($000)	March ($000)	April ($000)
Opening balance	(2)			
Cash inflows				
Cash sales	5	7	9	10
Payments by debtors	3	4	5	6
Total cash inflow				
Cash outflows				
Rent	1.5	1.5	1.5	1.5
Materials	3.5	4	5.5	6
Labour	3	3	3	3
Other costs	1	1.5	1.5	2.0
Total cash outflows				
Net cash flow				
Closing balance				

Table 19.2: Pro-printing: forecasted cash flow, January to April ($000)

Benefits of cash flow forecasts

Cash flow forecasting has a number of benefits, especially for start-up businesses:

- By showing periods of negative cash flow, plans can be put in place to provide additional finance – for example, arranging a bank overdraft or preparing to inject more owners' capital.
- If negative cash flows appear to be too great, then plans can be made for reducing these – for example, by cutting down on purchase of materials or machinery or by not making sales on credit, only for cash.
- A new business proposal will never progress beyond the initial planning stage unless investors and bankers have access to a cash flow forecast and the assumptions that lie behind it.

Limitations of cash flow forecasts

Although an entrepreneur should take every reasonable step to improve the accuracy of cash flow forecasts, it would be unwise to assume that they will always be accurate. So many factors, either internal to the business or in the external environment, can change and send a cash flow forecast off course. This does not make them useless, but they must be used with caution. Here are the most common limitations of cash flow forecasts:

- Mistakes can be made in preparing the revenue and cost forecasts or they may be drawn up by inexperienced entrepreneurs or staff.
- Unexpected cost increases can lead to major inaccuracies in forecasts. For example, fluctuations in oil prices can cause the cash flow forecasts of major airlines to be misleading.
- Incorrect assumptions can be made in estimating the sales of the business, perhaps based on poor market research, and this will make the cash inflow forecasts inaccurate.

19.3 The relationship between investment, profit and cash flow

To business managers the term 'investment' does not have the same meaning as when it is used in general speech. Many people consider their savings to be 'good investments'. However, business investment means capital expenditure – spending on projects, usually long term, requiring equipment, materials and resources of all kinds. These investments might include:

- building a new factory/offices/shop
- opening a new quarry or mine
- researching and developing a new product
- entering a new market by setting up offices and a sales force there
- taking over another business.

Private sector business-investment decisions are nearly always undertaken because management believes that, in time, profits will be earned as a consequence.

Investment spending leads to a cash outflow, often in the first year of the project. However, the cost of the project is not recorded at the time of the cash expenditure. Capital spending is recorded as a cost over a period of years as the benefit from it is also likely to be received over several years. To match the cost of the project to the expected revenue from it, the actual expense is recorded as annual depreciation (loss of value) over the useful life of the assets purchased.

Table 19.3 shows this process and the relationship between investment, cash flow and profit. The project lasts for two years and the assets purchased fall in value each year and are sold at the end of their useful life – the end of year two.

Year	Investment	Impact on cash flow	Impact on profit
0	$6 million	$6 million outflow	No impact
1	No further spending	Cash from sales – cash payments for operating expenses	Revenue – (operating expenses + annual depreciation)
2	No further spending; assets at end of useful life are sold	(Cash from sales + cash from sale of assets) – cash payments for operating expenses	(Revenue + income from sale of assets) – (operating expenses + annual depreciation)

Table 19.3: Investment, profit and cash flow

19.4 Strategies for dealing with cash flow problems

The strategies used to deal with cash flow problems depend on the main underlying cause of the cash flow difficulties, which can be as follows.

Lack of planning

Cash flow forecasts are a massive help in predicting future cash problems for a business. This form of financial planning can be used to predict potential cash flow problems so that business managers can take action to overcome or prevent them in plenty of time.

> ### TIP
> Remember, cash flow forecasts do not solve cash flow problems by themselves, but they are an essential part of financial planning and can help to prevent cash flow problems from developing.

Poor credit control

The **credit control** department of a business keeps a check on all customers' accounts – who has paid, who is keeping to agreed credit terms and which customers are not paying on time. If this credit control is inefficient and badly managed, then debtors will not be followed up and asked for payment, and potential **bad debts** will not be identified.

> ### KEY TERMS
> **credit control:** monitoring of debts to ensure that credit periods are not exceeded
>
> **bad debt:** unpaid customers' bills that are now very unlikely ever to be paid

Allowing customers too much credit

In many trading situations, businesses will have to offer trade credit to customers in order to be competitive. Assume a customer has a choice between two suppliers selling very similar products. If one supplier insists on cash payment 'on delivery' and the other allows two months' trade credit, then customers will go for credit terms because it improves their cash flow. However, allowing customers too long to pay means reducing short-term cash inflows, which could lead to cash flow problems.

> ### LEARNER PROFILE
> **Knowledgeable and caring**
>
> A local table manufacturer has just received a $200 000 order from a department store. The department store has been given a 30-day credit period on the tables. This is a profitable deal for the manufacturer, but the business's chief financial officer has some concerns.
>
> The department store has been making losses for the last two years and it has paid the manufacturer late twice this year. The manufacturer's salespeople who were in the store two weeks ago said there were gaps on the shelves and the store looked low on stock. There are rumours that the department store is struggling to manage its own cash flow.
>
> If the table manufacturer turns down the order from the department store, it will have to make up the sales from somewhere else. Alternatively, it could make the store pay in cash, but the department store does not want to do this and claim the business is in a sound cash flow position.
>
> The manufacturer has a good relationship with the department store that goes back many years.
>
> In pairs or as a group, discuss the importance of the managers at the table manufacturer being knowledgeable and caring in making their decision about the contract with the department store.

Expanding too rapidly

When a business expands rapidly, it has to pay for the expansion and for increased wages and materials months before it receives cash from additional sales. If insufficient finance has been arranged to pay for this cash requirement then the business can be said to be **overtrading**. This can lead to serious cash flow shortages even though the business is successful and growing.

Unexpected events

Unforeseen increases in costs (e.g., the breakdown of a delivery van that means it needs to be replaced, a dip in predicted sales income, or a competitor reducing prices unexpectedly) could lead to negative net monthly cash flows.

> **KEY TERM**
>
> **overtrading:** expanding a business rapidly without obtaining all the necessary finance so that a cash flow shortage develops

There are three main strategies that businesses can adopt to deal with cash flow problems:

- reducing cash outflows
- improving cash inflows
- sourcing additional finance.

Care needs to be taken here. The aim is to improve the cash position of the business, not just revenue or profits. These are different concepts. For example, a decision to advertise more in order to increase sales on credit, which will eventually lead to increased cash flows, may make the short-term cash position worse as the advertising has to be paid for. Only an increase in revenue that also leads to a simultaneous increase in net cash flow will improve the cash flow of the business.

Tables 19.4 and 19.5 outline the methods used to increase cash inflows (including finance options) and reduce cash outflows.

> **TIP**
>
> When answering an examination question about improving cash flow, just writing 'the firm should increase sales' will not demonstrate a true understanding of the difference between revenue and cash flow.

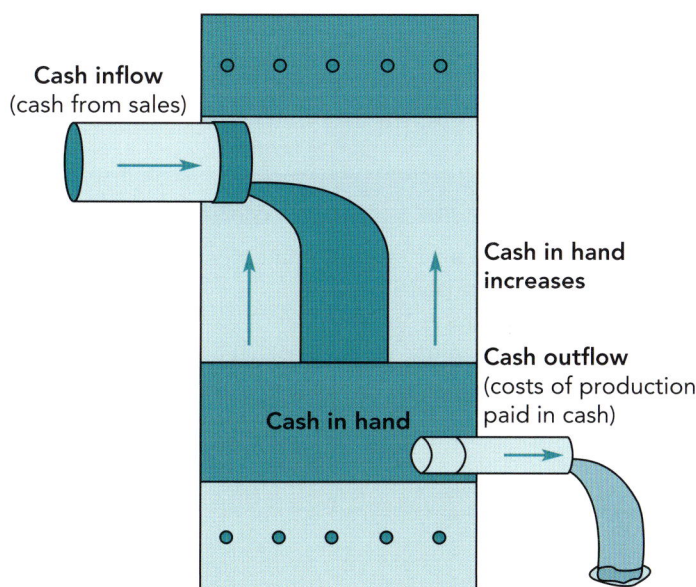

Figure 19.1: Symbolic drawing of cash-flow 'tank' with leakages and injections of cash

Method to increase cash inflow	How it works	Evaluation
Reduce credit terms to customers	Cash flow can be brought forward by reducing credit terms from, say, two months to one month	Customers may purchase products from firms that offer extended credit terms
Increase cash sales (with no increase in promotion costs)	Sale of inventories at lower-than-normal price; obtain free publicity, e.g., for community work	Sale of inventories at lower-than-normal price may improve cash flow, but it will worsen profit margins
Overdraft	Flexible loans can be arranged, which the business can draw on as necessary up to an agreed limit	Interest rates can be high and there may be an overdraft arrangement fee Overdrafts can be withdrawn by the bank and this often causes insolvency
Short-term loan	A fixed amount can be borrowed for an agreed length of time	The interest costs have to be paid The loan must be repaid by the due date
Sale of assets	Cash receipts can be obtained from selling off redundant assets, which will boost cash inflow	Selling assets quickly can result in selling them for a low price The assets might be required at a later date for expansion The assets could have been used as collateral for future loans
Sale and leaseback	Assets can be sold, e.g., to a finance company, but they can then be leased back from the new owner	The leasing costs add to annual overheads There could be loss of potential profit if the asset price increases The assets could have been used as collateral for future loans

Table 19.4: Ways to increase cash inflows (including additional sources of finance) and their possible limitations

ACTIVITY 19.3

You are running a small coffee shop business and your firm needs to raise short-term finance. In pairs or as a group, prepare a presentation on raising short-term finance and cover the advantages and disadvantages of each source of finance. In your presentation consider the following factors:

- reduce credit terms to customers
- increase cash sales
- overdraft
- short-term loan
- sale of assets
- sale and leaseback.

Method to reduce cash outflow	How it works	Evaluation
Delay payments to suppliers (creditors)	Cash outflows will fall in the short term if bills are paid after, say, three months instead of two months	Suppliers may reduce any discount offered with the purchase Suppliers can either demand cash on delivery or refuse to supply at all if they believe the risk of not being paid is too great
Delay spending on capital equipment	By not buying equipment, vehicles, etc., cash will not have to be paid to suppliers	The business may become less efficient if outdated and inefficient equipment is not replaced Expansion becomes difficult
Use leasing not outright purchase of capital equipment	The leasing company owns the asset and no large cash outlay is required	The asset is not owned by the business Leasing charges include an interest cost and add to annual overheads
Cut overhead spending that does not directly affect output, e.g., promotion costs	These costs will not reduce production capacity, and cash payments will be reduced	Future demand may be reduced by failing to promote the products effectively

Table 19.5: Methods to reduce cash outflows

CASE STUDY 19.3

Improving the working capital cycle at Chen

Chen Ltd is a Thailand-based business trading in frozen food. It is a small family run firm managed by the CEO, Hathai Chen, who is the granddaughter of the founder Parth Chen.

Hathai's main objective this year is to improve the company's working capital cycle. The business has an acid test ratio of 0.4 which is well below the industry average. She would like to convert as many customers to cash payment as possible, but several are reluctant to do this. She also wants to push three customers who are large supermarkets to pay more quickly, but they are reluctant do this. She is in the process of negotiating a longer payment period with Chen's major supplier, which they are willing to accept, but Chen will lose their 2% early payment discount if this happens.

Hathai is a strong believer in effective cash flow management because of the issues that can arise from cashflow problems.

1   Define the term 'working capital'. [2]

2   Outline how Hathai's approach of converting as many customers as possible to cash payment will improve Chen's cash flow position. [4]

3   Explain what an acid test ratio of 0.4 shows about Chen's liquidity position. [4]

4   Explain two benefits to Chen of effective cash flow management. [4]

5   Evaluate Hathai's decision to increase sales to cash customers and delay payment to creditors to improve Chen's cash flow. [10]

THEORY OF KNOWLEDGE

What is it like to be in a business when it goes bankrupt?

Here is first-hand account of what it is like for employees when a business goes bankrupt.

I was HR manager for a head office site of nearly 400 employees. I learned the full details of my employer's financial difficulties on the TV news after leaving work. Like every other employee, I did not know what to expect.

The next day delivered angst and doubt along with the arrival of the administrators onto site. They arrived and took up positions behind closed door management offices with formal introductions only to senior management. More administrators moved onto site gradually, from a handful the first day to around 20 unfamiliar, emotionless faces, silently working on their laptops in hushed groups in meeting rooms.

Long emails lacked clarity about what this really meant for the 26 000 employees as a buyer for business was sought and not found. There was obvious worry about impending job losses, the presence of the administrators on site created further apprehension. There was a lack of transparency. Meetings between the now new management team (the administrators) left employees nervously speculating on their next move.

Meetings with senior directors to gain necessary information about the day-to-day running and management of the company resulted in group emails containing employee lists which 'invited' the first dispensable employees to their pre-departure group briefing. Further lists of names and job roles set out who was needed at each stage of closure. In a well-oiled administration machine, it can be a brutal time.

The brevity of the administrator's announcements, the lack of opportunities for employees to ask questions or take time to say their goodbyes, was shocking. But the clinical nature of the process could not mask the very real display of human emotions of anger, fear and sadness.

Over the next eight weeks, employees left in 'waves' based on their perceived value as decided by the administrators. First, it was customer service agents, then operational teams clearing stock, and then facilities and estates teams which managed building closures and document archiving.

In pairs or as a group, discuss the importance of emotion in understanding the reality of a business going bankrupt.

19.5 Working capital and cash flow

The need for a business to hold working capital and its definition were explained in Chapter 14. Managing cash inflows and outflows effectively helps to minimise the need to hold working capital. As working capital is measured by current assets less current liabilities, reducing spending on current assets or cutting cash outflows by increasing current liabilities will have the effect of reducing working capital.

WORKED EXAMPLE 19.1

Current assets = $12 000; current liabilities = $8000

Working capital = $4000

Reducing current assets by $1000 and increasing current liabilities to $9000 will cut working capital to $2000

19.6 Liquidity and cash flow

The importance of liquidity, its definition and measurement were explained in Chapter 17. Negative net cash flows will be likely to reduce the liquidity of a business. The significance of this can be assessed by calculating the liquidity ratios.

SELF-EVALUATION CHECKLIST

After studying this chapter, complete this table.

I am able to apply and analyse:	Needs more work	Almost there	Ready to move on
the difference between profit and cash flow (AO2)			
cash flow forecasts (AO2)			
the relationship between investment, profit and cash flow (AO2)			
understanding and measuring working capital (AO2)			
liquidity (AO2)			
I am able to synthesise and evaluate:			
strategies for dealing with cash flow problems (AO3)			
I am able to use and apply:			
cash flow forecasts (AO4)			
understanding and measuring working capital (AO4)			

REFLECTION

To what extent is it ethical for a large business to improve its own cash flow by delaying payment to smaller businesses that supply it with goods and services?

PROJECT

The importance of managing cash flow

Running out of cash is the reason why over 80% of businesses fail. Effective cash flow management is not only crucial for a business to survive but also for its long-term success. These are some ways businesses can manage their cash flow effectively:

- collect cash at the point where a good or service is sold
- invoice customers quickly
- Remind customers if payments are late
- offer customers a discount for prompt payment
- hold an emergency cash reserve.

In pairs or as a group, prepare a presentation on how businesses can manage their cash flow effectively.

EXAM-STYLE QUESTIONS

Organiczny farm shop is trying to improve its cash flow

Organiczny Ltd is a Polish farm shop that specialises in organic produce from local farmers. The business has an excellent reputation locally where it attracts many domestic customers as well as retailers. However, it has a cash flow problem at certain times during the year and relies on a on a bank overdraft which has a high interest rate. This was partly caused by the bankruptcy of a major customer whose large outstanding debt went unpaid.

CONTINUED

Organiczny has a number of contracts with two large supermarkets who are very slow to pay. Organiczny's finance manager, Kamil Boruc, wants to improve Organiczny's cash flow situation. He would like to reduce the payment period for supermarkets from 30 days to 10 days, and he would like to stop giving credit terms to customers with a poor payment history. In addition, he would like to reduce stock levels in the shop and increase the time period Organiczny uses to pay its own suppliers.

The table shows Organiczny Ltd's cash flow forecast for the next four months.

- Rent for the shop is $32 000 quarterly and is due in August.
- $16 000 tax is due to be paid in July.
- The opening cash balance is ($3000).

	June ($000)	July ($000)	August ($000)	September ($000)
Opening balance				
Cash inflows				
Cash sales	60	75	62	87
Payments by debtors	22	24	21	28
Total cash inflow			83	
Cash outflows				
Rent			32	
Materials	41	47	42	65
Labour	15	15	12	17
Other costs	12	13	9	18
Tax				
Total cash outflow				
Net cash flow				
Closing balance				

1   Define the term 'bank overdraft'.   [2]
2   Outline the impact that the bankruptcy of one of Organiczny Ltd's customers would have on its cash flow.   [4]
3   Using the cash flow data calculate the following:
    a   the total cash inflow in each month   [2]
    b   the total cash outflow in each month   [2]
    c   the net monthly cash flow   [2]
    d   the opening cash balance at the beginning of each month   [2]
    e   the closing cash balance at the end of each month   [2]
4   Outline **two** sources of short-term finance other than a bank overdraft that Organiczny Ltd's could source to improve its cash flow position.   [4]
5   Evaluate Kamil Boruc's proposed decision to reduce the payment period for the supermarkets from 30 days to 10 days and to reduce the stock levels in the shop.   [10]

Investment appraisal

BUSINESS IN CONTEXT

Chips: a sustainable investment in wind power

McCain Foods is the world's largest producer of frozen chips. The company focuses on continuous innovation to give competitive advantage and to allow the brand to deliver value and quality. At one of its major European factories, McCain has invested in a big wind power project to generate electricity. This is used to cook and then freeze thousands of tonnes of chips each year. By reducing the cost of paying for energy, McCain's cash outflows are reduced. These cost savings meant that the **payback period** of the initial investment in wind power was just over four years. The rate of return is 8.6% per year. The discounted **net present value (NPV)**, after five years, is $0.17 million.

Although not very profitable, this investment fits in well with McCains' corporate social responsibility strategy. It will also be an important element of the company's social audit. The wind power has cut carbon dioxide emissions by 10 000 tonnes a year. Environmental groups claim that many more sustainable investment projects such as this are needed to reduce climate change.

Discuss in pairs or a group:

- To what extent is it possible to calculate the profitability of a future investment?

- Why might businesses focus more on the profitability of new investment than its environmental impact?

- Why might the time taken to pay back an investment be important to the business?

Investing in energy from wind turbines, used to cook and freeze McCain chips, is both a profitable and a sustainable investment

KEY TERMS

payback period: length of time it takes for the net cash inflows to pay back the original capital cost of the investment

net present value (NPV): today's value of the estimated net cash flows resulting from an investment

KEY CONCEPT LINK

Sustainability

In order to achieve energy independence, the Mexican government has invested in the Deer Park oil refinery in Texas. The government has paid $596 million for a controlling interest in the refinery with the aim of securing an increase in the supply of oil available to Mexico.

20.1 Investment appraisal

Investment means purchasing capital goods (such as equipment, vehicles and new buildings) and improving existing fixed assets. Many investment decisions involve significant strategic issues, such as relocation of premises or the adoption of computer-assisted engineering methods. Other investment plans are less important to the overall performance of the business, for example replacing worn-out photocopiers. Relatively minor investment decisions will not be analysed to the same degree as those that require substantial capital expenditure.

ACTIVITY 20.1

Investment decisions often involve businesses appraising the profitability of their decision by making an assessment of the net cash flows associated with a project. The most profitable project may well be the option the businesses chooses. However, suppose you are an energy business and the most profitable option for you is a coal-fired power station and not a solar energy plant. Perhaps sustainability should be the deciding factor and not profit.

In pairs or as a group, discuss the view that sustainability should always be as important as profit when a business makes investment decisions.

Investment appraisal is undertaken by using quantitative techniques that assess the financial feasibility of the project. Non-financial issues can also be significant, and therefore qualitative appraisal of a project might also be very important. In some businesses, especially those dominated by the founding entrepreneur, formal investment appraisal may not be applied. Instead, the owner may develop a 'feel' for what is likely to be most successful and go ahead with that project even though no formal analysis has been undertaken. The use of such intuitive or 'hunch' methods when taking investment decisions cannot be easily explained to other managers. It is an approach which is also difficult to justify unless the investment decisions turn out to be successful.

KEY TERM

investment appraisal: evaluating the profitability or desirability of an investment project

Quantitative investment appraisal

Quantitative investment appraisal requires the following information:

- the initial capital cost of the investment, including any installation costs
- the estimated life expectancy – for how many years can returns be expected from the investment?
- the residual value of the investment – at the end of their useful lives will the assets be sold, earning additional net returns?
- the forecast net returns or net cash flows from the project – these are the expected returns from the investment minus the annual running cost.

Methods of quantitative investment appraisal include:

- payback period
- average rate of return
- net present value using discounted cash flows.

Forecasting cash flows in an uncertain environment

All of the techniques used to appraise investment projects require forecasts to be made of future cash flows. These figures are referred to as **annual forecast net cash flows**.

KEY TERM

annual forecast net cash flow: forecast cash inflow minus forecast cash outflows

We can assume, rather simplistically, that the cash inflows are the same as the annual revenues earnt from the project and the cash outflows are the annual operating costs.

These net cash flow figures can then be compared with those of other projects and with the initial cost of the investment. Forecasting cash flows is not easy and is rarely likely to be 100% accurate. With long-term investments, forecasts several years ahead have to be made and there is the increased chance of external factors reducing the accuracy of the figures. For instance, when appraising the construction of a new airport, forecasts of cash flows many years ahead are likely to be required. Revenue forecasts may be affected by external factors such as:

- an economic recession that could reduce both business and tourist traffic through the airport

- increases in oil prices that could make air travel more expensive than expected, again reducing revenue totals

- the construction of a new high-speed rail link within the country, which might encourage some travellers to switch to this form of transport.

These future uncertainties cannot be removed from investment appraisal calculations. The possibility of uncertain and unpredicted events making cash flow forecasts inaccurate must be constantly borne in mind by managers. All investment decisions involve some risk due to this uncertainty.

ACTIVITY 20.2

The Gotthard base tunnel is 57 km and in some places 2.3 km from the surface. The project took 17 years to build and cost 12.2 billion Swiss francs. Teams excavated 28.2 million tonnes of rock in the process. Trains can cross the Gotthard group of mountains at a maximum speed of 250 km/h, taking about 20 minutes. The tunnel allows 260 freight trains to pass through the tunnel every day, as opposed to 180 in the old tunnel.

1   In pairs or as a group discuss the ways the next cash flow of such a large project would have been calculated.

2   Do you think the bridge could ever pay back its initial investment?

Quantitative techniques of investment appraisal

Payback method

If a project costs $2 million and is expected to pay back $500 000 per year, the payback period will be four years. This can then be compared with the payback on

alternative investments. It is normal to refer to 'year 0' as the time period in which the investment is made. The cash flow at this time is therefore negative – shown by a bracketed amount (see Table 20.1). This table shows the forecast annual net cash flows and cumulative cash flows. The cumulative cash flow figure shows the 'running total' of cash flows and becomes less and less negative as further cash inflows are received. Notice that in year 3 it becomes positive – so the initial capital cost has been paid back during this year. But when during this year? If we assume that the cash flows are received evenly throughout the year (this may not be the case, of course), then payback will be at the end of the fourth month of the third year (i.e. 2 years and 4 months). How do we know this? At the end of year 2, $50 000 is needed to pay back the remainder of the initial investment. A total of $150 000 is expected during year 3; $50 000 is a third of $150 000 and one-third of a year is the end of month 4. To find out the exact month this formula is used:

$$\frac{\text{additional cash inflow needed}}{\text{annual cash flow in year 3}} \times 12 \text{ months}$$

$$= \frac{\$50\,000}{\$150\,000} \times 12 \text{ months} = 4 \text{ months}$$

Year	Annual net cash flows ($)	Cumulative cash flows ($)
0	(500 000)	(500 000)
1	300 000	(200 000)
2	150 000	(50 000)
3	150 000	100 000
4	100 000 (including residual value)	200 000

Table 20.1: Cash flows of an investment

Importance of payback of a project

Managers can compare the payback period of a particular project with other alternative projects in order to put them in rank order. Alternatively, the payback period can be compared with a 'cut-off' time period that the business may have decided on. For example, it may not accept any project proposal that does not pay back within five years. The uses and benefits of the payback period technique include the following:

- A business may have borrowed the finance for the investment and a long payback period will increase interest payments.

- Even if the finance was obtained internally, the capital has an opportunity cost of other purposes for which it could be used. The speedier the payback, the more quickly the capital is made available for other projects.

- The longer into the future before a project pays back the capital invested in it, the more uncertain the whole investment becomes. The changes in the external environment that could occur to make a project unprofitable are likely to be much greater over ten years than over two.

- Some managers are 'risk averse'– they want to reduce risk to a minimum, so a quick payback reduces uncertainties for these managers.

- Cash flows received in the future have less real value than cash flows today, owing to inflation. The more quickly money is returned to an investing company, the higher its real value will be.

Virgin Atlantic invested £200 000 in a new technology communication system which provides direct contact with potential customers, giving details about special fare offers. The system earnt extra cash flow of £200 000 in three months – a very rapid payback

Evaluation of payback method

The payback method is often used as a quick check on the viability of a project or as a means of comparing projects. However, it is rarely used in isolation from the other investment appraisal methods (see Table 20.2).

Advantages	Disadvantages
It is quick and easy to calculate.	It does not measure the overall profitability of a project – indeed, it ignores all of the cash flows after the payback period. It may be possible for an investment to give a really rapid return of capital but then to offer no other cash inflows.
The results are easily understood by managers.	
The emphasis on speed of return of cash flows gives the benefit of concentrating on the more accurate short-term forecasts of the project's profitability.	This concentration on the short term may lead businesses to reject very profitable investments just because they take some time to repay the capital.
The result can be used to eliminate or 'screen out' projects that give returns too far into the future.	It does not consider the timing of the cash flows during the payback period – this will become clearer when the principle of discounting is examined in the other two appraisal methods (average rate of return and net present value).
It is particularly useful for businesses where liquidity is of greater significance than overall profitability.	

Table 20.2: Payback method – advantages and disadvantages

Accounting rate of return

The **accounting rate of return (ARR)** may also be referred to as the average rate of return. If it can be shown that Project A gives a return on the capital invested of, on average, 8% per year while Project B returns 12% per year, then the decision between the alternative investments will be an easier one to make.

KEY TERM

accounting rate of return (ARR): measures the annual profitability of an investment as a percentage of the capital cost)

The ARR (%) is measured by this formula:

> **KEY FORMULA**
>
> $$ARR = \frac{\text{average annual profit}}{\text{capital cost}} \times 100$$

The average annual profit is calculated by this formula:

> **KEY FORMULA**
>
> $$\text{average annual profit} = \frac{(\text{total returns} - \text{capital cost})}{\text{number of years}}$$

Table 20.3 shows the expected net cash flows from a business investment in a fleet of new fuel-efficient vehicles. They cost $8 million. The inflows for years 1 to 3 are the annual cost savings made. In year 4, the expected residual value of the vehicles is included.

Year	Net cash flow
0	($8 million)
1	$3 million
2	$3 million
3	$3 million
4	$3 million (including $2 million residual capital value)

Table 20.3: Net cash flows for fleet investment

The four stages in calculating ARR are shown in Table 20.4.

1	Add up all positive net cash flows	= $12 million
2	Subtract the capital cost	= $12 million − $8 million = $4 million (this is total profit or total net cash flow)
3	Divide by the life span to calculate the average annual profit	= $4 million/4 = $1 million
4	To calculate the ARR %, divide the result in stage 3 by the capital cost × 100	$\frac{\$1 \text{ million}}{\$8 \text{ million}} \times 100 = 12.5\%$

Table 20.4: The four stages in calculating ARR

Why is the ARR of a project important?

What does this result mean? It indicates to the business that, on average over the lifespan of the investment, it can expect an annual return of 12.5% on its investment. This could be compared with:

- The ARR on other projects.
- The minimum expected return set by the business. This is called the **criterion rate**. (In the example above, if the business refused to accept any project with a return of less than 10%, the new vehicle fleet would satisfy this criterion.)
- The annual interest rate on loans. If the ARR is less than the interest rate, it will not be worthwhile taking a loan to invest in the project.

> **KEY TERM**
>
> **criterion rate:** the minimum accounting rate of return (ARR) that a business would accept before approving an investment

Evaluation of average rate of return

ARR is a widely used measure for appraising projects, but it is best considered together with payback results. The two results then allow consideration of both profits and cash-flow timings (see Table 20.5).

Advantages of ARR	Disadvantages of ARR
It uses all of the cash flows, unlike the payback method. It focuses on profitability, which is the central objective of many business decisions. The result is easily understood and easy to compare with other projects that may be competing for the limited investment funds available. The result can be assessed quickly against the predetermined criterion rate of the business and with the interest on borrowed capital.	It ignores the timing of the cash flows. This could result in two projects having similar ARR results, but one could pay back much more quickly than the other. As all cash inflows are included, the later cash flows, which are less likely to be accurate, are incorporated into the calculation. The time value of money is ignored as the cash flows have not been discounted.

Table 20.5: Advantages and disadvantages of ARR

CASE STUDY 20.1

Investment appraisal of a new hotel

The Silver Leaf Hotel Group (SLHG) is based in Cambodia. The business is looking to expand and has produced financial data on a location near Siem Reap. The new hotel will be based on traditional Cambodian themes and will focus on sustainability. The initial cost of setting up the new hotel will be $22 million. The projected cash flow data for the proposed hotel is set out in Table 20.6.

Year	Annual net cash flows ($ million)
0	(22.0)
1	5.5
2	6.5
3	7.0
4	7.0
5	7.0

Table 20.6: Projected cash flow for the proposed hotel

1   Define the term 'payback'.   [2]

2   Outline how SLHG's net cash flow data is forecast.   [4]

3   Calculate the following from the data in Table 20.6:

   a   payback of the new hotel   [2]

   b   average annual rate of return of the hotel   [2]

4   Evaluate the usefulness of payback and average annual rate of return as methods of investment appraisal to support SLHG's investment decision about the new hotel.   [10]

LEARNER PROFILE

Communicators

When you are selling an investment project to a group of stakeholders you will need data on the potential costs and cash flow returns of your project. This will be in the form of figures for payback, ARR and NPV of the investment project you are trying to sell. But remember, when you are selling something it is more than the data you have got to 'sell'. Some of the people you are selling to may have little understanding of financial data.

Discuss in pairs or as a group the importance of effective communication when you are trying to sell an investment project.

20.2 Net present value (NPV)

Discounting future cash flows

You may be starting to realise that, when using two investment appraisal techniques, managers may be uncertain which project to invest in if the two methods give conflicting results. For example, if a project is estimated to pay back at the end of year 3 at an ARR of 15%, should this be preferred to an alternative project B with a payback of four years but an ARR of 17%?

Managers need another investment appraisal method, which solves this problem of trying to compare projects with different returns and payback periods. This additional method considers both the size of cash flows and the timing of them. It does this by discounting cash flows. If the effects of inflation are ignored, most people would rather accept a payment of $1000 today than a payment of $1000 in a year's time. Which would you choose?

The payment today is preferred for three reasons:

- It can be spent immediately and the benefits of this expenditure can be obtained immediately. There is no waiting involved.
- The $1000 could be saved at the current rate of interest. The total of cash plus interest will be greater than the offer of $1000 in one year's time. The real value of the sum in the future will also be impacted by inflation.
- The cash today is certain, but the future cash offer is always open to uncertainty.

This is called taking the 'time value of money' into consideration. Discounting is the process of reducing the value of future cash flows to give them their value in today's terms. How much less is future cash worth compared to today's money? The answer depends on the rate of interest. If $1000 received today can be saved at 10% interest, then it will grow to $1100 in one year's time. Therefore, $1100 in one year's time has the same value as $1000 today at 10% interest. This value of $1000 is called the present value of $1100 received in one year's time. Discounting calculates the present values of future cash flows so that investment projects can be compared with each other by considering today's value of their returns.

How to discount

The present value of a future sum of money depends on two factors:

- the higher the interest rate, the less value future cash has in today's money
- the longer into the future cash is received, the less value it has today.

These two variables – interest rates and time – are used to calculate discount factors. You do not have to calculate these, they are available in discount tables and an extract from one is given in Table 20.7. To use the discount factors to obtain present values of future cash flows, multiply the appropriate discount factor by the cash flow. For example, $3000 is expected in three years' time. The current rate of interest is 10%. The discount factor to be used is 0.75 – this means that $1 received in three years' time is worth the same as 75 cents today. This discount factor is multiplied by $3000 and the present value is $2250.

Year	6%	8%	10%	12%	16%	20%
1	0.94	0.93	0.91	0.89	0.86	0.83
2	0.89	0.86	0.83	0.80	0.74	0.69
3	0.84	0.79	0.75	0.71	0.64	0.58
4	0.79	0.74	0.68	0.64	0.55	0.48
5	0.75	0.68	0.62	0.57	0.48	0.40
6	0.71	0.63	0.56	0.51	0.41	0.33

Table 20.7: Extract from discounted cash flow table

Net present value (NPV)

This method once again uses discounted cash flows to calculate net present value. It is calculated by subtracting the capital cost of the investment from the total discounted cash flows. The three stages in calculating **NPV** are:

1 Multiply discount factors by the cash flows. Cash flows in year 0 are never discounted as they are today's values already.

2 Add the discounted cash flows.

3 Subtract the capital cost to give the NPV.

The working is clearly displayed in Table 20.8. The initial cost of the investment is a current cost paid out in year 0. Current cash flows are not discounted. A discount rate of 8% is used.

Year	Cash flow	Discount factors @ 8%	Discounted cash flows (DCF)
0	($10 000)	1	($10 000)
1	$5 000	0.93	$4 650
2	$4 000	0.86	$3 440
3	$3 000	0.79	$2 370
4	$2 000	0.74	$1 480

Table 20.8: Discounted cash flows

Net present value is now calculated.

total discounted cash flows = $11 940

original investment = ($10 000)

NPV = $1940

This result means that the project earns $1940 in today's money values. So, if the finance needed can be borrowed at an interest rate of 8% or less, the investment will be profitable. What would happen to NPV if the discount rate was increased, perhaps because interest rates have gone up? This will reduce NPV as future cash flows are worth even less when they are discounted at a higher rate. The choice of discount rate is, therefore, crucial to the assessment of projects using this method of appraisal.

Usually, businesses will choose a rate of discount that reflects the interest cost of borrowing the capital to finance the investment. Even if the finance is raised internally, the rate of interest should still be used to discount future returns. This is because of the opportunity cost of internal finance – it could be left on deposit in a bank to earn interest. An alternative approach to selecting the discount rate to be used is for a business to adopt a cut-off or criterion rate. The business would use this to discount the returns on a project and, if the net present value is positive, the investment could go ahead.

Evaluation of net present value

Net present value is a widely used technique of investment appraisal in industry, but, as it does not give an actual percentage rate of return (see Table 20.9), it is often considered together with the internal rate of return percentage, which is not an IB specification topic.

Advantages	Disadvantages
It considers both the timing of cash flows and their size in arriving at an appraisal.

The rate of discount can be varied to allow for different economic circumstances. For instance, it could be increased if there was a general expectation that interest rates were about to rise.

It considers the time value of money and takes the opportunity cost of money into account. | It is reasonably complex to calculate and to explain – especially to innumerate managers!.

The final result depends heavily on the rate of discount used, and expectations about interest rates may be inaccurate.

Net present values can be compared with other projects, but only if the initial capital cost is the same. This is because the method does not provide a percentage rate of return on the investment (internal rate of return). |

Table 20.9: Net present value – advantages and disadvantages

TIP

When calculating investment appraisal methods, set out your working carefully, using the same type of tables used in this chapter.

Qualitative investment appraisal

Quantitative investment appraisal techniques provide numerical results which assist managers in choosing between investment projects. An important limitation to all of these quantitative techniques is that they ignore qualitative (non-numerical) considerations. No manager can afford to ignore other factors which cannot be expressed in a numerical form but which could have

CASE STUDY 20.2

Using NPV to assess the expansion of a cinema

New Frame Cinema is looking to expand its existing cinema complex to grow its business. The business has been trading very successfully for three years.

The project will involve adding three new auditoriums, giving the business a total of nine screens. This is expected to significantly increase the cinema's revenues. However, the expansion will add to New Frame's costs and the initial investment in the project will cost $5.2 million. Table 20.10 sets out the projected cash flows for the cinema expansion project.

Year	Cash flow ($ million)	Discount factor
0	(5.2)	1
1	1.1	0.94
2	2.0	0.87
3	2.2	0.82
4	2.2	0.76

Table 20.10: Projected cash flow for the cinema expansion project

1 Define the term 'net present value'. [2]

2 Outline two items that might be included in New Frame Cinema's initial investment. [4]

3 Calculate the net present value of New Frame Cinema's expansion proposal. [4]

4 Evaluate the usefulness of net present value to help New Frame Cinema make its expansion decision. [10]

a crucial bearing on a decision. These are referred to as **qualitative factors** and include the following:

- The impact on the environment and the local community – bad publicity stemming from the announcement of some proposed investment plans may dissuade managers from going ahead with a project because of the long-term impact on image and sales. An example is the dispute over the building of a third runway at London's Heathrow airport.

- Planning permission – certain projects may not receive planning permission if they are against the interests of local communities. Local planners weigh up the social costs and benefits of a planned project. Community members will often have a direct role through a public enquiry or may set up a pressure group to make their views known and try to achieve a particular outcome.

- Aims and objectives of the business – for example, the decision to close bank branches and replace them with internet and telephone banking services involves considerable capital expenditure – as well as the

potential for long-term savings. However, managers may be reluctant to pursue these investment policies if there is concern that the aim of giving excellent and personal customer service is being threatened. Similarly, the decision to replace large numbers of workers with labour-saving machinery may be reversed if the negative impact on human relations within the business appears to be too great.

- Risk – different managers are prepared to accept different degrees of risk. No amount of positive quantitative data will convince some managers (perhaps as a result of previous experience) to accept a project that has a considerable chance of failure.

KEY TERM

qualitative factors: factors that cannot be measured in numerical or financial terms that are considered by managers before taking decisions

ACTIVITY 20.3

A small commercial art gallery has a decision to make. It could build an extension to its existing gallery which would cost $50 000. This is a large amount of money for the gallery and a major financial commitment. If the extension is built it would benefit the customers and employees of the gallery. More artwork could be presented as result of the extension, it would be a much better viewing experience for visitors and buyers, and it would be a better place to work.

In pairs or as group, prepare a presentation on the quantitative and qualitative factors that might affect the investment decision of the gallery.

TIP

Unless the question asks only for an analysis of numerical or quantitative factors, your answers to investment appraisal questions should include an assessment of qualitative factors too.

CASE STUDY 20.3

Elk Ltd is a small manufacturing business based in Costa Rica that specialises in ceramics. Eduardo Fernandes is the CFO who is considering the financial data related to an investment in a production line that will increase the firm's revenue. The financial data related to each system is set out in the table.

1   Define the term 'average rate of return'.   [2]

2   Outline what the payback of system A and system B shows.   [4]

3   Explain which system is likely to be more profitable for Elk.   [4]

System	Investment	Payback	Average rate of return	Net present value
A	$13.4 million	3 years 7 months	16%	$645 000
B	$15.6 million	4 years 1 month	18%	$677 000

THEORY OF KNOWLEDGE

Known as the 'tallest unfinished building in the world', the Ryugyong Hotel in North Korea was designed to compete against the Westin Stamford Hotel in Singapore built by a South Korean firm. A North Korean construction company broke ground in 1987, and started to build the pyramid-based design. Construction halted in 1992 after the Soviet Union collapsed and all potential funding ended, leaving a disused crane perched on its tip for over two decades. Today the Ryugyong Hotel remains empty with no interior decoration.

In pairs or as a class discuss the extent to which some of the world's biggest investment projects are more about emotion than reason.

SELF-EVALUATION CHECKLIST

After studying this chapter, complete this table.

I am able to apply and analyse:	Needs more work	Almost there	Ready to move on
payback and average rate of return (ARR) to appraise investment opportunities (AO3)			
net present value (NPV) to appraise investment opportunities (AO3)			
I am able to use:			
payback and average rate of return (ARR) to appraise investment opportunities (AO4)			
net present value (NPV) to appraise investment opportunities (AO4)			

REFLECTION

To what extent do you agree with the view that as the future is so uncertain there is no point in undertaking investment appraisal and managers should use their intuition to make 'hunch' investment decisions? Discuss your opinion with another learner.

PROJECT

The Burj Khalifa is an 829.8 metre high skyscraper in Dubai. The building was completed in 2009 at a cost of $1.5 billion. It houses offices, residential homes, hotels, leisure facilities and retail space. It is not a cheap place to live or to locate a business. Two-bedroom apartments are sold for around $2 million. Real estate is an important part of investment in a country where buildings increase the productive capacity of the economy.

In groups prepare a video presentation on the investment appraisal method you would use for the Burj Khalifa. It should include assessment of:

- the initial investment
- cash inflows
- cash outflows
- net cash flows
- payback
- ARR
- NPV.

Thinking about your project:

- Do you feel your understanding the different methods of investment appraisal has improved?
- How good was your video presentation compared to those of the other groups in the class?
- How could you improve your video presentation?

EXAM-STYLE QUESTIONS

Sun and Sand Ltd's investment decision

Sun and Sand Ltd is a tourism business based in the Bahamas that is looking to develop its portfolio of hotels and apartments to include yachts. The CEO of Sun and Sand, Gwyneth Best, has persuaded the business's board of directors to look at two yachts as investment opportunities. Yacht-based holidays are expensive, but it is a growing market amongst affluent consumers who visit the Bahamas. Gwyneth also believes development of the business into yachts will enhance the high-quality image of the Sun and Sand. The two yachts being considered are the *Royal Bird* at a cost of $19 million and *Endless Sunset* at a cost of $22 million. The cash flows generated by each yacht are set out in the table.

Year	*Royal Bird* net cash flows ($ million)	*Endless Sunset* net cash flows ($ million)	Discount rate 8%
0	(19)	(22)	1
1	2.5	2.7	0.93
2	4.9	5.3	0.86
3	5.7	5.9	0.79
4	6.2	6.3	0.74
5	6.3	6.4	0.68

Table 20.11:

1	State the equation for average rate of return (ARR).	[2]
2	Define the term 'payback'.	[2]
3	Outline how Sun and Sand Ltd might generate net cash flows from the yacht project.	[4]
4	Explain why projects like the Sun and Sands yacht need to have their net cash flow discounted.	[4]
5	Using the data in Table 20.11 calculate the payback and ARR of each yacht investment.	[4]
6	On the basis of each project's payback and ARR, explain which yacht performs better.	[4]
7	Outline the purpose of a discount rate on a project.	[2]
8	Using the data in Table 20.11 calculate the NPV of each yacht investment.	[4]
9	On the basis each project's NPV, explain which yacht performs better.	[4]
10	Explain two weaknesses of Sun and Sand relying on investment appraisal data to make its decision about the yachts.	[4]

Chapter 21

Budgets

LEARNING OBJECTIVES

On completing this chapter you should be able to:

Apply and analyse:

> The difference between cost and profit centres (AO2)

> The roles of cost and profit centres (AO2)

> Constructing a budget (AO2)

> Variances (AO2)

> The importance of budgets and variances in decision-making (AO2)

Use and apply:

> Constructing a budget (AO4)

> Variances (AO4)

BUSINESS IN CONTEXT

Mauritius Metro Express project – on budget and on time

Unlike around 80% of large projects, the new Mauritius Metro Express seems likely to be completed within the original **budget** of $565 million. This overall figure was divided into detailed financial plans for land purchase, construction, cost of the trains and testing of the system. A business analyst said, 'Given the complex and long-term nature of most large projects, to keep within budget is remarkable.'

Why do so many large-scale projects cost far more than their original budget or financial plan? Reasons include:

- political optimism before the project starts, to influence public opinion

- environmental factors such as extreme weather

- technical issues, especially when dealing with untried technologies.

Big projects that have been delayed and ended up costing far more than the original budget include:

- Navi Mumbai Airport (India) $1.5 billion over budget

- London Crossrail (UK) $4.9 billion over budget

- Berlin Willy Brandt Airport (Germany) $6.1 billion over budget

The Metro Express in Mauritius: this big infrastructure project is due to be completed within budget

- Flamanville Nuclear Power Station (France) $10 billion over budget.

Discuss in pairs or in a group:
- What are the benefits of a business having financial plans?

- How could budgets for very large projects be made more accurate?

KEY TERM

budget: a detailed financial plan for the future

KEY CONCEPT LINK

Change

At the end of December 2019, businesses of different sizes in different industries across the world would have set up their budgets for 2020. By March 2020 Covid-19 had taken hold and all of those budgets would have been rendered irrelevant. Like so many areas of business that involve making forecasts, budgets struggle to deal with unexpected change, and the impact of Covid-19 is probably the most consequential unexpected change most businesses have ever experienced.

21.1 The difference between cost centres and profit centres

An important element of understanding budgets and the purposes of budgeting is to be able to explain what cost centres and profit centres are. Budgets are allocated to these sections of a business.

Cost centres

Examples of **cost centres** are:

- in a manufacturing business – products, departments, factories, particular processes or stages in the production, such as assembly
- in a hotel – the restaurant, reception, bar, room letting and conference sections.

Different businesses will use different cost centres that are appropriate to their own needs.

Profit centres

Profit centres are sections or departments of a business which can have both costs and revenue allocated to them so that profit or loss can be calculated.

Examples of **profit centres** are:

- each branch of a chain of shops
- each department of a department store
- in a multi-product firm, each product in the overall portfolio of the business.

The key difference between cost centres and profit centres is therefore the allocation of revenue. Some sections or departments of a business will only incur costs and will not earn revenue – such as administration and research and development. Any budgets set for cost centres can only focus on cost levels. In contrast, it is possible to allocate both costs and revenue to profit centres. So, each branch of a chain of fast-food restaurants can set budgets for both costs and revenue – and these can be compared to give a budgeted profit figure.

21.2 The roles of cost centres and profit centres

If an organisation is divided into these centres, certain benefits are likely to be gained:

- Managers and other employees will have financial targets to work towards – if these are reasonable and achievable, this should have a positive impact on motivation.
- These targets can be used to compare with actual performance and help identify those areas performing best in terms of not exceeding cost budgets or exceeding profit budgets.
- The individual performances of sections/divisions and their managers can be assessed and compared.
- Work can be monitored and decisions made about the future. For example, should a profit centre be kept open or should the price of a product be increased?
- Members of each cost centre or profit centre might develop a sense of belonging to that section; a team spirit could become established which will act as a motivating influence.

However, the following problems might arise when using these centres:

- Managers and workers may consider their section of the business to be more important than the whole organisation. There could be damaging competition between profit centres to gain new orders.
- Some costs – indirect costs – can be impossible to allocate to cost and profit centres accurately and this can result in arbitrary and inaccurate overhead cost allocations.
- Reasons for the good or bad performance of one particular profit centre may be due to external factors not under its control.

> **KEY TERMS**
>
> **cost centre:** a section of a business, such as a department, to which costs can be allocated or charged
>
> **profit centre:** a section of a business to which both costs and revenues can be allocated

TIP

You may be asked to explain the roles of cost centres or profit centres.

CASE STUDY 21.1

Budgeting at L'Chique

L'Chique is a chain of clothing shops based in Asia. The business has been successful over the last three years and its revenues increased by more than 20% last year. The number of stores in the chain is growing and is planned to increase from 34 to 41 in the next 12 months. The business's target market segment is 18–35-year-olds and it focuses on sustainable fashion.

The business prides itself on effective budgeting and financial control. Each store within the L'Chique chain is a profit centre which is responsible for managing its own financial performance. A system of delegated budgeting is used to give individual store managers greater responsibility, and managers receive extensive training in setting up and managing budgets.

1   Define the term 'profit centre'.   **[2]**

2   Explain two advantages of L'Chique operating its stores as profit centres.   **[4]**

3   Explain two reasons why L'Chique might have delegated budgeting to its store managers.   **[4]**

4   Evaluate the importance to L'Chique of effective budgeting.   **[10]**

21.3 Constructing a budget

The financial planning process is known as budgeting. A budget is a detailed financial plan for a future time period. If no financial plans are made, an organisation drifts without real direction or purpose. Managers will not be able to allocate the scarce resources of the business effectively without a plan to work towards. Employees working in an organisation without plans for future action are likely to feel demotivated as they have no targets to work towards and no objective to be praised for achieving. If no targets are set, then an organisation cannot review its progress because it has no set objective against which actual performance can be compared. Therefore, financial planning requires the construction of budgets.

ACTIVITY 21.1

Producing a charity event budget

You are planning a school charity event such as a disco, dinner, cake sale, sponsored run, etc.

1   Produce a budget for the event based on initial expenses, running expenses and revenues. Set out your budgeted revenues and expenditure data in a spreadsheet.

2   Present your proposed charity event and its budget to the rest of the class.

A budget is not a forecast, although much of the data on which it is based will come from forecasts, since we are looking into the future. Budgets are plans that organisations aim to fulfil. A forecast is a prediction of what could occur in the future.

Budgets may be established for any part of an organisation as long as its performance is quantifiable. There may be sales budgets, capital expenditure budgets, labour cost budgets, etc.

Coordination between departments when establishing budgets is essential. This should avoid departments making conflicting plans. For example, the marketing department may be planning to increase sales by reducing prices, yet the production department may be planning to reduce output and the direct-labour cost budget. These targets will conflict and need to be reconciled.

Decisions about constructing and setting budgets should be made with the subordinate managers who will be involved in putting them into effect. Those who are to be held responsible for fulfilling a budget should be involved in setting it. This sense of 'ownership' not only helps to motivate the department concerned to achieve the targets but also leads to the establishment of more realistic targets. This approach to budgeting is called 'delegated budgets'.

> **KEY TERM**
>
> **delegated budgets:** control over budgets is given to less-senior management

The budget will be used to review the performance of a department, and the managers of that department will be appraised on their effectiveness in reaching targets. Successful and unsuccessful managers can therefore be identified.

Stages in constructing budgets

Figure 21.1 shows how budgets are commonly constructed. This involves seven stages as follows.

Stage 1

The most important organisational objectives for the coming year set by senior managers, based on:

- the previous performance of the business
- external changes likely to affect the organisation
- sales forecasts based on research and past sales data.

Stage 2

The key or limiting factor that is most likely to influence the success of the organisation must be identified – this is usually sales. The sales budget will be the first to be prepared. Accuracy is essential at this stage. An error in the key-factor budget will distort all other budgets. For example, if the sales budget proves to be inaccurate, e.g., it is set at a level that proves to be too high, then cash, production, labour budgets and so on will become inaccurate too.

Stage 3

The sales budget is prepared after discussion with sales managers in all branches and divisions of the business.

Stage 4

Subsidiary budgets are prepared based on the sales budget. These will include the cash budget, administration budget, labour cost budget, materials cost budget, and selling and distribution budget. The budget holders, e.g., cost- and profit-centre managers, should be involved in this process if the aim of delegated responsibility for budgets is to be achieved.

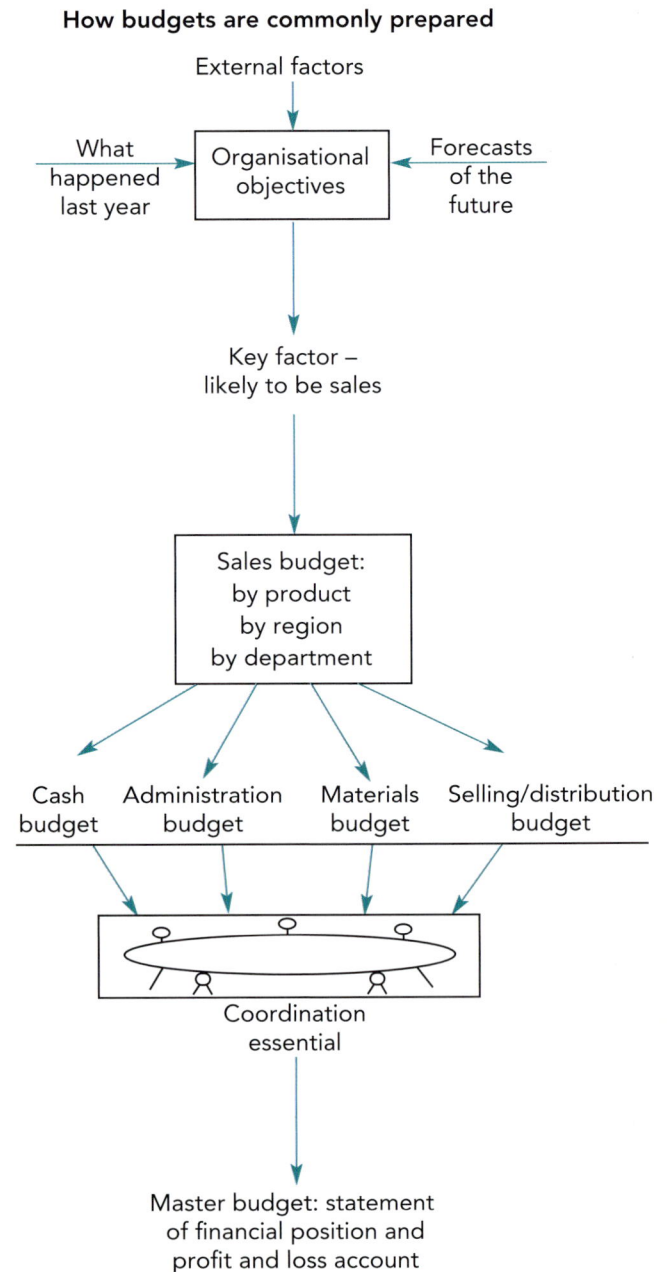

Figure 21.1: How budgets are commonly constructed

Stage 5

These budgets are coordinated to ensure consistency. This may be undertaken by a budgetary committee with special responsibility for ensuring that budgets do not conflict with each other and that the overall planned expenditure does not exceed the resources of the business.

Stage 6

A master budget is constructed that contains the main details of all other budgets. It includes a budgeted profit and loss account and statement of financial position.

Stage 7

The master budget is then presented to the board of directors for its approval.

Once approved, the budgets will become the basis of the operational plans of each cost centre and profit centre in the organisation.

> **TIP**
>
> When discussing delegated budgeting try to link this in your answer with the motivational approach of Herzberg – making work more challenging and rewarding.

Setting budget levels

Incremental budgeting and zero budgeting are the two methods most widely used to set budget levels.

Incremental budgeting

In many businesses that operate in highly competitive markets there may be plans to reduce the cost budget for departments each year, but to increase the sales budgets. This puts increased pressure on many staff to achieve higher productivity. **Incremental budgeting** does not allow for unforeseen events. Using the previous year's figures as a basis means that each department does not have to justify its whole budget for the coming year – only the change or 'increment'.

> **KEY TERM**
>
> **incremental budgeting:** uses last year's budget as a basis and an adjustment is made for the coming year

---

CASE STUDY 21.2

Importance of budgets

Many business owners begin their operation with a wave of optimism and enthusiasm, but the reality of business can soon dampen that positivity without a well thought out plan. It is not possible to create a successful business without an effective budget.

Budgeting sounds quite boring. However, successful businesses need to allocate time to create and manage budgets, prepare and review business plans and regularly monitor their financial situation and business performance.

Budgeting identifies current available working capital, provides an estimate of expenditure and anticipates incoming revenue. By referring to budgets, businesses can measure performance against forecast and ensure sufficient resources are available to support business functions. It enables the business owner to concentrate on cash flow, reducing costs, improving profits and increasing returns on investment. Budgets also provide a platform for future growth and development.

Budgeting is the basis for all business success. It helps with both planning and control of the finances of the business. If there is no control over spending, planning is futile and if there is no planning there are no business objectives to achieve.

1 Outline what a sales revenue budget shows. **[2]**

2 Outline the meaning of the coordination and controlling functions of budgets. **[4]**

3 Explain why budgeting cash flow is so important. **[4]**

Zero budgeting

This approach to setting budgets requires all departments and budget holders to justify their whole budget each year. **Zero budgeting** is time-consuming as a fundamental review of the work and importance of each budget-holding section is needed each year. However, it does provide added incentive for managers to defend the work of their own section. Also, changing situations can be reflected in very different budget levels each year.

> **KEY TERM**
>
> **zero budgeting:** setting budgets to zero each year and budget holders have to argue their case to receive any finance

> **THEORY OF KNOWLEDGE**
>
> There is only one rule of budgeting – 'don't exceed your budget'. So why do so many people break the rule?
>
> In pairs or as a group discuss the following question: To what extent do business people act rationally when making decisions?

Example of budget construction

The following example shows how the annual budget for a fast-food restaurant can be constructed.

> **WORKED EXAMPLE 21.1**
>
> In Table 21.1, 'this year' data refers to the actual performance of the restaurant. The budget for next year is based on incremental budgeting and this:
>
> - sales are forecast to increase by 8% following last year's increase in promotion and a reduction in the unemployment rate
> - labour costs are expected to increase by 2% following a wage increase
> - material costs are predicted to increase by 3% following discussions with major suppliers
> - overhead costs are expected to increase by 5% – interest rates have risen, business rents have increased and energy costs are influenced by the rising world price of gas.

More detailed budgets

In larger organisations it is usual to have more than one source of income and many different types of expenses. Table 21.2 shows the construction of a more detailed budget.

	Budget this year ($000)	Budget for next year ($000)
Revenue from sales	200	216
Total income	200	216
Labour costs	50	51
Material costs	40	41.2
Overhead costs	80	82
Total expenses	170	174.2
Profit/loss (or excess of revenues over (under) costs)	30	41.8

Table 21.1: Constructing a budget

	Budgeted figures ($ million)
Income	
Revenue from sales	225
Interest earned	4
Total income	229
Expenses	
Salaries and wages	122
Materials	35
Rent	25
Advertising	2
Electricity	6
Total expenses	190
Profit/loss	39

Table 21.2: The construction of a more detailed budget

21.4 Variances

During the period covered by the budget and at the end of it, the actual performance of the organisation needs to be compared with the original targets, and reasons for differences must be investigated. This process is known as **variance analysis**. A **variance** is the difference between budgeted and actual figures. Variance analysis is an essential part of budgeting for a number of reasons:

- It measures differences from the planned performance of each department, both month by month and at the end of the year.

- It assists in analysing the causes of deviations from budget. For example, if actual profit is below budget, was this due to lower sales revenue or higher costs?

- An understanding of the reasons for the deviations from the original planned levels can be used to change future budgets in order to make them more accurate. For example, if sales revenue is lower than planned as a result of market resistance to higher prices, then this knowledge could be used to help prepare future budgets.

- The performance of each individual budget-holding section may be appraised in an accurate and objective way.

If the variance has had the effect of increasing profit, for example sales revenue is higher than budgeted for, then it is termed a **favourable variance**. If the variance has had the effect of reducing profit, for example direct material costs are higher than budgeted, then it is termed an unfavourable or **adverse variance**. See Table 21.3.

Using variance analysis results

Managers may need to respond quickly to both adverse and favourable variances. Clearly, adverse variances will need to be looked at in some detail to see if cheaper supplies or working methods could be adopted. However, an adverse variance caused by an increase in output leading to higher raw material costs is of much less concern.

Favourable variances cannot be ignored either. They may reflect a poor and inaccurate budgeting process where cost budgets were set too high. A favourable

direct cost variance caused by output being much less than planned for is not very promising – why were sales and output lower than planned for?

LEARNER PROFILE

This is an advert for some budgeting software.

Our financial management software is rich in functionality, delivering a full suite of financial management modules and core and advanced functionality. More importantly, our proven solution automates many core accounting processes, making the solution efficient and easy to use. Through a range of mobile apps and Microsoft Office integration, people across your organisation will be able to input data, action approvals and view relevant reports, all helping improve business-wide efficiency and increase productivity.

In pairs or in a group, discuss how knowledgeable, open-minded business people might react to such advertising.

Financial variable	Budget ($)	Actual result ($)	Variance ($)	Favourable or adverse
Revenue	15 000	12 000	3 000	Adverse – this reduces profit
Direct costs	5 000	4 000	1 000	Favourable – this increases profit
Overhead costs	3 000	3 500	500	Adverse – this reduces profit
Net profit	7 000	4 500	2 500	Adverse – profit is below forecast

Table 21.3: West Indian Carpets variance calculations

WORKED EXAMPLE 21.2

Variance analysis for West Indian Carpets Ltd

The variance calculations for West Indian Carpets, shown in Table 21.3, can be verified by checking the net profit variance ($2500 adverse) against the net sum of the other variances ($3500 adverse − $1000 favourable = $2500 adverse). The benefits to be gained from regular variance analysis include:

- Identifying potential problems early so that remedial action can be taken. Perhaps, in this case, a new competing carpet retailer has opened up and West Indian Carpets will have to quickly introduce strategies to combat this competition.

- Allowing managers to concentrate their time and efforts on the major, or exceptional, problem areas. This is known as management by exception. In this case, it seems that managers should urgently investigate the likely causes of the lower than expected sales figures.

Table 21.4 identifies the possible causes of adverse and favourable variances.

More detailed variance analysis

When a more detailed budget has been prepared then variance analysis can be even more useful in identifying reasons why performance has been above or below budget.

Table 21.5 shows this more detailed variance analysis. Each variance has been indicated as being either favourable (F) or adverse (A).

	Budgeted figures	Actual figures	Variance
Income			
Revenue from sales	225	239	14 F
Interest earned	4	3	1 A
Total income	229	242	13 F
Expenses			
Salaries and wages	122	125	3 A
Materials	35	40	5 A
Rent	25	25	0
Advertising	2	3	1 A
Electricity	6	5	1 F
Total expenses	190	198	8 A
Profit/loss	39	44	5 F

Table 21.5: The construction of a more detailed budget and variance analysis ($ million)

Adverse variances	Favourable variances
Sales revenue is below budget *either* because units sold were fewer than planned for *or* the selling price had to be reduced due to competition	Sales revenue is above budget *either* due to higher than expected economic growth *or* problems with one of the competitors' products
Actual raw material costs are higher than planned for *either* because output was higher than budgeted *or* the cost per unit of materials increased	Raw material costs are lower *either* because output was less than planned *or* the cost per unit of materials was lower than budgeted
Labour costs are above budget *either* because wage rates had to be increased due to shortages of workers *or* the labour time taken to complete the work was longer than expected	Labour costs are lower than planned for *either* because of lower wage rates *or* quicker completion of the work
Overhead costs are higher than budgeted, perhaps because the annual rent rise was above the level forecast	Overhead costs are lower than budgeted, perhaps because advertising rates from TV companies were reduced

Table 21.4: Possible causes of adverse and favourable variances

21.5 The importance of budgets and variances in decision-making

Setting budgets and calculating variances from them are a central part of financial planning for any business. The budgeting process has the following benefits:

- Planning – it makes managers consider future plans carefully so that realistic targets can be set.

- Effective allocation of resources – it can be an effective way of ensuring that the business does not spend more resources than it has.

- Sets targets to be achieved – most work teams and the people within them work will be motivated to work effectively if they have a realisable target to aim for.

- Coordination – the allocation of resources to different cost and profit centres requires coordination between these departments and leads to a balanced resource allocation.

- Monitoring and controlling – budgets cannot be ignored once in place and constant checking is needed to monitor that the plan is being met.

- Modifying – if there is evidence to suggest that the budget is unrealistic, then either the plan or the way of working towards it must be changed.

- Assessing performance – variance analysis allows a comparison of actual performance with the original budgets.

Budgets and variances also play a key role in business decision-making in the following ways:

- **Raising finance.** Once budgets have been set for the next time period, management will know how much finance is required to meet the financial plans of the business. This helps with deciding on the sources of finance to be used. Budgeting will also help managers decide on the lowest-cost way to finance day-to-day business expenses. For example, it may not be necessary to take out loans (and incur interest charges) to pay for essential expenses if budgeting shows that these costs can be paid for out of revenue.

- **Deciding between projects.** Business growth requires investment in projects that will develop the business. Budgeting helps managers to see what forms of expansion would be realistic within available resources. Budgets and variances might reveal areas of wasteful spending that, if eliminated, could finance the business as it moves forward with long-term projects. Budgeting helps managers avoid the problem of starting projects that turn out to be beyond the resources of the business.

- **Restricting the role of emotion in decision-making.** Effective budgeting requires a logical and rational approach to target setting and resource allocation. It reduces the risk of managers making short-term decisions spurred on by emotion or irrational thinking. For example, if the annual promotion budget has been set for a retail clothing store, then the manager is unlikely to be influenced by an excited and apparently convincing advertising salesperson who claims that spending with his organisation will lead to huge sales increases. Referring to the original budget will allow any spending decision to be considered rationally in light of what is affordable.

- **Making decisions to adjust strategy.** Budgets and variances tell managers how the business, and all cost and profit centres within it, is performing. Significant variances from budget might require a change of strategic direction. The key factor in the budget is business revenue from sales. If managers find that actual income levels are missing targets then quick decisions might need to be made. Should some loss-making centres be closed? Should additional resources be allocated to marketing and promotion? Should ways be found to cut back on expenses? Decisions to adjust strategy will be made more effective by using the data made available by the budgetary process.

Potential limitations of budgets

There are potential limitations associated with budgets and these can restrict their effectiveness:

- Lack flexibility. If budgets are set with no flexibility built into them, then sudden and unexpected changes in the external environment can make them very unrealistic. These external changes include unplanned increases in materials and energy-cost inflation.

- Short-term focus. Budgets tend to be set for the relatively short term, for example the next 12 months. Managers may take a short-term decision to stay within budget that may not be in the best long-term interests of the business. For example, a decision to reduce the size of the workforce to stay within the labour budget may limit the firm's ability to increase output if sales were to increase more quickly than forecast in the future.

- May result in unnecessary spending. If the end of the budgeting period approaches and managers realise that they have underspent their budgets, unnecessary spending decisions might be made so that the same level of budget can be justified next year. If a large surplus exists at the end of the budget period, how could managers justify the same level of resources next year?

- Revised budgets are often needed for new projects. When a major new project is being undertaken, perhaps a one-off building scheme such as a large bridge or tunnel, it may be difficult to set realistic budgets, and frequent and substantial revisions to the budgets might be necessary.

ACTIVITY 21.3

Producing a gap year budget

You are planning a gap year during which you will travel around the world.

1 Produce a budget for your gap year based on initial expenses, everyday expenses and possible income from fundraising or working. Set out your budgeted income and expenditure data in a spreadsheet.

2 Present your proposed gap year plan and your budget to the rest of the class.

CASE STUDY 21.3

Variance analysis at Lighting Solutions Ltd

Lighting Solutions Ltd manufactures lighting products that are sold to retailers and commercial buyers. The company has been relatively successful this year in terms of sales, but it has struggled to control its costs. Component costs have increased significantly, and this has affected Lighting Solutions' direct costs. The accounting department at Lighting Solutions uses variance analysis to help management interpret the financial performance of different parts of the business.

Table 21.6 sets out Lighting Solutions budgeted profit and loss account for 2021.

1 Define the term 'variance analysis'. [2]

2 Outline two factors that determine how Lighting Solutions sets its sales revenue budget. [4]

3 Using the data in Table 21.6 calculate the following:

	Budget	Actual	Variance
Sales revenue	1400	1550	
Direct materials	400	488	
Direct labour	350	386	
Gross profit			
Overhead cost	370	395	
Net profit			

Table 21.6: Lighting Solutions budgeted profit and loss account, 2021 ($000)

a budgeted and actual net profit [2]

b sales, direct material cost, direct labour cost and indirect cost variances [2]

c gross and net profit variances [2]

4 Outline what the different variance figures show about Lighting Solutions' performance during the year. [4]

SELF-EVALUATION CHECKLIST

After studying this chapter, complete this table.

I know and understand:	Needs more work	Almost there	Ready to move on
the difference between cost and profit centres (AO2)			
the roles of cost centres and profit centres (AO2)			
constructing a budget (AO2)			
variances (AO2)			
the importance of budgets and variances in decision-making (AO2)			
I am able to use and apply:			
budgets (AO4)			
variances (AO4)			

REFLECTION

Make a budget of your personal income and expenditure for the next three months. After three months has passed compare your actual income and expenditure with your original budget. To what extent do you think personal finances can be improved with budgeting?

PROJECT

The top five budgeting problems most businesses face are:

- Time: budgeting is a very time-consuming process that requires huge amounts of staff time.

- Cost: if budgeting occupies large amounts of staff time it is going to be expensive to carry out.

- Communication: so many stakeholders are involved to the budgetary process that communicating it throughout the organisation is incredibly complex.

- Complexity: budget setters face a complex set of interrelated activities and deadlines, which have unpredicted changes.

- Accuracy: budgeting is about the future, and that means uncertainty.

In pairs or as a group, produce a presentation on how you would try to overcome the top five budgeting problems identified.

Thinking about your project:

- Once you have completed your presentation, do you think you have a clearer understanding of the problems of budgeting?

- How good was your presentation compared to those of the other groups in the class?

EXAM-STYLE QUESTIONS

Variance analysis at a hotel group

Staylef plc is an established hotel group based in Eastern Europe. Staylef has had a mixed year, with some areas of the business performing better than others. The business markets itself under three brands:

- Ecostay – A group of 2-star budget hotels where rooms are sold at a low price.
- Nightstay – A group of 3-star standard hotels where rooms are sold at average prices.
- Premierstay – A group of 4-star luxury hotels where room are sold at high prices.

Each of the hotel brands are operated as profit centres, and sales and net profit data budgeted for the year is shown in the table.

	Ecostay		Nightstay		Premierstay	
	Budget	Actual	Budget	Actual	Budget	Actual
Sales revenue	4.2	4.8	6.4	6.9	5.7	4.5
Total cost	3.2	3.5	4.1	4.5	4.4	4.2

The CEO of Staylef group is concerned about the performance of the Premierstay group which has struggled during the year. The CEO of Premierstay has stepped down and has been replaced. Some of the staff at Premierstay believe the CEO was treated unfairly because the market conditions were not that easy for this area of the business due to an economic recession in certain countries in Eastern Europe.

1   Define term term 'budget'.   [2]
2   Define the term 'favourable sales variance'.   [2]
3   Outline two factors that need to be accounted for to budget for each hotel brand's direct labour cost.   [4]
4   State how a sales variance is calculated.   [1]
5   Using the budget data in the table, calculate the following variances for each hotel brand.
    a   sales   [2]
    b   total cost   [2]
    c   net profit   [2]
6   Outline each hotel brand's net profit performance, based on the variances you have calculated.   [4]
7   Explain how a recession in certain countries in Eastern Europe might have affected the net profit variance of Premierstay.   [4]
8   Evaluate the usefulness of variance analysis to Staylef.   [10]

Marketing

> # Chapter 22
> # Introduction to marketing

BUSINESS IN CONTEXT

Marketing McDonald's

The global fast-food market is estimated to have total sales of over $700 billion and is growing at an annual rate of 4.6%. McDonald's **market share** is around 22 per cent of this total – three times greater than that of its closest rival. Clearly, McDonald's has taken some very effective decisions to reach this level of dominant market leadership. It also suggests that its strategy of **market orientation** is achieving success.

The company's directors are never complacent and each year new marketing innovations are introduced. McDonald's marketing is currently responding to the following:

- the global economic downturn, which started in 2020, created market opportunities for 'premium fast-food products' aimed at consumers who have limited incomes and cannot afford a meal in a three-star restaurant

- increasing concern about the bad health effects of fast food – especially youth obesity – means that healthier menu options are becoming much more widely available

- different consumer tastes and national cultures that exist in the international markets mean that products and promotions have to frequently adapt.

McDonald's claims:

We are constantly researching consumer wants, and as many people cannot now afford full restaurant meals, we are revising our menu to appeal to them with luxury beef and chicken products in specialist ciabatta bread. The company is also committed to increasing its range of salads and other healthy options.

McDonald's is also aware of the cash limits of its traditional customers and is targeting them with a new 'dollar-saver' menu. In India, it has opened its first 'vegetarian only' restaurant.

In Japan, the company's advertisements are focused on adults more than children, with some features that are unique to the local culture. As the appetite of the Japanese differs from that of average Americans,

Interior of a McDonald's restaurant in Japan

the serving sizes of burgers, fries and drinks in Japan are smaller. Only in Japan does McDonald's offer the Teritama Burger as a spring menu item while the Tsukimi Burger is offered in the autumn.

McDonald's is able to adapt its menu and marketing plans to each culture. It shows that it respects the differences between cultures and takes note of these as it develops additional menu items to maintain or increase market share as the total market is growing.

Discuss in pairs or a group:

- To what extent does the market share of a business indicate the success of the marketing of its products?

- Do you think it is important that McDonald's is responding to cultural and taste differences between countries? Explain your answer.

- Why is a strategy of market orientation achieved by 'researching consumer wants' important to a business such as McDonald's?

KEY TERMS

market share: the percentage of sales in the total market sold by one business

market orientation: an outward-looking approach basing product decisions on consumer demand, as established by market research

ACTIVITY 22.1

Marketing is the interface between a business organisation and its consumers. Ultimately, businesses succeed or fail based on the successful relationship they have with their consumers. This means that marketing has a leading role in a business's strategic decision-making. For example, when a mobile phone company is launching a new smartphone, its strategy will most likely be led by market research carried out by the firm's marketing department. The information produced by the department will shape the business's strategic decision-making on the product, its price, the place where it will be sold and how it is going to be promoted.

Research the marketing strategy of a business in the mobile phone market.

22.1 What is marketing

Most people think of **marketing** as just being about advertising and selling of products. However, this is a very limited view – marketing embraces much more than just telling people about a product and selling it to them. There are thousands of definitions of marketing. One of the shortest and clearest is from the Chartered Institute of Marketing:

> Marketing is the management process responsible for identifying, anticipating and satisfying consumers' requirements profitably.

Another definition comes from *Contemporary Marketing Wired*, by Boone and Kurtz (9th edition, 1998):

> Marketing is the process of planning and undertaking the conception, pricing, promotion and distribution of goods and services to create and maintain relationships that will satisfy individual and organisational objectives.

It seems from this definition that marketing involves a number of related management functions. These include:

- market research
- product design
- pricing
- advertising
- distribution
- customer service
- packaging.

So, marketing is a very important business activity! Marketing activities are all those associated with identifying the particular wants and needs of target-market customers and then trying to satisfy those customer needs better than your competitors do. This means that market research is needed to identify and analyse customer needs. With this knowledge, strategic decisions must then be taken about product design, pricing, promotion and distribution.

THEORY OF KNOWLEDGE

Imagination and emotion

What makes a good marketing slogan? Here are five of the top promotional slogans produced by some of the world's leading businesses. Some of the best slogans that are used by leading brands tend to be short, catchy, easy to recognise and simple to remember. They are a bit like hit songs – you can't get them out of your head!

'Just Do It' – Nike

'Think Different' – Apple

'Where's the Beef?' – Wendy's

'Open Happiness' – Coca-Cola

'Because You're Worth It' – L'Oréal

Examine the importance of imagination and emotion in developing a good marketing slogan.

KEY TERM

marketing: the management task that links the business to the customer by identifying and meeting the needs of customers profitably – it does this by getting the right product at the right price to the right place at the right time

Your favourite product

1 Working in pairs or in groups, think about a favourite product that each of you own.

2 Complete the table for your favourite product by using a few words to describe that product under each heading. For example, if the product was an Apple iPhone, under 'product design' it might say: aesthetic, high quality, nice to hold.

3 In the final section of the table, discuss why your product is a 'good product' and summarise this in a series of key words.

Activity	Your product
Product design	
Pricing	
Advertising	
Distribution	
Customer service	
Packaging	
Why it is a good product?	

Market size

Market size can be measured in two ways: volume of sales (units sold) or value of goods sold (revenue).

The size of a market is important for three reasons:

- a marketing manager can assess whether a market is worth entering or not
- businesses can calculate their own market share
- growth or decline of the market can be identified.

It is not always easy to measure market growth in an unambiguous way. Different results may be obtained depending on whether the growth and share rates are measured in volume or value terms. For example, if total

market size: the total level of sales of all producers within a market

sales in the market for jeans rose from 24 million pairs at an average price of $32 to 26 million pairs at an average price of $36, then market growth can be measured in two ways:

- by volume – the market has risen from 24 to 26 million units, an increase of 8.33%
- by value – the revenue has risen from $768 million to $936 million, an increase of 21.87%.

Which of these two figures – value or volume – should be used to measure the changing market share for any one jeans manufacturer? The manufacturer could use the measure that reflects better on its own position. So it may also be difficult to compare firms' changing market shares. A cosmetic company that specialises in selling low volumes of expensive products is likely to have a higher market share in value terms than when measured by volume.

22.2 Market orientation and product orientation

This is an important distinction. Most businesses would today describe themselves as being 'market-oriented' or 'market-led'. This approach requires market research and market analysis to indicate present and future consumer demand. The consumer is put first – the business attempts to produce what consumers want rather than try to sell them a product they may not really want to buy. It has advantages, especially in fast-changing, volatile consumer markets. In these cases, increasing consumer awareness of competitors' products, prices and image can result in significant fluctuations in popularity of goods and services. The benefits of market orientation are threefold:

- The chances of newly developed products failing in the market are much reduced (but not eliminated) if effective market research has been undertaken first. With the huge cost of developing new products, such as cars or computers, this is a convincing argument for most businesses to use the market-oriented approach.
- If consumer needs are being met with appropriate products, then they are likely to survive longer and make higher profits than those that are being sold following a product-led approach.

- Constant feedback from consumers (market research never actually ends) will allow the product and how it is marketed to be adapted to changing tastes before it is too late and before competitors 'get there first'.

The days of traditional **product-oriented** businesses, which assume there will always be a market for the products they make, are fast disappearing. However, product-led marketing still exists to an extent and the following instances help to explain why:

- Product-oriented businesses invent and develop products in the belief that they will find consumers to purchase them. The development of the WAP mobile phone was driven more by technical innovation than by consumer needs – consumers were not aware that such versatile products were

likely to be made available until the basic concept had been invented and developed into an innovative new product. Pure research in this form is rare but still exists, for example in pharmaceutical and electronic industries. Here there is still the belief that if they produce an innovative product of a good enough quality, then it will be purchased.

> ### KEY TERM
>
> **product orientation:** an inward-looking approach that focuses on making products that can be made – or have been made for a long time – and then trying to sell them

CASE STUDY 22.1

Xiaomi launches its first foldable phone and enters the market to take on Samsung

The smartphone manufacturer Xiaomi has launched its first foldable phone as it looks to increase its share of the premium mobile phone market. Xiaomi is seeing a rapid increase in sales with 31% growth in revenues. The business is now third behind Apple and Samsung in the mobile phone market with a market share of 11.1%.

Its latest foldable phone model has as an 8.01 inch display when fully open and it has a screen on the back when closed. The phone also has a state-of-the-art camera on the Mi 11 Ultra with its low-light photography and powerful zoom, which makes it one of the best phone cameras in the market.

The key to Xiaomi's success is effective marketing of its foldable phone. Xiaomi has used extensive market research during the process and has looked to develop a product that consumers really want to buy. It hopes this market-orientated approach is going to further grow its revenues and market share.

Xiaomi has tried to develop a sustainable strategy for its products with the aim to 'Develop hand in hand with customers and act responsibly to environment and products'. The business wants to

use circular concepts in product design to minimise environmental impact.

1. Define the term 'marketing'. [2]

2. Outline how Xiaomi has adopted a market-orientated approach to marketing its foldable smartphone. [4]

3. Explain why Xiaomi might have made sustainability part of its marketing strategy. [4]

4. Explain **two** weaknesses of Xiaomi using a market-orientated approach to marketing its foldable smartphones. [4]

- Product-oriented businesses concentrate their efforts on efficiently producing high-quality goods. They believe quality will be valued above market fashion. Such quality-driven firms still do exist, especially in product areas where quality or safety is of great importance, such as bottled-water plants or the manufacture of crash helmets.

Evaluation of these two approaches

The trend then is towards market orientation, but there are limitations. If a business attempts to respond to every passing consumer trend or market fashion, then it may well overstretch its resources and end up not doing anything particularly well. Trying to offer choice and range so that every consumer need is met can be expensive. In contrast, researching and developing an innovative product can be successful, even if there has been no formal market research – consider Dyson's hugely profitable cyclone vacuum cleaner for example.

ACTIVITY 22.3

Market orientation and product orientation in your school

Think about your school and whether it is market orientated or product orientated. In pairs or as a group discuss the aspects of your school activities which are market orientated and which aspects are product orientated. Do you think your school has got the balance right to market itself successfully?

22.3 Market share

This is an important relative measure of the success of a business against its competitors.

Market share is calculated by the following formula:

KEY FORMULA

$$\text{market share \%} = \frac{\text{sales of business in time period}}{\text{total market sales in time period}} \times 100$$

'Sales of business' and 'total market sales' can be measured in either units (volume) or sales value in this market. Market share, and increases in it, is often the most effective way to measure the relative success of one business's marketing strategy against that of its competitors. If market share is increasing, then the marketing of that business's products has been relatively more successful than most of its competitors.

The main reasons for a business being able to increase its market share are:

- lower prices than those of competitors
- better customer service leading to high levels of customer satisfaction
- innovations in product or customer service which have not yet been matched by competitors
- selling through new channels to reach more consumers
- increasing customer loyalty and encouraging these existing customers to buy more.

ACTIVITY 22.4

The following data represents the total revenues of the two largest firms in the budget airline industry in a country: Airline A $5.5 million, Airline B $3.7 million. Total market sales in the budget airline industry is $12.2 million.

1 Define the term 'market share'.

2 Calculate the market shares of Airline A and Airline B.

3 Explain the benefits Airline A might have because of its market share.

Market leadership

The product with the highest market share is called the 'brand leader'. Why might it be important for a brand or a manufacturer to have **market leadership** in this way?

KEY TERM

market leadership: when a business has the highest market share of all firms that operate in that market

---

22.4 Market growth

Market growth measures how rapidly a market is growing from one time period to the next. If total market sales last year were $500 million and this year they reached $600 million then the market has grown by 20%.

KEY TERM

market growth: the percentage change in the total size of a market (volume or value) over a period of time

---

KEY FORMULA

$$\text{annual market growth \%} = \frac{(\text{total market sales this year} - \text{total market sales last year})}{\text{total market sales last year}} \times 100$$

The main reasons why a market experiences growth are:

- technologically advanced products that appeal to a wider market

- increasing customer incomes in most of the countries where the products are sold

- increasing size of countries' populations which leads to increasing numbers of potential consumers

- international trade agreements which lower barriers to trade between countries

- legal changes – such as bans on petrol and diesel cars leading to increasing sales of electric vehicles

- consumer tastes changing towards the products being sold, e.g., trend towards buying organic and vegan food products.

The benefits to a business of operating in a growing market are based around the ability to increase sales without having to take market share from competitors. As the overall size of the market is growing, theoretically *all* businesses in the market could increase sales. However, if the sales of a business increase at a slower rate than overall market sales, then the market share of that business will decline. This might make the business vulnerable to a takeover from a larger and more competitive business.

If total market sales are falling over time then market growth is negative. This must mean that if a business is to avoid its own sales from falling, it must gain market share at the expense of its rivals.

22.5 Market share and market leadership

Market share is an important measure of business performance – especially relative performance as compared with rival companies. There are many 'internal' measures of marketing success such as customer satisfaction, brand awareness, loyalty and profit margins, but market share can be benchmarked against the competition. Other reasons why market leadership through having the highest market share is important are:

- Being 'market leader' with the highest market share can be used in advertising and promotional material. 'This is the most popular product in the market' can be a convincing argument influencing more consumers to buy it. Most consumers want to be associated with popular products.

- Market leaders are in a strong bargaining position with both suppliers and retailers. Suppliers will want to continue with long-term supply contracts with the most successful business in the market. This will help suppliers achieve high sales, and their reputation and status will be improved as a result of being a supplier to the biggest business in the industry. Market leaders are therefore in a strong bargaining position and might obtain special discounts on supplies.

- Retailers will be keen to stock the market-leading product as consumers would be disappointed not to find it in their stores. These strong bargaining positions could lead to lower costs and longer credit periods from suppliers as well as higher selling prices to, and shorter payment periods from, retailers.

- Recruitment of high-class employees is often easier for market-leading businesses as people would rather work for 'winners' than less-successful businesses.

- Financing might become easier if investors and banks become convinced that the status of being market leader with the highest market share adds to the stability and profit potential of the business.

However, aiming to become market leader can have some negative effects on a business too:

- It can put pressure on a business and key employees to continue to increase sales and to maintain market leadership once this is reached. The business media will look for any sign of slippage in position and will quickly report that a business is losing market share and, possibly, losing touch with its consumers.

- If too much emphasis is placed on market share then it could take attention away from profitability. Price cuts and lower profit margins are one way of increasing market share – but is this strategy financially sustainable in the longer term? The reasons why a business is market leader need to be assessed carefully before stakeholders can conclude that the business really does have a winning formula rather than just a 'sell-it-cheap-to-increase-share' strategy.

- In many countries, governments impose regulations and controls on businesses that have a dominant market leadership with a high market share. Governments often fear that this market dominance will lead to higher prices to consumers as a result of low competition. In addition, there will also be concern that businesses with a near monopoly position will exploit smaller, weaker supplier businesses.

- Relatively small businesses – perhaps family owned or sole trader businesses – might have no plans to become market leader as aiming to increase sales at all costs might conflict with other objectives such as retaining control of the business or focusing on quality goods or quality customer service.

CASE STUDY 22.2

The US TV news market

The US television market if dominated by three major news networks Fox News, CNN and MSNBC. Cable news is a growing market and annual revenues have increased by over 200% since 2007. The total market revenues in 2022 stand at nearly $6 billion. News coverage is profitable because it draws in significant revenues from customer subscriptions and advertising sales. There are concerns that news coverage being dominated by a small number of businesses is open to bias and has too much influence on the views of the people who watch the news channels.

1 Define the term 'market growth'. [2]

2 Outline two ways market growth can be measured in the TV news market. [4]

3 Explain two reasons why the TV news market in the USA might be growing. [4]

4 Evaluate the disadvantages of news coverage being dominated by three companies. [10]

TIP

It is very important to understand that market share can fall even when sales of the business are increasing. This is because, if the total market sales are increasing at a faster rate than one firm's sales, the market share will fall.

CASE STUDY 22.3

Sales of electric vehicles in Norway

All countries are experiencing market growth in electric vehicles (EVs) but the rise in EV sales in Norway that is particularly striking. Norway is the first nation where sales of EVs have overtaken sales of petrol and diesel vehicles. Total sales in the Norwegian car market are $3.2 billion and EVs have taken 54% of this market, up from 42% on the previous year.

Volkswagen is the EV market leader in Norway with sales of $0.71 billion in the EV market. Tesla is second with sales of $0.68 billion and BMW is third with sales of $0.59 billion.

The Norwegian government has committed to phasing out the sale of petrol and diesel cars by 2025 and the data that has been released on electric vehicle sales suggests the country is well on the way to achieving this target. Indeed, when you add hybrid sales to EVs the total market sales is 89%.

The political, economic and technological environment in Norway has created a business environment that has driven the growth of the EV market. While government policy has encouraged EV market growth, it is demand from environmentally conscious Norwegian consumers that has really affected the EV market.

1   Define the term 'market share'.   [2]

2   Using the information in the text calculate Volkswagen's market share of Norway's electric vehicle market.   [2]

3   Define the term 'market leadership'.   [2]

4   Explain two benefits to Volkswagen of being the market leader in Norway's EV market.   [4]

LEARNER PROFILE

Principled

Philip Morris International (PMI) is one of the largest tobacco firms in the world, producing five of the world's top 15 cigarette brands. It has a workforce of over 71 000 around the world. There are a large number of senior roles working for PMI.

Discuss in pairs or a group whether you would ever work for a business that marketed a product like cigarettes.

SELF-EVALUATION CHECKLIST

After studying this chapter, complete this table.

I am able to apply and analyse:	Needs more work	Almost there	Ready to move on
market orientation versus product orientation (AO2)			
market share (AO2)			
market growth (AO2)			
I am able to synthesise and evaluate:			
the importance of market share and market leadership (AO3)			
I am able to use and apply:			
market share (AO4)			
market growth (AO4)			

REFLECTION

Do you think all businesses manufacturing mobile phones should aim to increase market share to gain market leadership? Explain your answer. Compare your conclusions with those of other learners.

PROJECT

The sports goods business Nike is an example of a market-oriented company. As it has grown and developed, it has consistently added processes and features that clearly address concerns and desires expressed by its consumers.

Marketing-oriented companies are vibrant, communicative businesses that look for ways to understand what their customers want and create products specifically designed for those customers. Making sure there is a demand for their products and services is one of the most important elements of a marketing-oriented company.

A company using market orientation invests huge amounts to time researching current trends in a given market. Nike, for example, engages in market orientation. It will research what consumers most want and need in sports goods rather than producing products that are meant to follow the trends of other manufacturers.

In pairs or as a group, produce a presentation on how you would research the training shoe market for Nike to find out:

- how consumers use their training shoes
- what are the most important features that consumers look for in their training shoes
- how much consumers are willing to pay for training shoes
- where consumers like to buy their training shoes.

Thinking about your project:

- Once you have completed your presentation, do you feel your understanding of market orientation has improved?
- How good was your presentation compared to those of the other groups in the class?
- How could you improve your presentation?

EXAM PRACTICE QUESTIONS

Marketing desserts

M&C Desserts was one of the most successful producers in its market in 2012. This medium-sized family business was a leading producer of desserts in its region supplying supermarkets, smaller shops, restaurant and catering businesses. Its product range includes cheesecakes, hot puddings and mousses. M&C's products are seen as good quality, but there are new competitors in the market whose products are seen as premium quality. Although the competition's products are over 20% more expensive, they have taken market share away from M&C, particularly amongst higher income consumers and buyers in the 25–35 age group.

M&C has been criticised for being too product orientated and its management believes the business needs to adopt a more product-orientated marketing strategy. One area of concern for M&C is the growing awareness in society about food that has excess fat and the implication this has for obesity. To deal with this issue M&C has launched a reduced sugar and fat range, and consumption of these items is being promoted as part of a balanced diet.

1	Define the term 'market orientation'.	[2]
2	State the equation to measure market share.	[2]
3	Outline how M&C could become more product orientated.	[2]
4	Define the term 'market leader'.	[2]
5	Identify **two** benefits of M&C becoming a market leader.	[2]
6	Explain **two** ways M&C could increase its market share.	[4]
7	Outline how market growth is measured.	[2]
8	Describe **two** ways that M&C tries to differentiate its products.	[4]
9	Outline the difference between market share and growth in the dessert market.	[4]
10	Evaluate the view that M&C desserts should become more market orientated in order to increase the sales.	[10]

> Chapter 23

Marketing planning

LEARNING OBJECTIVES

On completing this chapter you should be able to:

Apply and analyse:

- The role of marketing planning (AO2)
- Segmentation, targeting (target market) and positioning (position maps) (AO2)
- The difference between niche market and mass market (AO2)
- The importance of having a unique selling point/proposition (USP) (AO2)

Synthesise and evaluate:

- How organisations can differentiate themselves and their products from competitors (AO3)

Use and apply:

- Segmentation, targeting (target market) and positioning (position maps) (AO4)

Select and apply the business management tools:

- Boston Consulting Group (BCG) Matrix

> Porter's generic strategies

BUSINESS IN CONTEXT

Marketing planning for the iPhone never ends

One of the most influential years for smartphone evolution was 2007. It was the year Apple revealed the very first iPhone. It was the smartest and slimmest touch screen device to hit the market and the first mobile that offered fully accessible internet via a touchscreen. Apple's mission has always been to lead the industry in innovative products that are very different from competitors' products. Its constant search for **unique selling points (USPs)** paid off with the original iPhone. It was a marketing sensation and it achieved all of the initial marketing objectives set for it, including:

- 2% market share in the USA and UK in the first year after launch (445 000 sales)

- 10% market share in the second year after launch

- 50% market share three years after launch.

The overall marketing strategy was, and remains, to differentiate the iPhone from other mobile phones. Apple aims at the primary **target market** of the upper-middle-class professional. Other, less-advanced versions of the iPhone, are targeted at other **market segments**. Pricing of the original iPhone was premium penetration for the first few months – and then it was reduced to establish quick market dominance.

Apple works hard to get each new version of the iPhone the reception it deserves, and apart from the traditional promotion media, there is now a much greater emphasis on social media promotions. The Apple CEO combines paid Twitter promotions with his own active promotion of the latest iPhone through his own Twitter account. This gets Apple fans and followers involved on one of the social media networks which arguably provides the best real-time engagement.

Constant market research is undertaken to make sure the promotion strategy is getting through to the target market.

Apple uses several sales channels including its website, company-branded stores, authorised sales partners and other e-commerce websites in various markets including Amazon and Flipkart. Its own website and retail stores play a central role in the distribution and sales of Apple products, including iPhones, around the world.

The iPhone continues to be a major player in the global smartphone market despite the rise of competitors such as Samsung and Huawei. Apple continues to focus on effective **marketing planning** to try to maintain or increase the global market share it has gained in recent years of between 21% and 23%.

Discuss in pairs or a group:

- Why is it important to set marketing objectives when planning to market a new product?

- How important is it to have a 'target market' when planning marketing?

- In your own experience of mobile phones, how successful is Apple in differentiating its products from those of competitors?

KEY TERMS

unique selling point (USP): the special feature of a product or customer service that makes it different from those of competitors.

target market: the segment of the market that a particular product is aimed at

market segment: a sub-group of a market made up of consumers with similar characteristics, tastes and preferences

marketing planning: the process of developing appropriate strategies and preparing marketing activities to meet marketing objectives

23.1 The role of marketing planning

A market plan is a formal written document which outlines in detail how the business unit intends to achieve the marketing objectives derived from the overall business objectives. Effective marketing planning is nearly always based on clear awareness of market trends, competitors' actions and consumer wants, so market research is vital.

The main elements of a marketing plan are:

- details of the company's (SMART) marketing objectives, e.g., increasing market share from 7.5% to 10% in three years
- sales forecasts to allow the progress of the plan to be monitored, e.g., the total market is forecast to have an annual growth rate of 2%
- marketing budget – how much finance the business plans to spend and how it is to be allocated e.g., $5 million per year on promotion and other marketing activities
- marketing strategies to be adopted to achieve the marketing objectives, e.g., use segmentation to develop products for different groups of consumers
- detailed action plans showing the marketing tactics to be used to implement the strategies, e.g., set prices for each product just below the average of competitors' prices in each segment.

A marketing plan is an essential component of any successful marketing campaign. Successful marketing does not just 'happen', it has to be planned and prepared for.

Table 23.1 shows the roles and limitations of marketing plans.

23.2 Segmentation, targeting and positioning

Very few markets are made up of consumers who want exactly the same type and design of product. Even the market for petrol for vehicles comprises consumers who want the lowest-price fuel and those prepared to pay more for 'premium' petrol with extra additives. Groups of consumers with similar tastes and characteristics are called market segments. If a business adopts only mass marketing (see 23.3) then it is not important to differentiate between market segments as the 'whole market' is being targeted with the same product. In the case of most businesses, attempts are made to aim their products at particular groups of consumers, believing that these groups demand slightly different products or 'offerings'. This is the process of 'segmentation'.

The first stage in the **market segmentation** process is to research the whole market and identify specific consumer groups within it. The individuals in a particular market segment respond to trends and market forces in similar ways and require similar products. Identifying the key segments and directing marketing activities towards them is the key to successful segmentation.

KEY TERM

market segmentation: identifying different segments within a market and targeting different products or services to them

Roles	Limitations
Marketing plans provide focus to the work of the marketing department and a 'road map' of the stages to be taken in implementing marketing strategies.	Marketing plans that are not revised to meet changing internal or external conditions – such as the arrival of new competitors – will become outdated.
Effective marketing planning will ensure that marketing strategies and tactics are linked to SMART objectives. This will increase the likelihood of the marketing campaign's success.	Marketing planning must be a constant process. An old plan will be ineffective when market conditions change. They need to be reviewed constantly and the final outcome of the planned strategy must be judged against the original objectives to aid future decision-making.
The marketing budget will be planned in advance with the finance department and should be adequate to achieve the campaign's objectives.	Marketing plans need to be based on an up-to-date assessment of the market and consumer preferences or it will be inappropriate for current conditions.
Marketing planning helps achieve the integration of different business functions as all departments will need to be involved in the planning process.	
Planning marketing ahead helps to ensure that the marketing mix (see Chapter 26) is appropriate and fully integrated.	

Table 23.1: Marketing plans – roles and limitations

In the clothing market, children make up one segment; males can be part of another segment while females form another segment. The 'youth clothing segment' could be further segmented into students and those in employment.

Once the market segments have been identified then businesses must decide which of these segments are going to become target markets. This is the key difference between these two concepts – target markets are the market segments that the business plans to aim its product at. A clothing business does not have to target all segments in the clothing industry. It might decide to target only males or females, the youth market segment, or more 'mature' consumers. Each target market will require its own marketing strategy and promotion mix.

Here are some examples of market segmentation:

- Computer manufacturers, such as Dell, produce PCs for office and home use, including games, but they also make laptop models for business people who travel.
- Coca-Cola not only makes the standard cola drink but also Diet Coke for slimmers, and flavoured drinks for consumers with particular tastes.
- Renault, the car maker, produces several versions of its Mégane model, such as a coupé, saloon, convertible and 'people carrier' – all appealing to different groups of consumers.

Sometimes businesses only market their goods or services to one segment and deliberately do not aim to satisfy other segments. Gap is a clothing retailer that aims only at the youth market; Nike shoes are intended for sports use; and Coutts Bank only offers banking services to the seriously rich. These businesses make a virtue out of concentrating on one segment and developing an image and brand that suits that segment.

Successful segmentation requires a business to have a very clear picture of the consumers in the target market it is aiming to sell in. This is called the consumer profile. The main characteristics of consumers contained in a consumer profile are income levels, age, gender, social class and region. Marketing decisions, such as price and types of promotion, need to be appropriate for the

KEY TERMS

marketing mix: the key decisions that must be taken in the effective marketing of a product

consumer profile: a quantified picture of consumers of a firm's products, showing proportions of age groups, income levels, location, gender and social class

consumer profile of the target market. A well-targeted product will need less advertising and promotional support than one which does not really meet the needs of the consumers it is aimed at.

Markets may be segmented in a number of different ways. The three commonly used bases for segmentation are as follows.

Geographic differences

Consumer tastes may vary between different geographic areas, for example the need for warmer clothing in Northern Europe compared to South-East Asia. So it may be appropriate to offer different products and market them in 'location-specific' ways.

ACTIVITY 23.1

In pairs or in groups, write a list of ten restaurants you know. This can be major chain restaurants such as McDonald's or a local independent restaurant. Prepare a product position map using restaurant price and restaurant quality. On your map, plot where you think each of your restaurants is on the product position map.

Prepare a presentation in your pair or group showing how you positioned your restaurants on your product position map.

CASE STUDY 23.1

Market segmentation at Louis Vuitton

Moët Hennessy Louis Vuitton (LVMH) is one of the most recognisable luxury brands in the world. The business also markets itself through a number of subsidiary brands such as Christian Dior, Givenchy, Stella McCartney and Bulgari.

A market research consultancy produced the following profile for a typical Louis Vuitton customer:

- women aged 35–54

- top 5% income group

- college educated

- fashion conscious

- status conscious.

1   Outline the difference between geographic market segmentation and demographic market segmentation.   [4]

2   Explain how profile of the typical Louis Vuitton customer might affect the price and place elements of the LVHM marketing mix.   [4]

3   Using a product position map based on quality and price illustrate where LVHM products would be positioned.   [2]

4   Discuss the usefulness of market segmentation to LVHM.   [10]

THEORY OF KNOWLEDGE

Challenges to the marketing of luxury goods: intuition and emotion

In 2020 the luxury goods market suffered major challenges all over the world. It experienced a $79 billion decline in sales – nearly a quarter of its market.

Much of the decline was due to consumers of luxury goods spending an extended period of time at home during the Covid-19 pandemic, with few opportunities to go shopping. Luxury brands had to use e-commerce as their only viable way of reaching their customers.

In pairs or as a group discuss the following questions.

- What is the role of intuition in making ethical judgements about the marketing of luxury goods?
- What role does emotion play in the way we feel about the success or failure of marketing luxury goods?

Demographic differences

These are the most commonly used basis for segmentation as age, sex, family size and ethnic background can all be used to separate markets. A house construction firm will use demographic data to help determine which segment of the market a new block of apartments should be aimed at. Should they be retirement flats with a resident caretaker? Should they be small studio flats for young, single people? Should they offer large reception rooms that will appeal to extended families? The construction firm may not attempt to attract all market segments – but having decided on the most appropriate one, it will be essential to gear the price and promotion strategies towards that segment.

An individual's social class may have a big impact on their expenditure patterns. This will be largely due to income differences between various classes of employment. The wealthy will have very different consumption patterns from the working class. The jobs people do are one of the main factors that influence people's income levels; however, other forces apart from income levels could also be a factor. For instance, top professional groups would be expected to spend more money on, say, power boating and golfing, as these tend to be class-related activities.

Many marketing acronyms exist as abbreviations for different demographic groups of consumers. Here are just three:

- DINKY – double income no kids yet
- NILK – no income lots of kids
- WOOF – well-off older folk.

LEARNER PROFILE

Memory and emotion

The nostalgia behind historic brands and trends has an impact in many consumer markets. Whether its vinyl records, the Mini car, the Instamatic Camera or Adidas Original trainers, many businesses have tried to draw on the successful brands of 30 or 40 years ago.

Studies suggest that nostalgia encourages consumers to spend their money by promising an immediate return in the form of happy memories. The reason why retro marketing has become increasingly popular is the linking of the brand and the customer at a deeper, emotional level. Along with emotional attachment, products like vinyl records draw on the positive memories many older consumers have of them.

In pairs or as a group, discuss a product you bought some years ago and talk about the strength of emotion and memory that affects your current view of the product.

Psychographic factors

These are to do with differences between people's lifestyles, personalities, values and attitudes. Lifestyle is a very broad term which often relates to activities undertaken, interests and opinions rather than personality. The huge increase in TV channels and TV viewing in many countries has contributed to the growth of 'TV dinners', which are pre-prepared meals that are quickly ready to eat so that the consumer does not miss any of their favourite programmes.

Table 23.2 summarises the advantages and limitations of market segmentation.

Advantages	Limitations
Businesses can define their target market precisely and design and produce goods that are specifically aimed at these groups, leading to increased sales.	Research and development and production costs might be high as a result of marketing several different product variations.
It helps to identify gaps in the market – groups of consumers that are not currently being targeted – and these might then be successfully exploited.	Promotional costs might be high as different advertisements and promotions might be needed for different segments – marketing economies of scale may not be fully exploited.
Differentiated marketing strategies can be focused on target market groups. This avoids wasting money on trying to sell products to the whole market – some consumer groups will have no intention of buying the product.	Production and stock-holding costs might be higher than for the option of just producing and stocking one undifferentiated product.
Small firms unable to compete in the whole market are able to specialise in one or two market segments.	By focusing on one or two limited market segments there is a danger that excessive specialisation could lead to problems if consumers in those segments change their purchasing habits significantly.

Table 23.2: Market segmentation – advantages and limitations

Product positioning

Once a market has been segmented and target markets identified, a business has to 'position' its product. Before deciding on which product to develop and launch, it is common for businesses to analyse how the new brand will relate to the other brands in the market, in the minds of consumers. This is called 'production positioning' and is often illustrated with a product position map. Once completed, the map allows the business to identify how competitors are positioned relative to its own products and to identify opportunities in the marketplace.

The first stage in preparing the product position map or product perception map is to identify the features of this type of product that are considered to be important to consumers – as established by market research. These key features might be price, perceived quality, perceived brand image, level of comfort offered (hotels) and customer service levels. They will be different for each product category, but the two attributes to be used must be chosen carefully to reflect the main factors influencing consumer decisions.

The second stage, based on qualitative market research, is to position each of the competing products on the graph according to consumers' perceptions of them.

Figure 23.1 illustrates the main cola products of Coca-Cola and PepsiCo and estimated consumer perceptions of each brand. The completed product position map uses two product attributes:

- male/female consumers
- sugar level/calories.

The chart suggests that there might be a market gap for a soft drink with high calories aimed at female consumers. However, neither company plans to offer new brands in this sector. Can you suggest why that is?

Both companies frequently introduce new products which are positioned to take advantage of what might be gaps in the existing market coverage. In 2021 PepsiCo brought out a limited edition cocoa flavoured cola (Cocoa Cola) which was looking to break into the market for people who want 'a delicious blend of cocoa (and hint of marshmallow!) mixed with Pepsi cola.' In 2019 Coca-Cola's new drink was 'Zero Raspberry' with no added sugar. According to Ana Amura, marketing manager at Coca-Cola Great Britain: 'We know how much our fans

> **KEY TERMS**
>
> **production positioning:** the process of designing the company's products and image to occupy a distinctive place in the perceptions of consumers in the target market
>
> **product position map or perception map:** a diagram that analyses consumer perceptions of competing brands in respect of two product characteristics

love new flavours and we're really excited to add Coca-Cola zero sugar Raspberry to the line-up.' Both Pepsi and Coke introduced mid-calorie colas back in 2001; Pepsi Edge was the original brand. However, due to slow sales, the product was taken off the market after five years.

A second example of a position map is shown in Figure 23.2.

Product-positioning analysis could be used in a number of ways:

- It identifies potential gaps in the market. This could be the segment that the business should aim for. Alternatively, the business could play safe and position the new product with others – this is likely to be less risky but could be less profitable too.

- Having identified the sector with the greatest 'niche' potential, the marketing manager is then made aware of the key feature(s) of the product that should be promoted most heavily.

Coca-Cola product line		Pepsi product line	
Coca-Cola		Pepsi	
Coca-Cola C2		Pepsi Max	
Diet Coke		Diet Pepsi	
Coca-Cola Zero		Pepsi One	

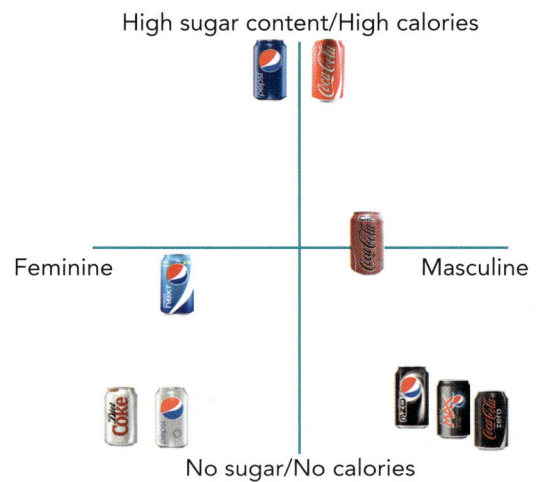

Figure 23.1: Product positioning of well-known cola drinks

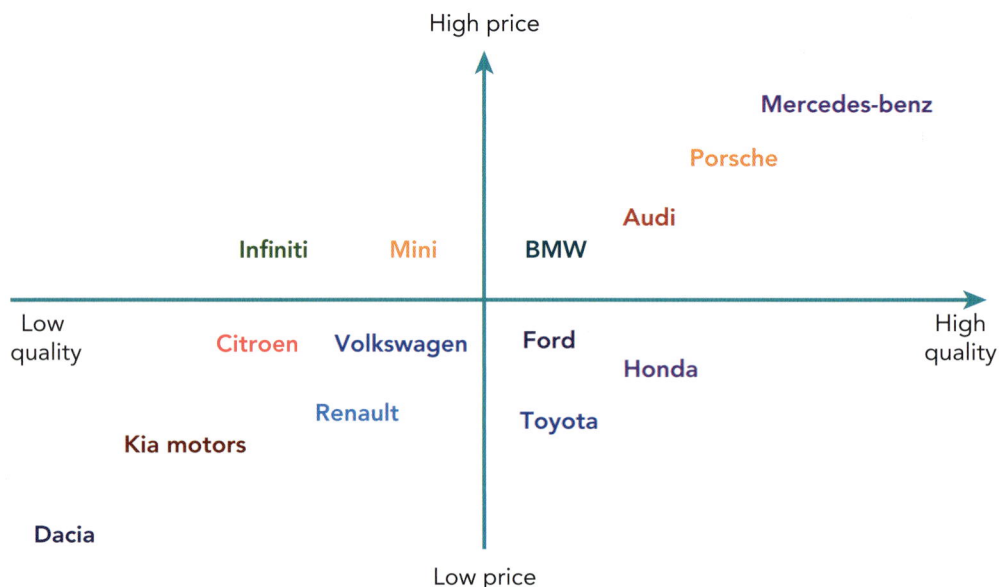

Figure 23.2: Position map for some brands of cars

ACTIVITY 23.2

An ice cream manufacturer markets the brands in the table. Draw a product position map and mark each brand on the chart in the correct location.

	Price 500 ml	Quality
Vanilla cup	1.89	Basic
Café latte	3.49	Medium
Strawberries and cream	3.49	Medium
Salted caramel	4.49	High
Chocolate cup	1.99	Basic

• Lastly, when this analysis is used to monitor the position of existing brands a marketing manager can easily see if a repositioning of one of them is required. This could involve a new advertising campaign or restyled packaging rather than a newly launched product.

23.3 Difference between niche market and mass market

Niche marketing can involve targeting products at a very small section of the whole market, and it may be one that has not yet been identified and filled by competitors. Examples of firms employing niche marketing include Versace fashion designs and Clinique perfumes. Both of these businesses sell only expensive, high-status products. Other niche markets exist for non-luxury products, such as 'extreme sports' clothing and '$-stretcher' retail shops that only sell very cheap items, attracting a low-income segment of the market.

Mass marketing is the exact opposite. 'One product for the whole market' is now becoming quite an unusual concept for firms to adopt, but it is still seen in, for example, the toothpaste and fizzy drinks markets. Hoover, the vacuum-cleaner manufacturer, used to sell a very limited range of products as most consumers wanted just a simple and effective cleaner. Now, with increased consumer choice and more competitors operating in the market, Hoover offers a much wider range of models of different sizes, power output and prices to appeal to different segments of the mass market.

KEY TERMS

niche marketing: identifying and exploiting a small segment of a larger market by developing products to suit it

niche market: a small and specific part of a larger market

mass marketing: selling the same products to the whole market with no attempt to target groups within it

mass market: a market for products that are often standardised and sold in large quantities

ACTIVITY 23.3

Niche marketing an environmentally friendly product

Bee's Wrap is an eco-friendly, reusable alternative to modern food wrap such as clingfilm and foil. Bee's Wrap is made from an organic muslin cloth steeped in beeswax, jojoba oil and tree resin. It comes in a variety of sizes and can be used to cover a food items such as sandwiches, fruit and vegetables, and cheese. The product avoids all of the downsides of using plastic wraps and it comes at a low price.

Working in pairs or as a group, research another sustainable niche product. Prepare a short video clip (maximum one minute) to promote your sustainable product.

Advantages of niche marketing	Advantages of mass marketing
Small firms may be able to survive and thrive in markets that are dominated by larger firms. If the market is currently unexploited by competitors, then filling a niche can offer the chance to sell at high prices and high profit margins – until the competitors react by entering too. Consumers will often pay more for an exclusive product. Niche market products can also be used by large firms to create status and image – their mass-market products may lack these qualities. **Note:** these can also be viewed as the disadvantages of mass marketing.	Small-market niches do not allow economies of scale to be achieved. Therefore, mass-market businesses are likely to enjoy substantially lower average costs of production. Mass-market strategies run fewer risks than niche strategies. As niche markets contain relatively small numbers of consumers, any change in consumer buying habits could lead to a rapid decline in sales. This is a particular problem for small firms operating in only one niche market with one product. **Note:** these can also be viewed as the disadvantages of niche marketing.

Table 23.3: Advantages of niche marketing and mass marketing

So, although it is not true niche marketing, the company is recognising the limits of pure mass marketing.

Both types of marketing – niche and mass – have their advantages, as outlined in Table 23.3.

23.4 Unique selling point/proposition (USP)

The most successful new products are those that are differentiated from competitors' products and offer something 'special'. Product differentiation can be an effective way of distancing a business from its rivals – the best form of product differentiation is one that creates a USP.

Examples of effective USPs include:

- FedEx – 'When it absolutely, positively has to be there overnight'.
- Dyson vacuum cleaners – 100% suction 100% of the time from bagless technology. Against all odds, the Dyson became the biggest-selling vacuum cleaner in Europe within four years, despite being an unknown name and costing more than competing products.
- Death Wish Coffee – 'The World's Strongest Coffee'. This USP instantly tells potential consumers that this coffee 'packs a punch' and is likely to taste very different from more mellow

coffee brands. Claiming to be the 'world's strongest' product in any category is a risky strategy. Death Wish Coffee supports its claim by using advertisements that show how the coffee is made and offering a full refund if consumers are not satisfied with its strength.

The benefits of an effective USP include:

- effective promotion which focuses on the differentiating feature of the product or service
- opportunities to charge higher prices due to exclusive design/service
- free publicity from business media reporting on the USP
- higher sales than undifferentiated products
- customers' willingness to be identified with the brand because 'it's different'.

USPs can be based on any aspect of the marketing mix. For example:

- **Product.** The TESLA electric car is now widely recognised as the best electrically driven car in the world. It incorporates a number of key patented innovations that make it faster and give it a longer range than other electric vehicles.
- **Price.** The Reject Shop group in Australia offers to match any competitors' prices for groceries 'less another 10%'. This, and other marketing strategies, contributed to profit increasing by 45% in the first six months of 2021.

CASE STUDY 23.2

Domino's unique selling point

Domino's Pizza is one of the most successful restaurant businesses in the world with a turnover of over $14 billion and a net profit of over $700 million. Many business analysts have focused on Domino's central unique selling points: 'Fresh, hot pizza delivered in 30 minutes or less, guaranteed.' This simple statement made by Domino's founder Tom Monaghan's made two crucial claims. He promised fresh, hot pizza delivered not quick, fast, or soon, but precisely in 30 minutes or less.

As a mass market product with a clear vision, Domino's continues its incredible growth with over 600 new outlets opening worldwide in 2021.

1 Define the term 'unique selling point'. [2]

2 Outline Domino's mass market approach to marketing its product. [4]

3 Explain why Domino's unique selling point might have been important in its marketing strategy. [4]

CASE STUDY 23.3

The impact of sustainability on marketing at H&M

H&M's new CEO Helena Helmersson doesn't believe that fast fashion should be a dirty word. 'Having people all over the world be able to express themselves through fashion and design – that should be something beautiful.'

One thing that's clear is that things can't go on as they are. The current system involves the production of more than 100 billion garments every year, with clothes being worn an average of just seven times before they're thrown away, according to one survey. Clothing production is not only an enormous drain on natural resources, but also hugely polluting, with the fashion industry as a whole contributing up to 10 per cent of global CO_2 emissions.

As part of its bid to become more eco-friendly, H&M has set a target of achieving 100 per cent recycled or other sustainably sourced materials by 2030, along with the ambitious goal of becoming climate positive by 2040. For Helmersson, it is the ultimate goal of moving to a 100 per cent circular model – one in which all products can be reused or fully decomposed – that's her main focus, although there's still a long way to go before that can be achieved.

1 Outline how ethics might have affected H&M's marketing objectives. [2]

2 Explain two advantages to H&M of setting a target of achieving the use of 100% recycled materials or other sustainably sourced materials by 2030. [4]

3 Explain two disadvantages for H&M of setting a target of achieving the use of 100% recycled materials or other sustainably sourced materials by 2030. [4]

- **Place.** Dell became the first computer manufacturer to focus almost exclusively on internet sales. Keeping its costs down allowed it to offer competitive prices.
- **Promotion.** 'When it absolutely, positively has to be there overnight' is one of the most famous promotional slogans of recent years (it relates to the FedEx courier service). It helped to establish in customers' minds the unique quality of service that this company claimed to offer.

23.5 Differentiation from competitors

In globalised markets with increasing competition, it is becoming increasingly important for businesses and their products to offer something substantially different to most of their competitors. This differentiation can take a number of different forms. The possible benefits and limitations of these are analysed in Table 23.4.

Form of differentiation	Benefits	Limitations
Low/lowest prices	Consumers have limited spending power. Low prices will always attract a high proportion of them towards the product.	Will total profit fall if the profit margin is reduced to very low levels? Do low prices integrate with the rest of the marketing mix? Could consumers perceive the product/brand to be of low quality too? Is quality image more important than low prices? Globalisation is increasing the number of low-priced products from low-cost countries, so effective differentiation on price is more difficult.
Trust	Customers are careful to spend their limited incomes wisely. They often research each purchase to make sure they're making a 'safe' decision. They want to buy from companies they trust and believe in. If a business successfully builds up customer relations based on trust, consumer loyalty will be high.	Trust is difficult for a newly formed business to establish, so other forms of differentiation might be necessary. Trust – and with it, company image – can be damaged by issues such as environmental disasters or a series of poor feedback on social media. It is always very difficult to re-establish trust.
Ethical stance	In some markets, consumers are very keen to support companies that adopt an ethical stance by purchasing their products. This ethical approach might lead to higher costs and prices, but some customers will 'pay the difference' because they share the company's values.	In some markets low prices are more important than ethical positions. A lack of genuine ethical position – rather than just an ethical promotion campaign, for example – could lead to a loss of trust if consumers discover that the business was really only adopting a misleading or false show of ethical behaviour.

Form of differentiation	Benefits	Limitations
Purchase convenience	Consumers' lack of time or dislike of the shopping experience means that more convenient ways to browse and purchase could create effective differentiation. Free delivery, click and collect, and streamlined online shopping processes are examples of convenient ways to shop.	These methods of 'convenient shopping' are now so widespread that it is difficult to gain true, long-lasting differentiation. If all businesses in the market offer online shopping, how can any one business differentiate the way it sells its products?
Innovation	If this is the result of research and development (R&D) that leads to patented products or processes, then it can be difficult for competitors to copy this form of differentiation. As with USPs it can lead to a reputation for innovative, cutting-edge products that can command premium prices.	R&D is an expensive and time-consuming process and does not always lead to successful innovative products. Constant development might be needed to stay ahead of competitors, so a business needs to continue to commit resources into developing innovative products that differentiate the business and its brands. The resources needed for successful R&D might be beyond many businesses.

Table 23.4: Forms of differentiation

23.6 Business management tools

Marketing planning has been studied by management analysts and several techniques have been developed to assist in the process. Two of these are analysed here.

Boston Consulting Group (BCG) matrix

This method of analysing the market standing of a firm's products and the product portfolio of a business was developed by the Boston Consulting Group. The **Boston Consulting Group (BCG) matrix** highlights the position of the products of a business when measured by market share and market growth (see Figure 23.3).

The Boston matrix allows an analysis, not only of the existing product portfolio, but also of what future marketing strategies the business could take next. The size of each circle on the matrix represents the total revenue earnt by each product. The four sectors created by the matrix can be analysed in the following ways.

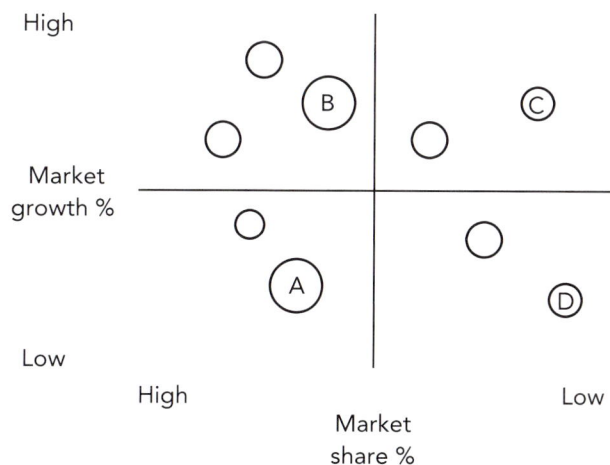

Figure 23.3: The Boston Consulting Group matrix

- **Low market growth – high market share: product A, cash cow.** This is a well-established product in a mature market. Typically, this type of product is profitable and creates a high positive cash flow. Sales are high relative to the market, and promotional costs are likely to be low as a result of high consumer awareness. The cash from this product can be 'milked' and injected into some of the other products in the portfolio. Hence, this product is often referred to as a cash cow. The business will want to maintain cash cows for as long as possible.

- **High market growth – high market share: product B, star.** This is clearly a successful product as it is performing well in an expanding market. It is often referred to as a star. The business will be keen to maintain the market position of this product in what may be a fast-changing market. Therefore, promotion costs will be high to help differentiate the product and reinforce its brand image. Despite these costs, a star is likely to generate high amounts of income.

- **High market growth – low market share: product C, question mark.** The question mark consumes resources but generates little return. If it is a newly launched product, it is going to need heavy promotion costs to help become established. This finance could come from the cash cow. The future of the product may be uncertain, so quick decisions may need to be taken if sales do not improve. These could include revising the design, relaunching with a new brand image or even withdrawal from the market. However, it should have potential as it is selling in a market sector that is growing fast.

- **Low market growth – low market share: product D, dog.** The dog seems to offer little to the business either in terms of existing sales and cash flow or future prospects because the market is not growing. It may need to be replaced soon with a new product development. The business could decide to withdraw from this market sector altogether and position itself into faster-growing sectors.

Impact of Boston matrix analysis on marketing planning

This analytical tool has relevance when:

- analysing the performance and current position of existing product portfolios
- deciding on what action to be taken with existing products
- planning for the introduction of new products.

By identifying the position of all products of the business, a full analysis of the portfolio is possible. This should help the business to focus on which products need marketing support or which need corrective action. This action could include the following marketing decisions:

- **Building** – supporting question-mark products with additional advertising or further distribution outlets. The finance for this could be obtained from the established cash cow products.

- **Holding** – continuing support for star products so that they maintain their good market position. Work may be needed to freshen the product in the eyes of the consumers so that high sales growth can be sustained.

- **Milking** – taking the positive cash flow from established products and investing it in other products in the portfolio.

- **Divesting** – identifying the worst-performing dogs and stopping the production and supply of these. This strategic decision should not be taken lightly as it will involve other issues, such as the impact on the workforce and whether the spare capacity freed up by stopping production can be used profitably on another product.

These strategies can only be undertaken if the business has a balanced portfolio of products. If there are too many dogs or question marks, then the overall shortage of cash may not allow the firm to take appropriate action.

Limitations of using the Boston matrix for marketing planning

No technique can guarantee business success. This will depend on the accuracy of the marketing managers' analysis and their skills in developing marketing plans and making marketing decisions. The Boston matrix helps to establish the current situation of the firm's products, but it is of little use in predicting future success or failure.

- On its own the Boston matrix cannot tell a manager what will happen next with any product. Detailed and continuous market research will help. However, at all times decision-makers must be conscious of the potentially dramatic effects of competitors' decisions, technological changes and the fluctuating economic environment.

- The Boston matrix is only a planning tool, and it has been criticised for simplifying the complex set of factors that determine product success.
- The Boston matrix assumes that higher rates of profit are directly related to high market shares. This is not necessarily the case when sales are being gained by reducing prices and profit margins.

CASE STUDY 23.4

Sintel markets online computer games. The company is based in Uruguay and is five years old. The company's turnover has reached $14 million and its net profit was $3.5 million. This is a young growing company that sees sales growth as a key objective. Sintel has four games and their market growth and market share are set out in the table.

	Market share	Market growth
Alien destructor	High	High
Battle star	Low	High
Deep sea	High	Low
Law enforcement	Low	Low

1 Outline what the Boston matrix shows. **[4]**

2 Draw a Boston matrix diagram and show where each of Sintel's products is in the matrix. **[4]**

3 Explain two ways the Boston matrix might be useful to Sintel in achieving its sales growth objective. **[4]**

TIP

If you are asked to discuss the usefulness of the Boston matrix for marketing decisions, remember that it does not provide strategic choices for a business. Explain that it analyses a business's product portfolio and highlights those products that might need strategic action to be taken.

Porter's generic strategies

Michael Porter is a well-known academic who has undertaken extensive research into the development of business strategies. Much of his work focuses on how business might be able to gain a long-term **competitive advantage** over its rivals.

KEY TERM

competitive advantage: an advantage that a business has over rivals gained by offering consumers greater value, either with low prices or by providing greater benefits and service to justify a higher price

Porter suggested four 'generic' business strategies that could be adopted in order to gain competitive advantage. The strategies relate to the extent to which the scope of a business's activities are narrowly or broadly focused, and the extent to which a business seeks to differentiate its products.

Porter referred to the four strategies with these titles (see Figure 23.4):

- **Cost leadership** – a business should follow a cost leadership strategy when:
  - it has a low-cost competitive manufacturing (or customer service) process, or low-cost raw materials
  - it targets the entire market (a broad approach) so its competitive advantage will apply to all of its products on the market.

Examples of the cost leadership strategy in practice include McDonald's and Bic products.

- **Differentiation** – a business should follow a differentiation strategy when:
  - its competitive advantage is its uniqueness due to the quality of its products or the image of the company
  - it targets an entire market (broad approach) as this uniqueness is applied to all of its products.

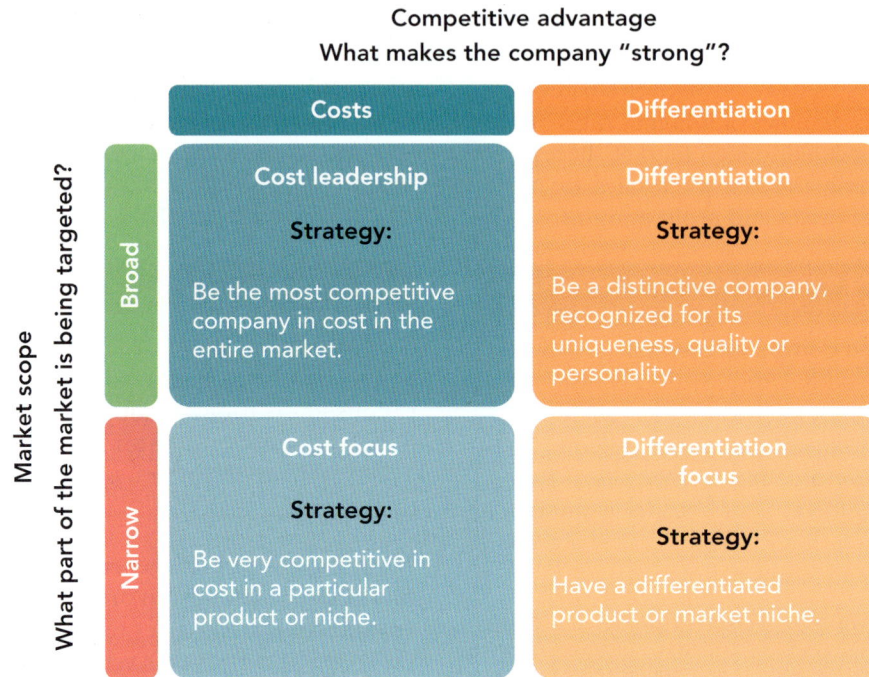

Figure 23.4: A summary of Porter's generic strategies

Examples of differentiation strategy in practice include Porsche cars and Burberry clothing.

- **Cost focus** – a business should follow a cost focus strategy when:
  - it has very low costs in a certain product or market niche
  - it targets a niche or a narrow market segment rather than entire markets.

Examples of cost focus strategies in practice include Pap Murphy's pizza (it makes the pizzas but they are baked at home) and Ryanair (short-haul airline).

- **Differentiation focus** – a business should follow a differentiation focus strategy when:
  - it has a very unique product or niche
  - it only sells in one narrow market (or its other products lack uniqueness so are sold in a broad market).

Examples of a differentiation focus strategy in practice include Breezes resorts which only offer holidays for couples without children, and Rolls Royce Cars.

Porter's generic strategies can also be incorporated into Unit 1 of the IB syllabus. It could be a useful business management tool for entrepreneurs planning to start their own business. It helps to identify the different strategies that start-up businesses could adopt to gain an early competitive advantage.

SELF-EVALUATION CHECKLIST

After studying this chapter, complete this table.

I am able to apply and analyse:	Needs more work	Almost there	Ready to move on
the role of marketing planning (AO2)			
segmentation, targeting (target market) and positioning (position maps) (AO2)			
the difference between niche market and mass market (AO2)			
the importance of having a unique selling point/proposition (USP) (AO2)			
I am able to synthesise and evaluate:			
how organisations can differentiate themselves and their products from competitors (AO3)			
I am able to use and apply:			
segmentation, targeting (target market) and positioning (position maps) (AO4)			
I am able to select and apply the business management tools:			
Boston Consulting Group (BCG) Matrix			
Porter's generic strategies			

REFLECTION

A new business start-up in your country plans to start selling bottled mountain spring water flavoured with natural ingredients. It aims for an exclusive image and will target the product at high income consumers. What do you think will be the most important elements of a successful marketing plan? Compare your ideas with those of another learner.

PROJECT

Changing the target market segment at Lidl

Lidl is changing the focus of its marketing communications to talk more about its quality and range and less about price in a bid to convince shoppers it can be a destination for their big weekly shop.

To get an idea of the customers who use Lidl we can look at the demographic of Lidl shoppers, along with how this has changed. Previously, people didn't see Lidl as a shopping destination and were reluctant to admit to shopping there. However, this has changed dramatically and people no longer feel this way.

In previous years one in ten people shopped at a discount supermarket like Lidl or Aldi, but this has now changed to become one in three. This change was partly down to the addition of the premium ranges within their stores which created an opening for the upper-middle class and middle-class professionals. Around a quarter (31%) of the shoppers at Lidl are from the upper-middle class and middle-class professionals socioeconomic market segment.

A new advertising campaign is markedly different from what we are used to seeing from the usually value-focused German discounter. The campaign does away with the idea of capturing the 'surprise' of real people when they discover the price of Lidl products that has been the central concept of its marketing for several years. Instead, there is an emphasis on both quality and range across all in-store categories, not just food.

'We want to make it really clear that we are big on quality, and it's a quality that can be found in everything that we sell, the things that people really care about, not just the occasional product,'

Lidl's marketing director, Claire Farrant, tells *Marketing Week*.

A 60-second TV ad will be supported by an integrated marketing campaign that includes activity in print, radio, digital and cinema. The campaign will also run on social media, as well as in-store and at point-of-sale as Lidl looks to bring it to life through the customer experience. Farrant believes, 'Our campaign's core value will bring with it an exciting environment to shop for our customers and work for our colleagues.'

Lidl's market share, like that of its discount rival Aldi, is still growing. Lidl's sales were up 8.5% year on year in the 12 weeks to the end of May, giving it a market share of 5.8%. Lidl has added 630 000 new shoppers in the last year alone.

In pairs or in a group, produce a marketing strategy that includes how you would change each aspect of Lidl's marketing mix to target the upper-middle class and middle-class professionals socioeconomic market segment.

On your proposed Lidl strategy, include:

- price
- product
- promotion
- place.

Thinking about your project:

- Once you have produced your strategy, do you feel your understanding of marketing strategy has improved?
- How good is your strategy compared to those of the other groups in the class?
- How could you improve your strategy?

EXAM-STYLE QUESTIONS

Marketing electric scooters

Lemon Electric is a Canadian-based manufacturer of high-quality electric scooters which it markets throughout the country. Lemon's marketing department have developed its products with the unique selling point: 'speed, flexibility and environmentally friendly'. Lemon has a big online presence and sells its scooters through the business's user-friendly website. The company also distributes its scooters through a retailer that specialises in high-quality electric scooters and electric bikes.

Lemon's product has a relatively high price compared to its competitors in the scooter market. The business uses exclusively online promotion with extensive use of social media to reach existing and potential customers. Lemon has worked hard at researching their target market and has demographic and psychographic market segmentation. The profile of a typical Lemon customer is:

* 20–40 years old
* lives in urban location
* professional employment
* environmentally conscious.

The CEO of Lemon Electric is concerned that marketing the product in a niche way limits the company's sales and would like to see it broaden the market it sells to by also producing a less expensive range of lower-quality electric scooters.

1   Define the term 'mass market'.   [2]
2   Define the term 'niche market'.   [2]
3   State **two** ways Lemon Electric might segment a market.   [2]
4   Explain how Lemon electric might develop its unique selling point.   [4]
5   Outline **two** elements of Lemon Electric's target market segment.   [4]
6   Describe the product and price elements of Lemon Electric's marketing mix.   [4]
7   Explain why an understanding of its target market segment is important to Lemon Electric when it is promoting and distributing its product.   [4]
8   Define the term 'product position map'.   [2]
9   Construct a product position map showing product quality and price that shows the position of Lemon Electric's existing and new product on the map.   [4]
10 Evaluate a proposal by Lemon Electric to broaden its market and sell a less expensive range of lower-quality electric scooters.   [10]

> Chapter 24

Sales forecasting

Higher-level

LEARNING OBJECTIVES

On completing this chapter you should be able to:

Synthesise and evaluate:

> The benefits and limitations of sales forecasting (AO3)

Select and apply the business management tools:

> Simple linear regression

> Scatter diagrams

> Line of best fit

> Correlation/Extrapolation

BUSINESS IN CONTEXT

Nintendo constantly adjusts its sales forecasts

In 2021, business media reported that Nintendo increased its full-year **sales forecast** for the Switch games console to 26.5 million units, from an original forecast of 24 million. The company's sales forecasts are based trends in actual sales and continuous analysis of market trends. Switch sales increased faster than expected in 2020 as a result of the increased demand for home entertainment during the Covid-19 pandemic, which led to the revised sales forecast for 2021.

Nintendo used the revised sales forecasts to help produce financial, operations and workforce plans. The expected increase in sales of Switch was also expected to lead to higher sales of related games software. In contrast, in 2022 Switch sales forecasts were lowered by 10%. This was not due to falling demand but a result of supply and logistics disruptions affecting the entire electronics and gaming industries.

These external factors over the last three years illustrate both the need for, and the difficulty of, making accurate sales forecasts.

Discuss in pairs or in a group:

- Do you think it is important for all businesses to make sales forecasts? Explain your answer.

- To what extent are sales forecasts based on current sales trends likely to be accurate?

- Examine three factors outside of Nintendo's control which could influence sales of the Switch console over the next 12 months.

KEY TERM

sales forecast: prediction of sales for the next time period

KEY CONCEPT LINK

Change

An important part of effective business decision-making is being able to measure, analyse and forecast change. The most successful businesses are able to react to and anticipate change as it takes place in the market. This means using data effectively to guide managers when they are making decisions. Sales forecasting is a big part of this.

24.1 The benefits and limitations of sales forecasting

It is impossible to predict the future with complete certainty, but most businesses will attempt to forecast future sales – if only for short periods of time in the future. There are several methods of sales forecasting. The benefits and limitations of sales forecasting should always be considered by managers when attempting to predict future sales or when analysing sales forecast data.

Benefits of sales forecasting

If marketing managers were able to predict future sales accurately, the risks of business operations and decision-making would be greatly reduced. If, for example, a precise forecast of monthly sales over the next two years could be made, the benefits to the whole organisation and all major functional areas would be immense.

- The operations department would know how many units to produce, what quantity of materials to order and the appropriate level of inventory to hold.
- The marketing department would be aware of how many products to distribute and whether changes to the existing marketing mix were needed to increase sales.
- The human resources workforce plan would be more accurate, leading to the appropriate number of workers being employed and the most appropriate employment contracts being used, i.e., permanent or temporary.
- The finance department could plan cash flows with much greater accuracy, make accurate profit forecasts and plan for any necessary finance that might be needed.

> **LEARNER PROFILE**
>
> **Inquirers**
>
> What is a going to happen in the future has a crucial influence over business decision-making and strategy. Inquiring about the future is an important part of understanding how the business environment is likely to change and how business decision-makers are going to respond to this. For example, Denmark has banned the use of all petrol and diesel vehicles by 2030.
>
> A manager who is an inquirer will consider as many possible future implications of this decision for their business as they can.
>
> In pairs or as a group, discuss technological changes that might take place over the next ten years that could completely change the sales of a business.

In addition, the strategic decision-making role of senior managers – such as whether to develop new products or enter new markets – would become much better informed with accurate sales forecasts. The risks entailed by such important decisions would be reduced.

Finally, sales forecasts form an essential part of the market planning process and of the screening process before new products are launched on to the market. These forecasts will be based on market research data, gained from both primary and secondary sources.

Limitations of sales forecasting

In reality, such precision in forecasting is impossible to achieve. This is largely due to two main factors:

- unforeseen external factors that have a substantial influence on future sales levels
- problems in the methods of sales forecasting that can result in inaccurate forecasts.

Consider the difficulties in forecasting the sales of diesel-powered cars, even for a short period. Apart from changes in the costs of making these cars (and therefore the prices of them), future demand will be impacted by the price and availability of electric vehicles, new laws controlling the use of diesel vehicles in urban areas, pressure group activity against such vehicles, as well as the general economic climate. Despite these problems, most businesses make sales forecasts in order to reduce to an acceptable minimum the unforeseen nature of future changes. A common way of assessing future demand for a product yet to be fully launched is to use test marketing in one particular area. For existing products, sales forecasts are commonly based on past sales data. This is called time series analysis.

ACTIVITY 24.1

Forecasting your own grades

As a student following the IB diploma you will study six subjects. You might be wondering what your Diploma score will be at end of the course.

In pairs or in a group, discuss the following questions:

1   What factors do you consider when you are forecasting your IB grades?

2   How is forecasting your IB grades useful to you and your school?

3   What are the difficulties of forecasting your IB grades?

THEORY OF KNOWLEDGE

Knowledge question: To what extent do intuition, emotion and reason influence the way business people make forecasts?

Forecasting in business is difficult. Time series analysis can help to make the forecasting process more scientific, but it means making judgements about the future – which is always uncertain. Consider these quotes on forecasting:

- 'I never think of the future – it comes soon enough.' Albert Einstein.

- 'Forecasts usually tell us more of the forecaster than of the future.' Warren Buffett.

- 'Forecasts create the mirage that the future is knowable.' Financial historian Peter L. Bernstein.

- 'We have two classes of forecasters: Those who don't know – and those who don't know they don't know.' Economist John Kenneth Galbraith.

- 'No amount of sophistication is going to allay the fact that all of your knowledge is about the past and all your decisions are about the future.' Former GE executive Ian Wilson.

24.2 Business management tools
Simple linear regression

TIP

'Simple' (as in 'simple linear regression') does not mean that the calculations are always easy! 'Simple' in this instance means that only two variables are being considered, e.g., level of sales and number of selling staff. If more than two variables are considered it becomes 'complex' regression analysis!

Simple linear regression is used to model the relationship between two variables. The aim is to predict the value of a dependent variable (e.g., sales) based on changes in the value of an independent variable (e.g., number of selling staff or the price level).

Consider the following data for past quarterly sales of furniture by a retail store and the amount it spends on advertising:

	Sales ($000)	Advertising spend ($000)
Year 1 Q1	120	6
Q2	200	12
Q3	240	14
Q4	200	10
Year 2 Q1	220	10
Q2	240	14
Q3	280	20
Q4	160	10
Year 3 Q1	200	14
Q2	240	20
Q3	280	24
Q4	300	24

Table 24.1: Sales and advertising expenditure

At first look, can you tell if there is a close relationship between sales and the amount spent on advertising? Is the relationship what you would **expect** to exist? What form does the relationship take?

- Is it positive – do sales broadly increase with more advertising and fall when advertising is reduced?

- Is it negative – do sales broadly fall when advertising is increased?

Obviously if we could determine the nature of this relationship between sales and advertising spending it would help the business determine the optimum level of advertising spending. Further research could then be undertaken to see which forms of advertising promotion are most and least effective in impacting on sales.

How can the data shown in Table 24.1 be made more useful for further analysis? One approach is to graph the data to achieve a scatter diagram of the coordinates. This is easy to do if spreadsheet software is used!

Scatter diagrams

These graphs are used to illustrate the relationship between two variables. They are easy to use and the relationship between the two variables can be more clearly identified than from a table of data. Figures 24.1 to 24.3 show three possible scatter diagrams and the relationship (if any) between the variables shown:

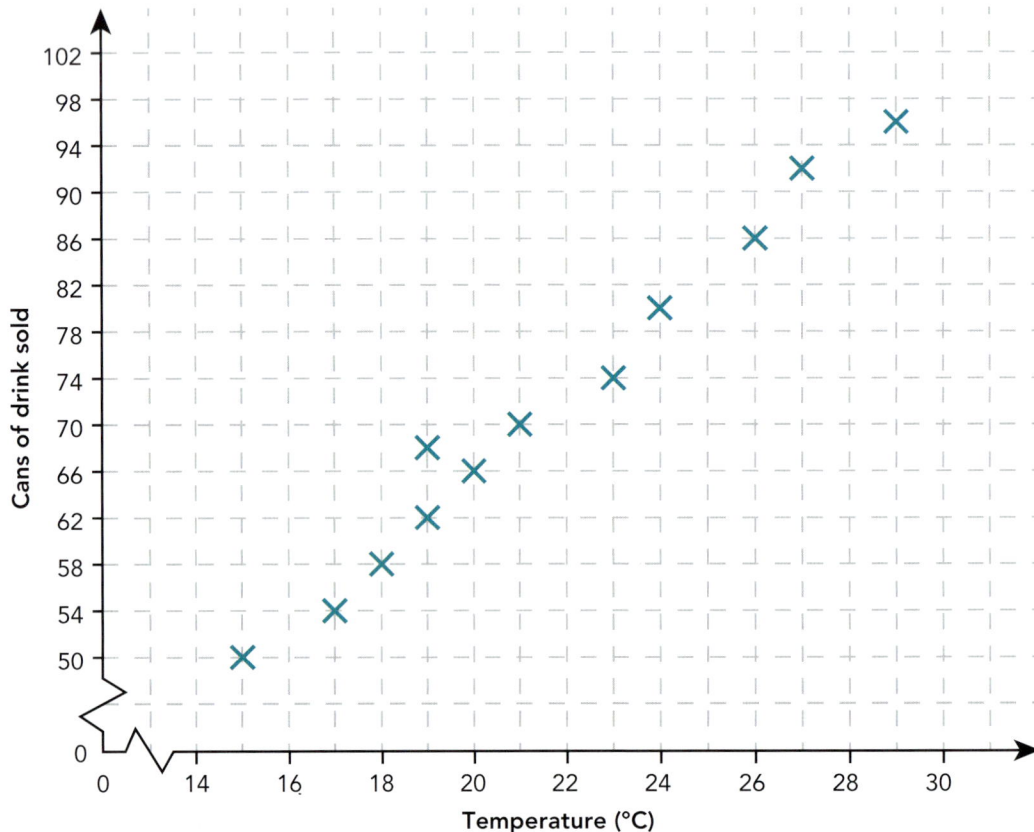

Figure 24.1: A positive relationship between two variables

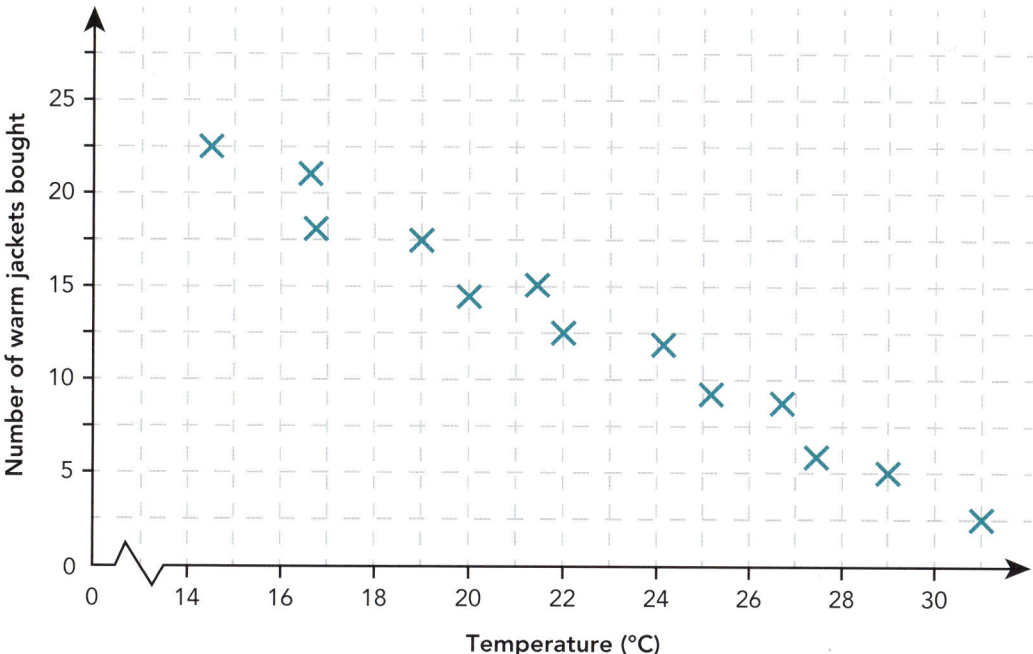

Figure 24.2: A negative relationship between two variables

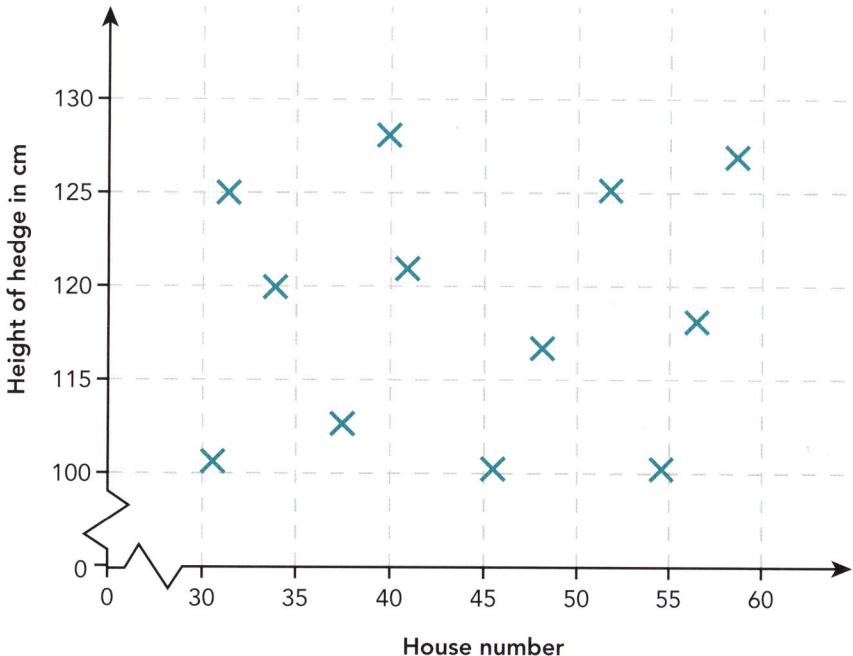

Figure 24.3: No connection between the two variables

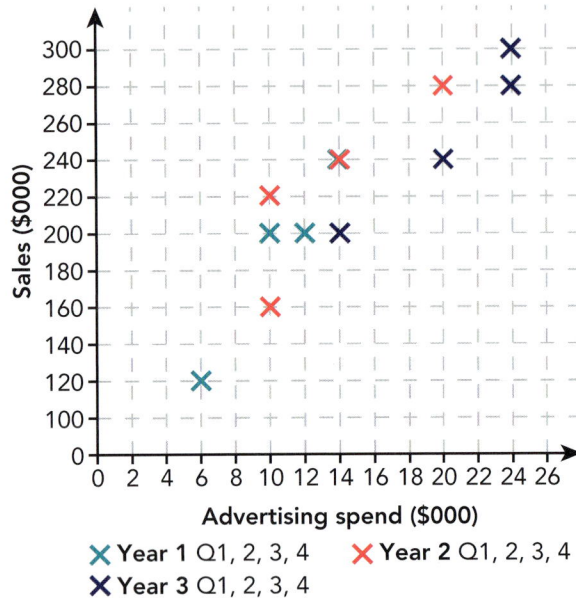

Figure 24.4: Scatter diagram for data in Table 24.1

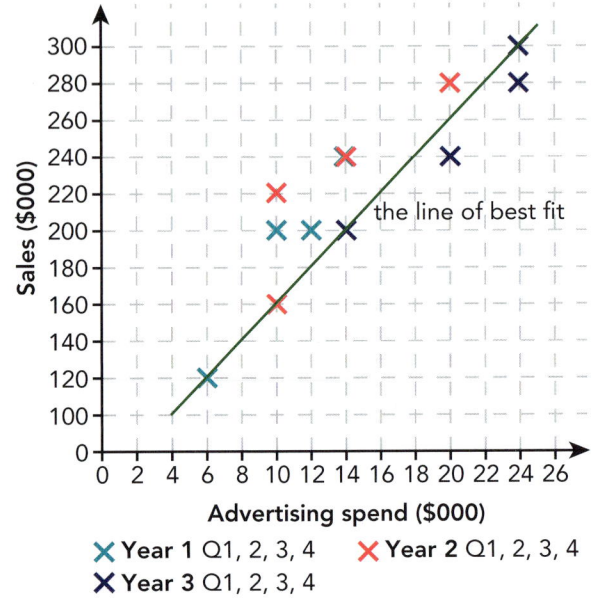

Figure 24.5: The line of best fit

Figure 24.4 shows the data from Table 24.1 in a scatter diagram. Note that the dependent variable is always on the y (vertical) axis.

Line of best fit

The nature of the relationship between the two variables becomes clear once a scatter diagram has been produced. The strength of this relationship can be clarified further by drawing a line of best fit. A line of best fit is a straight line that goes as centrally as possible through the coordinates plotted. It will then clearly indicate the trend of the relationship between the variables. The steeper the line of best fit then the stronger the relationship (positive or negative) is between the two variables. Figure 24.5 shows an estimated line of best fit showing the positive relationship between the two variables.

Correlation/extrapolation

Correlation means using statistical analysis to measure the strength of the relationship between two variables. Correlation can be measured in a number of different ways and the most widely used method is Pearson's correlation coefficient. The results of the correlation coefficient are always between −1 and 1. However, the correlation result does not tell us *why* and *how* the relationship exists; it just suggests that the relationship exists.

A correlation coefficient of 1 means that for every positive increase in one variable, there is a positive increase of a fixed proportion in the other. In business terms this result is unlikely. For example, the relationship between airline ticket prices and the price of oil will be very high, but other airline cost factors mean that the correlation between the two will never equal 1.

A correlation coefficient of −1 means that for every positive increase in one variable, there is a negative decrease of a fixed proportion in the other. Again, in business this result is unlikely, but a logistics business will understand that the amount of fuel remaining in a delivery truck's tank will reduce in negative correlation to its average speed.

Zero means that for every increase in the independent variable, there is not a positive or a negative change in the dependent variable. The two variables are just not related.

A word of warning: correlation is not causation! Many business managers make the common error of assuming that if there is strong correlation between two variables, then there must be strong causation between the two variables. A good example of the difference is when ice cream sales are compared to sales of sunglasses. There is a very strong correlation between these two variables. However, one does not cause the other! The cause of sales of both ice cream and sunglasses rising is most likely to be sunny, hot weather.

CASE STUDY 24.1

Understanding sales data in the Brazilian ice cream market

Fria-Gelo is a chain of Brazilian ice cream outlets. The company has been relatively successful over the last two years and its sales and profits have increased. The company's market share has also increased in this competitive market. Fria-Gelo believes strongly in qualitative market research, and it is continuously running focus groups to test new ice-cream flavours.

The table sets out Fria-Gelo's quarterly sales data over the last two years.

	Sales ($000)
Year 1	
Q1	1045
Q2	706
Q3	813
Q4	1029
Year 2	
Q1	1120
Q2	823
Q3	887
Q4	1265

1   Define the term 'sales forecast'. [2]

2   Explain to benefits to Fria-Gelo of sales forecasting. [4]

3   Plot a scatter diagram of Fria-Gelo's sales revenue against time and draw a line of best fit. [4]

4   Outline what the data shows about the trend in Fria-Gelo's sales. [2]

5   Explain **two** problems for Fria-Gelo of forecasting sales. [4]

Extrapolation involves making statistical forecasts by using historical trends that are projected for a specified period of time into the future. It is only used for time-series forecasts – where, for example, sales data has been gathered over a period of time. The simplest method of extrapolation is to extend the line of best fit (based on a scatter diagram) into future time periods. This line can then be used to read off forecasts for sales in future – although to be more accurate, these forecasted figures should be adjusted for regular seasonal and cyclical fluctuations. Using the graph in Figure 24.6, which is based on the data in Table 24.2, the extrapolated sales forecast for 2025 is $168 million.

Year	Sales ($ million)
2016	132
2017	134
2018	137
2019	141
2020	148
2021	152
2022	155
2023	159

Table 24.2: Sales data recorded for last eight years

Integrating these business management tools across the syllabus

All of these techniques of forecasting can be applied to other areas of the IB syllabus. They could be used by business managers when setting business objectives (Chapter 3). For example, if the sales forecasts for the next three years are for substantial increases in sales then new objectives and targets could be set for each division and region of the business based on these forecasts.

The importance of sales forecasts to the finance department cannot be under-estimated. Cash flow forecasts, for example, depend very much on the expected future sales performance of the business.

CASE STUDY 24.2

Measuring sales in a music school

Year	Sales ($000)
2020 Q1	34
2020 Q2	26
2020 Q3	35
2020 Q4	38
2021 Q1	33
2021 Q2	32
2021 Q3	36
2021 Q4	42

Stepping Out Tuition is an online music school that offers lessons via Zoom to students who live all over the world. The business uses a large number of online music tutors to offer guitar, piano, violin and cello classes. The business is growing, which means taking on more tutors and investing in an IT system to make the business run efficiently. The sales data for Stepping Out is set out in the table.

1   Plot a scatter diagram of Stepping Out's sales revenue against time and draw a line of best fit.   [4]

2   Outline what Stepping Out's sales data shows.   [2]

3   Explain **two** reasons why it might be difficult to make judgements about Stepping Out's sales performance based on the sales data.   [4]

CASE STUDY 24.3

The Hungry Guy Takeaway

Delima Kok is planning to start a takeaway business in Kuala Lumpur called the Hungry Guy. It is going to be a small takeaway business that specialises in Malaysian street food. In planning the business, Demila has been working hard to research the market and has produced detailed sales forecasts for the first trading year of the business.

1   Define the term sales revenue.   [2]

2   Outline **two** factors Delima will need to determine in order to produce a sales forecast.   [4]

3   Explain **two** benefits to the Hungry Guy of accurate sales forecasts.   [4]

SELF-EVALUATION CHECKLIST

After studying this chapter, complete this table.

I am able to synthesise and evaluate:	Needs more work	Almost there	Ready to move on
the benefits and limitations of sales forecasting (AO3)			
I am able to select and apply the following business management tools:			
simple linear regression			
scatter diagrams			
line of best fit			
correlation/extrapolation			

REFLECTION

How would you attempt to forecast the number of learners at your school or college who might choose to study IB Business Management over the next three years? Try to make such a forecast and compare your results with those of another learner.

Reflect on the problems of making such a forecast.

PROJECT

Sales forecast assumptions

There are many factors that can potentially affect sales that should form the basis of a business sales forecast, including:

- the economy – whether the economy is growing or in recession

- the industry – whether the market for a product is expending or contracting

- competition – the extent to which new competition is entering the market

- significant customers – whether the business is likely to attract or lose any major customers

- legal factors – whether there are any new laws or regulations that could affect a business's sales

- social factors – the extent to which trends in consumer taste, preferences and fashion are likely to affect future sales.

A business will also need to think about its own marketing: whether it is launching a new product, embarking on a promotional campaign, developing a new online presence and/or changing the price of the price of the product.

In pairs or as a group:

1 Choose a local business.

2 Brainstorm the factors affecting the future sales of the business using the ideas considered here, and forecast what you think is going to happen to your business's sales next year.

3 Prepare and deliver a presentation on how you prepared your business's sales forecast.

Thinking about your project:

- Now that you have prepared and delivered your presentation, do you feel you have a better understanding of the use of sales forecasting?

- How would you rate your group's presentation in comparison to those of the other groups?

- What changes would you make to your presentation if you could do it again?

EXAM-STYLE QUESTIONS

Falling sales in the Moroccan hotel market

The Mansour Elite is a chain four- and five-star hotels based in Morocco. The business is struggling with falling sales and the last two years have seen a significant fall in revenues and profits.

Ayat Alami has just be appointed the CEO of the business with the objective of trying to turn things around. Ayat believes the hotel group has lost focus on its core consumers and needs to be more market orientated. Her first job, however, is to look at the business's sales data which is set out in the table.

	Sales ($ million)
Year 1	
Q1	2.13
Q2	2.62
Q3	2.01
Q4	1.98
Year 2	
Q1	2.10
Q2	2.43
Q3	1.95
Q4	1.82

1   Define the term 'market orientated'.   **[2]**
2   Define the term 'linear regression'.   **[2]**
3   Outline what a scatter diagram shows.   **[2]**
4   Outline why a line of best fit is useful.   **[2]**
5   Define the term 'correlation'.   **[2]**
6   Plot a scatter diagram of Mansour Elite's sales revenue against time and draw a line of best fit. **[4]**
7   Outline what the trend in sales data for Mansour Elite shows.   **[2]**
8   Explain **two** problems for Mansour Elite of becoming more market orientated.   **[4]**
9   Explain **two** benefits for Mansour Elite of forecasting sales.   **[4]**
10 Explain **two** problems for Mansour Elite of forecasting sales.   **[4]**

> Chapter 25
Market research

LEARNING OBJECTIVES

On completing this chapter you should be able to:

Apply and analyse:
- The following methods/techniques of primary market research:
  - surveys
  - interviews
  - focus groups
  - observations (AO2)
- The following methods/techniques of secondary market research:
  - market analyses
  - academic journals
  - government publications
  - media articles
  - online (AO2)
- The difference between qualitative and quantitative market research (AO2)
- The following methods of sampling:
  - quota
  - random
  - convenience (AO2)

Synthesise and evaluate:
- Why and how organisations carry out market research (AO3)

Select and apply the business management tools:
- Mean; mode; median; bar charts; pie charts; infographics; quartiles; standard deviation

BUSINESS IN CONTEXT

Internet, mobile phones, apps and social media – market research in the 21st century

Market research – it is standing on a street corner with a clipboard and asking people questions, isn't it? Wrong! Facebook, Twitter and other social media are causing traditional market research surveys to decline in importance. The two-way engagement with businesses that social media offers means that people will become a lot less willing to take part in 'high-street surveys'. If consumers want to tell a company something there are now so many ways to say it!

Businesses are turning to social media as a relatively cheap way of gaining insight into the market, brand appeal, customers and reasons for their buying behaviour. Most platforms such as Facebook and Twitter allow simple searching of the latest posts and popular terms. Researchers can learn about emerging trends and see what customers are talking about in real time. By setting up a few searches on Twitter using hashtags related to a brand, industry or product, a business can receive instant notice when customers or competitors are discussing their products!

ADVERTISING SURVEY

Discuss in pairs or a group:

• What are the potential benefits of businesses using market research information gained through social media sites?

• Are there likely to be any problems with depending *only* on these sources for consumer information? Explain your views to others in the group.

KEY TERM

market research: process of collecting, recording and analysing data about customers, competitors and the market

KEY CONCEPT LINK

Ethics

The development of technology has allowed businesses to gain increasing amounts of information on their consumers and potential consumers. The cookies used by businesses on their websites are an innovation that have enhanced their market research. Cookies allow the web servers used by a business's website to identify and track users as they navigate different pages on the website, and to identify users returning to a website. Some observers question the ethics of gaining the information of users in this way.

25.1 Why and how organisations carry out market research

Market research is a broad and far-reaching process. It is concerned not just with finding out, as accurately as possible, whether consumers will buy a particular product, but also with trying to analyse their reaction to:

- different price levels
- alternative forms of promotion
- new types of packaging
- different methods of distribution.

The four main reasons for organisations to carry out market research are as follows.

To identify the main features of a market and reduce risks of market entry

Before entering a new market a business will need to establish some of that market's key features:

- Overall size – is it worthwhile for the business to be entering this market?
- Growth – is the market becoming bigger or smaller in terms of total sales?
- Competitors – how many other businesses are selling similar products, how much market power do they have, and is it easy for new rivals to enter the market?

By investigating potential demand for a new product or service the business should be able to assess the likely chances of that product achieving a profitable level of sales. Although research into the features of a market cannot guarantee success, market research is still a key part of new product development (NPD). Table 25.1 summarises how NPD is supported by market research.

The NPD process		The market research process
Identify consumer needs and tastes	→	Primary and secondary research into consumer needs and competitors
Product idea and packaging design	→	Testing of product and packaging with consumer groups
Brand positioning and advertising testing	→	Pre-testing of the product image and advertisements
Product launch and after launch period	→	Monitoring of sales and consumer response

Table 25.1: Summary of how new product development (NPD) is supported by market research

To predict future demand changes and market trends

A travel firm may wish to investigate social and other changes to see how these might affect the demand for holidays in the future. For instance, the growth in the number of single-person households may suggest that there could be a rising demand for 'singles' holidays. Using market research to try to establish future demand trends is often useful, but it can be risky to depend on the results. For example, the release by a competitor of a revolutionary new product is not something that can be predicted, but it will impact on the accuracy of any research undertaken about market shares and consumers' buying intentions.

To explain consumer buying patterns for existing products and market trends

Market research is not just undertaken for new or planned products; it needs to be conducted for existing products and brands too. This helps to assess current performance and creates a basis for future marketing objectives. The key role of consumer buying behaviour in determining sales patterns is crucial. This behaviour can be analysed by market research that focuses not just on 'numbers likely to be sold' but the reasons behind consumer decisions to purchase or not. For example, if, when researching into likely future demand trends for electric vehicles, it is found that 'range anxiety' is a much more important factor than price, design or brand image in consumer behaviour, then this conclusion needs to be shared with the product development team.

To assess the most favoured designs, flavours, styles, promotions and packaging

Consumer tests of different versions of a product or of the proposed social media campaigns to promote it will enable a business to focus on the aspects of design and performance that consumers rate most highly. These can then be incorporated into the final product. The importance to consumers of all features of a good or service can be examined through market research. 'Taste tests' can help determine the most popular ice cream flavours. 'Advertising recall' questionnaires can check on how memorable a promotion campaign was. 'Consumer feedback' emails can ask for the factors that a consumer found most and least satisfactory about a recently purchased good or service experience.

The main methods of market research

Primary research collects 'first-hand' data – it is being collected by the organisation for the first time for its own needs. In contrast, **secondary research** is the use and analysis of data that already exists. This data was originally collected by another organisation, often for a different purpose, and is often referred to as 'second-hand' data.

Tables 25.2 and 25.3 summarise the advantages and disadvantages of these two methods of research.

Initial secondary research will nearly always indicate the focus that subsequent primary research should have. However, on its own secondary research is rarely sufficient, which is why primary research is also usually undertaken. Table 25.3 summarises the advantages and disadvantages of secondary research. Secondary research gathers background data, but only primary research can provide detailed, up-to-date information from consumers within the firm's target market.

> ### KEY TERMS
>
> **primary research:** the collection of first-hand data that is directly related to a firm's needs
>
> **secondary research:** collection of data from second-hand sources

Advantages	Disadvantages
Up to date and therefore more useful than much secondary data	Costly – market research agencies can charge thousands of dollars for detailed customer surveys and other market research reports
Relevant – collected for a specific purpose – directly addresses the questions the business wants answers to	Time-consuming – secondary data could be obtained from the internet much more quickly
Confidential – no other business has access to this data	Doubts over accuracy and validity – largely because of the need to use sampling and the risk of sampling error
The increasing use of IT such as social media platforms is reducing the cost of primary research	

Table 25.2: Primary research – advantages and disadvantages

Advantages	Disadvantages
Often obtainable very cheaply – apart from the purchase of market intelligence reports	May not be updated frequently and may therefore be out of date
Identifies the nature of the market and assists with the planning of primary research	As it was originally collected for another purpose, it may not be entirely suitable or presented in the most effective way for the business using it
Obtainable quickly without the need to devise complicated data-gathering methods	Data-collection methods and the accuracy of these may be unknown
Allows comparison of data from different sources	Might not be available for completely new product developments
	Accuracy of source material must be checked

Table 25.3: Secondary research – advantages and disadvantages

25.2 The methods/ techniques of primary market research

Surveys

These involve asking consumers or potential consumers directly – usually by means of a questionnaire – for their opinions and preferences. They can be used to obtain both qualitative and quantitative research (see 25.4). For example, here are two questions asked in a recent **survey** of shoppers:

- 'How many foreign holidays did you take last year?'
- 'What do you look for in an ideal foreign holiday?'

> **KEY TERM**
>
> **survey:** detailed study of a market or geographical area to gather data on attitudes, impressions, opinions and satisfaction levels of products or businesses, by asking a section of the population

The first question will provide quantitative data, which can be presented graphically and analysed statistically. The second question is designed to find out the key qualitative features of a holiday that would influence consumer choice. There are four important issues for market researchers to consider when conducting consumer surveys:

- Who to ask: in most cases it is impossible or too expensive to survey all potential members of a target market (the survey population). A 'sample' from this population is therefore necessary. The more closely this sample reflects the characteristics of the survey population, the less chance there is of sampling error.

- What to ask: the construction of an unbiased and unambiguous questionnaire is essential if the survey is to obtain useful results.

- How to ask: should the questionnaire be self-completed and returned by post, or filled in by an interviewer in a face-to-face session with the respondent? Could a telephone, social media, chat app or online survey be conducted instead? Increasingly, businesses use IT to conduct surveys, which allows for quick responses and analysis of the data gathered.

- How accurate it is: assessing the likely accuracy and validity of the results is a crucial element of market research surveys.

Questionnaire design

It is not easy to write an effective questionnaire. The temptation is often to ask too many questions in the hope of gaining every last scrap of information. Yet people may become suspicious or bored if there are numerous questions. Unless it is absolutely essential to know the names and precise ages or income levels of respondents, these questions are best avoided, as there will be reluctance to answer them. If data about income is essential, one way around the reluctance to answer is to group income levels together, such as:

'Please indicate which of the following income levels you are in:
$10 000–$20 000
$20 001–$30 000 . . .'

Open questions lead to results which will be difficult to collate and present numerically, but they might provide a useful insight into consumers' 'thinking' about a product. **Closed questions** lead to results which are easy to present and analyse, but offer little scope for explaining the reasoning behind consumers' answers.

KEY TERMS

open questions: those that invite a wide-ranging or imaginative response

closed questions: questions to which a limited number of preset answers is offered

---

Asking all open questions is not a good idea, although questionnaires usually end with an open question. They allow respondents to give their opinion. For example: 'What do you really think of Jupiter perfume?' The answers to this will be so varied in length and content that the results will be difficult to compile and present statistically. A better option might be to use a closed question such as:

What most attracted you to buy Jupiter perfume?

- *price*
- *image*
- *packaging*
- *widely available*
- *smell.*

As the design of the questionnaire will greatly influence the accuracy and usefulness of the results, it is advisable to undertake an initial pilot survey to test the quality of the questions. Other principles to follow include:

- Make the objectives of the research clear so that questions can be focused on these.
- Write clear and unambiguous questions.
- Try to make sure that the questions follow each other in a logical sequence.
- Avoid questions that seem to point to one particular answer.
- Use language that will be readily understood.
- Include some questions that will allow a classification of results by gender, area lived in, occupation and so on.

ACTIVITY 25.1

1   Working in pairs or small groups, produce a questionnaire that aims to find about the music listening habits of students in your school. The brief for the questionnaire is to find out:

- the media students use to listen to music – streaming, radio, CD, vinyl, etc.
- where students listen to music – home, while travelling, at school, etc.
- genres of music students listen to – rock, rap, dance, etc.
- length of listening time
- favourite artists
- attendance at live music events.

2   Once you have produced your questionnaire, discuss your questions with the rest of your class. Now put your questionnaire to the test by publishing it on survey monkey or a similar survey website and sending it to a group of students at your school.

Interviews

The response rate to most forms of self-completed questionnaires is nearly always very poor. Questions could easily be misunderstood and the sample returned could be biased in favour of those respondents with the most spare time, for example retired people. Direct interviews are conducted by an interviewer, usually either in the street or in the respondent's home. Skilled interviewers will avoid bias in the way in which they ask questions, and detailed questions can be explained to the interviewee. Follow-up questions can be asked if required.

This can be an expensive method, but the interviewer will continue their work until the preset sample size has been reached – whereas the response to postal questionnaires is always uncertain.

ACTIVITY 25.2

Managing a focus group

Set up a focus group in your class to research into the food and refreshment provision at your school.

The research brief is: How can the food and refreshment provision at your school be improved?

1 Design research questions to discuss with your focus group.

2 Conduct a ten-minute focus group discussion to answer the questions you have formulated.

3 Write a summary of the findings of your focus group.

4 Discuss with your class the strengths and weaknesses of using focus groups as part of market research.

Focus groups

In focus discussion groups, questions are asked and the group are encouraged to actively discuss their responses about a product, advertising, packaging and so on. All members of the **focus group** are free to talk with other group members. These discussions are often filmed and this footage is then used by the market research department as a source of data. Information is often believed to be more accurate and realistic than the responses to individual interviews or questionnaires, where respondents do not have this discussion opportunity presented.

However, there might be the risk of researchers leading or influencing the discussion too much, ending up with biased conclusions.

Observations

This is one of the oldest techniques used in marketing research. Through direct observation of people, marketing specialists are able to identify actions and watch how customers or potential customers respond to various stimuli. For a small business, observational marketing research is one of the simplest ways that one can find out many things about their customers and clients. One of the most common ways researchers use **observational techniques** is through cookies on computers, used to track users' web views and visits. Focus groups use observational techniques, as do the Nielsen ratings used to track peoples' popular viewing habits of television programmes. Public transport companies use observational research to conduct traffic counts and usage patterns. Many retail businesses use observational techniques when they record purchasing behaviour through barcoded transactions and observe customers reading product packaging.

KEY TERMS

focus groups: a group of people who are asked about their attitude towards a product, service, advertisement or new style of packaging

observational technique: a qualitative method of collecting and analysing information obtained through directly or indirectly watching and observing others in business environments, e.g., watching consumers walk around a supermarket

---

This market research method is relatively inexpensive as the main cost is that of the observer's remuneration. During observation, if the observer is completely unseen, customers often behave naturally and do not try to demonstrate their 'ideal selves' instead of their true actions. Recall error is not a problem when conducting observational research. Observational research can be modified to obtain the best results possible, if necessary. For instance, if the observer cannot see clearly enough from a particular location, they may choose to move to a closer observing spot. Observational techniques often provide the only way to conduct certain research, such as determining the number of shoppers visiting a store or the behaviour of children when watching an advertisement.

However, observational research is time-consuming and does not provide qualitative evidence explaining consumers' behaviour. The observer must have patience and time to devote to watching a set number of individuals or settings to obtain the information necessary. Researchers may also become distracted while observing, which can distort the results of the research. There is also an ethical question – should customers, especially young children, be observed without their knowledge and permission?

THEORY OF KNOWLEDGE

Some years ago, Starbucks was involved in a joint venture with Pepsi to market a coffee-flavoured carbonated drink called Mazagran. The venture failed. The drink was not popular with consumers and sales declined after initial curiosity waned. The product was removed from the market within a year.

However this failure did lead to a different success. Market research had told Starbucks that customers wanted a cold, sweet, bottled coffee beverage. However, they wanted a milk drink rather than a soda. It is believed that the development of Mazagran helped Startbucks to later launch its successful range of bottled Frappuccino drinks.

How important are emotion and reason in making decisions based on market research?

To what extent do businesspeople act rationally when making decisions?

CASE STUDY 25.1

The importance of primary research

We live firmly in the age of big data. Every link we click is tracked and catalogued. We rate our Uber drivers and the things we buy on Amazon and the cleanliness of airport bathrooms. The films and TV shows we are prompted to stream on Netflix are based on algorithms that analyse everything we have ever watched before.

Technological development has continuously improved the quantitative market research techniques businesses use. But when designers and marketers need to come up with new ideas or vet products before trying to sell them, they still turn to the same 'low-tech' methods that have been used for decades: putting a group of people in a room and getting them to talk it through as part of a focus group.

Focus groups might seem like a throwback – they came to prominence in the middle of the 20th century – and their demise has been predicted many times over the years. But despite the number of times they have been declared dead (a victim of ever-improving digital analytics) they have gone nowhere. In 2018, $2.2 billion was spent worldwide on conducting focus groups.

1 Define the term 'quantitative market research'. [2]

2 Outline **two** methods of quantitative market research that businesses can use. [4]

3 Explain how focus groups might be better than quantitative market research when a business is developing a new product. [4]

25.3 Secondary market research

Secondary research is often undertaken before primary research – but only if the data exists, which it may not if the planned product is so different that no second-hand data exists. Why undertake secondary research first? A great deal of information can be gathered about a market and market trends from secondary sources at relatively low cost This research might indicate that the market being considered has very little growth potential so the business could save time and money by not proceeding with primary research. The results from secondary research can be used to give focus to the primary research that the business usually undertakes **after** secondary research. However, secondary data:

- is never completely up to date
- may not provide answers to specific questions that the business wants answers to
- is available to competitors too.

Secondary research is usually undertaken using the following methods.

Market intelligence analysis reports

These are extremely detailed reports on individual markets and industries produced by specialist market research agencies. They are very expensive, but they are usually available at local business libraries – though these might not be the most up-to-date versions, which are sold directly to businesses in the market being researched. Examples of market research analyses are:

- Mintel reports
- Key Note reports
- Euromonitor International.

If the owner of a small hotel planned to expand the business by opening a hotel in the capital city, one of these reports on the hotel and catering market would provide huge amounts of detail on market and consumer trends, eating and holiday habits of consumers, number of tourists and so on.

Academic journals

Several academic journals are published which focus on the science and techniques involved in market research. These would be of particular interest to the market research department of businesses – not so much for the market research data that they contain but for the discussion of market research methodology.

Government publications

In most countries, sources, such as the following from the UK, could be referred to:

- population census
- Social Trends
- Annual Abstract of Statistics
- Living Costs and Food Survey.

Therefore, if a furniture manufacturer was undecided whether to produce new designs for teenagers' bedrooms or electric reclining armchairs for the elderly, reference to government publications for the forecast age distribution of the population over the next ten years would be a useful starting point.

Trade organisations

Trade organisations produce regular reports on the state of the markets that their members operate in. For example:

- British Furniture Manufacturers
- Make UK (the engineering employers federation).

If an entrepreneur planned to start small-scale furniture-making business, then details of the most recent trends in consumer taste for furniture could be obtained from the first source in the list. Clearly, further research might then be needed to see if, locally, this national data was reflected in consumer demand in the entreprenuer's own area, if they planned to sell to through local markets.

Media articles and specialist publications

These are widely available although some can only be obtained via subscription. Before a business uses market evidence from these publications, questions should be asked about the primary resource of the data, who collected it and whether any potential for bias – intentional or not – exists. Examples include:

- *Marketing* – this journal provides weekly advertising spend data and consumer 'recall of adverts' results
- *The Grocer*
- *Motor Trader*
- *The Financial Times* – regular articles on key industries such as IT and detailed country reports – essential for potential exporters
- Society of Motor Manufacturers and Traders annual report.

Online

The internet has transformed secondary data collection. The internet allows a business to research competitors and analyse their website and online marketing strategy. Business websites can also reveal information about how a firm is promoting its products and services. The published accounts of public limited companies are available online and they usually include details of sales levels, sales growth and profit margins. Online secondary research is often a good starting point for analysing a market. Perhaps the biggest issue is the vast amount of data that is available online. It is important to use the most reliable and relevant sources only. Whenever secondary research is conducted just from the internet, the accuracy and reliability of the source should always be checked.

LEARNER PROFILE

Knowledgeable

Knowledge of their consumers and potential consumers is crucial in allowing business people to develop an effective marketing strategy. Market research is one way of building up this knowledge.

'The more market and consumer knowledge an organisation has, the more likely it is to make good decisions.'

In pairs or as a group, discuss the extent to which this statement is true.

CASE STUDY 25.2

Netflix and secondary market research

Lab42 is a market research business that has just produced a report on subscription video on demand. Lab42's findings were based on a survey of 500 US streaming consumers. A key finding for Netflix is that it is still the leading provider in the market with the highest percentage of all users, highest percentage of exclusive users, and the highest consumer retention rate.

Based on the data from those who took part in the research, Netflix accounts for 89% of streaming video subscribers. Many customers subscribe to more than one service, and many Netflix customers also subscribe to Amazon.

1   Define the term 'market research'. [2]

2   List **four** methods of secondary data that Netflix might use as part of its market research. [4]

3   Explain **two** ways secondary market research might help Netflix in developing marketing strategy. [4]

4   Evaluate the usefulness of secondary research to Netflix as a method of gaining information about the subscription video-on-demand market. [10]

25.4 Qualitative research and quantitative research

All market research investigations can be categorised as either being 'qualitative' or 'quantitative'. Finding out about the quantities that consumers might purchase and at what prices is clearly important information, but what is often even more revealing is why consumers will or will not buy a particular product. **Qualitative research** should discover the motivational factors behind consumer buying habits. For example, **quantitative research** might establish the size of the potential market for a new luxury ice cream. But will consumers buy it for its taste and the quality of its ingredients or because it will be promoted as a lifestyle product that will reflect on the consumers' image of themselves? Only qualitative research, perhaps by the use of focus groups, can establish the answer to the last question – and it is important because it will help the business in its pricing and promotional decisions for the new product.

> **KEY TERMS**
>
> **qualitative research:** research into the in-depth motivations behind consumer buying behaviour or opinions
>
> **quantitative research:** research that leads to numerical results that can be presented and analysed

25.5 Sampling

In most cases of primary data collection it is impossible or too expensive to ask the 'entire population'. In data collection, the term 'population' does not mean 'the population of the region/country/world' but the total number of people under study, as defined by the objectives of the market research. For example: 'All people aged 21–25 years old still in full-time education'.

Owing to the cost of gathering data from the whole population that is of potential interest to the business, as well as the time it would take, sampling is essential when using primary research methods. Generally speaking, the larger the sample, the more confidence

can be given to the final results. In surveying consumer reaction to a new advertising campaign for a major brand of chocolate, a **sample** of ten people is unlikely to be sufficient. The first ten people chosen might show a positive reaction to the new advertisement. Yet the next ten might show a negative reaction. A sample of ten is too small to be confident about the result, as variations from the views of the whole target population occur by chance because of the limited number of respondents. A sample of 100 or even 1000 will produce results that will reflect much more accurately the total preferences of the whole survey population. There will be much less risk of pure chance distorting the results and causing **sampling error**.

What prevents all primary research being based on a sample size of 1000? Cost and time are the two major constraints here – the bigger the samples, the greater the cost and the longer the time needed to collect and interpret results.

The three most frequently used methods of sampling are as follows.

Quota sampling

The population is first segmented into mutually exclusive sub-groups – such as part-time and full-time workers. Then the interviewer or researcher uses their judgement to select people from each segment based on a specified proportion. For example, an interviewer may be told to sample 200 part-time workers and 300 full-time workers between the ages of 45 and 60 years. In **quota sampling** the selection of the sample is non-scientific and it may therefore be biased. Interviewers might be tempted to interview those who look most helpful or most attractive. The main weakness of quota sampling is that not everyone gets a chance of selection.

> **KEY TERMS**
>
> **sample:** group of people taking part in a market research survey selected to be representative of the whole target market
>
> **sampling error:** mistakes in research caused by using a sample for data collection rather than the whole target population
>
> **quota sampling:** gathering data from a number of people chosen out of a specific sub-group

Random sampling

Each member of the target population has an equal chance of being included in the sample. To select a random sample the following are needed:

- a list of all the people in the target population
- sequential numbers (each member of this population is assigned a number)
- a list of random numbers generated by computer.

If a sample of 100 is required, then the first 100 numbers on the random number list are taken and the people who had these numbers allocated to them will form the sample – but it may take time to contact these specific people. Just asking the first 100 pedestrians who pass by during a survey on a main shopping street is *not* random sampling. That is called convenience sampling and will be biased because different groups of people tend to frequent the main shopping streets at different times. This means that a single convenience sample will not reflect the whole population in which the business is interested.

Convenience sampling

The advantages of convenience sampling are the availability and the speed with which data can be gathered. The disadvantages are the risk that the sample might not represent the population as a whole, and it might be biased by volunteers. For example, if a study to determine the average age and gender of customers at a supermarket is conducted for three hours on a weekday afternoon it might be over-represented by elderly people who have retired and under-represented by people of working age.

KEY TERMS

random sampling: every member of the target population has an equal chance of being selected

convenience sampling: drawing a representative selection of people because of the ease of volunteering or selecting people because of their availability or easy access

---

CASE STUDY 25.3

Sampling methods on major market research projects

Novák, Svoboda and Dvořák (NSD) is a market research agency based in the Czech Republic. For large-scale market research projects, NSD uses random sampling.

The samples are based on a random sample of adults aged 18 and older. A random sample is one in which everyone in the population has an equal chance of being selected. The sample sizes used by NSD for the biggest surveys normally consist of over 1000 respondents.

A random sampling approach is used by NSD to make a statistical adjustment of the data to allow for gender, age, education and ethnicity. The sampling approach is based on using phone numbers that are randomly generated. The research period for interviewing is five days and potential respondents are called between 6 p.m. and 9 p.m.

NSD is an expensive agency that prides itself on the most precise and accurate methods. It is used by some of the largest companies in world.

1   Define the term 'random sample'.   [2]

2   Outline how NSD produces a random sample for a market research project.   [4]

3   Explain **one** advantage and **one** disadvantage of NSD using random sampling.   [4]

25.6 Business management tools – quantitative data

Once market research data has been collected it must be used – otherwise, what was the point of gathering it? Before most data can be used effectively it needs to be presented and analysed.

Descriptive statistics: data presentation

The main methods of data presentation are examined in Table 25.4.

Method of presentation	Main uses
Bar charts	Used when the absolute size or magnitude of results needs to be presented and compared Component and percentage component charts can be used to show how the total figure is comprised of different sections. Figure 25.1 shows a simple component bar chart. Alternatively, the bars could have been drawn to represent the percentage of each category out of the total. 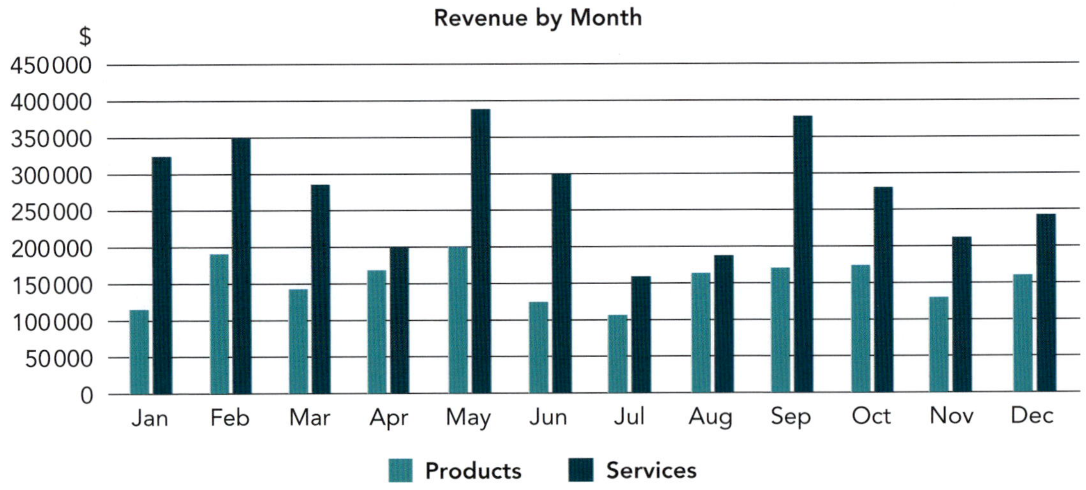 **Figure 25.1:** A bar chart

Method of presentation	Main uses
Pie charts	Used to show the relative importance of sections or segments out of a total result – these can then be visually compared with other time periods; they are less effective when comparisons between totals are needed or when precise comparisons of segments over time are required. 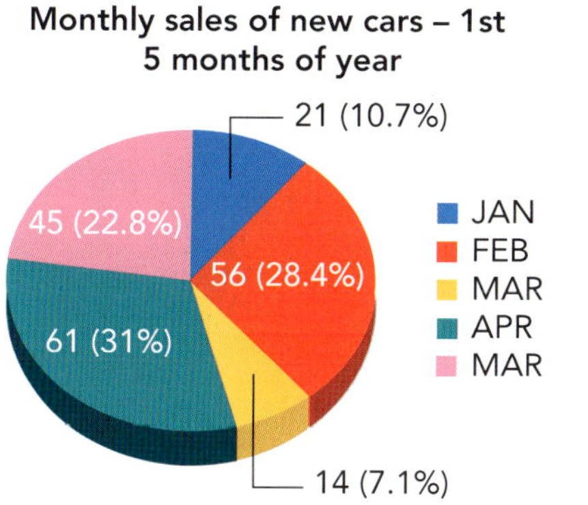 **Monthly sales of new cars – 1st 5 months of year** 21 (10.7%) 45 (22.8%) 56 (28.4%) 61 (31%) 14 (7.1%) JAN FEB MAR APR MAR **Figure 25.2:** A pie chart
Infographics	Used for graphic and visual representations of data which are intended to present information clearly. They improve understanding by using images to enhance peoples' ability to see patterns and trends. They can often be rather imprecise when using one symbol to represent a large number of results. 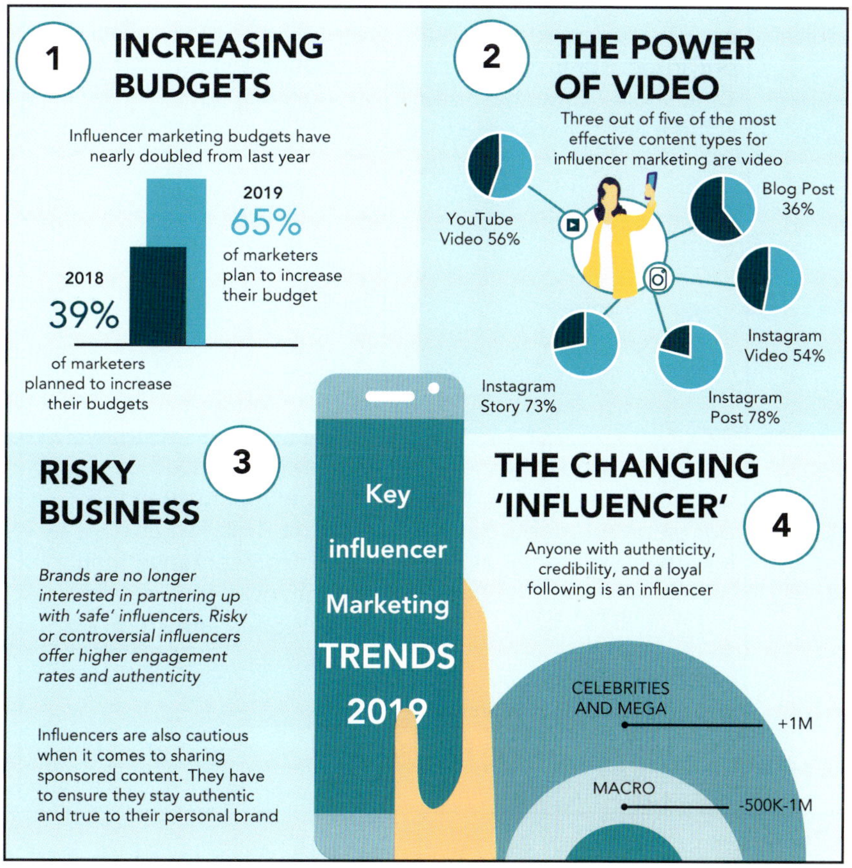 **1 INCREASING BUDGETS** Influencer marketing budgets have nearly doubled from last year 2019 **65%** of marketers plan to increase their budget 2018 **39%** of marketers planned to increase their budgets **2 THE POWER OF VIDEO** Three out of five of the most effective content types for influencer marketing are video YouTube Video 56% Blog Post 36% Instagram Video 54% Instagram Story 73% Instagram Post 78% **Key influencer Marketing TRENDS 2019** **3 RISKY BUSINESS** Brands are no longer interested in partnering up with 'safe' influencers. Risky or controversial influencers offer higher engagement rates and authenticity Influencers are also cautious when it comes to sharing sponsored content. They have to ensure they stay authentic and true to their personal brand **4 THE CHANGING 'INFLUENCER'** Anyone with authenticity, credibility, and a loyal following is an influencer CELEBRITIES AND MEGA +1M MACRO -500K-1M **Figure 25.3:** An infographic

Table 25.4: Examples of methods of data presentation

The most common way of analysing data is to calculate 'averages' of results. These measures tell a user something about the 'central tendency' of the data being analysed. Table 25.5 explains the uses and limitations of three commonly used measures of average.

Average measure	Uses	Advantages	Disadvantages
Mean – the mathematical average obtained by adding all results and dividing by number of results.	When the range of results is small, the mean can be a useful indicator of likely sales levels per period of time. This could be used to help determine reorder levels. Often used for making comparisons between sets of data, e.g., attendance at football clubs.	The mean includes all of the data in its calculation. It is well recognised as the average as it is so widely used – and therefore it is easily understood. It can be used to analyse data further in other ways that assist in understanding the significance of the results collected.	The main problem is that the mean is affected by one or two extreme results. For instance, a mean income figure for employees of a business is likely to be distorted by the high salary of the chief executive officer. It is commonly not a whole number. Is it really useful for stock-ordering purposes to know that the mean shoe size sold was 6.38?
Mode – the most frequently occurring result.	As the most frequently occurring, the result could be used for stock-ordering purposes. For instance, if a shoe shop knows that size 6 is the most popular size this will influence its stock orders.	It is easily observed and no calculation is necessary. The result is a whole number. It is easily understood.	For grouped distributions, the result is estimated from the modal group – a fairly complex calculation could be made if this estimate was not accurate enough. The mode does not consider all of the data. As a consequence, it cannot be used for further statistical analysis. There may be more than one modal result, which could cause confusion.
Median – the middle result when data is put in order.	Could be used in wage negotiations, e.g., 'Half of our union members earn less than $xx per week.' Often used in advertising, e.g., 'The reliability records show that our products are always in the best-performing 50% of all brands.'	It is less influenced by extreme results than the mean is. This makes it more representative than the mean when there are a few significantly high or low results.	Calculation from grouped data is not straightforward and there is an element of inaccuracy when doing this. When there is an even number of items in the results, its value is approximated. It cannot be used for further statistical analysis.

Table 25.5: The three types of averages

ACTIVITY 25.3

1   Use the data you derived from the survey you did in Activity 25.1 to carry out statistical analysis of the music-listening habits in your school. Use suitable software to produce one of the following charts to represent the data from your survey. For example, a pie chart could be used to illustrate the data on the proportion of students listening to music of different genres.

- table
- line graph
- bar chart
- pie chart
- histogram
- infographic.

2   Present the data you have produced to the rest of the class and summarise your conclusions for each question in the survey.

Quartiles and standard deviation

These are two measures of the 'spread' of data – how dispersed the data is from the 'middle point'. For example, assume two classes (of 20 students each) took a business test. The mean score in both classes was 52%. However, in class 1, 5 students scored above 70% and 5 students scored below 30%. In class 2, all students scored between 30% and 70%. The results in class 1 are much more dispersed from the mean.

What are the possible business uses of measures of 'dispersion'? Two examples help to illustrate the potential usefulness:

- Example 1: a clothes retailer has researched the waist sizes of men's jeans sold over the last 12 months. Half of the jeans sold were for waist sizes between 30 cm and 36 cm. The retailer should order more jeans in this size range than any other size range.

- Example 2: A yogurt manufacturer is controlling the volume of yogurt its machines put into each pot. The mean measure is 200 ml. The average amount by which the volume varies from this is 20 ml. Would the manufacturer be taking a risk of breaking consumer law if the pots were labelled with 'contain at least 180 ml'?

Quartiles are a measure that splits numerical data into four equal parts when the data is put in order. The inter-quartile range is the difference between the third quartile result and the first quartile result. Note that the value of the second quartile is the same as the median. Figure 25.4 illustrates how quartiles divide a set of data into four equal sections.

Using the data in Figure 25.4, the sales manager of the car showroom should expect in 25% of future periods to sell 26 new cars or fewer. This information might

KEY TERM

quartiles: splitting an ordered set of results into four equal parts

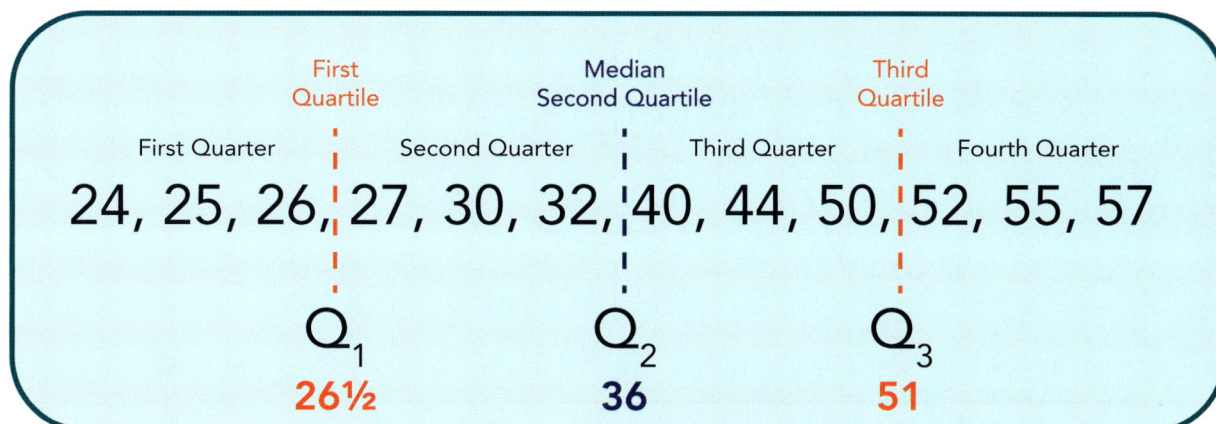

Figure 25.4: Twelve results for typical weekly sales of new cars divided into quartiles

encourage the sales manager to introduce a bonus if sales people exceed this figure each week.

Standard deviation is another measure of dispersion or spread of the data.

Business managers do not necessarily need to know how the SD is measured – but they should be aware of its significance for important business decisions. The key benefit of calculating the SD (which can be undertaken using a calculator or computer) is that its value indicates the spread of data around the mean. When sufficient data has been gathered (for example on the number of coffees bought per consumer each month or the weight of packets of biscuits produced on a production line) the results will be distributed evenly around the mean (symmetrically). These results can be presented in the form of a distribution curve as shown in Figure 25.5 and this is called a normal distribution curve.

The mean number of coffees bought in Figure 25.5 is 50 per month, and the average difference from this mean

result (the SD) is 10. The special feature of a normal curve is that the proportion of results within 1, 2 or 3 SDs of the mean will always be the same, no matter what is being measured. So, in the example in Figure 25.5, 68% of consumers bought 40–60 coffees each month, 1 SD either side of the mean. If we want to know what proportion of consumers bought more than 70 coffees per month (perhaps to calculate the cost of a discount scheme for those who consume a lot of coffee!) the graph shows us how to do that. The graph makes it clear that 95% of consumers bought between 30 and 70 coffees, so 5% bought *either* less than 30 *or* more than 70. As the curve is symmetrical, 2.5% bought more than 70 coffees so the discount scheme will be costed on the basis of only 2.5% of consumers being eligible for it.

Integrating these business management tools into the syllabus

Statistical data is likely to be gathered and analysed in all of the functional areas of a business. The following examples indicate how the presentation of statistics

> **KEY TERM**
>
> **standard deviation (SD):** measures the average dispersion of a set of data from its mean result

Standard deviations in a normal distribution

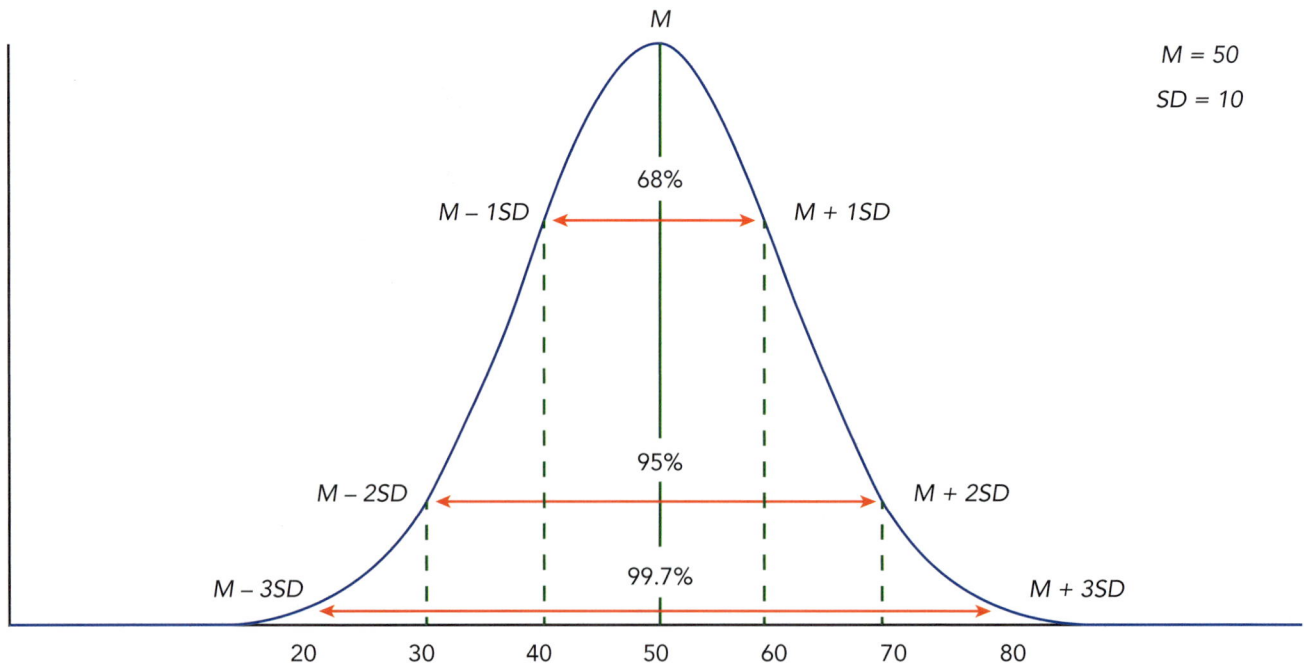

Figure 25.5: Number of coffees bought per consumer each month

could be important for managers in operations, human resources, finance as well as in marketing:

- comparing output levels from a factory over a period of 12 months
- showing how rates of employee absenteeism vary between different branch offices in a large business
- presenting to shareholders the sales and profit performance of the business over a period of several years.

Similarly, the analysis of statistical data could be important to all departmental managers. Knowing and

understanding the measures of central tendency and dispersion of data could be helpful when:

- an operations manager in a bakery has to stop production when there is more than a 2% risk of the weight of loaves falling below 350 grams – as this is the stated weight on the packaging
- a human resource manager is developing a bonus system for sales employees where only those achieving the top 5% of sales results will be eligible
- a finance manager is analysing the chance that the financial targets of different branches of the business will be exceeded by more than 80% of the branches.

SELF-EVALUATION CHECKLIST

After studying this chapter, complete this table.

I am able to apply and analyse:	Needs more work	Almost there	Ready to move on
The following methods/techniques of primary market research: surveys, interviews, focus groups, observations (AO2)			
the following methods/techniques of secondary market research: market analyses, academic journals, government publications, media articles, online (AO2)			
the difference between qualitative and quantitative market research (AO2)			
the following sampling methods: quota, random, convenience (AO2)			
I am able to synthesise and evaluate:			
why and how organisations carry out market research (AO3)			
I am able to select and apply the business management tools:			
mean, mode, median, quartiles, standard deviation, bar charts, pie charts, infographics			

REFLECTION

Think of a business you would like to start. Explain to another learner how you would plan and carry out effective market research for this business.

PROJECT

Market research through vending machines

Coca-Cola markets and sells its products in over 200 countries and has developed a global and universal image over 127 years. However, the brand needs to address different regional preferences such as flavour, calorie count, sugar content, consumer behaviour and of course competition. It is using information technology to drive its research.

The Freestyle 9100

Coca-Cola has reinvented the fountain beverage machine with the Coca-Cola Freestyle 9100. It includes optical and motion sensors, Bluetooth technology, real-time cloud connectivity and artificial intelligence. The Freestyle 9100 means vending machine data can be processed in real-time to analyse consumer purchasing decisions.

Introduction of AI

Each individual machine conducts real-time analysis of consumer data, responding in various helpful ways to improve customer experience. The AI algorithm means every establishment can use its machine to promote unique, bespoke beverages and trending flavours to its consumers.

AI also allows these machines to adjust to the 'mood' of their environment. In gyms, for example, the display screen will focus on performance-based sodas, the promotion of water and healthier beverages. Machines in shopping malls will display lively, colourful, trending sodas, and hospital machines will appear more functional. Globally, Coca-Cola has installed over 50 000 machines, serving over 14 million drinks per day, which creates a lot of research data.

Responding to the data

Coca-Cola's drinks machines gave data that suggested considerable consumption levels of Sprite and Cherry flavours. As a result, Coca-Cola released Sprite Cherry and Sprite Cherry Zero products in stores. In light of growing awareness of health and wellness, and increasing sales of diet beverages, the Freestyle 9100 was also adapted to include 117 low calorie/ no-calorie options and 130 no-caffeine options.

The app

The new drink dispenser also invites customers to download a 'pre-order app' allowing them to create drink mixes prior to collecting orders. The strategy appeals to Gen Z and Millennials in response to the rising use of smartphones and tech-savvy consumers. The app is expected to produce more accurate decision-making data since customers have more time to make their choices.

Coca-Cola remains the world's largest beverage company through continual innovation such as their latest adoption of AI. By using high-tech solutions to collecting consumer data, Coca-Cola optimised its product and sales processes. The dispensing machines have become real-time sources of market research, allowing it to identify opportunity and weakness before taking to the shelves. As consumer preferences evolve, winning brands will continually innovate to stay one step ahead.

1 Working in pairs or groups, research the ways other businesses have used AI and other IT-based data collection techniques as part of their market research.

2 Present your example to the class.

Thinking about your project:

- Now that you have prepared and delivered your presentation, do you feel you have a better understanding of the use of IT in market research?

- How would you rate your group's presentation in comparison to those of the other groups?

- What changes would you make to your presentation if you could do it again?

EXAM-STYLE QUESTIONS

The success of Energizze

The Banda family run a medium-sized soft-drinks manufacturing business in Zambia called Banda Beverages. The company has been successful over last five years because of its best-selling energy drink Energizze. The company launched Energizze two years ago in an attempt to exploit the fast-growing energy drink market and saw sales start well and then grow dramatically. The product is now one of top five selling soft drinks in Zambia.

Part of Banda Beverages' success as a business is effective primary market research. The business has a strong marketing team that worked with a specialist market research consultancy on the launch of Energizze. The marketing team used a quota sample to conduct a consumer survey that generated effective quantitative research. However, when it is doing initial reach it uses convenience sampling to save time. Once a sample group has been generated Banda uses a series of focus groups to build on the information from the consumer survey and produce qualitative research.

Banda Beverages has also tried to develop its approach to consumer data collection by using information technology and AI. This approach has produced very up-to-date consumer preference information which has helped Banda adapt its product mix.

1	Outline what a pie chart shows.	[2]
2	Define the term 'sampling'.	[2]
3	State **two** types of charts that Banda could use to display data.	[2]
4	Explain why Banda might choose to use pie charts rather than bar charts to display a particular piece of data.	[4]
5	Outline the difference between quantitative and qualitative market research.	[4]
6	Explain **two** benefits of quantitative research used by Banda.	[4]
7	Define the term 'convenience sampling'.	[2]
8	State **two** methods of secondary research.	[2]
9	Explain why Banda Beverages might have chosen to also use quota sampling.	[4]
10	Evaluate the view that the key to the successful launch of Energizze was effective market research.	[10]

> # Chapter 26
> # The seven Ps
> # of the
> # marketing mix

LEARNING OBJECTIVES

On completing this chapter you should be able to:

Apply and analyse:

- Product: The relationship between the product life cycle, product portfolio and the marketing mix (AO2)
- Product: The relationship between the product life cycle, investment, profit and cash flow (AO2)
- Product: The following aspects of branding awareness, development, loyalty, value (AO2)
- Product: The importance of branding (AO2)
- The following aspects of promotion: above-the-line promotion, below-the-line promotion, through-the-line promotion (AO2)

CONTINUED

Synthesise and evaluate:

- Product: Extension strategies (AO3)
- Price: The appropriateness of the following pricing methods: cost-plus pricing (mark-up), penetration pricing, loss leader, predatory pricing, premium pricing

> dynamic pricing, competitive pricing, contribution pricing, price elasticity of demand (AO3)

- Promotion: Social media marketing as a promotional strategy (AO3)
- Place: The importance of different types of distribution channels (AO3)
- People: The importance of employee–customer relationships in marketing a service and cultural variations in these relationships (AO3)
- Processes: The importance of delivery processes in marketing a service and changes in these processes (AO3)
- Physical evidence: The importance of tangible physical evidence in marketing a service (AO3)
- Appropriate marketing mixes for particular products or businesses (AO3)

BUSINESS IN CONTEXT

Which does best with digital promotion – Nike or Adidas?

These are two of the best-known companies and their brand logos – the 'swish' and 'three stripes' – are recognised globally. These rivals spend billions of dollars each year (Nike $3.59 billion and Adidas $3 billion) on competing promotions and point-of-sale displays. Increasingly, both brands are switching this expenditure to digital media to appeal to their main target markets. Brandwatch reported that Adidas features in over six million images and Nike in over five million on Instagram and Twitter each month. This means that they are highly popular and visible online.

Nike has more followers than Adidas on Instagram and YouTube, whereas Adidas has more followers on Facebook and Twitter.

Successful **digital promotions** depends on:

- using hashtags
- engaging with the audience
- using multiple social media channels

- generating conversations with consumers
- being innovative
- personalising communications with consumers.

Discuss in pairs or a group:

- Why is digital promotion so important to these two businesses?
- How can digital promotion be used to 'communicate personally' with consumers?
- Both companies spend about 10% of total revenue on promotions. Do you think it would be better to use this finance to offer lower prices instead?

KEY TERM

digital promotion: the use of the internet, mobile devices, social media, search engines and other channels to communicate with consumers to provide information about products and encourage the purchase of them

CONTINUED

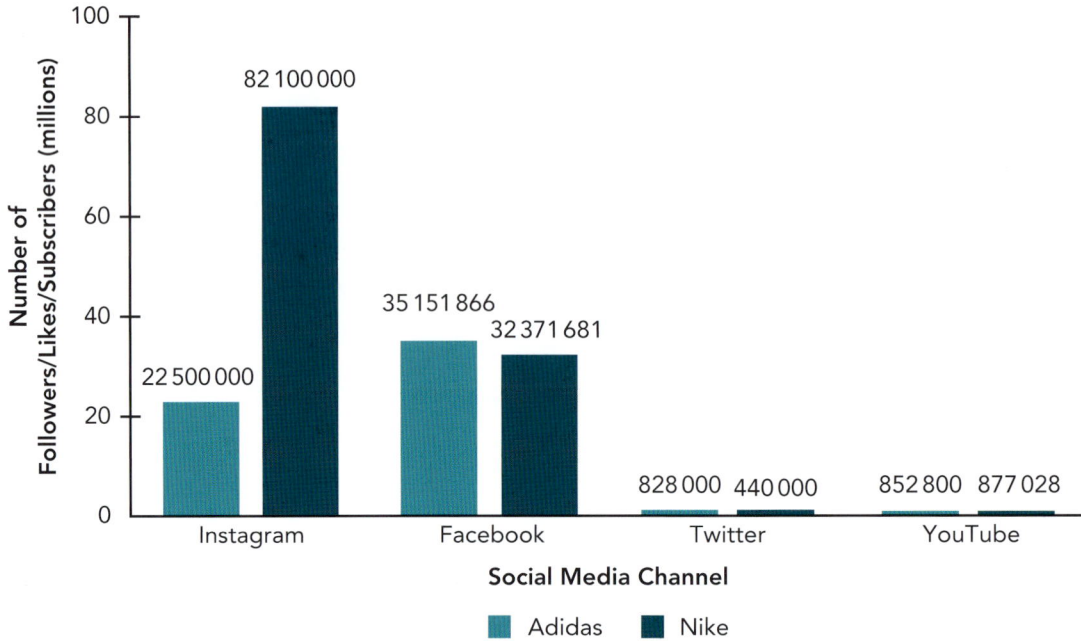

Which company is on top with social media platforms?

KEY CONCEPT LINK

Creativity

Flash mobs have become increasingly popular online over the years. Fitting with that trend is a flash-mob video of more than 250 people dancing at the Central Station in Antwerp, Belgium. The goal was to promote the *Grease* musical in Antwerp.

The video begins with one man dancing, but it progresses into an amazing act with hundreds of people. The video was captured during morning rush hour at the Belgian station. People were minding their own business. But a few moments later, suddenly the familiar music from *Grease* starts playing, and people start looking around. One man begins to dance. Four more join him and people free up the floor for them.

This flash mob is a an unusual marketing event, used to promote a product.

26.1 Marketing mix

The **marketing mix** for a product is a major factor in influencing whether a business can sell it profitably.

The marketing mix is made up of seven interrelated decisions – the seven Ps. The four Ps which are relevant for all products (goods and services) are **product, price, promotion** (including advertising and packaging) and **place** (where and how a product will be sold to consumers). The other three Ps relate to the marketing of services – **people, process** and **physical evidence**.

The four Ps which are relevant to all products are:

- **Product**. Customers require the right good or service. This might be an existing product, an adaptation of an existing product or a newly developed one.

- **Price** is important too. If set too low, then customers may lose confidence in the product's quality; if it is too high, then many will be unable to afford it.

- **Promotion** must be effective and targeted at the appropriate market – telling customers about the product's availability and convincing them that 'your brand' is the one to choose. Packaging is often used to reinforce this promotional image.

- **Place** refers to how the product is distributed to the consumer. If it is not available at the right time in the right place, then even the best product in the world will not be bought in the quantities expected.

Not all of the four Ps have the same degree of significance in every marketing mix. It is vital that these elements fit together into a coherent and integrated plan – targeted at clear marketing objectives. An appropriate marketing mix will ensure that these marketing decisions are interrelated. They must be carefully coordinated to make sure that customers are not confused by conflicting messages being given about the good or service being sold – this is called a **coordinated marketing mix**.

KEY TERMS

marketing mix: the key decisions that must be taken in the effective marketing of a product

coordinated marketing mix: key marketing decisions complement each other and work together to give customers a consistent message about the product

ACTIVITY 26.1

In pairs or as a group, produce a presentation about the marketing mix of your school. In your presentation consider the importance of product, price, promotion and place in the way your school is marketed.

ACTIVITY 26.2

1 Why are the products in the Table not using a coordinated marketing mix?

	Product	Price	Place	Promotion
Mix A	Exclusive range of watches	High – aiming at the affluent consumers	Exclusive shops in big city location	Advertised on a local television network
Mix B	Range of electrical goods targeted at low-income families	Low – low costs mean the products are accessible to low-income buyers	Sold only over the internet	Advertised on billboards and in free local newspapers
Mix C	Nail salon targeting mid-range consumers	High – premium prices set for consumers	Salon located in high street locations	Advertised in local newspapers and online
Mix D	High-quality coffee shop chain targeting high-income consumers	Premium or high-price strategy	Expensive business district locations	Advertised in local newspapers

2 For each product in the table, identify the element of its marketing mix that does not appear to fit in with the overall marketing mix.

3 For each product, analyse a change to the marketing mix that would make the mix better coordinated.

26.2 Product

It is sometimes said that 'you can sell any product to consumers once, but to establish loyalty and good customer relationships, the product must be right'. The product needs to meet customer expectations, as discovered by market research, regarding:

- quality
- durability
- performance
- appearance.

If it does not, then no matter how low the price or how expensive the advertisement, it will not sell successfully in the long term.

The term '**product**' includes consumer and industrial goods and services. Consumer goods can be both **consumer durables** (e.g., washing machines) and single use (e.g., chocolate bars). Industrial products such as mining equipment are purchased by businesses, not final consumers. Consumer services have no physical existence but they satisfy consumer needs in intangible ways, e.g., hairdressing, car repairs, childminding and banking.

> ### KEY TERMS
>
> **product:** the end result of the production process sold on the market to satisfy a customer need
>
> **consumer durables:** manufactured products that can be reused and are expected to have a reasonably long life, such as cars

26.3 The product life cycle, product portfolio and the marketing mix

The product life cycle

Knowing when to launch a new product or update an existing one can give a business a crucial advantage. Allowing existing models of cars or computers to struggle in the market when other businesses are introducing attractive new or revamped ones is a classic business error that has led to many failures. An awareness of the **product life cycle** principle can assist greatly in dealing with this problem. The life cycle of a product records the sales of that product over time. There are several stages in this life cycle and these are shown in Figure 26.1.

> ### KEY TERM
>
> **product life cycle:** the pattern of sales recorded by a product from launch to withdrawal from the market

Points to note on the first three stages:

- **Introduction.** This is when the product has just been launched after development and testing. Sales are often quite low to begin with and may increase only quite slowly – but there are exceptions, such as a newly launched download by a major rap artist.

- **Growth.** If the product is effectively promoted and well received by the market, then sales should grow significantly. This stage cannot last forever, although all firms wish that it would. Eventually (and this may take days, weeks or even years) sales growth will begin to slow and might stop altogether, which leads the product into the next stage. The reasons for declining growth include increasing competition, technological changes making the product less appealing, changes in consumer tastes and saturation of the market.

- **Maturity or saturation.** At this stage, sales fail to grow, but they do not decline significantly either. This stage can last for years, for example Coca-Cola. The saturation of consumer durables markets is caused by most consumers who want a certain product having already bought one. The best recent example is mobile phones. Although the world market has grown phenomenally in recent years, in sales growth ended altogether in 2020. This was partly because the vast number of consumers already possessed a mobile phone. Many consumers will only buy a new mobile phone if their existing one breaks down or is replaced by newer technology. This is why all phone companies are working so hard on the next generation of mobile phones using 5G.

This technology contributed to an increase in global mobile sales of 5.5% in 2021.

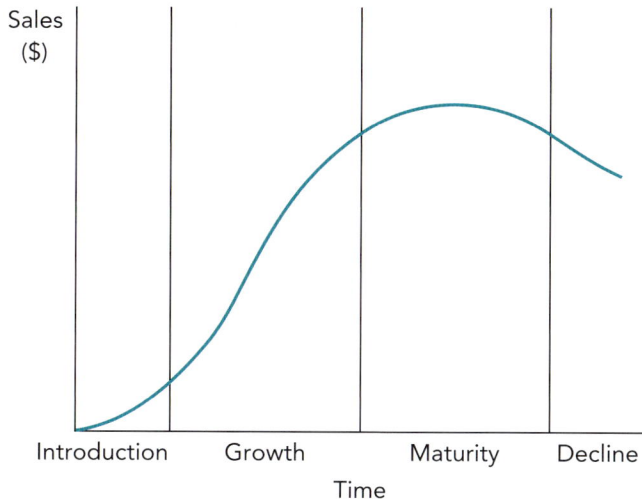

Figure 26.1: Product life cycle – the length of each stage will vary from product to product

---

ACTIVITY 26.3

In pairs or as a group, research a business on the internet and complete the following:

1 Make a list of 5–10 products that are part of the business's product portfolio.

2 Draw a product life cycle on your computer (you could also create a hand-drawn poster version).

3 Position the products you have selected in the places you think they are in the product life cycle.

4 Create a computer-generated presentation (or a poster version) that illustrates your businesses product portfolio in terms of the product life cycle.

This is partly a creativity exercise, so make your presentation as artistic as you can.

CASE STUDY 26.1

Tencent's product life cycle

Tencent is one of the largest video gaming companies in the world. As gaming has increasingly gone online, Tencent has developed its online product line aggressively with a series of games that have generated huge revenues. In 2020 Tencent launched Moonlight Blade, which achieved revenues of over $50 million in its first week of release. Other successful Tencent titles include League of Legends, Player Unknown's Battlegrounds, PUBG Mobile and Arche Age.

Video games tend to have relatively short product life cycles, which means Tencent has to have a whole series of new games in development to replace games as they go into the decline phase of the product life cycle.

1 Define the term 'product line'. [2]

2 Using a product life cycle diagram, outline the different phases of the marketing mix that a computer game might go through during its existence. [4]

3 Explain **two** reasons why products in the online video game market might have a short product life cycle. [4]

4 Discuss the usefulness of the product life cycle to Tencent in the management of its product portfolio. [4]

The product portfolio

Most businesses market more than one type of product, and this means that they have a **product portfolio**.

> ## KEY TERM
>
> **product portfolio:** the collection of all of the products (goods and services) offered for sale by a business

There are several advantages to a business having a range of products in its portfolio. They include:

- it reduces the business risk of consumer tastes or demand trends moving against a single product, such as the move away from DVDs to downloads

- it allows a balanced product portfolio to be developed, which provides for some diversification

- cash flow and profit peaks and troughs are likely to be smoothed out over long periods of time.

Businesses often take important decisions about underperforming and unprofitable products, a strategy that requires portfolio analysis (see the BCG matrix in Chapter 24).

Well-established businesses often have diversified product portfolios. New product developments, mergers and takeovers contribute to portfolio range and size over time. Large businesses can afford to market a range of different products using different marketing techniques. International marketing can also lead to an increase in the size of a product portfolio, with products being adapted or new ones added to meet the demand trends and cultures of difference countries (see Chapter 29).

In contrast, more recently established businesses with smaller portfolios are more exposed to market changes and the performance of their main products. This can result in variable cash flow and profit performance over time.

Ideally, a business should aim for a balanced product portfolio. As one product reaches the decline stage of its product life cycle, so other products are in their growth stage or are being prepared for launching onto the market. This approach will lead to a more balanced risk profile for the business as well as achieving smoother cash flow and profit results over time. Figure 26.2 illustrates an ideal balanced product portfolio.

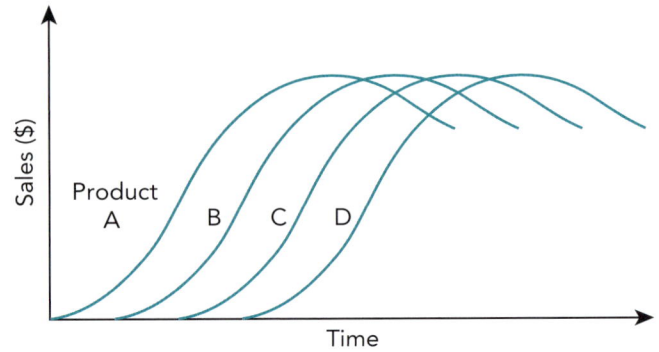

Figure 26.2: A balanced portfolio of products

How the product life cycle impacts on the marketing mix

- When would you advise a business to lower the price of its product – at the growth or at the decline stage?

- In which phase is advertising likely to be most important – during introduction or at maturity?

- When should variations be made to the product – during introduction or at maturity?

- At which stage of the product life cycle should new products be researched and developed to update and augment the product portfolio?

One of the key applications of the product life cycle concept is as a guide to making changes to elements of the marketing mix. Table 26.1 explains how marketing-mix decisions can be influenced through knowledge of the product life cycle.

> ## TIP
>
> When discussing the product life cycle it is important to remember that no two products are likely to have exactly the same pattern of sales growth/maturity and decline.

How product portfolio analysis impacts on the marketing mix

Boston Consulting Group matrix analysis of the product life cycle helps marketing departments to make key marketing mix decisions. If you refer back to Chapter 23 to reacquaint yourself with the key features of this matrix, it will help you understand the following possible strategies. For example, the matrix helps marketing managers to:

- analyse the performance and current position of existing product portfolios
- decide what marketing action to take with existing products
- plan for the introduction of new products.

By identifying the position of all products of the business on the matrix, a full analysis of the portfolio is possible. This should help focus on which products need marketing mix support or which need corrective action. This action could include the following marketing decisions:

- **Building** – supporting question mark products with additional advertising, sales promotion

or further distribution outlets. The finance for this could be obtained from the established cash cow products.

- **Holding** – continuing marketing support for star products so that they maintain their good market position. In time, adaptations of the product may be needed to freshen it in the eyes of the consumers so that high sales growth can be sustained.

- **Milking** – taking the positive cash flow from established products and investing it in other products in the portfolio. This investment could either be in terms of new product development or spending on promotion and other marketing activities to support the sales of other products in the portfolio.

Product life-cycle phase	Price	Promotion	Place (distribution outlets)	Product
Introduction	May be high compared to competitors (premium) or low (penetration)	High levels of above-the-line promotion (informative advertising to make consumers aware of the product's arrival on the market)	Restricted outlets – possibly high-class outlets if a premium pricing strategy is adopted	New model launched
Growth	If successful, an initial penetration pricing strategy could now lead to rising prices	Consumers need to be convinced to make repeat purchases – brand identification will help to establish consumer loyalty	Growing numbers of outlets in areas indicated by strength of consumer demand Online selling could be used	Planning product improvements and developments to maintain consumer appeal
Maturity	Competitors likely to be entering market. Business will need to keep prices at competitive levels	Brand reinforcement continues – growing need to stress the positive differences with competitors' products Use below-the-line promotion aimed at clearly identified target markets	Highest geographical range of outlets possible – developing new types of outlets where possible	New models, colours, accessories, etc. as part of extension strategies
Decline	Lower prices to sell off stock – or if the product has a small 'cult' following, prices could even rise	Advertising likely to be very limited – may just be used to inform of lower prices	Eliminate unprofitable outlets for the product	Prepare to replace with other products – slowly withdraw from certain markets

Table 26.1: The marketing mix and phases of the product life cycle

- **Divesting** – identifying the worst-performing dogs and stopping the production and supply of these. This strategic decision should not be taken lightly as it will involve other issues, such as the impact on the workforce and whether the spare capacity freed up by stopping production can be used profitably on another product. Divesting should, ideally, come at the same time as the introduction of a newly developed product into the market.

These marketing mix strategies can only be undertaken if the business has a balanced portfolio of products. If there are too many dogs or question marks, then the overall shortage of cash may not allow the firm to take appropriate action.

ACTIVITY 26.4

Consider the following four products and discuss in pairs or as a group what you think each of their product life cycles would look like.

- McDonald's Big Mac
- iPhone
- Minecraft computer game
- Kellogg's Cornflakes.

26.4 Extension strategies

These strategies aim to lengthen the product life cycle of products. They include developing new markets for existing products (e.g., export markets), new uses for existing products, and product relaunches involving new packaging and advertising (see Figure 26.3).

During the 'decline' phase, sales will fall steadily. Either no extension strategy has been tried, or it has not worked, or the product is so obsolescent that the only option is replacement. Newer products from competitors are the most likely cause of declining sales and profits – and when the product becomes unprofitable or when its replacement is ready for the market, it will be withdrawn. An evaluation of possible **extension strategies** is outlined in Table 26.2.

KEY TERM

extension strategies: marketing plans that extend the maturity stage of the product before a brand new one is needed

---

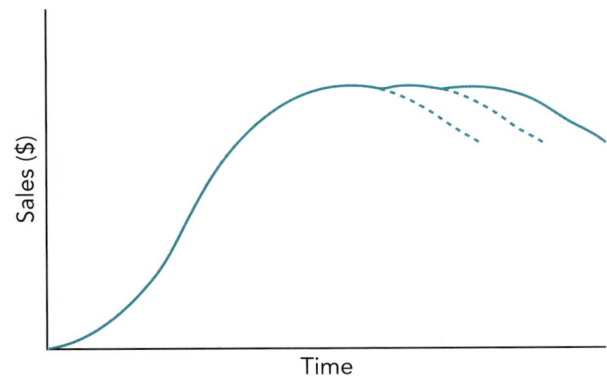

Figure 26.3: Product life cycle – showing the effect of extension strategies

Evaluation of extension strategies

Strategy	Example	Benefits	Limitations
Add features to the original product	Adding a camera and bigger screen to an old tablet computer design	Can usually be developed and marketed more quickly – and at lower cost – than a completely new product	The basic original product is still ageing and at maturity/decline, so consumers may not be interested in a slightly revised product
Repackage a product	Breakfast cereal box changes its design	Relatively cheap and quick method	Consumers may quickly realise that the product is the same and feel they are being misled
Discount the price	Reduce the price of an older model of smartphone before a new model is released	Lower-income consumers can now afford the product – product promotion might actually target different market segments	Impact on long-term image of the brand and the company – better to replace the product earlier to avoid discounting
Rebrand	Changing the name, packaging and promotion of a confectionery bar so it can be sold to different market segments	Opens up new market segments; can be presented as a substantially 'new product'	Expensive – is this rebranding strategy really worthwhile if a product has the perception of being old-fashioned and is shortly to be replaced?
Sell into new markets, e.g., export markets	Sell ageing model of car in a low-income country that has few manufacturers and limited choice of products	Market development can increase sales, especially if the product is not perceived as being too old or 'mature' in these markets	Product and promotion may need to be redesigned to meet local laws and cultural requirements

Table 26.2: Benefits and limitations of extension strategies

The relationship between the product life cycle, investment, profit and cash flow

Product life cycle and investment

Investment – capital spending which aims to return a profit – is likely to be heaviest towards the end of a product's life cycle. Newer replacement products will be needed to 'take over' when the existing products cease to sell in sufficient numbers and profits are falling or non-existent. The time period required to research and develop (R&D) new products will determine the timing of this new investment. With pharmaceutical products it may well be a continuous process as the R&D can take many years before a potentially profitable new drug is ready for launch.

Product life cycle and profit

The profitability of products will vary considerably during the life cycle. High profit margins are most likely during the growth and maturity phase – but towards the end of the latter stage, prices might have to be made more competitive and this might start to lead to lower margins. At the decline stage, prices could fall further, hitting gross profit margins. However, if the fixed costs of developing the product and the machinery required to produce it have been fully covered, sales of the product might still yield some net profit.

Product life cycle and cash flow

Cash flow is vital to business survival and ignoring the link between cash flow and product life cycles could lead to lack of liquidity for the business. Figure 26.4 shows this typical relationship.

Cash flow is negative during the development of the product as costs are high, but nothing has yet been produced or sold. At introduction, the development costs might have ended but heavy promotional expenses are likely to be incurred – and these could continue into the growth phase. In addition, there is likely to be much unused factory capacity at this stage which will place a further strain on costs. As sales increase, then cash flow should improve – precisely when will depend on the length of consumer credit being offered.

The maturity phase is likely to see the most positive cash flows, because sales are high, promotional costs might be limited and spare factory capacity should be low. As the product passes into decline, so price reductions and falling sales are likely to combine to reduce cash flows. Clearly, if a business has too many of its products either at the decline or the introduction phase then the consequences for cash flow could be serious. Firms will benefit from a balanced portfolio of products, at different stages of their life cycles, so that cash from those entering maturity can be used to provide investment funds for developing eventual replacement products.

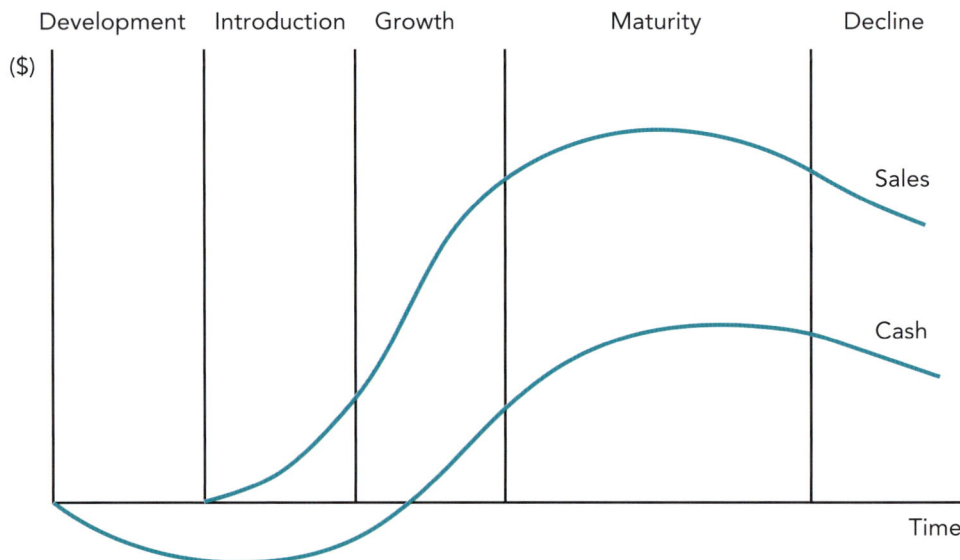

Figure 26.4: The link between cash flow and product life cycle

CASE STUDY 26.2

Branding in the outdoor clothing market

Rocky Path is a regional business that manufacturers outdoor clothing. The business uses corporate branding with each of its product lines carrying the Rocky Path brand name. The company's product mix includes waterproof jackets and trousers, walking boot and shoes, outdoor knitwear, and shirts and outdoor trousers.

Rocky path was founded eight years ago and has achieved average year-on-year growth of 7% since it was launched. The business's CEO, Aashi Bulan, believes the key to the company's success is maintaining a balanced product portfolio where existing products can support the

development of new products. Rocky Path has been very good at building a strong brand image for its products and extending the life of its most successful brands.

CONTINUED

1   Define the term 'extension strategy'.   [2]

2   Outline the profit and cash flow characteristics of the maturity phase of Rocky Path's product life cycle.   [4]

3   Explain why cash cows are important to Rocky Path when it is trying to maintain its long-term growth.   [4]

4   Discuss the usefulness of the Boston matrix for Rocky Path's brand management.   [10]

THEORY OF KNOWLEDGE

The Mars bar is one of the best-known brands of confectionery in world. It is produced by the American multinational Mars which also markets Wrigley's chewing gum and Pedigree Pet Food. Mars' commitment to its consumers is set out on its website and includes:

- investing $1 billion to build a new cocoa supply chain model centred on smallholder farmers

- creating more sustainable and resilient mint through plant science and investing in communities

- reducing its carbon footprint by using enough renewable energy to create all M&Ms® sold

- following the Nourishing Wellbeing commitment to advance science, innovation and marketing in ways that help billions of people and their pets lead healthier, happier lives.

Many people see a conflict between Mars' social commitment and the impact the Mars products might have on the health of its customers. The standard sized Mars bar has 20.8 grams of sugar (5 teaspoons) and the recommended daily intake is 30 grams.

In pairs or as a group discuss the extent to which ethics affects our trust in the marketing of confectionery such as the products produced by Mars.

26.5 Branding

Mobile phones are an example of a product, but Samsung is an example of a **brand**. What is the difference? The product is the general term used to describe the nature of what is being sold. The brand is the distinguishing name or symbol that is used to differentiate one manufacturer's products from another.

Branding can have a real influence on marketing. It can create a powerful image or perception in the minds of consumers – either negative or positive – and it can give one firm's products a unique identity. Successful brands can often charge premium prices as consumers are loyal to the product and the image that it generates. This helps to make the demand for products less price sensitive.

However, attempting to establish a new brand is often expensive. Increasing **brand awareness** and **brand loyalty** are primary goals of promotional activity in the early months or years of a product's launch. It can cost

millions of dollars to attempt to create an effective brand image, and success cannot be guaranteed. If a brand image receives bad publicity (such as Nestlé's

KEY TERMS

brand: an identifying symbol, name, image or trademark that distinguishes a product from its competitors

brand awareness: the extent to which a brand is recognised by potential customers and is correctly associated with a particular product – can be expressed as a percentage of the target market

brand loyalty: the faithfulness of consumers to a particular brand as shown by their repeat purchases irrespective of the marketing pressure from competing brands

marketing of powdered baby milk in developing countries) then the image of all products in the 'corporate brand' will be damaged.

If both brand awareness and **brand development** are high then the equity of the brand is likely to be substantial. **Brand value (or brand equity)** is the total amount that customers are prepared to pay extra for a branded product compared to what they would pay for a generic non-branded product.

KEY TERMS

brand development: measures the infiltration of a product's sales, usually per thousand population; if 100 people in 1000 buy a product, it has a brand development of 10

brand value (or brand equity): the premium that a brand has because customers are willing to pay more for it than they would for a non-branded generic product

---

The importance of branding

Effective branding can lead to the following benefits:

- it promotes instant recognition of the company and product – especially through the use of logos and images.

- it helps to differentiate the company and its products from rivals – this is especially important when the products themselves might be difficult to differentiate, e.g., petrol/gasoline.

- it aids employee motivation – they can become committed to the brand.

- It generates referrals from customers – especially through the use of social media.

- Customers know what to expect from the company and products.

- An emotional attachment can develop between the brand and customers, increasing customer loyalty.

- It increases the value of the business above the value of its physical assets (brand equity).

Branding is now increasingly an international process, not confined to one country or region. Establishing a successful brand image across national borders opens up the potential for increased sales and economies of scale – especially in terms of globally marketing products with the same range of promotions under the same name. It is increasingly important that businesses which have a multinational presence build up a consistent and recognisable brand image that is transferable between countries. UBS Bank has achieved this. Created by a series of mergers and takeovers that gave it many separate brand names and products, the bank lacked recognition in markets outside Switzerland. It merged many products under the UBS name and relaunched itself as a global bank serving local needs but with the prestige and image that come from being the sixth-largest bank in the world. Globalised branding and marketing can have substantial benefits, but there are limitations too if the international brand and image fail to link in with localised culture and customer tastes.

KEY TERM

trademark: a distinctive name, symbol, motto or design that identifies a business or its products – can be legally registered and cannot be copied

---

ACTIVITY 26.5

Characteristics of a brand

1   Working in pairs or as a group, consider the five branded products in the table. Complete the table by adding brand characteristics that match the products in the table.

2   In your pair or group discuss the logo/ **trademark** and slogan you might use for a new diet soft drink.

Product	Logo/ trademark	Slogan	Image description
Nutella			
Ralph Lauren			
Google			
McDonald's			
Disney			

CASE STUDY 26.3

Rebranding in social media

Facebook announced that it was rebranding. Facebook is now called Meta. The company is introducing a new company logo and further distinguishing the Meta name from the Facebook app.

1 Define the term 'brand'. [2]

2 Outline two ways that Facebook brands its product. [4]

3 Explain **two** benefits to Facebook of effective branding. [4]

4 Explain an advantage and a disadvantage to Facebook of rebranding itself. [4]

26.6 Price and pricing methods

Price is the amount paid by consumers for a product. Price is a vital component of the marketing mix as it impacts on the consumer demand for the product.

The pricing level will also:

- determine the degree of value added by the business to bought-in components
- influence the revenue and profit made by a business due to the impact on demand
- reflect the marketing objectives of the business and help establish the psychological image and identity of a product.

Get the pricing decision wrong and all of the hard work in market research, product development and branding can be put at risk.

Factors determining the price decision

There are a number of factors that will determine the pricing decision for a product:

- costs of production
- competitive conditions in the market
- competitors' prices
- marketing objectives

- price elasticity of demand
- whether it is a new or an existing product.

The significance of these is discussed in this chapter.

Cost-plus (mark-up) pricing

The **cost-plus pricing** method is often used by retailers. They take the price that they pay the producer or wholesaler for a product, and then just add a percentage **mark up**. The size of the mark up usually depends upon a combination of the strength of demand for the product, the number of competitors, and the age and stage of life of the product. Sometimes it also depends on traditional practice in the industry.

KEY TERMS

cost-plus pricing: adding a fixed mark up to the unit cost of a product to cover overhead costs and for profit

mark up: the extra amount or percentage added to the cost of goods to give the retail or selling price

---

WORKED EXAMPLE 26.1

Cost of bought-in materials: $40

50% mark-up on cost = $20

Selling price: $60

Penetration pricing

Firms tend to adopt **penetration pricing** because they are attempting to use mass marketing and gain a large market share. If the product gains a large market share, then the price could slowly be increased.

KEY TERM

penetration pricing: setting a relatively low price often supported by strong promotion in order to achieve a high volume of sales

---

Market penetration pricing aims to maximise short-term profits, before competitors enter the market with a similar product, and to project an exclusive image for the product. If rivals do launch similar products, it may be necessary for the price to be reduced over a period of time.

An example of this is pharmaceutical firms, which are often given a legal monopoly for a certain number of years for new drugs. They are able to charge high prices in order to recoup their considerable investments in research and to make high profits. It is not uncommon for them to reduce their prices in the last year of their legal monopoly in order to hold their market share when other companies enter.

The distinction between market penetration pricing and market skimming is illustrated in Figure 26.5.

Loss leaders

Loss leaders are widely used by supermarkets. Selling milk or bread at very low prices – perhaps below cost price – should encourage consumers into the stores to buy this low-priced product and, usually, other goods on which the supermarket makes a higher profit margin. Is this fair on smaller retailers of milk and bread who cannot buy in supplies as cheaply as the large supermarkets? Other examples include computer printers sold for $40 – but the replacement ink cartridges can cost $30 each.

KEY TERM

loss leader: product sold at a very low price to encourage consumers to buy other products

---

Predatory pricing

This is an illegal pricing strategy in the countries that make up the European Union and in other countries as it unfairly favours the strong, established companies compared to new entrants. In practice, it is very difficult to prove – businesses often claim that they are just adopting a loss-leader strategy.

A sign of **predatory pricing** is when the price of a product gradually gets lower, which can happen during a price war. It is difficult to prove that this is predatory pricing because it can be seen as price competition and not a deliberate act to eliminate competitors.

In the short term, a price war can be beneficial for consumers because of the lower prices. However, in the long term it is not beneficial as the company that wins a predatory price war (effectively putting its competitor out of business) will have a monopoly where it can set higher prices, offering consumers little option but to pay these (see Table 26.3 for a summary of pricing methods).

KEY TERM

predatory pricing: deliberately undercutting competitors' prices in order to try to force them out of the market

---

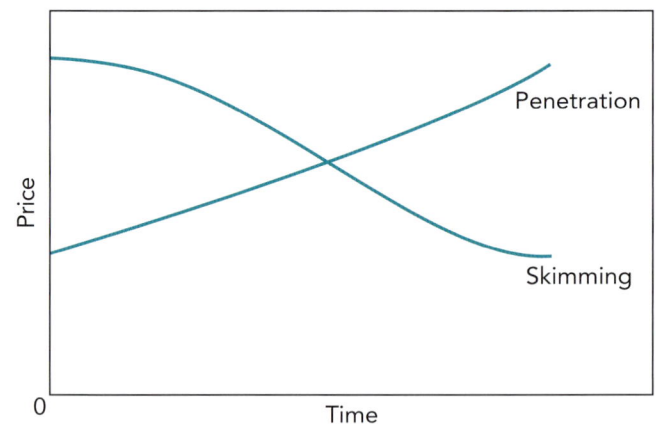

Figure 26.5: Market penetration pricing method compared with market skimming

Premium pricing

How do consumers judge the quality of a product and the value of a brand? One way is to compare the price of one product with its competitors. Many consumers assume that a higher-priced product will yield them greater satisfaction as it is either of higher quality (real or perceived) or has a brand image with greater appeal than that of its rivals. The psychological impact of price and pricing levels can be very strong and this encourages some businesses to use **premium pricing**.

The purpose of premium pricing is to give the sense that the product has a higher-quality image and reputation than competitors' products. It will only be effective if it is used as part of a coordinated marketing mix designed to reinforce that perception.

Premium pricing sets high prices and keep them high. The manufacturers of luxury brands often use premium pricing.

> **KEY TERM**
>
> **premium pricing:** setting a price above that of competitors with the aim of developing a superior image for the product.

CASE STUDY 26.4

Pricing high-quality furniture

The furniture maker Mahmoud Ltd is under competitive pressure from new firms that have entered the market in and around Cairo. Mahmoud makes high-quality dining furniture that is targeted at the luxury end of the furniture market.

There have been a significant number of new entrants to the market that have put Mahmoud under considerable pressure, and its total sales and market share are falling. The business's CEO, Anat, has sought the advice of a consultancy who have advised Mahmoud to reduce its mark-up from 50% to 30% in its cost-plus approach to pricing.

Total variable cost	$450 000
Total fixed cost	$330 000
Units produced	2400

1   Define the term 'cost-plus pricing'.   [2]

2   Using the cost data in the table calculate the price of a table at a 50% and 30% mark up.   [4]

3   Explain **two** disadvantages of Mahmoud reducing its mark up from 50% to 30%.   [4]

Methods	Advantages	Disadvantages
Cost-plus pricing	Price set will cover all costs of production Easy to calculate for single-product firms where there is no doubt about fixed-cost allocation Suitable for firms that are 'price makers' due to market dominance	Not necessarily accurate for firms with several products where there is doubt over the allocation of fixed costs Does not take market/competitive conditions into account Tends to be inflexible, e.g., there might be opportunities to increase prices even higher If sales fall, average fixed and average total costs rise – this could lead to the price being raised using this method
Penetration pricing	Low prices should lead to high demand – it is important to establish high-market share for new products If demand is high, the business may be able to raise prices after a period of time to increase profit margins	Profit margins might be very low – prices might have to increase in the future and there could be consumer resistance to this It could start a price war – and if competitors have more resources they might be able to survive this better Low price might be perceived as being an indicator of low quality
Loss leader	Makes a loss on one product but this is more than compensated for by profits on other products – perhaps complementary to the loss leader Increases market share	Cheaper generic alternatives might be sold by rival firms so the profit-making complementary products are not purchased from the loss-leading business
Predatory pricing	Drives down prices to benefit consumers and is likely to increase demand for the product May reduce the number of competitors in the long term and increase monopoly power of the 'predator'	It is illegal in many countries and, if proven, heavy fines can be imposed Consumers may try to find alternative products if the business achieves market power dominance and increases prices in the long term Consumers may perceive a lower quality product
Premium pricing	Helps to establish a perception of exclusivity and high brand image Consumers might associate high prices with high quality	Will only be effective if part of a coordinated mix which helps to establish a premium image for the product Could lead to low sales and revenue if consumers switch to lower-priced competitors

Table 26.3: Summary of main pricing methods

CASE STUDY 26.5

Premium pricing in the smartphone market

When the Apple, Samsung and Huawei introduce new smartphones into the market they look at attracting consumers called 'early adopters' to buy their latest phone. 'Early adopters' are buyers who like to be first to get the newest product and are willing to pay a high price for the privilege of doing this. The smartphone manufacturers understand this and use a pricing strategy called premium pricing. The table sets out launch prices of the latest phones produced by Samsung, Huawei and Apple.

	Samsung Galaxy S21	Huawei Psmart	iPhone 13
Release price ($)	988	955	1099

Later in a smartphone's product life cycle the initial attractiveness of the 'latest version' wears off and the manufacturers adopt a 'going-rate' pricing strategy.

1   Define the term 'premium pricing'.   **[2]**

2   Outline how smartphone manufacturers change their pricing strategy as their product moves through the product life cycle.   **[4]**

3   Explain **two** reasons why Apple might sell the iPhone 13 at a higher price than Huawei's Psmart and the Samsung Galaxy.   **[4]**

4   Evaluate the view that premium pricing is the most effective pricing strategy for smartphone manufacturers when they are launching a new phone.   **[10]**

Dynamic pricing

The **dynamic pricing** method involves setting constantly changing prices when selling products to different customers, especially online through e-commerce. E-commerce has become a hot spot for dynamic pricing models due to the way consumers can be separated by and communicated with over the internet. Consumers cannot tell what other buyers are paying. Businesses can vary the price according to demand patterns or knowledge that they have about a particular consumer and their ability to pay. Airlines often use this method of pricing. On a typical flight, it is rare to find any two passengers who have paid the same fare.

> **KEY TERM**
>
> **dynamic pricing:** offering products at a price that changes according to the level of demand and the customer's ability to pay

Competitive pricing

There are two main reasons why a business might adopt **competitive pricing** and price its products at the same or very similar level to that of its competitors:

- There is one dominant business in the market. This business often becomes the price leader. Once it sets its prices it would be very difficult for a smaller business to charge higher prices unless it sold a clearly differentiated product. It might be impossible to charge lower prices than the dominant business if the latter has the lowest costs of production per unit.
- Some markets have a number of businesses of the same size selling similar products. The prices are very

> **KEY TERM**
>
> **competitive pricing:** making pricing decisions based on the price set by competitors.

similar in order to avoid a price war which would reduce profit for all of the businesses. An example of this would be large petrol retail companies.

Contribution pricing

The **contribution pricing** method does not try to allocate the fixed costs to specific products. Instead, the business calculates a variable cost per unit of the product. It then adds an extra amount, which is known as a contribution to fixed costs. If enough units are sold, the total contribution will be enough to cover the fixed costs and to return a profit.

The advantage of contribution-cost pricing over cost-plus or mark-up pricing is that the level of competition can be considered when making the pricing decision. If competition is very high, a low contribution per unit

KEY TERM

contribution pricing: setting prices based on the variable costs of making a product, in order to make a contribution towards fixed costs and profit.

can be added to the variable cost per unit. This will give a lower price than mark-up pricing as the fixed costs have not been included. If there is little competition, then a higher contribution can be added to the variable cost per unit. (See also contribution costing Business management tool, Chapter 31).

WORKED EXAMPLE 26.2

A business produces a single product that has variable costs of $2 per unit. The total fixed costs of the firm are $40 000 per year. The business wants each unit sold to make a contribution of $1. The selling price is therefore $3. Every unit sold makes a contribution towards the fixed costs of $1. If the firm sells 40 000 units in the year, then the fixed costs will be covered. Every unit sold over 40 000 will mean the business makes a profit. If the firm sells 60 000 units, then the fixed costs will be covered and a $20 000 profit will be made.

Many businesses that have excess capacity use contribution-cost pricing to attract extra business that will absorb the excess capacity.

Methods	Advantages	Disadvantages
Dynamic pricing	Maximises revenue by setting different prices for different consumers	Requires advanced IT systems to adjust prices quickly according to changing demand levels
	Varies the price according to market conditions and the price elasticity at different times	Consumers dislike the system as it is viewed as a form of exploitation
	Can be used to improve stock management – cut prices to sell excess stock	Consumers may be alienated if they find out some buyers have paid a much lower price
Competitive pricing	Helps to maintain market share and even increase sales if all businesses in the market set low prices	May reduce profit margins if prices are set to respond to low-priced competitors
	Avoids setting prices which are much lower than rivals' prices, which will reduce profit margins	Some rivals might have lower average costs, and pricing competitively will risk the business making a loss
	Helps to build customer loyalty if they can be assured of receiving a competitive price	Setting competitive prices below cost will risk long-term survival
Contribution pricing	Sets prices that could be lower than the cost-plus method so makes the business more competitive	Does not include fixed costs in the pricing decision
	Avoids the inaccurate allocation of fixed costs which can lead to inappropriate prices	A loss will be made if total contribution is less than fixed costs
		Cannot be sustained in the long term if fixed costs are not being covered

Table 26.4: Advantages and disadvantages of pricing methods

Price elasticity of demand

Pricing decisions should be based on as much up-to-date and relevant information as possible. A key piece of information in pricing decisions is how demand is likely to respond to a change in price. Marketing departments try hard to assess the impact that changes in the price of a product will have on demand for it. A form of measurement has been developed to help in this assessment. It is called price elasticity of demand.

Look at the two demand curves in Figures 26.6 and 26.7. $D_2 D_2$ has a steeper gradient than $D_1 D_1$. What impact does the slope or gradient of the curves have on the demand levels for these two products when prices are changed? You will notice that, when the price of both products is increased by the same amount, the reduction in demand is greater for product B than it is for product A. This could be important information for the marketing manager because the total revenue for product A has actually increased, but for B it has fallen, as can be seen by the size of the shaded areas.

This relationship between price changes and the size of the resulting change in demand is known as **price elasticity of demand**.

> ### KEY TERM
>
> **price elasticity of demand (PED):** a measure of the responsiveness of demand for a product following a change in its price

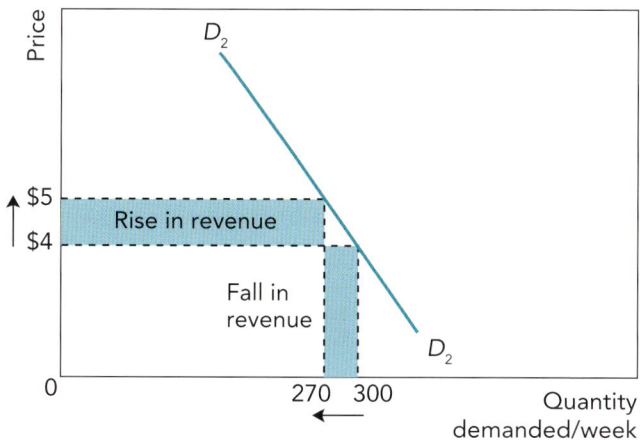

Figure 26.6: Demand curve for product A

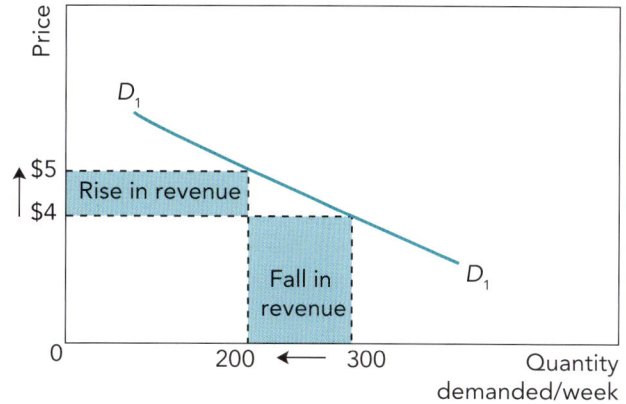

Figure 26.7: Demand curve for product B

This concept can be demonstrated on demand curves as shown in Figures 26.5 and 26.6. Product A's demand is less elastic or less responsive to a price change than product B's. This idea can also be measured mathematically, but calculation of PED is not required for IB Business Management.

The formula for price elasticity of demand (PED) is:

> ### KEY FORMULA
>
> $$PED = \frac{\text{percentage change in quantity demanded}}{\text{percentage change in price}}$$

The value of PED is normally negative because a fall in price (−ve) usually results in a rise in demand (+ve). Similarly, a rise in price (+ve) results in a fall in demand (−ve). This is called an inverse relationship. It is quite common to ignore the negative sign of the PED result, as it is the numerical value of the result that is important.

> ### WORKED EXAMPLE 26.3
>
> In Figure 26.6, the price increased from \$4 to \$5 and demand fell from 300 units per week to 270 units. What is the PED?
>
> **Step 1:** Calculate the percentage change in price.
>
> **Step 2:** Calculate the percentage change in demand.
>
> **Step 3:** Use the PED formula:
>
> % change in demand = 10
>
> % change in price = 25
>
> $PED = \dfrac{10}{25} = 0.4$ (remember, this result is negative)

CONTINUED

It is now important to explain this result. A PED of 0.4 (do not forget that we are overlooking the minus sign) means that demand changes by 0.4% for every 1.0% change in price. As this is *less than one*, it is described as being inelastic. Consumers do not respond much to a change in the price in this product. An increase in price will raise a firm's revenue, while a price reduction, because demand will change little, will reduce revenue.

Factors that determine price elasticity of demand

There are a number of factors that will determine the PED of a product:

- **How necessary the product is.** The more necessary consumers consider a product to be, the less they will react to price changes. This will tend to make the demand inelastic, as is the case with salt and cooking oil.

- **Number of close competitors.** If there are many competitors then there are a large number of substitutes. Consumers will quickly switch to another brand if the price of one manufacturer's product increases (e.g., fruit being sold by one seller in a large street market). Any decision by a business to reduce the number of competing products, such as a merger or takeover, will probably make demand for its own products less elastic.

- **Consumer loyalty.** If a firm has successfully branded its product to create a high degree of loyalty among consumers, like Coca-Cola, then the consumers will be likely to continue buying the product following a price rise. Another example of this is designer clothes that have a strong following among high income consumers, even when prices rise. All businesses attempt to increase brand loyalty with influential advertising and promotional campaigns and by making their products more distinct. This is called product differentiation.

- **Price of the product as a proportion of consumers' incomes.** A cheap product that takes up a small proportion of consumers' incomes, such as matches or batteries, is likely to have inelastic demand, as consumers will not be greatly affected by a 10% or 15% price increase.

Price elasticity of demand – uses in business

There are two main business uses of PED:

- **Making more accurate sales forecasts.** If a business is considering a price increase, perhaps to cover rises in production costs, then an awareness of PED allows a forecast of likely demand changes to be calculated. For instance, if PED is believed to be -0.8 and the price is increased by 10%, what will be the new weekly sales level if it is currently 10 000 per week? Demand will fall by 8% (check this out using the PED formula) and this will give a forecast sales level of 9 200 per week.

- **Impact on pricing decisions.** If an operator of bus services is considering changing its pricing structure, then knowing the PED on different routes will help. It could increase prices on routes with low PED (inelastic demand) and reduce them on routes with high PED (elastic demand). These decisions will increase the total revenue of the bus operator.

If a business is planning to use premium pricing, it would be assuming that demand is relatively price inelastic so that the high price will not result in a proportionately greater reduction in demand. Revenue should increase if demand is price inelastic.

If a business is planning to use penetration pricing, it would be assuming that demand is relatively price elastic so that the low price results in a proportionately greater increase in demand. Revenue should increase if demand is relatively price elastic.

Evaluation of price elasticity of demand

PED has its uses, but the concept and the results gained from it must be used with caution. It has three main limitations:

- PED assumes that nothing else has changed. If Business A reduces the price for a product by 10%, it will expect sales to increase because of this. However, if, at about the same time, a competitor leaves the industry and consumer incomes rise, the resulting increase in sales of Business A's product may be substantial, but *not just* because of the price reduction. Calculating PED accurately in these and similar situations where other changes occur will be almost impossible.

- A PED calculation, even when calculated when nothing but price changes, will become outdated quickly. It may need to be recalculated often, because over time consumer tastes change and new competitors may bring in new products. Last year's PED calculation may be very different to one calculated today if market conditions have changed.

- It is not always easy, or indeed possible, to calculate PED. The data needed for working it out might come from past sales results following previous price changes. This data could be quite old and market conditions might have changed. In the case of new products, market research will have to be relied upon to estimate PED. This is done by trying to identify the quantities that a sample of potential customers would purchase at different prices. This will be subject to the same kind of inaccuracy as other forms of market research.

26.7 Promotion

Promotion is about communicating with actual or potential customers. Effective promotion not only increases awareness of products, but can create images and product 'personalities' that consumers can identify with. Advertising is only one form of promotion and other techniques include direct selling and sales promotion offers. The combination of all forms of promotion used by a business for any product is known as the 'promotion mix'. The amount firms spend on promotion (the promotion budget) is often a key decision, but successful communication is not just about the total amount spent. It is also about how the budget is allocated between the competing forms of promotion available – and company budgets are increasingly being diverted to social media and other technology-based forms of promotion.

KEY TERM

promotion: the use of advertising, digital promotions, sales promotion, personal selling, direct mail, trade fairs, sponsorship and public relations to inform consumers and persuade them to buy

TIP

When writing about promotion of a product try to consider the marketing objectives of the business. Is the promotion being used likely to help achieve these objectives?

What is promotion trying to achieve?

Promotional objectives should aim to:

- increase sales by raising consumer awareness of a new product
- remind consumers of an existing product and its distinctive qualities
- encourage increased purchases by existing consumers or attract new consumers
- demonstrate the superior specification or qualities of a product compared to those of competitors – often used when the product has been updated or adapted in some way
- create or reinforce the brand image or 'personality' of the product
- correct misleading reports about the product or the business and reassure consumers after a 'scare' or an accident involving the product
- develop or adapt the public image of the business – rather than the product
- encourage retailers to stock and actively promote products to the final consumer.
- It is important to differentiate between the following aspects of promotion.

Above-the-line promotion

Advertising

Advertising is a form of **above-the-line promotion** which aims to communicate information about a product or business through mass media such as radio, TV and newspapers. These advertisements are usually directed towards the appropriate market by selecting the right media – but it is possible that many people who are unlikely to purchase the product may see the advertisements too. Successful advertising campaigns have led to substantial increases in consumer awareness and sales, and this effect can last for a considerable length of time if brand loyalty can be established.

KEY TERM

above-the-line promotion: a form of promotion that is undertaken by a business by paying for communication with consumers, e.g., advertising

Advertisements are often classified into two types, but in practice this distinction is often quite blurred.

- Informative advertising – these are advertisements that give information to potential purchasers of a product, rather than just trying to create a brand image. This information could include price, technical specifications or main features and places where the product can be purchased. This style of advertising could be particularly effective when promoting a new product that consumers are unlikely to be aware of or when communicating a substantial change in price, design or specification.

- Persuasive advertising – this involves trying to create a distinct image or brand identity for the product. It may not contain any details at all about materials or ingredients used, prices or places to buy it. This form of advertising is very common, especially in those markets where there might be little actual difference between products and where advertisers are trying to create a perceived difference in the minds of consumers.

In reality, there is little difference between these two styles of advertising: 'The more informative your advertising, the more persuasive it will be' (David Ogilvy, *Confessions of an Advertising Man*, New York: Ballantine Books, 1971).

Above-the-line advertising methods are used when a business wants to reach a wide audience and create awareness of a brand in a mass market. This is most likely to be the case when the product is new or has recently undergone a considerable update. The cost associated with this form of promotion means that it is unlikely to be used unless the business has a sizeable marketing budget. Above-the-line advertising helps to strengthen a brand image and give a memorable impression of the brand's central message.

For certain markets and products, above-the-line promotion is often the most effective way of communicating with potential consumers. For example, products that have a mass appeal are often advertised using above-the-line methods because the communication reaches a wide-ranging audience, helping to achieve awareness amongst potential consumers and creating brand recall.

However, it is also possible that mass advertising will fail to pinpoint the appropriate target market, and more focused methods of promotion will be needed in these cases.

CASE STUDY 26.6

Nike advert: 'You Can't Stop Us'

During the Covid-19 pandemic Nike released an online advert titled 'You Can't Stop Us', featuring footage of black, white, Asian, disabled and Muslim athletes. Shortly after being released the video had been viewed 20 million times on Twitter and more than 11 million times on YouTube. The video also gained critical acclaim for its message of inclusiveness and perseverance.

Throughout the 90-second video, an athlete on one half of the screen mirrors another athlete on the opposite side as if they were a single person. The video also reflects on the Covid-19 crisis, showing stadiums being deep-cleaned. There is also footage of athletes in different sports kneeling during their national anthem in protest at racial injustice.

1 Define the term 'social media marketing'. [2]

2 Outline **two** promotional objectives Nike might be trying to achieve with the 'You Can't Stop Us' advert. [4]

3 Explain why the Nike advert 'You Can't Stop Us' is an example of above-the-line promotion. [4]

4 Explain **two** reasons why 'You Can't Stop Us' advert has been so successful at reaching so many potential Nike customers. [4]

Below-the-line promotion

Below-the-line marketing is aimed specifically at targeted segments or individuals that have been identified as potential customers. Popular below-the-line marketing methods include sales promotion techniques, direct marketing including email and social media, and sponsorship of events. Sponsorship of events is growing in popularity as potential customers will have a memorable experience that they will then link with the brand name when they make buying decisions.

Below-the-line promotion is focused on targeting specific marketing messages to certain people. This helps to ensure the message and promotion method used are as closely related as possible to the age range, tastes and preferences of the target group. Below-the-line promotion is often aimed at achieving specific and measurable marketing goals such as converting consumers from one brand to another. Instead of simply raising awareness of the brand, below-the-line promotion is designed to allow direct communication with consumers about the product or brand. This form of marketing is usually easily quantifiable with the benefit of results that can be measured against target. It is a form of customer relationship management.

Examples of below-the-line promotion are as follows.

Sales promotion

Sales promotion generally aims to achieve short-term increases in sales. There is a huge range of incentives and activities that come under the umbrella term 'sales promotion' (see Table 26.5). They include:

- price deals – a temporary reduction in price, such as 10% off for one week only
- loyalty-reward programmes – consumers collect points, air miles or credits for purchases and redeem them for rewards
- money-off coupons – redeemed when the consumer buys the product
- point-of-sale displays in shops (e.g., 'aisle interrupter' – a sign that juts into the supermarket aisle from a shelf; and 'dump bin' – a free-standing bin centrally placed and full of products 'dumped' inside to attract attention)
- 'buy one get one free' (BOGOF)
- games and competitions, e.g., on cereal packets

- public relations
- sponsorship.

Sales promotion can be directed at either:

- the final consumer to encourage purchase (pull strategy), or
- the distribution channel, e.g., the retailer, to encourage stocking and display of the product (push strategy).

The methods of sales promotions and their possible limitations are shown in Table 26.5.

Through-the-line promotion

Through-the-line promotion is a combination of both above- and below-the-line promotion.

It is an overall attempt to raise brand awareness *and* target specific potential customers. The aim is to convert these customers into measurable and quantifiable sales.

KEY TERMS

below-the-line promotion: promotion that does not use directly paid-for means of communication but is based on targeting individual market segments or individual consumers with incentives to purchase, e.g., sales promotion techniques

customer relationship management: the strategies and techniques a business uses to interact and communicate with customers

sales promotion: incentives such as special offers or special deals directed at consumers or retailers to achieve short-term sales increases and repeat purchases by consumers

through-the-line marketing: an integrated marketing strategy that combines elements of both above-the-line and below-the-line promotion

One example of this is 360 degree marketing. This approach means using not only a national TV campaign but supporting it with mailshots and targeted offers to loyalty-card holders. An increasingly common promotion strategy is to use digital marketing, combining online banner advertisements with social media posts and blogs.

Method explained	Possible limitations
Price promotions – these are temporary reductions in price, also known as price discounting. They are aimed at encouraging existing customers to buy more and attracting new customers to buy the product.	Increased sales gained from price reductions will affect gross profit on each item sold. There might be a negative impact on the brand's reputation from the discounted price.
Money-off coupons – these are a more versatile and better-focused way of offering a price discount. Coupons can appear on the back of receipts, in newspaper advertisements or on an existing product pack.	They may simply encourage consumers to buy what they would have bought anyway. Retailers may be surprised by the increase in demand and not hold enough stocks, leading to consumer disappointment. Proportion of consumers using the coupon might be low if the reduction it offers is small.
Customer loyalty schemes such as air miles or customer loyalty cards – focused on encouraging repeat purchases and discouraging consumers from shopping with competitors. Information stored through loyalty cards provides a great deal of information about consumers' buying preferences.	The discount offered by such schemes cuts the gross profit on each purchase. There are administration costs to inform consumers of loyalty points earned and these may outweigh the benefits from increased consumer loyalty. Most consumers now have many loyalty cards from different retailers, so their 'loyalty' impact is reduced.
BOGOF – 'buy one get one free' – this encourages multiple purchases, which reduces demand for competitors' products too.	There could be substantial reduction in gross profit margin. Consumers may consider that if this scheme is able to operate, are they paying a 'normal' price that is too high? Is the scheme being used to sell off stock that cannot be sold at normal prices – impact on reputation? Current sales might increase, but future sales could fall as consumers have stocked up on the product.
Point-of-sale displays – maximum impact on consumer behaviour is achieved by attractive, informative and well-positioned displays in stores.	The best display points are usually offered to the market leaders – products with high market share. New products may struggle for best positions in stores – unless big discounts are offered to retailers.
Public relations – the use of free publicity provided by newspapers, TV and other media to communicate with and achieve understanding of the public.	This is not easily controllable as some 'free publicity' might not be positive towards the company or its products, e.g., newspaper reviews.
Sponsorship – payment by a company to team owners or event organisers so that the company's name becomes associated with the team or event.	The success of the sponsorship is largely out of the company's control. If the team loses every match or the event is a failure, this might reflect badly on the sponsor.

Table 26.5: Common methods of below-the-line promotion

CASE STUDY 26.7

Promotional mix at McDonald's

The fast-food giant McDonald's uses a wide variety of above-the-line and below-the-line methods of promotion to highlight its business activities. A central theme of its advertising is the 'I'm loving it' campaign, which was the business's first global promotional campaign.

McDonald's global approach to promotion can also be seen in its sponsorship of world events such as the football World Cup and the Olympic games. At a local level you can also see how active McDonald's can be, from the roadside billboard direction sign to its outlets to its golden arch signage on the stores itself.

You can also see some interesting applications of marketing used by McDonald's. These range from a streetlamp with a McDonald's coffee pot on the end of it to a zebra crossing where the road is marked out by French fries.

All of these promotional methods come at a significant cost, with McDonald's spending $1.62 billion on promotion in the USA in 2021.

1   Define the term 'below-the-line promotion'.   **[2]**

2   Outline **two** types of below-the-line promotion used by McDonald's.   **[4]**

3   Explain **two** reasons why McDonald's might be sponsoring the World Cup and the Olympic games.   **[4]**

4   Evaluate the view that spending $1.62 billion on its promotional mix is an effective way to increase its sales.   **[10]**

With this combined strategy, through-the-line promotion should increase general awareness of a product or brand as well as focusing offers on those most likely to buy it.

However, a through-the-line strategy is likely to be more expensive than using either of the other two approaches alone. For this reason, it is normally only widely used by large, established companies with the marketing budget to support such a strategy.

TIP

Do not confuse advertising and sales promotion – they are both forms of promotion, but they are not the same.

26.8 Social media as a marketing strategy

It is not an exaggeration to state that the internet is transforming the ways in which businesses market and promote their products.

Promotion using social media sites is an example of **online marketing** and it can have some significant benefits and limitations. These are examined in Table 26.6.

KEY TERM

online marketing: advertising and marketing activities that use the internet, email and mobile communications to encourage direct sales via electronic commerce

Benefits	Limitations
Improved audience reach – Social media platforms have a global reach and this reduces the unit cost of reaching potential consumers compared to traditional forms of promotion.	**Lack of skill** – Large businesses will have dedicated teams of people monitoring social media. Small businesses or newly set up enterprises may be led by people who do not have the skills to choose the appropriate social media or engage with customers in the most effective ways.
Targeted marketing – Social networking websites give advertisers the ability to target audiences based on site users' personal interests and what their friends like. If a consumer lists rock music as one of their interests on a social networking site, then they will see advertisements about rock concerts and artists. Some sites' advertising will also highlight which rock artists their friends like, to provide a personal connection. This is called 'smart' marketing. Companies effectively reach the people who are most interested in what they have to offer. In addition, social networking enables word of mouth to promote products beyond what advertising alone does – and many consumers trust this type of referral more than traditional advertising.	**Time investment** – Setting up a social media account takes less than 30 minutes, but managing a social media account day to day is a time investment many small businesses do not make. A successful social media campaign counts on almost constant interaction between a company and its customers. This means time has to be set aside each day to post engaging information, ideas and tips and respond to comments left by consumers and followers. Not responding to customers' questions can be damaging to reputation and followers could quickly lose interest.
Interactivity – One benefit of social network marketing is that businesses can interact with potential customers using conversation threads and forums. Engaging customers in conversation makes them more likely to take a deeper interest in the product.	**Negative feedback** – While it is beneficial for businesses to get feedback from their customers, social media makes the feedback public. If a customer has a bad experience with a product, he or she is likely to share the experience on the social network profile. This could quickly damage the brand's image unless it is responded to quickly and satisfactorily.
Performance metrics – Some IT-based promotional services provide feedback and assessment services to their advertisers. With these forms of measurement, businesses can track which type of advertisements are attracting the most web traffic. Also, consumer profile and demographic information such as the age of people most interested in the company's product can help direct future promotional efforts.	**Performance metrics** – When a business uses an email marketing program such as MailChimp or ConstantContact, the business can track how many emails are sent, how many people opened the email and the number of sales generated as a result. Social media does not offer the same measurability. Business owners find themselves wondering if it is worth investing time and dedicating human resources. Business owners who want immediate marketing results may have to accept that if they use social media as a tactic, they may not be able to track results until months later.
Speed of transmission – The speed at which social media transmits news about a business and its products can be an advantage. One well-placed, critical feedback comment can be responded to almost immediately with instant updates. Social networking also gives businesses the ability to notify followers instantly about product updates, new product launches and even product recalls. Live, current content through social media makes business advertising seem dynamic and makes products more attractive, especially to younger consumers.	**Security issues** – Not everyone is a fan of social media – either they lack time or they are concerned about issues around security of information. Therefore, social media cannot be the only form of promotion used by businesses if they want to contact the widest range of potential consumers possible.

Table 26.6: Benefits and limitations of using social media for promotion

Social media and viral marketing

This is a recent marketing phenomenon that facilitates and encourages people to pass on a marketing message to others. Viral promotions can be in the form of video clips, interactive flash games, e-books and text messages. It is claimed that a customer tells an average of three people about a product or service they like and 11 people about a product or service which they do not like. **Viral marketing** is based on this form of communication. Marketing managers try to identify individuals with high social-networking potential – called 'influencers'. They create viral messages that appeal to them and have a high chance of being passed on to many people, some of whom will be impressed that the 'influencer' has contacted them about the product.

KEY TERM

viral marketing: the use of social media sites or text messages to increase brand awareness or sell products

ACTIVITY 26.6

Through-the-line promotion

Putting the focus on the 'invisible' homeless

RaisingTheRoof is a Canadian charity that focuses on the plight of homeless people and looks for ways to fight homelessness.

The NGO's marketing team came up with hard-hitting posters that were placed in locations where homeless young people would typically sit, often ignored. RaisingTheRoof's poster message was stark and clear: 'If this poster were a homeless youth, most people wouldn't even bother to look down.' This says it all. Is there any doubt about what people should do? This is a guerrilla campaign at its best.

1   In pairs or in a group, discuss a through-the-line promotion campaign that you would use to raise awareness of a social issue such as homelessness.

2   Write a short report on the through-the-line promotion campaign you have chosen.

CASE STUDY 26.8

Promoting guitars

Strum and Pick Guitars is a Chilean business that manufactures high-quality acoustic guitars. Strum and Pick was close to bankruptcy two years ago and was bought by a large Chilean manufacturing business called ACM Music that specialises in musical instruments. ACM appointed Sofia Rojas as CEO of Strum and Pick to turn the business around by increasing sales and profits and growing its market share.

Sofia Rojas believes that Strum and Pick makes very good guitars, and she thinks they can be sold at a premium price, but she feels they are badly promoted. Sofia has worked closely with the marketing team at ACM to develop an effective promotional mix. Along with the normal promotional methods that businesses in this market use, Sofia has also put a lot of effort into sponsoring several high-profile Chilean performers who endorse the Strum and Pick instruments.

Sofia has set up a YouTube channel for Strum and Pick guitars which offers free online tuition. Another significant below-the-line method Sofia has used is to offer free new and reconditioned guitars to music schools. Sofia also wants to use an event-based marketing campaign as part of the firm's below-the-line promotion where some high-profile artists are involved in spontaneous performances in city centre locations.

1   Define the term 'promotional mix'.   [2]

CONTINUED

2   Outline the difference between above-the-line and below-the-line promotion. **[4]**

3   Explain an advantage and a disadvantage of Strum and Pick using events based on spontaneous performances as part of their below-the-line promotion. **[4]**

4   Discuss the strengths of the below-the-line methods of promotion that Sofia Rojas has chosen to promote Strum and Pick Guitars. **[10]**

26.9 Place

'Place' decisions are concerned with how products should pass from manufacturer to the final customer. Several different **channels of distribution** are available for firms to use.

KEY TERM

channel of distribution: the chain of intermediaries a product passes through from producer to final consumer

The main reasons why the choice of distribution channel is an important element of the marketing mix are:

- Consumers may need easy access to a firm's products to allow them to see and try them before they buy, to make purchasing easy and to allow for the return of goods if necessary.

- Manufacturers need outlets for their products that give the widest market coverage possible, whilst retaining the desired image of the product.

- Retailers – firms that sell goods to the final consumer – will sell producers' goods but will demand a mark-up to cover their costs and make a profit. So, if price is very important, using few or no intermediaries would be an advantage.

Channel strategy

When deciding on an appropriate channel strategy, a business must answer these questions:

- Should the product be sold directly to consumers?
- Should the product be sold through retailers?
- How long should the channel be (how many intermediaries)?
- Where should the product be made available?
- Should electronic methods of distribution be used?
- How much will it cost to keep the stock of products on store shelves and in channel warehouses?
- How much control does the business want to have over the marketing mix?
- How will the distribution channel selected support the other components of the marketing mix?

Factors influencing choice of distribution channel include the following:

- Industrial products tend to be sold more directly with fewer intermediaries than consumer goods.
- Geographical dispersion of the target market – if the target market is large but widely dispersed throughout the country, then the use of intermediaries is more likely.
- The level of service expected by consumers, e.g., after-sales servicing of a car means that internet selling is not appropriate for most manufacturers.
- Technical complexity of the product, e.g., business computers are sold directly as they require a great deal of technical sales staff know-how and a supporting service team.
- Unit value of the product – it may be worth employing sales staff to sell directly to customers if the unit cost is high. For example, employing sales staff would be worthwhile for selling a luxury yacht worth $5 million, but would not be worthwhile for jewellery being sold for $5.
- Number of potential customers – if the number of potential customers is few, as with commercial aircraft, direct selling might be used, but Nike or Reebok with their millions of customers for sports shoes worldwide would use intermediate channels to distribute their products.

The channel strategy must be integrated with the marketing objectives of the business. For example, if the aim is to secure a niche market with a high-quality image product (e.g., branded cosmetics), then selling it through street vendors will not achieve this objective. If, however, the marketing aim is to achieve maximum sales and distribution coverage (e.g., sweets), then selling through a few carefully selected and exclusive food retailers will not be successful. As with all components of the marketing mix, distribution channel strategy must be clearly linked to marketing objectives and to the other components of the mix in order for an effective and convincing overall marketing strategy to be developed.

> ### TIP
>
> Do not confuse 'place' or 'distribution' decisions with transportation methods. Place is about how and where the product is to be sold to a customer; transportation is about how the product is to be physically delivered.

Distribution channels

The most commonly used distribution channels are shown in Figures 26.8 to 26.10. Figure 26.8 shows the direct route which gives the producer full control over marketing of products. This is sometimes known as direct selling or direct marketing. The growth of online marketing has led to a rapid rise in the popularity of this channel of distribution.

With the increasing size of many modern retailers, the 'single-intermediary channel' depicted in Figure 26.9 is becoming more common. These huge retailers have strong purchasing power. They are able to arrange their own storage and distribution systems to individual stores.

In Figure 26.10 we see what is often known as the traditional two-intermediaries channel as, until recent developments in retailing and the internet, it was the most common of all channels of distribution.

See Table 26.7 for the benefits and drawbacks of distribution channels.

Trends in distribution channels in recent years include:

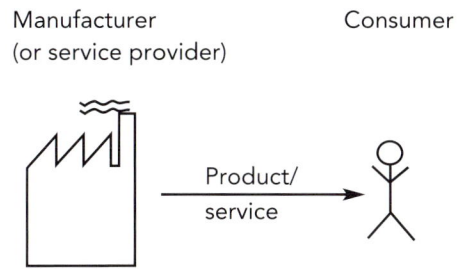

Figure 26.8: Direct selling to consumer

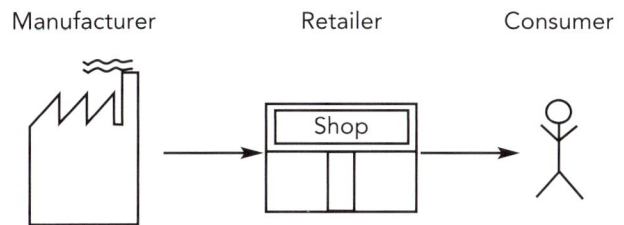

Figure 26.9: Single-intermediary channel

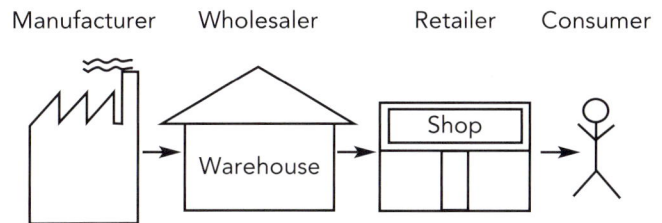

Figure 26.10: Two-intermediaries channel

- The increased use of the internet for direct selling of goods and services. In the service sector this can be seen with internet banking and direct selling of insurance policies online.

- Large supermarket chains performing the function of wholesalers as well as retailers, as they hold large stocks in their own central warehouses. By owning another link in the distribution chain, the business is engaging in vertical marketing.

- Businesses increasingly using a variety of different channels – for example, an ice-cream manufacturer may have its own ice-cream vans to sell directly to consumers as well as supplying retailers. Hotels may sell accommodation directly as well as through travel agents and holiday companies.

- Increasing integration of services where a complete package is sold to consumers – for example, air flights, car hire, hotel accommodation all sold or distributed to consumers at the same time.

Type and main features	Examples of products or services often using this channel	Possible benefits	Possible drawbacks
Direct selling: no intermediaries – sometimes referred to as 'zero intermediary' channel	Online ordering from manufacturer Airline tickets and hotel accommodation sold over the internet by the service providers Farmers' markets – selling produce directly to consumers	No intermediaries so no mark-up or profit margin taken by other businesses Producer has complete control over the marketing mix – how the product is sold, promoted and priced to consumers Quicker than other channels May lead to fresher food products Direct contact with consumers offers useful market research Online selling can be used to reach a very wide market	All storage and stock costs have to be paid for by producer No retail outlets limits the chances for consumers to 'see and try' before they buy, and this is a major limitation of online selling Online selling raises security issues in the minds of some consumers No advertising or promotion paid for by intermediaries and no after-sales service offered by shops Can be expensive to deliver each item sold to consumers
Single-intermediary channel – normally used for consumer goods but could also be an agent for selling industrial products to businesses	Holiday companies selling holidays via travel agents Large supermarkets that hold their own stocks rather than using wholesalers Where the whole country can be reached using the one-level route, e.g., a single agent in a small country	Retailer holds stocks and pays for cost of this Retailer has product displays and offers after-sales service Retailers often in locations that are convenient to consumers Producers can focus on production – not on selling the products to consumers	Intermediary takes a profit mark-up and this could make the product more expensive to final consumers Producers lose some control over marketing mix Retailers may sell products from competitors too, so there is no exclusive outlet Producer has delivery costs to retailer
Two-intermediaries channel – wholesaler buys goods from producer and sells to retailer	In a large country with long distances to each retailer, many consumer goods are distributed this way, e.g., soft drinks, electrical goods and books	Wholesaler holds goods and buys in bulk from producer Reduces stock-holding costs of producer Wholesaler pays for transport costs to retailer Wholesaler 'breaks bulk' by buying in large quantities and selling to retailers in small quantities May be the best way to enter foreign markets where the producer has no direct contact with retailers	Another intermediary takes a profit mark-up – may make final goods more expensive to consumer Producer loses further control over marketing mix Slows down the distribution chain

Table 26.7: Distribution channels – main benefits and potential limitations

CASE STUDY 26.9

The marketing mix at Costa Coffee

Obviously, coffee is the main product offered by Costa Coffee. But Costa also offers a range of other beverages such as hot chocolate, ice blends, sandwiches and cakes. The management at Costa believe product is the most important factor in the business's marketing mix because the complete marketing strategy of the firm depends on their customers' 'loving their food and drink'.

Costa Coffee uses a premium pricing approach because it sees itself as a high-quality brand and the price needs to reflect this. Costa sees the best experience for its customers, in terms of the food and drink they consume, as crucial and this can only be achieved at a high price.

There are over 1000 Costa Coffee outlets in the UK located in variety of locations such as town centre high streets, shopping malls, train stations, motorways services, universities and hospitals. The breadth of the place element of its marketing mix opens the business up to a huge number of customers.

Costa Coffee uses very little advertising as part of its marketing mix. It relies on word-of-mouth publicity as a key element in the way it promotes itself. Costa believes 'happy customers' will always be the biggest draw to its outlets.

1   List the **four** elements of the marketing mix. [4]

2   Outline Costa Coffee's approach to the price and place elements of its marketing mix. [4]

3   Explain why Costa sees the business's product as the most important element of the marketing mix. [4]

4   Explain **two** disadvantages to Costa Coffee of setting a low price for its products. [4]

5   Explain **two** advantages for Costa Coffee of using word-of-mouth promotion. [4]

CASE STUDY 26.10

Distribution and Tesla

Tesla's announcement in 2021 to shift most of its sales to online had investors and analysts questioning everything, from the company's cash flow to its ability to grow market share without physical showrooms.

The automaker plans to cut back on its showroom staff and direct customers to order its electric vehicles through their phones. CEO Elon Musk said all purchases will come with a seven-day, money-back guarantee in case anyone has second thoughts about the purchase.

CONTINUED

Numerous studies show that more and more drivers are doing most of their research online before even stepping into a car dealership. Some are skipping dealers altogether or opting for sellers like Tesla that offer 'no-haggle' pricing where the buyer knows exactly what they will pay when they leave the showroom.

The move to online sales is also likely to create more competition between Tesla and conventional car dealers, which have spent decades fighting the electric car maker to prevent it from selling directly to consumers through its company-owned stores.

Auto analysts suggest that online sales will weigh on traditional car dealerships in the near future and may put many out of business. Just 35% of US car dealers say they are 'likely' or 'very likely' to sell their cars online, according to a survey by Roots & Associates.

While Musk's decision may baffle some now, 'ultimately, this will be a very strong competitive strength for Tesla.' According to the National Automobile Dealers Association in the USA, going to a car lot is still 'by far the best way to sell, distribute and service new vehicles.'

1   Define the term 'distribution channel'. [2]

2   Outline the method of distribution used by Tesla. [2]

3   Outline an alternative method of distribution that Tesla could use. [2]

4   Explain **two** possible advantages to Tesla of using its chosen method of distribution. [4]

5   Explain **two** possible disadvantages to Tesla of using its chosen method of distribution. [4]

LEARNER PROFILE

Principled/caring

Large soft -drinks manufacturers such as PepsiCo and Coca-Cola sell a product that many people would describe as unhealthy. Added sugar in soft drinks such as Coca-Cola (the average 330 ml can has 32 g of sugar in it) is probably the unhealthiest ingredient in the modern diet. It provides calories and has no added nutrients. Consuming too much sugar is linked to weight gain, obesity, type 2 diabetes, and heart disease.

'How can principled, caring employees work for organisations that knowingly sell unhealthy food to their customers?'

Discuss this question in pairs or with your class.

Could you work for an organisation that sold an unhealthy product?

ACTIVITY 26.7

The UK-based sustainable retailer, The Wild Tree, offers low-price, stylish, sustainable shopping.

CONTINUED

The shop specialises in contemporary and stylish alternatives to the everyday items that people assume can only be made in plastic. Wild Tree's plastic-free product mix includes reusable bags, bottles, cups, kitchen utensils and household cleaning products. All of the products sold through The Wild Tree are delivered in recyclable packaging and sealed with paper tape.

1   In pairs or as a group discuss the influence of sustainability on the marketing mix of a business.

2   Do you think sustainability should be a factor in all marketing decisions?

26.10 People

The three additional Ps that are relevant to the marketing of services are:

- people
- process
- physical evidence.

The people element of the marketing mix refers to the employees and managers of a business and how they relate to customers and communicate with them. The people employed by a business – especially service businesses where customers cannot judge a company by the attributes of physical products – can either give it a competitive advantage **or** can lead to poor customer reaction and reduced consumer loyalty. Poor customer experiences can soon be posted on social media and then the whole world knows about it!

Customers make judgements about service provision and delivery based on the people representing the organisation. This is because people are one of the few elements of the service that customers can see and interact with.

People online

Even online retailers must think about their 'people'. When they employ people who genuinely believe in the products or services that the online business sells then it is much more likely that they will perform the best that they can. In addition, they are more likely to give managers honest feedback and input into the types of products the business is producing and selling.

Getting good people

Well-trained, confident and well-motivated employees who deal with customers in an efficient, speedy manner also help to create customer loyalty – and it is always much cheaper to keep existing customers than to find and attract new ones. Employees require appropriate interpersonal skills and training, an aptitude for dealing with people, and service knowledge in order to deliver a quality service.

In his best-selling book, *Good to Great*, Jim Collins claimed that the most important factor applied by the best companies was that they first of all 'got the right people on the bus, and the wrong people off the bus'. Once these companies had hired the right people, the second step was to 'get the right people in the right seats on the bus'.

Managers need to plan carefully when deciding exactly who is going to carry out each task and responsibility. An important part of any business is having the right people to support the company's products and/or service. Excellent customer-service personnel who can provide support with clearly known expectations, such as hours of operation and average response time, is key to maintaining a high level of customer satisfaction.

ACTIVITY 26.8

Good salespeople should be honest from the start and should only want to sell you something that you need for your personal and professional success. And yes, that means being honest — even if being honest means losing a sale.
Be honest with the customer about what the company can truly provide.

Lydia Vargo

1   Salespeople are considered an important part of the people element of the extended marketing mix. In pairs or as a group make a list of five attributes that make a good salesperson.

2   Design a roleplay exercise that involves an interaction between a salesperson and a customer.

CASE STUDY 26.11

Enhancing the people at Apple

Apple is making a radical switch in the way they're going to sell the new Apple Watch: enter in the era of the Fashionista at Apple.

That's right. Apple employees will be trained on giving fashion and style advice to customers to help them choose the right Apple Watch to purchase. . . .

CONTINUED

Purchasing a watch is a completely different experience from purchasing an iPad or a computer. Most people choose a watch based on their personal style and look, one that complements their fashion sense and projects a certain image they desire.

[The principles of Apple's employee training:]

- Bring in experts. Apple is savvy enough to realize that their current sales program is lacking in fashion education, so they've hired experts from Burberry, Yves St. Laurent, Tag Heuer, and Louis Vuitton to build that knowledge into their sales structure. . . .

- Build relationships through trust. Apple want their sales staff to build relationships with customers based on trust so that customers see salespeople as valuable fashion advisors. . . .

- Ask plenty of questions. Apple employees are being trained on the types of questions to ask

customers to find out exactly what they want and need in a new Apple Watch. . . .

- Educate their customers. Apple wants their sales staff to determine how much customers know about the functionality of the Apple Watch. . . .

- Up-sell newer models. Apple wants their sales staff to upsell customers to the latest version of the iPhone to get the most out of the Apple Watch.

1 List the **three** extra factors in the extended marketing mix. [2]

2 Outline Apple's approach to the people aspect of the extended marketing mix to increase the sales of its Apple watches. [4]

3 Explain **two** problems Apple might face in trying to enhance the people aspect of the extended marketing mix. [4]

THEORY OF KNOWLEDGE

Many industry experts believe The Walt Disney World Resort based in Florida is the number one theme park in the world. The 25 000 acre site is home to four theme parks: Magic Kingdom, Epcot, Disney's Hollywood Studios and Disney's Animal Kingdom. The site also has two water parks and 27 resort hotels.

The quality of Disney's resort is crucial in relation to customer experience and the extended marketing mix (people, process and physical evidence). One of the keys to Disney's success is how its attractions appeal to children, which is hugely important in the way it designs all aspects of the park. This means the designers of the rides and attractions at Disney's resort have to use their imagination and see the park through the eyes of a child in order to produce a product that is so successful.

In pairs or as a group, present an example that illustrates the importance of imagination in bringing about innovation in the Walt Disney World Resort. Your example could be a picture or a video clip.

26.11 Process

The sixth factor to consider within the marketing mix is the system used to deliver the goods or services – the **process**. What processes has McDonald's put in place to ensure that if a customer walks into one of its restaurants and orders a Big Mac Meal it is delivered within two minutes? What were the stages in the process that allowed the customer to obtain this service delivery? Could it be made even more speedy? The speed and efficiency of service delivery are determined by the 'process' that has been put in place.

KEY TERM

process: procedures and policies that are put in place to provide the service or the product to the consumer

Banks that send out debit cards automatically when their customers' old one has expired require an efficient process to identify expiry dates and renewal. An efficient service that replaces out-of-date debit cards will be likely to create consumer loyalty and confidence in the company. All services need to be underpinned by clearly defined and efficient processes. This will avoid delays in providing the service and promote a consistent customer experience. In other words, processes mean that everybody in the organisation knows what to do and how to do it.

Short waiting times, quality information given to customers and the helpfulness and knowledge of employees are all expectations of customers that should be met if the process is effective and well tested.

The importance of changing process

Processes must change in order for businesses to remain competitive. Online shopping offers customers a much quicker and more convenient ordering/payment/delivery process than traditional retail shopping. If a business selling goods did not embrace this technology then its processes would seem outdated.

The rapid growth of internet and 'mobile' banking have allowed customers access to their accounts and banking services 24/7. The use of mobile phones to make cashless payments is helping to transform commerce in less-developed economies that have relatively poor physical infrastructure. Banks or financial service providers that fail to adopt these technologically advanced processes will not attract customers (perhaps younger customers, in particular) who are demanding changing processes to fit in with their lifestyles and expectations.

ACTIVITY 26.9

Here is a list of five of the top music and video streaming sites on the internet:

- Netflix
- Disney Plus
- Amazon Prime Video
- Spotify
- Apple music.

1   In pairs or as a group, choose one or more of these sites and investigate how effective the process element is in using the site/s.

2   Discuss in your pairs or group what makes an effective process on an internet streaming site.

26.12 Physical evidence

This element of the mix was defined by Booms and Bitner (1981) as:

> the environment in which the service is delivered and where the firm and customer interact, and any tangible components that facilitate performance or communication of the service.

This refers to the way the business's goods or service 'appears from the outside'. **Physical evidence** includes where the service is being delivered from, such as the location, and the appearance and state of repair/decoration of retail shops. This element of the marketing mix can help distinguish a company from its competitors. Physical evidence can be used to support the charging of a premium price for a service and establish a positive customer experience. For example, all hotels provide a bed to sleep in, but one of the things that affects the price charged is the condition of the room containing the bed. Customers will make judgements about the organisation based on the physical evidence.

KEY TERM

physical evidence: the ways in which the business and its products are presented to customers

---

Physical evidence – examples

Customers who walk into a restaurant expect a clean and friendly environment. If the restaurant is smelly or dirty, customers are likely to walk out before they have even ordered or received the service. Physical evidence can also refer to the appearance of employees and how they dress and act. If the waiting staff in the restaurant appear unclean or dishevelled, this will not inspire customer confidence!

Services are examples of **intangible products** as they provide a benefit to the customer but they do not have

---

KEY TERM

intangible product: a non-physical product (a service) provided to a consumer, such as an insurance policy or a car repair

---

a physical form. With **tangible products**, the packaging is a key part of physical evidence. Decisions need to be made about the size, shape, colour, material, printed information for customers, bar code and label of the packaging. This should be customer-tested and updated when needed. Visual packaging of a tangible product can make or break a purchase. Small improvements in the packaging or external appearance of a product or service can lead to completely different reactions from customers.

> ### KEY TERM
>
> **tangible product:** a physical object that can be touched, such as a building, car, tablet computer or clothing

Physical evidence – consistency with other elements of the mix

It is important that the physical environment is consistent with the other elements of the marketing mix. For example, it is difficult to justify the high-quality status of a restaurant that has excellent food, a strong positive brand image and a price to match if the premises themselves are of poor quality.

To the customer or potential customer, the physical environment has to feel right and be in line with their expectations. Customers have expectations of an airline when a ticket is booked based on other aspects of the marketing mix – for example price, promotional activities and the route and timings being offered. However, customer expectations of the physical environment may well differ depending upon which airline the booking is with. Customers may be prepared to accept an aircraft that is perhaps in need of some internal refurbishment if they booked with a budget airline. They would be less understanding if they had paid a higher price to book with a prestigious airline. This is another example of where the physical environment is inconsistent with other aspects of the marketing mix, leading to customer dissatisfaction.

Customers use other senses apart from sight to make judgements about the physical environment they find themselves in. The smell of freshly baked bread is now a common feature of supermarkets and this helps to convince customers that food is freshly prepared for them. Similarly, customers expect to smell food in a food establishment, not cleaning products. Company vehicles are another example of physical evidence that customers take note of. The WEGO courier business uses only electric vans for its deliveries – does this help to inspire customer confidence in the social responsibility of the business and the services that it offers?

CASE STUDY 26.12

Mandarin Oriental Hotel Group International Ltd – We Care

Mandarin Oriental Hotel Group International Limited (MOHG) is a Hong Kong hotel investment and management business. Its main business is luxury hotels and resorts. MOHG has more than 30 properties worldwide. The business's mission is to 'completely delight and satisfy our guests. We are committed to continual improvement, to making a difference every day and to being the best.' To achieve this MOHG aims to give its customers the very best hotel rooms and the highest-standard hotel facilities which are delivered by the highly trained and motivated staff.

The Covid-19 pandemic has raised many challenges for MOHG, and it has sought to tackle these challenges through the 'We care' programme. This has involved putting the following procedures in place in its hotels:

CONTINUED

- health declaration forms on arrival, as appropriate

- temperature checks as a standard protocol

- increased cleaning measures across all hotel areas

- Mandarin Oriental 'We Care' personal protective equipment (PPE) provided for all guests.

1 Define the physical evidence in the context of the extended marketing mix. **[2]**

2 Outline how the MOHG has used the 'We Care' programme as part of the hotel's physical evidence. **[4]**

3 Explain **two** benefits to MOHG of achieving the best possible physical evidence element of the extended marketing mix. **[4]**

4 Evaluate the view that physical evidence is the most important aspects of MOHG's extended marketing mix. **[10]**

26.13 Seven Ps model in a service-based market

The combined seven Ps marketing mix now forms the overall strategy that a service-based business will adopt to win and keep customers. Each element of the mix must be integrated with all other elements to ensure a consistent image of the business and its services (see Figure 26.11). For example, customers will be confused if they are charged high prices for what they are told is 'the best and fastest internet service available' but they find it almost impossible to communicate with the business through its own website.

26.14 An appropriate marketing mix

- If an expensive, well-known brand of perfume was for sale on a **market stall**, would you be suspicious?
- If the most exclusive shop in your town sold expensive gifts and wrapped them in **newspaper**, would you be surprised?
- If a cheap range of children's clothing was advertised in a glossy **colour magazine** aimed at professional women, would this advertisement lead to many sales?

These are all examples of poorly integrated and inappropriate marketing-mix decisions. The marketing decisions – shown in bold – lack integration with the rest of the marketing mix and are therefore inappropriate. If the messages that consumers receive about a product are confused or lack focus, they may fail to recognise the true identity or 'personality' of the product. Consumers are likely to reject products where the marketing mix has not communicated a clear and unambiguous message, resulting in fewer long-term sales.

If just one part of the marketing is inconsistent or does not integrate with the rest, it may lead to the failure of even the best marketing plan.

As businesses must be constantly aware of changes in their external environment, what was an 'appropriate marketing mix' last year may be unsuitable this year if economic or market conditions have changed. An economic recession, the development of new technology products by competitors or significant changes in consumer tastes will all need to be evaluated when adapting a marketing mix over time.

The most appropriate marketing-mix decisions will therefore be:

- based on marketing objectives that are achievable within the marketing budget
- coordinated and consistent with each other
- targeted at the appropriate consumers
- adapted in response to changes in economic and market conditions.

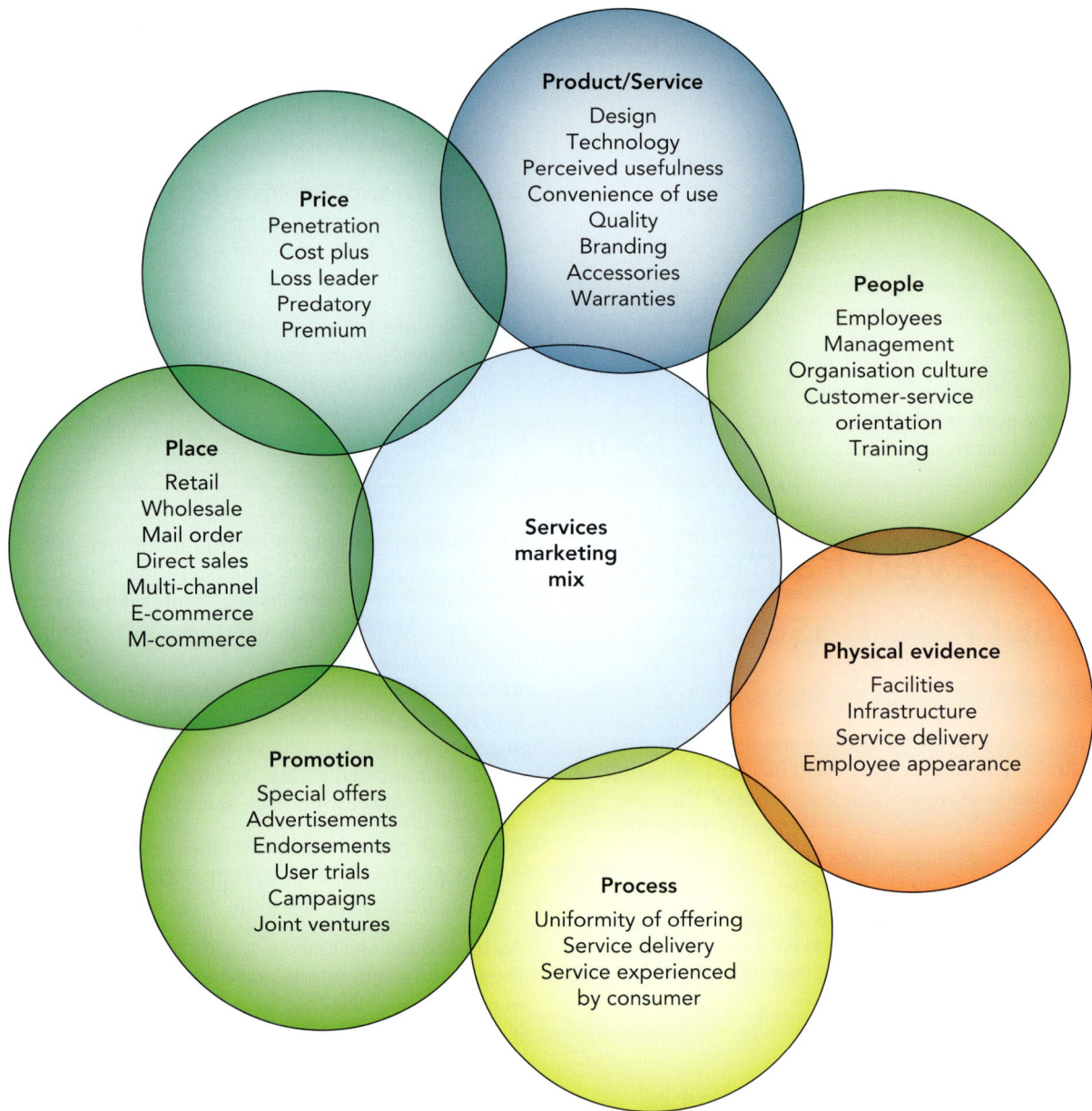

Figure 26.11: Services marketing mix

LEARNER PROFILE

Some cultural norms in eating in restaurants around the world

In Thailand, dishes arrive all at once and not in any particular order. Arriving on time for meals and being well dressed is important in Japan, as is ensuring that you serve others before yourself. In Ghana and Morocco, as food is usually eaten with your hands, a wash basin is passed around before a meal. In Japan, make sure that you do not cross or lick your chopsticks or pass food with them. In India, certain areas within the Middle East, Ghana and Ethiopia, eating with your left hand is often considered unclean and everything should be eaten with the right hand (and without cutlery). This is contrary to Japanese custom where eating anything with your hands is inappropriate. Forks in Thai restaurants are meant to push food onto spoons, and in Russia, Italy and Colombia, knives should be held in the right hand and forks in the left. A common practice in France is using your bread to move food onto your fork during meals – especially great for mopping up those rich French sauces!

Discuss in pairs or as whole class the importance of the being open-minded and knowledgeable when using the extended marketing mix to market products globally.

SELF-EVALUATION CHECKLIST

After studying this chapter, complete this table.

I am able to apply and analyse:	Needs more work	Almost there	Ready to move on
product: the relationship between the product life cycle, product portfolio and the marketing mix (AO2)			
product: the relationship between the product life cycle, investment, profit and cash flow (AO2)			
product branding: awareness, development, loyalty, value (AO2)			
product: the importance of branding (AO2)			
promotion: above-the-line, below-the-line and through-the-line (AO2)			
I am able to synthesise and evaluate:			
product: extension strategies (AO3)			
price: the appropriateness of the following pricing methods. cost-plus pricing (mark-up), penetration pricing, loss leader, predatory pricing, premium pricing dynamic pricing, competitive pricing, contribution pricing, price elasticity of demand (AO3)			
promotion: social media marketing as a promotional strategy (AO3)			
place: the importance of different types of distribution channels (AO3)			

CONTINUED

people: the importance of employee–customer relationships in marketing a service/cultural variation in these relationships (AO3)			
processes: the importance of delivery processes in marketing a service and changes in these processes (AO3)			
physical evidence: the importance of tangible physical evidence in marketing a service (AO3)			
appropriate marketing mixes for particular products or services (AO3)			

REFLECTION

Think about the times you have received very good customer service. Analyse why you consider the service to have been exceptional. Was it because of 'processes' or 'people'? Compare your experiences with those of another learner.

PROJECT

Marketing the Impossible Burger?

There is a plant-based burger that looks, tastes and cooks like a burger produced using beef. The Impossible Burger is made using a compound ingredient called 'heme' which copies the 'meaty' characteristics of beef. Because it is plant-based, the impossible burger has a smaller environmental footprint than its beef alternative.

When it was offered to diners in a London burger restaurant it was received incredibly well. Customers couldn't believe the taste, texture and smell of the product, that they believed was a regular beef burger. Blind taste test after blind taste test produced the same response from customers. Given the environmental and health concerns of beef burgers, why would you ever want to choose one over the 'impossible burger'?

Imagine you have opened a vegetarian burger restaurant selling the Impossible Burger.

1   In pairs or as a group, prepare a marketing strategy for your restaurant that includes:

- product – what will be on your menu

- price – how much you will charge for your food

- promotion – the type of promotion you will use

- place – where you will locate your restaurant.

2   Prepare a presentation of your strategy to give to your class.

Thinking about your project:

- How would you rate your group's strategy in comparison to those of the other groups?

- What changes would you make to your strategy in light of the other groups' efforts?

EXAM-STYLE QUESTIONS

Extract 1: Branding at L'Oréal

The multinational beauty and cosmetics company L'Oréal is the leading company in the personal care market. With a turnover of just under $30 billion and around 88 000 employees it has significant influence over its market. L'Oréal breaks its product mix into four divisions which are shown in the table.

Division	Brands
Active cosmetics	Vichy, Inneov, Sonaflore
Luxury products	Diesel, Ralph Lauren, YSL
Professional products	Technique, Matrix Essentials, Mizani, Kerastase
Personal care	Ombrelle, Maybelline, Essie, Garnier, Magic, Colorama

Like many large businesses selling a wide product mix, L'Oréal looks to balance the brands its sells, and the Boston matrix is a useful tool to achieve effective brand management.

1	Define the term 'brand'.	[2]
2	Outline how L'Oréal is an example of product branding.	[4]
3	Using a Boston matrix diagram, explain what the matrix shows.	[4]
4	Discuss the usefulness of the Boston matrix to L'Oréal in its brand management.	[10]

Extract 2: Marketing one of the world's most expensive restaurants

Developing a marketing strategy for one of the world's most expensive restaurants is a challenge. But Sublimotion is so much more than just one of the world's most expensive restaurants. It's dining at its most surreal, futuristic, and thought-provoking. Under the helm of double Michelin starred chef Paco Roncero, this one-of-a-kind establishment pushes the dining experience in bold new directions by combining food, art, and illusionism into a novel, revolutionary concept that ventures far beyond the palate.

During this theatrical gastronomic show, 12 lucky diners feast on avant-garde cuisine in a high-tech, interactive space called 'capsule', which serves as a blank canvas ready to be transformed into almost anything imaginable!

Every year, chef Paco Roncero partners with some of the greatest names in the culinary world to offer guests at Sublimotion an unprecedented gastronomic experience, worthy of countless Michelin stars.

The show-stopping multisensory adventure is masterminded by famous film directors and its soundtrack put together by award-winning composers. To complete the experience, diners are handed a Samsung Gear VR (virtual reality headset) that immerses them in a mind-blowing fantasy world during their meal. A staggering 20-course tasting menu accompanied by wine and champagne is €1500 per person, but some say it's a small price to pay for such a dramatic gastronomy-meets-virtual-reality experience.

1	Define the term 'marketing strategy'.	[2]
2	Outline the physical evidence and people elements of Sublimotion's extended marketing mix.	[4]
3	Explain why physical evidence is an important part of Sublimotion's extended marketing mix.	[4]
4	Evaluate the view that people is the most important aspect of Sublimotion's extended marketing mix.	[10]

> Chapter 27

International marketing

Higher-level

LEARNING OBJECTIVES

On completing this chapter you should be able to:

Synthesise and evaluate:

> The opportunities and threats posed by entering and operating internationally (AO3)

BUSINESS IN CONTEXT

IKEA adapts to Chinese market

Set up in Sweden in 1943, IKEA has grown to become the world's largest furniture retailer with almost 500 stores, including 35 in China. The products sold in each of these stores are remarkably similar. IKEA has largely ignored the retailing 'rule' that international success involves tailoring product lines to national tastes and consumer preferences. Ikea's founder – Ingvar Kamprad – had the vision that stores should sell a product range that is 'typically Swedish'. This has led to substantial cost benefits as huge production runs of identical products lead to economies of scale. These cost savings have helped to cancel out the high transport costs that international furniture retailers experience. The company sells largely 'flat-pack' furniture that has to be assembled at home, further reducing the cost of supplying stores around the globe.

Some consumers object to the standardised product formula. IKEA did have to make some product design changes in the highly competitive US market where furniture such as beds and wardrobes tend to be larger. Materials used for some furniture sold in India and China is adapted to humid climatic conditions.

The displays in IKEA showrooms in China are culturally relevant. They include an section on

New IKEA store in Henan province, China

balconies, which are common in Chinese homes. In southern China, balconies are shown being used to dry clothes, while in northern Chinese IKEA stores, the display balconies are shown as another place for food storage. These different uses reflect the customs in each region.

Discuss in pairs or a group:

- What are the potential opportunities and threats to IKEA of adopting the same or similar marketing strategies for all of the countries it operates in?

- How important is it that international retailers are seen to be 'culturally relevant' in each country they operate in?

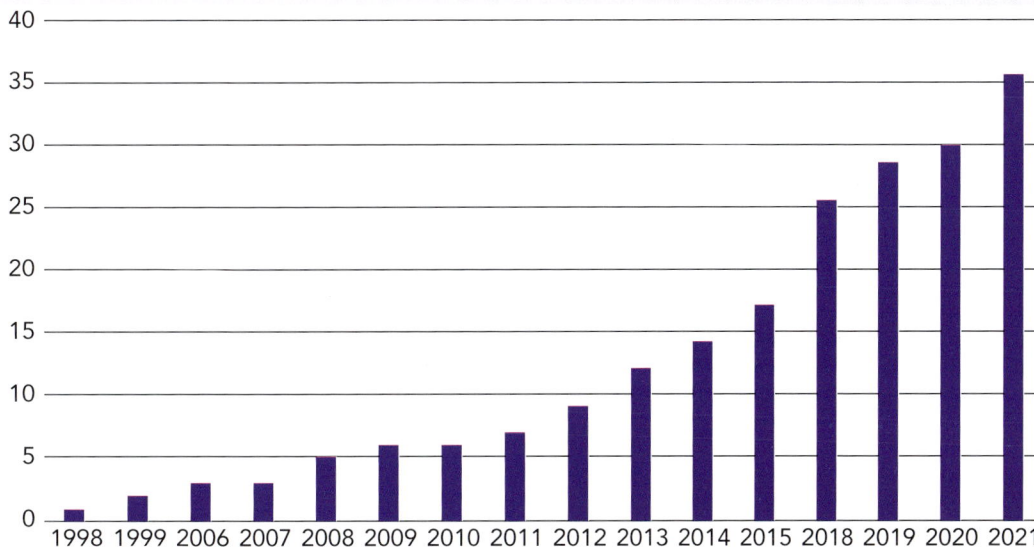

Number of IKEA stores in China (1998-2021)

ACTIVITY 27.1

A great deal of international marketing involves businesses exporting goods to other countries, which has a significant impact on a country's carbon footprint. This comes in the form of fossil fuel used to power ships, aeroplanes and lorries. The more a company exports, the bigger the carbon impact. Obviously, there are significant benefits for stakeholders associated with businesses involved in international marketing, but the trade-off in terms of the environmental cost to the global society is significant.

In pairs or as a group discuss whether international marketing involving the movement of goods is worth the environmental cost.

27.1 The opportunities and threats of international marketing

Selling in foreign markets was once too risky and expensive for most firms, so only large businesses that were growing too big for their national markets did it. Improved communications, access to e-commerce, better transport links and freer international trade – all key features of globalisation – have changed this. For many businesses, **international marketing** is now an opportunity to profitably expand their sales, and indeed for some companies it is no longer an option but a necessity.

KEY TERM

international marketing: selling products in markets other than the original domestic market

ACTIVITY 27.2

Rank 2021	Brand	Brand Value 2021 ($ million)
1	Amazon	683 852
2	Apple	611 997
3	Google	457 998
4	Microsoft	410 271
5	Tencent	240 931

The table sets out the five most valuable global brands in 2021.

In pairs or as a group, prepare a presentation that sets out:

- the nature of the product they sell

- the characteristics of brand image (logo, trademark, slogan)

- reasons why the business exists as an international brand

- the nature of a successful global brand.

Opportunities

Deciding to market products internationally has potential rewards in terms of more sales, greater global market share and higher profit. The main opportunities posed by international marketing are:

- Develop marketing operations in expanding markets when the domestic market is saturated, mature or badly affected by external events such as a pandemic. For example, in 2021 sales of cars in Germany fell by 10% but in India they rose by 27%.

- Take advantage of the potential to increase profits through rapid sales growth and low costs in emerging markets. In 2020, the GDP growth rate of Guyana was 43.4% and in Egypt it was 6.7%, but in the USA it fell by 3.5%.

- Take advantage of higher consumer spending power in countries with a higher per capita GDP. Higher incomes can result in consumers' disposable incomes being high, and these conditions create the opportunity to increase sales by using international marketing in those countries. For example, in 2021, per capita GDP was \$131 781 in Luxembourg but only \$265 in Burundi.

- Spread risks between different markets at different stages of the economic cycle. In any one year, not every country is at the same stage of the economic cycle. For example, selling luxury products in 2020 in Belize (where GDP fell by 16%) was much more difficult than in Guyana which recorded a growth rate of 26%.

- Diversify into other markets when there are poor trading conditions in the home market (perhaps due to the entry of new rivals). This means that international marketing can allow sales to continue to grow despite increased competition in the domestic market.

- Take advantage of increased economies of scale by expanding through selling to international markets.

Threats

If setting up marketing operations was easy and risk free, many more businesses would attempt international marketing. The fact that many businesses fail to successfully exploit new markets abroad suggests that there are some serious threats involved with this strategy. They include:

- Differences in consumer needs and wants and in usage patterns for products in international markets can lead to increased costs to adapt and market them to address these differences. Failure to respond to the differences on the grounds of cost can lead to expensive marketing failures.

- Transportation costs might be greater than the potential profit to be made from selling products in international markets.

- Differences exist in the legal environment of countries. For example, some products might be banned altogether, or safety regulations might be tougher in some countries than others. Businesses will have to meet all legal requirements in the markets they decide to operate in and they will need to obtain specialist knowledge of these legal constraints for each market.

- There are likely to be high levels of competition from national producers, some of which may receive subsidies or 'special treatment' from national governments.

- Counterfeit goods are a big risk in some countries. The 'grey market' – either copies of branded products or branded products sold through unauthorised channels – can undermine the reputation and profit margins of well-known global brands.

- Failure to research and respond to cultural differences in international markets is perhaps the greatest threat of all. Cultural differences are a key factor in international marketing, but they are often difficult to define and measure. Failure to recognise cultural and language differences can have a disastrous effect on the marketing strategy of a business. Cultural differences exist because of many reasons. People from different cultures have:
  - different perceptions
  - different values and ideologies
  - different tastes, attitudes, lifestyles, religious beliefs, customs and rituals.

Maximising opportunities and reducing threats of international marketing

How can businesses that are engaged, or planning to engage, in international marketing optimise the returns from this strategy?

1 Select an appropriate method of entry

Table 27.1 outlines the advantages and disadvantages of different ways in which a business can adopt international marketing. Choosing an *inappropriate* method will increase the threats and reduce the opportunities of selling abroad.

Method	Advantages	Disadvantages
Direct exporting	Selling directly via e-commerce has the same benefits as all online selling – see Chapter 26 Profit is not 'shared' with another business unless an agent in the importing country is used to promote/distribute the products Complete control of marketing strategy rests with the exporting business	No knowledge gains from businesses/partners based in international markets Exporting business bears all the risks May be import tariffs imposed by governments to protect markets for products produced nationally
International franchising	Using franchisees based 'in country' gives each franchised unit local knowledge Franchisees contribute to the capital cost by purchasing a franchise licence Some operational issues are now the responsibility of the local franchisee	Some loss of centralised control Careful selection of each franchisee is essential as damage to business brand name in one country could spread globally
Joint ventures	Venture partner is likely to be based in the international market being targeted so local knowledge will be obtained – customs, laws, culture, etc. Capital injection will be shared Management responsibilities and risk will be shared May be the only means of entering some markets if governments insist on 'local partners'	Management problems due to clash of business cultures or personalities Profits will be shared Local partner needs to be chosen carefully to avoid risk of fraudulent operations Loss of complete control of operations and marketing strategy
Licensing	Reduces capital costs of setting up own operations Licensee will benefit from local knowledge	Loss of control over quality and marketing strategy Profit margin may be reduced compared to maintaining complete control and eliminating a third party in the production/marketing of products
Direct investment in subsidiaries	Gives complete control over the operations of the subsidiary Local subsidiary will have managers with local knowledge Existing operations will allow quicker entry to the market than setting up new facilities	Culture clash is possible between the parent company and the management of the subsidiary May be strict local laws regarding takeovers and retrenchment of local employees Valuation of foreign subsidiaries may be difficult – parent company must avoid 'overpaying' for local knowledge and existing facilities

Table 27.1: Advantages and limitations of international-market entry methods

2 Recognise the importance of cultural differences

Using Hofstede's cultural dimensions (Chapter 10) marketing managers might be able to make the following adjustments to marketing strategy to reflect cultural differences.

- **Power distance.** Cultures with a high power distance have strong hierarchies and powerful leaders. Decisions tend to be made by heads of families and senior managers. Discussion and teamwork are more important in low power distance cultures. To reflect these differences, marketing in high power distance countries should be directed towards and appeal to people in leadership roles. Perhaps it could be stressed that the products create benefits for the whole family or company, which could make the leader appear to be more successful.

- **Individualism/collectivism.** For countries with high individualism, promotional campaigns could target individual consumers by emphasising how the products will directly benefit them. Individual freedom, saving time and self-gratification are important messages. For markets with low individualism and strong community ties, the whole community should be addressed by promotions. These could explain how, if its members buy these products, the community will benefit.

- **Masculinity and femininity.** Markets with high masculinity differentiate between the roles of men and women. International marketing businesses should research the culture of the countries they sell to and make sure that marketing activities target the correct gender for each product as defined by the nation's culture. Markets with low masculinity promote sexual equality, so there could be negative reactions to gender-specific promotions.

- **Tolerance of ambiguity/uncertainty.** Cultures with high ambiguity avoidance will prefer very clear and unambiguous marketing messages. For example, promotions could focus on product characteristics, its benefits and any unique features. Cultures that are more willing to tolerate ambiguity accept lifestyle-based promotions, persuasive (as opposed to informative) advertising and marketing messages with implied product benefits.

- **Long-term/short-term orientation.** Eastern cultures tend to have high long-term orientation scores while Western societies score lower on this cultural characteristic. Marketing campaigns could recognise these orientations by using promotions that stress traditional structures for markets with high long-term orientation scores and reinforcing short-term benefits for low-scoring markets.

- **Indulgence and quick gratification.** People who live within high indulgence cultures value leisure time and pastimes and have relaxed sexual standards. Low indulgence cultures tend to have rigid social restrictions with fewer individual freedoms. Where an advertisement could feature attractive people on a beach to appeal to high indulgence cultures, it could result in negative consequences in restrained societies. In these low indulgence cultures, businesses might be advised to focus on the social benefits of the products, their usefulness or how well adapted they are to the existing social order.

3 Adopt the most appropriate marketing strategy in each country

According to some analysts (e.g., Levitt) the world is becoming more standardised in the goods and services that it is demanding. This suggests that the same standard products can be marketed successfully throughout the world. If this is true, then the opportunities for companies to use technology to gain massive economies of scale by selling the same product across the globe are huge.

Other writers (e.g., Douglas and Wind) suggest that substantial differences still exist in consumer needs in different countries' markets. Standardisation is only one option for entering these markets, and this will sometimes fail owing to national and regional differences in consumer tastes. The alternative is for businesses to adapt a global marketing mix to local needs and conditions – this is called localisation.

The two broad approaches to selling goods and services internationally are known as 'pan-global marketing' and 'global localisation'. See Table 27.2 for the advantages and disadvantages of a pan-global marketing strategy.

KEY TERMS

pan-global marketing: adopting a standardised product across the globe as if the whole world were a single market – selling the same goods in the same way everywhere

global localisation: adapting the marketing mix, including differentiated products, to meet national and regional tastes and cultures

---

Pan-global marketing may continue to be important for two groups of products in particular:

- Upmarket brands with international appeal for their exclusivity such as Rolex watches, Rolls-Royce cars and Versace dresses. The opportunity to buy the same product as international celebrities is the key promise made by these brands. Consumers do not want them adapted to their markets.

- Mass-appeal brands, such as Levi's, Apple and Nike, have substantial opportunities for global campaigns and standardised products – and the economies of scale that result from these.

Global localisation

Global localisation is the opposite of standardisation and is the business strategy that responds to the drawbacks of a pan-global or pan-regional strategy.

'Thinking global – acting local' is sometimes how this approach to international marketing is summed up. Yum! Brands, the world's largest fast-food organisation that includes top brands such as KFC and Pizza Hut, has adopted this approach with great success. It offers all of its franchisees and branches around the globe the benefits and security offered by a giant multinational corporation. However, it differentiates most aspects of its marketing mix between different countries and markets. For example:

- In China, it sells products that are not available in other countries to suit local consumers' tastes. So, although it was the first company to introduce the Chinese to pizzas, its best-selling lines today include 'KFC Dragon Twister'.

Advantages	Disadvantages
A common identity for the product can be established. This aids consumer recognition, especially in a world of increasing international travel by consumers and the widespread use of satellite TV channels with 'international' advertising.	Despite growing similarity between consumer tastes in different countries, it might still be necessary to develop different products to suit cultural or religious variations. Market opportunities could be lost by trying to sell essentially the same product everywhere.
Cost reduction can be substantial. The same product can be produced for all markets allowing substantial economies of scale. This is particularly important for businesses that have to spend huge sums on developing new products that may have only a short product life cycle. The same marketing mix can be used. This allows just one marketing agency and advertising strategy to be used for the whole world or region rather than different ones for each country.	Legal restrictions can vary substantially between countries. This does not just apply to product restrictions, e.g., it is illegal to use promotions involving games or gambling in certain countries. There may also be restrictions on what can be shown in advertisements.
It recognises that differences between consumers in different countries are reducing – it is often said that teenagers in different countries have more in common with each other than they have with their parents! Therefore, a pan-global strategy for a product aimed at teenagers could be developed.	Brand names do not always translate effectively into other languages. They might even cause offence or unplanned embarrassment for the company if the selection of the brand name to be used in all markets is not made with care.
	Setting the same price in all countries will fail to take into account the substantially different average income levels that exist.

Table 27.2: Pan-global marketing strategy – advantages and disadvantages

- Price levels are varied between different countries to reflect different average incomes.

- Advertisements always contain local 'ethnic' people.

- Its distribution and place decisions are tested for local markets too. In China, it tried out 14 new Chinese

quick-service restaurants offering authentic Chinese food in surroundings designed in a local style.

Table 27.3 explains the benefits and limitations of global localisation.

Benefits	Limitations
Local needs, tastes and cultures are reflected in the marketing mix of the business and this could lead to higher sales and profits	The scope for economies of scale is reduced
There is no attempt to impose foreign brands/products/advertisements on regional markets	The international brand could lose its power and identity if locally adapted products become more popular than the 'international' product
The products are more likely to meet local, national and legal requirements than if they are standardised products	There will be additional costs of adapting products, advertisements, store layouts, etc. to specific local needs – these costs might lead to higher prices than a global marketing strategy would result in
There will be less local opposition to multinational business activity	

Table 27.3: Benefits and limitations of global localisation

LEARNER PROFILE

Communicators

A crucial aspect of international marketing is for a business to be able to communicate with existing and potential buyers in different languages. Facebook, for example, allows its users to create adverts in multiple languages so they can reach customers throughout the world. Businesses that create promotional messages that are short and easily recognisable will have an advantage in global markets.

In pairs or in groups, discuss the importance of effective communication in international marketing.

CASE STUDY 27.1

UPS has confirmed an expansion across 40 countries

United Parcel Service is a US-based multinational shipping and delivery business. UPS is committed to further expansion overseas in 40 new countries. UPS express services are now available to businesses across more than 140 different countries. Continued expansion by UPS means guaranteeing morning or midday service for companies in all of the countries where UPS is based. As a result of this, UPS can get shipments efficiently to all of its customers, whether they are domestic or commercial users.

'Cross-border trade continues to present growth opportunities for us and for our customers of all sizes,' said Nando Cesarone, president of UPS International. 'Our time-sensitive services are faster, they speed up time-to-market in high-growth economies and they offer another way for our customers to optimise their cross-border supply chains.'

One method UPS uses to expand in overseas markets is franchising through UPS Store, which is the world's largest franchisor of retail shipping and posting. In using this approach UPS wants to maintain a pan-global approach to the way it markets its services.

With businesses requiring guaranteed time-of-day delivery that can be relied upon, UPS is growing

its express services footprint within key markets by adding new postal codes in 14 European countries, in addition to other markets in Asia, the Americas, the Indian subcontinent, Russia, Nigeria and Vietnam.

1 Define the term 'international marketing'. [2]

2 Outline how UPS uses international franchising to expand in overseas markets. [4]

3 Explain why UPS has used a pan-global approach to marketing its service in overseas markets. [4]

4 Evaluate the benefits to UPS of expanding its service in overseas markets. [10]

THEORY OF KNOWLEDGE

Consider the following advertising slogans:

- To advertise their leather seats, American Airlines used the slogan 'Fly in leather', which translated into Spanish for the market in Mexico as 'Fly naked'.

- HSBC used the slogan 'we assume nothing' to promote its banking service, which translated to 'we do nothing' in many countries.

- General Motors struggled to promote the 'Nova' model of car in Spain because Nova translates to 'No go' in Spanish.

In pairs or as a group, discuss the importance of language in international marketing.

CASE STUDY 27.2

The global holiday market

Reserve.com is a global travel business. This is a large successful company with a turnover of over $10 billion and a net profit of $3 billion. Reserve markets itself under a number of leading online brands including:

- Reserve it – accommodation
- One deal – package holidays
- Pick up and go – car rental
- Highline – flights
- Order it – restaurant booking.

Reserve.com has huge global reach, operating websites in nearly 200 countries. The company is very good at marketing itself online. When anyone puts a holiday-related search into their web browser a Reserve.com brand will be at the top of the potential customer's search.

One of the challenges Reserve.com has is marketing its business at a local level where people identify local or regional factors in making holiday decisions. An example of this is when Reserve.com launched Taiyang, which is an online travel business that specialises in the Asian market. This global localisation approach could help Reserve.com break into regional markets.

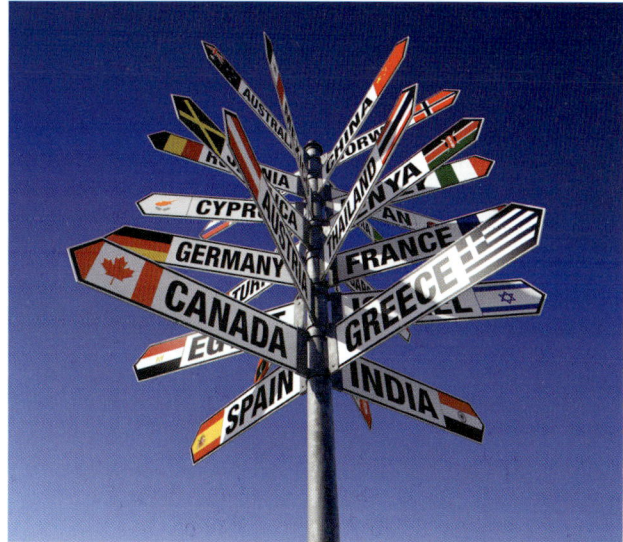

1   Define the term 'global localisation'.   [2]

2   Outline how it uses its product mix to target different segments of the holiday market.   [4]

3   Explain **two** problems Reserve.com might experience when marketing its product mix internationally.   [4]

4   Evaluate the benefits of Reserve.com of marketing its travel products online.   [10]

ACTIVITY 27.4

Nike and its agency, Yard, ventured into the greater Paris region, known as 'Grand Paris', for the unveiling of its latest sneaker, the Air Max 270. Rather than setting up in the chicest parts of Paris, they headed out to the suburbs in search of the brand's true fans. Working with French influencers, the activation, which was staged last month, featured pop-up shops in building entrances in neighbourhoods just outside Paris, giving residents an exclusive sneak peek at the Air Max before it hits stores. With the help of two icons who grew up in Grand Paris, actor Lucas, who is also an affiliate of the rap group PNL and rapper/entrepreneur Mac Tyer, the brand and its agency ventured beyond city lines to target today's trendsetters.

The Paris event used Grand Paris as its theme and featured a special contest with the rare opportunity of becoming a brand designer. Participants could design their own version of the Air Max shoe, using their city as inspiration. In addition to the pop-up stores, Yard launched a parallel national print and digital campaign for Nike featuring French trailblazers from Grand Paris.

1   In pairs or as a group research another company that has used a global local approach for a promotion campaign.

2   Discuss the effectiveness of using this as an approach to international marketing.

SELF-EVALUATION CHECKLIST

After studying this chapter, complete this table.

I am able to synthesise and evaluate:	Needs more work	Almost there	Ready to move on
the opportunities and threats posed by entering and operating internationally (AO3)			

REFLECTION

Assume that you are the CEO of an international food processing business which is not currently selling in your own country. What would be the most important cultural factors that you would have to consider if the business planned to start marketing food products in your country? Would you consider cultural difference to be an opportunity or a threat to your business? Compare your ideas with those of another learner.

PROJECT

Top tips for an international online marketing campaign:

- Think global, act local. In international communication you need to show customers you are responsive to their local language, culture and needs.

- Choose the right internet domain. The domain name you choose should be a .com domain. This is a worldwide domain and the firm's website will appear everywhere in the world.

- Find a niche. You need to be a specialist in certain areas or product offerings because ultimately this will attract the most suitable potential customers to you.

- Offer linguistic choice on your website. It is important you translate your website into other keys languages to target your customers, incite their trust and show you care for them.

- Make contacting you easy. On your website it must be as easy as possible to contact you. Include your phone number, email address, links to social media.

- Empathise with your customers. Be sympathetic to the language, customs and culture of the countries you are marketing your product in.

- Trust. At the heart of business and especially business communication is trust. You need to show your customers you are trustworthy so they trust your company and its products.

- Adapt to the language of the buyer. In an ideal scenario the buyer or potential customer should be addressed in their own language. By doing so they are more likely to take the time to listen to you, to have a look at your products and to trust you.

CONTINUED

- Always plan. Define a clear strategy; choose your target; think about the layout, colours and content of your website. Choose a strategic domain, translate it into relevant languages.

1 In pairs or as a group you need to develop an online international marketing campaign for a product in a particular country, using the tips discussed above. In your campaign you need to:

- choose a product

- choose a country to market your product in

- set a price

- develop a promotional theme

- choose a method of delivery

- develop a web page.

2 Make a presentation about your marketing campaign.

Thinking about your project:

- Now that you have delivered your presentation, do you feel you have a better understanding of international marketing?

- How would you rate your group's presentation in comparison to those of the other groups?

- What changes would you make to your presentation if you could do it again?

EXAM-STYLE QUESTIONS

Marketing desserts

Red and Blue plc consider expanding into Europe

Red and Blue Plc is a North American-based steak restaurant. The business is very established in the USA, but it wants to expand into several countries in Europe. Red and Blue markets itself as a medium-priced restaurant, and it is looking to achieve high volumes through its outlets. The menu is based on steaks and there is limited choice.

The company has been very successful in North America, but the management feels the market is saturated and for the business to grow it needs to expand overseas. The challenges it has are dealing with different tastes in different countries, and growing numbers of consumers who are moving away from beef either as vegetarians or people who have environmental concerns.

Red and Blue is thinking of rebranding itself in Europe and offering a more chicken-based menu in response to these concerns. Red and Blue might even change the name of its business if it expands into Europe to move away from its US image. There is some resistance amongst the Red and Blue's directors who feel the American image is key to the brand's identity and are resistant to this global localisation approach.

1	List two examples of international marketing.	[2]
2	Define the term 'pan-global marketing'.	[2]
3	State **two** methods of international marketing.	[2]
4	Outline **two** benefits of international marketing.	[4]
5	Outline **two** threats of international marketing.	[4]
6	Explain how a joint venture can be used in international marketing.	[4]
7	Define the term 'global localisation'.	[2]
8	Outline **two** ways Red and Blue might use global localisation in its approach to expanding into Europe.	[4]
9	Explain how changes in consumer taste might be a threat to Red and Blue.	[4]
10	Evaluate Red and Blue's decision to expand into Europe.	[10]

Operations management

> # Chapter 28

Introduction to operations management

BUSINESS IN CONTEXT

Sustainable energy operations – a reasonable objective?

Total Oil is a major oil and gas producer. The burning of these fossil fuels is claimed to be a major cause of global warming and climate change. The company argues that low-cost energy from all sources – including oil and gas – is needed to promote economic growth. It points out that almost one billion people in the world today have no access to electricity. So how can energy be provided to everyone without destroying the planet for future generations?

Total is committed to a policy of **sustainable operations**. It has set the objective of reducing the carbon footprint of the business with more efficient refining equipment and well-insulated business premises. It aims to double its low-carbon electricity production in five years. It is developing solar power generating capacity and wind and hydraulic power. It has bought a company called Saft that is developing efficient batteries to allow solar power to be stored efficiently and cheaply.

The CEO wants to reinvent the business as much more than an oil and gas company. His ambition is for 'low-carbon' operations to account for nearly 20% of the company's activities in 20 years.

Discuss in pairs or in a group:

- Can an oil and gas business ever be fully sustainable?

- To what extent will the measures taken by Total Oil benefit the company as well as the environment?

KEY TERM

sustainable operations: business operations that can be sustained in the long term, e.g., by protecting the environment and not damaging the quality of life of future generations

KEY CONCEPT LINK

Change

Shell is working to provide more renewable and low-carbon energy options for customers through investments in wind, solar, electric vehicle charging, hydrogen, and more.

Many energy company companies worldwide are undergoing significant change as they move away from fossil fuels towards renewable energy sources.

TIP

Sustainability is now an important element of operational decisions. An effective way to evaluate the operational decision of any business is to consider whether or not it is likely to result in sustainability.

28.1 The role of operations management

'Operations' or 'operations management' is concerned with the use of resources called inputs – land, labour and capital – to provide outputs in the form of goods and services. In doing this, operations managers must be concerned with:

- **efficiency of production** – keeping costs as low as possible will help to give competitive advantage
- **quality** – the good or service must be suitable for the purpose intended
- **flexibility and innovation** – the need to develop and adapt to new processes and new products is increasingly important in today's dynamic business environment.

Essentially, operations managers are aiming to produce goods and services of the required quality, in the required quantity, at the time needed, in the most cost-effective way. To do this, operations managers must understand the transformation process.

ACTIVITY 28.1

Think about your school or college as an organisation that needs to be managed effectively as an operation. Consider how it manages:

- the efficiency of its operation
- the cost of its operation
- the quality of the education
- new innovation in education.

1 In pairs or as a group, discuss how effective you think operations management is in your school.

2 Discuss the challenges your school faces when it is trying to manage its operations efficiently.

The production or transformation process

In all businesses at all stages of production, the production process is basically the same. 'Inputs' are converted or transformed into 'outputs', and this is sometimes called the 'transformation' process. This can be illustrated quite simply (see Figure 28.1).

This process applies to both manufacturing and service industries. By 'production', we mean the making of tangible goods, such as computers, and the provision of intangible services, such as banking. The aim in all cases is to 'add value' to the inputs that are bought in by the business so that the resulting output can be sold at a profit.

The degree of value added to the inputs will depend on a number of factors (not all of which are operations management issues):

- **The design of the product or the nature of the service.** Does this allow for economic manufacture, whilst appearing to have quality features that will enable a high price to be charged? Some customers are prepared to pay higher prices for products that offer better quality than cheaper substitutes.
- **The efficiency with which the input resources are combined and managed.** For example, by reducing waste, the operations management department will increase the value added by the production process. Increasing productivity will reduce costs per unit and this will increase **added value** if the customer prices remain unchanged. So efficient operations processes and operations decisions are closely linked to value added.

KEY TERM

added value: the difference between the cost of purchasing raw materials and the price the finished goods are sold for

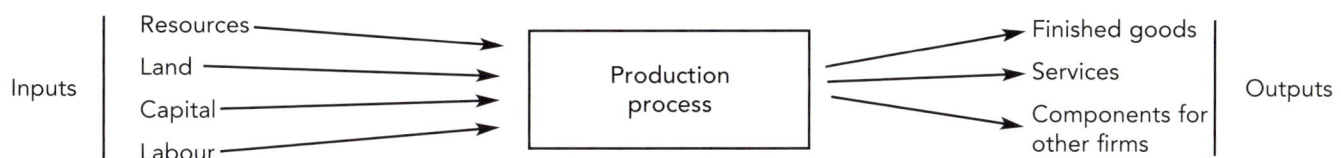

Figure 28.1: The transformation process

- **Being able to convince consumers to pay more for the good or service than the cost of the inputs.** A good example is the market for luxury ice creams, where the marketing campaigns increase the willingness of consumers to pay far in excess of input costs for the product.

The operations process can involve many stages before physically selling the good or service. These include:

- converting a consumer need into a product that can be produced efficiently
- organising operations so that production is carried out efficiently, e.g., ordering stocks to arrive on time
- deciding on suitable production methods
- setting quality standards and checking they are maintained.

Resources used in operations

All business operations require resources – these are the production inputs.

- **Land.** All businesses need somewhere to operate from, even if it is the bedroom of a sole trader operating an internet-based website design service. Of course, some businesses require large sites for the extraction of minerals or the manufacture of finished products.
- **Labour.** All business activity requires some labour input. This could be the manual labour of a gardener or the mental skills of a research scientist. The quality of the labour input will have a significant impact on the operational success of a business. The effectiveness of labour can usually be improved by training in specific skills – but trained workers will become sought after by other businesses and may leave.
- **Capital.** This refers to the tools, machinery, computers and other equipment that businesses use to produce the goods and services they sell. The term 'capital' can also mean the amount the owners of a business invest to set it up. Efficient operations often depend on capital equipment, and, in competitive markets, the more productive and advanced the capital, the greater the chance of business success.

The role of operations management in linking with other business functions

Operations management decisions can never be taken in isolation from the rest of the business. Coordination between business functions is essential if obvious problems are to be avoided. These are some examples that illustrate why it is important for operations management to link with other business departments:

- Operations managers need to ensure that the appropriate quantity of the good or service is made available so that the **marketing** department may successfully sell it profitably.
- Operations managers need to work closely with the **human resources** department so that appropriate numbers of suitably qualified workers are employed.
- Operations decisions, such as expanding capacity, often require funding, so frequent liaison with the **finance** department is essential.

These are both examples of capital inputs to the production process

The importance of close cooperation and interdependence between business functions (departments) can be illustrated by the following situations where these links did not exist:

- Operations continue to manufacture a product at the same output level even though it is experiencing declining sales.

- Operations have a new product innovation but it fails to be developed effectively owing to a shortage of finance.

- Operations' plan to increase output in a factory by introducing a third daily shift of workers is not communicated to the human resources department.

- Operations identify a new location for the production facilities but the human resources department is not consulted.

LEARNER PROFILE

Caring/principled

You are the CEO of a European-based car manufacturer and you are faced with more European Union (EU) rules telling you that your company's new cars from 2025 have to be completely recyclable. This is going to add €2500 to the cost of each car you produce. If your business absorbs the cost it means less profit for already unhappy shareholders who have seen their dividends fall over the last three years, or your business has less profit to reinvest in the new environmentally friendly electric cars you want to produce. If you add the cost to the selling price of the firm's cars it means the less well-off car buyers are the hardest hit by the drive for sustainability.

As a caring, principled CEO, do you increase the selling price of your cars or settle for lower profits on each car you sell?

The role of operations management in sustainability

'Planet, people, profit' – this is how the commonly held view that businesses have a wider role in the local, national and global communities than just 'making money' is often summarised. It is also known as the 'triple bottom line' – suggesting that business performance should be assessed not just in terms of financial surplus (profit) but also by measuring the impact on the environment and society.

Social enterprises are those that are set up with the specific aim of achieving the 'triple bottom line'. However, other businesses (from large multinationals to smaller local businesses) are becoming increasingly focused on satisfying environmental and social goals as well as financial ones. Some cynical observers suggest that they do this because 'it is good for business to be seen to be doing good'.

Ecological sustainability

Operations management can achieve greater **ecological sustainability** by:

- reducing waste at all levels of the organisation (see lean production and quality management (Chapter 30))

- using less energy and sourcing it from renewable sources where possible

- reducing water use and recycling water

- reducing the use of non-renewable resources in production

- designing products that use recycled materials or allow materials to be recycled at the end of their useful life

- designing products that use less-harmful energy sources, e.g., electric cars.

KEY TERM

ecological sustainability: the capacity of ecosystems to maintain their essential functions and processes, and retain their full biodiversity over the long term

Social sustainability

Operations management can achieve greater **social sustainability** by:

- designing production systems that are safe and healthy for employees
- designing work and workplaces to allow for social interaction
- creating jobs in low-income or deprived areas – this may mean relocation of operations facilities
- reducing the negative impact of production on communities, e.g., cutting harmful pollution.

KEY TERM

social sustainability: the ability of a community to develop processes and structures which not only meet the needs of its current members but also support the ability of future generations to maintain a healthy community

ACTIVITY 28.2

LUSH Fresh Handmade Cosmetics is a business that makes ethical trading one of the key focuses of its operations. Its vision is that business should be ethical, and individual companies should not stand out simply because they are not damaging the environment or being unfair. They believe that no company should be trading from an unethical position and society has a right to expect fairness as the normal course of business.

As a cosmetics business, LUSH has been fighting animal testing for over 30 years and it boycotts all suppliers who test any of their products or ingredients on animals. The LUSH website links prominently to literature about animal testing, humane alternatives and activist opportunities.

1   In pairs or as a group, research another business that takes such a strong ethical position.

2   Prepare a presentation on the ethical position of the business you have chosen.

Economic sustainability

Operations management can achieve greater **economic sustainability** by:

- Managing and maintaining operational assets (equipment, machinery and buildings) so that they have extended lifespans and do not need to be replaced due to damage or unnecessary wear and tear.
- Increasing the efficiency of the production process to improve business competitiveness. This will usually involve increasing labour and capital productivity. High-productivity businesses tend to have low unit costs and have a better chance of future profitability (economic sustainability) than businesses with low-productivity rates.
- Researching and developing products and processes that create customer interest and create value. For example, the future of Apple should be secure if it can continue to develop and launch innovative products that have a clear USP.

KEY TERM

economic sustainability: in a business context, economic sustainability involves using the assets of the company efficiently to allow it to continue functioning profitability over time

You should notice a common theme running through the three definitions given above – the long term. Sustainability means undertaking activities today that do not damage the ability of future generations to undertake the same activities. Clearly, using up the world's supply of fossil fuels is not a sustainable form of energy generation as future generations will not be able to do this. Throwing rubbish into landfill sites is not sustainable as there are fewer and fewer available sites and they can cause damaging, polluting side effects. You should be able to think of many more unsustainable business and non-business activities. The next section on business management tools considers some of the techniques being adopted by businesses to increase the sustainability of their operations.

CASE STUDY 28.1

Operations management at Adidas

Adidas is the largest sportswear business in Europe with a sales revenue of $22 billion in 2021. It is also a high 'value added' business with net profits of $2.3 billion. Like many organisations it has become increasingly focused on sustainability in its operations management. Sustainability is a holistic initiative for Adidas that runs throughout its business. This stretches from the offices and stores that their employees work in, to the innovative products it creates for its customers. The sustainable solutions it develops target the entire life cycle of sport; how apparel, footwear or equipment is made, sold, played and eventually disposed of.

Adidas manufacturing sites have the following goals in production:

- Water: they set strong targets to reduce water consumption in production. They also commit to water conservation practices and ensure that 100% of their cotton is from sources that use recycled water for irrigation.

- Chemicals: Adidas works with chemical experts, environmental organisations and industry federations to upgrade their approach to reduce chemicals usage in production.

- Energy: Adidas has achieved energy reduction targets of 20% year on year and have committed to being carbon neutral by 2050.

- Labour: Adidas is committed to fair labour practices, fair compensation and safe working conditions in production and throughout its supply chain.

1   Define the term 'valued added'.   [2]

2   Outline **two** resources Adidas uses in its production process.   [4]

3   Describe how Adidas manages water and energy in its operations to be more sustainable.   [4]

4   Discuss the view that achieving greater sustainability in production can only be good for Adidas.   [10]

THEORY OF KNOWLEDGE

Trust

In 2013, meat processing businesses were accused of using horsemeat in place of beef to reduce their costs.

For example, it was found that Tesco Everyday Value Spaghetti Bolognese contained 60% horsemeat.

The product was withdrawn from all its stores immediately. The ready meal product came from a French factory that was using horsemeat rather than beef.

In pairs or as a group, discuss the extent to which trust is important when we buy products from the world's leading businesses.

CASE STUDY 28.2

Producing with reusable packaging

Humans produce more than 300 million tonnes of plastic a year. Half of it is single use, and more than 8 million tonnes finds its way into the ocean.

A European based start-up is doing its part to break our global plastic addiction with an eco-friendly casing that can be used for ketchup, mustard, mayonnaise or any condiment. Made from seaweed, Ooho sachets from the business Notpla are biodegradable, compostable and even edible. Seaweed farmed in northern France is dried out and ground into powder before undergoing a patented process that turns it into a clear substance which can be moulded like plastic. Notpla's Ooho sachets can be used in place of plastic packaging. Seaweed is an effective base material for packaging because it uses natural material as an input that is a carbon recycler, rather than plastics which comes from non-renewable oil.

1   Define the term 'sustainable production'.   [2]

2   Outline why Notpla is considered a sustainable business.   [4]

3   Explain **two** benefits to Notpla of being a sustainable business.   [4]

4   Explain **two** disadvantages to a food business of choosing to use Notpla's packaging for their product.   [4]

28.2 Business management tools for sustainable operations

All of the following circular business models contribute towards the concept of the circular economy, which has the aim of making production and consumption more ;sustainable.

KEY TERMS

circular business model: a business approach that creates product value whilst at the same time improving resource efficiency by extending the useful life of products and components

circular economy: a model of production and consumption which involves sharing, leasing, reusing, repairing, refurbishing and recycling existing materials and products for as long as possible

---

Circular supply models

The aim of the circular supply business model is to achieve fully renewable, recyclable, or biodegradable resource inputs that serve as essential materials for a different production process. The overall goal of this business model is to reduce an organisation's dependence on new raw materials and other resources. This approach is especially important for companies that depend on scarce resources or commodities. Figure 28.2 illustrates the concept.

A key element of circular supply models is to maximise the recycling element of each production process and, consequently, reduce the 'raw materials' and 'residual waste' elements.

Resource recovery models

The resource recovery model is based on the idea of converting waste into secondary raw materials. The objective of this model is to obtain additional use from resources and to extract more value from them by delaying final disposal for as long as possible.

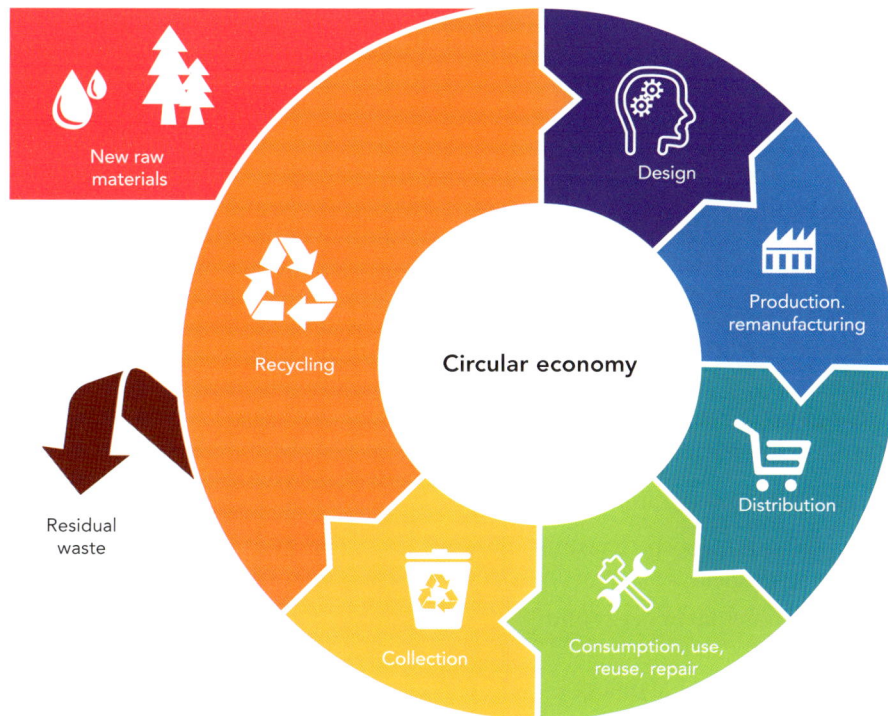

Figure 28.2 The circular economy

By reducing the need for newly exploited natural resources, production is made more sustainable in the long term. Sorting and processing waste and converting it into a useable resource for further production is a good example of the circular economy in operation. A key step in order for this model to be successful is to identify ways of recovering products that have reached the end of their 'original lives' so that the valuable materials and the energy that went into producing them can be reused.

The resource recovery model can result in additional revenue for businesses that use it. For example:

- extracting more added value from existing resources
- creating less dependence on high-cost new raw materials
- selling the resources retrieved from waste to other businesses for use in their operations.

Some current examples are as follows.

Heat from waste products

Fuel blending is often the safest and most efficient option for destroying both hazardous and non-hazardous waste. The heat generated from the combustion of this waste can be recovered in some operations and used in the manufacturing of concrete for example.

Reusing organic waste from food or farm products

Many countries use landfill sites for waste from these sources. Modern processes are now able to convert this waste into biomethane gas. This is then used as an energy source to create electricity or hydrogen for battery or fuel cell electric vehicles.

Extracting precious metals and other valuable materials from mobile phones and other electronic goods

The rising prices of many naturally occurring metals such as copper and palladium mean that it can now be profitable to extract these and other metals from electronic devices and car exhaust systems. These reused materials help to reduce the need for ecologically damaging new mine workings.

Recovering oil and waste water

During the refining of petrol and other fuel products, oily sludge is produced as a by-product. An innovative recycling process now allows refineries to recover value from this sludge by using a treatment process that separates the oil, water and solids. Once separated, the recovered oil and water is returned to the refinery for reuse in the refining of crude oil.

Benefits of resource recovery programmes:

- They provide a source of lower-cost materials and newly exploited ones.
- If processed waste materials can be sold, a new income stream is created.
- They improve the public relations image of the business by developing a socially responsible operations process.
- Environmentally conscious consumers may be attracted to the business and its products.

Possible limitations of resource recovery programmes:

- There may be high initial capital costs in resource recovery locations and equipment.
- The extraction process may require energy and other resources.
- They may not be economically viable unless government support is provided – or newly exploited resources are taxed and that increases their cost.
- Recycling sites may need to be carefully located, away from areas of habitation.

Product life extension models

How long is a product designed to last? This might depend on what it is and its selling price. Most consumers would expect a new car to last in good reliable condition for a great deal longer than a simple torch or pocket lamp for example. Consumers want products to last for as long as possible – even if they might sell them at some stage of their useful lives.

If businesses made consumer durable products that lasted for many years there would be fewer 'repeat sales' as the item will not need replacing as quickly, and revenue and profit could fall in the long term. So there is a conflict around the question of how long a product should last.

Some business analysts argue that manufacturers often operate on the basis of planned obsolescence, that is, deliberately designing products to fail after a certain period of time. However, reputation and business image will be damaged if the products stop working sooner than most customers expect.

The rapid pace of technological development has led to many consumers replacing products before their useful and serviceable life has ended. Modern consumer society encourages us to buy the 'latest gadget' and the 'new improved models' despite having a perfectly functioning older model. This practice leads to vast amounts of products being thrown into landfill or other disposal sites. In addition, some of the world's scarce resources are used to manufacture the newer products.

The product life extension model focuses on lengthening the time period that a product can be used before it needs to be disposed of. The objective is to maximise the lifespan of the product and reduce waste levels and exploitation of new sources of raw materials.

Benefits of product life extension models:

- They may reduce the costs of production as new resources become scarcer and more expensive; it will cost less in the long term to produce higher-quality and more durable products.
- The brand image of quality will improve as many environmentally aware consumers will place a higher value on more durable products and the businesses that make them.
- They improve the corporate social responsibility image of the business and attract eco-minded consumers towards its products.
- They reduce the risk of not meeting increasingly restrictive consumer protection laws in many countries that are insisting on products that perform effectively for longer.
- Businesses may sell more spare parts and maintenance materials to allow older products to be serviceable for longer.

Limitations of product life extension models:

- In some markets this approach will not succeed unless enough consumers prefer 'longevity' over image of the 'latest model'.
- The initial manufacturing cost is likely to increase as higher-quality and more durable materials and components will be required.
- Consumer expectations of the life span of a product will increase, so if a business has a problem with the quality and performance of one batch of products, negative publicity could damage image and sales.

Sharing models

Many products purchased by consumers and businesses are not used constantly. A product which is not used most of the time is a waste of the Earth's resources. If it could be shared with other potential users, fewer new products would need to be manufactured. A sharing model or sharing platform is a circular business model in which a business encourages owners of products to increase the usage and value derived from them by sharing them with others.

Sharing platform businesses aim to connect the things people own that are underutilised with other people who are willing to pay to use them. It is important to understand that the sharing platform business does not actually make or own any of these underutilised products. It simply creates the opportunity for consumers to take advantage of the unused potential of products.

Examples of business initiatives which use the sharing model are:

- **Ridesharing or car sharing** instead of owning a car or relying on public transport. Uber is a well-known example.

- **Coworking.** Individuals or businesses share an office with people or businesses that need more space, and they each pay a proportion of the expenses such as rent, utilities, office support and office supplies.

- **Couchsurfing** allows individuals who have houses or apartments to give travellers somewhere to sleep such as in unused rooms or even just on a couch.

- **Peer to peer lending** provides a means whereby individuals who need to raise finance can be put in touch with those having surplus funds. This allows those with underused resources to put them to an effective use.

Benefits of sharing models:

- Owners of goods: homeowners, car owners or owners of surplus office space gain from sharing platforms because they receive payment for allowing others to use their goods or products when they are not using them.

- The sharers but not owners of goods: people sharing the assets and resources of others benefit because they can make use of them without the fixed cost of buying and owning them. This encourages small business start-ups by cutting overhead costs and the responsibilities of owning assets.

- Sharing platform companies: they receive a fee for connecting owners and sharers. They do not need to own or produce the products they sell.

Limitations of sharing models:

- The sharing platform can make substantial fees (Airbnb is an example) which may leave the asset owner will limited returns.

- Some consumers see a potential safety risk with car sharing, and privacy issues remain a problem with online sharing platforms.

- There tends to be less government control and regulation of the 'sharing economy' than the traditional forms of purchase, and this adds to the risks for both asset owners and those sharing them.

CASE STUDY 28.3

The car-sharing market has grown significantly since 2012, maintaining an annual growth rate of around 16.4% since 2010. With this sustained growth, it is expected that 36 million users will be using car-sharing for business and domestic use by 2025.

1   Outline how car sharing works.   [2]

2   Explain two benefits of car sharing.   [4]

3   Explain two limitations of car sharing.   [4]

ACTIVITY 28.3

In pairs or as a group, research the way co-working operates and prepare a presentation on your findings.

Product service system models

The basis of this type of model is that the customer (consumer or business) is more concerned with obtaining the benefit from a product than actually owning it. A product service system (or servitisation) therefore starts from the point that companies must offer the function of the product to customers, not the product itself. This concept adds to the circular economy model by encouraging customers to only buy the services of a product as and when they need them, and not to actually own the product which might involve not using it for long periods. In this way, the economy needs to use less as products are being more fully utilised more of the time – so fewer products will need to be produced. This results in less energy use and less raw material resource use.

Business examples include the contract Philips has with Schiphol airport to provide all of its lighting requirements over a long-term period. Any replacement LED lights or any improved versions of lights will be provided at Philips' expense as the supplier (not the airport) will own the lights. Similarly, Rolls Royce aero engines are now frequently supplied on a 'product service' basis and not sold outright. The company claims that in the longer term these service contracts are much more profitable whilst giving airline customers the benefits of long-term servicing and maintenance without the initial cost of buying the jet engines.

Figure 28.3 illustrates the reduction in conflict between supplier and customer with product service agreements. The traditional 'purchase' model shows that the supplier wants to maximise resource use to produce and sell as many cleaning machines as possible, whereas the customer wants to reduce purchases to lower costs. In the product service model the supplier offers the product as a service but will only have to produce what the customers can use – so reducing resource usage and removing conflict between them.

It is also claimed that the product service system improves sustainability over the lifespan of assets as the contracts include arrangements for the maintenance of these product services, recycling and, when necessary, product replacement.

Benefits of product service system models:

- A more sustainable economy with fewer products manufactured as fewer will be left idle for long periods.
- Increased employment in the service sector, e.g., workers to maintain products.

Product-Service System Example: Cleaning machines

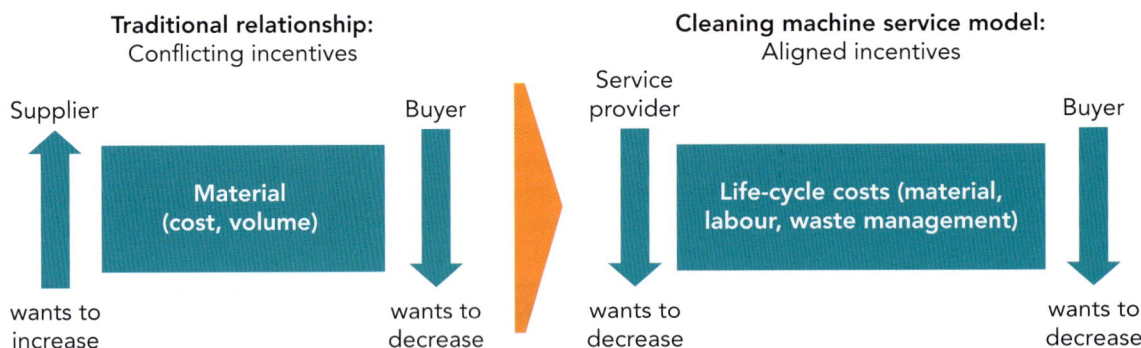

Formerly conflicting incentives for seller and buyer are aligned, resulting in potential cost savings and environmental gains for both parties.

Figure 28.3: The gains from a product service system for a cleaning machine contract compared to purchasing cleaning machines

- Less conflict between the interests of the supplier and consumers.
- The risk of poor performance of the product is passed from the consumer to the supplier of the product or service.
- Long-term relationships are built between the supplier and the consumer based on long-term service contracts.

Limitations of product service system models:

- Customer resistance to not owning and controlling the asset.
- May be locked in to long-term service contracts which could be a disadvantage if the product and/ or business prove to be unreliable.

Links between business management tools and other units of the IB syllabus

These business management tools can be applied and integrated into other units of the IB syllabus. For example:

- Unit 1 – corporate social responsibility can be demonstrated by adopting the circular economy models.
- Unit 4 – the marketing mix will need to be adapted to switch successfully from a product-based mix (that is, selling the product) to a produce service mix (selling customers a long-term service).

SELF-EVALUATION CHECKLIST

After studying this chapter, complete this table.

I am able to apply and analyse:	Needs more work	Almost there	Ready to move on
The role of operations management (AO2)			
I am able to select and apply the business management tools:			
circular supply models			
resource recovery models			
product life extension models			
sharing models			
product service system models			

REFLECTION

Do you think it is ever possible to argue that one business function is more important than the others, or do they all depend on each other? Discuss your ideas with another learner.

PROJECT

Working in a sweatshop in Bangladesh

The factory is small with no windows, and the walls and ceiling are covered in dirt. There are over twenty sewing machines around the room. Each sewing machine has a bench for the worker but there is very little space. There are no welfare facilities and the toilet is little more than a hole in the ground. The workers start work at 9 o'clock in the morning and work for twelve hours with only a short lunch break. The work is described as back-breaking, repetitive and boring.

1   You are a management consultant. Write a report to the directors of a clothing retailer buying clothing sourced from Bangladesh that is produced using sweatshop labour.

In your report set out the advantages and disadvantages of moving to a more expensive supplier that is more socially sustainable.

2   Share your report with other students in your class.

Thinking about your project:

- How good is your report compared to those of others in your class?

- Assess the strengths and weaknesses of your report.

- How would you improve your report?

EXAM-STYLE QUESTIONS

A sustainable Mexican restaurant

Veg-Mexicana is one of most popular sustainable restaurants in Mexico City. This vibrant restaurant, owned and managed by the Hernandez family, serves meat-free Mexican food with a strict vegetarian and vegan menu. Ana Hernandez is the restaurant manager, and she believes passionately in marketing a sustainable product and using sustainable production methods. By having sustainability as a core part of their vision and mission statement the business hopes to create an image of social responsibility.

By sourcing all its ingredients locally, it tries to manage its transport carbon footprint and reduce it to the lowest level possible. Much of the energy it uses is produced by solar power, and it cooks all of the food using the latest energy-efficient equipment. The business also hires staff who are committed to social responsibility in their work.

Ana Hernandez regularly speaks out on social issues such as the benefits of being a vegan or vegetarian and the disadvantages of eating meat from a health, animal welfare and environmental standpoint.

1	Define the term 'social sustainability'.	[2]
2	Define the term 'ecological sustainability'.	[2]
3	List **two** ways Veg-Mexicana tries to use sustainable production methods.	[2]
4	Define the term 'value-added'.	[2]
5	Explain **two** ways Veg-Mexicana can add value to its product.	[4]
6	Outline **two** resources used by Veg-Mexicana in production.	[4]
7	Explain **two** reasons why the relationship between Veg-Mexicana's operations management and human resources management might be important.	[4]
8	Outline **two** ways Veg-Mexicana can be considered to be a socially sustainable business.	[4]
9	Explain how Veg-Mexicana's approach to sustainability might allow it to achieve greater added value.	[4]
10	Evaluate the view that Veg-Mexicana's approach to sustainability will make it a successful business.	[10]

Chapter 29

Operations methods

LEARNING OBJECTIVES

On completing this chapter you should be able to:

Synthesise and evaluate:

- The following operations methods:
  - job production
  - batch production
  - mass/flow production
  - mass customisation (AO3)

BUSINESS IN CONTEXT

Is mass customisation the way forward for production?

Consumers are increasingly able to customise products or services to meet their own requirements. This trend has been particularly well exploited by car, computer, smartphone and clothing manufacturers. Now the latest technology is increasing the potential for **mass customisation** to build unique products for each consumer.

Online configuration technologies can now easily and cost-effectively generate images of customers' preferences, and 3D modelling allows shoppers to envisage the final product. In manufacturing, 3D printing and dynamically programmable robotic systems can switch between different models and variants with almost no loss of efficiency from traditional flow line production of standardised products.

Opportunities exist in the following industries, but this list could easily be added to:

- food – personalised menus and ingredients to meet specific dietary requirements

- clothing – customised clothing designs which should fit perfectly as scanning technology gives accurate body measurements

- health care – DNA-based personalised medications

- cars – consumers can choose from a vast range of options, colours, interiors and even bodywork shapes.

Mass customisation brings benefits for consumers – but businesses seek to make the process profitable as well.

Chocri is a small German chocolate manufacturer business that has expanded online sales by 30% since starting up its website createmychocolate.com.

The website gives customers the ability to choose from over 100 different types of ingredients and toppings for their personalised chocolate bars.

NikeiD allows consumers to customise the design of sports shoes with a huge variety of colours, decals and materials used in construction. This has enabled Nike to retain the highest market share in the global sports shoe market.

Discuss in pairs or in a group:

- Are there any goods and services that could not, in your opinion, be customised profitably to meet individual consumer's tastes? Explain your answer to your partner or others in your group.

- To what extent have advances in technology transformed the way products are made?

KEY TERM

mass customisation: the use of flexible computer-aided technology on flow production lines to configure products that meet individual customers' requirements for customised products.

29.1 Job production

This method of organising production is normally used for single, one-off products. These products may be small or large and are often unique. Good examples of **job production** would be a specially designed wedding ring, or made-to-measure suits for each consumer, or conversions of rare classic cars to run on battery power. In order to be called job production, each individual product has to be completed before the next product is started. At any one time, there is only one product being made. New, small businesses often use labour-intensive job production before they get the chance to expand and purchase advanced equipment. Job production enables specialised products to be produced and tends to be motivating for workers, because they produce the whole product and can take pride in it. It is sometimes referred to as customised production.

Job production – every Aston Martin engine is built by hand

However, this production method tends to result in high unit costs, it often takes a long time to complete, and it is usually labour intensive. The labour force also needs to be highly skilled, and this is not always easy to achieve. Aston Martin is an example of an expensive car that is individually produced for the needs of each customer. Each engine is hand built and carries a plate with the engineer's name on it.

29.2 Batch production

Batch production makes products in separate groups and the products in each batch go through the whole production process together. The production process involves a number of distinct stages and the defining feature of batch production is that every unit in the batch must go through an individual production stage before the batch as a whole moves on to the next stage.

A good example of this form of production is a baker making batches of rolls. First, the dough is mixed and kneaded. Then, after being left for a time, the dough is separated into individual amounts, the right size for rolls. After this the rolls are baked together, and then they are left to cool. When they have cooled, they are put on display in the shop and another batch can be prepared. Each roll has gone through the process with the other rolls in the batch and all the rolls have undergone each stage of the process before going on to the next stage.

Batch production allows firms to use division of labour in their production process and it enables economies of scale if the batch is large enough. It is usually employed in industries where demand is for batches of identical products – such as 500 school uniforms for the students at one school. It also allows each individual batch to be specifically matched to the demand, and the design and composition of batches can be easily altered.

The drawbacks are that batch production tends to have high levels of work-in-progress stocks at each stage of the production process. The work may well be boring and demotivating for the workers. If batches are small, then unit costs are likely to remain high. There is often a need to clean and adjust machinery after each batch has passed through.

Batch production should not be confused with flow production. Some businesses produce 'batches' of products using a flow production system. For example, a soft-drinks firm may bottle a batch of 20 000 cans of orange drink before resetting the line and producing a 'batch' of another drink. This is **flow production** rather than batch production because the individual items are free to move through the process without having to wait for others.

Batch production

29.3 Mass/flow production

These methods are very similar so they will be discussed together. The main difference is that with flow production (sometimes referred to as 'continuous flow production') output is produced 24 hours a day continuously, often with a minimum of labour input. They both produce large quantities of identical products – although see section 29.4 for mass customisation.

Mass production and flow production are structured so that individual products move from stage to stage of the production process as soon as they are ready, without having to wait for any other products. Flow production systems are capable of producing large quantities of output in a relatively short time and so it suits industries where the demand for the product in question is high and consistent. It also suits the production of large numbers of a standardised item that only requires minimal alterations. Flow/mass production usually takes place on a production line – hence the use of the term 'line production'. This production method often involves the

KEY TERMS

flow production: producing items in a continually moving production line – also known as line production. This can be a continuous 24-hours-a-day method

mass production: producing large quantities of a standardised product

assembly of a number of sub-assemblies of individual components. Parts may be bought from other companies. There is usually some automation of tasks (e.g., by using computer-aided manufacturing (CAM)) and this enables a smaller number of workers to produce more products.

An example of flow/mass production would be a Coca-Cola production plant like the one in Ho Chi Minh City, Vietnam.

Flow production at the Coca-Cola plant in Ho Chi Minh City, Vietnam

Here, the product is standardised in that it is a can of soft drink of a standard size. The system is flow production because the cans move through the various stages independently. However, the firm can make changes to the contents of the cans and the labelling on them without having to alter the flow production system. It is capable of producing Coke, Sprite and Schweppes Soda Water on the same production line. It is essential that the flow production process is planned carefully so that there are no disruptions in the system. In a perfect system, the production process would be broken down so that all of the stages are of equal duration and produce equal output levels.

Flow/mass production has a number of advantages over other types of production. Labour costs tend to be relatively low, because much of the process is mechanised and there is little physical handling of the products. The constant output rate should make the planning of inputs relatively simple and this can lead to the minimisation of input stocks through the use of just-in-time (JIT) stock control. Quality tends to be consistent and high, and it is easy to check the quality of products at various points throughout the process. The main disadvantage is the high initial set-up cost. Capital-intensive, high-technology production lines are going to cost a great deal of money. In addition, the work involved tends to be boring, demotivating and repetitive.

CASE STUDY 29.1

Different production methods

Here are three examples of businesses from across the world that use different production methods.

Mumbai Maestro was founded in 2018 and prides itself on being the best tailor in Mumbai. The business's USP is detail, service and quality. Maestro uses highly experienced cutters and tailors to make very highest quality made-to-measure suits.

Des Gâteaux et du Pain is a bakery business that specialises in Artisan breads, breakfast pastries and pâtisseries. Des Gateaux produces it products in small production runs normally producing 20-40 units at a time.

Molinos Río de la Plata is Argentina's largest food manufacturing company. The company is a major manufacturer of sunflower oil which it produces on large production runs in its factory in Buenos Aires.

1   Define the term 'flow production'.   [2]

2   Outline the difference between the production methods used by Mumbai Maestro and Des Gâteaux et du Pain.   [4]

3   Explain why Molinos Río de las Plata uses flow production to manufacture its sunflower oil.   [4]

Process production

The production of goods using this method usually requires inputs for continuous conversion into finished products. These inputs, such as heat, time and pressure, can undergo thermal or chemical conversion in producing finished products. A good example of this is the continuous flow of crude oil into an oil refinery, which uses heat, gases and chemicals to produce a range of industrial products as well as gasoline. The product typically cannot be disassembled into its constituent parts. For example, once it is produced, a tin of paint cannot be broken down into its ingredients. Process manufacturing industries include chemicals, food and beverage, petrol and paint.

The way **process production** systems are designed means that to achieve effective and efficient operation, output must be continuous over a long period of time. Disruptions or accidents can force production to halt, and it is expensive and time-consuming to restart production.

> **KEY TERM**
>
> **process production:** producing standardised goods, typically in bulk quantities, by using a continuous input of materials and other resources

29.4 Mass customisation

The search for production methods that combine the advantages of job production (flexibility and worker satisfaction) with the gains from flow/mass production (low unit costs) has led to the development of mass customisation. This method is only possible because of tremendous advances in technology such as computer-aided design (CAD) and computer-aided manufacturing (CAM). These have allowed much quicker developments of new products, designs that feature many common components and robotic machinery that can be switched to making different parts. Developments in the organisation of the production flow lines have also reduced the alienating effects of typical mass production. The emphasis on

repetitive, boring tasks has been a major factor in poor worker motivation.

The mass customisation process combines the latest technology with multi-skilled labour forces to use production lines to make a range of varied products. This allows the business to move away from the mass-marketing approach with high output of identical products. Instead, focused or differentiated marketing can be used which allows for higher added value – an essential objective of all operations managers. So, for example, Dell Computers can make a customised computer to suit the customer's specific needs in a matter of hours. By changing just a few of the key components, but keeping the rest the same, low unit costs are maintained with greater product choice.

> **LEARNER PROFILE**
>
> **Principled/caring**
>
> The Lacrosse helmet maker, Cascade, is experienced in making protective sports equipment, but it has turned its hand to producing protective equipment for those on the frontlines of the fight against Covid-19. The New York-based business stopped manufacturing lacrosse equipment when its work was deemed non-essential and switched its resources to start producing face shields, putting some of Cascade's approximately 75 employees back to work.
>
> Research another business that had to switch production to manufacturing personal protective medical equipment during the Covid-19 crisis.
>
> In pairs or in groups, produce a presentation on your example. Focus on the extent to which your example is of a principled/caring business decision.

Production methods – summary

Table 29.1 summarises the main features, advantages and limitations of the production methods considered here, i.e., batch, mass/flow and mass customisation.

	Main feature and essential requirements	Main advantages	Main limitations	Some practical applications
Job production	Single one-off items, often to customer's specific design or requirements Highly skilled workforce Close contact with customers to understand their requirements	Able to undertake specialist projects or jobs, often with high value added High levels of worker motivation as skills are being fully employed	High unit production costs as much production will be labour-intensive Time-consuming – customers will usually have to be prepared to wait for completion of the product Wide range of tools and equipment needed	Works of art, special fashion dresses, one-off furniture designs and construction projects
Batch production	Group of identical products pass through each stage together Labour and machines must be flexible to switch to making batches of other designs	Some economies of scale Faster production with lower unit costs than job production Some flexibility in design of product in each batch	High levels of stocks at each production stage as work in progress is high Unit costs likely to be higher than with flow production Large batches could lead to unsold stock of consumer tastes change	Products with high seasonal demand (e.g., ice cream) or products that are only seasonal (e.g., freezing of vegetables) School uniforms and popular clothing items of most demanded sizes
Flow/mass production	Large-scale production of standardised products Specialised, often expensive, capital equipment – but can be very efficient High steady demand for standardised products	Low unit costs due to constant working of machines, high labour productivity and economies of scale	Inflexible – often very difficult and time-consuming to switch from one type of product to another Expensive to set up flow-line machinery as it often requires high technology equipment Inflexibility causes problems if consumer tastes change often	Mass-market cars, basics computer models, TVs, low-priced clothing

	Main feature and essential requirements	Main advantages	Main limitations	Some practical applications
Mass customisation	Flow production of products with many standardised components but customised differences too Many common components Flexible and multi-skilled workers Flexible equipment – often computer controlled to allow for variations in the product	Combines low unit costs with flexibility to meet customers' individual requirements High levels of consumer retention since products are tailored to individual requirements Efficient production process with latest computer-controlled equipment	Expensive product redesign may be needed to allow key components to be switched to allow variety Expensive flexible capital equipment needed Cannot hold stocks of customised products, so it is difficult to satisfy surges in demand Customers may need to be prepared to wait for completion of their customised order	Products aimed at niche market segments – often at higher prices than standardised products, e.g., special sports shoes, unique paint finishes for cars, mainstream computer programs adapted to the needs of one business

Table 29.1: Summary of the main production methods

THEORY OF KNOWLEDGE

3D printing is the construction of a three-dimensional object from a computer-generated model. As an innovation, it is believed that 3D printing will challenge the traditional mass manufacturing model and revolutionise production systems. For example, Nike, IKEA and Ford have all made use of 3D printing in their manufacturing processes. The American Football cleats used at the Superbowl were manufactured using 3D printing.

Research a business that uses 3D printing.

In pairs or in a group, discuss the extent to which changes in technology in business are the result of imagination, intuition or reason.

29.5 Production method choice

The following factors will influence which production method is appropriate for a particular business/product:

- **Size of the market.** If the market is very small, such as for designer clothes, then job production is likely to be used. Flow production is most efficiently adopted when the market for similar or identical products is very large and consistent throughout the year. If mass production is used in this way, then mass-marketing methods will also have to be adopted to sell the high output levels that can be manufactured. Even in a market for mass-produced items, such as cars, there may be market niches that will allow smaller manufacturers to survive by making one-off products or batches of identical goods before changing the design or style for another model. If the market demands a large number of units, but at different times of the year (e.g., textbooks at the start of the academic year) then batch production might be most appropriate.

- **The amount of capital available.** A purpose-built flow production line is difficult and expensive to construct. Small businesses are unlikely to be able to afford this type of investment and are more likely to use job or batch production.

Production system in a service organisation

Production still occurs in service organisations, but unlike manufacturing businesses, service organisations are producing their product at the point where it is going to be consumed. This is particularly the case in fast-food businesses.

1   In pairs or as a group, research the production system used by a business such as McDonald's, KFC, Burger King, Starbucks or Pret A Manger.

2   In pairs or as group discuss:

  • the production system the business is using

  • the differences between producing in a service environment and in a manufacturing environment

• **Availability of other resources.** Large-scale flow production often requires a supply of relatively unskilled workers and a large, flat land area. Job production needs skilled craftspeople. If any of these resources are unavailable, or very limited in supply, then the production method may have to be adapted to suit available resources.

• **Market demand exists for products adapted to specific customer requirements.** If businesses want the cost advantages of high volumes combined with the ability to make slightly different products for different markets, then mass customisation or a form of flexible cell manufacturing might be most appropriate. Technology is giving businesses increasing flexibility to produce a variety of models from one basic design and production process.

Using more than one method

Most businesses do not just use one production method. It is quite common to use more than one production method to gain the benefits that they offer. A French restaurant might have a continuous supply of staple items on the menu – such as frites – but make batches of a dish that can be kept hot for a long time (or even frozen and reheated) such as boeuf bourguignon. Specialist dishes to be cooked at the table, such as flambés, will use job production. Standard Land Rover models are made on a line production system of mass production. Orders for military versions with special features in common will be made together in one batch. One-off orders, such as a bulletproof, gold-plated model, would be hand-assembled and finished.

Mass customisation in the production of skis

Austrian company, Fischer Sports, is a long-established manufacturer of ski equipment. The business is now offering a customisation feature from five selected top models in its range, giving customers the opportunity to transform their new skis into a one-of-a-kind product. When a customer purchases a pair of Fischer skis from a specialist retailer, they can make use of a customisation system which allows them to have the skis designed to their own specification. Customers are sent customisation options available in the form of a badge that can be inserted into the skis to make them unique. The badge is then ordered via Fischer's software and fulfilment partner, Mylabel. The customised badges are sent to the customer and can be inserted into the rear portion of the skis. Fischer Sports' customers thus get the opportunity to transform their premium skis into something which is personal to them.

1   Define the term 'mass customisation'.   [2]

2   Explain why Fisher sports has chosen to use mass customisation in its production.   [4]

3   Explain a disadvantage to Fischer Sports of using mass customisation.   [4]

SELF-EVALUATION CHECKLIST

After studying this chapter, complete this table.

I am able to synthesise and evaluate:	Needs more work	Almost there	Ready to move on
the following operations methods: • job production • batch production • mass/flow production • mass customisation (AO3)			

REFLECTION

Using your knowledge of both employee motivation and production methods, how might you explain the link between production methods and the level of employee motivation?

PROJECT

Kangovou is a US based manufacturing business, launched in 2012 by two entrepreneurs, Pretty Govindji and Tess Brennan. The business manufactures a children's dishware set which is ethically manufactured and reasonably priced.

Kangovou's mission statement is: 'Our mission at Kangovou is to provide you and your family with a superior, healthy option for storing and transporting your food.'

Kangovou products are designed for eco-friendly on-the-go families who are very health conscious. The business's users are recyclers and re-users who make homemade food for their children.

As an ethical business it ensures all parts of its product production is safe and focused on the health of the workers. As an ethical business, in addition to safety procedures that are legally required Kangovou enforces safety procedures that are in the best interests of workers. It does not sacrifice worker safety or worker health for increased productivity. Workers are treated fairly, with balanced work hours, appropriate compensation, and thorough protection against injury.

In pairs or in a group, research Kangovou and prepare a presentation on:

• how the business is ethical in all aspects of its production

• the advantages and disadvantages of its ethical approach.

Thinking about your project:

• Has your understanding of ethics and production been improved?

• How good was your group's presentation in comparison to those of the other groups?

• What changes would you make to your presentation if you were to do it again?

EXAM-STYLE QUESTIONS

Chocolate production in Nigeria

Musa Ltd is a Nigerian-based confectionery manufacturer specialising in palm oil-free chocolate. Musa limited is a large regional chocolate producer and approximately 30% of its production is exported. Musa has always been well-known for the use of batch production, but it also uses job production for certain specialist products. The business batch produces its main chocolate brands, which is how it is able to create a variety of flavour combinations and introduce limited edition chocolate on a regular basis. Musa is often approached by individual customers for specialist chocolate products, which it produces using job production.

Musa Ltd is thinking about buying another chocolate manufacturing business that mass produces a leading brand of chocolate in Nigeria. This business uses flow production, and Musa Ltd is concerned about the impact this has on workforce motivation. One way around this is to invest in new machinery and switch to batch production.

1   Define the term 'job production'.   [2]
2   Define the term 'batch production'.   [2]
3   Explain **two** disadvantages of Musa using job production for specialist chocolate products. [4]
4   Outline **two** characteristics of flow production.   [4]
5   Outline **two** characteristics of mass customisation.   [4]
6   Define the term process production.   [2]
7   List **two** types of industry that might use process production.   [2]
8   Outline how Musa Ltd uses batch production and job production.   [4]
9   Explain **two** advantages of Musa using job production for specialist chocolate products. [4]
10 Evaluate the advantages of Musa Ltd switching the production method from flow production
    to batch production.   [10]

Chapter 30

Lean production and quality management

LEARNING OBJECTIVES

On completing this chapter you should be able to:

Know and understand:

> The following features of lean production:
> • less waste
> • greater efficiency (AO1)

Apply and analyse:

> The following methods of lean production:
> • continuous improvement (kaizen)
> • just-in-time (JIT) (AO2)

> Features of cradle-to-cradle design and manufacturing (AO2)

> Features of quality control and quality assurance (AO2)

CONTINUED

> The following methods of managing quality:
>   - quality circle
>   - benchmarking
>   - total quality management (TQM) (AO2)
>
> The importance of national and international quality standards (AO2)

Synthesise and evaluate:

> The impact of lean production and TQM on an organisation (AO3)

BUSINESS IN CONTEXT

Lean production

Laura Wilshire, an employee on the assembly line at Toyota's giant assembly plant in Kentucky, USA, is not happy. There is something wrong with the seat-belt fitting on the car she is working on. She pulls a cord, stopping production and her five fellow workers on that production line crowd round. They soon see that the belt is not screwed in properly and fix the problem. 'I don't like to let something like that go,' Laura says. 'Quality's really important for people who buy our cars.'

Workers pull the cord 2000 times a week at this car factory. Employees then become involved in solving quality problems and reducing waste. This helps make Toyota one of the most reliable and desired brands in the USA. In contrast, in a typical Ford factory, workers pull the cord only twice a week, a legacy of poor worker–manager relations in the past. Using workers to solve problems is part of Toyota's **lean production** system. This has been copied around the world. The company can produce cars more cheaply and to a higher quality than its US rivals. Just-in-time (JIT) deliveries are insisted on from suppliers. Production changes are now so flexible that consumer needs for a different car specification can be met much more quickly than decades ago. The average lifespan of a new model, before it is revised or replaced, is just over two years. At the start of the 21st century, the average lifespan was five years.

Toyota's CEO in the USA says: 'Being customer focused is really important. We can react to changes so quickly.' Toyota claims that with simultaneous engineering and flexible production systems, it can develop a brand new model in just 18 months. It takes some other car companies three years. Toyota's president has said that he does not care if Toyota remains the largest car-maker in the world: 'What is important is to be number one for quality.'

KEY TERM

lean production: producing goods and services with the minimum of wasted resources while maintaining high quality

CONTINUED

Discuss in pairs or in groups:

- Based on this article, what benefits could lean production offer a business?

- Do you think it is an advantage to be able to develop new products more quickly than competitors? Justify your answer.

KEY CONCEPT LINK

Ethics

Lean production can reduce waste and improve production efficiency, but it has human costs. Stories of employees working long hours, having short breaks and being exposed to demanding physical tasks under time pressure take a toll on the mental and physical health of a business's workforce.

30.1 The features of lean production

In competitive global markets, businesses have to focus on improving operational efficiency. Increasingly, businesses are using techniques of lean production to help them achieve this improvement.

Lean production is closely associated with Japanese production methods that are now widely adopted throughout much of the industrialised world. This concept is closely linked with other operations and human resource practices – such as quality circles, empowerment of workers, efficient use of capacity and JIT. It is also linked with the objective of achieving quality output – being lean should involve 'getting it right first time' to reduce wastage of resources.

The overall objective of this production method is to produce quality output with fewer resources – that is, less waste, higher efficiency and elimination of non-added-value activities. Lean means cutting out anything in the production process that adds complexity, cost and time, and does not add value to the customer. Figure 30.1 illustrates this principle.

Figure 30.1: Lean production: eliminating buffers, reducing transfer distance and streamlining processes will mean products will be delivered to customers more quickly and will be of a higher quality

Less waste

The eight main sources of waste in industry have been identified as:

- excessive transportation of components and products

- excessive inventory/stock holding

- too much movement by working people, e.g., to get supplies of components

- waiting time – delays in the production process

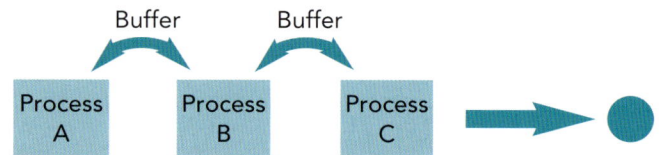

- overproduction – producing ahead of demand which may be lower than expected

- over-processing – making goods that are too complex as they could have been designed more simply

- defects – products that do not come up to quality standards and have to be rejected or corrected
- unutilised talent – not using all of the potential skills and abilities of employees.

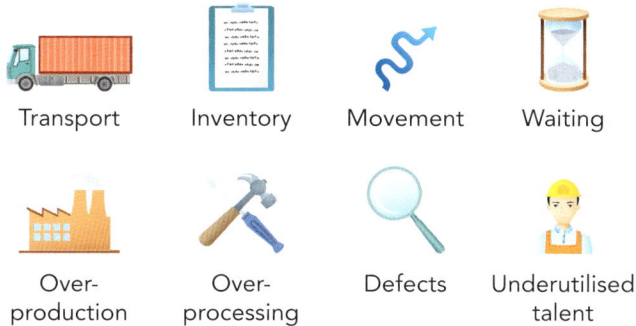

Figure 30.2: The different causes of waste

Greater efficiency

Business efficiency is measured by comparing the ratio of 'inputs to outputs'.

The most common measure is productivity – labour and capital – which measures output per unit of labour or capital input.

Productivity is not the same as the level of production and the two should not be confused. Production is an absolute measure of the quantity of output that a firm produces in a given period of time. Productivity is a relative measure and is concerned with how efficiently inputs are converted into outputs.

> **KEY TERM**
>
> **productivity:** the ratio of outputs to inputs during production, e.g., output per worker per time period

Efficiency and productivity can be increased by:

- improving employees' skill levels
- improving workers' motivation
- purchasing more technologically advanced equipment
- more effective management of labour and other resources.

30.2 Methods of lean production

Continuous improvement (kaizen)

The philosophy behind **kaizen** is that all workers have something to contribute to improve the way their business operates and the way the product is made. Traditional styles of management never give workers the opportunity to suggest improvements to the way things are done because the assumption is that trained managers 'know best'. The objective of managers adopting this autocratic approach is to keep production up to the mark and then look for one-off improvements in the form of inventions or to make investments in machines to increase productivity.

> **KEY TERM**
>
> **kaizen:** Japanese term meaning 'continuous improvement'

> **ACTIVITY 30.1**
>
> Kaizen is a Japanese term that can be roughly translated into 'good change'. The original work on this management theory came from Professor William Edwards Deming (1900–1993) an American engineer, statistician and management consultant. Deming worked with many Japanese businesses after World War II applying the principle of Kaizen – continuous improvement. The first business to fully adopt the principles of Kaizen was Toyota.
>
> In pairs or as a group, research Deming's 14 key principles. Discuss how applicable these principles are in today's operations management.

The continuous improvement philosophy suggests that, in many cases, workers actually know more than managers about how a job should be done or how productivity might be improved. Someone who works at a task every day is more likely to know how to change it to improve either quality or productivity than a manager with, perhaps, no hands-on experience of production at all. Another key feature of this idea is that improvements in productivity do not just result from massive one-off investments in new technology. A series of small improvements, suggested by staff teams, can, over time, amount to as big an improvement in efficiency as a major new investment. This idea is illustrated in Figure 30.3.

Conditions necessary for continuous improvement and kaizen groups to operate:

- Management culture must be directed towards involving staff and giving their views and ideas importance. Managers must accept that, in many areas of the business, work experience will count for as much as theoretical knowledge.

- Team-working – suggesting and discussing new ideas to improve quality or productivity is best done in groups. These kaizen groups are likely to be drawn from the work team – or cell – operating in the place of work. Kaizen groups should meet regularly to discuss problems that they have identified. This requires management to provide the time and necessary training. Recommendations for change could then be put forward to managers, or each group may be empowered to put their own ideas into practice.

- Empowerment – giving each kaizen group the power to take decisions regarding workplace improvements allows speedier introduction of new ideas and motivates employees to come up with even more ideas. This suggestion is linked with the work of Herzberg and the concept of job enrichment.

- All employees should be involved.

Many firms now use the continuous improvement approach, but it needs to be adopted throughout an organisation. Indeed problems can occur if some work groups within the business do not make small improvements in this way. The continuous improvement process has a knock-on effect and improvements in one part of the production system will require improvements further down the line. For example, if a worker on a production line that assembles cars finds a way to save five seconds from the time it takes to weld the roof panels on to the support struts, then the workers who are responsible for the next process must also find a way to save five seconds or there will be a bottleneck and an increase in work in progress. There would be no overall increase in production levels. This example highlights the need for all workers to be involved in a continuous improvement programme if the firm is to fully benefit from its success.

> ## TIP
>
> In an examination answer, it would be good analysis to link the continuous improvement principle to the work of Herzberg on job enrichment (see Chapter 10).

Continuous improvement (kaizen) – an evaluation

Although now a widely used practice, there are some limitations to the kaizen approach:

- Some changes cannot be introduced gradually and may need a radical and expensive solution, e.g., the need for Kodak to invest heavily in the manufacture of digital cameras rather than 'paper-film' based cameras when the new technology was introduced.

- There may be very real resistance from senior managers to such a programme due to their existing culture. Kaizen will only work effectively if there is genuine empowerment of the groups involved – authoritarian managers would find this impossible to accept.

- At least in the short term there may be tangible costs to the business of such a scheme, such as staff training to organise meetings and lost output as a result of meeting time.

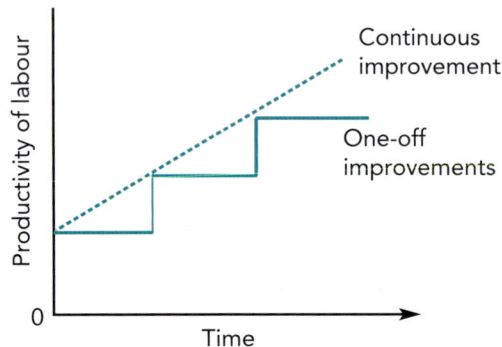

Figure 30.3: Continuous improvement (kaizen) compared to 'one-off' changes

CASE STUDY 30.1

Lean production in Cable Manufacturing

RZY plc is a Columbian-based cable manufacturing company that wants to increase its operational efficiency. To do this it wants to reduce set-up times on the machinery used to produce cables and shorten the lead time it takes to gets its product to market.

It employed a firm of management consultants to look at ways of using lean production to improve RZY's productive efficiency. The consultancy found ways to streamline machine set-up and changeover requirements, which increased machinery production time by 5 hours per day. The consultancy also suggested changes to the dispatch system for RZY's cables by using JIT which would reduce delivery times by 8%. The consultancy advised RZY's management to use a continuous improvement so that the gains in the business's improvements in productivity and efficiency can be sustained in the long term.

1   Define the term 'productivity'.   [2]

2   Outline **two** characteristics of continuous improvement.   [4]

3   Explain **two** benefits to RZY of using lean production to improve its productive efficiency.   [4]

4   Evaluate the possible problems that RZY might have in introducing lean production.   [10]

Just-in-time (JIT)

Originating in Japan, this approach to stock control is now influencing stock-holding decisions in businesses all over the world. **JIT (just-in-time)** requires that no buffer stocks are held, components arrive just as they are needed on the production line and finished goods are delivered to customers as soon as they are completed. The principle is easy to understand, but much less easy to put into practice.

KEY TERM

JIT – just-in-time: this stock-control method aims to avoid holding stocks by requiring supplies to arrive just as they are needed in production, and completed products are produced to order

For JIT to work effectively these conditions must be met:

- **Relationships with suppliers have to be excellent.** Suppliers must be prepared and able to supply at very short notice – short lead time. Suppliers have to see that being reliable and consistent is of great long-term benefit to them as well as the business adopting JIT. This often means that a firm will have only one, or at most two, suppliers for each component, so that a relationship of mutual benefit can be built up.

- **Production staff must be multi-skilled and prepared to change jobs at short notice.** There is no point in a worker continuing to produce the same item all the time if this leads to stocks building up. Each worker must be able to switch to making different items at very short notice so that no excess supplies of any one product are made. For example, if a worker in a clothing factory usually makes men's denim jeans, but demand is falling, then the worker should be able to switch to making other garments that are still in demand.

- **Equipment and machinery must be flexible.** Old-fashioned manufacturing equipment tended to be designed to produce one range of very similar products. It might have taken days to adapt it to making other types of products. This equipment would be most unsuitable for JIT-based systems. The machinery would have to produce large batches of one type of component before being converted to making another item. Stocks of each item produced would be needed to cope with demand while it was producing other goods. Modern, computer-controlled equipment is much more flexible and adaptable – often able to be changed with no more than a different software program. In this way, very small batches of each item can be produced, which keeps stock levels to an absolute minimum. However, such equipment is expensive and, as a result, JIT may not be so appropriate for small or under-financed firms.

- **Accurate demand forecasts will make JIT a much more successful policy.** If it is very difficult for a firm to predict likely future sales levels, then keeping zero stocks of materials, parts and finished goods could be a very risky strategy. Demand forecasts can be converted into production schedules that allow calculation of the precise number of components of each type needed over a certain time period.

- **The latest IT equipment will allow JIT to be more successful.** Accurate data-based records of sales, sales trends, reorder levels and so on will allow very low or zero stocks to be held. Similarly, if contact with suppliers can be set up with the latest electronic data exchanges, then automatic and immediate ordering can take place, when it is recorded that more components will shortly be required.

- **Excellent employer–employee relationships are essential for JIT to operate smoothly.** Any industrial-relations problem could lead to a break in supplies and the entire production system could grind to a halt. It is no coincidence that many of the businesses that have adopted JIT in Japan and in Europe have a no-strike deal with the major trade unions.

- **Quality must be everyone's priority.** As there are no spare stocks to fall back on, it is essential that each component and product must be right first time. Any poor-quality goods that cannot be used will mean that a customer will not receive goods on time. The advantages and disadvantages of JIT are summarised in Table 30.1.

Advantages	Disadvantages
Capital invested in stock is reduced and the opportunity cost of stock-holding is reduced	Any failure to receive supplies of materials or components in time caused by, for example, a strike at the supplier's factory, transport problems or IT failure will lead to expensive production delays
Costs of storage and stock-holding are reduced. Space released from holding of stocks can be used for a more productive purpose	Delivery costs will increase as frequent small deliveries are an essential feature of JIT
There is much less chance of stock becoming outdated or obsolescent. Having fewer goods held in storage also reduces the risk of damage or wastage	Order-administration costs may rise because so many small orders need to be processed
The greater flexibility that the system demands leads to quicker response times to changes in consumer demand or tastes	There could be a reduction in the bulk discounts offered by suppliers because each order is likely to be very small
The multi-skilled and adaptable staff required for JIT to work may gain from improved motivation	The reputation of the business depends significantly on outside factors such as the reliability of supplying firms

Table 30.1: The advantages and disadvantages of JIT stock control

> **TIP**
>
> When possible, try to make this link: efficient management of stock can help to reduce waste levels and this can create added value for a business.

> **TIP**
>
> Any question about JIT that involves discussing how appropriate it is in different business cases should lead to an answer that considers the potential drawbacks of the approach as well as its more obvious benefits.

JIT evaluation

JIT may not be suitable for all firms at all times:

- There may be limits to the application of JIT if the costs resulting from production being halted when supplies do not arrive far exceed the costs of holding buffer stocks of key components.

- Owners of small businesses could argue that the expensive IT systems needed to operate JIT effectively cannot be justified by the potential cost savings.

- In addition, rising global inflation makes holding stocks of raw materials more beneficial as it may be cheaper to buy a large quantity now than smaller quantities in the future when prices have risen. Similarly, higher oil prices will make frequent and small deliveries of materials and components more expensive.

CASE STUDY 30.2

Crest of Wave Ltd

Crest of Wave is a South African business than manufactures surfboards. The company uses JIT principles extensively to improve its manufacturing process. One of the important aspects of Crest of Wave's approach to JIT is the relationship it has with its suppliers. The business carries minimal levels of stock and relies on the very shortest lead time for delivery from its suppliers. This means it can meet customer demand immediately without having to carry significant levels of stock.

Crest of Wave's successful application of JIT is based on:

- reliable suppliers with the ability to meet Crest of Wave's lead-time requirements

CONTINUED

- very efficient component assembly so that Crest of Wave can meet consumer demand

- accurate sales forecasts so that Crest of a Wave can anticipate the need for stock.

1   Define the term 'lead time'.   [2]

2   Outline **two** characteristics of JIT used by Crest of aWave.   [4]

3   Explain **two** advantages to Crest of Wave using JIT stock management.   [4]

4   Explain **two** disadvantages to Crest of Wave using JIT stock management.   [4]

THEORY OF KNOWLEDGE

Here are three examples of businesses that have applied Kaizen in the way they manage their businesses:

- CEO of a hospital: 'We are a 220-bed community hospital and we just want to make it simple. We get the people closest to the work involved in looking after patients and focus on making every aspect of their care as good as it can be. We do this over and over again because we want to get better at getting better.'

- Manager of an architecture business: 'It's a goal that everyone feels empowered and prepared to question their work processes and implement change. We want to be a culture of structured improvement every day.'

- Production manager of a transport firm: 'We made a project to reduce our fuel costs, which is probably one of our largest expenses in the company. What was important was not only the negotiations but also getting our drivers to go to the right fuel stations.'

In pairs or as a group discuss the extent to which the application of Kaizen is effective because it involves intuition.

CASE STUDY 30.3

Lean production in a service business

McDonald's uses the 'Made-for-You' production system in the way it serves its food, which is an application of just-in-time production. The 'Made-for-You' production system gives customers the ability to order what they want on their sandwiches, and have it delivered 'hot and fresh' instead of eating something already prepared and pulled from a warming tray.

Each sandwich is prepared when the order is received from the customer. This 'Made-for-You' production system has a target of under 90 seconds from order to delivery. This gives the customer the freedom to choose their own fresh sandwich with only limited waiting time.

Customers place their order at touch screens, and then receive a number with a 'digital locator', which tells staff where the customer is sitting. Once the order is ready to serve, a McDonald's employee delivers the food to the customer's table.

1 Define the term 'lean production'. [2]

2 Outline **two** ways that McDonald's has applied lean production in its restaurants. [4]

3 Explain **two** advantages of lean production for McDonald's. [4]

4 Explain **two** disadvantages for McDonald's of using lean production. [4]

30.3 Cradle to cradle design and manufacturing

This term was first used by Walter R. Stahel in the 1970s and popularised by William McDonough and Michael Braungart in their 2002 book of the same name. In this book, McDonough and Braungart encourage people to:

> Imagine a world in which all the things we make, use, and consume provide nutrition for nature and industry – a world in which growth is good and human activity generates a delightful, restorative ecological footprint.

The basic concepts of **cradle to cradle (C2C)** are:

- **Waste = Food:** leftover materials from production can be an input (or 'food') into another process or product. There are two types of nutrients:
  - **technical nutrients** – inorganic or synthetic materials that can be infinitely reused
  - **biological nutrients** – organic materials that decompose naturally and provide food for microbiological life.
- **use of renewable energy**
- **reduce water usage**

In cradle-to-cradle design and manufacturing all material inputs and outputs are seen either as technical or biological resources or nutrients. Technical resources – such as scrap steel – can be recycled or reused with no loss of quality. Biological resources – such as waste products from food processing – can be composted and reused in an environmentally friendly way.

In contrast, the expression 'cradle to grave' refers to a business taking responsibility for the disposal of goods it has produced (e.g., by safe disposal of waste or unwanted products) but not putting the products' constituent components back into the production process.

KEY TERM

cradle to cradle (C2C): a design and manufacturing model where products are safe, enriching to the environment or user, and leave no waste for future generations

ACTIVITY 30.2

The Norwegian furniture manufacturer Vestre has been making furniture for over 70 years. Vestre's new factory will be one of the most sustainable production facilities ever built. It will be powered 250 000 kWt of renewable energy thanks to the 1200 solar panels situated on its roof. And, with a 90–95% process water recycling rate from the factory's production line itself, this development will set a new environmental benchmark in global manufacturing.

1 In pairs or as a group, research into another manufacturing businesses with sustainability as a central objective.

2 Prepare a presentation on the business you have researched.

Potential benefits of C2C are:

- The synthetic materials required in the production process can be reused with no reduction in product integrity. The biological nutrients can be disposed of harmlessly and decompose into the soil. When adopted correctly C2C ensures the smallest possible environmental impact.

- In a well-designed C2C system, since manufacturing resources, or technical nutrients, are often reused, it can reduce business costs.

- Once a C2C plan has been established and the materials have been sourced, the manufacturing model can be repeated indefinitely as long as the biological and technical nutrients are available and correctly sourced.

Potential limitations of C2C are:

- Just one variation by a supplier of either a technical or biological nutrient can result in a disturbance in the C2C plan as the revised nutrient might be less recyclable.

- Supply chain disruptions are particularly significant for C2C business models as finding alternative suppliers and nutrients might prove to be impossible.

- The best C2C designed manufacturing systems are so tightly defined that manufacturers may find it difficult to vary or adapt the final product if it means the mix of technical and biological ingredients changes. So, the flexibility of product variety might be much reduced.

CASE STUDY 30.4

Cradle-to-cradle production

Here are three examples of products that are based on cradle-to-cradle production:

- **MODS** is a modular shoe, in response to the millions of pairs of shoes that end up in landfills each year, where they can take 30–40 years to decompose. MODS shoes can be customised and updated. They are made from bamboo and wool textiles and recycled fibre, and without using glue.

- **Banana Stem Fibre Packaging** transforms a geographically abundant material in Columbia into sustainable food packaging. Bananas are farmed across several regions of Colombia, yet farmers currently perceive banana stem fibre as waste. Drawing upon traditional food preparation methods, Banana Stem Fibre Packaging offers a sustainable alternative to plastic and paper food packaging.

- **OLI** is an intelligent solution for food waste. With the average US household generating 474 pounds of food waste per year on average, OLI offers a practical solution to increasing the percentage of our landfill waste that is composted and returned to the biosphere.

1 Define the term 'cradle-to-cradle production'. [2]

2 Explain **two** advantages to a business of using cradle-to-cradle production. [4]

3 Explain **two** disadvantages to a business of using cradle-to-cradle production. [4]

30.4 Quality control and quality assurance

What is meant by 'quality'?

A **quality product** does not necessarily have to be the 'best possible'.

Consumer expectations will be very different for goods and services sold at different prices. So we have to make clear from the outset that a quality product does not *have* to be made with the highest-quality materials to the most exacting standards – but it must meet consumer requirements.

In certain cases, a product must meet the highest quality standards and the high cost of it becomes almost insignificant. Internal parts for a jet engine used on a passenger plane will be expected to have a failure rate of less than one in one million. However, if fashion clothing was made to the same exacting standards (with regard to stitching, buttons, zips, etc.) how much would a pair of jeans cost then? Designing too much quality into a product that consumers do not expect to last for many years can make the product very expensive and uncompetitive.

A quality product does not have to be expensive. If low-cost light bulbs and clothes pegs last for several years in normal use, then they have still met consumer expectations and have been of the required quality. So a highly priced good may still be of low quality if it fails to come up to consumer requirements. A cheap good can be considered of good quality if it performs as expected. It should now be clear that quality is a relative concept and not an absolute one – it depends on the product's price and the expectations of consumers.

It is easy to think of **quality standards** in terms of manufactured goods, e.g., the reliability of cars or the wear rate of clothes. However, quality is a crucial issue for service providers too. For example, the quality of service offered by UK banks is claimed to be inferior to those in other countries in terms of:

- time taken to answer the telephone
- no indication of waiting time on the telephone
- queuing time in branches
- contact with the same person on each occasion
- number of accounts errors made
- quality of financial advice given.

The advantages of producing quality products and services are:

- easier to create customer loyalty
- saves on the costs associated with customer complaints, e.g., compensation, replacing defective products and loss of consumer goodwill
- longer life cycles
- less advertising may be necessary as the brand will establish a quality image through the performance of the products
- a higher price (a price premium) could be charged for such goods and services. Quality can, therefore, be profitable.

TIP

Quality is often viewed by students as an absolute concept and not a relative one. Quality must be explained with reference to the expectations of the target market consumers. The level of quality selected by any business must be based on the resources available to it, the needs of the target market and the quality standards of competitors.

KEY TERMS

quality product: a good or service that meets customers' expectations and is therefore 'fit for purpose'

quality standards: the expectations of customers expressed in terms of the minimum acceptable production or service standards

---

ACTIVITY 30.3

Measuring quality in a school

1   In pairs or as a group, think about each aspect of your school's operations. This could include activities such as:

- lessons
- co-curricular activities such as drama music and sport

CONTINUED

- pastoral care

- facilities such as dining and medical care.

2 In your pair or group, write a report on how you would measure quality in each of these activities in your school.

What are the differences between quality control and quality assurance?

These two terms are used to classify two very different approaches to managing and achieving quality in any business.

Quality control is based on inspection or checking, usually of the completed product or of the service as it is being provided to a consumer.

Examples of quality control are:

- an iPad being tested at the end of the production line for battery-charging capability.

- a supervisor listening to, and recording, a telephone-banking adviser speaking to a customer.

KEY TERM

quality control: this is based on inspection of the product or a sample of products

Quality-control techniques

There are three stages to effective quality control:

1 **Prevention** – This is the most effective way of improving quality. If the design of the product follows the requirements of the customer and allows for accurate production, then the other two stages will be less significant. Quality should be 'designed into' a product.

2 **Inspection** – Traditionally this has been the most important stage, but it has high costs and these could be reduced by 'zero-defect' manufacturing which is the aim of total quality management.

3 **Correction and improvement** – This is not just about correcting faulty products, it is also concerned with correcting the process that caused the fault in the first place. This will improve quality in the future.

Inspecting for quality

Traditionally, quality has been checked by inspecting products at the end of the production process. Some checking might take place at different stages of the process, but the emphasis was on the quality of the finished article. Quality inspection is expensive – qualified engineers have to be used – and such checks can involve damaging the product, e.g., dropping computers to see if they still work afterwards. As a result, a sampling process must be used and this cannot guarantee that every product is of the appropriate quality. When quality checks are used during the production process, then statistical techniques are used to record and respond to results.

Weaknesses of inspecting for quality

The key point about inspected quality is that it involves a group of quality-control inspectors who check the work of workers. There are several problems with this approach:

- It is looking for problems and is, therefore, negative in its culture. It can cause resentment among workers, as inspectors believe that they have been 'successful' when they find faults. In addition the workers are likely to look upon the inspectors as management employees who are there just to check on output and to find problems with the work. Workers may consider it satisfying to get a faulty product passed by the team of inspectors.

- The job of inspection can be tedious, so inspectors become demotivated and may not carry out their tasks efficiently.

- If checking takes place only at specific points in the production process, then faulty products may pass through several production stages before being picked up. This could lead to a lot of time being spent finding the source of the fault between the quality checkpoints.

- The main drawback is that it removes workers' responsibility for quality. The inspectors have full authority for checking products so the workers will not see quality as their responsibility and will not feel that it is part of their task to ensure that it is maintained. Ultimately, this lack of responsibility is demotivating and will result in lower-quality output.

Quality assurance

Quality assurance is based on setting agreed quality standards at all stages in the production of a good or service in order to ensure that customers' satisfaction is achieved. It does not just focus on the finished product. This approach often involves self-checking by workers of their own output against these agreed quality standards. The key differences between the two methods are that quality assurance:

- puts much more emphasis on prevention of poor quality by designing products for easy fault-free manufacture, rather than inspecting for poor-quality products – 'getting it right the first time'
- stresses the need for workers to get it right the first time and reduces the chances of faulty products occurring or expensive reworking of faulty goods
- establishes quality standards and targets for each stage of the production process – for both goods and services
- checks components, materials and services bought into the business at the point of arrival or delivery – not at the end of the production process, by which stage much time and many resources may have been wasted.

The quality assurance department will need to consider all areas of the firm. Agreed standards must be established at all stages of the process, from initial product idea to it finally reaching the consumer. These stages include:

- **Product design** – Will the product meet the expectations of consumers?
- **Quality of inputs** – Quality must not be let down by bought-in components. Suppliers will have to accept and keep to strict quality standards.
- **Production quality** – This can be assured by total quality management (TQM) and emphasising with workers that quality levels must not drop below preset standards.

- **Delivery systems** – Customers need goods and services delivered at times convenient to them. The punctuality and reliability of delivery systems must be monitored.
- **Customer service including after-sales service** – Continued customer satisfaction will depend on the quality of contact with consumers after purchase.

Examples of quality assurance are:

- Nissan car factories have predetermined quality standards set and checked at each stage of the assembly of vehicles by the workers accountable for them.
- First Direct, a European telephone-banking organisation, sets limits on waiting times for calls to be answered, average times to be taken for meeting each customer's requests, and assurance standards to monitor that customer requests have been acted on correctly.

Quality assurance has the following claimed advantages over quality-control systems based on final inspection:

- It makes everyone responsible for quality – this can be a form of job enrichment.
- Self-checking and making efforts to improve quality increase motivation.
- The system can be used to 'trace back' quality problems to the stage of the production process where a problem might have been occurring.
- It reduces the need for expensive final inspection and correction or reworking of faulty products.

TIP

Quality is not just an issue for large businesses. Small and medium-sized firms also need to give consideration to this vital operations-management area. They must ensure that the quality level selected and the quality-assurance methods used are within their resources. In fact, by using quality assurance with the emphasis on reducing wasted faulty products and on staff self-checking quality levels, these businesses can save money in the long term.

LEARNER PROFILE

Being a good communicator in operations management

Setting out the rules for staff in the Covid-19 crisis was a challenge for all businesses. These were the rules for staff a Kentucky Fried Chicken (KFC):

- Taking all reasonable measures, including signage, posters and floor markings to ensure that a distance of 2 metres is maintained wherever possible between team members working in the restaurants.

- All team members must complete Covid-19 training before they come back to work.

- Staff must follow increased hand hygiene measures including sanitising of touch points.

- Provision of gloves which must be worn by cashier team members.

- Provision of masks for all team members that must be worn at all times.

- Provision of protective screens at hand-off points, including front counter and drive-thru window.

In pairs or in a group, discuss how important you think being a good communicator is for a manager trying to get their staff to follow these rules.

CASE STUDY 30.5

Caribbean Farm Machinery Ltd (CFM)

A meeting between the sales and operations directors of CFM was very heated. They blamed each other for the disappointing rise in customer complaints and the fall in unit sales. The sales director complained that the number of machines leaving the factory with faults had increased. He went on to say the reputation was being damaged by consumers' concerns about CFM's product reliability, and the business risks losing many customers. CFM just lost a government order for 15 tractors to a competitor that was able to promote their ISO 9000 certificate.

The operations director replied by saying that customers were becoming much more demanding, and it was up to the sales department to provide better after-sales service. The operations director said CFM has increased the number of quality-control engineers from five to eight and they are correcting more faults in finished products than ever before.

Year	CFM customer complaints	CFM sales revenue ($ million)
2019	127	17.3
2020	134	16.5
2021	167	14.6

Table 30.2: Customer complaints and revenues at CFM

1 Define the term 'quality assurance'. [2]

2 List **four** elements of the quality assurance process. [4]

3 Explain **two** consequences of poor quality for CFM. [4]

4 Evaluate the benefits to CFM of improving its quality assurance. [10]

30.5 Methods of managing quality

Quality circles

This is a Japanese-originated approach to quality. It is based on employee involvement in improving quality, using small groups of employees to discuss quality issues. As well as leading to quality improvements, using team-working and participation can result in greatly increased worker participation. The overall aim of the groups is to investigate quality problems and present solutions to management or, if a group is fully empowered, to put the improvements into effect itself.

> **KEY TERM**
>
> **quality circles:** groups of employees who meet regularly to discuss ways of resolving problems and improving production and quality in their department/organisation

Main benefits	Main conditions determining success
Improves quality through joint discussion of ideas and solutions	Circle members must be committed to improving quality
Improves motivation through participation	Training given in holding meetings and problem-solving
Makes full use of the knowledge and experience of the staff	Full support from management
	The team should be empowered to implement the recommendations

Table 30.3: Quality circles – main benefits and necessary conditions

> **ACTIVITY 30.4**
>
> In Activity 30.3 you were asked you to think about quality in the different aspects of your school's operations.
>
> As a group, form a quality circle and discuss the following:

> **CONTINUED**
>
> 1 identify six operational activities in your school that could be improved
>
> 2 how the six operational activities you have identified could be improved
>
> 3 how you would communicate your operational improvement to the school management
>
> 4 the challenges of implementing the improvements you have identified.

Benchmarking

The full title for **benchmarking** is 'best practice benchmarking'.

This comparison will identify areas of the business that need to be improved to meet the standards of quality and productivity of the best firms.

Stages in the benchmarking process are:

1 **Identify the aspects of the business to be benchmarked** – this could be decided by interviewing customers and finding out what they consider to be most important. For example, research may reveal that the most important factors are reliability of the product, speed of delivery and after-sales service.

2 **Measure performance in these areas** – for example, reliability records, delivery records and the number of customer complaints.

3 **Identify the firms in the industry that are considered to be the best** – this process might be assessed by management consultants or by benchmarking schemes operated by government or industry organisations.

4 **Use comparative data from the best firms to establish the main weaknesses in the business** – this data might be obtained from firms by mutual agreement, from published accounts, specialist industry publications and contact with customers/suppliers.

> **KEY TERM**
>
> **benchmarking:** involves management identifying the best firms in the industry and then comparing the performance standards (including quality) of these businesses with those of their own business

Benefits	Limitations
Benchmarking is a faster and cheaper way of solving problems than firms attempting to solve production or quality problems without external comparisons.	The process depends on obtaining relevant and up-to-date information from other firms in the industry. If this is difficult to obtain, then the benchmarking exercise will be limited.
The areas of greatest significance for customers are identified and action can be directed to improving these.	Merely copying the ideas and practices of other firms may discourage initiative and original ideas.
It is a process that can assist the firm to increase international competitiveness.	The costs of the comparison exercise may not be recovered by the improvements obtained from benchmarking.
Comparisons between firms in different industries, for example customer service departments in a retailer compared with a bank, can encourage a useful crossover of ideas.	
If the workforce participates in the comparison exercise this can result in better ideas for improvement and increased motivation.	

Table 30.4: Benefits and limitations of benchmarking

5   **Set standards for improvement** – these might be the standards set by the best firms or they could be set even higher to create a competitive advantage.

6   **Change processes to achieve the standards set** – this may require nothing more than a different way of performing one task, but more substantial changes may be necessary.

7   **Re-measurement** – the changes to the process need to be checked to see if the new, higher standards are being reached. Benchmarking is not a one-off exercise and to be effective it should become a continuous process to achieve long-term improvements in productivity and quality.

Total quality management (TQM)

This approach to quality requires the involvement of all employees in an organisation. It is based on the principle that everyone within a business has a contribution to make to the overall quality of the finished product or service.

Total quality management (TQM) often involves a significant change in the culture of an organisation. Employees can no longer think that quality is someone else's responsibility. Instead, the search for quality must affect the attitudes and actions of every employee. When adopting this concept, every worker should think about the quality of the work they are performing because another employee is, in effect, their **internal customer**.

Every department is obliged to meet the standards expected by its customer(s). These departmental relationships are sometimes known as quality chains. All businesses can, therefore, be described as a series of supplier and customer relationships.

Examples of TQM are:

- A truck driver who drops off supplies to retailers is the internal customer of the team loading the vehicle – goods must be handled carefully and loaded in the right order. The truck driver has to face the retailer if goods are damaged or the wrong ones are delivered.

- A computer assembly team is the internal customer of the teams producing the individual components – a fault with any of these means the assembled computer will not meet quality standards.

KEY TERMS

total quality management (TQM): an approach to quality that aims to involve all employees in the quality-improvement process

internal customers: people within the organisation who depend upon the quality of work being done by others

The TQM concept has revolutionised the way all workers are asked to consider quality. To be effective the concept must be fully explained and training given to all staff. TQM is not a technique; it is a philosophy of quality being everyone's responsibility. The aim is to make all workers at all levels accept that the quality of the work they perform is important. In addition, they should be empowered with the responsibility of checking this quality level before passing their work on to the next production stage.

This approach fits in well with the Herzberg principles of job enrichment. TQM should almost eliminate the need for a separate quality-control department with inspectors divorced from the production line itself.

TQM aims to cut the costs of faulty or defective products by encouraging all staff to 'get it right first time' and to achieve 'zero defects'. This is in contrast to traditional inspected quality methods that considered quality control as being a cost centre of the business. Under TQM, if quality is improved and guaranteed, then reject costs should fall and the demand for the products rises over time. However, TQM will only work effectively if everyone in the firm is committed to the idea. It cannot just be introduced into one section of a business if defective products coming from other sections are not reduced. The philosophy requires a commitment from senior management to allow the workforce authority and empowerment, as TQM will not operate well in a rigid and authoritarian structure.

> **KEY TERM**
>
> **zero defects:** the aim of achieving perfect products every time

30.6 The impact of lean production and TQM on an organisation

The impact of lean production methods can help to transform the competitiveness of both manufacturing and service-based businesses. However, they cannot be introduced overnight and, as with any major business change, they will have to be introduced with an understanding of their impact on different functions within a business. This section considers these impacts.

But firstly, here is a summary of the potential benefits of lean production.

Main advantages of lean production

- Waste of time and resources is substantially reduced or eliminated.
- Unit costs are reduced, leading to higher profits.
- Working area is less crowded and easier to operate in.
- There is less risk of damage to stocks and equipment.
- New products are launched more quickly.

Impact of lean production on business functions

Finance

The purchase of new and advanced capital equipment is expensive. Without machinery that can be quickly adapted to different products, lean production will be impossible. Small production runs and fast switch-over times are essential to make waste and stock reduction a real possibility. This technology does not come cheaply and some firms, particularly smaller manufacturers with limited resources, may decide not to take up this option. By specialising in niche-market products, which are less price sensitive, firms may still be able to maintain competitiveness without adopting lean production. In addition, the retraining of staff in the multi-skills needed to produce a range of different products will be expensive.

Human resources

If lean production is being introduced into a traditional business, then the existing workforce and management team will need to be prepared to accept the necessary changes in working conditions and levels of empowerment. The new culture will need to accept much more worker involvement, for example through kaizen groups and more worker empowerment. Staff need to realise the crucial importance of their reliability and dedication. As so few stocks are held and no 'buffers' exist, the commitment of the workers to the success of lean production is essential. Real lean production depends just as much on flexible and cooperative employees as it does upon machines.

Lean production is not always the 'solution'

Lean production might not be suitable when:

- Businesses have real difficulty in forecasting demand and so are running on virtually zero stocks. This would be a major problem if demand rose unexpectedly.

- Production processes are very expensive to start up after a break in production. For example, if a steel works ran out of stocks of coke or iron ore, the resulting cool-down in the blast furnace could lead to a huge repair bill because cooling causes cracking of the internal linings.

- Firms use lean production as a device for making extensive redundancies. Lean production can result in job losses – this is one aspect of increased efficiency. However, a faltering business that attempts to adopt lean production merely as an attempt to cut job numbers will be unlikely to gain the much-needed support of the workforce.

- Businesses depend on customer service as their USP. In these situations, a less 'lean' approach might give customers more choice of finished product and more certain delivery dates.

- The costs of new technology and retraining are so substantial that some businesses might have to survive on making existing systems more efficient rather than fully embracing lean production principles.

Impact of TQM

Quality is not an 'option'. It is a fundamental aspect of all successful businesses. Quality is an issue for all firms, not just those in the secondary sector or service-sector firms, such as those in tourism and insurance, for whom it is important to put the quality of their 'products' and customer service at the top of their priorities to survive in competitive markets. Improving quality has obvious cost advantages if the rate of defective products is reduced. The marketing and 'people' benefits should not be overlooked either. Satisfying customers will give clear advantages when seeking further sales. Involving all employees in quality-improvement programmes can lead to a more motivated workforce. Improving quality needs to be the driving force throughout an organisation – it is not just an issue for the factory floor or the bank clerk. At the same time, the meaning of quality must not be forgotten – it is not necessary to produce the best product or service 'at all costs', but to achieve the quality of product or service that the customer expects, and that will encourage them to return in the future.

30.7 National and international quality standards

Quality standards aim to give stakeholders a form of assessing the product quality, performance or behaviour of businesses. Each country has its own standards organisations but increasingly international standards are becoming more significant as they aim to achieve consistency between national standards. The most important international standards body is the International Organization for Standardization (ISO).

The ISO is the world's largest developer of voluntary international standards. International standards give state-of-the-art specifications for products, services and good practice, helping to make industry more efficient and effective. These standards have been developed through global agreement and they help to break down barriers to international trade.

Founded in 1947, the ISO has published more than 19 500 international standards covering almost all aspects of technology and business. From food safety to computers, and agriculture to healthcare, ISO international standards impact on business activity and customer satisfaction.

ISO 9000

This award is given to firms that can demonstrate that they have a quality-assurance system in place that allows for quality to be regularly measured and for corrective action to be taken if quality falls below these levels. This award does not prove that every good produced or service provided by the business is of good quality. It is an indication that a business has a system of quality in place that has relevant targets set and activities ready to deal with a quality problem.

To obtain the **ISO 9000** certificate the firm has to demonstrate that it has:

- employee training and appraisal methods
- methods for checking on suppliers
- quality standards in all areas of the business
- procedures for dealing with defective products and quality failures
- after-sales service.

The benefits for a business of being forced to establish a quality-assurance framework and to have this monitored externally are clear. However, there are drawbacks such as costs of preparing for inspection and bureaucratic form-filling to gain the certificate.

ISO 9000 is one of a series of international guidelines for quality assurance. ISO 9000 relates specifically to the criteria that need to be met during the manufacturing process. It is not a guarantee of good quality, however.

> **KEY TERM**
>
> **ISO 9000:** an internationally recognised certificate that acknowledges the existence of a quality procedure that meets certain conditions

SELF-EVALUATION CHECKLIST

After studying this chapter, complete this table.

I am able to know and understand:	Needs more work	Almost there	Ready to move on
the following features of lean production:			
• less waste			
• greater efficiency (AO2)			
I am able to apply and analyse:			
the following methods of lean production:			
• continuous improvement (kaizen)			
• just-in-time (JIT) (AO2)			
features of cradle-to-cradle design and manufacturing (AO2)			
features of quality control and quality assurance (AO2)			
the following methods of managing quality:			
• quality circle			
• benchmarking			
• total quality management (TQM) (AO2)			
the importance of national and international quality standards (AO2)			
I am able to synthesise and evaluate:			
the impact of lean production and TQM on an organisation (AO3)			

REFLECTION

Using the techniques you have studied in this chapter, how could you advise the head or principal of your school/college to do the following?

- Make the organisation 'leaner'.

- Measure the quality of education and of the 'student experience'.

Compare and discuss your ideas with those of another learner.

PROJECT

Total quality management at Cadbury

The UK-based confectionery manufacturer owned by Mondelez International uses total quality management (TQM) extensively in its production process. By using TQM, Cadbury ensures that the chocolate/products that are produced are of a high quality and meet the needs of the customers. Confectionery is such a competitive market that it is crucial for Cadbury to produce chocolate products in the most efficient way possible.

To enforce total quality management, Cadbury has supervisors that monitor the production process throughout its production plants. Cadbury also monitors the quality of its products by using a quality assurance system. TQM ensures that the products made by Cadbury are of the highest quality.

There are four steps in Cadbury's TQM cycle:

- **Step 1** – Planning improvements in production based on the evaluation of production data collected.

- **Step 2** – Applying any improvements in an experimental way to see how effective they are.

- **Step 3** – Studying the effects of any operational changes to see how effective they are.

- **Step 4** – Putting operational improvements into practice by communicating them with the different teams affected.

The culture at Cadbury is that all employees are jointly responsible for monitoring quality and identifying any issues relating to quality. This gives its workers responsibility for self-checking and inspection of all the confectionery products produced by Cadbury.

1   In pairs or as a group research a business that uses TQM.

2   Prepare a video presentation that sets out how the business you have researched uses TQM and the advantages and disadvantages of the business using TQM.

Thinking about your project:

- Once you have produced and watched your video, do you feel your understanding of TQM has improved?

- How good is your video compared to those of the other groups in the class?

- How could you improve your video presentation?

EXAM-STYLE QUESTIONS

Exam style question

Aiko Tech

Aiko is a South Korean computer manufacturer that specialises in PCs and laptop computers for the business market. Aiko has a very good reputation for producing high-quality, reliable products that Aiko's buyers can really trust. The computers that the business produces are priced at a high level to reflect the quality of the product.

One of the strengths of Aiko is its application of lean production. Its use of JIT means the business can hold minimum stock levels and the whole factory space can be used for revenue generation rather than holding stock.

The philosophy of total quality management runs throughout Aiko's operations and has enabled it to achieve the very highest production standards. It is a business with a faulty return rate of less than 0.2%. The business makes extensive use of quality circles to continuously improve the quality of its products.

Aiko employs the very best people and it pays them high wages and offers excellent working conditions such as free health care and childcare. All employees at Aiko are expected to contribute to quality management.

There are threats to Aiko. Two new competitors have entered the market offering a product that is not as good as Aiko's but is being sold at a significantly lower price. The management at Aiko are looking seriously at the new entrants and are considering how to respond to this competition.

1	Define the term 'quality circle'.	[2]
2	Explain **two** factors that might make quality circles effective.	[4]
3	Outline **two** ways Aiko uses total quality management to improve the quality of its products.	[4]
4	Explain **two** advantages of lean production for Aiko.	[4]
5	Explain **two** benefits of improving labour productivity at Aiko.	[4]
6	Outline characteristics of continuous improvement (Kaizen).	[4]
7	Define the term 'just-in-time'.	[2]
8	Explain **two** factors that are important for the effective use of just-in-time stock management.	[4]
9	Explain **two** ways Aiko's use of JIT can increase its profits.	[4]
10	Evaluate the view that Aiko's success is down to its use of lean production.	[10]

> Chapter 31

Location

LEARNING OBJECTIVES

On completing this chapter you should be able to:

Apply and analyse:

- The reasons for a specific location of production (AO2)

Synthesise and evaluate:

- The following ways of reorganising production, both nationally and internationally:
  - outsourcing/subcontracting
  - offshoring
  - insourcing
  - reshoring (AO3)

Select and apply the business management tools:

- Decision trees (AO4)

BUSINESS IN CONTEXT

Locating in Trinidad and Tobago

Several big international corporations including Microsoft, IBM and Unilever, have taken advantage of the expanding economy of Trinidad and Tobago to locate their regional operations there. The country is situated very close to major shipping routes and has two major international ports. INVESTT is the national investment agency for Trinidad and Tobago and offers important incentives to businesses locating there.

PR Trinidad Ltd extracts anise oil, which is used as flavouring for the distinctive drinks it makes. Its anise bushes are planted on land leased at a reasonable rent from the government. Before deciding on Trinidad as the best location, the company analysed the economic and political stability of the country. Trinidad also enjoys the right climate for anise production. Other reasons given by the company for its location decision were the well-trained workforce with a good supply of qualified technicians from the local university. Some joint ventures with other local businesses are planned. The existence of other businesses in the same supply chain was an important factor in moving to Trinidad too.

Trinidad is the most important island for manufacturing within the regional free-trade area known as CARICOM. Being a member of this organisation allows free trade between members for goods manufactured on the island.

Discuss in pairs or in a group:

- Assess the benefits of Trinidad and Tobago as a location for businesses to move to.

- Do you think that the location decision is important for all businesses? Explain your answer by referring to soft-drink manufacturers and hairdressing businesses.

KEY CONCEPT LINK

Sustainability

Some of the most famous brand names in the world have gone carbon neutral. Companies such as Google, Sky, Marks & Spencer and Avis have set sustainability as a leading business objective and have followed this through by going carbon neutral.

31.1 Specifying a production location

Deciding on the 'optimal' location for a new business – or for relocation of an existing one – is often crucial to its success. Location decisions (i.e., choosing new sites for expansion or relocation of the business) are some of the most important decisions made by management teams. Selecting the best site will have a significant effect on many departments of the business and, ultimately, on the profitability and chances of success of the whole firm.

Location decisions have three key characteristics:

- They are strategic in nature as they are long term and have an impact on the whole business.
- Due to the costs of relocation, they are difficult to reverse if an error of judgement is made.
- They are taken at the highest management levels and are not delegated to subordinates.

An optimal location decision is one that selects the best site for expansion of the business or for its relocation, given current information. This best site should maximise the long-term profits of the business.

KEY TERM

optimal location: a business location that gives the best combination of quantitative and qualitative factors

ACTIVITY 31.1

Sustainability is increasingly one of the key factors in location decisions. Sweden one of the leading countries in the world for sustainable manufacturing, and achieving the right location is an important part of this. Sweden has achieved its 2020 zero waste vision. It is also on target to run entirely on renewable energy by 2040, and it ranks among Europe's top five countries for circular economy legislation.

In pairs or as a group, discuss the factors a business would need to take into account when it is choosing a sustainable location.

The optimal site is nearly always a compromise between conflicting benefits and drawbacks. For example:

- A well-positioned retail location in a high-class shopping mall will have the potential for high sales but will have higher rental charges than a similar-sized shop away from the centre.
- A factory location which is cheap to purchase because of its distance from major towns might have problems recruiting staff due to the lack of a large and trained working population.

An optimal location is likely to be a compromise that balances:

- high fixed costs of the site and buildings with convenience for customers and potential sales revenue
- the low costs of a remote site with limited supply of suitably qualified labour
- **quantitative factors** with qualitative ones
- the opportunities of receiving government grants in areas of high unemployment with the risks of low sales as average incomes in the area may be low.

KEY TERM

quantitative factors: these are measurable in financial terms and will have a direct impact on either the costs of a site or the revenues from it and its profitability

TIP

Do not assume that the 'best' location for a business will never change. Cost and other factors can change over a period of time and this accounts for many firms 'relocating' to new sites – but this can be expensive.

The problems resulting from a non-optimal location are outlined in Table 31.1.

Problem	Disadvantages to business
High fixed site costs	High break-even level of production; Low profits – or even losses; If operating at low-capacity utilisation, unit fixed costs will be high
High variable costs, e.g., labour	Low contribution per unit produced or sold; Low profits – or even losses; High unit variable costs reduce competitiveness
Low unemployment rate	Problems with recruiting suitable staff; Labour turnover likely to be a problem; Pay levels may have to be raised to attract and retain employees
High unemployment rate	Average consumer disposable incomes may be low – leading to relatively low demand for income-elastic products
Poor transport infrastructure	Raises transport costs for both materials and finished products; Relatively inaccessible to customers; Difficult to operate a just-in-time (JIT) stock management system due to unreliable deliveries

Table 31.1: Disadvantages to a business of non-optimal location decisions

Quantitative reasons for a specific location

Site and other capital costs such as building or shop-fitting costs

These vary greatly from region to region within a country and between countries. The best office and retail sites may be so expensive that the cost of them is beyond the resources of all but the largest companies. The cost of building on a greenfield site (one that has never previously been built on) must be compared with the costs of adapting existing buildings on a developed site.

Labour costs

The relative importance of these as a locational factor depends on whether the business is capital intensive or labour intensive. For example, an insurance company's telephone-based customer support centre will need many employees, but the labour costs of a nuclear power station will be a very small proportion of its total costs. The attraction of much lower wage rates overseas has encouraged many European businesses to set up operations in other countries, e.g., bank and insurance company call centres.

Transport costs

Businesses that use heavy and bulky raw materials (such as factories that make steel) will incur high transport costs if suppliers are a long way from the steel plant. Goods that increase in bulk during production will, traditionally, reduce transport costs by locating close to the market. Service industries, such as hotels and retailing, need to be conveniently located for customers, and transport costs will be of less significance.

Market potential

The level of sales made by a business can depend directly on location. Convenience stores have to be just that – convenient to potential customers. In addition to this, certain locations can add status and image to a business, and this may allow value to be added to the product in the eyes of the consumers. This is true for high-class retailers situated in London's Bond Street or Ngee Ann City in Singapore, but also for financial specialists operating from an address in New York's Wall Street.

Government grants

Governments across the world are very keen to attract new businesses to locate in their country. Grants may be offered to act as an incentive. Existing businesses

---

CASE STUDY 31.1

Locating a new battery plant

BerSport Ltd has opened a new lithium battery plant just outside Leipzig. The new high-tech factory has a production area totalling 60 000 square metres. The CEO, Albert Weber, sees BerSport's expansion as an important step in the company's growth strategy and essential to ensuring Germany is a location for battery technology development.

The new factory had significant support from the regional government who provided a grant to help finance initial capital costs. The new building was constructed with low carbon emissions as an important factor, and production will be carbon neutral within one year. Leipzig is seen as good location because there are plenty of highly skilled workers and land in the region is relatively low cost. Leipzig is also close to many car manufacturers who are increasingly switching production to electric vehicles and will use the batteries in their cars.

1 Define the term 'optimal location'. [2]

2 Outline **two** quantitative factors that might have influenced BerSport's location decision in Leipzig. [4]

3 Explain why the proximity of a skilled workforce might be an important factor in BerSport's decision. [4]

---

operating in a country can also receive financial assistance to retain existing jobs or attract new employment to deprived areas of high unemployment.

Once these quantitative factors have been identified and costs and revenues estimated, the following techniques can be used to assist in the location decision.

Profit estimates

By comparing the estimated revenues and costs of each location, the site with the highest annual potential profit may be identified.

When the management team have to decide between several possible locations, each with different chances of being successful and different degrees of risk, then the decision tree technique can be used (see the section 31.6).

Investment appraisal

Location decisions often involve a substantial capital investment. Investment appraisal methods can be used to identify locations with the highest potential returns over a number of years. The simplest of these, the payback method, can be used to estimate the location most likely to return the original investment most quickly. This could be of particular benefit to a business with a capital shortage or in times of economic uncertainty. Calculating the annual profit as a percentage of the original cost of each location is another useful measure. See Chapter 20.

Break-even analysis

This is a straightforward method of comparing two or more possible locations. The lower the break-even level

CASE STUDY 31.2

Locating a paint factory

ARP paints is a Vietnamese-based paint manufacturer. Its main site is located near Ho Chi Minh City but it is considering a new factory location near Hanoi in the north of the country. This new production facility will allow ARP to expansion its market share of the domestic paint market in Vietnam. A location in the north will strengthen its presence in that region and it will be close to many potential retail and industrial buyers.

ARP is considering three locations and the financial data on each location is set out in Table 31.2.

ARP has hired a consultancy firm to consider each location and the consultancy has the following findings on each location.

Location	Initial investment ($ million)	Payback time	Average rate of return (%)
A	16	3 years 7 months	8.3
B	13	2 years 10 months	7.9
C	18	4 years 2 months	9.1

Table 31.2: Investment appraisal for ARP's three locations

- Location A has very good access to local road infrastructure.
- Location B is near an area where skilled labour could be easily recruited.
- Location C is close to an area of natural beauty and there is opposition from environmentalists.

1 Define the term 'payback'. [2]

2 Outline what the average rate of return of 7.9% on location B shows. [4]

3 Explain which location is likely to be most profitable in the long term. [4]

4 Discuss the view that the best location for ARP is always the most profitable. [10]

of output the better the site is (provided all other factors are the same). This information might be particularly important for businesses that face high levels of fixed costs and which may benefit from a location with lower overheads. See Chapter 32.

Qualitative factors

There are other important reasons why a business might choose a specific location that cannot be measured in financial terms. These are called qualitative factors.

Safety

To avoid potential risk to the public and damage to the company's reputation as a consequence of an accident that risked public safety, some industrial plants will be located in remote areas, even though these may increase transport and other costs.

Room for further expansion

It is expensive to relocate if a site proves to be too small to accommodate an expanding business. If a location has room for further expansion of the business, then this might be an important long-term consideration.

Managers' preferences

In small businesses, managers' personal preferences regarding desirable work and home environments could influence location decisions of the business. In larger organisations, such as a plc, this is unlikely to be a factor, as earning profits and increasing returns to shareholders will be key objectives that will take priority in location decisions.

Labour supply

Apart from the cost of labour, the availability or non-availability of workers with appropriate skills will be an important factor for most business location decisions.

Ethical considerations

A business deciding to relocate is likely to make workers redundant. This will cause bad publicity. It could also be contrary to the ethical code of the business and may be viewed by stakeholders as being immoral. In addition, if the relocation is to a country with much weaker controls over worker welfare and the environment, there could be further claims that the business is acting unethically.

Environmental concerns

A business might be reluctant to set up in an area that is particularly sensitive from an environmental viewpoint, as this could lead to poor public relations and action from pressure groups.

Infrastructure

The quality of the local infrastructure, especially transport and communication links, will influence the choice of location. Singapore's huge port facilities have encouraged many of the world's largest shipping firms to set up a base there. The quality of IT infrastructure varies considerably around the world and this is an important consideration for companies that need quick communication with their different sites or customers, for example call centres or selling via the internet. The growing popularity of online shopping in developed countries may lead to some retailers opening fewer high-street stores and more warehouse operations to supply consumers.

CASE STUDY 31.3

Qualitative location factors

The Newmark Group is an American commercial property business that specialises in sourcing office space for service-based organisations. It has produced a report that focuses on five important location factors for tech companies. These are the five factors driving the location decisions:

- Retention of employees – by locating an office presence in a desirable city where the cost of living is lower, the tech businesses are more

likely to retain their workers and can attract new talent.

- Diversity – many tech companies realise that the diversity of their current workforces is a competitive strength. Building a team that draws from a variety of cultural, ethnic, LGBTQ and linguistic backgrounds is a highly weighted factor driving many of these location decisions.

- Politics and culture – many companies look at the political and cultural environment of

CONTINUED

a location to determine whether a market will be a match with the company's home markets and corporate culture.

- Eating and drinking – a common theme of these site searches is a focus on what life is like outside the workplace. A large part of this relates to experiences surrounding food and drink.

- Weather and climate – weather conditions can be a key component of the search for a new location. Many companies look to avoid not only overly cold climates but also those locations that have limited sunshine.

1   Define the term 'qualitative location factor'.   **[2]**

2   Outline the ethical and environmental factors that might affect a tech business's location decisions.   **[4]**

3   Explain why qualitative factors are important in the location decision of a tech business.   **[4]**

4   Evaluate the view that qualitative factors are the most important factors in the location decision of a service businesses.   **[10]**

Other locational issues

The pull of the market

This is less important than it once was due to the development of transport and communication industries and with the world becoming increasingly a single market. The internet has helped to make the location of a retailing business less important. But the market is still very important for some consumer service industries. The increase in car ownership has led to many of these being located out of town and city centres and on ring roads. The cinema is a good example. Once the centrepiece of a town, cinemas are now often located away from town centres on sites that offer plenty of parking. Superstores and other retail stores have relocated in a similar way.

Planning restrictions

Local authorities have a duty to serve the interests of their populations. On the one hand, they want business and industry because they provide employment. On the other hand, they want to protect the environment of the towns and villages. In some areas, large development corporations have been set up to develop a town or city into a much more successful combination of dwellings and industrial activity. In most countries, local or central government has set up industrial estates and business parks that both businesses and consumers find very attractive.

External economies of scale

These are cost reductions that can benefit a business as the industry 'clusters' and grows in one region. It is common for firms in the same industry to be clustered in the same region. Silicon Valley in the USA and Bangalore in India have very high concentrations of IT-focused businesses. All IT firms in these regions will benefit from the attraction of a pool of qualified labour in the area, local college courses focused on IT, and a network of suppliers whose own economies of large-scale production should offer lower component costs. In addition, it will be easier to arrange cooperation and joint ventures when the businesses are located close to each other.

ACTIVITY 31.2

Location of your school

In pairs or as a group, discuss the factors that might have affected the location of your school. Structure your discussion in the following way:

- quantitative factors

- qualitative factors

- market pull-factors

- other factors.

1   Produce a list of the top **five** location factors and try to rank them in order.

2   Present the reasoning for your top **five** factors to the rest of the class.

Advantages	Disadvantages
Greater convenience for consumers, e.g., McDonald's restaurants in every town	Coordination problems between the locations – excellent two-way communication systems will be essential
Lower transport costs, e.g., breweries can supply large cities from regional breweries rather than transport from one national brewery	Potential lack of control and direction from senior management based at head office
Production-based companies reduce the risk of supply disruption if there are technical or industrial relations problems in one factory	Different cultural standards and legal systems in different countries – the business must adapt to these differences
Opportunities for delegation of authority to regional managers from head office – help to develop staff skills and improve motivation	If sites are too close to each other, there may be a danger of 'cannibalism' where one restaurant or store takes sales away from another owned by the same business
Cost advantages of multi-sites in different countries	

Table 31.3: Multi-site locations – advantages and disadvantages

Multi-site locations

See Table 31.3 for the advantages and disadvantages of multi-site locations.

LEARNER PROFILE

Knowledgeable

Freed from the design restrictions of a head office in Seattle, USA, Starbucks Asia cafés have redefined and personalised the coffee-drinking experience for local communities. Engaging with the local community and creating spaces that fit the culture and the lifestyle is a key part of the design process in Asia. To achieve that, Scott Keller (head store designer at Starbucks) and his team have to work with a variety of partners in different markets. One of the largest is Hong Kong's Coffee Concepts, a subsidiary of Maxim's, which operates Starbucks stores in Hong Kong, Macau, Singapore, Vietnam and Cambodia – and it will double its store count to nearly 800 when it takes over 372 Thailand locations.

Discuss is pairs or as a group the importance of local knowledge when Starbucks is locating in overseas markets.

31.2 Ways of reorganising production

If a business receives orders that it cannot easily fulfil because of lack of capacity, it is common to contract another business to undertake some or all of the additional work. However, the growth of **outsourcing** and **subcontracting** by many businesses in recent years has not necessarily been driven by shortage of capacity.

These are the other major reasons for outsourcing:

- **Reduction and control of operating costs.** Instead of employing expensive specialists that might not be fully used at all times by the business it could

KEY TERMS

outsourcing: using another business (a 'third party') to undertake a part of the production process rather than doing it within the business using the firm's own employees

subcontracting: the practice of assigning to another business (the subcontractor) part of a contract, e.g., a specialist activity that makes up part of a construction contract

be cheaper to 'buy in' specialist services as and when needed. These specialist firms may be cheaper because they benefit from economies of scale, as they may provide similar services to a large number of other businesses. Much outsourcing involves offshoring – buying in services, components or completed products from low-wage economies.

- **Increased flexibility.** By removing departments from the employee payroll and buying in services when needed, fixed costs arc converted into variable costs. Additional capacity can be obtained from outsourcing only when needed and if demand falls contracts can be cancelled much more quickly than closing down whole factories owned by the business. The advantages of using subcontractors to 'take the strain' during periods of full capacity removes the need for expensive long-term capacity expansion projects.

- **Improved business focus.** By outsourcing 'peripheral' activities, the management of a business can concentrate on the main aims and tasks of the business. These are called the 'core' parts of the business. So a small hotel might use management time to improve customer service and outsource the accounting function completely.

- **Access to quality service or resources** that are not available internally. Many outsourcing firms employ quality specialists that small to medium-sized businesses could not afford to employ directly.

- **Releases internal resources** for use in other areas. If the HR section of an insurance company is closed and the HR functions are bought in, then the office space and computer facilities that were formerly used by this department could be made available to other departments.

There are potential drawbacks to outsourcing and subcontracting too:

- **Loss of jobs within the business.** This can have a negative impact on employee motivation. Workers who remain directly employed by the organisation may experience a loss of job security. Bad publicity may result from redundancies too, especially if the business is accused of employing very low-wage employees in other countries in place of the jobs lost. This could lead to the firm's ethical standards being questioned.

- **Quality issues.** Internal processes will be monitored by the firm's own quality-assurance system. This will not be so easy when outside contractors are

performing important functions. A clear contract with minimum service-level agreements will be needed. The company contracting out the functions may have to send quality-assurance staff out to the business undertaking the tasks to ensure that product quality and customer-service standards are being met.

- **Customer resistance.** This could take several forms. Overseas telephone call centres have led to criticism about inability to understand foreign operators. Customers may object to dealing with overseas outsourced operations. Bought-in components and functions may raise doubts in the customers' minds over quality and reliability.

- **Security.** Using outside businesses to perform important IT functions may be a security risk – if important data was lost by the business, who would take responsibility for this?

TIP

You may be asked for your advice on outsourcing an activity. Generally, the more important an activity is to the overall aims and reputation of the business, the less likely it is that outsourcing will be appropriate.

Outsourcing evaluation

The trend towards outsourcing will continue as firms seek further ways of improving operational effectiveness and as more opportunities arise due to globalisation. The process is not without its risks, however. Before any substantial **business-process outsourcing** of complete functions is undertaken or before any stage of the production process is outsourced, the company must undertake a substantial cost–benefit analysis of the decision. Having closed or run down a whole department to outsource its functions, it would be time-consuming and expensive to reopen and reestablish it if it was found that the outsourcing had failed.

KEY TERM

business-process outsourcing (BPO): a form of outsourcing that uses a third party to take responsibility for complete business functions, such as HR and finance

One of the key factors in any business decision on outsourcing is to decide what is a truly core activity that is so important that it must be kept within the direct control of the business. The nature of these core activities will vary from business to business.

ACTIVITY 31.3

1   In pairs or as a group discuss the services your school might be able to outsource. You could structure your discussion based on the following areas:

- teaching
- HR
- finance
- catering
- administration
- photocopying and reprographics
- cleaning
- medical services
- marketing.

2   Prepare a presentation on the school activity you are most likely to outsource and why.

Offshoring

The arguments for and against offshoring are very similar to those for outsourcing within the same country. However, there are some additional factors to consider:

- Low-cost countries offer substantial benefits. This is undoubtedly the major reason explaining most business **offshoring** decisions.
- The potential for higher profits will benefit the finance department despite the high setup costs of overseas operations or the transport and communication costs of using subcontractors in overseas locations.
- With labour wage rates in India, Malaysia and Eastern Europe being a fraction of those in Western Europe and the USA, it is not surprising that **multinationals** that wish to remain competitive have to seriously consider offshoring at least some of their production to low-wage economies. Examples include Norwich Union Insurance call centres (India); Audi automobiles (Mexico); Dyson vacuum cleaners (Malaysia).

- In developing countries, because of the shortage of jobs, the subcontracting businesses will find it easy to recruit unskilled or semi-skilled workers. Many of these workers are well educated with good English-language skills.

KEY TERMS

offshoring: the relocation of a business process done in one country to the same or another company in another country

multinational: a business with operations or production bases in more than one country

---

TIP

Do not confuse offshoring with outsourcing, although they may be linked. Outsourcing is transferring a business function, such as human resources, to another company. It is only offshoring if this company is based in another country.

Look at the data in Table 31.4 for legal minimum wage rates in several countries. The substantial differences in these wage rates per hour help to explain the cost advantages that multinational corporations could benefit from by locating production in low-wage economies.

Country	2021 legal minimum wage rate per hour ($)
Pakistan	0.63
Mexico	0.88
Brazil	1.1
Slovakia	3.8
South Korea	7.7
United Kingdom	11.2
Luzembourg	15.8

Table 31.4: Legal minimum hourly wage rates, 2021 ($)

TIP

Do your own research on major location decisions (both at home and abroad) of businesses based in your country.

The first thing you'll notice when you look at the massive complex designed by Danish design firm C.F. Møller Architects is an eye-catching yellow rectangular structure on the roof that looks a lot like one of the brand's iconic building bricks, but look closer and you'll see an even more literal nod to the company's handiwork: giant LEGO blocks constructed into the walls themselves.

Part of the new 54 000-square-foot LEGO campus, the design was inspired by a painting that hangs in LEGO Group owner Kjeld Kirk Kristiansen's office and strives to serve as a source of ingenuity for the brand's employees. 'Our mission is to inspire children, so it's important we provide our talented colleagues with an environment that is playful and inspires creativity and innovative thinking,' CEO Niels B. Christiansen recently said in a press statement.

There are references to the company's beloved products everywhere you look, from the parking garage, whose exterior takes inspiration from LEGO road playmats, to the interiors, which feature bricked-out walls, vibrant colours, and geometric forms, as well as sculptures pieced together with the blocks themselves.

Of course, this being Scandinavia, the buildings are also sustainably built. Solar panels on the site's parking garage provide energy for half of the campus, while the rooftops of the buildings themselves are covered with sedum plants, which absorb water and carbon dioxide; collected rainwater will also be employed in the irrigation of the site's landscaped parks. Inside, the designers have chosen a resilient gypsum fiberboard, minimizing steel needs and thereby reducing carbon emissions by 650 tons.

In pairs or as a group prepare a presentation which has the following theme: The importance of imagination and emotion in locating and designing a factory or office.

Potential limitations of offshoring

International locations can also add to the number of drawbacks that might result from an inappropriate location decision. Here are some of the major additional issues that need to be weighed up carefully before going offshore.

Language and other communication barriers

Distance is often a problem for effective communication. This human resources problem is made worse when company employees, suppliers or customers use another language altogether. This is one of the reasons for India's success in attracting offshoring companies – English is one of the official languages.

Cultural differences

These are important for the marketing department if products are being sold in the country concerned – consumer tastes and religious factors will play a significant role in determining what goods should be stocked. Cultural differences also exist in the workplace and impact on human resource management. Toyota found that the typical Mexican worker is self-reliant and independent, yet the Toyota manufacturing system depends greatly on team work and cooperation. Effective staff training may be necessary to ensure that cultural differences do not prevent successful overseas expansion. For example, Oscar Rodriguez was only 20 when he was employed by Toyota's new Tijuana factory. 'I was self-reliant and I would conceal production problems and try and fix them myself,' he said. 'But I was taught how to communicate and I have learnt that there is never a stupid question. The company supervisors teach us well and they are patient.'

Level of service concerns

This operations management issue applies particularly to the offshoring of call centres, technical support centres and functions such as accounting. Some consumer groups argue that offshoring of these services has led to inferior customer service due to time difference problems, time delays in phone messages, language barriers and different practices and conventions, for example with accounting systems.

Supply-chain concerns

The operations management department will also be concerned about the loss of control over quality and reliability of delivery with overseas manufacturing plants. This reason is always cited by Zara, the clothing company, for its decision not to offshore clothing production to cheaper countries, as 'fast fashion' requires very close contact with suppliers. Using just-in-time (JIT) manufacturing may become much riskier if important supplies have to be shipped thousands of miles to an assembly plant.

Ethical considerations

There may be a loss of jobs when a company locates all or some of its operations abroad. In the case of Burberry clothing, this led to a consumer boycott as there were claims that the company's decision to close its Welsh factory was not 'the right thing to do'. In addition, there have been several reports of high-street clothing retailers sourcing supplies from Asian factories using child labour and very low-wage labour. Could this negative publicity cancel out the competitive advantage of low-cost supplies? Will the marketing department experience lost sales due to negative publicity, and will human resources find it more difficult to recruit well-qualified staff if the business is viewed as being unethical?

TIP

Remember, the lowest-cost location may not always be the optimal location. If quality suffers or if there is negative public reaction to products being made by low-wage workers, then low costs may be outweighed by even lower revenue!

Is it right to sell clothing in European shops that has been made by low-wage labour in Asian countries?

CASE STUDY 31.4

Offshoring at Google

Google is an example of a tech business that has used offshoring successfully. The corporation launched its research and development centre in Eastern Europe using the local business, CloudSimple. Acquisition of CloudSimple by Google illustrates that there is always a place for advancement and innovation, even if you already have the world's largest team of developers. CloudSimple is now a part of Google Cloud, and it improves the sharing of ideas online. There is also no doubt that the decision to offshore was not made of the basis of a lack of expertise at Google in the US. Offshoring meant Google was able reduce its labour cost in research and development because of the lower wage level amongst software developers in Ukraine.

1   Define the term 'offshoring'.   [2]

2   Outline how Google has used offshoring in Ukraine.   [4]

3   Explain **two** benefits to Google of offshoring.   [4]

Insourcing

The problems associated with outsourcing have led to some businesses starting to undertake more projects or manufacturing 'in-house'. The process of **insourcing** is effectively the opposite of outsourcing.

> **KEY TERM**
>
> **insourcing:** the reverse of outsourcing as it is undertaking a business function or process within the business rather than contracting it to another business

Insourcing allocates projects or specific units of work to a person or department within the company instead of contracting an outside business to undertake it. For example, an organisation might insource the marketing campaign development for a new product if the business has already recruited marketing and promotion specialists for another product within the organisation.

The insourcing process often involves recruiting new personnel and developing operations and processes into the organisation. It can also require training and upskilling existing employees to perform tasks that would otherwise require outsourcing.

The business has full control of the insourced project or production unit but the additional costs – especially the set-up costs – can be substantial.

Reshoring

An increasing number of businesses are reversing the offshoring process. A prime example of **reshoring** is that of General Motors (GM) in the USA which switched from being 90% dependent on offshoring of its IT services to just 10%. The process of manufacturing 'returning home' is explained by the following factors:

- The cost savings from manufacturing in some Asian countries have halved since 2010, compared to many Western economies, as Asian labour costs have risen.

- Quality control issues with suppliers from other countries have cost some companies more than they were saving.

- Businesses have to fill a whole shipping container to reduce shipping costs per unit, and they had to put goods waiting for transport in expensive warehouses.

- Working conditions in factories in many low-cost countries break the strict ethical codes of Western businesses, so production is being scaled back.

- US shale gas production has cut manufacturing energy costs in US factories.

- Reshoring is claimed to be more sustainable than offshoring. Inshored production is undertaken in tightly regulated production facilities in the USA and other Western economies that have greater environmental safeguards compared with those in less regulated low-cost countries.

- The pandemic, which started in 2020, caused supply chain breakages and disruption to production which reshoring, by keeping suppliers more local, might have prevented.

It is claimed that an estimated half a million jobs could return to the USA if companies evaluate the problems, and full business and environmental costs, of outsourcing to Asian countries.

The essential difference between insourcing and reshoring is:

- insourcing is when the business undertakes a formerly outsourced project itself

- reshoring is when the business contracts another business to undertake the project – but in its own original or home country.

> **KEY TERM**
>
> **reshoring:** ending offshoring contracts with overseas suppliers and returning functions or processes to businesses in the original or home country

31.3 Business management tools

Decision trees

A **decision tree** is a technique that considers the value of the options available and the chances of them occurring.

This technique is based on a diagram that is drawn to represent four main features of a business decision:

- all the options open to a manager
- the different possible outcomes resulting from these options
- the chances of these outcomes occurring
- the economic returns from these outcomes.

By comparing the likely financial results from each option, the manager can minimise the risks involved and maximise the potential returns.

KEY TERM

decision tree: a diagram that sets out the options connected with a decision and the outcomes and economic returns that may result

Constructing decision trees

The tree is a diagram which has the following features:

- It is constructed from left to right.
- Each branch of the tree represents an option together with a range of consequences or outcomes and the chances of these occurring.
- Decision points are denoted by a square – these are decision nodes.
- A circle shows that a range of outcomes may result from a decision – a chance node.
- Probabilities are shown alongside each of these possible outcomes. These probabilities are the numerical values of an event occurring – they measure the 'chance' of an outcome occurring.
- The forecast economic returns (or values) are the likely financial gains or losses of a particular outcome – the 'pay-offs'.
- Expected values are the likely average return from any particular outcome. They are calculated by using this formula:

Expected value = probability of outcome × forecast economic return

Working out 'expected values'

Using the formula shown in the list, the **expected value** of tossing a coin and winning $5 if it comes down heads is $0.5 \times \$5 = \$2.50$. In effect, the average return, if you repeated this a number of times, would be to win $2.50 – this is the expected value. The purpose of a decision tree is to show the option which gives the most beneficial expected value.

For example, the manager of an events-organising business has to decide between holding a fundraising auction indoors or outdoors. The financial success of the event depends not only on the weather, but also on the decision to hold it indoors or outdoors.

Table 31.5 shows the expected financial returns or 'economic returns' from the event for each of these different circumstances. From past weather records for August, there is a 60% chance of fine weather and a 40% chance of it being poor. The indoor event will cost $2000 to arrange and the outdoor event will cost $3000.

Weather	Indoors	Outdoors
Fine	$5000	$10000
Poor	$7000	$4000

Table 31.5: The possible economic returns from the alternative options

The decision tree of the event is shown in Figure 31.1. This diagram demonstrates the main advantages of decision trees:

- They force the decision-maker to consider all the options and variables related to a decision.
- They put these on an easy-to-follow diagram, which allows for numerical considerations of risk and economic returns to be included.
- The approach encourages logical thinking and discussion among managers.

KEY TERM

expected value: the likely financial result of an outcome obtained by multiplying the probability of an event occurring by the forecast economic return if it does occur

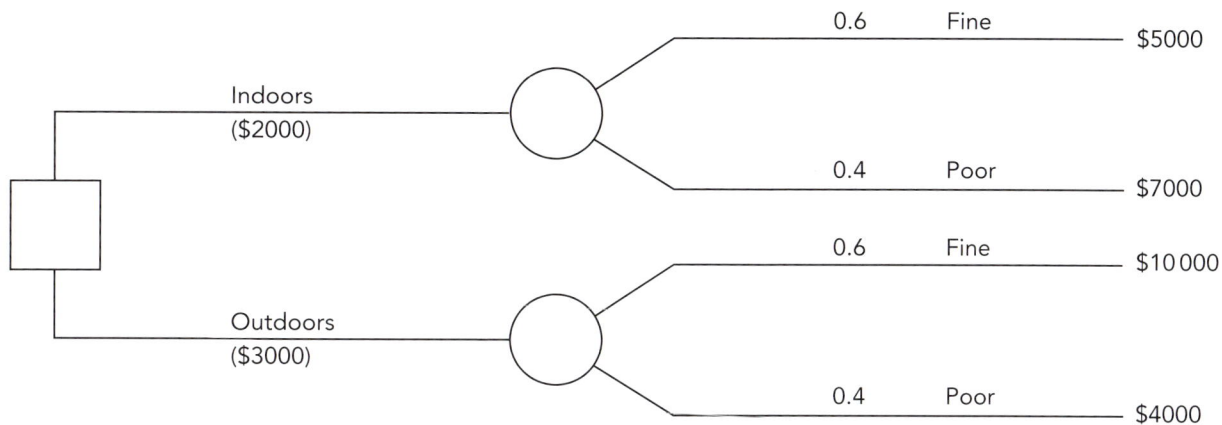

Figure 31.1: Decision tree for the fundraising auction

Using the tree diagram in Figure 31.2, which option would give the highest expected value – holding the event indoors or outdoors? The answer is gained by calculating the expected value at each of the chance nodes. This is done by multiplying the probability by the economic return of both outcomes and adding the results. The cost of each option is then subtracted from this expected value to find the net return.

This is done by working through the tree from right to left, as follows (see Figure 31.2):

- The expected value at node 1 is $5800.
- The expected value at node 2 is $7600.
- Subtract the cost of holding the event either indoors or outdoors.
- Indoors = $5800 − $2000 = $3800
- Outdoors = $7600 − $3000 = $4600

Therefore, the events manager would be advised to hold the event outdoors as, on average, this will give the highest expected value. The other option is 'blocked off' with a double line in the figure to indicate that this decision will not be taken.

THEORY OF KNOWLEDGE

Decision trees are fantastic as a mathematical model that gives the decision-maker a precise outcome on a decision at the mercy of future uncertainty. Where would you be without such mathematical models?

Consider the statement: 'Mathematical models enable us to make sense of future chaos.'
To what extent do you think this is true?

Decision trees – an evaluation

This technique has many benefits:

- It allows the visual representation of decisions and possible outcomes from them.
- It forces managers to consider not only the possible financial outcomes from a decision but also the likely chances of success or failure.
- The calculation of expected monetary values is a good starting point for the quantitative assessment of different options.

However, when decision-making is planned there are limitations to using decision trees too:

- The primary limitation concerns the accuracy of the data used. Estimated economic returns may be quite accurate when they concern projects where experience has been gained from similar decisions. In other cases, they may be based on forecasts of market demand or 'guestimates' of the most likely financial outcome. In these cases, the scope for inaccuracy of the data makes the results of decision-tree analysis a useful guide, but no more.
- The probabilities of events occurring may be based on past data, but circumstances may change. What was a successful launch of a new store last year may not be repeated in another location if the competition has opened a shop there first.

The conclusion is that decision trees aid the decision-making process, but they cannot replace either the consideration of risk or the impact of qualitative factors on a decision. The latter could include the impact on the environment, the attitude of the workforce and the approach to risk taken by the managers and owners of the business. There may well be a preference for fairly certain but low returns, rather than taking risks to earn much greater rewards.

Finally, remember that the expected values are average returns, assuming that the outcomes occur more than

once. With any single, one-off decision, the average will not, in fact, be the final result. Decision trees allow a quantitative consideration of future risks to be made – they do not eliminate those risks.

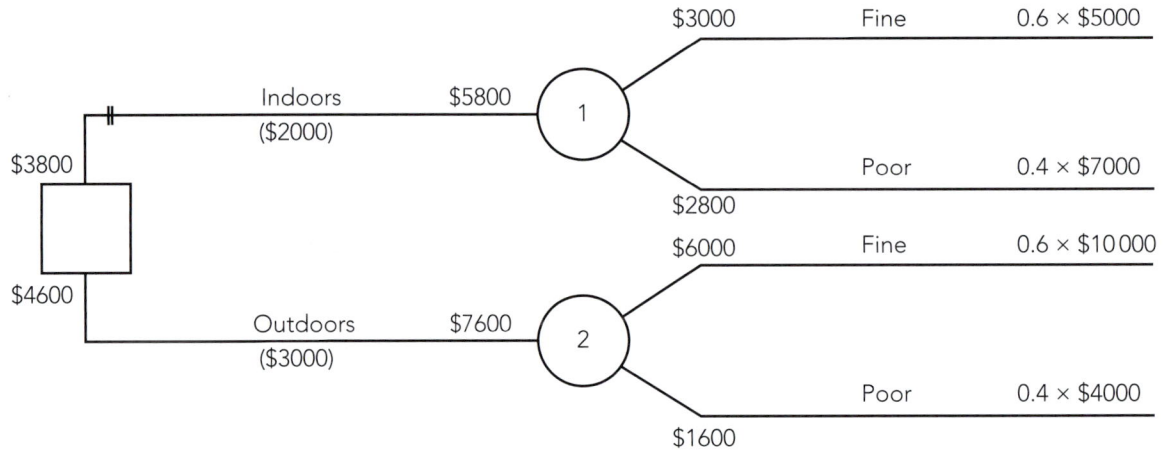

Figure 31.2: Calculating expected values – working from right to left

CASE STUDY 31.5

Choosing a place to locate a market stall

Amit Chotai has an important decision to take. Amit owns and manages a mobile market stall selling cooking pans and kitchen equipment in Mumbai. He has to decide which market to visit next Saturday. There are four options in and around Mumbai but, of course, he can only go to one market. He has estimated the revenues he could earn from each location by using past records and by consulting with other stallholders. His estimates in dollars ($), together with the chances of earning them, are shown in the table.

1 Define the term 'expected value'. [2]

2 Using the data given, construct a decision tree of the options Amit has, and add the probabilities and forecasted economic returns. [4]

3 Calculate the expected values of the four options that Amit could choose from. [4]

4 On the basis of quantitative factors, explain which market Amit should visit on Saturday. [4]

5 Outline **two** factors that could influence the accuracy of Amit's forecasts. [4]

Town A		Town B		Town C		Town D	
Probability	Revenue ($)	Probability	Revenue ($)	Probability	Revenue ($)	Probability	Revenue ($)
0.4	5000	0.3	3000	0.4	3000	0.3	5000
0.6	8000	0.5	4000	0.5	6000	0.3	6000
		0.2	8000	0.1	10000	0.4	9000

SELF-EVALUATION CHECKLIST

After studying this chapter, complete this table.

I am able to apply and analyse:	Needs more work	Almost there	Ready to move on
the reasons for a specific location of production (AO2)			
I am able to synthesise and evaluate:			
the following ways of reorganising production, both nationally and internationally: • outsourcing/subcontracting • offshoring • insourcing • reshoring (AO3)			
I am able to select and apply the business management tools:			
decision trees (AO4)			

REFLECTION

To what extent do you think the location decisions of multinational corporations might be affected by a global pandemic? Discuss your conclusions with another learner.

PROJECT

Would you locate a business in Venezuela?

Entrepreneurs: The next time you feel overwhelmed or frustrated, stop for a second and imagine what it would be like to build your company in Venezuela. Let me assure you that your daily challenges pale in comparison with a day in the life of a Venezuelan founder.

I recently spent a week working with entrepreneurs in Caracas, Venezuela's capital city. I travelled there with some trepidation, as the country is currently experiencing a full-blown humanitarian crisis. Basic goods, including critical medical supplies, are scarce, so most citizens line up for hours a day in order to get food, toothpaste, and many other necessities that are taken for granted in the rest of Latin America. Meanwhile, the currency has collapsed. There is hyperinflation and you need a carrier bag full of bolivars to buy your groceries. There are pervasive shortages of water and electricity, and perhaps worst of all, Caracas is now ranked as the world's most violent city.

In the absence of a functioning economy, political strife and the constant threat of crime why would anyone locate a business in Venezuela. Well here are three examples. CityWallet, a fintech (financial technology) startup whose app lets users make micropayments for services like parking and public transport that typically require cash. 'Locally, we're a solution to the daily problems of a Venezuelan, like the lack of paper money and the absence of payment alternatives,' says co-founder Atilana Piñón.

Here is another example. OnSpotMe is an app that allows people and companies to leave virtual messages for friends or customers at a variety of locations. While they currently operate in Venezuela, Spain, and Curaçao, and plan to expand throughout Latin America, executing internationally is tough when you are based in a highly volatile country. 'The bureaucracy, the limitations to exchanging money, and the difficulty of staying competitive with international companies,' are each daily battles for Ricardo Sanabria, CEO of OnSpotMe.

At times, Sanabria has struggled 'to pay the salaries of programmers and designers, who are regularly offered higher salaries in dollars by international companies.' When he was searching for an iOS programmer, a candidate in Valencia, a three-hour drive from Caracas, expressed serious interest, until she received an offer from a Boston-based company for 20 times OnSpotMe's budget. 'The weakness of the Venezuelan bolivar makes it almost impossible to compete,' Ricardo laments, 'but, there are strategies that you can use to retain key employees in an organisation. You have to find people who believe in entrepreneurship – or who are entrepreneurs themselves – and give them sweat equity.'

Telefonica-backed business, Wayra is housed in a funky, industrial space in Caracas. Wayra offers capital, mentorship, technical support, and a global network of like-minded entrepreneurs. When I visited their offices, I quickly realised that Wayra is an oasis in a sea of chaos. When you are there, you almost forget about the challenges that exist in the rest of the country. Then a trip to the bathroom, where water is regularly turned off due to shortages, gives you a sharp dose of reality.

- In pairs or as a group prepare a video presentation about locating a business in a challenging location like Venezuela. You could also choose another example of a challenging location.

Thinking about your project:

- How well have you understood the ideas you covered?

- How would you rate your group's video compared to those of other groups in your class?

- Think about the changes would you make to your video presentation to improve it.

EXAM-STYLE QUESTIONS

An overseas location decision

Clearwrite pens is an Australian pen manufacturer that has decided open a production plant in Bolivia in an attempt to establish its market position in South America. Clearwrite is looking at two locations in Bolivia. The financial profile of each location is set out in the table.

	Investment ($ million)	Average rate of return (%)
Location X	16.7	8.9
Location Y	21.4	7.8

Location X is an industrial development zone that is heavily supported by the government because it is in a town that has suffered from industrial decline in recent years. The plant is close to the airport, so it is good for the management staff that Clearwrite expect to relocate to Bolivia. The road infrastructure is also good in the area, which will help when bringing in components and moving out finished products. Crime is a major problem in location X. It is a dangerous area, particularly for foreigners.

Location Y is in a coastal area of Bolivia and is one of the nicest places to live in the country. There is a good supply of highly skilled workers. The local infrastructure is not as good as at location X and it is a three-hour drive from the airport. There will be no government support for Clearwrite if it locates in this area and there will be some local opposition from environmentalists if Clearwrite opts for location Y.

Clearwrite could also consider offshoring production of its pens to a Bolivian manufacturer. The management at Clearwrite have some concerns about this approach, particularly because the ARR is lower than Clearwrite locating in Bolivia.

1 Outline an example of how Clearwrite might use offshoring. [2]

2 Explain **two** possible problems to Clearwrite of using outsourcing as an approach to producing in Bolivia. [4]

3 Define the term optimal location. [2]

4 Define the term 'qualitative factor' in a location decision. [2]

5 List **two** qualitative factors that might affect Clearwrite's location decision. [4]

6 Explain how infrastructure and environmental concerns might affect Clearwrite's location decision. [4]

7 List **four** set-up costs which might be included in the initial investment in both locations. [2]

8 Using the information in the table, calculate the average annual profit for location X and location Y. [4]

9 Explain why Clearwrite should choose location X based on financial factors. [4]

10 Evaluate the view that quantitative factors such as government support and good infrastructure are the most important in Clearwrite's location decision if it chooses location X. [10]

Chapter 32

Break-even analysis

BUSINESS IN CONTEXT

Airlines need to break-even in the long term

Calculating the level of output of sales needed for revenue to cover costs is an important management tool. It is called the **break-even point** and indicates that, if sales increase above this level, the business will start to make a profit. Pakistan International Airlines is at the break-even point. Over a recent accounting period, revenue has increased because four repaired planes have come back into service. At the same time, ticket reservation costs have been greatly reduced due to an efficient new IT-based system. The combination of rising revenue and lower costs has helped the business achieve break even.

The story at Malaysian Airlines is similar, but break even has not yet been reached. Higher passenger numbers, attracted by the airline's famous customer service, have boosted revenue. Prices for add-ons such as seat selection have been reduced to just above the cost of providing these extra services. Other costs are under control, especially for jet fuel and airport check-in.

It has been calculated that most US airlines need to fill 75% of their aircraft seats, on average, to break even. In 2020, American Airlines failed to reach this figure; it was forced to retire 150 aircraft early and reduce the number of management employees in order to increase the chances of becoming profitable again.

Discuss in pairs or in a group:

- Why do you think the break-even point is important for businesses?

- Examine two ways in which a loss-making airline could achieve the break-even point.

Efficient check-in systems can reduce costs and the break-even point

KEY TERM

break-even point: the level of output at which total costs equal total revenue

KEY CONCEPT LINK

Change

Changes in the internal and the external environment force businesses to adapt their strategies to remain competitive in the market. For example, technological evolution may lead businesses to buy new equipment, and a new competitor in the market may force a firm to reconsider its pricing strategy. However, while they are undertaking these changes, businesses must ensure that they cover the costs and return enough profit to shareholders. Thus, break-even analysis is a basic tool to support managers with strategic decisions taken to manage change.

32.1 Total contribution and contribution per unit

Contribution is a very important concept in business and management. The **contribution per unit** is the amount each unit of production contributes towards the fixed costs and profit of the business. Each item produced will incur direct costs (mainly variable costs). If the selling price of each unit is *greater than* this direct cost, then a contribution is being made. This contribution is *not* profit – because the fixed costs have not yet been covered.

Total contribution is the total contribution of all units sold. If total contribution of a product *exceeds* the fixed costs for the period, then the surplus is profit. If total

contribution is *less* than fixed costs, then a loss has been made.

These two concepts are important when calculating the break-even quantity for a business and when using break-even analysis to help make business decisions. These issues are explained in the following sections.

LEARNER PROFILE

Risk takers

The Covid-19 pandemic increased the financial pressures of businesses around the world. Many organisations, especially small to medium-sized ones, were forced out of the market. Others had to take the risk of relocation to increase their chance of survival in the long term. The chart shows the factors behind owner-occupiers' movement and sales in South Africa, based on third-quarter data from the FNB Commercial Property Broker Survey, which is based on a sample of commercial property brokers in the six major areas of the country.

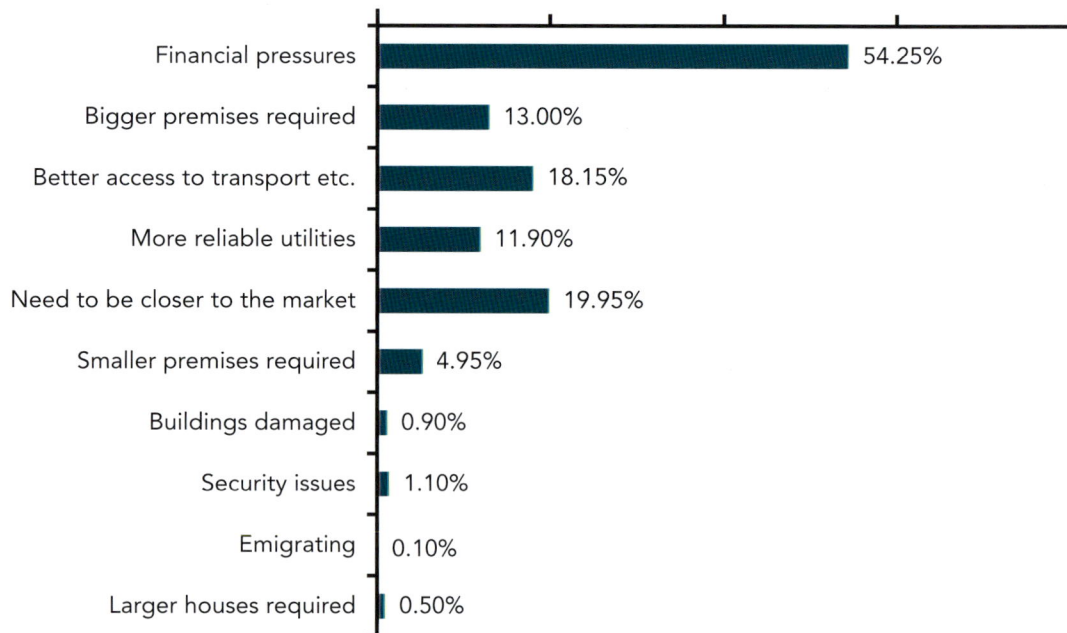

Factor	Percentage
Financial pressures	54.25%
Bigger premises required	13.00%
Better access to transport etc.	18.15%
More reliable utilities	11.90%
Need to be closer to the market	19.95%
Smaller premises required	4.95%
Buildings damaged	0.90%
Security issues	1.10%
Emigrating	0.10%
Larger houses required	0.50%

More than half of owners or occupiers of commercial property (54.25%) in South Africa decided to relocate, looking for a more affordable solution to achieve a lower break-even output. Such as decision would help them to cover their costs with a lower level of output, which would be important in periods of economic uncertainty and unstable consumer demand, such as the conditions created during the pandemic.

Of course, relocation decisions are not only driven by the need to achieve a lower break-even quantity and a higher margin of safety. Some businesses relocate for other reasons, such as to improve their market positioning and to increase their capacity and total profit in the long term.

- Why is relocation often the main solution for a business to achieve a lower break-even level of output? Discuss how relocation could affect revenues or costs and thus the break-even quantity of a business.

- Why is relocation described as a risky decision, even if it helps a business to cover its costs more easily? Suggest the kind of risks that a business takes when relocating.

Quantity sold	Fixed costs ($)	Variable costs ($)	Total costs ($)	Revenue (Price × quantity) ($)	Profit/(Loss) ($)
0	500	0	500	0	(500)
100	500	100	600	200	(400)
200	500	200	700	400	(300)
300	500	300	800	600	(200)
400	500	400	900	800	(100)
500	500	500	1000	1000	0
600	500	600	1100	1200	100
700	500	700	1200	1400	200

Table 32.1: Cost and revenue data for the sale of hamburgers

32.2 Break-even analysis

If a business is able to calculate the break-even point then it will know the quantity that must be sold to cover all costs. This will be important data to assist in making important production and marketing decisions. At the break-even level of output and sales, profit is zero. This must mean that at break-even:

total costs = total revenue and no profit or loss is made

Break-even analysis can be undertaken in three ways:

- table of costs and revenues method
- graphical method
- formula method.

The table method

Table 32.1 shows the cost and revenue data for a hamburger stall at a Premier League football match. The stall has to pay the club $500 for each match day – these are the fixed costs. Each hamburger costs $1 in ingredients and labour (variable costs) and they are sold for $2 each.

The break-even level of sales for the operator of the hamburger stall is 500 units. At this level of sales, total costs equal total revenue.

The graphical method – the break-even chart

The break-even chart requires a graph with the axes shown in Figure 32.1. The chart itself is usually drawn showing three pieces of information:

- fixed costs, which, in the short term, will not vary with the level of output and which must be paid whether the firm produces anything or not

- total costs, which are the addition of fixed and variable costs; we will assume, initially at least, that variable costs vary in direct proportion to output

- sales revenue, obtained by multiplying selling price by output level.

Figure 32.2 shows a typical break-even chart. Note the following points:

- The fixed costs line is horizontal, showing that fixed costs are constant at all output levels.

- The variable costs line starts from the origin (0). If no goods are produced, there will be no variable costs. It increases at a constant rate and, at each level of output shows that total variable costs= quantity × variable cost per unit. The line is not necessary to interpret the chart and is often omitted, as the variable costs are included in the total cost line.

- The total costs line is obtained by adding fixed costs to variable costs. It begins at the level of fixed costs, but then follows the same slope/gradient as variable costs. The difference between the variable cost line and the total cost line is always constant – as this difference is equal to fixed costs.

- Sales revenue starts at the origin (0) as if no sales are made, there can be no revenue. It increases at a constant rate, and at each level of output shows that total revenue = quantity × price.

- The point at which the total cost and sales revenue lines cross (*BE*) is the break-even point. At production levels below the break-even point, the business is making a loss; at production levels above the break-even point, the business is making a profit.

- Profit is shown by the positive difference between sales revenue and total costs – to the right of the *BE* point.

- Maximum profit is made at maximum output and is shown on the graph.

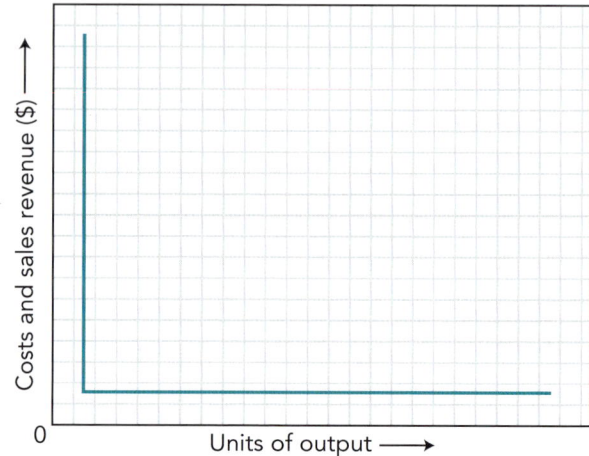

Figure 32.1: The axes for a break-even chart

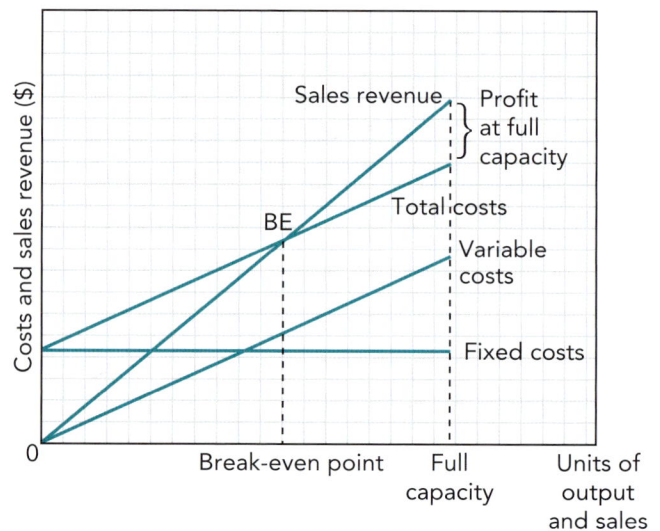

Figure 32.2: A typical break-even chart

Margin of safety

This is a useful indication of how much sales could fall without the business starting to make a loss. For example, if break-even output is 400 units and current production is 600 units, the **margin of safety** is 200 units. This can be expressed as a percentage of the break-even point. For example: production in excess of break-even point = 200 = 50.0% of break-even output

> **KEY TERM**
>
> **margin of safety:** the amount by which the current output level exceeds the break-even level of output

If a business is producing below break-even point, it is in danger. This is sometimes expressed as a negative margin of safety. Hence, if break-even output is 400 and the firm is producing at 350 units, it has a margin of safety of −50. The minus sign simply tells us that the production level is below break-even.

The margin of safety is shown in Figure 32.3.

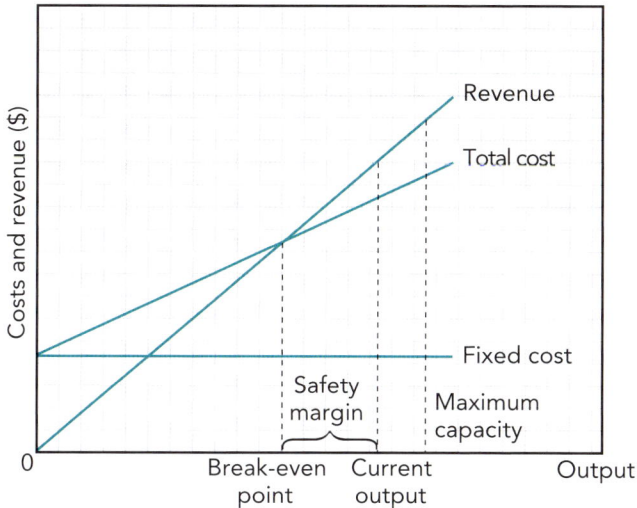

Figure 32.3: A break-even chart showing the safety margin

The calculation of break-even method

The break-even formula can be used to calculate the break-even point. It uses the concept of contribution per unit introduced in section 32.1.

Using contribution per unit to calculate break-even output

The following formula can be used to calculate break-even:

KEY FORMULA

$$\text{break-even level of output} = \frac{\text{fixed costs}}{\text{contribution per unit}}$$

If fixed costs are $200 000 and the contribution per unit of output is $50, then the break-even level of production is:

$$\frac{\$ 200 000}{\$ 50} = 4000 \text{ units}$$

This is an exact answer and, therefore, it is likely to be more accurate than many break-even graphs.

CASE STUDY 32.1

Can Zcook achieve break even?

Zhen is starting Zcook, a small business in Hong Kong, producing homemade meals for business executives. The meals will be delivered to the customers' offices by bicycle. Zhen will hire one part-time employee for the delivery. She hopes that she will be able to sell at least 250 meals per month. The maximum capacity of her kitchen is 300 meals per month. But she is afraid that she might face problems achieving break even in the first months of operations.

The following data is a summary of Zcook's key forecasted financial information. Zhen knows that apart from the standard costs, as a start-up she may have to pay some extra one-off expenses as well.

Salaries	$1000 per month
Raw materials	$5 per meal
Transportation costs and other variable costs	$2 per meal
Other fixed costs	$600 per month
Price	$15 per meal

Table 32.2: Zcook's forecast financial data in $

1   Define the term 'break even'. [2]

2   Suggest **two** reasons why Zhen may have difficulties achieving 'break even' as a start-up business. [4]

3   Prepare a fully labelled break-even chart, to scale, also indicating the margin of safety of Zcook at 250 meals per month. [6]

4   Calculate the maximum monthly profit for Zcook. [2]

ACTIVITY 32.1

The following monthly break-even chart is being prepared by Jonah, a junior assistant in the operations management department of a business producing chairs.

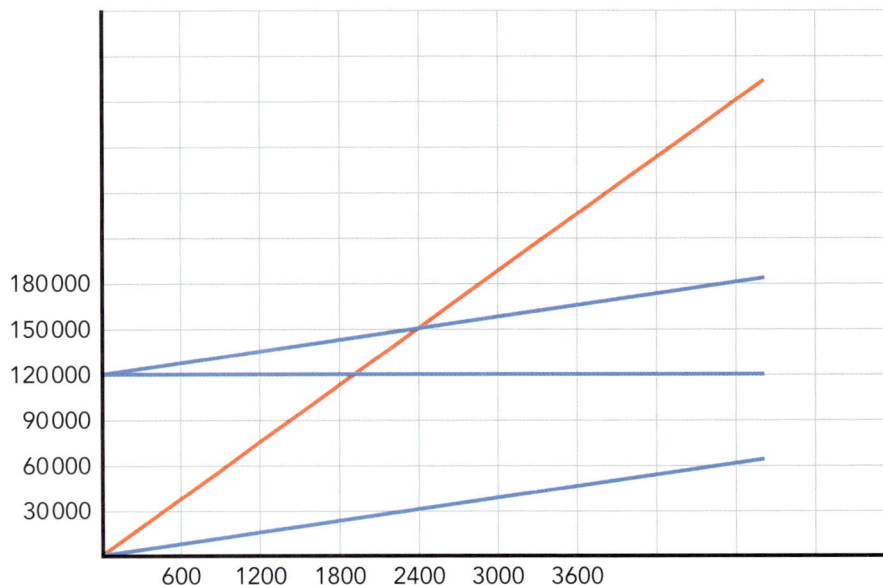

1   Help Jonah to:

    a   fully label the diagram. Assume all business transactions are in $.

    b   identify the break-even output on the diagram

    c   show the margin of safety at 3600 chairs per month

    d   calculate the profit at 4800 chairs per month

    e   show the effect of an increase in the fixed costs by $30 000 per month on the break-even quantity.

2   Suggest one sudden change in the external environment of the business that would force Jonah to do all the calculations and the graphical representation of the break-even analysis from scratch.

3   Why do businesses such as the chair firm still prepare break-even analysis, even though the underlying assumptions may change? Discuss this in class.

Reflection: In question 3, did you consider all the different information that a business can take from a break-even chart, apart from the break-even quantity?

32.3 Break-even analysis – the effect of changes in price and costs

In addition to obtaining break-even levels of production and margins of safety, break-even techniques can also be used to help managers make key decisions which impact on price and costs.

The charts can be redrawn showing a potential new situation, and this can then be compared with the existing position of the business. If the formula method is used, new price or cost data can be inserted into the formula to allow for a comparison of break-even points before and after the price or cost change. Care must be taken in making these comparisons, as forecasts and predictions are usually necessary and these could prove to be inaccurate. This and other limitations of break-even analysis are explained in section 32.4.

Here are two examples of how the break-even techniques can be adapted to show the impact of important changes:

1 A marketing decision to increase the price of the product: The effect of this is shown in Figure 32.4. The higher price raises the sales revenue line at each level of quantity sold. The assumption made in this example is that maximum sales will still be made. With a higher price level, this may well be unlikely and will depend on price elasticity of demand. The impact of this higher price is to:

   a   lower the break-even point because the contribution per unit is now higher

   b   increase the safety margin

   c   increase profit made at maximum output/sales.

The same results will be obtained if the break-even formula is used because higher prices, with all other factors such as variable costs remaining unchanged, will result in a higher contribution per unit and a lower break-even point. Refer back to the previous example (where fixed costs were $200 000 and the contribution per unit of output was $50). If the contribution per unit is increased to $52 as a result of a $2 price increase, the break-even point now becomes:

$$\text{break-even point} = \frac{\$200\,000}{\$52} = 3846 \text{ units}$$

2 An operations management decision to lease more efficient new equipment with much lower variable costs. This will reduce the gradient of the variable cost line. However, the leasing charges will increase fixed costs so the fixed cost line will rise horizontally at each level of output. The combined effect of these changes on total cost is shown in Figure 32.5. The impact of this decision, will be to:

   a   lower the break-even point

   b   increase the safety margin

   c   increase profit made at maximum output/sales.

This can be calculated by referring back to the numerical example in point 1. If the new equipment adds $50 000 to annual fixed costs but reduces variable costs by $20 per unit then the break-even point becomes (with the price unchanged):

$$\text{break-even point} = \frac{\$250\,000}{\$70} = 3571 \text{ units}$$

This lower break-even point would suggest that this operations management decision is advisable as the variable cost reduction outweighs the higher fixed costs.

However, the assumption made here is that the higher fixed costs have had a smaller impact on total costs than the lower variable costs. If the reverse was the case and the reduction in variable costs was very small, the impact on break-even point, safety margin and profit would all be reversed.

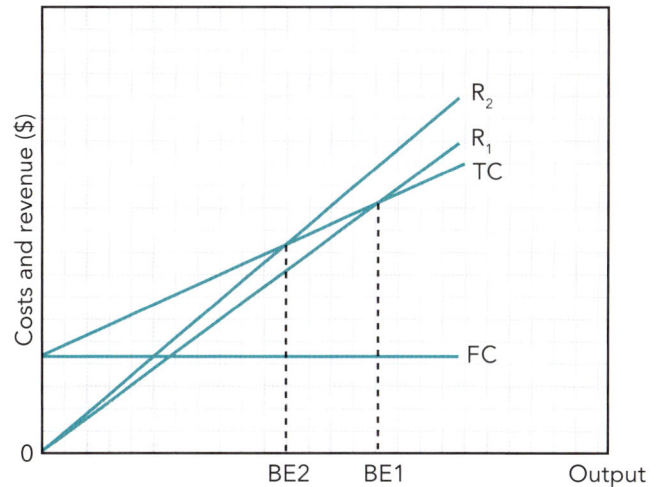

Figure 32.4: A break-even chart showing the effect on the break-even point and maximum total profit of a price rise (BE$_2$)

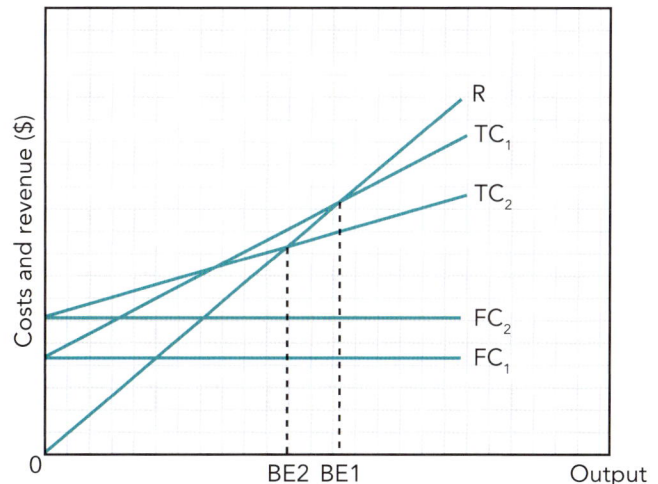

Figure 32.5: A break-even chart showing the possible impact of new equipment (raising fixed costs), but offering substantially lower variable costs (BE$_2$)

Calculating target profit output

An adapted version of the break-even formula can be used if a business wants to use a target profit level to establish the level of output required to achieve it. This might be used by a business or a division of a business that has set a fixed rate of return as an objective and the purpose is to calculate what level of output/sales will be needed to achieve this aim.

The formula now becomes:

KEY FORMULA

$$\text{target profit level of output} = \frac{\text{fixed costs + target profit}}{\text{contribution per unit}}$$

WORKED EXAMPLE 32.1

We will assume that the target profit is $25 000, fixed costs are $200 000 and contribution per unit is $50. The level of output needed to earn the target profit is:

$$\frac{\$200\,000 + \$25\,000}{\$50} = \frac{\$225\,000}{\$50} = 4500 \text{ units}$$

This can now be referred to as the 'target output' because, if this level of sales is reached (assuming the price and costs do not change) then the target profit and rate of return will be achieved.

Calculating revenue to achieve target profit

The revenue that must be earnt to achieve target profit can be calculated using the following formula:

KEY FORMULA

$$\text{revenue to achieve target profit} = \frac{\text{fixed costs + target profit}}{1 - \text{direct cost / price}}$$

WORKED EXAMPLE 32.2

In service businesses in particular, such as lawyers or surveyors, it is useful to know how much income the business needs to cover all of its costs and make a target profit. Assume that the monthly fixed costs of a law practice are $60 000.

CONTINUED

It aims to make a profit of $20 000 per month. Lawyers are paid $50 per hour (variable costs) and clients are charged $100 per hour, the **revenue to achieve target profit** will be:

$$\text{revenue to achieve target profit} = \frac{(\$60\,000 + \$20\,000)}{1 - (\$50\,/\,\$100)} = \$160\,000$$

KEY TERM

revenue to achieve target profit: the amount of revenue needed to cover both fixed and variable costs and earn the business a target profit

Calculating target price

If a business wants to break even at a level of production of 1000 units each month and direct costs are $3 per unit and fixed costs $6000 per month, what price must it charge? This is quite a common question for business managers to ask if they want to set the break-even point quite low and if they believe that, to a certain extent, demand is relatively unresponsive to price.

The solution is to adapt the original break-even formula.

KEY FORMULA

$$\text{break-even target price} = \left(\frac{\text{fixed costs}}{\text{production level}}\right) + \text{direct cost}$$

WORKED EXAMPLE 32.3

$$\text{break-even target price} = \left(\frac{\$6000}{1000}\right) + \$3 = \$9 \text{ per unit}$$

CASE STUDY 32.2

OMG shoes

The following break-even chart has been prepared by the operations manager of OMG shoes.

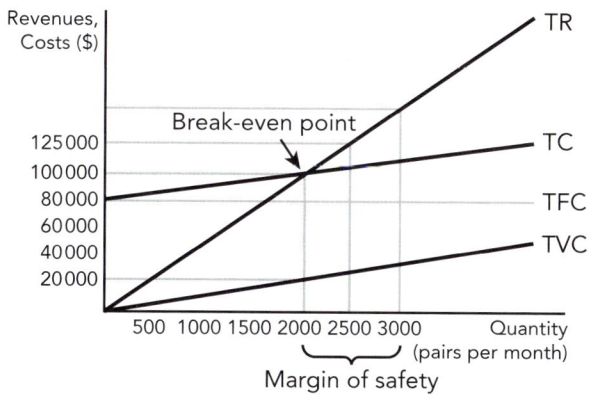

1 Define the term 'margin of safety'.   [2]

2 Calculate the selling price per pair of shoes.   [2]

3 Calculate the profit at 2000 pairs per month.   [2]

4 Calculate the variable cost per pair of shoes.   [2]

5 Calculate the total contribution at 2500 units.   [2]

6 Explain what will happen to the break-even point if the price rises to $60 per pair.   [2]

7 Explain one assumption that you have made in answering Q6.   [2]

ACTIVITY 32.2

A firm producing cookies achieves break-even at 5500 units (packs) per month.

1 Analyse what is likely to happen to this quantity if:

   a The business hires a secretary for the office and pays her a fixed monthly salary.

   b The business relocates to other premises where the rent is lower.

CONTINUED

   c The price of sugar per kilo rises

   d The business buys technologically advanced energy-saving machines, which produce items faster.

   e The business grows and enjoys bulk-buying economies of scale.

2 Can a business producing cookies reduce its break-even level of output, even if it does not enjoy economies of scale? If yes, how? Discuss.

32.4 Uses and limitations of break-even analysis as a decision making tool

So far we have examined the following benefits of break-even analysis:

- Charts are relatively easy to construct and interpret.

- It provides useful guidelines to management on break-even points, safety margins and profit/loss levels at different rates of output.

- Comparisons can be made between different options by constructing new charts to show changed circumstances. In the example above, the charts could be amended to show the possible impact on profit and break-even point of a change in the product's selling price.

- The equation produces a precise break-even result.

- Break-even analysis can be used to help managers when taking important decisions, such as price changes, location decisions, whether to buy new equipment and which project to invest in.

TIP

It is very important to remember that a break-even chart or calculation is only accurate for a limited period of time, for example because of cost changes or changes in market conditions that mean the price has to be changed.

When using break-even analysis and making cost and revenue projections for the future, it is important for managers not to assume that future forecasts about sales and costs are completely accurate. Managers must consider these limitations of break-even analysis when interpreting its results:

- The assumption that costs and revenues are always represented by straight lines is unrealistic. Not all variable costs are direct costs which change directly or 'smoothly' with output. For example, labour costs may increase as output reaches maximum

due to higher shift payments or overtime rates. The revenue line could be influenced by price reductions made necessary to sell all units produced at high output levels. The combined effects of these assumptions could be to create two break-even points in practice (see Figure 32.6).

- Not all costs can be conveniently classified into fixed and direct or variable costs. The introduction of semi-variable costs will make the technique much more complicated.

- No allowance is made for stock levels on the break-even chart. It is assumed that all units produced are sold. This is unlikely to always be the case in practice so it cannot be assumed that maximum output, for example, will always be converted into sales.

- Cost and revenue data are often estimated when break-even analysis is undertaken and the actual data might vary from those used in the break-even calculation.

- Also, fixed costs will remain unchanged at different output levels up to maximum capacity. For example, machinery may require additional and costly maintenance as it is used more intensively.

- When making a price change, demand is unlikely to remain constant. This means that an assumption has to be made about the impact on demand and revenue. This needs an assessment about price elasticity and this estimate could be inaccurate.

- When buying or leasing new equipment, the impact on variable costs must be estimated and this might not be accurate. This means that the impact on break-even, safety margin and profit might be very different once the equipment is operating.

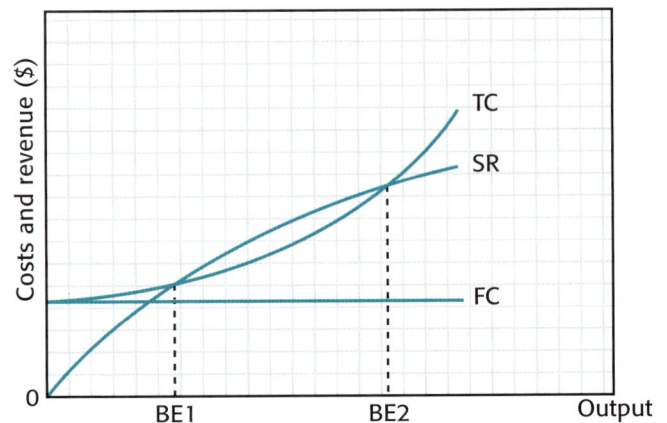

Figure 32.6: A break-even chart showing how non-linear assumptions can lead to two break-even points

---

CASE STUDY 32.3

Posh Paws targets a higher profit

Posh Paws Ltd produces an innovative 'teaser ball' toy for dogs. The selling price is $25 per unit and Posh Paws sells the product only online. In 2020, the business sold 10 000 units, the direct cost of which was $15 per ball. To run Posh Paws, the fixed costs per year amount to $90 000. For 2021, the finance director targets a profit 20% higher than 2020.

1 Define the term 'target profit'. [2]

2 Calculate the quantity to be produced in order for Posh Paws to reach the 2021 target profit. [2]

3 Calculate the price that must be charged if the business wants to break even at 8000 units. [2]

4 Explain the effect that the change in price (calculated in question 3) would have on the firm's margin of safety, at any given level of output. [2]

THEORY OF KNOWLEDGE

Knowledge question: To what extent can the human sciences provide accurate predictions?

Break-even analysis is an important tool that helps a business to identify its break-even level of output and margin of safety, as well as the expected profit at any given level of output. Moreover, the tool can help the business to predict the effect of marketing decisions (such as changes in prices) on the quantity that needs to be produced to reach a given targeted profit.

However, to what extent are such predictions accurate, given the numerous factors that may suddenly change in dynamic markets, especially amid fast-changing external conditions?

In 2021, the price of natural gas surged to record highs and this affected the production planning process of many businesses, including those producing fertilisers in the UK. Carbon dioxide is an important by-product of fertiliser production, and it is used widely as part of the production and packaging of meat products. With natural gas prices soaring, two large UK fertiliser factories owned by US firm CF Industries Holdings stopped operations. The sudden, extreme increase in the variable cost per unit for reasons outside the control of the industry made any break-even analysis practically useless. The impact was so severe that the industries had to stop production overall until the price of natural gas returned to normal levels. The effect was extreme across the food industry because, due to the lack of adequate carbon dioxide (a basic raw material), their production plans were also destroyed.

Can a human science such as business management rely on predictions? To what extent can businesses make decisions based on a break-even analysis that involves predictions based on mathematical assumptions? Discuss in class.

CASE STUDY 32.4

Break-even charts

The following data has been provided by the finance director of La Pitch which manufactures high-quality tents for the specialist outdoor market. The marketing director wants to reduce the price of the tents to $39.99 to increase sales volume (he considers this to be a psychologically attractive price to consumers). But there are concerns about reducing unit contribution and covering costs. There are also concerns about exceeding La Pitch's factory capacity.

- Direct labour per unit $17

- Direct materials per unit $18

- Fixed costs $200 000 per year

- Current selling price $45

- Maximum capacity of the factory is 30 000 units

1   Define the term 'unit contribution'.   [2]

2   Based on La Pitch's financial information construct a fully labelled break-even chart. Calculate the break-even point, the margin of safety and profit from the sale of 25 000 tents.   [8]

3   Examine the advantages and disadvantages of the marketing director's proposal to reduce the price of the tents to $39.99.   [10]

ACTIVITY 32.3

Beata is ready to buy a franchise agreement to open a shop of a popular and growing chain selling perfumes. She needs to choose between two possible locations.

Location A:

Size of the store: 50 square metres, in a busy shopping mall

Rent: $2000 per month

Break-even quantity: 100 litres per month

Maximum capacity: 200 litres per month

Location B:

Size of the store: 100 square metres, in a growing shopping area, with no established competitors yet

Rent: $2400 per month

Break-even quantity: 130 litres per month

Maximum capacity: 400 litres per month

Which location should Beata choose? Discuss in class.

Reflection: When discussing the locations, did you consider qualitative factors along with the break-even analysis information? Have you thought of the limitations of the break-even analysis as a tool for decision-making?

SELF-EVALUATION CHECKLIST

After studying this chapter, complete this table.

I am able to apply and analyse:	Needs more work	Almost there	Ready to move on
total contribution and contribution per unit (AO2)			
break-even charts and break-even analysis: • break-even quantity/point • profit or loss • margin of safety • target profit output • target profit • target price (AO2)			
the effects of changes in prices or costs on the break-even quantity, profit and margin of safety, using graphical and quantitative methods (AO2)			
I am able to synthesise and evaluate:			
limitations of break-even analysis as a decision-making tool (AO3)			

CONTINUED

I am able to use and apply:	Needs more work	Almost there	Ready to move on
a break-even chart and the following aspects of break-even analysis: • break-even quantity/point • profit or loss • margin of safety • target profit output • target profit • target price (AO4)			
the effects of changes in prices and costs on the break-even quantity, profit and margin of safety, using graphical and quantitative methods (AO4)			

REFLECTION

Do you think break-even analysis is of equal value to all businesses in all situations? Explain your answer to another learner.

PROJECT

When a tech startup fails, it's inevitably a harsh time for the founder, the employees, the investors and the customers.

But when a social enterprise shuts down, its failure also affects those populations or ecosystems that the business was supposed to serve, increasing both the stakeholders' sense of responsibility and the real-world consequences of their failure.

Although that's likely why so many social entrepreneurs are reluctant to talk about their business failures, it's also the reason they should share them more openly.

In other words, the failure of a social enterprise is much more sensitive than that of a traditional company, and for that reason it is very important to understand the factors that led to failure.

1   Do some personal research on the reason why for-profit social enterprises often fail, and find a few real-world examples.

2   Bring your findings to class and prepare a poster which lists the five most important reasons behind the failure of for-profit social enterprises. Identify how these reasons affect the ability of the businesses to break even, and thus to survive in the long term.

3   Discuss in class: Why is it often more difficult for for-profit social enterprises to break even compared to conventional for-profit organisations? How do you think social entrepreneurs could try to solve this problem?

EXAM-STYLE QUESTIONS

Windcheater Car Roofracks

Paolo and Stefano are partners owning Windcheater Car Roofracks (WCR) which needs to expand output as a result of increasing demand from motor accessory shops. The business uses batch production to produce its roof racks. The current output capacity has been reached at 5000 units per year. Each rack is sold to the retailers for $40. Production costs are:

- direct labour $10
- direct materials $12
- fixed costs $54 000.

Paolo, who is the operations manager, is considering two options for expansion:

- **Option 1:** extend the existing premises but keep the same method of production. This would increase fixed costs by $27 000 per year and direct costs would remain unchanged. Capacity would be doubled.

- **Option 2:** purchase new machinery, which will speed up the production process and cut down on wasted materials. Fixed costs would rise by $6000 per year, but direct costs would be reduced by $2 per unit. Output capacity would increase by 50%.

Stefano, who is a finance graduate, does not agree with the expansion options, as both require heavy investment. He believes that the problem is the low price at which the products are sold in the market. 'Our competitors sell to retailers at $50 per rack, and their quality is not as good as ours. We should increase our price to $45, leading to a higher unit contribution. I believe that such a decision would reduce our sales to 4500 units per year, but we will experience a higher profit than we do now by selling 5000 units at $40 per year.

1	State **two** types of fixed costs that could be relevant to WCR.	[2]
2	Construct a fully labelled break-even diagram for Option 1, showing the break-even output and the margin of safety at full capacity	[6]
3	Calculate the maximum profit for WCR in Option 1.	[2]
4	Construct a fully labelled break-even diagram for Option 2, showing the break-even output and the margin of safety at full capacity.	[6]
5	Calculate the maximum profit for WCR in Option 2.	[2]
6	Outline what will happen to the break-even output of Option 2, if Paolo is wrong in his estimations and the fixed costs would rise by more than $6000 per year.	[2]
7	Calculate the profit for WCR at 4500 units based on Stefano's proposal to increase the selling price.	[2]
8	Outline **one** possible advantage and **one** disadvantage for WCR from increasing the selling price of roof racks	[4]
9	Explain **one** advantage and **one** limitation for WCR from using break even as a tool to make decisions.	[4]
10	Based on your calculations, recommend which of the solutions proposed by the two owners might be more suitable for WCR	[10]

> Chapter 33

Production planning

Higher-level

LEARNING OBJECTIVES

On completing this chapter you should be able to:

Apply and analyse:

> The local and global supply chain process (AO2)

Analyse, apply and use:

> Stock control charts based on the following: lead time; buffer stock; re-order level; re-order quantity (AO2 and AO4)

> Capacity utilisation rate (AO2 and AO4)

> Defect rate (AO2 and AO4)

> Labour productivity, capital productivity, productivity rate, operating leverage (AO2 and AO4)

Synthesise and evaluate:

> The difference between JIT and just-in-case (JIC) (AO3)

CONTINUED

Synthesise and evaluate, use and apply:

> Cost to buy (CTB) (AO3 and AO4)

> Cost to make (CTM) (AO3 and AO4)

Analyse, apply and use the following business management tools:

> make or buy analysis; contribution costing; absorption costing; critical path analysis; Gantt charts

BUSINESS IN CONTEXT

The shocking cost of holding stock

On average the cost to a business of holding **stock** is between 4% and 10% of the value of the inventory. So, if an average stock level is $1 million, the annual cost of keeping and looking after the goods could be up to $100 000. However, research has shown that the figure could be as high as 40%. These costs include:

- storage costs – the rent on the warehouse
- stock-handling costs
- loss and damage of stock
- obsolescence
- opportunity cost of capital tied up in stock.

When all of these costs are analysed, the figure of 30–40% as the total cost of holding stock does not seem so outrageous after all.

But how can these costs be reduced? Could businesses manage their operations with lower stock levels – or even no stock at all? The experience of a large Scottish supermarket group suggests that it is possible to move away from holding large amounts of stock 'just in case' there is a demand for the products.

The managers of Scotmid decided on an IT-driven stock-ordering system that reordered goods from suppliers automatically as remaining goods on the shelves were purchased by customers. According to business analysts, the business now has much tighter control of stock and wastage and improved cash flow. Stock-holding has reduced dramatically with huge benefits throughout the supermarket group.

Discuss in pairs/groups:

- Why do businesses hold stock?
- Could a business manage with 'zero' stock? Explain your answer.

KEY TERM

stock (inventory): materials and goods required to allow for the production and supply of products to the customer

KEY CONCEPT LINK

Ethics

Businesses are often faced with a dilemma when they are buying inputs from suppliers. The cheapest places to source your inputs might have the most unethical business practices. This could be the use of s`weatshop or child labour or the worst environmental standards in the production process.

33.1 The supply chain process

The supply chain encompasses all the businesses involved in ensuring a product is manufactured and supplied to the final customer. Supply chain management is an important process for most businesses, especially with the increasing trend towards outsourcing/offshoring. Businesses will strive to have an optimised supply chain because it usually translates into lower costs for the company.

Supply chains need to be managed to reduce costs, minimise transportation, eliminate bottlenecks and maximise customer value. According to the Council of Supply Chain Management Professionals (CSCMP), supply chain management encompasses the planning and management of all activities involved in sourcing, procurement, stock and logistics management. Modern supply chain management requires IT links with all suppliers and distribution companies and the constant monitoring of deliveries and dispatches of parts/components/finished goods.

Local supply chains use only regional suppliers and manufacturers in an area close to the business's own area. This can be beneficial to small businesses that cannot easily build links and relationships with global suppliers. The 2020 pandemic contributed to supply problems for those businesses using non-local suppliers. Production delays, material shortages, rising transport costs and increasing transport unreliability affected many countries and highlighted another advantage of having local suppliers for all key parts, components and business services.

Before 2020, many businesses focused on developing global supply chains with the lowest-cost suppliers. Globalisation, freer international trade, low shipping costs and improved global communications all contributed towards the trend for using low-cost global suppliers.

> **TIP**
>
> Do not confuse the term 'logistics' with 'supply chain'. Logistics refers to the physical distribution process of parts/components and finished goods whereas the supply chain includes relationships and trading terms with multiple companies such as suppliers, manufacturers and the retailers.

> **KEY TERM**
>
> **supply chain:** every business that comes into contact with a particular product, including manufacturing and supplying parts for the product, assembling it, delivering it and selling it

> **CASE STUDY 33.1**
>
> ### Samsung's sustainable supply chain
>
> Samsung Electronics endeavours to build strategic partnerships with best-performing suppliers based on mutual trust in their sustainable supply chain. This is why they adopt a fair and transparent process when taking on new suppliers. Any company that wants to be a Samsung supplier can post its new business proposals on the supplier portal. Samsung has an international procurement centre (IPC) that serves as the procurement hub, and the IPC enables Samsung to identify outstanding suppliers in strategically important regions across the globe.
>
> Samsung have three important criteria that they use when taking on new suppliers:
>
> - Environment and safety: Suppliers need to satisfy the criteria set out in 22 articles, such as fire prevention equipment, occupational health and environmental standards.
>
> - Labour rights: Suppliers need to satisfy criteria set out in 20 articles, such as prohibition of child labour, guaranteed minimum wage and equal opportunities.
>
> - Eco-partner: Suppliers needs to satisfy criteria on product environmental policy, environmental education and training, and sole use of inputs sourced from eco-certified suppliers.
>
> 1   Define the term 'supply chain'.   [2]
> 2   Outline **two** elements of an effective supply chain.   [4]
> 3   Explain **two** advantages to Samsung of adopting a sustainable supply chain.   [4]
> 4   Explain **two** disadvantages to Samsung of adopting a sustainable supply chain.   [4]

33.2 The difference between just-in-time and just-in-case

These are two approaches to stock management. One, JIC (just-in-case), focuses on the importance of always having sufficient stock to meet nearly all eventualities. The other, JIT (just-in-time), focuses on reducing stock-holding costs to a minimum.

The benefits and aims of JIT – the just-in-time stock control principle – were explained in Chapter 30. Traditionally, businesses tended to rely on the JIC principle of stock control – 'just-in-case'. Failure to hold enough stocks of parts and components could result in production being halted when stock runs out. Failure to hold enough stocks of finished goods could mean customer dissatisfaction if demand cannot be met immediately or in the short term.

Virtually all businesses hold stock of some kind. Banks and insurance companies will hold stock of stationery, and retailers have stock of goods on display and in their warehouses. Manufacturing businesses will hold stock in three distinct forms:

- **Raw materials and components**. These will have been purchased from outside suppliers. They will be held in stock until they are used in the production process.
- **Work in progress**. At any one time the production process will be converting raw materials and components into finished goods and these are 'work in progress'. For some firms, such as construction businesses, this will be the main form of stock held. Batch production tends to have high work-in-progress levels.
- **Finished goods**. Having been through the complete production process, goods may then be held in stock until sold and dispatched to the customer.

Read section 33.1 again to understand the important principles on which JIT is based and the requirements for it to operate effectively. These requirements – such as close relationships with suppliers and excellent transport links – are less important with JIC and these are some of the differences between the two systems. However, the essential difference between the JIT and JIC strategies is that with JIT stock is minimised or, if possible, eliminated whereas in JIC, stock is held at a sufficient level to act as a buffer if there are production problems or delays with the delivery of component parts. The operation of JIC is usually represented by the stock control graphs which are analysed in section 33.3.

Table 33.1 summarises the advantages and disadvantages of the just-in-case stock management approaches.

TIP

Any question about JIT that involves discussing how appropriate it is in different business cases should lead to an answer that considers the potential drawbacks of the approach as well as its more obvious benefits.

Advantages	Disadvantages
Stocks of raw materials can be used to meet increases in demand by increasing the rate of production quickly	There are high opportunity costs of working capital tied up in stock
Raw-material supply hold-ups will not lead to production stopping	There are high storage costs such as security and insurance
Economies of scale from bulk discounts will reduce average costs	There is a risk of goods being damaged or becoming outdated, which means they might have to be sold for less than they cost
Stocks of finished goods can be displayed to customers and increase the chances of sales	

Advantages	Disadvantages
Stocks of finished goods can be used to meet sudden, unpredicted increases in demand – customer orders can be filled without delay Firms can stockpile completed goods to meet anticipated increases in demand as with seasonal goods or products such as toys at festival times	Less significance is given to 'getting it right first time' – a key component of lean production – as if there are faulty products, other supplies are kept in stock to replace them Space used to store stock cannot be used for productive purposes

Table 33.1: Just-in-case stock management approach – advantages and disadvantages

CASE STUDY 33.2

JIT at Walmart

Walmart uses just-in-time inventory in the application of the just-in-time (JIT) method of stock management. This method involves measures and activities that have the operational objective of minimising stock levels and related costs. At Walmart, the just-in-time inventory method is applied in the form of cross-docking. This means that suppliers' trucks and Walmart's trucks meet at the company's warehouses and distribution centres. Goods are transferred from the suppliers' trucks directly to Walmart's trucks, which deliver the goods to the stores.

The main benefit of cross-docking at Walmart's warehouses is the minimisation of stock levels.

CONTINUED

Fewer goods are stored at the warehouses. A smaller stock level is less costly to manage. Also, cross-docking enables Walmart to deliver goods to the stores quickly. This enables the firm to respond rapidly to fluctuations in demand and related changes in the market. The application of JIT stock management supports Walmart's operational efficiency objectives.

1   Outline the difference between just-in-case and just-in-time stock management. [4]

2   Describe how Walmart uses cross-docking to as part of its approach. [4]

3   Explain **two** advantages to Walmart of using JIT stock management. [4]

4   Explain **two** disadvantages of Walmart using JIT stock management. [4]

ACTIVITY 33.1

This is an extract from a trade union report on the application of JIT and lean production methods on a production line.

'Multi-skilling and elimination of waste in the production process can have detrimental effects on the working conditions of production line workers. JIT, for example, puts huge pressure on employees and is at odds with the concept of job enrichment. JIT serves as a system which increases workload and there is clear evidence it negatively affects the mental health of employees.'

In pairs or as a group, prepare a presentation on the ethics of applying JIT on a production line if it has a negative effect on the mental health of a business' employees.

TIP

Remember to apply your answer to the business in the Case study question when writing about stock and stock-handling systems. For example, if the business sells toys, it is likely to hold high stocks of toys at festival times.

33.3 Stock control charts

Stock control charts or graphs are widely used by businesses adopting the JIC strategy to monitor stock levels. These charts record stock levels, stock deliveries, buffer stocks and maximum stock levels over time. They help a stock manager to determine the appropriate order time and order quantity (see Figure 33.1).

Figure 33.1 has certain key features:

- **Buffer stocks.** The more uncertainty there is about delivery times or production levels, the higher the buffer stock level will have to be. Also, the greater the cost involved in shutting production down and restarting, the greater the potential cost savings from holding high buffer stocks.

- **Maximum stock level.** This may be limited by space or by the financial costs of holding even higher stock levels. One way to calculate this maximum level is to add the most cost-effective number of units to be ordered (the 'economic order quantity' or EOQ) of each component to the buffer stock level for that item.

- **Re-order quantity.** This will be influenced by the economic order quantity concept referred to here.

- **Lead time.** The longer this period of time, then the higher the re-order stock level will have to be. The less reliable suppliers are, the greater the buffer stock level might have to be.

KEY TERMS

buffer stocks: the minimum stocks that should be held to ensure that production could still take place should a delay in delivery occur or production rates increase

re-order quantity: the number of units ordered each time

lead time: the normal time taken between ordering new stocks and their delivery

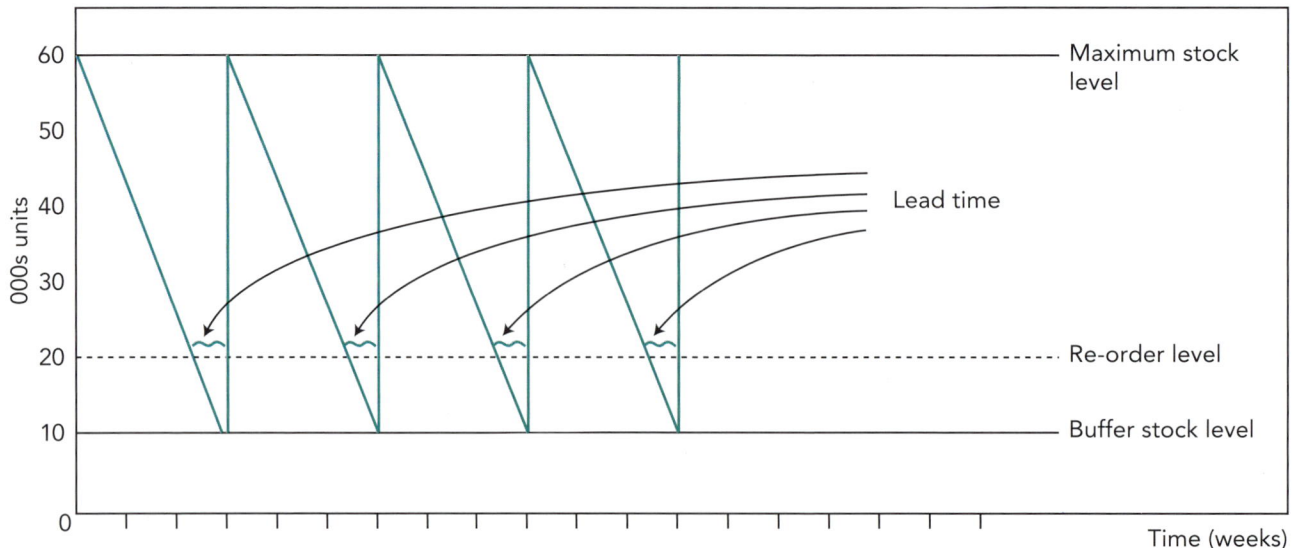

Figure 33.1: A typical stock control chart

- **Re-order stock level.** It is now very common for computers to be used to keep a record of every sale and every delivery of stock. The re-order quantity and re-order stock level can be programmed into the computer, then it can re-order automatically from the supplier when stocks fall to the re-order stock level. The stock control chart can also be prepared by the computer. Figure 33.2 shows the sale of Popsquash soft drinks by one retailer over a ten-week period.

As can be seen from Figure 33.2, the stock level does not always follow the regular and consistent pattern shown in Figure 33.1. The sales have been affected by two important factors, shown by the more steeply sloping lines, and deliveries were sometimes delayed so the lead time is not the same after every order. This is a more realistic situation and helps to illustrate the usefulness of this type of chart for future decision-making regarding stocks.

> **KEY TERM**
>
> **re-order stock level:** the level of stocks that will trigger a new order to be sent to the supplier

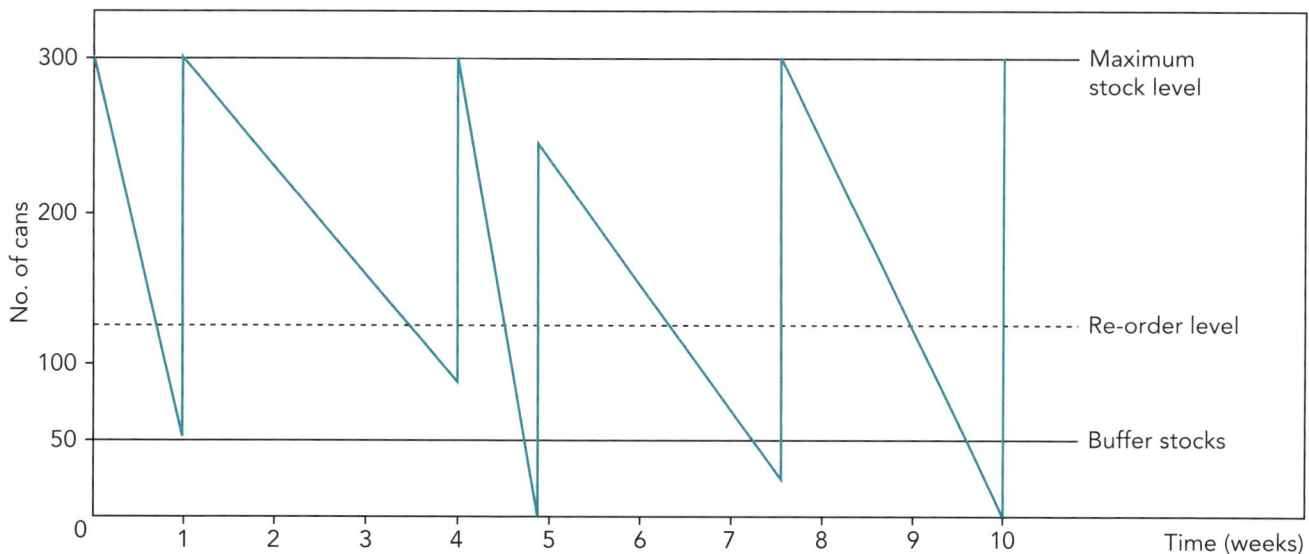

Figure 33.2: Stock control chart for Popsquash soft drinks

CASE STUDY 33.3

Stock control at a skateboard manufacturer

Edge of the Kerb Ltd (EoK) is an Australian based skateboard manufacturer. The business is only two years old, and it is looking to improve its stock management system. EoK is concerned about the reliability of one of its main suppliers. This supplier has let EOK down in the past which has led to costs due to running out of stock. EoK has decided to use another supplier who is more reliable and supplies a better-quality input. However, the cost of the stock from the new supplier is 10% higher.

The diagram shows EoK's stock control chart.

1   Define the term 're-order level'.   [2]

2   Define the term 'lead time'.   [2]

3   On 1 February EoK stock was at 146 250 and on 3 March EoK ran out of stock for 14 days despite a reorder taking place on 21 February.

Using this information and the stock control diagram calculate the following:

a   how much stock was used between 1 February and 3 March   [2]

b   the stock re-ordered for delivery on 1 February   [2]

CONTINUED

c the lead time after EoK reordered on 21 February (remember there are 28 days in February) [2]

4 Evaluate EoK's decision to choose a new supplier. [10]

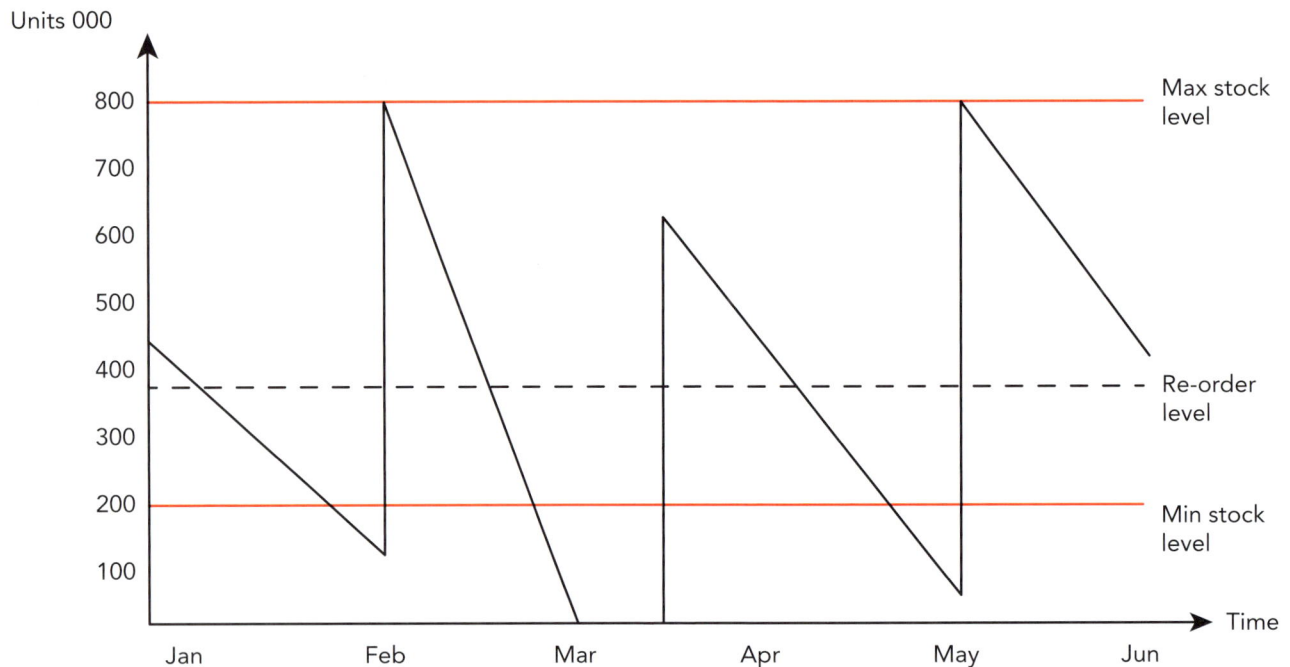

THEORY OF KNOWLEDGE

Theory of knowledge

Having an effective stock management system brings significant benefits to all manufacturing companies. It provides important and timely information in real time to help better planning and to make informed operational decision.

By establishing the optimum level of stock that a business needs, managers can set up an ordering and stock system based on the stock control diagram. This guides the re-ordering stock level and the timing of orders.

The benefits of having a stock control system in a business are:

- lost sales due to running out of stock are reduced

- customer service is better

- cash flow is improved

- space in the business's warehouse is optimised

- the company has greater control of its production system.

Effective use of the stock control chart can give a business all of these advantages.

In pairs or as a group, discuss the knowledge issues of reason and memory associated with a model like the stock control chart.

Evaluate the importance of business models such as stock control charts as a tool to help managers be successful.

33.4 Capacity utilisation rate

An important responsibility of senior operations employees is to manage the **capacity utilisation** rate of the business. There could be serious consequences for a business of recording a rate of capacity utilisation that is consistently low or consistently very high.

Capacity utilisation for any particular time period is calculated by the formula:

KEY FORMULA

$$\text{capacity utilisation rate} = \frac{\text{actual output}}{\text{productive capacity}} \times 100$$

Productive or maximum capacity is the total level of output that a business can achieve in a certain time period. So, for a hotel, monthly total capacity will be the number of 'room nights' available during that period. For a factory, it will be the total level of output that all of the existing resources can produce. If a business is working flat out, i.e., at **full capacity**, it is achieving 100% capacity utilisation with no spare capacity.

WORKED EXAMPLE 33.1

In any one week a hotel has 500 room nights available for visitors to book. Last month the hotel had 50 rooms booked to visitors.

Capacity utilisation last month $= \dfrac{350}{500} \times 100 = 70\%$

KEY TERMS

capacity utilisation: the proportion of maximum output capacity currently being achieved

full capacity: when a business produces at productive capacity or maximum output

Impact on average fixed costs

When capacity utilisation is at a high rate, average fixed costs will be spread out over a large number of units – unit fixed costs will be relatively low. When capacity utilisation is low, fixed costs will have to be paid for by fewer units and unit fixed costs will rise (see Table 33.2).

100-bed hotel	All bedrooms occupied (100% of capacity)	50 bedrooms occupied (50% of capacity)
Hotel fixed costs per day, e.g., rent and salaries	$2500	$2500
Average fixed costs per room per day	$25	$50

Table 33.2: How unit fixed costs for a hotel vary with capacity utilisation

Full capacity working

Do all businesses aim to produce at 100% capacity all of the time? In theory, the cost advantages of this would appear to be great. Unit fixed costs will be at their lowest possible level and this should help to increase profits. The business will be able to claim that it is so successful that it has no spare capacity. For example, hotels will put up 'No vacancy' signs and airlines will have no unsold seats. Employees will have a sense of job security too.

But there are potential drawbacks to operating at full capacity for a long period of time:

- Employees may feel under pressure due to the workload and this could raise stress levels. Operations managers cannot afford to make any production-scheduling mistakes, as there is no slack time to make up for lost output.
- Regular customers who want to increase their orders will have to be turned away or kept waiting for long periods. This could lead them to use other suppliers with the danger that they might be lost as long-term clients.

- Machinery will be working flat out and there may be insufficient time for maintenance and preventative repairs, which could lead to increased unreliability in the future.

So many firms attempt to maintain a high level of capacity utilisation, but to keep some spare capacity for unforeseen eventualities.

ACTIVITY 33.2

Imagine you are a running a small restaurant. The business is incredibly successful and is fully booked for three months in advance. Potential customers are constantly calling the restaurant and sending emails trying to book tables, but you often have to disappoint them. You have tried to rearrange the way you use table space to increase capacity, but it is not possible to expand capacity any more. You have a decision to make. There are three possible options:

- Expand the restaurant by building an extension. This would be disruptive because your restaurant would have to shut for four months.

- Move the restaurant to a new location. There is a building available but at a much higher rent.

- Stay at the current location, but each day you know you are losing a large amount of revenue from customers you turn away.

In pairs or as a group:

1 Discuss the issues for the restaurant of operating at capacity.

2 Produce a presentation showing which option you would choose for the restaurant and why.

TIP

When making decisions about how to deal with excess capacity it is important to consider both the length of time that the spare capacity might exist for and the causes of the problem.

Should a business be worried about a low rate of capacity utilisation?

Fixed costs per unit sold will be high and it could be a sign of declining demand for the products of the business. However, the impact on the business depends on the following:

- Is this a seasonal, short-term issue or has low-capacity utilisation been experienced for some time?

- Are competitors also experiencing low-capacity utilisation? If this is the case, the problem is likely to be industry-wide and may be caused by eternal factors such as an economic recession.

- Is the business currently making a loss and how long can this be financed by the business?

Depending on the answers to these questions, the business might respond in a number of ways when experiencing low rates of capacity utilisation:

- Reduce prices or offer short-term discounts to attract more consumers, e.g., hotels reduce prices during off-peak times of the year.

- Consider other changes to the marketing mix such as products aimed at consumers less affected by an economic recession (if this is the cause of the problem).

- Consider reducing capacity if the problem seems to be a long-term one. This is a form of rationalisation and will almost certainly involve redundancies, so this decision needs to be managed and communicated to employees effectively.

How might a business respond to long-term full capacity working?

The potential problems connected with operating at full capacity have been referred to. When a business is operating close to or at full capacity, then other decisions have to be considered:

- Should the business increase its scale of operation by acquiring more production resources? This will involve capital expenditure, and if demand falls in future, there will be excess capacity.

- Should it maintain existing capacity but outsource or subcontract more work to other businesses? This would make production levels more responsive to consumer demand, but would suppliers be reliable and would quality be affected?
- Should it keep working at full capacity and not expand? High demand for products could be managed by increasing prices and, as a result, profit margins. This decision would depend on the predicted price elasticity of demand.

33.5 Defect rate

There is little point in aiming for high levels of capacity utilisation if many of the products are below the standards of quality that the business aims to reach. It is important for operations managers to measure, record and monitor the **defect rate**.

> **KEY TERM**
>
> **defect rate:** the proportion of output in a time period which fails to reach quality standards

The formula for the defect rate is:

> **KEY FORMULA**
>
> $$\text{defect rate (\%)} = \frac{\text{number of defective products}}{\text{total output in time period}} \times 100$$

Management action will be necessary if this defect rate rises above the level that is considered acceptable. If 'zero defects' is the aim, then any defective items will require managers to investigate the likely causes, which could include:

- faulty supplies, e.g., of components
- machinery which fails to reach acceptable tolerance limits
- poorly trained employees
- low employee motivation levels.

33.6 Productivity and operating leverage

Productivity is not the same as the **level of production** and the two should not be confused. The level of production is an absolute measure of the quantity of output that a firm produces in a given period of time. Productivity is a relative measure and is concerned with how efficiently inputs are converted into outputs. There are several measures of productivity.

> **KEY TERMS**
>
> **productivity:** the ratio of outputs to inputs during production, e.g., output per worker per time period
>
> **level of production:** the number of units produced during a time period

Labour productivity

> **KEY FORMULA**
>
> Labour productivity (number of units per worker)
> $$= \frac{\text{total output in a given time period}}{\text{total workers employed}}$$

Nearly all businesses are trying at all times to increase **labour productivity**, even if total production is not increasing. A business can do this by employing fewer but better-skilled workers and by using fewer but more technologically advanced machines. Improvements in productivity usually lead to a reduction in the unit costs of production. If the costs of labour and capital inputs do not change, then any increase in output per worker or output per machine will lead to a fall in unit costs. In competitive markets, this could give firms a crucial advantage.

> **KEY TERM**
>
> **labour productivity:** the number of units produced per employee during a time period

	Number of units produced	Number of workers employed	Labour productivity = output/workers	Annual pay per worker	Labour cost per unit
Company A	5 000	10	500	$2 000	$4.00
Company B	12 000	20	600	$2 000	$3.33

Table 33.3: The higher the level of labour productivity, the lower the labour cost per unit produced (assuming the pay per worker is the same)

Table 33.3 shows the annual output and employment levels in two companies producing kitchen cupboards.

Raising labour productivity levels

There are four main ways in which productivity levels could be increased:

- **Improve the training of employees to improve skill levels**. Employees with higher and more flexible skill levels should be more productive. As well as being able to perform tasks more efficiently, they could become more interested in work due to their ability to do different jobs. However, training can be expensive and time-consuming, and highly qualified staff could leave to join another, perhaps rival, business.

- **Improve employee motivation**. There are many different views on the most appropriate ways to do this. Increasing pay is unlikely to have a permanent impact on productivity (as identified by Herzberg and as explained in Chapter 10). There may be little point in increasing pay by 10% if labour productivity only rises by 5%. After all, it is unit costs that firms want to drive down. Most businesses now put the emphasis on non-financial methods of motivation. These include involvement in decision-making, kaizen groups, delegation and quality circles. If these increase productivity without an increase in labour pay, unit costs will fall.

- **Purchase more technologically advanced equipment**. Modern machinery – from office computers to robot-controlled production machines – should allow increased output with fewer staff. But such expensive investment will only be worthwhile if high output levels can be maintained. In addition to the capital cost, staff may need to be retrained and there may be genuine fear amongst the workers about lost jobs and reduced security of employment.

- **More effective management**. There are many ways in which ineffective management can reduce the overall productivity of a business. Failure to purchase the correct materials, poor maintenance schedules for machines or heavy-handed management of staff are just some of these. More efficient operations and people management could go a long way to improve productivity levels.

Capital productivity

This measure is used to show how efficiently the capital assets of a business, such as machinery, are being used to produce output.

The formula often used for **capital productivity** is:

> **KEY FORMULA**
>
> $$\text{capital productivity} = \frac{\text{value of output in time period}}{\text{value of capital employed}}$$

> **KEY TERM**
>
> **capital productivity:** a measure of how efficiently capital input is used to produce output

> **WORKED EXAMPLE 33.2**
>
> A factory produced output valued at $4 million last year. Capital assets are currently valued at $8 million.
>
> Capital productivity = 4 million/8 million = 0.50

A measure of capital productivity that can be used for a particular piece of capital equipment, such as a robotic welding machine is:.

> **KEY FORMULA**
>
> $$\text{machine productivity} = \frac{\text{output in time period}}{\text{total machine hours}}$$

CASE STUDY 33.4

Improving efficiency: Mumbai Kitchen Products Ltd (MKP)

MKP manufactures kitchens for the industrial market and supplies many catering companies and restaurants. Aashi Khan is the CEO of MKP. She took over as CEO six months ago and has observed a number of operation management issues in the business which could be improved. The business's operations director is Rohit Chandra, and he has come under considerable pressure because of perceived inefficiencies in production.

Aashi is concerned about MKP's capacity utilisation data. Rohit Chandra claims capacity utilisation is more to do with marketing than production. Aashi is also concerned about the fact that investment in new machinery has not brought improvements in productivity. She is a big believer in effective employee training to improve productivity, and she plans to invest significantly in this.

Production data for the last three years is set out in the table.

	2019	2020	2021
Maximum annual capacity units (000)	310	330	350
Actual annual output units (000)	268	276	283
Workers employed	220	245	258

1   Define the term 'capacity utilisation'. [2]

2   a   Calculate MKP's capacity utilisation over the last three years. [2]

b   Outline what has happened to MKP's capacity utilisation over the last three years. [2]

c   Explain why Rohit Chandra has blamed the marketing department for MKP's capacity utilisation. [4]

3   Define the term 'labour productivity'. [2]

4   a   Calculate the labour productivity figures for MKP over the last three years. [2]

b   Outline what has happened MKP's labour productivity over the last three years. [2]

c   Explain **two** reasons why MKP's labour productivity might have fallen. [4]

5   Evaluate the methods that Aashi could use to increase labour productivity. [10]

WORKED EXAMPLE 33.3

A flow production line produced 50 000 bottles last week. It was in operation for 45 hours.

Machine productivity $= \dfrac{50\,000}{45} = 1111.1$ bottle per hour

Managers will be concerned if either of these measures is declining as it might indicate unreliable capital equipment or poorly trained employees who cannot maximise the output from any given piece of equipment.

Productivity

These measures of productivity confirm that it is a relative concept that relates output to inputs. Overall factor productivity can also be measured by comparing total inputs during a period with total output.

KEY FORMULA

Overall productivity $= \dfrac{\text{total output}}{\text{total inputs}}$

or

$$\dfrac{\text{total output}}{(\text{labour} + \text{capital input})}$$

All measures of productivity are more useful to managers if:

- the results are compared over time to recognise any trends in the efficiency of operations
- the results are compared with those of other similar businesses, perhaps through a benchmarking exercise.

Operating leverage

The **degree of operating leverage** is an important indicator of the proportion of fixed costs to total costs and the impact this can have on operating profit when sales levels change.

KEY TERM

degree of operating leverage: measures how much a company's operating changes in response to a change in sales

Operating leverage can be used to assess the degree to which a business can increase operating profit by increasing revenue. A business that generates sales with a high gross margin and low variable costs is described as having high operating leverage.

Businesses with high operating leverage must cover a larger amount of fixed costs during each time period whether they sell any products or not. The business may make a large gross profit on each extra item sold, but it must reach enough sales volume to cover its substantial fixed costs. If it can do this, then the business will earn a significant profit on all sales after it has paid for its fixed costs. However, profit will be more sensitive to changes in sales volume.

Businesses with low operating leverage have high variable costs per unit that vary directly with the number of units sold, but they have relatively low fixed costs to pay each time period. In a business with low operating leverage, a large proportion of total costs are variable costs. In this case, the business makes a relatively small profit on each extra unit sold, but it does not have to achieve a high sales volume in order to cover its relatively low fixed costs. It is easier for this type of business to earn a profit at low sales levels, but it will not earn very high profits if it generates additional sales.

To calculate operating leverage, the following formula is used:

KEY FORMULA

degree of operating leverage $= \dfrac{(\text{revenue} - \text{total variable costs})}{\text{operating profit}}$

XYZ Company records the following financial results for one month:

Revenue	$100 000
Variable costs	$30 000
Fixed costs	$60 000
Operating profit	$10 000

Using the formula shown gives:

$$\text{degree of operating leverage} = \frac{\$70\,000}{\$10\,000} = 7$$

This results means that for every 1% change in revenue, operating profit will increase by 7%

If XYZ's sales increase by 20% next month, the financial results are now:

Revenue	$120 000
Variable costs	$36 000
Fixed costs	$60 000
Operating profit	$24 000

With XYZ's high degree of operating leverage, the 20% increase in sales translates into a 140% increase in its operating profit.

Understanding operating leverage

The higher the degree of operating leverage, the greater the potential risk from forecasting. Relatively small errors in forecasting sales can be multiplied into large errors in profit and cash flow projections.

The operating leverage result indicates how well a business is using its fixed-cost capital assets, such as its warehouse and machinery and equipment, to generate profits. The more profit a business can earn from the same value of fixed assets, the higher its operating leverage.

One important management lesson that can be gained from operating leverage is that if efforts are made to minimise fixed costs, operating profit will increase without making any changes to the selling price, contribution margin, or the number of units sold.

33.7 Cost to buy (CTB) and cost to make (CTM)

Should a business undertake all operations in the production of a product itself or should it 'buy in' some parts, components or services? This is a key operations question and can only be answered by measuring the cost to buy of a component part of the production process and the cost to make it within the business. The make or buy decision is further considered in section 33.8. This section is concerned with how to calculate CTB and CTM.

The following data is required:

* expected volume (V)
* the fixed costs associated with making the product (FC)
* the unit direct costs of making the product (UDC)
* the unit cost from an external supplier (including transport costs) (UCS).

This data can then be inserted into the following formulae:

KEY FORMULA

cost to buy (CTB) = V × UCS

and

cost to make (CTM) = FC + (UDC × V)

An example can be used to demonstrate the two formulae:

* **Cost to buy**: An operations manager of a computer assembly firm has obtained an estimate from a specialist supplier of keyboards: To supply 10 000 (V) keyboards each month at $5 (UCS) each = total cost, including transport, of $50 000 (CTB).
* **Cost to make**: The manager has estimated the internal direct costs of making keyboards in-house at $5.20 (UDC) each. The fixed costs that can be directly allocated to the production of these keyboards amount to $6000 per month (FC). Total cost of making the products is [$6000 + ($5.20 × 10 000)] = $58 000 (CTM).

33.8 Business management tools

Make or buy analysis

One of the key factors for operations managers to consider when making the 'make ourselves or buy-in' decision is the relative costs of these two options. In quantitative terms, if it can be shown that the long-term costs of outsourcing (buying-in) a component or product are less than the cost of making that component or product then outsourcing might be the better option. However, qualitative factors should also be considered, such as the impact of redundancies on worker morale, social responsibility objectives and quality issues.

If cost to make (CTM) exceeds cost to buy (CTB), then it is more financially advantageous to buy-in or outsource. If CTB exceeds CTM, the opposite is true and the business will benefit financially from making the product in-house. The unit cost from suppliers of a component or service can be obtained from estimates given by potential suppliers.

Using the calculations from section 33.7: obtaining 10 000 keyboards from an outsourcing company would save the computer business $8000 per month. The cost to buy is less than the cost to make – assuming the expenditure on the fixed costs can be stopped immediately when production of the component ceases.

Make-or-buy decisions are not just about numbers, however. Other questions that an operations manager should ask before outsourcing an operation include:

- Is this the organisation's core competency – and would the business be losing key skills by outsourcing?
- Could the business risk losing a competitive advantage by disclosing detailed information about production designs and methods to an outsourcing business?
- What will the impact on quality and perceived image be?
- Can the outsourcing business be relied upon to deliver as and when required? This is an especially important consideration if the purchasing business operates JIT.
- What additional risks would the business be taking?

- How irreversible is the decision? Could the business return to making the product if a supplier lets them down completely?

Contribution costing

Contribution costing solves the problem of deciding on the most appropriate way to allocate or share out overhead costs between products – it does not allocate them at all. Instead, the method concentrates on two very important accounting concepts:

- **Marginal cost** is the cost of producing an extra unit of output. For example, if the total cost of producing 100 units is $4000 and the total cost of producing 101 units is $4050, the marginal (or extra) cost is $50.
- The contribution of a product is the revenue gained from selling a product less its marginal cost. For example, if the 101st unit with a marginal cost of $50 is sold for $70, it has made a contribution towards indirect costs of $20. The unit contribution is the difference between the sale price ($70) and the marginal cost ($50) = $20. This is not the same as profit. Profit can only be calculated after overheads have also been deducted.

KEY TERM

contribution costing: costing method that allocates only direct costs to cost centres and profit centres, not overhead costs

marginal cost: the additional cost of producing one more unit of output.

Contribution costing has very important advantages over absorption costing when management plans to take important decisions based on cost data. An example contribution costing statement is shown in Table 33.4.

	Novel ($000)	Textbook ($000)
Revenue	50	100
Direct materials	15	35
Direct labour	20	50
Other direct costs	10	5
Total direct costs	45	90
Contribution	5	10

Table 33.4: Contribution costing statement for Cairo Printers Co.

This statement does not allocate overhead costs between the two products. However, overheads cannot be ignored altogether. They are needed to calculate the profit or loss of the business:

- Total contribution for Cairo Printers Co. = $15 000
- Total indirect/overhead costs amounted to $12 000
- Profit = contribution less overheads
- Therefore, the business has made a profit of $3000.

This link between contribution to overheads and profit is a crucial one.

CASE STUDY 33.5

Seaview Hotel

The direct cost of each hotel guest at the Seaview hotel is $15 per night. The room price is $50 per night. The total indirect cost per week is $1000. On average, 100 guests stay each week.

1   Calculate the contribution per guest per night. **[2]**

2   Calculate the weekly contribution from 100 guests. **[2]**

3   Calculate the profit made in one week with 100 guest nights. **[2]**

4   A group of 50 people has asked to spend one night at the hotel during a week when only 30 other guests are booked. The group has offered to pay a price of $20 each.

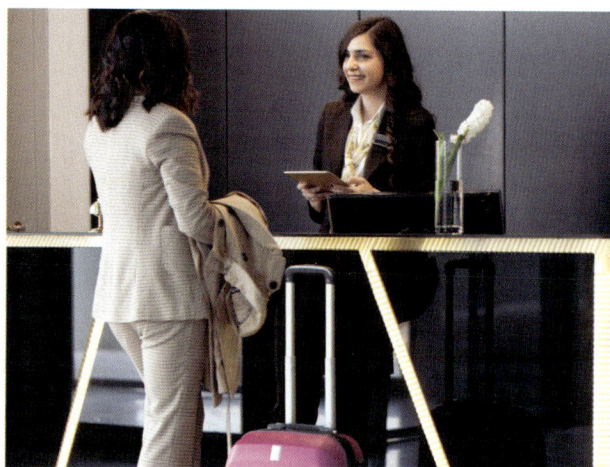

Discuss whether the manager should accept this offer. **[10]**

ACTIVITY 33.3

Researching costs and prices

1   In pairs or as a group, research the cost situation at your school.

   a   Identify and list four possible cost centres within your own school or college. Discuss with the managers or heads of these cost centres the benefits and drawbacks of using this form of organisation. Check the accuracy of your answer with your bursar/college accountant.

   b   Estimate the annual costs of one of the cost centres identified.

   c   Explain whether any of the cost centres identified in question a are, in fact, profit centres. Explain your answer.

2   In pairs or as a group, look up airline ticket prices for a popular local air route.

   a   How many different prices can you find?

   b   Do you think the lowest-cost airline is using contribution costing to calculate the price of air tickets or full cost pricing? Explain your answer.

Case study 33.5 and Activity 33.3 illustrate how contribution costing can be useful.

If a business sells more than one product, contribution costing shows managers which product is making the greatest or least contribution to overheads and profit. If all the relevant costs were allocated to each product instead, the manager could decide to stop producing a product that seemed to be making a loss. However, if it is still making a positive contribution, what would happen to profit if production was stopped? In cases such as this, stopping production of a product while it is earning a positive contribution will reduce the overall profits of the business. This is because the fixed overhead costs will still have to be paid, but there will be reduced contribution to pay them.

Contribution costing and special order decisions

If a business has spare capacity or if it is trying to enter a new market segment, contribution costing assists managers in deciding whether to accept an order at a price below the full cost of the product. For example, hotels often offer very low rates to customers in off-peak seasons. It is better to earn a contribution from additional guests than to leave rooms empty.

If a customer offers a special order contract at a price below full unit cost, this can lead to an increase in the total profits of the business. This is because the fixed overhead costs are being paid anyway and any extra contribution earnt will increase profit. But there are risks with this policy:

- Existing customers may realise that lower prices are being offered to new customers and demand a similar price. If all goods or services being sold by a business are sold at just above marginal cost, then this could lead to an overall loss being made.
- When high prices are a key feature in establishing the exclusivity of a brand, then to offer some customers lower prices could destroy a hard-won image.
- Where there is no excess capacity, sales at a price based on contribution cost may be reducing sales based on the full cost price.
- In some circumstances, lower-priced goods or services may be resold into the higher-priced market by customers themselves.

Situations when contribution costing would be used

- Contribution costing avoids inaccuracies and arbitrary indirect cost allocations and gives a contribution, not a profit total. Contribution costing can therefore be used in setting prices that just cover the direct costs of production.
- Decisions about a product or profit centre are made on the basis of its contribution to indirect costs – not profit or loss based on what may be an inaccurate allocation of all relevant costs, direct and indirect. Contribution costing can therefore be used to make a decision about whether to close a cost/profit centre.
- Excess capacity is more likely to be effectively used if special orders or contracts that make a positive contribution are accepted. Contribution costing can therefore be used in decision-making on special-order decisions.

Situations when contribution costing would not be used

- By ignoring indirect costs, contribution costing does not take into account that some products may result in much higher indirect costs than others. In addition, single-product firms have to cover the fixed costs with revenue from this single product, so using contribution costing would not be used in this case.
- Contribution costing would not be used when making decisions about business expansion or developing new products. All costs of these developments will need to be considered, not just the direct costs.
- Contribution costing may lead managers to choose to maintain the production of goods just because of a positive contribution. Perhaps a brand-new product should be launched instead that could, in time, make an even greater contribution.
- As in all areas of decision-making, qualitative factors may be important too, such as the image a product gives the business.

Absorption costing

Absorption costing allocates all costs to each product and is sometimes referred to as 'full costing'. If the business is only producing one type of product, then this is not a problem. In this case, the stages in full costing are:

KEY TERM

absorption costing: a method of costing in which all indirect and direct costs are allocated to the products, services or divisions of a business

---

- identify and add up all of the direct costs
- calculate the total of overheads of the business for a given time period
- add the total direct costs of making the product
- calculate the average cost of producing each product by dividing total costs by output.

WORKED EXAMPLE 33.5

A pump manufacturer produces 5000 pumps per year.

Total direct costs = $100 000

Total overhead costs = $50 000

Full cost of producing pumps = $150 000

Average (or unit) full cost per pump = $30

Comment: This is a straightforward calculation as there is just one product being made. The main problem arises when a business produces two or more products. How should indirect expenses then be divided up between the two (or more) products?

The division of indirect costs is called an allocation of indirect costs. The easiest way is to divide total overhead costs by the number of different products being produced.

In Example 2, a manufacturer produces both Product A and Product B. Can you see the problem with this allocation of overhead costs? Example 2 demonstrates the problem (see Table 33.5).

WORKED EXAMPLE 33.6

	Product A	Product B
Direct costs for each product	$45 000	$5 000
Allocated overheads (total overheads = $20 000)	$10 000	$10 000
Total or full cost	$55 000	$15 000
Annual output	10 000	500
Average full cost	$5.50	$30

Table 33.5: Simple absorption costing

Comment: This is an inaccurate division of indirect costs as Product A is obviously much more important to the business and incurs a much higher proportion of direct costs. This way of dividing overheads might lead to some very poor decisions, such as the pricing of Product B. As it has been allocated 50% of indirect costs then the final price, based on average cost, will be high and uncompetitive. Another way of allocating indirect costs must be used. Look at Example 3 (see Table 33.6).

WORKED EXAMPLE 33.7

	Product A=	Product B
Direct costs for each product	$45 000	$5 000
Proportion of total direct costs	90%	10%
Allocated overheads (total overheads = $20 000)	90% of $20 000 = $18 000	10% of $20 000 = $2 000
Total or full cost	$63 000	$7 000
Annual output	10 000	500
Average full cost	$6.30	$14

Table 33.6: Using direct cost information to allocate overheads

---

Comment: Now the indirect costs have been allocated differently. They have been allocated between the two products in the same proportion as they incur direct costs. Product A incurs 90% of direct costs and is allocated 90% of indirect costs. Product B incurs 10% of direct costs so is allocated 10% of indirect costs. More accurate full cost figures are obtained, which will be much more useful for decision-making such as setting prices.

This method is not perfect. One reason is that Product B might take up just as much factory floor space as A or use as much electricity because it is more dependent on machinery than A. An allocation of indirect costs such as rent and electricity based on direct costs might still not be accurate.

Absorption costing – additional points

- A method of allocating indirect costs has to be selected and used.

- This method should not change over time, or cost comparisons will be difficult.

- Indirect costs can be allocated using several methods. Proportion of total direct costs was used above, but other methods include:

  - proportion of total factory space taken up by each product

  - proportion of total labour costs incurred

  - proportion of the output of each product to total output.

Uses of absorption costing

- Absorption costing is particularly relevant for single-product businesses. In these businesses there is no uncertainty about the share of overheads to be allocated to the product.

- All costs are allocated, so no costs are left out of the calculation of total full cost or unit full cost.

- Absorption costing is a good basis for pricing decisions in single-product firms. If the full unit cost is calculated, this could then be used for mark-up pricing.

- Absorption costing data can be compared from one time period to another to assess performance, as long as the same method of allocating overheads is used.

Limitations of absorption costing

- There is no attempt to allocate each overhead cost to cost centres or profit centres on the basis of actual expenditure incurred. For example, a product may take up a large proportion of factory space but use low-cost and easy-to-maintain machinery. Should all overheads be allocated on the basis of factory space?

- Inappropriate methods of overhead allocation can lead to inconsistencies between departments and products.

- It can be risky to use this cost method for making decisions. The cost figures arrived at can be misleading and this can lead to inappropriate decisions being made about products or profit centres.

- If absorption costing is used, it is essential to allocate overheads on the same basis over time, otherwise sensible year-on-year comparisons cannot be made.

- The full unit cost will only be accurate if the actual level of output is equal to that used in the calculation. A fall in output will push up the allocated overhead costs per unit.

CASE STUDY 33.6

A make or buy decision

Cutting Machines Ltd is an established family busing that manufacturers lawnmowers. The market is a competitive one and Cutting Machines is looking to reduce its costs so that it can stay price competitive in the market. One way of doing this is for the business to buy in some components rather than manufacturing the components themselves. Cutting Machines has been offered the roller component of a lawnmower by another business at a competitive price.

Consider the costs data.

Product data for the roller component	
Direct labour costs per unit	$2.50
Direct material costs per unit	$3.80
Fixed factory costs directly allocated to each product (monthly)	$11 000
Current monthly output (units)	5 000
Unit cost of the roller if bought in from an outside supplier	$7.50

1   Define the term 'direct labour cost'.   [2]

2   Using the data, calculate:

    a   the total cost if Cutting Machines makes the roller component itself.   [2]

    b   the total cost of Cutting Machines buying in the component.   [2]

CONTINUED

3 Outline what difference it would make if Cutting Machines bought in the roller component. **[2]**

4 Explain **two** factors other than cost that might affect Cutting Machine's decision to buy in or make the roller itself. **[4]**

Critical path analysis

This is an important operations planning technique used widely in project management. Consider the construction of a house:

- The builder only wants to employ specialist workers on a subcontract basis when the job is ready for their particular skills.

- The builder also wants to order bricks and other materials to arrive just as they are needed. If they arrived weeks before they would block up the site, tie up working capital and encourage theft. He certainly does not want them to arrive three days late, with bricklayers kept waiting.

- Specialist equipment is often hired, and to keep this a day more than necessary will increase costs and hit cash flow.

How can all of the different tasks involved in building a house be put into order so that the right goods and labour can be employed just at the right time? The answer for many businesses is to use a technique known as **critical path analysis** (CPA) (also known as network analysis).

Critical path analysis – an introduction

CPA or network analysis indicates the shortest possible time in which a project can be completed. The activities that must be completed to achieve this shortest time

make up what is known as the **critical path**. The process of using critical path analysis involves the following steps:

1 Identify the objective of the project (e.g., building a factory in six weeks).

2 Put the tasks that make up the project into the right sequence and draw a **network diagram**.

3 Add the durations of each of the activities.

4 Identify the critical path – those activities that must be finished on time in order for the project to be finished in the shortest time.

5 Use the network as a control tool when problems occur during the project.

KEY TERMS

critical path analysis: a planning technique that identifies all tasks in a project, puts them in the correct sequence and allows for the identification of the critical path

critical path: the sequence of activities that must be completed on time for the whole project to be completed by the agreed date

network diagram: the diagram used in critical path analysis that shows the logical sequence of activities and the logical dependencies between them, so the critical path can be identified

Network diagrams

A network diagram can be drawn to help identify the critical path.

Figure 33.3 is a worked example of a network diagram is for a business with the objective to install a new machine and train the employees to operate it within three weeks (assume a five-day working week).

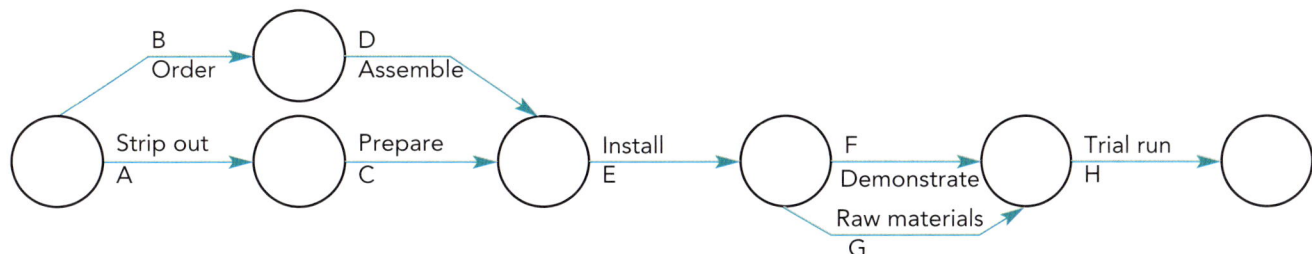

Figure 33.3: Installing a new machine – the network

A network diagram uses the following notation:

- An arrow indicates each activity or one stage of the project, which will take up time and resources.
- A node (circle) indicates the end of each activity.

The activities involved in this project and the estimated time for each activity (duration) are:

- strip out old machine (A) – three days
- order new machine and await arrival (B) – one day
- prepare site for new machine (C) – two days
- assemble new machine (D) – two days
- install new machine (E) – one week
- demonstrate to workers (F) – two days
- obtain necessary raw materials (G) – one day
- trial test run (H) – three days.

You will notice from the diagram that two activities start from the first node. This is because stripping out the old machine and ordering the new one are independent activities. They can be done simultaneously and do not have to be done in sequence.

- Clearly, this is a relatively simple project and, if these durations are added to the network diagram (Figure 33.4), it is possible to determine visually:
- which is the critical path of activities – these activities are indicated with pairs of short parallel lines
- that the project can be completed within three weeks.

It is clear that the critical activities are A, C, E, F and H. If these should be delayed in any way, for example if the preparation of the site takes more than two days, then the whole task will take longer than three weeks. It is clear that the other activities are not critical. These, in fact, may have some spare time. This is called float time. In more complex projects, this can be useful for achieving an even more efficient use of resources.

How the critical path is determined: a more complex example

The objective is to construct a house in 42 days. To create the network diagram, the tasks to be performed in order to build the house have been broken down into ten main activities, such as digging foundations and tiling the roof. These activities must be done in a certain order (e.g., the roof cannot be tiled before the walls are built) and this order of tasks is as shown in Table 33.7. The network diagram for these activities is shown in Figure 33.5.

You will notice that each of the nodes has been numbered for ease of reference. The duration times for each activity (Table 33.8) can now be added to the network diagram (Figure 33.6).

Activity	Preceding activities
A	–
B	–
C	A
D	B and C
E	A
F	E
G	F and D
H	B and C
I	G and H
J	I

Table 33.7: The order of tasks in building a house – the objective is to build a house in 42 days

These durations are very important. They allow us to calculate both the critical path and the spare time (or float time) for the non-critical activities. The critical path is indicated by calculating, at each node, the earliest start time (EST) and the latest finish time (LFT). These have already been added to the nodes in Figure 33.6.

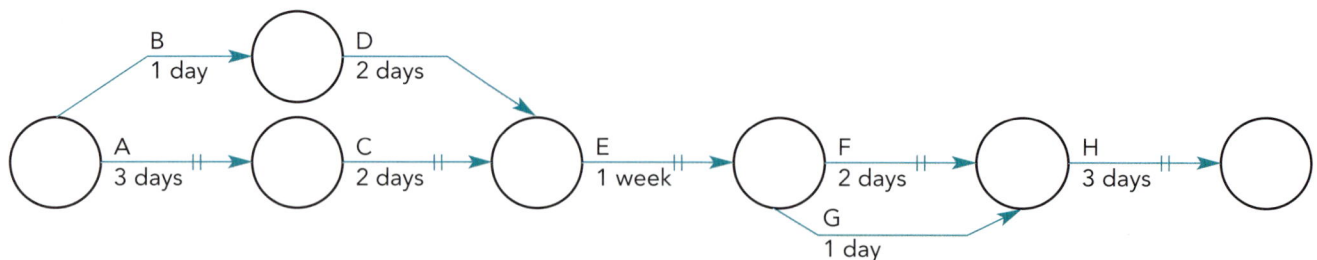

Figure 33.4: Adding durations to find the critical path

Activity	Duration (days)
A	8
B	6
C	12
D	6
E	14
F	10
G	3
H	14
I	3
J	4

Table 33.8: Duration times of the tasks involved in building a house

- **What is the earliest start time and how is it calculated?** It is the earliest time each activity can begin, taking into account all of the preceding activities. So activity E cannot start before day 8 because A will not be finished before then. And D cannot start before day 20 because both A and C have to be completed first.

- **What is the latest finish time and how is it calculated?** It is the latest time an activity can finish without delaying the whole project. So I (and all preceding activities) must be finished by day 38 or the entire project will take longer than 42 days (because four days must be allowed to finish J). Task F (and all preceding activities) must finish by day 32 or the time taken to complete G, I and J will take the total project time over 42 days.

The easiest way to calculate the LFTs is to work from right to left. The LFT at node 8 must be 42: the total project time. The duration of activity J is now subtracted from this to give 38. This is the LFT at node 7.

Where there is a choice of routes back to a node, the aim is to achieve the lowest number for LFT. The LFT for node 4 is therefore 21, achieved by working back through J, I and H, even though a higher number could be reached by working through J, I, G and D. Remember, the lowest number at each node is what is required for the LFT.

Calculating float times for non-critical activities

Look at the network diagram for building a house in Figure 33.5. Non-critical activities B, C, D and H will have float time. All of the non-critical activities, those not on the critical path, will have a certain amount of spare time. This spare time is called 'float'. There are two types of float.

Total float: the amount of time an activity can be delayed without delaying the whole project duration. This is calculated by the formula:

total float = LFT − duration − EST

Take task D as an example:

The LFT of D is 32.

The duration is 6.

The EST of D is 20 and therefore:

total float for D = 32 − 6 − 20 = 6 days

D could be delayed by up to six days without extending the total project duration or changing the critical path.

Free float: the length of time an activity can be delayed without delaying the start of the following activities. This is calculated by the formula:

free float = EST (next activity) − duration − EST (this activity)

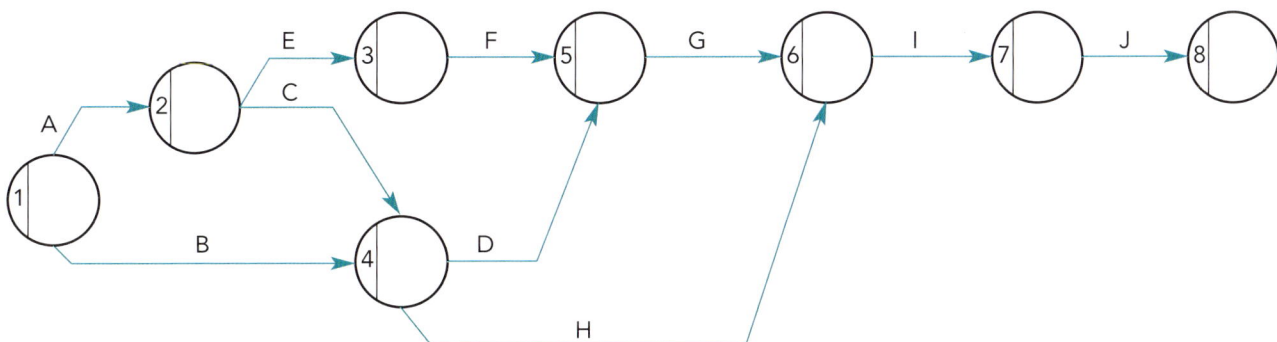

Figure 33.5: The main stages of building a house

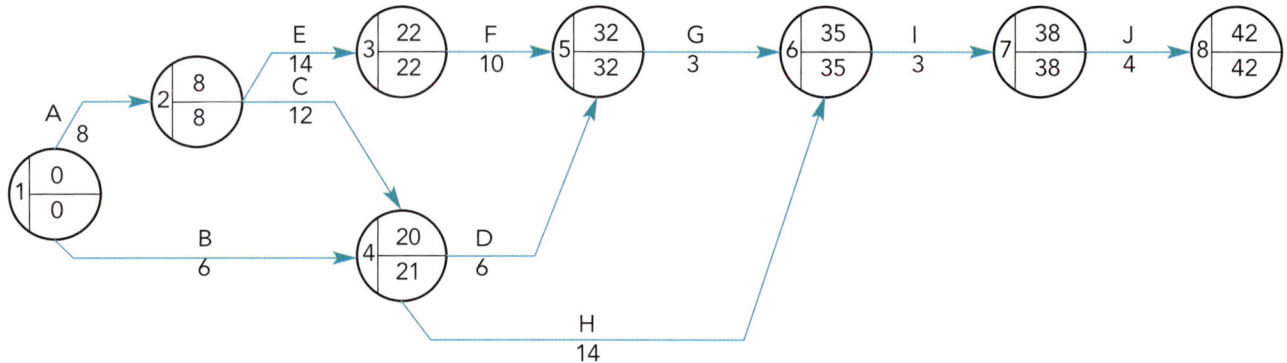

Figure 33.6: Adding in the activities and durations

Take task B as an example:

The EST of the next activity after B is 20.

The duration of B is 6.

The EST at the start of B is 0 and, therefore:

free float for B = 20 − 6 − 0 = 14

B could be delayed by 14 days without delaying the start of either H or D, the following activities (see Table 33.9).

Activity	Total float	Free float
B	15	14
C	1	0
D	6	6
H	1	1

Table 33.9: Float time for all non-critical activities

What is the critical path for this project?

Those activities that have no spare time are the critical ones. These activities are shown by those nodes where EST and LFT are equal. Take node 3 as an example. The EST of F is 22. This is the same as the LFT of E. Therefore no delay is possible: F must start on time or the whole project will overrun. Therefore, the critical path is made up of activities A, E, F, G, I and J. These will take 42 days to complete, so this becomes the project duration. Float times have significant applications in managing resources: see the advantages of critical path analysis.

The advantages of critical path analysis (CPA)

It has already been stated that network analysis can be used to assist the planning and management of complex projects. The following are some of the advantages that result from using the technique:

- Using the diagram to calculate the total project duration allows businesses to give accurate delivery dates. Customers may insist on a particular completion date and the critical time shows whether the firm can make this date or not.

- Calculating an EST for each activity allows the operations manager to order special equipment or materials needed for that task at the correct time. This ties the use of network analysis in with JIT strategies and assists in the control of cash flow and working capital.

- Calculating the LFT of each activity provides a useful control tool for the operations manager. The manager will be able to see whether the project is on schedule by checking the actual completion times of activities against the network LFT.

- Knowing the critical path can be very useful. If there is a delay on a critical activity, there is no float because it is critical and any delay will put back the whole project. This could lead to expensive damage claims from the customer. By knowing the critical path, the operations manager can see which other activities need to be speeded up if one has been delayed. For instance, in the network to build the house, if E was delayed by two days due to bad weather or non-arrival of equipment, the operations manager would know that one of the following critical activities needs to be accelerated to catch up the time lost.

- The additional resources for speeding up a critical activity could come from the non-critical ones. To use the house-building example, if F is to be reduced to eight days to counter the delay on E, the resources of labour, materials and machinery could be taken from D or H, as they both have spare time. This will allow a better and more efficient use of the firm's resources. This shows how the existence of float times on D and H allows resources to be allocated more efficiently.

- The sequential and logical structure of the diagram lends itself well to computer applications, and nearly all business applications of network analysis are now run on computer.

- The need to put all activities into sequence in order to structure the diagram forces managers to plan each project carefully by putting activities in the correct order.

- There is a huge need for rapid development of new products in today's fast-changing consumer markets. Network analysis gives design and engineering departments an advantage by showing them the tasks that can be undertaken simultaneously in developing a new product. Reducing the total time taken by the new project is based on the principle of simultaneous engineering.

> **TIP**
>
> A good way to evaluate the CPA techniques in your answers is to suggest that no planning technique, however good, can ensure that a project will reach a successful conclusion.

Critical path analysis – evaluation

CPA or network analysis is a planning and control technique that helps with project management. It cannot guarantee a successful project by itself and, as with any plan, it requires skilled and motivated employees to put it into effect.

A plan is only as good as the management behind it. If management of the project is poor, then even a good CP network diagram will not ensure success. This is particularly true when attempting to make up for lost time on a critical activity. Experienced managers will need to identify the cheapest option for using and switching resources from non-critical activities.

Workers will feel more committed to the plan of operation if they have been consulted during its construction, for example over likely duration of each activity.

When using CPA for a new project, there may be considerable guesswork involved in estimating the durations of each activity. There will be no previous experience to refer to. Although the drawing of the network and the addition of duration and float times is likely to be helped by using a computer, it can take

skilled labour hours to put a complex project on to a computer. This time and cost must be justified by the efficiency savings of applying the technique.

Gantt charts

A **Gantt chart**, frequently used in project management, is one of the most effective ways of showing activities (tasks or events) displayed over time. On the left of the chart is a list of the activities and along the top is a timescale. Each activity is represented by a bar; the position and length of the bar shows the start date, the duration of each activity and the end date of the activity. This allows managers to see quickly:

- what the main activities are
- when each activity begins and ends
- how long each activity is scheduled to last
- where activities overlap with other activities – these are simultaneous activities which can be 'done together' to save the business time in completing the project
- the start and end date of the whole project. This allows the business to inform customers when the project, such as a new building, is likely to be completed.

> **KEY TERM**
>
> **Gantt chart:** a visual representation of a project schedule in which a series of horizontal lines shows the amount of work planned in certain periods of time

A Gantt chart therefore shows managers what has to be done (the activities) and when (the schedule).

How to create a Gantt chart

- Step 1: Identify the most important activities or tasks. Gantt charts only give useful information if they include all the activities needed for a project to be completed. Then, for each task, the earliest start date and its duration must be estimated. This can be done with some accuracy if similar projects have been undertaken before, but if the project is a one-off then these estimates may prove to be inaccurate.

- Step 2: Identify relationships between the activities/tasks. Gantt charts show the relationship between the tasks in a project. Some tasks will need to be

Task name		Q1 2022				Q2 2022			Q3 2022	
	Dec. '21	Jan. '22	Feb. '22	Mar. '22	Apr. '22	May '22	Jun. '22	Jul. '22	Aug. '22
Planning		▨▨▨							
Research			▨▨						
Design				▨					
Implementation					▨▨▨▨				
Follow up								▨	

Figure 33.7: A simple Gantt chart

completed before the next one can be started and others cannot start until preceding ones have ended. For example, if a magazine is being prepared, the design must be completed before it can be sent to print.

These dependent activities are called 'sequential' or 'linear' tasks. Other tasks will be 'parallel' or simultaneous – i.e., they can be done at the same time as other tasks.
Management must identify which of the project's tasks are parallel and which are sequential. Where tasks are dependent on others, the relationship between them must be noted as this will help when management starts scheduling activities on the Gantt chart.

- Step 3: Input activities into software or a template. Gantt charts are now rarely drawn by hand and specialist software (e.g., Gantto, Matchware or Microsoft Project) is used. Some of these tools are cloud-based, meaning that the project team can access the document simultaneously, from any location. This helps greatly in discussing, optimising and reporting on a project.

Advantages of Gantt charts

When a Gantt chart is created, it is necessary to think through all of the tasks required in the project. As part of this process managers will:

- assign responsibility for each task
- work out the duration of each task
- assess potential problems.

This kind of detailed planning helps ensure that the schedule is actually achievable, that the right people are given responsibility for each task, and that the impact of potential problems or delays is understood and can be planned for.

Gantt charts enable managers to schedule projects to achieve the best possible completion date. They allow managers to review all necessary tasks and the most efficient order for successful completion. Managers can also use the charts to recognise the route of the critical path. The critical path is the sequence of tasks that must be completed on time if the entire project is to be finished on schedule.

Finally, Gantt charts can be used to keep employees and customers informed of the day-to-day developments. The chart can be updated at any point to show changes in the schedule and their implications. They can also be used to communicate when key tasks have been completed.

Gantt charts – an evaluation

Although widely used as a planning tool, Gantt charts have potential limitations:

- For projects that require many tasks, the Gantt chart may become very complex and difficult to interpret.
- A Gantt chart also requires frequent updates during the project if some activities are completed later than expected.
- The 'work breakdown structure' – the list of activities and their interrelationships – has to be complete and accurate otherwise the Gantt chart will have limited value. If an activity is left out or a duration is poorly estimated then the Gantt chart will have to be redrawn.
- Finally, Gantt charts do not offer a good solution when dealing with the triple constraints of time, cost and scope. The cost of a project is not depicted on a Gantt chart, nor the full scope of a project. No matter how detailed the Gantt chart is, the full complexity is not depicted. This is because the main focus of the Gantt chart is time.

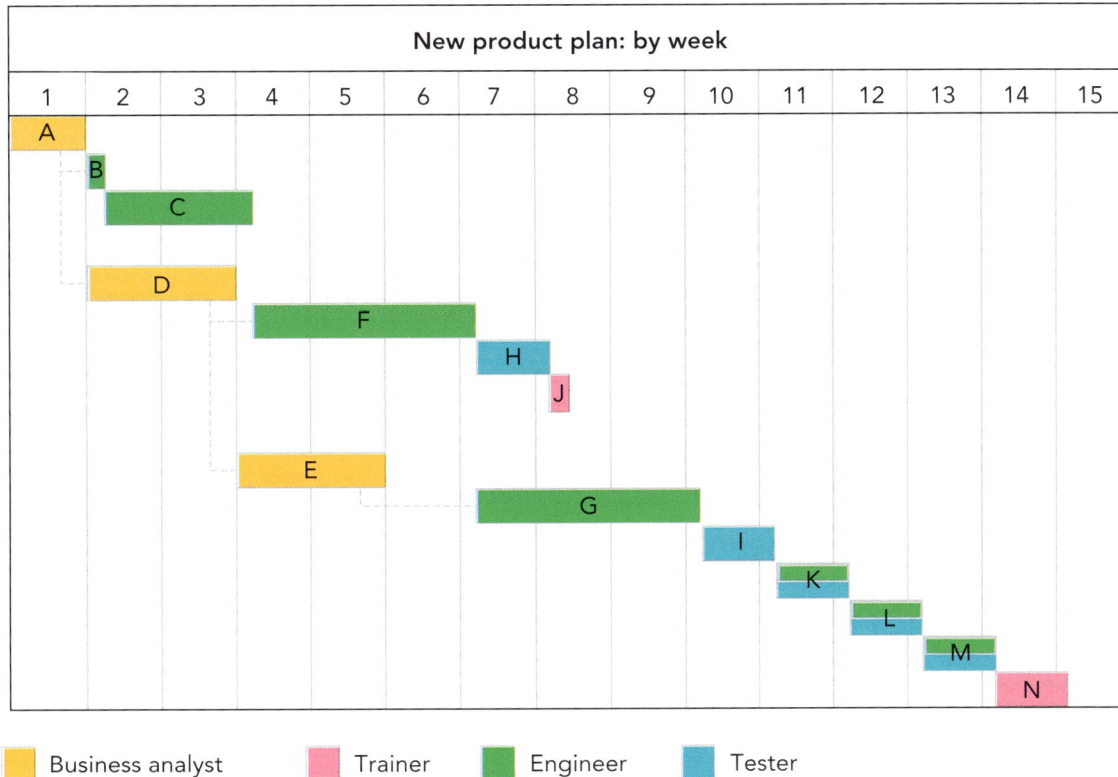

Figure 33.8: Gantt chart showing parallel and sequential activities

SELF-EVALUATION CHECKLIST

After studying this chapter, complete this table.

I am able to apply and analyse:	Needs more work	Almost there	Ready to move on
the local and global supply chain process (AO2)			
I am able to analyse, apply and use:			
stock control charts based on the following:			
• lead time • buffer stock • re-order level • re-order quantity (AO2 and AO4)			
capacity utilisation rate (AO2 and AO4)			
defect rate (AO2 and AO4)			
labour productivity, capital productivity, productivity rate, operating leverage (AO2 and AO4)			

CONTINUED

I am able to apply and analyse:	Needs more work	Almost there	Ready to move on
I am able to synthesise and evaluate:			
the difference between JIT and just-in-case (JIC) (AO3)			
I am able to synthesise and evaluate, use and apply:			
cost to buy (CTB) (AO3 and AO4)			
cost to make (CTM) (AO3 and AO4)			
I am able to select and apply the following business management tools:			
• make or buy analysis • contribution costing • absorption costing • critical path analysis • Gantt charts			

REFLECTION

Which aspect of production planning is likely to be of most importance to the success of an automobile manufacturing business? Be prepared to explain and defend your answer in presenting your ideas to the class.

PROJECT

Does money and prestige increase labour productivity?

Having complained about long working hours, first-year investment bank analysts at Goldman Sachs will get a pay rise in 2021 from $86 000 to $110 000.

But not everyone is sympathetic. Xavier Rolet believes the younger generation of bankers should stop complaining about long working hours or find another job. Early in his career Mr Rolet worked at Goldman Sachs in New York and in London. He says that he would regularly work 130 hours a week, seven days a week in the 1980s. He claimed: 'We'd work the whole New York trading day in the office, have dinner on the desk then trade Asia and Tokyo from 8.00 p.m. until 10.00 p.m., go home during the half-day recess and trade the Tokyo afternoon session from home from 12.00 p.m. to 2.00 a.m. We'd then grab some shut-eye until 4.00 a.m. Then it was back to the office to put our orders in time for the European markets to open.'

In 2021, some of the young Goldman Sachs bankers complained about 95-hour working weeks. They asked for their working week to be capped at 80 hours. Not only did they complain about sleep deprivation, they said that the treatment by senior bankers and the mental and physical stress were not tolerable. One young banker said, 'this is beyond the level of hard-working and is verging on abuse.' Earlier in 2021, the young Goldman Sachs bankers

CONTINUED

warned that if conditions did not improve they would have to leave.

1   In pairs or as a group, research what it is like to work in an investment bank like Goldman Sachs.

2   Produce a 5–10-minute video presentation on the advantages and disadvantages of using pay to increase labour productivity.

Thinking about your project:

•   How well have you understood the ideas you covered in your video?

•   How would you rate your group's video compared to those of other groups in your class?

•   How could you improve your video?

EXAM-STYLE QUESTIONS

Svoboda Ltd takes over Blue Ltd

Svoboda Ltd has just taken over a glass-making business called Blue Ltd on the outskirts of Prague. The business had gone into administration and Svoboda bought it at a very low price. However, Blue Ltd had significant operational problems and it needed plenty of structural changes to the way it operated.

Anton and Anna Novák are the brother and sister who own and manage Svoboda. Anton is the CEO and Anna is the operations director. Anna and Anton believe there are real strengths in Blue Ltd's brand name in the glass market, but the business has suffered from poor management for a number of years. Anna has identified the following operational problems at the glass-making business:

•   the business carries too much stock

•   employee motivation levels are low

•   labour productivity has been falling for three years

•   the business is operating at 62% capacity utilisation, which is well below the industry average.

•   the number of returns of faulty products has increased by 20% this year.

Anton and Anna want to introduce TQM and JIT as operational methods to turn the business around. They believe they can achieve the same level of output by making 20% of the current workforce redundant, and this would increase productivity. They plan to pay the remaining workers 20% higher wages to increase employee motivation. Anton feels that more effective marketing should increase capacity utilisation.

1   Define the term 'capacity utilisation'.   [2]

2   Outline **two** factors that might limit capacity utilisation at Blue limited.   [4]

3   Blue Ltd has a maximum output level a year of 900 000 units. Calculate the current output of the business.   [2]

4   Outline how improved marketing by Blue Ltd might increase capacity utilisation.   [4]

5   Explain what falling labour productivity at Blue Ltd means.   [4]

6   Define the term labour productivity.   [2]

7   State how labour productivity is measured.   [1]

8   Explain how making 20% of the staff redundant might increase Blue Ltd's labour productivity.   [4]

9   Explain **two** disadvantages of Blue Ltd carrying too much stock.   [4]

10   Evaluate the proposals Anton and Anna have put together to improve Blue Ltd's operational efficiency. [10]

> Chapter 34

Crisis management and contingency planning

LEARNING OBJECTIVES

On completing this chapter you should be able to:

Apply and analyse:

> The difference between crisis management and contingency planning (AO2)

> The factors that affect effective crisis management: Transparency; Communication; Speed; Control (AO2)

Synthesise and evaluate:

> The impact of contingency planning for a given organisations or situation in terms of: Cost; Time; Risks; Safety (AO3)

BUSINESS IN CONTEXT

Southwest Airlines' first in-flight fatality

On 17 April 2018, Southwest Airlines' Flight 1380 took off from LaGuardia airport in New York. It was forced to make an emergency landing in Philadelphia after an engine exploded and ripped open the fuselage (the main body of the aircraft). One passenger was killed. Other passengers were able to film their experience, bringing the real fear of being in trouble in the air to those on the ground.

Further crisis was avoided thanks to the well-trained air crew landing the aircraft safely without any other fatalities or serious injuries. While that was happening, CEO Gary Kelly and his team started responding to the crisis.

They made sure that passengers in Philadelphia had everything they needed. This included travel and accommodation arrangements and trauma counselling. Southwest Airlines also started investigating the cause of the incident immediately.

Southwest's employees had clear guidelines and checklists allowing them to respond to and manage the crisis speedily and effectively. In the two days following the fatal accident, Southwest took the following action:

- Kelly made a sincere and concise statement to the passengers and their families.

- All advertising on social media was suspended.

- Passengers staying in Philadelphia hotels had notes slipped under their doors reminding them that support was available 24/7.

- All passengers received personal phone calls and emails offering support and counselling.

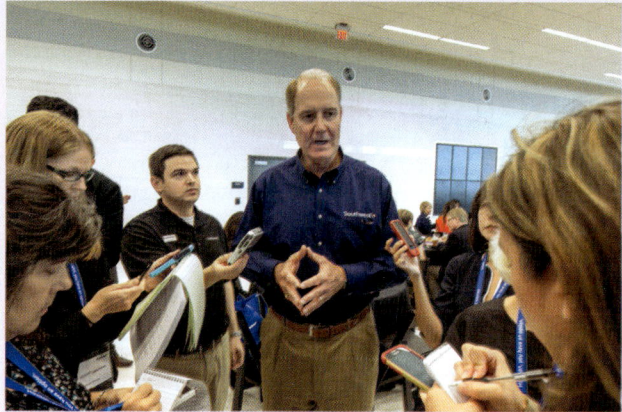

Gary Kelly, CEO of Southwest Airlines, managed the crisis well

- They were also sent $5000 to help ease the burden of any immediate costs and a $1000 Southwest travel voucher.

- Southwest's social media team kept monitoring online sites for real-time information to find out exactly what people were saying, posting and expressing.

The media responded positively to Southwest's actions with many news reports praising the bravery of the pilot, the calm authority of the cabin crew and the response of the CEO. The accident turned out to be a public relations success for the company.

Discuss in pairs or in a group:

- Is this crisis an example of a situation that could have been planned for?

- To what extent is it important that senior managers take a leading role in communicating the response of a business to a major crisis?

KEY CONCEPT LINK

Change

Managing change is a vital part of business management. Sometimes the change is brought about by the business itself, such as the opening of a new factory or the launching of a new product. But often businesses have to manage results of an event that dramatically changes the business environment. For example, the Covid-19 pandemic brought a market shock to travel companies, restaurants, concert venues, etc. that was incredibly difficult to deal with.

34.1 Crisis management and contingency planning

Contingency planning is also known as 'business continuity planning' or 'disaster-recovery planning', which perhaps gives a better idea of what it is for. Unplanned events can have a devastating effect on businesses of any size. Crises such as pandemics, fire, floods, damage to stocks , illness of key staff, IT system failure or accidents on the business's premises or involving its vehicles could all make it difficult or impossible to continue operating. At worst, important customers could be lost to competitors. Contingency planning helps with **crisis management** by enabling an organisation to prepare with a series of procedures to be put into effect if an emergency occurs. In this way the organisation will be better able to manage most negative situations when they occur.

KEY TERMS

contingency planning: preparing the immediate steps to be taken by an organisation in the event of a crisis or emergency

crisis management: steps taken by an organisation to limit the damage from a significant, damaging event by handling, containing and resolving it

ACTIVITY 34.1

'If you do not have a contingency plan or never perform risk analysis and mitigation activities it is like not having insurance.'

In pairs or as a group discuss the extent to which this statement is true.

Contingency planning and crisis management are not conflicting ideas but instead work in tandem. Contingency planning is the process of preparing for potential emergencies, while crisis management is the overall management of emergencies when they do occur. Smart and diligent contingency planning is an important aspect of crisis management because it ensures that individuals and organisations make the necessary preparations to be ready when serious problems arise.

ACTIVITY 34.2

In pairs or as group, investigate a crisis management situation that your school or another school has been in. Consider the following:

- the issues raised by the crisis

- how the school dealt with the crisis

- how effectively the school managed the crisis

- any future lessons for the school in terms crisis management.

34.2 Effective crisis management

A crisis is something which poses a genuine threat to the reputation or even survival of the organisation. This could be anything from an employee who has behaved inappropriately, to an accident that closed the business down temporarily. It might be that a customer is unhappy with how the organisation has behaved and used the media, often social media, to tell as many others as possible about their experience. Often, it is when a bad news story about an organisation becomes public that it becomes a real crisis.

THEORY OF KNOWLEDGE

Faith

Consider the following IT problems that different businesses experienced:

- RBS Group bank outages: RBS customers were affected by the technical glitch, which left 600 000 people without their wages or other payments.

- Nest thermostat glitch: the smart thermostat company, owned by Google, had a software update that went wrong and drained the batteries of all thermostats, leaving customers without heating or hot water in the middle of winter.

CONTINUED

- Co-op charges double: the Co-op supermarket chain had a one-off issue with software that meant customers ended up paying twice for their goods.

- Amazon 1p hiccup: during the busiest shopping season of the year, some products on Amazon's site ended up being sold for just 1p for a whole hour.

In pairs or as a group discuss the question: To what extent does our belief in IT systems functioning effectively mean we are always susceptible to a crisis?

The power of the media, particularly social media, means that news spreads quickly – especially bad news. Whatever the crisis, managing it effectively is crucial to minimising damage to the organisation.

Effective crisis management depends on the following factors.

Transparency

This means being honest and open about the crisis, its causes and consequences – and what the organisation intends to do in response to it. Keeping back any information or trying to manipulate it to the benefit of the business will almost always backfire and lead to an even more negative reaction than if the truth was communicated in the first instance.

Communication

The way the organisation communicates during a crisis can make the difference between the crisis escalating out of control and it being a minor setback. It is important to gain control of communications in a crisis by being proactive. If there is public interest in the crisis, then information needs to be given clearly, fully and promptly. If this is not done, the media will write their own stories and rumours will spread, especially through social media. The aim of successful crisis communications is to show that the organisation is:

- going about its normal work
- controlling and responding to the crisis
- retaining the support of the media, employees and customers, who matter most.

Mishandling crisis communications can make the whole situation much worse. If the message or media used is wrong, or the organisation appears to be in chaos, this reflects badly on the organisation and it makes another negative story for the media.

Speed

It is sometimes called the golden hour. This refers to how much time there is to respond to a crisis or incident before it is reported in the media. The time taken for events to become widely known has been greatly reduced by digital and social media. Eyewitness accounts of events or rumours about incidents appear on Twitter and other platforms at a speed once unimaginable.

The advice from Jane Jordan-Meier, author of *The Four Stages of Highly Effective Crisis Management: How to Manage the Media in the Digital Age* is: crisis management and communication plans are irresponsible or worse unless they include digital and social media. News used to be released by radio scanners, which pick up police and other emergency services messages. Twitter is now the 'scanner' of the 21st century. Twitter breaks the news and adds instant updates.

The impact of Twitter, Facebook, Instagram and LinkedIn cannot be overstated. A share price can drop quickly thanks to Twitter, which not only breaks news and gives updates but is also full of rumours and misconceptions. The share price in Qantas plummeted when it was thought an airliner had crashed in Indonesia. Once the airline communicated the facts about an engine failure, however, its share price recovered.

Speedy and careful monitoring can stop a hot issue in its tracks before it explodes into a crisis. Such rumour management is critical and can be established through something as simple as a Google Alert. Establishing listening posts to monitor social media messages also helps to record the existence and location of likely friends and potential enemies.

Jordan-Meier says that for every $1 spent on this careful preparation before a crisis, $9 is saved in the response.

Control

Keeping control of the crisis and not being swept along by events helps to present an image of calm and confidence. This will help to restore the image of the organisation once the crisis has passed. The chance of keeping control of a crisis situation will be helped greatly by having prepared a contingency plan and using this in rehearsals of potential crisis situations.

CASE STUDY 34.1

PR problem for The North Face

The North Face is an American outdoor recreation company that specialises in outdoor clothing, footwear and related equipment.

It is well known in digital marketing that getting to the top of the page on Google searches is a real advantage to a business. In 2019, a marketing agency for The North Face revealed that in order to do just that, it had covertly replaced Wikipedia photos of popular places with its own shots. They showed people wearing North Face products in the destinations. Within hours, Wikipedia's army of editors noticed. They changed the images back and told Wikipedia. It did not take long for the information to go viral on the internet and it became a PR crisis for The North Face who quickly apologised.

1   Define the term 'crisis management'.   [2]

2   Outline **two** elements of crisis management that The North Face could have used when the incident with Wikipedia went viral.   [4]

3   Explain **two** advantages to The North Face of effective crisis management.   [4]

One aspect of 'control' is for the organisation to start a media log. This should have details of all the newspapers and other media that have contacted the organisation, what information was sent and when they are expected to get back to you. If there is more than one individual on the crisis coordination team it should be clear who the media should contact and who has responsibility for each aspect of managing the crisis. Dealing with a crisis should be the responsibility of the most senior manager available. This is not a task that should be delegated as this makes it look like the senior management team do not care about the crisis or its consequences.

Finally, perhaps the crisis management advice of Lanny Davis, an adviser to former US president Bill Clinton, is relevant to all senior managers when faced with a disaster situation:

'Tell it Early, Tell it All, Tell it Yourself.'

34.3 The impact of contingency planning

Effective contingency planning allows a business to take steps to minimise the potential impact of a disaster and ideally prevent it from happening in the first place. The key steps to take in developing contingency plans are:

1   **Identify the potential disasters** that could affect the business. Some of these are common to all businesses, but others will be specific to certain industries. For example, the oil industry must plan for oil tankers sinking, explosions at refineries and leaks in oil and gas pipelines.

2   **Assess the likelihood of these occurring.** Some incidents are more likely to occur than others and the degree of impact on business operations varies too. It seems obvious to plan for the most 'common' disasters, but the most unlikely occurrences can have the greatest total risk to a business's future. These issues need to be balanced carefully by managers when choosing which disaster events to prepare for most thoroughly.

3   **Minimise the potential impact of crises.** Effective planning can sometimes remove a potential risk altogether. When this is not possible, the key is to minimise the damage a disaster can do. This does not just mean protecting fixed assets and people, but also the company's reputation and public goodwill, as far as possible. This is often best achieved by the publicity department telling the truth, indicating the causes when known

and giving full details of how to contact the business and the actions being taken to minimise the impact on the public. Staff training and practice drills with mock incidents are often the most effective ways of preparing to minimise negative impact.

4   **Plan for continued operations of the business.** Prior planning can help with alternative accommodation and IT data – the sooner the business can begin trading again, the less the impact is likely to be on customer relations.

Table 34.1 analyses the potential positive and negative impacts of contingency planning.

LEARNER PROFILE

Balanced

You are the owner of medium-sized trading business. Your cash flow is always tight and you need customers to pay on time so that you can pay your own debts. Any cash flow problem you have could lead to bankruptcy if it lasts for more than one month.

You walk into the office and all of your staff are upset and arguing. One of the business's largest customers has gone bankrupt and cannot pay the $500 000 debt they owe. If you cannot raise the $500 000 your business will also go bankrupt. The uproar in the office is making it hard for you to think of a crisis management strategy.

Discuss in pairs or with your class the importance of being calm and balanced when dealing with crisis situations.

ACTIVITY 34.3

In pairs or as a group, research a crisis management situation involving a business and produce a presentation on the crisis that answers the question: What is the best way for a business to deal with a crisis?

Advantages	Disadvantages
Reassures employees, customers and local residents that concerns for safety are a priority. Minimises negative impact on customers and suppliers in the event of a major disaster, and this can reduce the costs of recovering from a major incident. The time taken to respond to disasters or crises will be greatly reduced as training and practice sessions have been undertaken by employees. Promotes a culture of preparedness within the organisation and reduces the risks of accidents causing serious damage or injuries. By reducing risks of incidents occurring and minimising the dangers that might result, a culture of safety as a priority is encouraged in the organisation. The public relations response is more likely to be speedy, transparent and appropriate, especially if senior managers are used to communicate what the company intends to do, by when and how.	Costs of the planning process and the need to train employees and undertake practice drills of what to do in the event of a range of crises occurring, will add to business costs. This may discourage small businesses in particular not to commit resources to contingency planning. It needs to be updated constantly as the number and range of potential disasters can change, and this adds to the management time that needs to be devoted to contingency planning. If the planning is a reactive process (responding to negative events) and not a proactive one (reducing the likelihood of these events occurring) then the risk reduction of contingency planning will be much less. Contingency planning for disasters is often still more focused on safety issues than on planning for what to do if they occur.

Table 34.1: The impact of contingency planning

CASE STUDY 34.2

Contingency planning by the Royal Sol hotel

Tourists have been evacuated from beaches in south-western Turkey, where raging wildfires are now threatening hotels and homes. Turkish Coastguard vessels were deployed to bring holidaymakers to safety, according to local media. The Turkish fire service have been battling almost 100 separate blazes in resorts and villages on Turkey's Mediterranean and Aegean coasts – a major tourist region. The Royal Sol is a four-star hotel that has been evacuated because of the fire. The manager of the Royal Sol, Ayeleen Acar, has put the business's contingency plan into operation. She fears that the hotel could be shut for several weeks and will lose revenue as a result of this. She is also worried about future bookings because consumers are concerned about a similar incident happening next year.

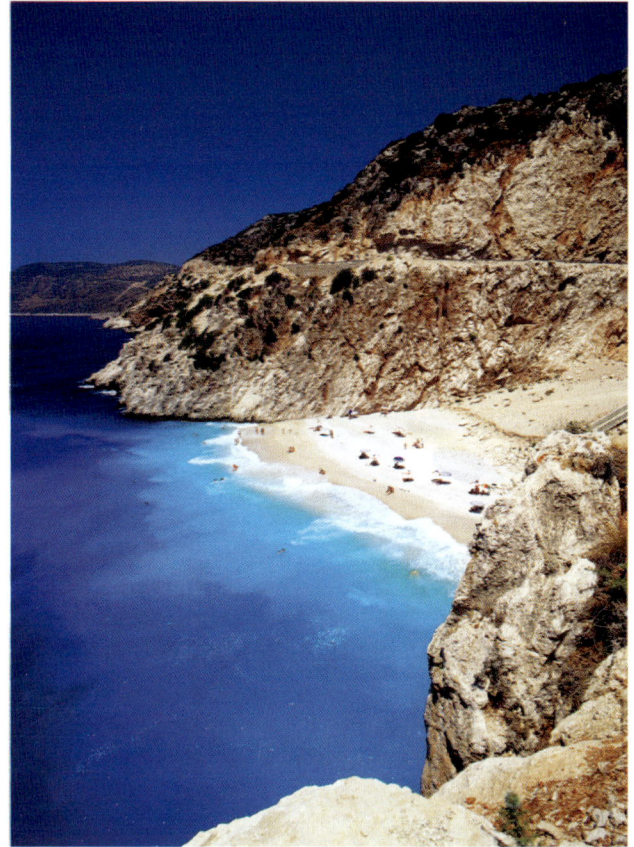

1   Outline **two** elements of a contingency plan. [4]

2   Explain **two** advantages to the Royal Sol hotel of contingency planning. [4]

3   Explain **two** difficulties for the Royal Sol hotel of enacting a contingency plan. [4]

SELF-EVALUATION CHECKLIST

After studying this chapter, complete this table.

I am able to apply and analyse:	Needs more work	Almost there	Ready to move on
the difference between crisis management and contingency planning (AO2)			
the factors that affect effective crisis management: • transparency • communication • speed • control (AO2)			

CONTINUED

After studying this chapter, complete this table.

I am able to synthesise and evaluate:	Needs more work	Almost there	Ready to move on
the impact of contingency planning for a given organisations or situation in terms of:			
• cost			
• time			
• risks			
• safety (AO3)			

REFLECTION

How would you advise a senior manager to use social media following a major disaster within their business, such as a fire?

PROJECT

Crisis in the airline industry

When an airline takes a plane out of use it gets sent to a 'boneyard'. This is a storage facility where unused planes are kept outdoors in a giant parking lot. Europe's largest 'boneyard' is an airfield in Teruel, Spain. Many planes are here in short-term storage waiting for maintenance work and to be sold to a new airline.

The Covid-19 pandemic has had a big impact. In a few short weeks the Teruel storage facility was completely full, as airlines cancelled flights due to the dramatic fall in air travel. By late March 2020, one of the world's biggest and fastest-growing industries was collapsing as airlines grounded their fleets due to the pandemic. The mood amongst everyone in the airline business was bad. To many, it felt like a tragedy.

In pairs or as a group, produce a presentation on the effect of the Covid-19 pandemic on the airline industry. In your presentation cover the following elements:

- how different stakeholders in the airline industry were affected

- how different airlines responded to the crisis

- the future of the airline industry.

Thinking about your project:

- Do you feel your understanding of crisis management has improved?

- How good was your presentation compared to those of the other groups in the class?

- How could you improve your presentation?

EXAM-STYLE QUESTIONS

VW's emission crisis

In an effort to sell diesel cars in the USA, VW launched a huge marketing campaign proclaiming the low emissions of its cars. But in September 2015 the US Environmental Protection Agency (EPA) found that many VW cars being sold in America had a so-called 'defeat device' in their diesel engines. The device could detect when a test was being carried out, and it changed the performance in order to improve results.

That was the start of the Volkswagen vehicle emissions crisis. The EPA's findings covered 482 000 cars in the USA alone. Affected vehicles included the VW Golf, Passet, Jetta and Beetle models as well as the VW-manufactured Audi A3, but the company admitted that the device had been fitted in approximately 11 million cars worldwide, including eight million in Europe.

Early in 2016 VW started recalling millions of cars worldwide. It set aside €6.7 billion to cover costs, which resulted in the company posting its first quarterly loss for 15 years, amounting to €2.5 billion.

VW America boss Michael Horn said, 'We've totally screwed up.' Martin Winterkorn, the group's chief executive at the time, said his company had 'broken the trust of our customers and the public'. Mr Winterkorn resigned following the scandal, replaced by the former boss of Porsche, Matthias Mueller.

1	Define the term 'contingency plan'.	[2]
2	Outline **two** reasons why crisis management is important.	[2]
3	List factors that affect effective crisis management at Volkswagen.	[2]
4	Outline **two** factors that affect effective contingency planning at Volkswagen.	[4]
5	Explain why transparency is important in contingency planning.	[4]
6	Explain why public relations is important in crisis management.	[4]
7	Outline **two** ways Volkswagen has tried to minimise the impact of the crisis.	[4]
8	Explain why speed and honesty might be important for Volkswagen in deal with the crisis.	[4]
9	Explain why managing risk is important for Volkswagen in producing a contingency plan.	[4]
10	Evaluate the view that an effective contingency planning was critical for Volkswagen in dealing with emissions crisis.	[10]

Chapter 35

Research and development

Higher-level

LEARNING OBJECTIVES

On completing this chapter you should be able to:

Apply and analyse:

> The importance of developing goods and services that address customers' unmet needs (of which the customers may or may not be aware) (AO2)

> Intellectual property protection: copyrights, patents, trademarks (AO2)

> Incremental innovation, innovation and disruptive innovation (AO2)

Synthesise and evaluate:

> The importance of research and development for a business (AO3)

BUSINESS IN CONTEXT

Alphabet invests most on research and development (R&D)

Alphabet, the parent company of Google, spent the most money – €23 billion – on **research and development** in 2019, according to the 2020 'EU Industrial R&D Investment Report'. This report found that R&D in the ICT, health and automotive industries increased for the tenth year in succession.

Europe-based companies increased research and development in 2019 by 5.6%. In the same year, USA-based companies increased their R&D investment by 10%.

Alphabet, which has its headquarters in Mountain View, California, has been the biggest spender in monetary terms on R&D since 2017, according to the European Commission. In 2019, Alphabet reported a third-quarter profit of $11.25 billion, which compared with a profit of $7.07 billion for the 12 months before. Revenue rose 14% to $46.17 billion.

When commenting on the financial result, Alphabet CEO Sundar Pichai said it was 'a testament to the deep investments we've made in artificial intelligence and other technologies, to deliver services that people turn to for help, in moments big and small.' Along with other computer and internet service-based businesses, Alphabet increased its revenue substantially during the global Covid-19 pandemic. The business continues to invest increasing amounts in R&D on developments that improve the interconnectedness of the world to improve, for example, the 'work from home' experience.

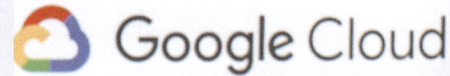

Alphabet CEO Sundar Pichai

The company's biggest revenues streams are: YouTube, Google Cloud and Google Play Store.

Discuss in pairs or a group:

- Why do you think the CEO of Alphabet believes that increased revenue and profit result from increased investment in R&D?

- Do you think all R&D spending will lead to higher profits? Explain your answer.

KEY TERM

research and development (R&D): scientific innovations and their technical improvement to create new products and processes

KEY CONCEPT LINK

Sustainability

A new development in office space is mobile, solar-powered, co-working offices. The Nova Pod has been developed by Cape Town-based Work & Co.

The pods can house up to six people and offer solar-generated electricity, Wi-Fi, bathrooms, fridges, charging stations and smart TVs – all powered by solar-generated electricity.

35.1 The importance of research and development

In most industries, change is the only constant. Change can result in new products or new ways of making existing products. Some industries are more likely to undergo substantial changes brought about by new technologies and new adaptations of existing technologies. The IT, computer and mobile-phone markets are experiencing more **innovation** than most. How do businesses benefit from introducing radical new products and processes, and what factors influence the range and pace of innovation?

KEY TERM

innovation: the practical application of new inventions into marketable products

Spending on research and development (R&D) is growing globally and in most industrial sectors.

LEARNER PROFILE

Thinkers

Five whys analysis

If someone is being questioned by a young child, they know what the 'Whys' sound like. Any answer to a question, is followed by an increasingly urgent series of 'Why? Why? Why? Why? Why?'

'Whys analysis' was created by Taiichi Ohno at Toyota, and the '5 Whys analysis' was made popular at the Japanese car manufacturer as a standard 'brainstorming' process to generate new ideas. This approach could then be used as a platform for R&D by a business.

The technique encourages an open dialogue that can trigger new ideas about a problem, whether done individually or with a group. Each 'why' leads on from the answer to the previous 'why'.

In pairs or as a group, discuss the importance of 'thinking' as part of the research and development process.

ACTIVITY 35.1

1 Form a brainstorming group in your class to answer the following question: What new innovation could help my learning at school?

2 As a group come up a with a potential product that could enhance student learning at school. Think about the process and the challenges it poses.

3 Prepare a presentation on your brainstormed idea for a product to help student learning.

The benefits of successful R&D spending to business include:

- **Competitive advantage** over competitors which enables them to increase sales at a faster rate than rivals, e.g., Dyson has become one of the world's leading vacuum-cleaner manufacturers in 20 years as a result of its 'dual cyclone' technology.

- It can create **intellectual property rights** for a business and these can become valuable assets which yield income for many years, such as patents (see section 35.3).

- **Customer loyalty** – Microsoft's continuous development and improvement programme for its computer-operating systems help to keep customers loyal to the brand even though competitors are growing in number.

- **High, premium prices** – being first into a market with an innovative product can allow high prices to be charged, e.g., the Hyundai Nexo is one of the first hydrogen-powered cars available for consumers to buy and it is sold in relatively small numbers at a premium price.

- **Publicity** – Apple receives free worldwide publicity for each new innovative product it releases; senior managers invite the world's media to huge launch events.

- **Lower costs** – Zara has revolutionised the process of designing, producing and marketing the latest fashions. It is able to design, manufacture, transport and retail new clothes more quickly than any other fashion businesses and this gives it substantial cost savings through supply chain management, data tracking and stock control.

So, the benefits gained from successful R&D spending can be considerable. Why else would Volkswagen, for example, be spending over $1.9 million an hour on developing new products and processes? The companies with the largest R&D budgets in 2020 are shown in Table 35.1. Despite the global downturn between 2020 and 2021, most business analysts claimed that innovation was still critical in preparing companies for the economic upturn. An economic downturn is often the best time to build advantage over competitors with R&D spending, especially weaker ones that may have to reduce their own investment on R&D for financial reasons.

Company	Industry	R&D spend ($ billion)
Amazon	Internet retail	42.7
Alphabet	Internet/technology	27.6
Huawei	Communications	21.7
Apple	Consumer electronics	19.4
Samsung	Consumer electronics	19.4
Microsoft	Technology software	19.3
Facebook	Social media	18.4
VW	Vehicles	16.9
Merck	Pharmaceuticals	13.6
Intel	Semiconductors	13.6

Table 35.1: Top global R&D spenders in 2020

TIP

Never confuse research and development (scientific research and technical development) with market research.

CASE STUDY 35.1

Research and development spending in the tech sector

These are three leading R&D companies in the global tech sector:

- Samsung (R&D spending: $19.4 billion). Samsung has R&D centres in 12 countries around the world which help the company to find new ways to captivate users. One of its leading products, the Galaxy smartphone, was a major success partly because of innovations like an intelligent7 camera and up to 1 TB of storage.

- Microsoft (R&D Spending: $19.3 billion). Microsoft is one of the leading innovation companies in the world. It has a research subsidiary which specialises in developing new products and employs over 100 people. On top of this, Microsoft owns research centres all over the world. Microsoft's research focuses on activities such as machine learning, data mining, linguistics and social networking.

- Huawei (R&D Spending: $21.7 billion). Huawei dominates the global market for mobile phones and the development of wireless networks. The company focuses its research funds in creating superfast 5G networks. Huawei is also investing significantly in the technology needed to support the introduction of self-driving cars.

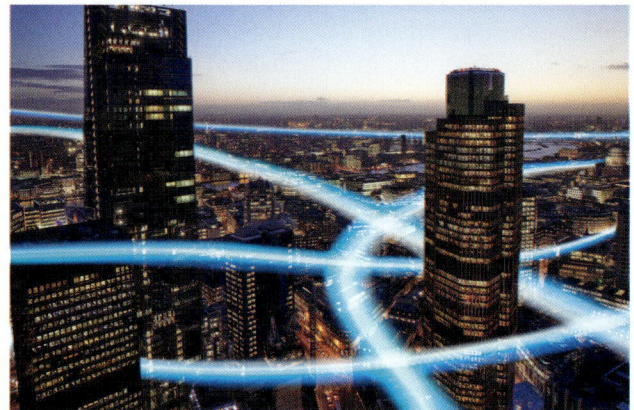

1 Define the term 'innovation'. [2]

2 Outline an example of R&D that each of the tech companies in the example are involved in. [4]

3 Explain **two** reasons why R&D is important to the companies listed here. [4]

Research and development – limitations

Although R&D spending has the potential to provide a competitive advantage, it may also have limitations:

- R&D **does not always lead to an invention or discovery**. Billions of dollars have been spent by pharmaceutical companies to develop a cure for the common cold – so far they have all failed.

- R&D is **expensive and has an opportunity cost**. Would the money spent on R&D be more wisely invested in marketing existing products more intensively?

- Inventions **do not always lead to successful innovative products**. Examples of product failures after extensive R&D spending include Crystal Pepsi, yoghurt shampoo, New Coke and disposable paper clothing.

- **Competitors' R&D spending** may result in even more successful products. Toshiba lost millions of dollars that it had invested in HD-DVD technology when it was knocked out of the market by Sony's Blu-ray system.

- **Ethical issues** can sometimes outweigh the potential commercial benefits. Many consumers still reject genetically modified (GM) food crops, and there is no certainty that big GM R&D spenders such as DuPont will receive a return on their investments.

- **Nature of the business** – R&D spending will either be of limited value or beyond the resources of many businesses largely because of their size and the nature of the market they operate in. If the market is not subject to significant change and the focus is on traditional job production techniques or high levels of consumer service, then R&D spending would be ineffective and would take resources from more important sections of the business.

KEY TERM

invention: the discovery of new ideas for products or processes

THEORY OF KNOWLEDGE

The critical piece of R&D – developing the Oxford-AstraZeneca vaccine

The development of the Oxford-AstraZeneca vaccine was one of the most significant pieces of research and development of the last 100 years. The team that developed the vaccine used a new method of vaccine design. The central piece of their plan was a revolutionary style of vaccine known as 'plug and play'. It has two highly desirable traits when facing the unknown – it is both fast and flexible. Conventional vaccines – including the whole of the childhood immunisation programme – use a killed or weakened form of the original infection and inject fragments of it into the body. But these vaccines are slow to develop. The world needed something much faster.

The Oxford scientists took a common cold virus that infected chimpanzees and engineered it to become the building block of a vaccine against almost anything. The virus from chimps is genetically modified so it cannot cause an infection in people. It can then be modified again to contain the genetic blueprints for whatever you want to train the immune system to attack. This target is known is an antigen. ChAdOx1 is in essence a sophisticated, microscopic postman. All the scientists have to do is change the package to suit the virus that was challenging them. And it worked.

In pairs or in groups, discuss the following questions:

- What is the relationship between imagination and reason in bringing about innovation?

- To what extent is the claim that the Oxford-AstraZeneca vaccine is one of the most significant pieces of research and development of the last 100 years true?

35.2 Unmet needs

Customers have needs that are unmet by the existing goods and services available on the market. Businesses can find out about these unmet needs by using market research. If research established that some consumers would like to be able to purchase tablet computers with larger screens, then manufacturers could respond to this unmet need by developing new products – probably by adapting existing tablets in this case.

Some innovations are so different and original that customers may not even be able to perceive that they could exist before they are marketed. If they prove to be sales successes, then these customers were not even aware of these unmet needs! Light-emitting diode (LED) lighting was a radical product development. These lights use less power and last longer, even when compared to low-energy bulbs. But consumers may not have been aware of their needs for such lighting before they were released on the market. The sales success of LED lights suggest that this product innovation is effectively meeting needs that were previously not being satisfied. Some unmet consumer needs, such as for LED lighting, are more important and less satisfied than others. This makes them potentially more profitable and important growth targets for businesses to focus on.

Not all innovations satisfy unmet needs – in which case they will be marketing failures.

The razor phone

A phone with an electric shaver built in was developed and manufactured by Tondemoketai. The company believed that this was a viable product when it was launched. The phone featured an electric shaver head at the bottom, hidden away under a plastic cover, and was able to power a 'full shave' when the battery was fully charged. It was not successful because it failed to satisfy a sufficiently substantial unmet consumer need.

Possibly a better system for Tondemoketai to have adopted would have been one driven by marketing and putting the customers' needs first. Producing innovative goods that are, according to market research, likely to sell is a more effective strategy. R&D is usually directed towards developing products that market research indicates will meet an unmet need – unless consumers are unaware of their future needs!

This is a list of five technology-based products that have been developed in schools since 2017 to help student learning:

- interactive whiteboards
- school-based intranet learning platforms
- tablet computers
- document sharing software such as Onenote
- videoconferencing software such as Zoom.

1 In pairs or as a group discuss the impact these technological innovations have had on your learning.

2 To what extent do you think technological innovation enhances student learning?

35.3 Intellectual property rights

As a type of asset, **intellectual property** is intangible, a creation of the mind, with no physical existence. With a tangible object – such as a computer – property rights cease when the object is destroyed. With intellectual property, since there is nothing physical, property rights only exist for as long as the law says they do.

This does not mean that intellectual property rights – the rights to possess, use, license, sell and financially benefit from property – are not worth anything. Far from it, as they can:

- set a business apart from its competitors and result in increased sales as a result of this distinctiveness

KEY **TERM**

intellectual property: refers to creations of the mind such as inventions, literary and artistic works and symbols, names, images and designs used in business

- be sold or licensed to provide an important revenue stream
- form a key part of the branding process and assist in the marketing of products
- be given a financial value on a business statement of financial position which increases its net assets
- give the business market power – a degree of monopoly control – as the **intellectual property rights** make copying of the idea or design illegal. This often allows the business to charge premium prices.

There may be problems protecting intellectual property. Copying without the permission of the **copyright** holder has always been a problem, but the ability to download digital versions of music, films and other material, which has led to illegal downloading, has made the task of protecting revenue earnt by the intellectual property even more difficult. In addition, brand names and trademarks can be damaged by bad publicity and this can 'write off' a great deal of value from a statement of financial position or the value of the business. Some countries do little to stop their domestic producers infringing the **patents** of foreign-based businesses, although international agreements mean that these 'copied' products cannot easily be sold abroad.

ACTIVITY 35.3

Disruptive technology

Cryptocurrency is a form of innovation in the payment system market that could revolutionise the financial service industry. Examples of cryptocurrency include Bitcoin, Ethereum and Solana. Other examples of disruptive technology in finance include PayPal, crowdfunding and mobile phone payment systems.

In pairs or as a group, prepare a presentation on disruptive technology in another market.

KEY TERMS

intellectual property rights: legal property rights over the possession and use of intellectual property

copyright: legal right to protect and be the sole beneficiary from artistic and literary works

patent: legal right to be the sole producer and seller of an invention for a certain period of time

35.4 Types of innovation

Innovation by businesses can be classified in several ways.

Incremental innovation

As its title suggests, this form of innovation involves small steps in improving an existing product or process.

The changes brought about by **incremental innovation** are usually focused on improving an existing product's design, performance, attractiveness to consumers, efficiency of manufacture or competitive differentiation. Many businesses use incremental innovation as a strategy to maintain or improve a product's market share. Incremental innovation is common in many industries such as cars and consumer technology where businesses aim to improve, on a regular basis, the appeal and features of an existing product. This approach is much less costly than trying to achieve disruptive innovations, but some well-resourced businesses will adopt both approaches.

KEY TERM

incremental innovation: a series of small improvements or upgrades made to a company's existing products, services or processes.

Innovation – 4Ps innovation model

The 4Ps innovation model makes the following distinctions in the process of innovation by businesses:

- **Product innovation:** new, marketable products such as hybrid/electric cars, or developing and improving existing products such as the Apple iPad Air. These products are trying to satisfy consumers' unmet needs – even if they are not aware of them!
- **Process innovation:** new methods of manufacturing a product or providing a service that offers benefits to the business/customer. For example, Pilkington's float glass process that cut the cost of making glass. In digital publishing and selling, books can now be purchased instantly and downloaded with processes such as 'one-click' buying on Amazon, which then automatically downloads the title to the user's Kindle.

- **Positioning innovation:** this involves 'relocation' of the customer's perception about a certain product. Today, in the global marketplace, position is everything. What makes the organisation profitable is not necessarily how good its products or services are, but what its customers' perception of them is. For example, an old established product in the UK is Lucozade – originally developed as a glucose-based drink to help children and invalids during convalescence. This link with illness was abandoned by the brand owners, GlaxoSmithKline and, later, Suntory, when the product was relaunched as a health drink aimed at the growing fitness market. It is now presented as a performance-enhancing aid to healthy exercise. This shift is a good example of position innovation. Mobile phones used to be marketed as devices used by business managers. Only later did they start to be perceived as essential gadgets for teenagers who would often look upon them as a fashion accessory as well as a communication device.

- **Paradigm innovation:** a distinct change in what a business does or in the nature of goods/services available. The creation of social media sites has been described as paradigm innovation. Replacing existing publishing businesses with 'online self-publishing' would be another paradigm innovation. The use of mobile phone apps to make financial transactions is having a huge impact on how banks provide services and relate with customers, and this is a paradigm innovation.

Disruptive innovation

The opposite of incremental innovation is radical or **disruptive innovation**. This concept was first developed by Clayton Christensen in 1995. It is similar to the concept of paradigm innovation. Disruptive innovation often requires major investment of time and resources, making it a much riskier and longer-term strategy than incremental innovation. However, some analysts argue that for an innovation to be truly 'disruptive' it has to be introduced by a new competitor – perhaps even a start-up business – entering a market with a completely different idea that forces existing competitors to respond to confront the new challenge. Another approach to classifying this type of innovation is to only recognise as being truly disruptive those innovations that produce substantial cost savings over existing products. By upsetting the existing high cost and high price business models, they force businesses already in the market to adapt quickly in response.

Examples of disruptive innovation include the development of electric 'flying taxis'; the original digital cameras; video streaming; Airbnb; 3D printing; and 'no checkout' food stores.

CASE STUDY 35.2

Innovation in driverless cars

Artificial intelligence giant Baidu has launched a driverless robotaxi service. Baidu's Apollo Go Robotaxi service is the first paid autonomous vehicle service where users can take a ride in a taxi without a backup driver to intervene. Customers will be able to hail a ride using an app, which allows them to locate a taxi nearby. If they are unable to spot the car, users can remotely sound the horn to find their ride.

Unlocking the vehicle will require customers to scan a QR code to verify their identity. When they get in, passengers can simply tap on the 'start the journey' button. When the car has made sure that the doors are closed and seat belts are fastened it will start moving. The vehicle will take passengers to their destination and payment is made through a smart app.

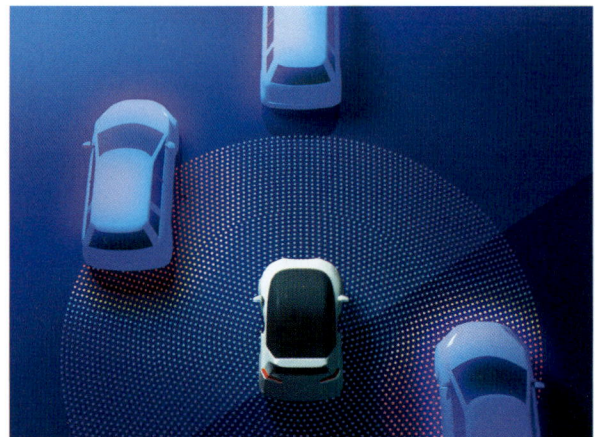

CONTINUED

1   List **four** types of innovation.   [2]

2   Outline why autonomous vehicle are an example of product innovation.   [4]

3   Explain **two** risks for Baidu of R&D into a driverless taxi service.   [4]

Adaptive creativity and innovative creativity

The 4Ps distinction is one way of analysing innovative change. A second dimension to innovation is the degree of change involved. Updating the styling on a model of car is not the same as coming up with a completely new concept car which has an electric engine and is made of new carbon fibre materials rather than steel and glass. Similarly, increasing the speed and accuracy of a welding machine is not the same thing as replacing it with a computer-controlled welding robot. There are degrees of novelty in these, running from minor incremental or adaptive improvements right through to radical changes involving innovative creativity which transform the products and services available.

Adaptive creativity examples	Innovative creativity examples
Cameras in mobile phones	Music and media streaming services
ATMs	Online banking and insurance
iPad mini	Alexa – virtual assistant AI technology
Airbus A350	Jet airliners
Flat beds in business class	Low-cost airlines

Table 35.2: Examples of adaptive creativity and innovative creativity

CASE STUDY 35.3

Gillette: managing product innovation

Product development is a key part of Gillette's success. Innovation in new products allows Gillette to differentiate from its competitors. The business's identity as 'innovation is Gillette' is based on the way it has introduced some of the most successful and widely acclaimed innovative products in the consumer products industry. Gillette's brands include Sensor, SensorExcel, Mach3 and Gillette for Women Venus.

The company's aim is to achieve 40% of its sales from products launched within the last five years.

Gillette's innovation into new products have added significantly to the brand value of the business. It has made razors a branded consumer product for which customers will pay a premium price.

1   Outline the difference between adaptive creativity and innovative creativity.   [2]

2   Outline **two** examples of adaptive creativity in the razor market.   [4]

3   Explain a benefit to Gillette's brand image of its high levels of expenditure in research and development.   [4]

4   Evaluate the view that increasing profits is the most important reason for innovation at Gillette.   [10]

SELF-EVALUATION CHECKLIST

After studying this chapter, complete this table.

I am able to apply and analyse:	Needs more work	Almost there	Ready to move on
the importance of developing goods and services that address customers' unmet needs (AO2)			
intellectual property protection: copyrights, patents, trademarks (AO2)			
incremental innovation, innovation and disruptive innovation (AO2)			
I am able to synthesise and evaluate:			
the importance of research and development for a business (AO3)			

REFLECTION

How important is research and development likely to be for a small customer service-based business?

PROJECT

The future of live performance?

In April 2020 the publishers of the game 'Fortnite' produced a live event in the game and more than 27 million people logged in to attend. The event allowed players to dance using their avatars and explore a psychedelic game world, while an animated version of the rapper Travis Scott performed live.

WaveXR Inc. and TikTok have also worked together on a live event that attracted 3 million viewers. Featuring the singer The Weeknd, the even included songs accompanied by animations and viewers could influence the event by voting in polls.

Analysts suggest that these events are an indication of how concerts and other live events might develop into a fully virtual format in future. The Covid-19 pandemic meant that most live events had to be cancelled, so musicians and concert promoters have been keen to find alternative ways to engage with fans. It appears likely that these type of events may continue even after the Covid-19 pandemic.

In pairs or as a group, produce a presentation on innovation in the streaming of live events. In your presentation cover the following elements:

- how different live events have been streamed

- the innovative features of the live event

- the way the live event has generated revenues

- the implications of the streamed event for conventional live events

- the extent to which external shocks like the pandemic lead to innovation.

Thinking about your project:

- Do you feel that your understanding of innovation has improved?

- How goof was your presentation compare to those of the other groups in the class?

- How could you improve your presentation?

EXAM-STYLE QUESTIONS

Energy innovation

Proxima Energia plc is a Paraguayan energy company that supplies electricity. The business is trying to diversity its sources of energy into the renewable sector. Proxima has established energy provision using wind and solar, but it is considering investment in anaerobic digestion. This is a food waste method of energy generation where waste food is converted into energy. Proxima Energia is considering a special plant that uses anaerobic digestion where food waste is broken down so that it gives off biogas. This methane-rich gas is then used to create new energy.

Anaerobic digestion is an effective way to prevent food waste from going to landfill and emitting greenhouse gases and at the same time producing renewable energy. The sludge material left over from the anaerobic digestion process can be sold off as fertiliser.

Proxima Energia has the following finance data.

	Proxima Energia	Industry average
Initial investment cost	$43 million	NA
Payback	6 years 7 months	7 years 6 months
Average annual rate of return (ARR)	9%	11%
Net present value (NPV)	$3.2 million	NA

1	Define the term 'innovation'.	[2]
2	State **two** types of innovation.	[2]
3	Explain the types of innovation that Proxima Energia is involved in.	[4]
4	Define the term invention.	[2]
5	Outline what payback shows.	[4]
6	State how ARR is calculated.	[2]
7	State how net present value is calculated.	[2]
8	Outline why anaerobic digestion is an example of process innovation.	[4]
9	Explain how Proxima Energia's investment in an anaerobic digestion plant is an example of sustainable innovation.	[4]
10	Evaluate whether Proxima Energia should invest in anaerobic digestion as a method of energy provision.	[10]

> Chapter 36

Management information systems

Higher-level

LEARNING OBJECTIVES

On completing this chapter you should be able to:

Know and understand:

> Data analytics (AO1)

> Database (AO1)

> Cybersecurity and cybercrime (AO1)

Apply and analyse:

> Critical infrastructures, including artificial neural networks, data centres and cloud computing (AO2)

CONTINUED

> Virtual reality (AO2)

> The internet of things (AO2)

> Artificial intelligence (AO2)

> Big data (AO2)

Synthesise and evaluate:

> Customer loyalty programmes (AO3)

> The use of data to manage and monitor employees; Digital Taylorism (AO3)

> The use of data mining to inform decision-making (AO3)

> The benefits, risks and ethical implications of advanced computer technologies and technological innovation on business decision-making and stakeholders (AO3)

BUSINESS IN CONTEXT

Big data and decision-making in supermarkets

Supermarkets produce a huge volume of data. There are millions of transactions per week, so data managers can measure the impact of even small changes, such as a small price increase to one product.

Every product purchased, along with its price, is recorded in huge databases, with tables exceeding hundreds of billions of rows. Loyalty card schemes, allow the supermarket businesses to create a complete picture of a customer's entire history of transactions. The richness of this data provides support for management decision-making on pricing levels, promotions, personalised communications to consumers, new products and ranging.

Ranging is about which products to sell in each store. Every square metre of each aisle is potentially worth thousands of dollars of sales per year. Supermarkets go to great lengths to make sure none of it is wasted on products that do not perform well. But 'performing well' is not as easy as picking the highest selling products or those with the biggest profit margins. Stores have to cater to all of the different customers who come into them. For example, a particular type of sauce might not be a big-selling item, but if it is important to the older demographic, then to stop stocking it might force them to shop elsewhere. Also, imagine someone is planning to make burritos this evening. If they can get most of the ingredients in one store, but it does not sell tortillas, shoppers may end up taking all of that potential revenue to a competitor.

CONTINUED

At the same time, a diverse product range costs money. There are complex logistics of managing a large range of different products. More products mean more supply chains to manage. Consumers in a budget supermarket like Aldi, will notice it often has a smaller choice of products for each product type, but it maintains higher stock levels in store. This is to cut down on the costs of a diverse product range, enabling lower prices at the expense of choice, before reducing quality.

This all makes for a very complex optimisation problem in which data analysis plays a key role. Products are regularly assessed against a number of criteria, such as sales, profitability, number of customers who purchase them and the loyalty of those customers to a product when it is not on promotion. Machine learning models (using the principles of artificial intelligence), trained on past examples of range changes can be used to predict how customers will react to proposed changes in the future. By taking store characteristics into account, such as size, local demographics and proximity to competitors, ranges can be optimised on a store-by-store basis.

Whilst supermarkets are already big users of data analytics and AI, there are many interesting concepts that may become more mainstream in future. Customer tracking is imperfect in its current form. Using loyalty cards to identify customers will bias the 'identified customers' towards those with a more frugal mindset. Another problem is that if someone enters the store but leaves without buying, their visit is unrecorded. Facial recognition technology and blue-tooth beacons could be used to plug these gaps and even provide data on how people move around the store. Having data on what a person walked past, what they paused at and how long they spent in store will bring further refinements in the layout of the store and the effectiveness of in-store promotions.

Obviously, there are major ethical implications with these new technologies which may slow their roll-out in liberal societies.

Discuss in pairs or in a group:

- How could a supermarket use the data it collects to help with pricing decisions? Try to use the concept of price elasticity in your discussion.

- To what extent do you think the collection and analysis of vast amounts of data has 'major ethical implications'?

KEY CONCEPT LINK

Change

The retail sector of the economy is subject to constant change both instore and online. Businesses that can use big data effectively can use it to support their marketing strategies in response to this change. If information tells a clothing retailer such as Ralph Lauren about changes in consumers' preferences in terms of colour, material and design, then the retailer can alter the products it sells in response to this. In this sense, big data helps businesses manage change.

36.1 Data analytics

Operating a business of any size can lead to the generation of vast amounts of data from all functional areas such as operations performance, cost and profit centre performance, HR data and marketing data such as consumer buying habits. The purpose of **data analytics** is to analyse data to identify trends,

KEY TERM

data analytics: the science of analysing raw statistical data to make conclusions about that information to inform business decision-making

correlations and insights that can be used to help make informed business decisions.

Data analytics is significant as it plays an important role in helping businesses to optimise their performance. A company can also use data analytics to make better business decisions and help analyse consumer trends and levels of customer satisfaction, which can lead to new (and improved) products and services.

Data analytics is usually based on the data collected by an effective **management information system (MIS)**. This is a set of systems (nearly always IT based) and reporting processes that gather data from a range of sources. The data is then sorted and compiled in meaningful ways and presented in an accessible and usable format. The data collected and presented from an MIS can then be subject to detailed data analytics

> **KEY TERM**
>
> **management information system (MIS):** the computerised databases and procedures that managers use to collect data to measure the effectiveness of their organisations, departments, teams, specific projects, or even individual employees

36.2 Database

Our personal details are almost certainly recorded on countless business and government IT-accessed **databases**. The storing and use of this data is regulated by law in most countries.

IT databases are vast stores of organised information from which data can be sorted, collated and delivered to a business user with a click of a mouse. Business databases help small-business owners and managers of larger businesses to organise and track their customers, stock and employees. The data they contain allows, for example, up-to-date customer relationship management techniques to be used, stock tracking of each item used or sold by the business, HR records on every employee and operations database for accurate scheduling of production to meet demand.

> **KEY TERM**
>
> **database:** a store of information that is organised for easy access, management and updating

36.3 Cybersecurity and cybercrime

The internet has provided businesses, governments and people with opportunities to communicate, download images and films, buy and sell products globally, and even just keep in touch. The internet has also provided huge opportunities for criminals too, and it has assisted in the birth and development of crimes using computers or aimed at computers. These actions are referred to as **cybercrime**. In 2020, businesses, governments and individuals spent an estimated $145 billion on systems designed to reduce the risk of cybercrime attacks – these systems are known as **cybersecurity**.

> **KEY TERMS**
>
> **cybercrime:** any criminal activity that involves a computer, networked device or a network
>
> **cybersecurity:** measures taken to protect against the criminal or unauthorised use of electronic data and illegal access to computer systems or internet-connected devices

The five main forms of cybercrime are:

- **Phishing scams:** emails sent from an internet criminal disguised as a communication from a legitimate, trustworthy source with the aim of tricking victims into handing over sensitive information or installing malware.

- **Website spoofing:** creating an exact copy of a trusted website with the aim of leading visitors to a phishing site. What appear to be 'legitimate' logos, fonts, colours and functionality are used to make the spoofed site look realistic.

- **Ransomware:** a form of malicious software designed to block access to a computer system until a sum of money is paid to the criminals.

- **Malware:** software that is specifically designed to disrupt, damage or gain unauthorised access to a computer system.
- **IOT hacking:** gaining illegal access to internet-connected devices such as VOIP phones, Wi-Fi office printers, Siri and Alexa units.

Most cybercrimes are carried out in order to generate profit for the cybercriminals. However, some cybercrimes are carried out against computers or devices directly in order to damage or disable them. Other criminals use computers or networks to spread malware, illegal information, images or other materials. Some cybercrimes do both by targeting computer systems to infect them with a virus, which is then spread to other machines and entire networks.

The primary impact on businesses of cybercrime is financial. The costs include:

- lost sales if a website is infected or suspended due to illegal action
- the cost of cybersecurity measures
- payment of ransoms
- reputational damage, reducing trust in the business if, for example, customers' data is hacked and published.

Cybercrime impacts on the global economy. According to Atlas VPN, when the cumulative cost of cyber incidents was added to the economic outlay of putting security measures in place, the cost of cybercrime was more than $1 trillion in 2020. This estimate suggests that around 1% of global GDP is lost to cybercrime.

ACTIVITY 36.1

The increasing cost of cybercrime

If it continues to grow at 15% a year it is estimated that cybercrime could cost the world economy $10.5 trillion annually by 2025. This is a huge cost to businesses, individuals and governments. In fact, the costs of cybercrime are greater than those of natural disasters and the illegal drugs market.

The top five cybercrimes are: phishing; cyber extortion; data breach; identity theft; harassment.

CONTINUED

The costs of cybercrime come in the form of data destruction, lost productivity, stolen intellectual property, data theft, fraud and reputational harm. If you add the cost of developing systems to protect businesses against cybercrime it is clear how expensive it is.

Research a cybercrime incident involving a business and prepare a presentation that sets out all of the possible costs to the business.

36.4 Critical infrastructures

Critical infrastructures are the systems, networks and assets that are so essential that the security of the organisation – perhaps even the nation – is at risk if there is largescale failure of them. For a business, its IT system is undoubtedly part of its 'critical infrastructure'.

Artificial neural networks

Artificial neural networks (ANNs) are created to make a series of programmed computers operate like a human brain.

KEY TERM

artificial neural network (ANN): programming computers to behave like interconnected brain cells

ANNs can be created to recognise handwriting or people (facial recognition) in just the same way that humans can. We use the interaction between our eyes and millions of brain cells to achieve recognition. ANNs can be programmed to be around 99% accurate when identifying handwriting and recognising people's identity from an image.

One business use of ANNs is to improve marketing strategies. The systems can process masses of information very quickly. This includes consumers'personal details, shopping patterns, and their responses to special offers and promotions. Using this information, businesses can identify and target the customers most likely to purchase a specific product by communicating information about it to them. Focusing marketing campaigns in this way saves time and money that would otherwise be wasted advertising to customers who are unlikely to respond.

THEORY OF KNOWLEDGE

Emotion

Facial recognition technology offers businesses the opportunity to measure the reaction of consumers to marketing content. By identifying individuals based on their facial characteristics, facial recognition systems can be used to analyse facial expressions. This information is used to measure an individual's emotional responses to areas of marketing such as product design, packaging and promotion. Software in the system can be used to detect human reactions such as fear, joy, anger and surprise.

In pairs or as a group discuss the extent it is possible to measure human emotion using facial recognition technology.

Data centres

Traditionally, businesses with substantial IT assets used a dedicated **data centre** to house them.

KEY TERM

data centre: a physical facility that organisations use to accommodate and make secure their critical IT equipment, applications and data

Data centres provide the following important services to a business:

- **computing:** the memory and processing power to run the applications, usually provided by high-specification servers
- **storage:** important business data is kept in a data centre, on media such as solid-state drives, with multiple backups

- **networking:** interconnections between data centre components and the outside world, including routers, switches and application-delivery controllers.

In addition to IT equipment, a data centre will need substantial investment in hardware and processes to ensure that it can provide continuous operation to the business. This equipment will include: power subsystems, uninterruptable power supplies, ventilation and cooling systems, backup generators, and cabling to connect to external network operators. The importance of data centres to the efficient and continuous operation of a business cannot be overstated, and software and hardware security measures are essential.

Cloud computing

The high cost of building, maintaining and updating data centres has led to many businesses using **cloud computing** either to support their data centres or to replace them. Since 2006, cloud computing service providers, such as Google, have been offering businesses data storage and management services on remote servers with access to data via the internet.

KEY TERM

cloud computing: using a network of remote servers hosted on the internet to store, manage and process data, rather than a data centre or a personal computer

Basically, a cloud data service is a remote version of a data centre, that is located somewhere away from the physical premises of the business. It lets a business access data via the internet. The cloud service provider undertakes maintenance and updates. These providers often own multiple data centres in several geographic locations to safeguard data during power outages and other failures.

A business that is considering using cloud computing services rather than its own data centre is likely to consider three major factors:

- **Cost:** The construction and equipping of a new data centre can cost millions of dollars. A cloud service provider will charge annual fees or subscriptions for the services it provides but it is likely to be more cost-effective, especially for smaller businesses. As the data needs of a business are likely to change over time, the cloud provider should be able to scale the level of service offered up or down quickly.

- **Capacity:** A data centre might still be preferable for a business that needs a dedicated system giving full control over data and the hardware. A dedicated data centre could be more suited for a business that needs to run many types of applications and complex workloads.

  However, a data centre has limited capacity unless substantial further capital is invested. A cloud data system has potentially unlimited capacity. But unless the user pays to have a private cloud within the provider's network, they will be sharing hardware resources with other cloud users.

- **Security:** Using a cloud service provider means entrusting it with all of the business's data. The level of security will be decided by the cloud provider. The data held in the cloud can be accessed by anyone with the proper credentials from anywhere that has an internet connection. This is convenient, but it creates many access points, all of which need a high level of security to ensure that data transmitted through them is secure.

36.5 Virtual reality (VR)

This application of technology in the form of creating **virtual reality** is having a significant impact on several functional business areas.

Business applications of virtual reality include:

- Retailing. Virtual reality heat mapping can track the products and displays that most attract consumers' attention as they walk round a store. VR can allow shoppers to explore products in a lifelike way, such as Ikea's virtual reality kitchen experience which helps shoppers discover kitchen features and imagine how they would feel in their own home. VR stores are never crowded, they have highly attentive assistants, and can contribute to a personalised shopping experience. During the pandemic many estate agents used VR to promote the interiors of properties for sale which could not be viewed in person.

- Training. VR training packages can be individually designed to meet the training needs of each employee. They can save on the cost of off-the-job training. Some retailers use VR packages to help prepare staff for very busy periods such as Black Friday. Immersing employees in a lifelike environment of long queues and possibly threatening crowds of people prepares them for an environment which is not an everyday occurrence. It also means that day-to-day business operations do not have to be disturbed for training purposes.

- Manufacture and product design. VR can help manufacturers cut costs of designing new products and building detailed prototypes by creating a VR simulation of the product. With the development of a new aeroplane, for example, the precise location of safety features such oxygen masks and life jackets can be tested and optimised through VR.

> **KEY TERM**
>
> **virtual reality:** computer-generated simulations of a three-dimensional image or environment that can be interacted with by a person using special electronic equipment, such as a helmet with a screen inside

36.6 The internet of things (IOT)

Although the term was first used in 1999, according to Cisco Internet Business Solutions Group (IBSG), the **internet of things** came into existence between 2008 and 2009 as that was the point in time when more 'things or objects' were connected to the internet than people in the world.

One of the first examples of an internet of things is from the early 1980s, and it was a Coca-Cola machine, located at the Carnegie Melon University. Programmers in the university could connect to the refrigerated appliance via the internet, and check to see if there was a drink available, and if it was cold, before making the trip to buy it. It is estimated that by 2025 there could be 42 billion devices connected to the internet. With no internationally agreed central security standards or compliance procedures underpinning this proliferation of IOT devices, individuals and businesses are likely to be exposed to IOT hacking for the foreseeable future.

> **KEY TERM**
>
> **internet of things (IOT):** consists of any device with an on/off switch connected to the internet

In the consumer market, IOT technology is closely associated with products that claim to make homes 'smart'. These include devices and appliances such as lighting fixtures, thermostats, home security systems, cameras, and other home appliances that can be controlled by smartphones and smart speakers. The IOT can also be used in health care, and one example illustrates the potential security risks of this. The US Food and Drug Administration (FDA) issued a warning in 2017 about implantable cardiac devices which are at risk of attack by hackers. These implants are used to monitor and control heart function, including heart attacks, and because they are accessible to hackers, unscrupulous people could control shocks, alter pacing and deplete the battery.

36.7 Artificial intelligence (AI)

Research into machines which can simulate human thought processes has been undertaken since the days of the very earliest electrical computers. With the huge increases in computing power that have been achieved in recent years, **artificial intelligence (AI)** has now become a reality.

Here are some common examples of AI in action:

- Siri, Alexa and other smart assistants
- self-driving cars
- robot financial advisers
- conversational bots in customer service environments
- email spam filters
- manufacturing robots that use AI
- AI recruitment and selection of candidates applying for a job
- AI assessment by a bank of loan risks to business customers.

KEY TERM

artificial intelligence (AI): a branch of computer science focusing on building smart machines capable of performing tasks that typically require human intelligence

---

Impact of AI on business

In a business, AI can:

- save time and money by automating routine processes and tasks such as recording of financial transactions and analysing market research data
- increase productivity and operational efficiencies, for example by using AI-controlled manufacturing processes
- avoid data analysis mistakes and 'human error', provided that AI systems are set up properly
- use insight gained from analysing masses of customer spending data to predict customer preferences and offer them a better, personalised experience
- mine vast amounts of data on potential customers to generate new contacts with them and increase the customer base
- increase revenue by identifying and maximising sales opportunities
- offer intelligent advice and support, for example with customer service focused chat bots.

AI and the future

There is little doubt that AI is far better at data analysis than a human brain is. Artificial intelligence software can analyse massive sets of data and make suggestions to the human users about how to respond to the results of data analysis. Managers can use AI to help assess the possible consequences of each possible course of action. This improves the accuracy of decision-making, but could a business be managed completely using AI?

With the many automated tasks that AI can currently perform, some people are certain that AI-controlled technology will lead to all business jobs – including senior management decision-making – being undertaken by machines. Several business analysts disagree, however. They recognise that many jobs will be replaced by machines, even some accounting, legal and HR positions, but that the human element in decision-making will be required for years to come. Also, the growing trend towards AI-based systems will require many people to be employed in programming and providing business support to AI-focused businesses.

A well-known firm of business analysts, McKinsey, has suggested that 50% of today's work activities could be automated by 2055. Integrating more AI and process automation into the workplace will change the nature of many people's jobs. Those that are displaced by AI may be able to find other employment, and many workers will have to change careers, so flexibility and access to appropriate training will be essential.

ACTIVITY 36.2

Data mining

The personal information of 533 million users of a social media site was found posted online by a hacker. It included names, birthdays, phone numbers, locations and email addresses. According to the company, the stolen data had originally been taken a few years before due to a vulnerability that the company put right in 2019.

Cybercriminals could use the revealed data to impersonate people and access their banking details and other important personal information.

In pairs or as a group, research other major security breaches that have occurred because of business data mining. Prepare a presentation on your findings.

36.8 Big data

Big data refers to vast quantities of complex data that is difficult or impossible to process using traditional methods. The amount of data that businesses now have access to is increasing each year. Only the latest data analytics systems can cope with interpreting and analysing it.

KEY TERM

big data: extremely large sets of data that may be analysed by computers to establish trends, patterns and associations which can help to inform business decisions

---

Where does all of this data come from that is flowing into businesses? There are many sources including:

- details of transactions between the business, its suppliers and customers
- IOT devices
- social media
- feedback from cost and profit centres
- feedback from AI-controlled machines
- feedback from customers.

Not only is the volume of data increasing, but the speed with which it arrives is getting faster. This requires a very fast system for analysing and responding to the data. Another factor that has made big data so essential to business managers is that the variety of formats in which information is received has also grown. Some examples include: numerical data, structured database data, unstructured text documents and messages, social media messages, emails and stock movement data.

Here are just some of the potential uses and benefits of big data for business:

- **Recruiting the right employees** Recruiting agencies can scan candidates' CVs (resumes) and LinkedIn profiles for keywords that would match the job description. The recruitment process is no longer based on what the candidate looks like on paper and how they are perceived at interview.

- **Increasing sales** The digital footprints that customers create when browsing online or posting to social media channels can tell a business a great deal about shopping preferences, beliefs, response to promotions and so on. This data allows businesses to adapt products to exactly what the customer wants.

- **Increasing productivity and efficiency** Quicker data analysis will increase the personal productivity of the specialists employed within a business. The business can also gain a lot of information about its own operations, productivity of each work team, feedback on customer experiences and variances from budget for each profit centre. This data allows management to gain insights into its own operations and to recognise areas where it could be more productive and effective.

- **Reducing costs** The use of big data to help make forecasts about future material and commodity cost movements could encourage a business to source cheaper materials. More efficient preventative maintenance programmes could be assessed using output and breakdown records from thousands of pieces of equipment. Rapid analysis of operations data about quality control levels should lead to rapid action to cut wastage rates.

Big data is not without its potential problems, however:

- Questionable data quality – perhaps from potentially unreliable consumer surveys or social media platforms – will make the resulting analysis of the data potentially risky for the business. Decisions taken on the basis of the analysis of unreliable data could prove damaging for the business.

- The huge amount of data has to be kept very securely, especially if it includes sensitive data about customers' personal details. The data is at risk from attack as cybercriminals could use this data illegally to their own advantage.

- Data centres are costly to purchase, manage and maintain. Cloud-based analytics and specialist providers of data management solutions could partly overcome these problems, but their services will involve subscription costs.

- High salaries are demanded by experts in the field of big data analysis and by professionals who know how to design and manage the necessary infrastructure. Collecting and analysing big data is not a low-cost course of action, but if it is undertaken effectively, the benefits could outweigh the costs.

CASE STUDY 36.1

Highly strung tennis (HTT) is a medium-sized business based in Madrid that manufactures high-quality tennis racquets. Whilst the game's major stars are tied to the world's leading sports good manufacturers, HTT has developed a niche market selling to leading amateur players in Europe and to tennis clubs and academies.

HTT has used AI extensively in its manufacturing processes, particularly in product design and quality control. HTT's use of data in the production of its racquets has enabled it to reduce product faults by 15%. Machine-based digital diagnostics has enabled HTT to pinpoint machinery errors and improve maintenance on the production line.

AI has helped HTT target consumers more effectively. By using intelligent systems, the business has been able to understand its customers better and track their buying patterns. This has been particularly important in guiding product design and advertising.

1 Define the term 'big data'. [2]

2 Outline **two** ways HTT uses AI. [4]

3 Explain **two** ways the use of AI might help HHT reduce its costs. [4]

4 Evaluate the usefulness of AI to increase HTT's profits. [10]

36.9 Customer loyalty programmes

Developing **customer loyalty** to ensure that they buy from the business in the future is closely related to **customer relationship marketing (CRM)**. Studies have shown that it can cost between four and ten times as much to gain new customers (with expensive promotions) as it does to keep existing ones. Increasing the loyalty of existing customers makes sense for another reason. If a business can secure repeat purchases from many customers with **customer loyalty programmes**, it means that there will be fewer customers buying products from competitors.

KEY TERMS

customer loyalty: a positive relationship between the business and customer which leads to a willingness by the customers to make repeat visits and purchases

customer relationship marketing (CRM): using marketing activities to build and establish good customer relationships so that the loyalty of existing customers can be maintained

customer loyalty programme: a marketing strategy that rewards loyal customers who frequently buy the brand's products

---

Customer loyalty programmes are designed to encourage repeat purchases by providing the customers (often called 'programme members') with discounts, unique offers, VIP events, points-based reward systems and free trials or tasting of new products. When it is well managed and appropriately focused, a customer loyalty programme should:

- retain existing customers
- encourage them to increase their spending
- encourage 'dormant' customers to return
- attract new customers.

At the heart of customer loyalty programmes is communication with the customer to gain information. Hence the need for 'big data' analysis. The aim is to gain as much information as possible about each existing customer. This includes income, product preferences, buying habits and so on. Using this information, marketing tactics can be adapted to meet the customers' needs. This is virtually segmenting each customer, and it is the opposite of mass marketing. Now that technology has made the collection and analysis of customer data so much easier and cheaper, customer loyalty programmes are becoming a widely adopted marketing strategy.

Developing effective long-term relationships that lead to customer loyalty can be achieved by:

- **targeted marketing** – giving each customer the products and services they have indicated, from records of past purchases, that they most need
- **customer service and support** – after-sales service and effective call centres are good examples of the support that is essential to build customer loyalty

Costs	Benefits
IT systems and data analytics software needed, and training of employees to respond to customer feedback.	For businesses with an existing customer base it has proven to be cost effective. Higher sales from effective loyalty programmes nearly always exceed the cost of analysing customer data and offering suitable rewards.
Effective customer loyalty campaigns may require the use of an external marketing consultancy at high cost.	It is a sustainable strategy for creating long-term customers, unlike 'low price offers' or similar promotions which tend to be short term in impact.
Customer loyalty programmes require an existing customer base. This needs to be established first before investing in loyalty programmes. If this is not done the costs will not lead to higher sales.	Loyal customers often recommend the business to friends and family, providing additional marketing benefit at no cost.
May be costly to respond to each customers' feedback which might contain special requests or requirements.	Lower cost per customer than trying to attract new customers.

Table 36.1: The potential costs and benefits of customer loyalty schemes

CASE STUDY 36.2

Four great customer loyalty programmes

Here are four famous brands that offer their customers loyalty schemes:

- Starbucks will give you a free drink on your birthday and offers you free in-store refills on coffee and tea. The Starbucks Rewards programme also provides convenience. Customers in the reward scheme can skip the line and order their personalised beverage before getting to the store.

- Reebok provides members of its loyalty programme VIP experiences such as training and wellness programmes, and members receive reward points for every transaction.

- Disney has teamed up with different retailers to offer its members reward points for purchasing movie tickets. Members also can also redeem rewards for exclusive experiences such as the Walt Disney Studios private tours.

- Baskin-Robbins Ice Cream offers customers a free scoop of ice cream for signing up to its loyalty scheme. The business offers its members the opportunity to order and pay with their phones, view the latest flavours, and buy customisable ice-cream cakes.

1   Define the term 'customer relationship marketing' (CRM).   [2]

2   Outline **two** pieces of consumer information that loyalty programmes can provide to businesses.   [4]

3   Explain **two** ways customer loyalty schemes can increase a business's sales.   [4]

4   Evaluate the effectiveness of customer loyalty programmes to increase a business's profits.   [10]

- **regular communication with customers** – to give frequent updates on new products, special offers, new features, new promotions and support services

- **using social media** – obtaining data and feedback from customers via social media sites, which allows tracking of, and communication with, customers.

Feedback management software platforms such as Confirmit and Satmetrix combine a company's internal survey data with trends identified through social media. This allows businesses to make more accurate decisions about which products to supply to satisfy customers' needs.

The costs and benefits of customer loyalty programmes need to be considered before a business adopts this strategy. See Table 36.1.

36.10 The use of data to manage and monitor employees

The data increasingly available to managers does not just cover production rates, machine reliability, customer loyalty rates and so on. It also monitors the performance of each individual employee. The use of data gathered and analysed electronically is referred to as **electronic performance monitoring (EPM)**.

> **KEY TERM**
>
> **electronic performance monitoring (EPM):** using data gathered and analysed electronically to measure and monitor employee performance

What data can HR managers gather and analyse about employee performance? Here are common examples:

- rate of working or productivity
- degree of work accuracy
- customer satisfaction/complaints feedback
- log-in and log-off times
- days absent/late
- number and duration of breaks
- social media activity.

These data sets can be compared with those of other employees and, if benchmarked data is available, with employees in other businesses. If there are a series of results which show declining performance then managers can focus on improving standards from the employees concerned. It could lead to focused training, target setting and detailed appraisal schemes, all with the objective of improving performance to, at least, above the current average on all measures.

The big question to ask about EPM is: Who benefits?

Opponents of EPM argue that, as with F. W. Taylor's original ideas, the aim of EPM is to improve every aspect of employee performance for the benefit of the business with higher output, lower costs and increased profit. In fact, this approach to using employee data to improve performance is often referred to as 'digital Taylorism'. It is argued that workers are treated like machines, and that the only factors that managers consider important about employees' work and achievements are those that can be measured. This approach could be very demotivating.

KEY TERM

digital Taylorism: building on Taylor's original work and adding to it by suggesting that digitally collected and analysed data is used to monitor and improve employee performance

Taylor originally argued that the best way to boost productivity was to enforce three rules in the workplace:

- break complex jobs down into simple ones
- measure everything that workers do
- link pay to performance, giving bonuses to high achievers and replacing underachievers.

Modern digital Taylorism builds on these three rules with the application of big data about employee performance.

In an article about Amazon in the *New York Times* it was suggested that Taylorism is thriving. The article claimed that the internet retailer uses classic Taylorist techniques to achieve efficiency: workers are constantly measured, the data is analysed digitally and those who fail to reach performance targets are ruthlessly eliminated. Amazon's CEO, Jeff Bezos, insisted that he did not recognise the company portrayed in the article.

Supporters of this use of HR employee performance data suggest that the measures taken to improve employee performance could result in benefits to both the business and the employee. They claim that:

- improving employee performance can improve business competitiveness and increase job security as a result
- pay levels could increase if targets are continually met
- bonuses could be paid for certain levels of improved performance
- training to improve performance can be rewarding and motivating
- effective appraisal schemes can encourage employees to suggest ways in which they could improve their own performance, giving them a sense of responsibility to improve performance.

The evaluation of the impact of digital Taylorism must depend on how the HR data is used, the relationship between managers and employees and whether the business aims to help workers achieve self-fulfilment at work. Failing to communicate the reasons for data collection and the mutual benefits that could result from improved employee performance will almost certainly result in fear, demotivation and uncooperative attitudes from employees – to the detriment of workers and the business.

36.11 The use of data mining to inform decision-making

Data mining is used to establish information from huge amounts of data that could be useful for decision-making.

KEY TERM

data mining: the process of analysing a large batch of information to establish trends and patterns which could be useful for business decision-making

There are several types of data mining, including pictorial data mining, text mining, social media mining, web mining, and audio and video mining. Data mining can help to solve business problems and answer business questions that traditionally were too time consuming to resolve manually. Using a range of statistical techniques to analyse data in different ways, managers can identify patterns, trends and relationships that would otherwise not be obvious. They can apply these trends and relationships to predict what is likely to happen in the future, and they can take decisions to influence business outcomes.

Data mining is used in many areas of business and research, including sales and marketing, product development, health care and education.

Potential uses include:

- Promotion – establishing the relationships between marketing and promotion campaigns and consumer responses to them. This helps marketing managers use appropriate marketing campaigns to target consumers.

- Marketing strategies – using data mining techniques, businesses can create data models to test new ideas. Managers can more easily identify the customers who will be interested in their products. New products that the businesses launch on the market will have a greater chance of being successful.

- Banking and finance – patterns of credit card activity can be monitored, which helps to highlight illegal fraudulent activity.

- Manufacturing – using operations data manufacturers can detect faulty equipment and determine optimal quality-control parameters. This helps to reduce wastage and achieve high levels of acceptable quality.

- Decision-making – by analysing data from previous business decisions such as locating new retail franchises, managers can determine the most important factors that lead to profitable level of sales. The relationships between these factors and sales performance will help in future decisions about where to locate new branches.

Potential limitations include:

- Privacy issues – concerns about personal privacy are increasing and this might limit in future the amount of personal data that consumers are willing to provide to businesses.

- Security issues – security is a big potential problem. The data that a business gathers and stores about its employees and customers (including social security numbers, dates of birth, payroll and other information) needs to be held securely to avoid damaging confidence and trust in the organisation.

Past relationships and trends may not apply in future

Basing business decisions on the analysis of past data is always risky, no matter how effective the mining and analytical techniques. Consumer spending patterns may be affected by external events such as an economic recession which did not feature in the data already gathered. Competitors' actions such as the launch of an advanced product will influence the relationship between promotion and sales for another business. Operations data in the past might not have been affected by supply chain issues, such as those that existed during the pandemic, but these will impact on major operations decisions taken now.

CASE STUDY 36.3

Supermarkets use data mining and business intelligence extensively. Supermarket loyalty card programmes are driven by the desire to gather comprehensive data about customers for use in data mining.

The US retailer, Target, used a data mining program to predict if its shoppers were likely to be pregnant. By looking at the contents of its customers' shopping baskets, it could spot customers that it thought were likely to be expecting a baby and begin targeting promotions for nappies, wipes and other baby-related products. The prediction was so accurate that Target made the news by sending promotional coupons to people who did not yet realise (or who had not yet announced) they were pregnant!

1 Define the term 'data mining'. [2]

2 Explain how Target could make use of data mining in its promotion and product elements of the marketing mix. [4]

3 Outline **two** limitations of data mining. [4]

36.12 The benefits, risks and ethical implications of advanced IT

We have already analysed the benefits of using advanced computer technologies in creating management information systems. Using big data and data mining, for example, informs and improves business decision-making.

However, there are serious moral or ethical issues that must be recognised and discussed as IT advancements make the gathering, storing and analysis of masses of data easier and less costly.

Here are some of these ethical issues:

- Information rights and obligations. What access rights do individuals and organisations have with respect to information that has been collected about them? What can they protect? What can they demand to see? What can they demand to be destroyed?

- Property rights and obligations. How will traditional intellectual property rights be protected in a digital society? It has become more difficult to trace and identify the ownership of such rights.

- Accountability and control. Who can and will be held accountable and legally liable for any harm done to individuals and organisations by the misuse of data held about them?

- Levels of security. What standards of data storage and system security should society demand to protect individual rights and the safety of society?

- Protecting values. What values should be preserved in an information- and knowledge-based society? Which cultural values and practices are supported by the newest information technology?

Some examples of ethical questions raised by technological advances

A new data analysis technology called non-obvious relationship awareness (NORA) has given governments and the private sector powerful profiling capabilities. NORA can take information about people from many unrelated sources, such as employment applications, mobile phone records, customer loyalty data and police records, and establish relationships to find obscure hidden connections that might help to identify criminals. For example, NORA can instantly discover, before he boards the plane, that the man at the airline ticket counter shares a phone number with a known terrorist. The technology helps in making society safer, but it does have ethical implications because it can provide detailed profiles of the activities and associations of individuals.

Advances in networking are greatly reducing the costs of moving and accessing huge quantities of data. They mean that large data pools can be mined remotely,

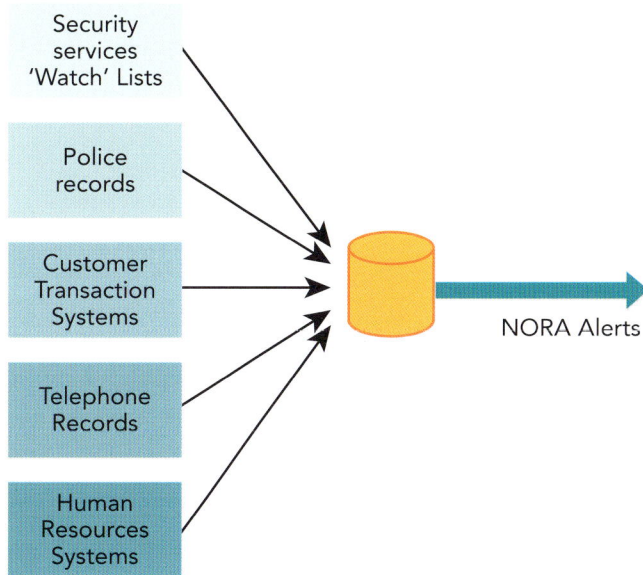

Figure 36.1: Non-obvious relationship awareness (NORA)

permitting an invasion of privacy on a large scale. The development of global digital superhighway communication networks raise many ethical and social concerns. Who will be held accountable for the flow of information over these networks? Will it be possible to trace information collected about each individual? What will these networks do to the traditional, formerly private, relationships between family, work and leisure?

NORA technology can take information about people from unrelated sources and find obscure, non-obvious relationships.

Governments are responding to the potential risks and threats posed by big data. Most national or state governments have passed laws that give individuals rights to know what data is held about them and how to access it to check it. For example, in the US,

the 2018 California Consumer Privacy Act (CCPA) and the supplementary 2020 California Privacy Rights Act (CPRA) are data protection laws that are being copied in many other US states. The European Union is considering banning the use of artificial intelligence for a number of purposes, including mass surveillance and social credit scores which can be used to reward or punish citizens for their behaviour.

What are the key principles that these laws should aim to protect?

- **Private customer data and identity should remain private:** private data obtained from a person with their consent should not be able to be used by other businesses or individuals if it allows tracing back to the individual's identity.

- **Shared private information should be treated as confidential:** other user businesses ('third parties') often share sensitive data – medical, financial or locational – and restrictions should be in place regarding whether and how that information can be shared further.

- **Consumers should have transparency** around how data on them is being used or sold, and the right to manage the flow of private information between powerful, third-party analytical systems.

- **Big data should not make choices for us:** big data analysis can influence and even determine who we are before we make our own choices. Businesses should think about which predictions and inferences they make about us should be allowed and which should not.

- **Big data should not reinforce unfair biases** like racism or sexism. Machine learning algorithms can absorb unconscious biases in a population and reinforce them in the courses of action proposed by the data analysis.

SELF-EVALUATION CHECKLIST

After studying this chapter, complete this table.

I know and understand:	Needs more work	Almost there	Ready to move on
data analytics (AO1)			
database (AO1)			
cybersecurity and cybercrime (AO1)			
I am able to apply and analyse:			
critical infrastructures, including neural networks, data centres and cloud computing (AO2)			
virtual reality (AO2)			
the internet of things (AO2)			
artificial intelligence (AO2)			
big data (AO2)			
I am able to synthesis and evaluate:			
customer loyalty programmes (AO3)			
the use of data to manage and monitor employees: Digital Taylorism (AO3)			
the use of data mining to inform decision-making (AO3)			
the benefits, risks and ethical implications of advanced computer technologies and technological innovation on business decision-making and stakeholders (AO3)			

REFLECTION

With at least one other student, prepare a report to the head/principal of your school/college on the:

- benefits to the school/college of gathering, retaining and analysing data on every student and the performance of every teacher

- risks and ethical implications of gathering, storing and analysing this data.

PROJECT

McDonald's has spent hundreds of millions of dollars developing artificial intelligence and machine learning. It has set up a new tech hub called the McD Tech Labs, where engineers and data scientists work on voice-recognition software.

Sales of fast food have slowed down in the USA as consumers have looked for healthier meal options.

As with many fast-food chains, McDonald's has seen customer numbers reduce and it has had to close restaurants.

In an attempt to reverse the trend, McDonald's has turned to technology. It has developed more strategic product marketing on digital boards, programmed to take into account factors such as

CONTINUED

the popularity of the menu item, waiting times, the time of day and even the weather. Customers are also tempted to order more at the end of their transaction when the screen displays a list of recommended items that they might enjoy.

At some drive-throughs, the company has tested technology that recognises licence-plate numbers so that it can tailor a list of suggested purchases to the customer's previous orders.

In pairs or as a group, research another business that uses AI in its operations. Produce a video presentation on the business's use of AI in marketing its product. In your presentation cover the following elements:

- the type of AI technology used
- the impact of the AI technology on consumers
- how the use of AI technology increases sales
- any weaknesses of using the AI technology.

Thinking about your project:

- Do you feel your understanding of the use AI has improved?
- How good was your video presentation compared to those of the others in the class?
- How could you improve your presentation?

EXAM-STYLE QUESTIONS

Technology and fashion

The Leaf is a fashion retailer based in Sydney, Australia. The business was started three years ago by Aashi Khan who was looking to establish an innovative fashion business that combined the latest fashion ideas with ground-breaking technology. Aashi has a background in fashion and also data analytics. Her management team uses big data extensively to develop all aspects of The Leaf's marketing strategy.

One aspect Aashi has focused on is the customer shopping experience. The Leaf's customers can use virtual reality in the store. When a customer goes to buy a garment, they have the opportunity to use the shop's 'state-of-the-art' headsets to give them the experience of wearing something in a variety of social situations.

Aashi has also been keen to use AI to predict what people will want to buy and wear in the future. The Leaf has used AI to map clothes onto the bodies potential customers and upload their photos to an app. This technology can be used by customers remotely and in-store.

1	State **two** characteristics of big data.	[2]
2	Outline **two** ways The leaf could use big data to improve the product element of its marketing mix.	[4]
3	Explain **two** benefits to The Leaf of using AI with its customers.	[4]
4	Define the term 'database'.	[2]
5	Define the term 'data analytics'.	[2]
6	Outline **two** reasons why The Leaf might use a data analytics.	[4]
7	Define the term 'cybercrime'.	[2]
8	Explain **two** reasons cybersecurity might be important to The Leaf.	[4]
9	List **two** forms of cybercrime that The Leaf might face.	[2]
10	Evaluate the benefits to The Leaf of using new technology to support its marketing strategy.	[10]

> # Unit 6
Examination skills

Examination skills

The assessment components

The Business Management course combines internal and external assessment to examine your performance over the two-year IB Diploma course.

Tables 37.1 and 37.2 illustrate the assessment requirements for standard level (SL) and higher level (HL) students, respectively.

	Paper 1	Paper 2	Internal assessment
	Based on a **pre-released statement** that specifies the scope for the **unseen case study**, in terms of context and background	Based on the **unseen stimulus material**. The focus is **quantitative**	**Business research project** This component is internally assessed by the teacher and externally moderated by the IB
Method	**Section A** (Units 1–5 excluding HL extension topics) Students answer all structured questions *(20 marks)*	**Section A** (Units 1–5 excluding HL extension topics) Students answer all structured questions in this section *(20 marks)*	Students produce a research project about a real business issue or problem facing a particular organisation using a conceptual lens. Maximum 1800 words *(25 marks)*
	Section B (Units 1–5 excluding HL extension topics) Students answer one out of two extended response questions *(10 marks)*	**Section B** (Units 1–5 excluding HL extension topics) Students answer one out of two questions comprised of structured questions and an extended response question material *(20 marks)*	
Total marks	30	40	25
Time	1 hour 30 minutes	1 hour 30 minutes	20 hours
Weighting	35%	35%	30%

Table 37.1: Standard level assessment components

	Paper 1	Paper 2	Paper 3	Internal assessment
	Based on a **pre-released statement** that specifies the scope for the **unseen case study**, in terms of context and background	Based on the **unseen stimulus material**. The focus is **quantitative**	Based on **unseen stimulus material** about a **social enterprise**	**Business research project** This component is internally assessed by the teacher and externally moderated by the IB
Method	**Section A** (Units 1–5 excluding HL extension topics) Students answer all structured questions *(20 marks)*	**Section A** (Units 1–5 including HL extension topics) Students answer all structured questions in this section *(30 marks)*	Students answer one compulsory question based on the unseen stimulus material *(25 marks)*	Students produce a research project about a real business issue or problem facing a particular organisation using a conceptual lens. Maximum 1800 words *(25 marks)*
	Section B (Units 1–5 excluding HL extension topics) Students answer one out of two extended response questions *(10 marks)*	**Section B** (Units 1–5 including HL extension topics) Students answer one out of two questions comprised of structured questions and an extended response question material *(20 marks)*		
Total marks	30	50	25	25
Time	1 hour 30 minutes	1 hour 45 minutes	1 hour 15 minutes	20 hours
Weighting	25%	30%	25%	20%

Table 37.2: Higher level assessment components

Command terms

The treatment of examination questions and the depth of analysis depends on the following command terms.

AO1: Knowledge and understanding			In which assessment component
Demonstrate knowledge and understanding of business management tools and theories, course topics and concepts, business problems/issues/decisions			**AO1**
Assessment objective (AO)	Meaning	Example of application in Business Management questions	Paper 1 (SL and HL) Section A and B
AO1 Define	Give a clear, precise statement of the meaning of a business term, word or concept	Define the term 'current asset'	Paper 2 (SL and HL) Section A and B Paper 3 HL Internal assessment
AO1 Describe	Give an account of the characteristics of an object or idea	Describe the CEO's leadership style	
AO1 List	Give a list of characteristics/features of an object or idea with no explanation	List two features of a partnership	
AO1 Identify	Give an answer from a number of possible options	Identify a reason for a fall in company Z's market share	
AO1 Outline	Give a brief summary of the points raised on an issue or idea	Outline the different types of secondary market research	
AO1 State	Give a specific name, value or other brief answer	State the net profit business XYZ made in 2021	

AO2: Application and analysis			In which assessment component
Apply and analyse business management tools and theories, course topics and concepts, business problems/issues/decisions through the selection and use of appropriate data			**AO2**
Assessment objective (AO)	Meaning	Example of application in Business Management questions	Paper 1 (SL and HL) Section A and B
AO2 Explain	Describe, giving reasons, a business idea, observation or issue	Explain how XYZ plc has increased its sales	Paper 2 (SL and HL) Section A and B
AO2 Comment	Give a judgement on a given statement or result of a calculation	Comment on the rise in ABC plc's market share	Paper 3 HL
AO2 Analyse	Separate business material or information into its constituent parts and determine its essential features	Analyse the factors that have led to a rise in business B's profits	Internal assessment
AO2 Apply	Use an idea, equation, principle, theory or law in relation to a given problem or issue	Apply the Boston Consulting Group matrix to analyse ABC plc's product portfolio	
AO2 Distinguish	Make clear the differences between two or more concepts or ideas	Distinguish between a democratic and autocratic leadership style	
AO2 Suggest	Give a solution, reason, hypothesis or another possible answer to a business situation	Suggest a ratio that could be used to measure the liquidity position of business Y	
AO2 Demonstrate	Use reasoning, evidence or examples to explain a business decision or situation	Demonstrate why company C has increased spending on advertising	

AO3: Synthesis and evaluation			In which assessment component
Synthesise and evaluate business management tools and theories, course topics and concepts, business problems/issues/decisions, stakeholder interests, strategy recommendations			AO3
Assessment objective (AO)	Meaning	Example of application in Business Management questions	Paper 1 (SL and HL) Section B
AO3 Compare and contrast	Explain similarities and differences between two (or more) ideas or concepts, referring to both (all) of them throughout	Compare and contrast Herzberg's and Taylor's approaches to motivating workers	Paper 2 (SL and HL) Section B
AO3 Examine	Look at an argument, decision or concept in a way that considers its assumptions and interrelationships	Examine ABC plc's decision to open new outlets in Indonesia	Paper 3 HL Internal assessment
AO3 Discuss	Give a balanced review of a variety of arguments, factors or theories. The view developed should be based on a reasoned argument supported by evidence	Discuss business XYZ's decision to cut prices to increase its market share	
AO3 Evaluate	Consider the advantages and disadvantages of a business decision or proposal	Evaluate the use of JIT stock management by ABC Ltd	
AO3 Justify	Provide evidence or reasons to support an argument, conclusion or decision	Justify ABC's decision to open a new factory	
AO3 Recommend	On an issue or decision, put forward a plan of action supported by reasoning and evidence	Recommend a promotional strategy to retailer A	
AO3 To what extent	Consider the relative strength of an argument based on reasoning and evidence	To what extent is the decision by business A to adopt profit-related pay a successful way to improve staff motivation?	

AO4: Use and application of appropriate skills			In which assessment component
Select and apply relevant business management tools, theories and concepts to support research into a business issue or problem. Select, interpret and analyse business materials from a range of primary and secondary sources. Create well-structured materials using business management terminology. Communicate analysis, evaluation and conclusions of research effectively			AO4
			Paper 1 (SL and HL) Section A and B
			Paper 2 (SL and HL) Section A and B
			Paper 3 HL
			Internal assessment
Assessment objective (AO)	Meaning	Example of application in Business Management questions	
AO4 Plot	Mark the position of points on a graph, chart or diagram	Plot the position of company Y's product on the product position map	
AO4 Complete	Add information or data	Complete the asset and liability figures in XYZ's statement of financial position diagram	
AO4 Construct	Present business data or information in the form of a diagram or table	Construct a decision tree for XYZ's different options	
AO4 Annotate	Add information or notes to a diagram, chart or graph	Draw and annotate an Ansoff's matrix for company Y	
AO4 Draw	Represent by means of a labelled, accurate diagram or graph	Draw a product life cycle for product Y	
AO4 Label	Add labels to a diagram	Label the position map provided	
AO4 Determine	Decide the appropriate course of action/ solution, get the only possible answer	Determine which of the two options is the most appropriate	
AO4 Prepare	Look at an argument, decision or concept in a way that considers its assumptions and interrelationships	Prepare a cash flow table for business X for 2023	
AO4 Calculate	Give a precise numerical value	Calculate XYZ's payback period on its new machine	

The requirements of the assessment components

Paper 1

In Paper 1, which is common for SL and HL students, you will be assessed on your knowledge and understanding of contemporary businesses issues. The IB will release a statement with the context of the case study, along with the first two paragraphs of the case study itself, to help students prepare.

During the examination you will be given the full case study of 800–1000 words. The questions are mostly qualitative.

Sample Paper 1 case study

Line 1 **M&G3D** was established in 2020 as a **private limited company** by Marta Garcia and George Bolt. The business was set up after Marta and George graduated from studying Business and technology (BT) at a postgraduate level. Initially, M&G3D, an online 3D printing business, specialised in producing collectable toys for the 3D figurine market. Today, Marta and George are looking for growth options.

Line 6 Marta and George discovered the endless opportunities of 3D printing at university. 3D printing, also known as 'desktop fabrication additive printing technology', involves using a digital file to develop objects for customers upon request. 3D printing uses raw materials such as metals, ceramics and polymers. The global market for 3D printing products and services was valued at roughly $12.6 billion in 2020. The industry is expected to grow at a compound annual growth rate of 17% between 2020 and 2023.[1]

Line 12 M&G3D was an immediate success. Even though the business was launched in the middle of the Covid-19 pandemic, it appealed to its targeted niche market segment. Its mission statement is: 'We exist to allow you to create the objects of your dreams, limited only by imagination.' The business has ethical objectives as well. It wants to be socially sustainable and create many personal and professional development opportunities for its 14 employees.

Line 17 M&G3D's targeted consumers are mainly hobbyists who like vintage toys. Some of them order parts for items such as model trains. The business is also targeting gamers who print objects for role-playing campaigns. Marta, the marketing and operations director, performed primary research to understand M&G3D's consumer profile. Secondary market research indicated that consumers in this niche are mainly males with high disposable income to spend on their hobbies. M&G3D's services are promoted through social media. A mark-up of 180% is used to price the 3D objects sold online only. But the market is becoming increasingly competitive, and Marta is currently reconsidering the pricing strategy used by M&G3D.

Line 25 George is the finance and human resources director of the business. He acknowledges that the marketing strategy approach led by Marta allowed M&G3D a high profit and high profitability from the first year of operation. Yet he believes that the business should diversify outside collectable toys. Marta is afraid of the risks of diversification. She believes that success in the 3D industry depends on specialisation and the ability of 3D producers to create added value for consumers that traditional manufacturing cannot provide. Apart from the collectable toys market, some industries where such customisation is often required are shoes, decorative items and jewellery. However, she agrees with George that there is a lot of potential for further growth outside the 3D figurine applications by shifting from prototyping to functional part manufacturing in markets such as the automotive industry. In recent years, some competitors successfully diversified in this market because 3D figurine technology helps to produce lightweight vehicle components. Therefore, when using 3D manufactured car parts, car manufacturers can reduce the vehicle's weight and improve performance. Nonetheless, Marta believes that 3D printing in automotives will not replace common mass production methods.

Line 39 While deciding appropriate growth options for the business, the two owners must consider both the capital and the revenue expenditure of 3D printers. The price of 3D printers is still high, and so is the software required to run them. Such software needs to be updated regularly to keep abreast of technological advancements. Moreover, 3D printing requires a lot of energy, making the production of certain items cost-ineffective.

Line 44 George has been approached by Carla, the CEO of Deco&More3D, a 3D printing business that is twice the size of M&G3D, specialising in the production of 3D jewellery and decorative items. Carla suggested that the two businesses should horizontally integrate by merging into a new entity under a new name. Integration in the industry, which is very fragmented, is a trend. It could allow the two businesses significant benefits such as economies of scale and creating opportunities for professional development for the employees of both businesses. Marta does not favour the idea of external growth. She believes that the brand name of M&G3D is enjoying increasing awareness and preference, and that it is an intangible asset that should not be sacrificed for quick growth. She is also afraid of potential cultural clashes.

[1] *https://www.statista.com/markets/418/technology-telecommunications/*

Section A sample questions

1   Define the term 'revenue expenditure' (line 40).   [2]

2   Describe **two** elements of M&G3D's marketing mix.   [4]

3   Suggest **one** reason why Marta should probably change its pricing strategy and one reason why she should not.   [6]

Section B sample question

4   Discuss whether M&G3D should diversify into the automotive market.   [10]

Tips for Paper 1

- The IB will release a statement with the context and background of the case study before the examination. Make sure you familiarise yourself with the industry that Paper 1 will focus on.

- Paper 1 will typically address a given industry. You are advised to collect secondary information in the form of newspaper articles, market intelligence reports, academic journals and national statistics on this market. Most of this information will probably be available online at no cost. You could also consider conducting primary research, for example by interviewing managers in businesses operating in the industry in question. Your teacher will guide and support you throughout your research process.

- The time available for Paper 1 is 90 minutes for 30 marks, so it is 3 minutes per mark. It may be wise to allocate less than 3 minutes per mark on Section A to allow you more time for Section B (as Section B requires planning). As a general rule, try to allocate roughly 60% of your time to Section A and 40% of your time to Section B.

- Your aim throughout the Paper 1 examination is to demonstrate good knowledge of the syllabus and the ability to apply theory on a given contemporary business issue.

- In Section A, sharp and focused answers are needed. Focus on the exact demands of the question based on the command term used. Do not write extensive responses.

- In Section B you need to address an evaluative question. You should demonstrate the ability to critically discuss an issue faced or decision to be made by the business appearing in the case study. Make sure that you provide a balanced, in-depth discussion by making good use of the data provided in the case study and based on management theory. In this part of the examination, you need to demonstrate your ability to effectively apply theory on the stimulus material to support an argument. Examiners will be looking for substantiated and balanced arguments. This is where you need to show your critical ability skill to discuss and synthesise the material provided in the case study through the help of appropriate management theory and tools. Plan your answer before writing. This will help you to focus better and to ensure that you adopt a balanced approach in your response. Planning involves appropriate paragraphing, including a conclusion. An effective conclusion is more than a simple summary of the points discussed in the main body. It could include an insightful comment about future decisions or problems to be faced by the organisation.

Paper 2

In this part of the examination, students are assessed for their syllabus knowledge. Most but not all questions will be quantitative.

Sample question

Jose and Piedra set up a partnership under the name Bubbles, a soft play park for children. Apart from offering childminding and supervision services in the park, Bubbles also organises birthday parties. Jose and Piedra share all responsibilities and capital expenditure. Bubbles wants to offer soft play equipment of excellent quality. The market is very competitive, and customers have a wide variety of similar parks to choose from. For the second quarter of the current year, Jose forecasts a cash flow problem for Bubbles.

Capital expenditure on new soft play equipment	$5000 in the first month
Estimated revenue per month	$7000 for the first month, increasing 5% each following month
Monthly rent	$2000
Opening cash balance	$1500
Utilities	$700 paid in the second month
Salaries	$3000 per month
All other expenses	$500 per month

Table 1: Bubbles' forecast cash flow figures (April–June)

Piedra suggested that both partners should use their personal savings to improve the cash flow position of Bubbles. Jose suggested that they should ask the bank for an overdraft instead. However, he knows that the bank might be unwilling to offer an overdraft to an unincorporated business like Bubbles.

1   State **two** advantages of partnerships.   [2]

_____

_____

_____

_____

2   Using Table 1, prepare a cash flow forecast for Bubble for months April to June.   [6]

3   Suggest **one** way **other than** personal savings to improve the cash flow position of Bubbles   [2]

_____

_____

_____

_____

4   Using information from the stimulus, discuss appropriate sources of finance for the cash flow problem faced by Bubbles   [10]

Tips for Paper 2

- In Paper 2, the stimulus material will include diagrammatic information such as charts and infographics. This information is just as important as the written stimulus and you should make use of it when answering the question.

- Section A: Compulsory structured questions. SL students answer fewer questions than HL students. Section A is worth 20 marks for SL and 30 marks for HL.

- Section B (the same for SL and HL): one question based on the stimulus material from a choice of two, worth 20 marks. Suggested time allocation: SL: 40% on Section A, 60% on Section B. HL: 55% on Section A, 45% on Section B.

- Section A involves structured questions based on the stimulus material. The focus of this section is primarily quantitative. Record your workings, use a ruler to draw tables and graphs. Answer questions precisely and in full, but do not write more than required. If you write excessively, you will waste time and you may lose focus.

- Section B examines structured questions like Section A, but it also examines AO3 through a 10-mark evaluative question. Make sure that you synthesise parts of the stimulus material to successfully answer this question (the question may explicitly require the use of charts or tables from the stimulus material provided). Use appropriate paragraphing (see tips for Section B, Paper 1).

- Using the business management toolkit as a basis to structure a balanced argument in the evaluative question of Section B is highly recommended.

Paper 3 (HL only)

This paper is based on a stimulus about a social enterprise. You will be asked to identify the human need behind social enterprise activities and the challenges faced by this business. You will also need to write a decision-making document, including a business recommendation.

Sample stimulus material Paper 3

Read the resources and answer the questions that follow.

Resource 1: News article

Food for All (FFA) winner of the Social Enterprise Award for 2021

The winner of the Social Enterprise Award for 2021 is FFA Social Supermarkets, which stood out for its clear vision and valuable contribution across our city. By creating excellent relationships with suppliers, it offers surplus food and consumer products at very low prices to people in need. But its contribution is not limited to low-priced offerings. FFA gives employment opportunities to people typically excluded from the labour market, such as the chronically unemployed. It also helps to improve the long-term employability skills of its staff through excellent training opportunities.

Social supermarkets (SSMs) differ from conventional supermarkets mainly in their marketing mix choices, primarily regarding the price strategy followed. Most items sold through FFA retail outlets are unsellable by the manufacturers (for example, because there is a problem with their packaging or because they are close to their expiry date, etc.). Therefore, SSMs help to reduce food waste as well. FFA stores sell products at 60%–70% of the price found in conventional supermarkets, in a way that each item sold will contribute to paying the firm's fixed costs. In FFA stores, distribution is restricted to financially disadvantaged consumers who have the required identification cards.

'We are so proud to receive this award,' said Maurice Dheere, FFA's founder and CEO. 'We had to overcome numerous problems to make FFA what it is today. Social supermarkets are difficult to operate, especially from a supply chain management and quality control perspective,' he added.

Resource 2: Internal communication (email)

From: Sandra Peters, finance director

To: Maurice Dheere, CEO

Subject: Financial Results 2021

Dear Maurice

Further to our recent discussion, please find attached the variance analysis between the actual results of the financial year 2021 compared to the budgeted figures.

Budget for FFA for the period ended 31/12/2021 ($ million)

	Budgeted figures	Actual figures	Variance
Income			
Sales revenue	26	22	−4
Total income	**26**	**22**	**−4**
Expenses			
Salaries and wages	7	7.5	0.5
Training	1	1	0
Cost of goods sold	12	11	−1
Rent	2	2	0
Advertising	1	1	0
Utilities	2	2.5	0.5
Total expenses	**25**	**25**	**0**
Net income	**1**	**−3**	**−4**

Our sales this year were lower than expected. Due to inflation, we had to take some price increases across our product portfolio. Unfortunately, most of our goods are price inelastic, excluding basic food products. To improve our sales performance, we could look for new revenue streams. Otherwise, we will need to cut some costs, starting with salaries and wages and training. The contracts of some of our employees are coming to an end next month. I think that we should not renew them.

To improve the accuracy of our budget next year, I plan to treat our five stores as separate profit centres.

Best wishes

Sandra

Sample Paper 3 questions

1   Identify the pricing strategy used by FFA to satisfy its customer needs.   [2]

2   Using the concept of the 'triple bottom line', explain two ways FFA tries to be a sustainable business.   [6]

3   Using all the resources provided and your knowledge of business management, recommend a possible plan of action to ensure economic sustainability for FFA in the following years.   [17]

Tips for Paper 3

- This paper aims to examine the ability of students to apply business theory and analyse and evaluate strategic decisions about a social enterprise. This part of the examination is forward-looking. You should demonstrate an ability to evaluate decisions acting as change agents.

- Suggested time allocation: 33% for the AO1 (2-mark) and AO2 (6-mark) questions, 67% for the AO3 (17-mark) question.

- AO1 questions in Paper 3 will typically require you to identify a particular human need in the case study.

- AO2 questions in Paper 3 are about your ability to explain the challenges faced by the social enterprise in question through the application of appropriate theory.

- AO3 questions involve the creation of a structured and balanced recommendation for the organisation to meet its objectives. Your ability to discuss and synthesise information based on management theory will be examined.
  The difference between AO3 17-mark questions and the 10-mark questions in Papers 1 and 2 is that the 17-mark questions require a strategic and forward-looking approach and not just a balanced discussion. To achieve that, a plan involving a careful re-reading of the case study is recommended. Nonetheless, the question is broad enough to allow full marks for many different responses, as long as these demonstrate sufficient strategic focus.

Internal assessment (IA)

Both HL and SL students must produce a business research project about a real issue or problem facing an organisation using a conceptual lens.

The business research project must be based only on **one** key concept – change, creativity, ethics or sustainability.

Word count: 1800 words (moderators will not read above this limit)

Structure: The IA should have:

- an introduction that sets the context and demonstrates some knowledge about the business organisation

- a main body with subtitles to present the finding from the supporting documents, analysed based on management theory/tools and discussed in a balanced and evaluative manner

- a conclusion that explicitly answers the research question.

Tips for a successful IA

- Choose your research question with the help of your teacher. If the research question is not the appropriate one, you will not be able to access all levels of the IA criteria.

- A successful IA question is likely to have two main characteristics:
  - not too wide, because wide questions do not allow in-depth analysis
  - not too narrow, so that 3–5 relevant supporting documents can be found to support it.

- Research questions should not be simplistic and their answer should not be obvious to the student before even conducting research.

- Choose your 3–5 supporting documents carefully, in a way that these would present a range of varied ideas. Supporting documents can be from both primary and secondary sources. If you phrase a forward-looking question, you are recommended to base your analysis mainly on primary sources. A backwards-looking question should be mostly based on secondary sources. The supporting documents must be relevant and sufficiently in-depth, and they need to provide a range of ideas and views.

  Examples of primary sources: surveys (face-to-face or online); interviews (face-to-face or online); focus groups.

  Examples of secondary sources: newspaper articles; final accounts/annual reports; business plans; management journals; market research analysis; transcripts of audio-visual files; government statitsics; official business webpages.

- Choose the appropriate business theories/tools that will help you critically analyse your research question based on your findings from the supporting documents. You need a range of theories/tools, but if you decide to apply too many you will not be able to apply them in sufficient depth.

- Follow the IA criteria closely, as these appear in the Business Management Guide.

Examples of appropriate IA research questions

1 **How can company X successfully grow in market Y?**

   Such a project could examine business management topics such as growth and marketing strategy and measure of financial success using **sustainability** as a conceptual lens.

2 **Should company X change its production method from batch to mass production?**

   The project could then examine areas within business management such as operations management, human resource management and investment appraisal using **change** as a conceptual lens.

The seven criteria for the internal assessment are:

Description	Total marks available
Criterion A: Integration of a key concept	5
Criterion B: Supporting documents	4
Criterion C: Selection and application of tools and theories	4
Criterion D: Analysis and evaluation	5
Criterion E: Conclusions	3
Criterion F: Structure	2
Criterion G: Presentation	2
Total:	25

> Glossary

above-the-line promotion: a form of promotion that is undertaken by a business by paying for communication with consumers, e.g., advertising

absorption costing: a method of costing in which all indirect and direct costs are allocated to the products, services or divisions of a business

accountability: the obligation of an individual to account for his or her activities and to disclose results in a transparent way

accounting rate of return (ARR): measures the annual profitability of an investment as a percentage of the average investment (average capital cost)

acid test ratio: this compares the liquid assets of a business with its current liabilities

acquisition: when a company buys at least 50% of the shares of another company and becomes the controlling owner – with the agreement of the existing owner(s)/managers

added value: the difference between the cost of purchasing raw materials and the price the finished goods are sold for

adverse variance: exists when the difference between the budgeted and actual figures leads to a lower than expected profit

annual forecast net cash flow: forecast cash inflow minus forecast cash outflows

Ansoff matrix: a model used to show the degree of risk associated with the four growth strategies of: market penetration, market development, product development and diversification

arbitration: resolving an industrial dispute by using an independent third party to judge and recommend an appropriate solution

artificial intelligence (AI): a branch of computer science focusing on building smart machines capable of performing tasks that typically require human intelligence

artificial neural network (ANN): programming computers to behave like interconnected brain cells

autocratic leadership: a style of leadership that keeps all decision-making at the centre of the organisation

backward vertical integration: integration with a business that is in the same industry but a supplier of the existing business

bad debt: unpaid customers' bills that are now very unlikely ever to be paid

bankruptcy: a legal proceeding carried out to allow individuals or businesses freedom from their debts, while simultaneously providing creditors an opportunity for repayment

batch production: producing a limited number of identical products – each item in the batch passes through one stage of production before passing on to the next stage

below-the-line promotion: promotion that does not use directly paid-for means of communication but is based on targeting individual market segments or individual consumers with incentives to purchase, e.g., sales promotion techniques

benchmarking: involves management identifying the best firms in the industry and then comparing the performance standards – including quality – of these businesses with those of their own business

big data: extremely large sets of data that may be analysed by computers to establish trends, patterns and associations which can help to inform business decisions

Boston Consulting Group (BCG) matrix: a method of analysing the product portfolio of a business in terms of market share and market growth

brand: an identifying symbol, name, image or trademark that distinguishes a product from its competitors

brand awareness: the extent to which a brand is recognised by potential customers and is correctly associated with a particular product – can be expressed as a percentage of the target market

brand development: measures the infiltration of a product's sales, usually per thousand population; if 100 people in 1000 buy a product, it has a brand development of 10

brand loyalty: the faithfulness of consumers to a particular brand as shown by their repeat purchases irrespective of the marketing pressure from competing brands

brand value (or brand equity): the premium that a brand has because customers are willing to pay more for it than they would for a non-branded generic product

break-even point: the level of output at which total costs equal total revenue

budget: a detailed financial plan for the future

buffer stocks: the minimum stocks that should be held to ensure that production could still take place should a delay in delivery occur or production rates increase

bureaucracy: an organisational system with standardised procedures and rules

business angels: individual investors who put in their own money in a variety of businesses and are seeking a better return than they would obtain from conventional investments

business objectives: short- or medium-term goals or targets – usually specific in nature – which must be achieved for an organisation to attain its overall corporate aim

business plan: a written document that describes a business, its objectives and its strategies, the market it is in and its financial forecasts

business-process outsourcing (BPO): a form of outsourcing that uses a third party to take responsibility for complete business functions, such as HR and finance

capacity utilisation: the proportion of maximum output capacity currently being achieved

capital employed: the total value of all long-term finance invested in the business = non-current liabilities + equity

capital goods: physical goods that are used by industry to aid in the production of other goods and services such as machines and commercial vehicles

capital productivity: a measure of how efficiently capital input is used to produce output

cash flow: the sum of cash payments to a business less the sum of cash payments from

cash flow forecast: estimate of a firm's future cash inflows and outflows

cash inflows: payments in cash received by a business, such as those from customers (debtors) or from the bank, e.g., receiving a loan

cash outflow: payments in cash made by a business, such as those to suppliers and workers

cell production: flow production split into self-contained work groups that are responsible for a complete unit of work

centralisation: keeping all of the important decision-making powers within head office or the centre of the organisation

chain of command: this is the route through which authority is passed down an organisation – from the chief executive and the board of directors

change management: planning, implementing, controlling and reviewing the movement of an organisation from its current state to a new one

channel of distribution: the chain of intermediaries a product passes through from producer to final consumer

charity: an organisation set up to raise money to help people in need or to support causes that require funding

circular business model: a business approach that creates product value whilst at the same time improving resource efficiency by extending the useful life of products and components

circular economy: a model of production and consumption which involves sharing, leasing, reusing, repairing, refurbishing and recycling existing materials and products for as long as possible

closed questions: questions to which a limited number of preset answers is offered

closing balance: cash held at the end of the month becomes next month's opening balance

cloud computing: using a network of remote servers hosted on the internet to store, manage and process data, rather than a data centre or a personal computer

collective bargaining: the negotiations between employees' representatives (trade unions) and employers on issues of common interest such as pay and conditions of work

command economy: economic resources are owned, planned and controlled by the state

commission: a payment to a sales person for each sale made

communication barrier: something that gets in the way of a message being received

communication methods: the media used to convey a message

competitive advantage: an advantage that a business has over rivals gained by offering consumers greater value, either with low prices or by providing greater benefits and service to justify a higher price

competitive pricing: making pricing decisions based on the price set by competitors

conciliation: the use of a third party in industrial disputes to encourage both employer and union to discuss an acceptable compromise solution

conglomerate integration: merger with or takeover of a business that is in a different industry

consumer durables: manufactured products that can be reused and are expected to have a reasonably long life, such as cars

consumer goods: the physical and tangible goods sold to final users, these include cars, food and clothing

consumer profile: a quantified picture of consumers of a firm's products, showing proportions of age groups, income levels, location, gender and social class

consumer services: non-tangible products that are sold to final users, these include hotel accommodation, insurance services and train journeys

contingency planning: preparing the immediate steps to be taken by an organisation in the event of a crisis or emergency

contribution costing: costing method that allocates only direct costs to cost centres and profit centres, not overhead costs

contribution per unit: selling price of a product minus direct costs per unit

contribution pricing: setting prices based on the variable costs of making a product, in order to make a contribution towards fixed costs and profit

convenience sampling: drawing a representative selection of people because of the ease of volunteering or selecting people because of their availability or easy access

cooperative: a group of people acting together to meet the common needs and aspirations of its members, sharing ownership and making decisions democratically

coordinated marketing mix: key marketing decisions complement each other and work together to give customers a consistent message about the product

copyright: legal right to protect and be the sole beneficiary from artistic and literary works

corporate aims: the long-term goals which a business hopes to achieve

corporate social responsibility: this concept applies to those businesses that consider the interests of society by taking responsibility for the impact of their decisions and activities on customers, employees, communities and the environment

cost centre: a section of a business, such as a department, to which costs can be allocated or charged

cost of sales (or cost of goods sold): this is the direct cost of purchasing the goods that were sold during the financial year

cost-plus pricing: adding a fixed mark up to the unit cost of a product to cover overhead costs and for profit

cradle to cradle (C2C): a design and manufacturing model where products are safe, enriching to the environment or user, and leave no waste for future generations

credit control: monitoring of debts to ensure that credit periods are not exceeded

creditor days: the average length of time taken to pay suppliers

creditors: suppliers to a business who have not yet been paid

crisis management: steps taken by an organisation to limit the damage from a significant, damaging event by handling, containing and resolving it

criterion rate: the minimum accounting rate of return (ARR) that a business would accept before approving an investment

critical path: the sequence of activities that must be completed on time for the whole project to be completed by the agreed date

critical path analysis: a planning technique that identifies all tasks in a project, puts them in the correct sequence and allows for the identification of the critical path

culture clash: a conflict arising from the interaction of people with different values, attitude and beliefs

current assets: the value of all assets that could reasonably be expected to be converted into cash within one year

current liabilities: debts of the business that will usually have to be paid within one year

current ratio: this compares the current assets with the current liabilities of the business

customer loyalty programme: a marketing strategy that rewards loyal customers who frequently buy the brand's products

customer loyalty: a positive relationship between the business and customer which leads to a willingness by the customers to make repeat visits and purchases

customer relationship management: the strategies and techniques a business uses to interact and communicate with customers

customer relationship marketing (CRM): using marketing activities to build and establish good customer relationships so that the loyalty of existing customers can be maintained

cybercrime: any criminal activity that involves a computer, networked device or a network

cybersecurity: measures taken to protect against the criminal or unauthorised use of electronic data and illegal access to computer systems or internet connected devices

data analytics: the science of analysing raw statistical data to make conclusions about that information to inform business decision-making

data centre: a physical facility that organisations use to accommodate and make secure their critical IT equipment, applications and data

data mining: the process of analysing a large batch of information to establish trends and patterns which could be useful for business decision making

database: a store of information that is organised for easy access, management and updating

debentures (or corporate bonds): bonds issued by companies to raise debt finance, often with a fixed rate of interest

debtor days: how long, on average, it takes the business to recover payment from customers who have bought goods on credit

debtors: customers who have bought products on credit and will pay cash at an agreed date in the future

decentralisation: decision-making powers are passed down the organisation to empower subordinates and regional/product managers

decision tree: a diagram that sets out the options connected with a decision and the outcomes and economic returns that may result

defect rate: the proportion of output in a time period which fails to reach quality standards

degree of operating leverage: measures how much a company's operating income changes in response to a change in sales

delayering: removal of one or more of the levels of hierarchy from an organisational structure

delegated budgets: control over budgets is given to less-senior management

delegation: passing authority down the organisational hierarchy

democratic leadership: a leadership style that promotes the active participation of workers in taking decisions

digital promotion: the use of the internet, mobile devices, social media, search engines, and other channels to communicate with consumers to provide information about products and encourage the purchase of them

digital Taylorism: building on Taylor's original work and adding to it by suggesting that digitally collected and analysed data is used to monitor and improve employee performance

direct costs: costs that can be clearly identified with each unit of production and can be traced back or allocated to a cost centre

disruptive innovation: when a substantially different a product or service using initially simple applications enters at the bottom of a market and then forcefully moves up the market, eventually displacing established competitors

diversification: the process of selling different, unrelated goods or services in new markets

dividends: the share of the profits paid to shareholders as a return for investing in the company

dynamic pricing: offering products at a price that changes according to the level of demand and the customer's ability to pay

ecological sustainability: the capacity of ecosystems to maintain their essential functions and processes, and retain their full biodiversity over the long term

economic sustainability: in a business context, economic sustainability involves using the assets of the company efficiently to allow it to continue functioning profitability over time

effective communication: the exchange of information between people or groups, with feedback

electronic performance monitoring (EPM): using data gathered and analysed electronically to measure and monitor employee performance

emerging market economy: a country with an economic system which results in low to middle income per head of population

employee appraisal: the process of assessing the effectiveness of an employee judged against pre-set objectives

empowerment: delegating to an employee or group of employees the authority to perform a task and to take appropriate decisions to be able to complete it

entrepreneur: someone who takes the financial risk of starting and managing a new venture

entrepreneurial culture: encourages management and workers to take risks, to come up with new ideas and test out new business ventures

equity finance: permanent finance raised by companies through the sale of shares

ethical code (code of conduct): a document detailing a company's rules and guidelines on staff behaviour that must be followed by all employees

ethics: moral guidelines that determine decision-making

expected value: the likely financial result of an outcome obtained by multiplying the probability of an event occurring by the forecast economic return if it does occur

extension strategies: marketing plans that extend the maturity stage of the product before a brand new one is needed

external diseconomies of scale: factors causing units costs for a business to rise as an industry expands, especially in a given region

external economies of scale: reductions in unit (average) costs of production of a business that result from growth of the industry, often in one particular region

external finance: raised from sources outside the business

external growth: business expansion achieved by means of merging with or taking over another business, from either the same or a different industry

external recruitment: filling vacant posts by appointing candidates from outside of the organisation

extrinsic motivation: comes from external rewards associated with working on a task, for example pay and other benefits

favourable variance: exists when the difference between the budgeted and actual figures leads to a higher than expected profit

feedback: information given by the receiver in response to a message

final accounts: the end of year financial accounts produced by a business

fixed costs: costs that do not vary with output or sales in the short term

flat (horizontal) organisational structure: one with few levels of hierarchy and wide spans of control

flexi-time: a flexible way of working that allows employees to fit their working hours around their individual needs to allow for other commitments outside of work

flow production: producing items in a continually moving production line – also known as line production. This can be a continuous 24-hours-a-day method

focus groups: a group of people who are asked about their attitude towards a product, service, advertisement or new style of packaging

force field analysis: an analytical process used to map the opposing forces within a business where change is taking place

formal communication: information that flows through well-defined official channels

forward vertical integration: integration with a business that is in the same industry but a customer of the existing business

franchise: a business that uses the name, logo and trading systems of an existing successful business

free-market economy: economic resources are owned largely by the private sector with very little state intervention

full capacity: when a business produces at productive capacity or maximum output

Gantt chart: a visual representation of a project schedule in which a series of horizontal lines shows the amount of work planned in certain periods of time

gearing ratio: measures the proportion of long-term capital invested in the business that is borrowed

geographical mobility of labour: extent to which workers are willing and able to move geographical region to take up new jobs

gig economy: a labour market characterised by the widespread use of short-term contracts or freelance work rather than jobs with permanent contracts

global localisation: adapting the marketing mix, including differentiated products, to meet national and regional tastes and cultures

globalisation: the growing interaction and integration between markets, businesses, people and governments worldwide

goodwill: arises when a business is valued at or sold for more than the statement of financial position value of its assets

gross profit: equal to sales revenue less cost of sales

gross profit margin: this ratio compares gross profit (profit before deduction of overhead expenses) with revenue

hierarchical structure: a structure in which power and responsibility are clearly specified and allocated to individuals according to their standing or position in the hierarchy

hire purchase: an asset is sold to a company which agrees to make fixed repayments over an agreed time period; the asset belongs to the company once the final payment is made

horizontal integration: integration with a business that is in the same industry and at the same stage of production

hourly wage rate: payment to a worker made for each hour worked

human resource management (HRM): the strategic approach to the effective management of an organisation's workers so that they help the business achieve its objectives and gain a competitive advantage

human resource planning: also known as workforce planning – analysing and forecasting the numbers of workers and the skills of those workers that will be required by the organisation to achieve its objectives

hygiene factors: aspects of a worker's job that have the potential to cause dissatisfaction, such as pay, working conditions, status and over-supervision by managers

incremental budgeting: uses last year's budget as a basis and an adjustment is made for the coming year

incremental innovation: a series of small improvements or upgrades made to a company's existing products, services or processes

indirect costs: costs which cannot be identified with a unit of production or allocated accurately to a cost centre – also known as overhead costs

induction training: introductory training programme to familiarise new recruits with the systems used in the business and the layout of the business site

industrial action: measures taken by the workforce or trade union to put pressure on management to settle an industrial dispute in favour of employees

informal communication: the sending of unofficial messages between informal groups within an organisation

information overload: so much information and so many messages are received that the most important ones cannot be easily identified and quickly acted on – most likely to occur with electronic media

initial public offering (IPO): the process of offering for sale the shares of a privately held company to financial institutions and the general public

innovation: the practical application of new inventions into marketable products

insolvency: a state of financial distress in which a person or business is unable to pay their debts. This can lead to liquidation

insourcing: the reverse of outsourcing as it is undertaking a business function or process within the business rather than contracting it to another business

intangible product: a non-physical product (a service) provided to a consumer, such as an insurance policy or a car repair

intellectual property: an intangible asset that has been developed from human ideas and knowledge

intellectual property rights: legal property rights over the possession and use of intellectual property

internal customers: people within the organisation who depend upon the quality of work being done by others

internal diseconomies of scale: factors that cause unit (average) costs of production to rise when the scale of operation of a business is increased

internal economies of scale: reductions in a unit (average) costs of production that result from an increase in the scale of operations of a business

internal finance: raised from the business's own assets or from profits left in the business (ploughed-back or retained profits)

internal growth: expansion of a business by means of opening new branches, shops or factories (also known as organic growth)

internal recruitment: filling vacant posts by appointing existing employees

international marketing: selling products in markets other than the original domestic market

internet of things (IOT): consists of any device with an on/off switch connected to the internet

interpersonal communication: exchange of information between two or more people

intrinsic motivation: comes from the satisfaction derived from working on and completing a task

intuitive management: decision making based on the hunches and subconscious expertise of managers

invention: the discovery of new ideas for products or processes

investment appraisal: evaluating the profitability or desirability of an investment project

ISO 9000:   an internationally recognised certificate that acknowledges the existence of a quality procedure that meets certain conditions

JIC – just-in-case stock control: stock management strategy that businesses use when they hold a high level of stocks because there is a risk of 'stock-out'

JIT – just-in-time stock control: this stock-control method aims to avoid holding stocks by requiring supplies to arrive just as they are needed in production, and completed products are produced to order

job enlargement: attempting to increase the scope of a job by broadening or deepening the tasks undertaken

job enrichment: aims to use the full capabilities of workers by giving them the opportunity to do more challenging and fulfilling work

job production: producing a one-off item specially designed for each customer

job rotation: the practice of moving employees between different tasks to promote experience and variety

joint venture: two or more businesses agree to work closely together on a particular project and create a separate business division to do so

just-in-time (JIT):   this stock-control method aims to avoid holding stocks by requiring supplies to arrive just as they are needed in production and completed products are produced to order

kaizen: Japanese term meaning 'continuous improvement'

labour productivity: the number of units produced per employee during a time period

labour turnover: measures the rate at which employees are leaving an organisation

laissez-faire leadership: a leadership style that leaves much of the business decision-making to the workforce – a 'hands-off' approach and the reverse of the autocratic style

lead time: the normal time taken between ordering new stocks and their delivery

leadership: the act of motivating a group of people towards achieving a common objective

lean production: producing goods and services with the minimum of wasted resources while maintaining high quality

leasing: obtaining the use of equipment or vehicles and paying a rental or leasing charge over a fixed period. This avoids the need for the business to raise long-term capital to buy the asset; ownership remains with the leasing company

level of hierarchy: a stage of the organisational structure at which the personnel on it have equal status and authority

level of production: the number of units produced during a time period

liabilities: financial obligations of a business that it is required to pay in the future

limited liability: the only liability – or potential loss – a shareholder (or partner in a limited liability partnership) has if the company fails is the amount invested in the company, not the total wealth of the shareholder

liquidation: the process of bringing a business to an end and distributing its assets to claimants such as creditors – usually done by selling the assets of the business and distributing the cash raised

liquidity: the ability of a business to pay its short-term debts

long-term loans: loans that do not have to be repaid for at least one year

loss leader: product sold at a very low price to encourage consumers to buy other products

management: directing and controlling a group of people or an organisation to reach a goal by using the resources available to the organisation

management buy-out: the existing managers of a business purchase it from the owners to take full control

management information system (MIS):   the computerised databases and procedures that managers use to collect data to measure the effectiveness of their organisations, departments, teams, specific projects, or even individual employees

manager: responsible for setting objectives, organising resources and motivating employees so that the organisation's aims are met

margin of safety: the amount by which the current output level exceeds the break-even level of output

marginal cost: the additional cost of producing one more unit of output

mark up: the extra amount or percentage added to the cost of goods to give the retail or selling price

market development: the strategy of selling existing products in new markets

market growth: the percentage change in the total size of a market (volume or value) over a period of time

market leadership: when a business has the highest market share of all firms that operate in that market

market orientation: an outward-looking approach basing product decisions on consumer demand, as established by market research

market penetration: achieving higher market shares in existing markets with existing products

market research: process of collecting, recording and analysing data about customers, competitors and the market

market segment: a sub-group of a market made up of consumers with similar characteristics, tastes and preferences

market share: sales of the business as a proportion of total market size, in a given period

market size: the total level of sales of all producers within a market

market value: the estimated total value of a company if it were taken over

marketing: the management task that links the business to the customer by identifying and meeting the needs of customers profitably – it does this by getting the right product at the right price to the right place at the right time

marketing mix: the key decisions that must be taken in the effective marketing of a product

marketing planning: the process of developing appropriate strategies and preparing marketing activities to meet marketing objectives

mass customisation: the use of flexible computer-aided technology on flow production lines to configure products that meet individual customers' requirements for customised products

mass market: a market for products that are often standardised and sold in large quantities

mass marketing: selling the same products to the whole market with no attempt to target groups within it

mass production: producing large quantities of a standardised product

matrix structure: an organisational structure that creates project teams from across traditional functional departments

merger: an agreement by shareholders and managers of two businesses to bring both businesses together under a common board of directors with shareholders in both businesses owning shares in the newly merged business

microfinance: the provision of very small loans by specialist finance businesses, usually not traditional commercial banks

mission statement: a statement of the business's core aims, phrased in a way to motivate employees and to stimulate interest by outside groups

mixed economy: economic resources are owned and controlled by both private and public sectors

motivating factors (motivators): aspects of a worker's job that can lead to positive job satisfaction, such as achievement, recognition, meaningful and interesting work and advancement at work

motivation: the factors that stimulate people to take actions that lead to the achievement of a goal

multinational: a business with operations or production bases in more than one country

multinational company or business: business organisation that has its headquarters in one country, but with operating branches, factories and assembly plants in other countries

net book value: the current statement of financial position value of a non-current asset = original cost – accumulated depreciation

net cash flow: the sum of cash payments to a business (inflows) less the sum of cash payments made by it (outflows)

net monthly cash flow: estimated difference between monthly cash inflows and outflows

net present value (NPV): today's value of the estimated net cash flows resulting from an investment

network diagram: the diagram used in critical path analysis that shows the logical sequence of activities and the logical dependencies between them, so the critical path can be identified

niche market: a small and specific part of a larger market

niche marketing: identifying and exploiting a small segment of a larger market by developing products to suit it

non-governmental organisation (NGO): a legally constituted body that functions independently of any government and that has a specific humanitarian or social aim/purpose, e.g., supporting disadvantaged groups in developing countries or advocating the protection of human rights

non-profit organisation: any organisation that has aims other than making and distributing profit and which is usually governed by a voluntary board

no-strike agreement: unions sign an agreement with employers not to strike in exchange for greater involvement in decisions that affect the workforce

observational technique: a qualitative method of collecting and analysing information obtained through directly or indirectly watching and observing others in business environments' e.g., watching consumers walk around a supermarket

occupational mobility of labour: extent to which workers are willing and able to move to different jobs requiring different skills

offshoring: the relocation of a business process done in one country to the same or another company in another country

online marketing: advertising and marketing activities that use the internet, email and mobile communications to encourage direct sales via electronic commerce

on-the-job training: instruction at the place of work on how a job should be carried out

open questions: those that invite a wide-ranging or imaginative response

opening cash balance: cash held by the business at the start of the month

optimal location: a business location that gives the best combination of quantitative and qualitative factors

organisational (corporate) culture: the shared values, attitudes and beliefs of the people working in an organisation that influence how they interact with each other and with external stakeholder groups

organisational structure: the internal, formal framework of a business that shows the way in which management is organised and linked together and how authority is passed through the organisation

outsourcing: using another business (a 'third party') to undertake a part of the production process rather than doing it within the business using the firm's own employees

overdraft: a bank agrees to a business borrowing up to an agreed limit as and when required

overtrading: expanding a business rapidly without obtaining all the necessary finance so that a cash flow shortage develops

pan-global marketing: adopting a standardised product across the globe as if the whole world were a single market – selling the same goods in the same way everywhere

partnership: a business formed by two or more people to carry on a business together, with shared capital investment and, usually, shared responsibilities

patent: legal right to be the sole producer and seller of an invention for a certain period of time

paternalistic leadership: a type of fatherly/motherly style typically used by dominant leaders where their power is used to control and protect subordinate employees who are expected to be loyal and obedient

payback period: length of time it takes for the net cash inflows to pay back the original capital cost of the investment

penetration pricing: setting a relatively low price often supported by strong promotion in order to achieve a high volume of sales

performance-related pay: a bonus scheme to reward staff for above-average work performance

person culture: when individuals are given the freedom to express themselves and make decisions

person specification: a detailed list of the qualities, skills and qualifications that a successful applicant will need to have

physical evidence: the ways in which the business and its products are presented to customers

piece rate: a payment to a worker for each unit produced

power culture: concentrating power among a few people

predatory pricing: deliberately undercutting competitors' prices in order to try to force them out of the market

premium pricing: setting a price above that of competitors with the aim of developing a superior image for the product

price elasticity of demand (PED): a measure of the responsiveness of demand for a product following a change in its price

primary research: the collection of first-hand data that is directly related to a firm's needs

primary sector business activity: businesses engaged in farming, fishing, oil extraction and all other industries that extract natural resources to be used and processed by other firms

private sector: comprises businesses owned and controlled by individuals or groups of individuals

privately held company: a business that is owned by shareholders who are often members of the same family; this company cannot sell shares to the general public

privatisation: the sale of public sector organisations to the private sector

process: procedures and policies that are put in place to provide the service or the product to the consumer

process production: producing standardised goods, typically in bulk quantities, by using a continuous input of materials and other resources

product: the end result of the production process sold on the market to satisfy a customer need

product development: the development and sale of new products or new developments of existing products in existing markets

product life cycle: the pattern of sales recorded by a product from launch to withdrawal from the market

product orientation: an inward-looking approach that focuses on making products that can be made – or have been made for a long time – and then trying to sell them

product portfolio: the collection of all of the products (goods and services) offered for sale by a business

product position map or **perception map:** a diagram that analyses consumer perceptions of competing brands in respect of two product characteristics

production positioning: the process of designing the company's products and image to occupy a distinctive place in the perceptions of consumers in the target market

productivity: the ratio of outputs to inputs during production, e.g., output per worker per time period

profit after tax: profit made after corporation tax has been deducted

profit and loss account: records the revenue, costs and profit (or loss) of a business over a given period of time

profit before interest and taxation: gross profit minus overhead expenses

profit centre: a section of a business to which both costs and revenues can be allocated

profit margin: this ratio compares operating profit with revenue

profitability: a relative measure of a business's ability to make a profit from sales or a capital investment

profit-related pay: a bonus for employees based on the profits of the business – usually paid as a proportion of basic salary

project based organisation (PBO): undertake most of their activities through temporary project teams, often with a small central administrative department overseeing them

project champion: a person assigned to support and drive a project forward and who explains the benefits of change and assists and supports the team putting change into practice

project groups: these are created by an organisation to address a problem that requires input from different specialists

promotion: the use of advertising, digital promotions, sales promotion, personal selling, direct mail, trade fairs, sponsorship and public relations to inform consumers and persuade them to buy

public corporation: a business enterprise owned and controlled by the state – also known as nationalised industry or public sector enterprise

public sector: comprises organisations accountable to and controlled by central or local government (the state)

publicly held company: a limited company with the legal right to sell shares to financial institutions and the general public; its share price is quoted on the national stock exchange

qualitative factors: factors that cannot be measured in numerical or financial terms that are considered by managers before taking decisions

qualitative research: research into the in-depth motivations behind consumer buying behaviour or opinions

quality assurance: a system of agreeing and meeting quality standards at each stage of production to ensure consumer satisfaction

quality circles: groups of employees who meet regularly to discuss ways of resolving problems and improving production and quality in their department/organisation

quality control: this is based on inspection of the product or a sample of products

quality product: a good or service that meets customers' expectations and is therefore 'fit for purpose'

quality standards: the expectations of customers expressed in terms of the minimum acceptable production or service standards

quantitative factors: these are measurable in financial terms and will have a direct impact on either the costs of a site or the revenues from it and its profitability

quantitative research: research that leads to numerical results that can be presented and analysed

quartiles: splitting an ordered set of results into four equal parts

quaternary sector business activity: this focuses on information technology (IT) businesses and information service providers such as research and development, business consulting and information gathering

quota sampling: gathering data from a group chosen out of a specific sub-group, e.g., a researcher might ask 100 individuals between the ages of 20 and 30 years

random sampling: every member of the target population has an equal chance of being selected

recruitment: the process of identifying the need for a new employee, defining the job to be filled and the type of person needed to fill it, attracting suitable candidates for the job and selecting the best one

re-order quantity: the number of units ordered each time

re-order stock level: the level of stocks that will trigger a new order to be sent to the supplier

research and development (R&D): scientific innovations and their technical improvement to create new products and processes

reshoring: ending offshoring contracts with overseas suppliers and returning functions or processes to businesses in the original or home country

retained profit: the profit left after all deductions, including dividends, have been made; this is invested back into the company as a source of finance

return on capital employed: this compares operating profit and the capital employed in the business

revenue (or sales turnover): the total value of sales made during the trading period = selling price × quantity sold

revenue stream: a source of income received over time from the sale of a product

revenue to achieve target profit: the amount of revenue needed to cover both fixed and variable costs and earn the business a target profit

rights issue: existing shareholders are given the right to buy additional shares at a discounted price

role culture: each member of staff has a clearly defined job title and role

salary: annual income that is usually paid on a monthly basis

sales forecast: prediction of sales for the next time period

sales promotion: incentives such as special offers or special deals directed at consumers or retailers to achieve short-term sales increases and repeat purchases by consumers

sample: group of people taking part in a market research survey selected to be representative of the whole target market

sampling error: mistakes in research caused by using a sample for data collection rather than the whole target population

scale of operation: the maximum output that can be achieved using the available inputs (resources) – this scale can only be increased in the long term by employing more of all inputs

scientific management: management of a business which follows the principles of efficiency derived from scientific experiments to improve productivity, especially those based on time-and-motion studies

secondary research: collection of data from second-hand sources

secondary sector business activity: businesses that manufacture and process products from natural resources, including furniture, brewing, baking, clothing and construction

self-actualisation: a sense of self-fulfilment reached by feeling enriched and developed by what a person has learned and achieved

share: a certificate confirming part ownership of a company. Most types of share entitle shareholders to dividends paid from profits

share capital: the total value of capital raised from shareholders by the issue of shares

shareholder value: the financial gains received by the owners of a company's shares

shareholders: individuals or institutions that buy/own shares in a limited company

shareholders' equity: total value of capital invested in the business by shareholders either in the form of share capital or retained profits

single-union agreement: an employer recognises just one union for purposes of collective bargaining

situational leadership: effective leadership varies with the task in hand and situational leaders adapt their leadership style to each situation

social audit: an independent report on the impact a business has on society. This can cover pollution levels, health and safety record, sources of supplies, customer satisfaction and contribution to the community

social enterprise: a business with social and/or environmental objectives that reinvests most of its profits into benefiting society rather than maximising returns to owners

social entrepreneur: a person who establishes an enterprise with the aim of solving social problems or achieving social change

social sustainability: the ability of a community to develop processes and structures which not only meet the needs of its current members but also support the ability of future generations to maintain a healthy community

sole trader: a business that is exclusively owned by one person who has full control of it and is entitled to all of the profit (after tax)

span of control: the number of subordinates reporting directly to a manager

spoken communication: oral way of sending information between two or more people

stakeholder concept: the view that businesses and their managers have responsibilities to a wide range of groups, not just shareholders

stakeholders: people or groups of people who can be affected by, and therefore have an interest in, any action taken by an organisation

standard deviation (SD): measures the average dispersion of a set of data from its mean result

start-up capital: capital needed by an entrepreneur to set up a business

statement of financial position (balance sheet): an accounting statement that records the values of a business's assets, liabilities and shareholders' equity at one point in time

STEEPLE analysis: the strategic analysis of the macro-environment in which a business operates including social; technological; economic; environmental, political, legal, ethical factors

stock (inventory): materials and goods required to allow for the production and supply of products to the customer

stock turnover: measures the number of times inventory is converted into sales in a period of time, usually one year

straight-line depreciation: a constant amount of depreciation is subtracted from the value of the asset each year

strategic alliances: arrangements between businesses in which each agrees to commit resources to achieve an agreed set of objectives

strategic analysis: conducting research into the business environment and into the business itself to help identify future strategies

strategic objective: a long-term target for the whole organisation, designed to achieve the corporate aim

strategy: a plan of action designed to help achieve an objective

strike: a form of industrial action in which workers, often trade union members, withdraw their labour services

subcontracting: the practice of assigning to another business (the subcontractor) part of a contract, e.g., a specialist activity that makes up part of a construction contract

supply chain: every business that comes into contact with a particular product including manufacturing and supplying parts for the product, assembling it, delivering it and selling it

survey: detailed study of a market or geographical area to gather data on attitudes, impressions, opinions and satisfaction levels of products or businesses, by asking a section of the population

sustainable operations: business operations that can be sustained in the long term, e.g., by protecting the environment and not damaging the quality of life of future generations

SWOT analysis: a form of strategic analysis that identifies and analyses the main internal strengths and weaknesses and external opportunities and threats that will influence the future direction and success of a business

synergy: the concept that, following a merger or acquisition, the combined value and performance of two businesses will be greater than the sum of the separate individual businesses.

tactical objective: a short-term target aimed at resolving a particular problem or meeting a specific part of a longer-term strategic objective

takeover: when a business wishes to acquire another company but this is opposed by that company's managers and is often referred to as a 'hostile takeover''

tall (vertical) organisational structure: one with many levels of hierarchy and, usually, narrow spans of control

tangible product: a physical object that can be touched, such as a building, car, tablet computer or clothing

target market: the segment of the market that a particular product is aimed at

task culture: based on cooperation and teamwork

team working: production is organised so that groups of workers undertake complete units of work

tertiary sector business activity: businesses that provide services to consumers and other businesses, such as retailing, transport, insurance, banking, hotels, tourism and telecommunications

through the line marketing: an integrated marketing strategy that combines elements of both above the line and below the line promotion

total contribution: unit contribution × output

total quality management (TQM): an approach to quality that aims to involve all employees in the quality-improvement process

total revenue: total income from the sale of all units of a product

trade union (labour union): an organisation of working people with the objective of improving the pay and working conditions of its members and providing them with support and legal services

trademark: a distinctive name, symbol, motto or design that identifies a business or its products – can be legally registered and cannot be copied

training: work-related education to increase workforce skills and efficiency

triple bottom line: the three objectives of social enterprises: economic, social and environmental

unique selling point (USP): the special feature of a product or customer service that makes it different from those of competitors

units of production method: depreciating an asset on the basis of its usage

variable costs: costs which vary with output

variance: difference between a budget and actual performance

variance analysis: the process of investigating any differences between budgeted figures and actual figures

viral marketing: the use of social media sites or text messages to increase brand awareness or sell products

virtual reality: computer-generated simulations of a three-dimensional image or environment that can be interacted with by a person using special electronic equipment, such as a helmet with a screen inside

vision statement: a statement of what the organisation would like to achieve or accomplish in the long term

window dressing: presenting the accounts of a business in the best possible, or most flattering, way which could potentially mislead users of accounts

workforce audit: a check on the skills and qualifications of all existing employees

workforce plan: numbers of workers and skills of those workers required over a future time period

working capital: the capital needed to pay for raw materials, day-to-day running costs and credit offered to customers. In accounting terms: working capital = current assets – current liabilities

zero budgeting: setting budgets to zero each year and budget holders have to argue their case to receive any finance

zero defects: the aim of achieving perfect products every time

> Key formulae

acid test ratio: $\dfrac{\text{current assets} - \text{stock}}{\text{current liabilities}}$

annual forecasted net cash flow: forecasted cash inflow minus forecasted cash outflows

ARR (%): $\dfrac{\text{average annual profit}}{\text{capital investment}} \times 100$

where the average annual profit $= \dfrac{\text{total returns} - \text{capital cost}}{\text{number of years}}$

break-even level of output: $\dfrac{\text{fixed costs}}{\text{contribution per unit}}$

break-even target price: $\left(\dfrac{\text{fixed costs}}{\text{production level}}\right) + \text{direct cost}$

capacity utilisation rate: $\dfrac{\text{actual output}}{\text{productive capacity}} \times 100$

capital employed: non-current liabilities + equity

capital productivity: $\dfrac{\text{value of output in time period}}{\text{value of capital employed}}$

contribution per unit: selling price of a product minus direct costs per unit

cost to buy (CTB): V × UCS

cost to make (CTM): FC + (UDC × V)

creditor days: $\dfrac{\text{creditors}}{\text{cost of sales}} \times 365$

current ratio: $\dfrac{\text{current assets}}{\text{current liabilities}}$

debtor days: $\dfrac{\text{debtors}}{\text{total revenue}} \times 365$

defect rate (%): $\dfrac{\text{number of defective products}}{\text{total output in time period}} \times 100$

degree of operating leverage: $\dfrac{(\text{revenue} - \text{total variable costs})}{\text{operating profit}}$

gearing ratio (%): $\dfrac{\text{non-current liabilities}}{\text{capital employed}} \times 100$

gross profit: equal to sales revenue minus cost of sales

gross profit margin%: $\dfrac{\text{gross profit}}{\text{sales revenue}} \times 100$

labour productivity: $\dfrac{\text{total output in a given time period}}{\text{total workers employed}}$

labour turnover: $\dfrac{\text{number of employees leaving in 1 year}}{\text{average number of people employed}} \times 100$

machine productivity: $\dfrac{\text{output in time period}}{\text{total machine hours}}$

market share%: $\dfrac{\text{sales of business in time period}}{\text{total market sales in time period}} \times 100$

net cash flow: the sum of cash payments to a business (inflows) minus the sum of cash payments made by it (outflows)

overall productivity: $\dfrac{\text{total output}}{\text{total input}}$

or

$\dfrac{\text{total output}}{(\text{labour} + \text{capital input})}$

price elasticity of demand (PED):

$$\frac{\text{percentage change in quantity demanded}}{\text{percentage change in price}}$$

profit after tax: operating profit minus interest costs and corporation tax

profit before interest and taxation: gross profit minus overhead expenses

profit margin%: $\frac{\text{profit before interest and tax}}{\text{sales revenue}} \times 100$

return on capital employed (%):

$$\frac{\text{profit before interest and tax}}{\text{capital employed}} \times 100$$

revenue (or sales turnover): selling price × quantity sold

revenue to achieve target profit: $\frac{\text{fixed costs + target profit}}{1 - \text{direct cost / price}}$

stock turnover: $\frac{\text{cost of sales}}{\text{average value of stock}}$

straight-line method of depreciation:

annual depreciation charge =

$$\frac{\text{historic cost of asset} - \text{residual value}}{\text{useful life of asset (years)}}$$

target profit level of output: $\frac{\text{fixed costs + target profit}}{\text{contribution per unit}}$

total contribution: unit contribution × output

units of production method:

Firstly, the depreciation per unit of output is calculated by using the following formula:

depreciation per unit $= \frac{\text{cost of asset} - \text{residual value}}{\text{total units of production}}$

Then, the annual depreciation is calculated by using the following formula:

annual depreciation = depreciation per unit × annual units produced

> Acknowledgements

The authors and publishers acknowledge the following sources of copyright material and are grateful for the permissions granted. While every effort has been made, it has not always been possible to identify the sources of all the material used, or to trace all copyright holders. If any omissions are brought to our notice, we will be happy to include the appropriate acknowledgements on reprinting.

Unit 1: Excerpt from Daimler Annual Report 2019, used by permission of Mercedes-Benz Group AG; Adapted from 'Coca-Cola's efforts to diversify are paying off as beverage maker tops forecast' by Christopher Doering, Senior Reporter at Industry Dive, © Oct. 25, 2017 used by permission of Industry Dive; **Unit 2:** Zhao, B. and Pan, Y. (2017) 'Cross-Cultural Employee Motivation in International Companies. Journal of Human Resource and Sustainability Studies', 5, 215-222. doi:10.4236/jhrss.2017.54019; Excerpt from '10 of the Most Successful Business Leaders Share Their Secret to Discovering Great Talent' Authored by Maxwell Huppert, Senior Creative Copywriter at Zoro.com, February 17, 2020; Excerpt from 'The Best Leaders Are Great Communicators Says Former Discover Financial CEO David Nelms' in a conversation with best-selling author and futurist Jacob Morgan, May 26, 2020 article published in Medium, used by permission of Jacob Morgan ©2020; Excerpt from 'Brazilian oil workers continue with strike; output unaffected' by Jeff Mower on SP Global, used by permission of S&P Global Commodity Insights, ©2022 by S&P Global Inc.; Excerpt from 'ScotRail passengers face fresh services disruption as engineering workers vote for strike action' By Martin Williams, First appeared in The Herald newspaper, used by permission of the author; **Unit 3:** Excerpt from '6 Crowdfunded Businesses That Became Million Dollar Companies', 29.03.2022 by Albert Chobanyan, used by permission of The Crowdfunding Formula, https://blog.thecrowdfundingformula.com/crowdfunded-businesses/; Adapted from NIMIR Chemicals Annual Report 2019, Running Financing (RF), used by permission of Nimir Industrial Chemicals Limited; Excerpt from 'About us' section - International Standards Board used by the permission of International Federation of Accountants; Adapted excerpt from 'Why Are U.S. Companies Delaying Payments to Suppliers?' by Conor McGlade July 17, 2018; Extract taken from: Rivers, L. (Manchester Metropolitan University, University of Huddersfield), 'Here's what it's like to work at a company that goes into administration', (2016), The Conversation, used by permission of the author, https://theconversation.com/heres-what-its-like-to-work-at-a-company-that-goes-into-administration-58430; Excerpt from 'Bizarre Politics: The 7 Worst Vanity Projects in Modern History' by Peter Mossack August 26, 2017, taken from crowdh.com; Excerpt from 'The Importance of Budgeting in Business' Posted on February 28th, 2018 by Karen Banks, used by permission of WLF Accounting & Advisory – authored by Karen Banks, Advisor; The Access Group; **Unit 4:** Excerpt from 'H&M's New CEO Wants To Fix Fast Fashion. Is That Possible?' 14 October 2020 By Emily Chan, Vogue UK, © Condé Nast, used by permission of Condé Nast; Excerpt from 'Lidl on its new marketing campaign: We want to be as famous for quality as we are for price' By Ellen Hammett 2 Jun 2019, Centaur Media plc; Excerpt from 'Focus groups shape what we buy. But how much do they really say about us? Even in the age of big data, brands can't quit the focus group' By Joseph Stromberg, Jan 22, 2019 © Vox Media, LLC; Excerpt from 'How is Apple Selling the Apple Watch?' by Matt © Natural Training; Adapted from 'Dining at Sublimotion in Ibiza Is a Mind-Blowing Multisensory Experience' By Meeroona, March 27, 2022 ©Veebrant.com; Adapted from 'How Nike created a buzz in the suburbs of Paris' by Kim Benjamin © May 18, 2018, used by permission of Haymarket Media Group Ltd; **Unit 5:** Article 'What is Kaizen? A Description and Examples' Posted by KaiNexus, Nov 8, 2019, Published in KaiNexus site, used by permission of KaiNexus, https://blog.kainexus.com/insights/improvement-disciplines/%20kaizen/what-is-kaizen/what-is-kaizen-a-description-and-examples; Excerpt from 'The LEGO Headquarters Is Made with—What Else?—Giant LEGOs, Leave it to the Danish to come up with something playful and practical' By Jennifer Fernandez, Nov 1, 2019 © Hearst Magazine Media, Inc; Excerpt from '3 reasons why social enterprises fail – and what we can learn from them' © Jun 8, 2017, used by permission of World Economic Forum; Excerpt adapted from 'The 6 Best PR Crisis Management & Communication Examples' © 2018 published on Prezly. Used by permission of Prezly; Adapted from 'Alphabet spends more on research and development than any other company' By Ian Horswill, 14 January 2021 © The CEO Magazine; Adapted from 'China launches first autonomous taxis in Beijing by Matthew Crisara, © 04 May 2021, used by permission of Motor1.com; Table 35.1 data compiled from company statement and YCharts via fdiintelligence.com; Adapted from 'How Data Science and AI are changing Supermarket shopping' by Richard Farnworth 2020, Medium, used by permission of the author.

Thanks to the following for permission to reproduce images:

Cover Viaframe/GI; *Inside* **Unit 1:** Nikolay Pandev/GI; By Chakarin Wattanamongkol/GI; Group4 Studio/GI; Bloomberg/GI; Aleksei Naumov/GI; Hakule/GI; Siwabud Veerapaisarn/GI; Mint Images/GI; Mihailomilovanovic/GI; Nurphoto/GI; Activity 2.1 Graph- Stock Performance since Tesla's IPO Date of June 29, 2010 - CNBC, Data From Factset; Figure 2.2 From The Article 'No Going Back – State

> Index

Note: Page numbers in *italic* refer to figures, page numbers in **bold** refer to tables.